THE OXFORD HANDBO

AQUINAS

THE OXFORD HANDBOOK OF

AQUINAS

Edited by

BRIAN DAVIES
AND ELEONORE STUMP

OXFORD
UNIVERSITY PRESS

OXFORD
UNIVERSITY PRESS

Oxford University Press is a department of the University of Oxford.
It furthers the University's objective of excellence in research, scholarship,
and education by publishing worldwide.

Oxford New York
Auckland Cape Town Dar es Salaam Hong Kong Karachi
Kuala Lumpur Madrid Melbourne Mexico City Nairobi
New Delhi Shanghai Taipei Toronto

With offices in
Argentina Austria Brazil Chile Czech Republic France Greece
Guatemala Hungary Italy Japan Poland Portugal Singapore
South Korea Switzerland Thailand Turkey Ukraine Vietnam

Published in the United States of America by
Oxford University Press
198 Madison Avenue, New York, NY 10016

First issued as an Oxford University Press paperback, 2014.

Library of Congress Cataloging-in-Publication Data
The Oxford handbook of Aquinas / edited by Brian Davies and Eleonore Stump.
p. cm.—(Oxford handbooks)
ISBN 978-0-19-532609-3 (cloth : alk. paper); 978-0-19-935198-5 (paperback)
1. Thomas, Aquinas, Saint, 1225?–1274—Handbooks,
manuals, etc. I. Davies, Brian, 1951–
II. Stump, Eleonore, 1947–
B765.T54O94 2011
189'.4—dc22
2010029796

Contents

Part III The Divine Nature

Part IV Ethics and Action Theory

Part V Epistemology and Philosophy of Mind

Part VI Theory of Language

Part VII Philosophical Theology

Abbreviations

CG	Aquinas, *Contra errores Graecorum*
CT	Aquinas, *Compendium theologiae*
DEE	Aquinas, *De ente et essentia*
Diu. nom.	Aquinas, *Expositio super Dionysium De divinis nominibus*
DPN	Aquinas, *De principiis naturae*
DSS	Aquinas, *De substantiis separatis*
DUI	Aquinas, *De unitate intellectus*
In BDH	Aquinas, *Expositio in librum Boethii De hebdomadibus*
In BDT	Aquinas, *Expositio super librum Boethii De trinitate*
In CA	Aquinas, *Expositio super librum De causis*
In DA	Aquinas, *Sententia Libri De anima*
In DC	Aquinas, *Sententia super librum De caelo et mundo*
In DMR	Aquinas, *Sententia de memoria et reminiscentia*
In Gal	Aquinas, *Expositio et Lectura super Epistolam Pauli Apostoli ad Galatas*
In Heb	Aquinas, *Lectura super Epistolam Pauli Apostoli ad Hebraeos*
In Meta	Aquinas, *Sententia super Metaphysicam*
In NE	Aquinas, *Sententia Libri Ethicorum*
In PA	Aquinas, *Sententia Libri Posteriorum Analyticorum*
In Peri herm.	Aquinas, *Expositio Libri Peri hermeneias*
In Phy	Aquinas, *Sententia super Physicam*
In Rom	Aquinas, *Lectura super Epistolam Pauli Apostoli ad Romanos*
In I Cor	Aquinas, *Lectura Super Primam Epistolam Pauli Apostoli ad Corinthios*
In II Cor	Aquinas, *Lectura super Secundam Epistolam Pauli Apostoli ad Corinthios*
Met.	Aristotle, *Metaphysics*
NE	Aristotle, *Nicomachean Ethics*
Pol.	Aristotle, *Politics*
QDA	Aquinas, *Quaestio disputata de anima*
QDC	Aquinas, *Quaestio disputata de caritate*
QDM	Aquinas, *Quaestiones disputatae de malo*
QDP	Aquinas, *Quaestiones disputatae de potentia*
QDSC	Aquinas, *Quaestio disputata de spiritualibus creaturis*
QDUVI	Aquinas, *Quaestio disputata de unione verbi incarnati*

QDV	Aquinas, *Quaestiones disputatae de veritate*
QDVCard	Aquinas, *Quaestio disputata de virtutibus cardinalibus*
QDVCom	Aquinas, *Quaestio disputata de virtutibus in communi*
Quodl	Aquinas, *Quaestiones de quodlibet I–XII*
SCG	Aquinas, *Summa contra Gentiles*
ST	Aquinas, *Summa theologiae*
Super Johan	Aquinas, *Lectura super Ioannem*
Super Sent	Aquinas, *Scriptum super libros Sententiarum*

Contributors

Michael Baur is Associate Professor of Philosophy, Adjunct Professor of Law, and Director of the Natural Law Colloquium, at Fordham University. He is the translator of Fichte's *Foundations of Natural Right* (2000) and Series Editor of "Cambridge Hegel Translations" (Cambridge University Press).

James Brent currently teaches at the Catholic University of America in Washington, D.C. His primary area of research is Aquinas's account of the relation between faith and reason. His article "Natural Theology" can be found in the *Internet Encyclopedia of Philosophy*.

Jeffrey Brower is Associate Professor of Philosophy at Purdue University. He is the author of a number of articles in medieval philosophy, metaphysics, and philosophy of religion, and is co-editor of *The Cambridge Companion to Abelard* (2004).

David Burrell is Theodore Hesburgh Professor emeritus in Philosophy and Theology at the University of Notre Dame and Professor of Ethics and Development at Uganda Martyrs University. His efforts since 1982 in comparative issues in philosophical theology in Judaism, Christianity, and Islam are evidenced in *Knowing the Unknowable God: Ibn-Sina, Maimonides, Aquinas* (1986), *Freedom and Creation in Three Traditions* (1993), *Original Peace* (with Elena Malits, 1998), *Friendship and Ways to Truth* (2000), and two translations: *Al-Ghazali on the Ninety Nine Beautiful Names of God* (1993) and *Al-Ghazali on Faith in Divine Unity and Trust in Divine Providence* (2001). Most recently he has published *Faith and Freedom* (2004), *Learning to Trust in Freedom* (2009), and a theological commentary on Job: *Deconstructing Theodicy* (2008).

Brian Davies is Professor of Philosophy at Fordham University, New York. His publications include *An Introduction to the Philosophy of Religion* (3rd edition, 2004), *The Thought of Thomas Aquinas* (1992), *Aquinas* (2002), *The Reality of God and the Problem of Evil* (2006), and *Thomas Aquinas on God and Evil* (2011).

James Doig is Emeritus Professor of Philosophy, Clayton College and State University, Morrow, GA. His publications include *Aquinas on Metaphysics* (1972) and *Aquinas's Philosophical Commentary on the* Ethics: *A Historical Perspective* (2001).

Gilles Emery, O.P. is Professor of Dogmatic Theology at the University of Fribourg, Switzerland. He is a member of the International Theological Commission of the Catholic Church and a member of the editorial board of the *Revue Thomiste*. His publications include: *La Trinité créatrice* (1995), *Trinity in Aquinas* (2003), *Trinity, Church, and the Human Person: Thomistic Essays* (2007), *The Trinitarian Theology of Saint Thomas Aquinas* (2007), and *The Trinity: An Introduction to Catholic Doctrine on the Triune God* (2011). He is co-editor, with Matthew Levering of *The Oxford Handbook of the Trinity* (2011).

Alexander Fidora is ICREA Research Professor in the Department of Ancient and Medieval Studies at the Universitat Autònoma de Barcelona. His recent publications include *Vincent Ferrer, Quaestio de unitate universalis—Ma'amar nikhbad ba-kolel* (Latin and Hebrew texts with English translation), ed. with M. Zonta (2010), *Domingo Gundisalvo y la teoría de la ciencia arábigo-aristotélica* (2009), *Raimundus Lullus: An Introduction to his Life, Works and Thought*, ed. with J. E. Rubio (2008). He is co-director of several series, such as Herders Bibliothek der Philosophie des Mittelalters and Bibliotheca Philosophorum Medii Aevi Cataloniae.

Michael Gorman is Associate Professor of Philosophy at the Catholic University of America in Washington, D.C. He has authored over twenty articles in philosophy and theology, among them "Questions Concerning the Existences of Christ" (2011 in K. Emery, R. Friedman, and A. Speer, eds., *Philosophy and Theology in the Long Middle Ages: A Tribute to Stephen F. Brown*), "On a Thomistic Worry about Scotus's Doctrine of the esse Christi" (2011 in *Antonianum*), and "The Essential and the Accidental" (*Ratio* 18 [2005]: 276–89).

Wayne Hankey is Carnegie Professor of Classics at King's College and Dalhousie University, Halifax, Nova Scotia, Chairman of Classics with the Dalhousie Program in Religious Studies, and Editor of *Dionysius*. His many publications include *God in Himself: Aquinas' Doctrine of God as expounded in the* Summa Theologiae (1987).

Tobias Hoffmann is Associate Professor of Philosophy at the Catholic University of America, Washington, D.C. He is the author of *Creatura intellecta: Die Ideen und Possibilien bei Duns Scotus mit Ausblick auf Franz von Mayronis, Poncius und Mastrius* (2002). He is co-editor of *The Problem of Weakness of Will in Medieval Philosophy* (2006), editor of *Weakness of Will from Plato to the Present* (2008), and editor of *A Companion to Angels and Medieval Philosophy* (2012).

Dominic Holtz O.P. is Professor of Philosophy at the Pontifical University of St. Thomas Aquinas in Rome. He was previously Assistant Professor of Church History and Thomistic Studies at the Aquinas Institute of Theology in St. Louis, Missouri. His "Carnal Knowledge and Contemplation: *Luxuria* and the Intellectual Virtues in St. Thomas Aquinas" appears in *In Medio Ecclesiae: Essays in Honor of Benedict M. Ashley* (2007).

Ludger Honnefelder is Otto Warburg Senior Research Professor of Philosophy at the Humboldt University at Berlin and Director of the Albertus-Magnus-Institut at Bonn. He is author of *Ens inquantum ens: Der Begriff des Seienden als solchen nach der Lehre des Johannes Duns Scotus* (1979), of *Scientia transcendens: Die formale Bestimmung der Seiendheit und Realität in der Metaphysik des Mittelalters und der Neuzeit (Duns Scotus—Suárez—Wolff—Kant—Peirce)* (1990), of *La métaphysique comme science transcendantale entre le Moyen Âge et les Temps modernes* (2002), of *Johannes Duns Scotus* (2005), and of *Was sollen wir tun, wer will ich sein? Vernunft und Verantwortung, Gewissen und Schuld* (2007) and *Woher kommen wir? Ursprünge der Moderne im Denken des Mittelalters* (2008). He has written a number of articles in medieval philosophy, metaphysics, and ethics and is the main editor of the *Editio Coloniensis* of the works of Albert the Great.

PETER KING is Professor of Philosophy and of Medieval Studies at the University of Toronto. The author of many articles on and translations of medieval philosophy, his most recent book is *Augustine: On Free Choice of the Will, On Grace and Free Will, and Other Writings* (2010). He has written several studies of cognitive and affective psychology in the Middle Ages, with particular attention to the role of Thomas Aquinas; most recently he has written on the history of medieval theories of the emotions for *The Oxford Handbook of the Emotions* (2010).

GYULA KLIMA is Professor of Philosophy at Fordham University, New York, and author of ARS ARTIUM: *Essays in Philosophical Semantics, Medieval and Modern* (1988), *John Buridan: Summulae de Dialectica, an annotated translation with a philosophical introduction* (2001), and *Readings in Medieval Philosophy* (2007). His most recent book is *John Buridan* (2009).

BRIAN LEFTOW is the Nolloth Professor of the Philosophy of the Christian Religion, Oxford University. He is the author of *God and Necessity* (OUP forthcoming), *Aquinas on Metaphysics* (OUP forthcoming), *Time and Eternity* (1991), and numerous articles in medieval philosophy, metaphysics, and the philosophy of religion.

BRUNO NIEDERBACHER, S.J. is Assistant Professor of Philosophy in the Department of Christian Philosophy at the University of Innsbruck. His main research interests are in medieval philosophy and in metaethics. He is the author of *Glaube als Tugend bei Thomas von Aquin* (2004), and the co-editor of *Theologie als Wissenschaft im Mittelalter* (2006).

THOMAS M. OSBORNE, Jr. is Associate Professor of Philosophy at the Center for Thomistic Studies, University of St. Thomas (Houston). He has written many articles on medieval and late scholastic philosophy and is the author of *Love of Self and Love of God in Thirteenth-Century Ethics* (2005).

ROBERT PASNAU is Professor of Philosophy at the University of Colorado at Boulder. His many publications include *Theories of Cognition in the Later Middle Ages* (1997), *Thomas Aquinas on Human Nature* (2002), and *The Philosophy of Aquinas* (2003, co-authored with Christopher Shields).

Timothy Pawl is Assistant Professor of Philosophy at the University of St. Thomas (Minnesota). His main research interests include metaphysics, philosophy of religion, and the thought of Thomas Aquinas. Some of his recent work has appeared in *Faith and Philosophy* and *The Australasian Journal of Philosophy*.

Martin Pickavé is Associate Professor of Philosophy and Medieval Studies at the University of Toronto. He is currently working on a monograph on medieval theories of the emotions, and with Russell L. Friedman (Catholic University Leuven) he is editing a *Companion to Cognitive Theory in the Later Middle Ages*. His recent publications include "Nicomachean Ethics 7.3 on Akratic Ignorance," *Oxford Studies in Ancient Philosophy* 34 (2008) (with Jennifer Whiting) and *Heinrich von Gent über Metaphysik als erste Wissenschaft* (2007).

Giorgio Pini is Associate Professor in the Philosophy Department at Fordham University, New York. His main research interests are in the thought of John Duns Scotus and later medieval metaphysics, philosophy of religion, and cognitive and moral psychology. He is the author of *Categories and Logic in Duns Scotus* (2002) and *Scoto e l'analogia* (2002). He is also the author of a number of articles in journals such as *Medieval Philosophy and Theology*, *Vivarium*, *The History of Philosophy Quarterly*, and *Journal of the History of Philosophy*.

Andrew Pinsent is Research Director of the Ian Ramsey Centre for Science and Religion at Oxford University, a member of the Theology Faculty there, and a Senior Research Fellow at Harris Manchester College. His principal research interests are in metaphysical problems pertinent to contemporary science and theology. He is the author of *The Second-Person Perspective in Aquinas's Ethics: Virtues and Gifts* (Routledge, 2012).

Jean Porter is the O'Brien Professor of Theological Ethics at the University of Notre Dame. She previously taught at Vanderbilt Divinity School. She is the author of numerous articles and four books on aspects of medieval moral thought and its contemporary significance including, most recently, *Nature as Reason: A Thomistic Theory of the Natural Law* (2005), and *Ministers of the Law: A Natural Law Theory of Legal Authority* (2010).

Michael Rota is Associate Professor of Philosophy at the University of St. Thomas (Minnesota). In addition to his work on Aquinas and on the metaphysics of causation, he is the author of articles relating to the fine-tuning argument, the cosmological argument, the problem of human freedom and divine foreknowledge, providence and evolution, and the problem of animal suffering. His papers have appeared in the *American Catholic Philosophical Quarterly*, *Faith and Philosophy*, *History of Philosophy Quarterly*, *The Monist*, *Pacific Philosophical Quarterly*, *Religious Studies*, and other journals.

Eleonore Stump is the Robert J. Henle Professor Philosophy at Saint Louis University. She has published extensively in medieval philosophy, philosophical theology, and metaphysics. Among her books are *Boethius's De topicis differentiis*

(1978; second printing, 1989), *The Cambridge Companion to Aquinas* (co-edited with Norman Kretzmann, 1993), *Aquinas's Moral Theory: Essays in Honor of Norman Kretzmann* (with Scott MacDonald, 1999), *Aquinas* (2003), and *Wandering in Darkness: Narrative and the Problem of Suffering* (2010).

JEAN-PIERRE TORRELL, O.P. is a former member of the Leonine Commission for the critical edition of the works of Aquinas. He is Professor Emeritus at the University of Fribourg (Switzerland). His many publications (as translated into English) include *Saint Thomas Aquinas: The Person and His Work* (1996), *Saint Thomas Aquinas: Spiritual Master* (2003), and *Aquinas's* Summa: *Background, Structure, and Reception* (2005).

CHRISTOPHER UPHAM is currently a research student, pursuing a Ph.D. in philosophy at Fordham University, New York.

RIK VAN NIEUWENHOVE is Lecturer in Theology at Mary Immaculate College, Limerick. His main areas of research are medieval theology and spirituality, theology of the Trinity, and soteriology. He is the author of *Jan van Ruusbroec: Mystical Theologian of the Trinity* (2003), and co-editor of *The Theology of Thomas Aquinas* (2005). He is co-author (with Declan Marmion) of *An Introduction to the Trinity* (2011).

JOSEPH WAWRYKOW is Associate Professor of Theology at the University of Notre Dame. His publications include *God's Grace and Human Action: "Merit" in the Theology of Thomas Aquinas* (1996) and *The Westminster Handbook to Thomas Aquinas* (2005). He is co-editor of *Christ among the Medieval Dominicans* (1998) and *The Theology of Thomas Aquinas* (2005).

THOMAS WILLIAMS is Professor of Catholic Studies and Professor of Philosophy at the University of South Florida. He is the co-author, with Sandra Visser, of *Anselm* (2008), translator of *Anselm: Basic Writings* (2007) and *Augustine: On Free Choice of the Will* (1993), editor of *The Cambridge Companion to Duns Scotus* (2003), and co-editor, with Arthur Hyman and James J. Walsh, of *Philosophy in the Middle Ages*, 3d ed. (2010). He has contributed to the *Cambridge History of Medieval Philosophy* (2009), the *Blackwell Companion to the Philosophy of Action* (2010), and the *Cambridge Companions* to Augustine (2001), Anselm (2005), Abelard (2004), and Medieval Philosophy (2003).

JOHN WIPPEL is the Theodore Basselin Professor of Philosophy at The Catholic University of America. He is the author of *The Metaphysical Thought of Godfrey of Fontaines* (1981), *Metaphysical Themes in Thomas Aquinas* (1984), *Boethius of Dacia: "On the Supreme Good," "On the Eternity of the World," "On Dreams"* (1987), *Mediaeval Reactions to the Encounter between Faith and Reason* (1995), *The Metaphysical Thought of Thomas Aquinas* (2000), *Metaphysical Themes in Thomas Aquinas* (2007). John Wippel is also co-author and co-editor (with Allan B. Wolter) of *Medieval Philosophy: From St. Augustine to Nicholas of Cusa* (1969) and co-author (with B. C. Bazán, G. Fransen, and D. Jacquart) of *Les Questions disputées et les questions quodlibétiques dans les facultés de théologie, de droit et de medicine* (1985).

THE OXFORD HANDBOOK OF

AQUINAS

INTRODUCTION

BRIAN DAVIES
ELEONORE STUMP

Thomas Aquinas (1224/25–1274) lived an active, demanding academic and ecclesiastical life that ended while he was only fifty (or a bit younger). He nonetheless produced many works, varying in length from a few pages to a few volumes. Because his writings grew out of his activities as a teacher in the Dominican Order and as a member of the theology faculty of the University of Paris, most are concerned with what he and his contemporaries thought of as theology. However, much of academic theology in the Middle Ages consisted in a rational investigation of the most fundamental aspects of reality in general and of human nature and behavior in particular. That vast domain obviously includes much of what is now considered to be philosophy and is reflected in the broad subject matter of Aquinas's theological writings.

The scope and philosophical character of medieval theology as practiced by Aquinas can be easily seen in his two most important works, *Summa contra Gentiles* (*SCG*) and *Summa theologiae* (*ST*). However, many of the hundreds of topics covered in those two large works are also investigated in more detail in the smaller works resulting from Aquinas's numerous academic disputations (something like a cross between formal debates and twentieth-century graduate seminars), which he conducted in his various academic posts. Some of those topics are taken up differently again in his commentaries on books of the Bible and/or works by Aristotle and other authors. Although Aquinas is generally remarkably consistent in his several discussions of the same topic, it is often helpful to examine parallel passages in his writings when fully assessing his views or the development of his views on any issue.

Aquinas's most obvious philosophical connection is with Aristotle. Besides producing commentaries on Aristotle's works, he often cites Aristotle in support of a thesis he is defending, even when commenting on Scripture. Although he dissents from Aristotle's views in many places, most notably those connected to ethics or metaphysics and theology, there are also in Aquinas's writings many implicit Aristotelian elements, which he had thoroughly absorbed into his own thought. He also often adopts Aristotle's critical attitude toward theories associated with Plato, especially the account of ordinary substantial forms as separately existing entities. Nonetheless, although Aquinas, like other medieval scholars of western Europe, had almost no access to Plato's works, he was influenced by the writings of Augustine and the pseudo-Dionysius. Through them he absorbed a good deal of Platonism as well.

On the other hand, Aquinas is the paradigmatic Christian philosopher-theologian, fully aware of his intellectual debt to religious doctrine. He was convinced, however, that Christian thinkers should be ready to dispute rationally on any topic, especially theological issues, not only among themselves but also with non-Christians of all sorts. Since in his view Jews accept the Old Testament and heretics the New Testament, he thought Christians could argue some issues with both groups on the basis of commonly accepted religious authority. However, because other non-Christians, "for instance, Mohammedans and pagans, do not agree with us about the authority of any scripture on the basis of which they can be convinced . . . it is necessary to have recourse to natural reason, to which everyone is compelled to assent—although where theological issues are concerned it cannot do the whole job" (since some of the data of theology are initially accessible only in Scripture).[1] Moreover, Aquinas differed from many of his thirteenth-century Christian colleagues in the breadth and depth of his respect for Islamic and Jewish philosopher-theologians, especially Avicenna and Maimonides. He saw them as valued coworkers in the vast project of philosophical theology, clarifying and supporting religious doctrine by philosophical analysis and argumentation. His own commitment to that project involved him in contributing to almost all the areas of philosophy recognized since antiquity, omitting only natural philosophy (the precursor of natural science).

A line of thought with such strong connections to powerful antecedents might have resulted in no more than a pious amalgam. Aquinas's philosophy avoids eclecticism, however, because of his own innovative approach to organizing and reasoning about all the topics included under the overarching medieval conception of philosophical Christian theology, and because of his special talents for systematic synthesis and for identifying and skillfully defending, on almost every issue he considers, the most sensible available position.

Because Aquinas developed most of his thought within the formal confines of thirteenth-century theology, and because this has in turn affected his place in the history of philosophy and the assessment of his work, some attention must be paid to the ways in which much of what we recognize as philosophy was an essential component of what he thought of as theology.

Aquinas devotes the first three books of *Summa contra Gentiles* to a systematic development of natural theology, which he saw as part of philosophy.[2] As part of philosophy, natural theology must be based entirely on "principles known by the natural light of intellect,"[3] principles of the sort that underlie Aristotle's metaphysics, which Aristotle himself thought of as culminating in theology (see Aquinas's interpretation of that thought in the prooemium to his *Sententia super Metaphysicam* [*Commentary on Aristotle's Metaphysics*]). In fact, the way Aquinas works in *SCG* I–III strongly suggests that he may have thought of natural theology as a science subordinate to metaphysics, somewhat as he would have understood optics to be subordinate to geometry.

There is something odd about that project of his that scholars have sought to understand. By Aquinas's day, the churchmen governing universities had overcome most of their initial misgivings about the recently recovered works of the pagan Aristotle and had acknowledged officially that the study of Aristotelian physics and metaphysics was compatible with the then universally recognized availability of revealed truths about God. Medieval Christians had come to appreciate the ancient philosophers' attempts to uncover truths about God on the basis of observation and reasoning alone as having been justified, even commendable, given their ignorance of revelation. Although no philosopher in Aquinas's circumstances could have justifiably undertaken a new project of natural theology heuristically, nonetheless, from their point of view no opprobrium would attach to natural theology taken up expositionally. The aim of such an enterprise would be not to develop theology from scratch but rather to show, in the spirit of Romans 1:20, the extent to which what had been supernaturally revealed could, in theory, have been naturally discovered. Such an enterprise is what *SCG* I–III seems to represent, in the view of some contemporary scholars.

What Aquinas himself says about his purpose in writing *Summa contra Gentiles* suggests that what he wrote had at least its formal cause in his consideration of the interrelation of philosophy and Christianity. He begins by writing about the concerns of a wise person, one of those "who give things an appropriate order and direction and govern them well."[4] Obviously, such a person has to be concerned with goals and sources, and so the wisest person will be "one whose attention is turned toward the universal goal, which is also the universal source," which Aquinas takes to be God.[5] Because this natural theology is oriented as it is, "it must be called the greatest wisdom itself, as considering the absolutely highest cause of all."[6] Therefore, the highest, most universal explanatory truth must be wisdom's concern.

Anyone aspiring to wisdom will attend to metaphysics, since, Aquinas reports, Aristotle rightly identified metaphysics as "the science of truth—not of just any truth, but of the truth that is the origin of all truth, the truth that pertains to the first principle of being for all things."[7] And, as Aquinas says in an observation that suits his own enterprise, "sometimes divine wisdom proceeds from human philosophy's starting points."[8] Nonetheless, since it is the business of one and the same science "to pursue one of two contraries and to repel the other... the role of the wise person is to meditate on the truth, especially the truth regarding the first principle, and to discuss it with others, but also to fight against the falsity that is its contrary."[9] The truth regarding the first principle will be the truth about God, supposing natural theology can show that God exists; and so the explanatory truth associated here with metaphysics is the truth associated also with theology.

In this pursuit by way of reason, Aquinas must and does shun "authoritative arguments" of any sort, but he shows good sense in not restricting himself to "demonstrative arguments" in developing natural theology. He does, of course, use demonstrative arguments when he thinks that he has them, but, like almost all philosophers of any period, he recognizes philosophy's need for "probable arguments" as well. A demonstrative argument takes as its premises propositions that explain the fact in the argument's conclusion by elucidating its causes (or, sometimes, its effects), and so it produces, or presents, scientific understanding. A probable argument, the sort that has always been most prevalent in philosophy, is one based on premises of any sort that are accepted widely or by experts in the relevant field; and so one group may be convinced by a probable argument that another group rejects.

In addition, Aquinas also frequently engages in what has come to be called philosophical theology, the application of reason to revelation. Philosophical theology shares the methods of natural theology broadly conceived—in other words, analysis and argumentation of all the sorts accepted in philosophy—but it lifts natural theology's restriction on premises, accepting as assumptions revealed propositions. This includes those that are initially inaccessible to unaided reason, such as the "mysteries" of Christian doctrine. In his many works of philosophical theology, Aquinas tests the coherence of doctrinal propositions (including the mysteries), attempts explanations of them, uncovers their logical connections with other doctrinal propositions, and so on, in order to bear out his conviction that the doctrines themselves are eminently understandable and acceptable, and that the apparent incoherence of some of them is only a feature of our initial, superficial view of them.

Aquinas's *Summa theologiae* is the paradigm of philosophical theology. The very first Article of the very first Question makes it clear at once that it is not natural theology of which *Summa theologiae* is a summa, since it begins by asking whether we need any "other teaching, besides philosophical studies," which in Aquinas's usage means the studies that medieval beginners in theology would have just completed in the arts faculty. The question arises because philosophical studies are characterized not only as dealing with "the things that are subject to reason" but also as encompassing "all beings, including God," as a consequence of which there is a part of philosophy that is theology.

Although Aquinas accepts this characterization of philosophy's subject matter as universal and as including a part that is properly called theology, he offers several arguments to support his claim that revealed theology is nonetheless not superfluous. In one of those arguments, he claims that a thing's "capacity for being cognized in various ways brings about a difference between sciences." By this he means that different sciences can reason to some of the same conclusions on the basis of different premises or evidence. In his example, he points out that in order to support the proposition that the earth is round a naturalist uses empirical observations, while a cosmologist might support that same conclusion on a strictly formal basis.

"And for that reason," he concludes, "nothing prevents the same things from being treated by philosophical studies insofar as they can be cognized by the light of natural reason, and also by another science insofar as they are cognized by the light of divine revelation. That is why the theology that pertains to *sacra doctrina* [in other words, revealed theology] differs in kind from the theology that is considered a part of philosophy."[10]

In this argument, Aquinas might appear willing to concede that revealed and natural theology differ only in this methodological respect, that they simply constitute two radically different ways of approaching the very same propositions about God and everything else. However, he would not actually concede this. There are propositions that belong uniquely to revealed theology's subject matter, simply because the different premises with which revealed theology begins can also lead to conclusions not available to unaided reason. And, of course, no doctrinal proposition that is initially available to human beings only in virtue of having been revealed by God can be part of natural theology's subject matter.

On the other hand, no propositions appropriate to natural theology are excluded from *ST*'s subject matter. The propositions that belong to natural theology form a proper subset of those that belong to revealed theology:

> It was necessary that human beings be instructed by divine revelation even as regards the things about God that human reason can explore. For the truth about God investigated by a few on the basis of reason [without relying on revelation] would emerge for people [only] after a long time and tainted with many mistakes. And yet all human well-being, which has to do with God, depends on the cognition of that truth. Therefore, it was necessary for human beings to be instructed about divine matters through divine revelation so that [the nature of human] well-being might emerge for people more conveniently and with greater certainty.[11]

When he sums up his examination of *sacra doctrina*, or revealed theology, Aquinas says that its "main aim ... is to transmit a cognition of God, and not only as he is in himself, but also as he is the source of things and their goal, especially of the rational creature."[12] Thus, the subject matter of *sacra doctrina*, the theology presented in this *summa* of theology, is the most basic truths about everything, with two provisos: first, it is about God and about things other than God as they relate to God as their source and goal; second, among the things other than God with which it deals, it is especially about human beings, whose study of theology should be motivated by the fact that their well-being depends specially on their grasp of certain theological truths. And, Aquinas insists, universal scope is just what one should expect in a rational investigation of the truth about God: "All things are considered in *sacra doctrina* under the concept of God, either because they are God, or because they have an ordered relationship to God as to their source and goal. It follows from this that the subject of this science is really God," even though the intended explanatory scope of the science is universal.[13]

In referring to *sacra doctrina* as a "science," Aquinas means to characterize it as a systematic, reasoned presentation of an organized body of knowledge consisting of general truths about some reasonably unified subject matter. In that broadly Aristotelian sense, it is not obviously wrong to think of theology as a science (as it would be in the narrower, twentieth-century sense of "science"). It is in that sense that the science of theology as Aquinas develops it in *ST* would now be called philosophical theology, the enterprise of employing the techniques and devices of philosophy in clarifying, supporting, and extending the propositions that are supposed to have been revealed for theology's starting points. Thus, some of the work of philosophical theology is an attempt to explain revealed propositions and systematically work out their implications. Like natural theology, which is subordinate to metaphysics, philosophical theology is a subordinate science. However, because it begins its work on divinely revealed propositions, Aquinas identifies the science to which it is subordinate as God's knowledge of himself and everything else, available to human beings directly only in the afterlife.[14] As he says earlier, "For us, the goal of faith is to arrive at an understanding of what we believe—[which is] as if a practitioner of a subordinate science were to acquire in addition the knowledge possessed by a practitioner of the higher science. In that case the things that were only believed before would come to be known, or understood."[15]

Not even the doctrinal mysteries are impervious to rational investigation, although unaided reason could never have discovered them. Regarding one central mystery, for example, Aquinas says: "It is impossible to arrive at a cognition of the Trinity of the divine persons by means of natural reason."[16] However, he says this in the twenty-second of a series of seventy-seven Articles of *ST* devoted to analyzing and arguing about the details of Trinity, in other words, in the midst of subjecting this mystery to philosophical theology. As he explains in the very Article in which he rules out the possibility of rationally discovering that there are three divine persons:

> There are two ways in which reason is employed regarding any matter... in one way to provide sufficient proof of something fundamental... in the other way to show that consequent effects are suited to something fundamental that has already been posited.... It is in the first way, then, that reason can be employed to prove that God is one, and things of that sort. But it is in the second way that reason is employed in a clarification of Trinity. For once Trinity has been posited, reasonings of that sort are suitable, although not so as to provide a sufficient proof of the Trinity of persons by those reasonings.[17]

Aquinas is also careful to point out that it is not mere intellectual curiosity or even a defense of the faith that is served by a rational clarification of the doctrine of the Trinity. In his view, this application of philosophical theology—confirming faith by reason, showing that belief in the Trinity is not after all irrational, exposing the intricate connections between these and other doctrinal propositions—aids one's understanding of creation and salvation.

The present volume is intended as a guide to Aquinas's thinking on almost all the major topics on which he wrote. In 1993 one of us (Eleonore Stump), together with Norman Kretzmann († 1998), edited a comparable volume, which appeared as *The Cambridge Companion to Aquinas.*[18] That well-received volume, however, consisted of only ten essays, contained comparatively little on Aquinas's treatment of wholly theological issues, and had almost nothing to say about Aquinas's life and influence. The present book is much fuller. In addition to documenting Aquinas's life and work, it includes contributions that explain the Greek, patristic, Jewish, and Islamic influences on Aquinas's thought, and it also contains entries that show the historical reception and development of Aquinas's views. There are many more essays exploring the philosophical and theological topics discussed by Aquinas.

The book begins with a part devoted to historical background. This part includes an account of Aquinas's life and works by Jean-Pierre Torrell, whose *Saint Thomas Aquinas: The Person and His Work* is the currently most authoritative biography of Aquinas.[19] It also contains a series of essays that set Aquinas in his intellectual context. These essays focus on the sources that are likely to have influenced his thinking, the most prominent of which (apart from the Bible, of course) were certain Greek philosophers (chiefly Aristotle), Latin Christian authors, such as Augustine, and Jewish and Islamic writers, such as Maimonides and Avicenna. The subsequent parts of the book address topics that Aquinas himself discussed. These include metaphysics, the existence and nature of God, ethics and action theory, providence and evil, epistemology, philosophy of mind and human nature, the nature of language, and an array of topics in philosophical theology, including Trinity, Incarnation, sacraments, and resurrection, among others. These parts include more than thirty contributions on topics central to Aquinas's own worldview. The final parts of the volume address the development of Aquinas's thought and its historical influence.

Although the volume thus aims at being comprehensive, readers familiar with Aquinas will undoubtedly find that some part of Aquinas's thought that strikes them as particularly important is not represented here. Sadly, it is not possible to do everything in one volume, even a fat one. At any rate, it is abundantly clear that some compromise is necessary between the ideal plan of presenting all of Aquinas's thought and any practicable plan for one book. We have tried to pick those issues and topics that allow a reader to see Aquinas's whole worldview in broad outline and to appropriate in particular some of its richest and most powerful parts.

Aquinas's philosophy includes reflection on some basic metaphysical topics while extending to discussions of what can be known by reason when it comes to the existence of God.[20] He has views to offer on questions such as "What is it for something to exist?" "How should we distinguish between things in the world?" "What is it for something to be an individual in the world?" and "How should we understand causation?" He also has views to offer on questions such as "Can we know that God exists?" and "Can we give some account of God's nature?" Parts II and III of this book try to explain and comment on what Aquinas has to say by way of answer to such questions.

Yet Aquinas's intellectual interests range beyond metaphysics and natural theology. As the list of topics given above shows, he also had a concern with many other areas of philosophy as well. Aquinas often insists that moral philosophy would be redundant if people lack freedom of choice. So Part IV begins with an account of

Aquinas's views on human freedom and agency, and it continues with consideration of Aquinas's approach to happiness, law, natural law, conscience, virtue and vice, and the theological virtues, among other things. Part V deals with Aquinas's theories of human knowledge and the nature of mind, as well as the relation of reason to faith. Part VI traces Aquinas's account of the nature of language and its limits when it comes to God.

The next part covers topics in philosophical theology. It includes an account of Aquinas's views on the problem of evil. Other chapters present Aquinas's account of the Trinity, the Incarnation, life after death, prayer, and the work of the Holy Spirit, among other things. Part VIII focuses on the progress of Aquinas's thought and its influence. It includes accounts of the ways in which Aquinas's ideas developed over time and the different ways in which subsequent thinkers have viewed and interpreted Aquinas's thought.

Finally, any attempt to present the views of a philosopher in an earlier historical period that is meant to foster reflection on that thinker's views needs to be both historically faithful and also philosophically engaged. So the present book combines both exposition and evaluation insofar as it is appropriate for any particular contributor to engage in both. It is our hope, therefore, that this *Handbook* will prove useful to someone wanting to learn about Aquinas's philosophy and theology while also looking for help in philosophical interaction with it.[21]

For invaluable assistance in preparing this volume for publication we are much indebted to Barb Manning, Stephen Chanderbhan, Zita Toth, and Gideon Jeffrey. We are also grateful to Peter Ohlin of Oxford University Press for helpful advice and for his patience in waiting for a work that was longer in the making than we originally expected it to be.

NOTES

1. *Summa contra Gentiles*, I.2.11; hereinafter *SCG*.
2. Cf. *Summa theologiae*, I q.1 a.1 ad 2; hereinafter *ST*.
3. *ST* I q.1 a.2.
4. *SCG* I.1.2.
5. *SCG* I.1.3.
6. *SCG* II.4.874.
7. *SCG* I.1.5.
8. *SCG* II.4.875.
9. *SCG* I.1.6.
10. *ST* I q.1 a.1 ad 2.
11. *ST* I q.1 a.1.
12. *ST* I q.2, intro.
13. *ST* I q.1 a.7.
14. *ST* I q.1 a.2.
15. *Expositio super librum Boethii De trinitate* 2.2, ad 7.

16. *ST* I q.32 a.1.

17. *ST* I q.32 a.1.

18. Cambridge: Cambridge University Press.

19. Jean-Pierre Torrell, *Saint Thomas Aquinas: The Person and His Work* (Washington, D.C.: Catholic University of America Press, 1996).

20. It is often said that Aquinas thinks that he can prove the existence of God. But he does not. For Aquinas, God's existence is identical with his essence, which Aquinas takes to be incomprehensible to us. He does, however, argue that we might make a philosophical case for "God exists" being true (on a certain understanding of "God"). For the distinction between "the existence of God" and "God exists," see Lubor Velecky, *Aquinas' Five Arguments in the "Summa Theologiae" 1a 2, 3* (Kampen: Pharos, 1994).

21. Parts of this introduction are revised versions of sections in the entry "Thomas Aquinas," by Norman Kretzmann and Eleonore Stump, *Encyclopedia of Philosophy* (London: Routledge Press, 1998) and a small section of the prefatory material taken from Eleonore Stump's *Aquinas* (London and New York: Routledge, 2003).

PART I

HISTORICAL BACKGROUND

CHAPTER 1

LIFE AND WORKS

JEAN-PIERRE TORRELL, O.P.

The Early Years

Thomas Aquinas was born in 1224/25 in the family castle of Roccasecca in southern Italy between Rome and Naples. Of minor nobility, his family was related to that of the counts of Aquino, from which he would be given his name. At the age of five or six years, being the youngest son of a large family, he was offered as an oblate to the Benedictine abbey of Monte Cassino. His biographers agree that his parents cherished the wish that he would someday be the Abbot. Aside from a good formation in Latin letters, the child acquired at the abbey a profound understanding of the Bible and a solid initiation in the study of Augustine and Gregory, whose influence is apparent in all of his works. He maintained above all a contemplative orientation that remains the distinctive mark of his theology.[1]

Due to troubles caused by the war between Pope Gregory IX and Frederick II, the young monk was sent to Naples in 1239 at the age of fourteen or fifteen to begin there his studies at the *studium generale* founded fifteen years earlier by Frederick II. Sicily and the south of Italy were, at that time, the seat of an intense intellectual life that was encouraged by the emperor. Thanks to the numerous translations of Michel Scot and his school, Aristotelian science, Arabic astronomy, and Greek philosophy and medicine were flourishing at Palermo, Salerno, and Naples. Little is known precisely on these years of Aquinas's studies at Naples except the names of two of his professors: Master Martin and Peter of Ireland. They are known well enough that we can deduce that Aquinas could have familiarized himself very early with the natural philosophy of Aristotle and his metaphysics, as well as with the work of the Arabic commentator Averroës and probably also with that of the Jew Maimonides.[2]

At Naples, Aquinas made the acquaintance of the Order of Preachers (Dominicans) who had been there since 1231; he took their habit in the spring of

1244. This initiative on his part was met with strong family opposition that was manifested by the kidnapping of the novice and his imprisonment at Roccasecca for about fifteen months (spring 1244 to summer 1245).[3] Tocco reports that he turned the forced leisure to profit by praying, reading the Bible in its entirety, and studying the *Sentences* of Peter Lombard.[4] Two shorts treatises that have long been attributed to this period, *De fallaciis* and *De propositionibus modalibus*, are now known to be inauthentic. The persistence of Aquinas in his choice succeeded in convincing his obstinate family. This episode highlights a spiritual characteristic of Aquinas that would mark him profoundly in his life and his work. In his writings on religious life, his attachment to the intellectual ideal (study, teaching, preaching) and to the mendicant poverty of his order is evident.[5]

Having been released by his family, the young Dominican was sent to Paris (1245–48), to the convent of St. James, to continue his studies under the direction of Albert the Great, who introduced him, most notably, to the work of Pseudo-Dionysius. He deepened his knowledge of the *Ethics* of Aristotle and appropriated the methods of the masters of the arts, whose courses he appears to have frequented. Sent with Albert to Cologne to found a new Dominican *studium*, Aquinas completed his formation as an assistant to his teacher (1248–52). At the end of that time (or shortly thereafter),[6] he taught *Super Isaiam* and *Super Ieremiam*, the first and precious witnesses of his spiritual approach to the Bible.[7]

First Assignment to Paris (1252–1259)

Sent back to Paris by his superiors to take his masters in *sacra doctrina*, Aquinas stayed there seven years (1252–59). At first as a bachelor of the sentences under the master Eli Brunet, he spent two years (1252–54) commenting on the *Sentences* of Peter Lombard but did not manage to write his text until 1256. This "manual," which had been used in Paris since Alexander of Hales, groups into four books the divers opinions (*sententiae*) of the Fathers of the Church and of the medieval theologians according to the major subjects of sacred doctrine: (1) the triune God is indivisible in His essence and in His three Persons; (2) God considered as Creator and His works; (3) the Incarnation and the Redemption; and (4) the sacraments and the last things. The commentary of Aquinas is shot through with his personal views and he does not hesitate to distance himself from Lombard or to disagree with him. Still a young theologian, he had borrowed a good deal from his master, Albert, and from his contemporary, the Franciscan Bonaventure. His concern for documentation, however, can already be observed by the frequency of his quotations: Aristotle (2,000; *Nicomachean Ethics:* 800; *Metaphysics*: 300; *Physics* and *De Anima*: approximately 250), Augustine (1,500), Denis the Areopagite (500), Gregory the Great (280), John Damascene (240), and so on. These numbers highlight a feature that remains constant: Aquinas does not think in a closed box but rather maintains a dialogue with all of the thinkers available to him. *De principiis naturae* and especially *De ente et essentia* must be attributed to this period. They both display a strong Avicennian influence.[8]

Once a master in theology (1256), Aquinas found himself engaged in the quarrel with the secular masters at Paris (William of Saint-Amour and his partisans), who were opposed to allowing mendicant religious into the university.[9] Aquinas refuted their arguments in *Contra impugnantes Dei cultum et religionem* (1256), where he takes up the defense of his order and reclaims for religious the rights to study and to teach. This conflict was prolonged for a while with new adversaries (Gerard of Abbeville and Nicolas of Lisieux) under different aspects and provoked the publication of two other works: *De perfectione spiritualis vitae* (1269–70) and *Contra doctrinam retrahentium a religione* (1270–71). Little known, these books uncover the doctrine of the religious life of the author and throw some light on the combative character of his personality.[10]

The primary obligation of Aquinas consisted, nevertheless, in composing his magisterial commentaries on the Bible; *legere* was the first charge of the *Magister in Sacra pagina*. It is not known exactly which of the books of the Bible Aquinas commented on during this period (probably some epistles of Paul), but he was faithful to this obligation during his life and several of his commentaries have been conserved: aside from *Isaiah*, *Jeremiah*, and *Lamentations*, the following courses must be mentioned: (*Lecturae* or *Expositiones*) *On Job* (Orvieto: 1261–65), *On Matthew* (Paris: 1269–70), *On John* (Paris: 1270–72), *On the Psalms* (Naples: 1273). It is difficult to know exactly the dates for the commentaries on the epistles of Paul.[11] Long neglected, these thousands of pages of biblical theology have recently become the object of growing attention for both their exegetical technique and their bearing on speculative theology.[12] Comprising an important part of his work, these commentaries must be read and used alongside the systematic expositions. These latter also give a decisive role to the Scriptures (25,000 biblical citations in the *Summa theologiae* alone) as they are not merely an authority amongst others, but the very source and structure of theological exposition.[13] Conscious of the limits of allegorical exegesis, Aquinas privileged the literal sense, which he judged to be the only sense suited to theological argumentation. He did not reduce it, though, to the philosophical sense but included in it the spiritual sense.

The second great obligation of a Master was to hold Disputed Questions (*disputare*), either ordinary or public.[14] The questions *De ueritate* belong to the first category. Each day, after having given the morning lesson, the master and his bachelor would rejoin their students in the afternoon to "dispute" on a chosen theme. As the three hours allowed for this active pedagogy were insufficient to exhaust the subject, they would proceed article by article; eventually, certain very short articles could be regrouped into one meeting and, inversely, a longer or more delicate subject could be broken up into several meetings. The result (objections, replies, and magisterial determinations) were reassembled later into one text and published together in final form: a question with a unified answer. The elaboration of *De ueritate* was thus spread out over three academic years (1256–59) at about eighty articles per year, which correspond roughly to the number of days of teaching. Without being able to give a detailed account of its contents, it can at least be said that the whole is divided into two sections: (1) truth and knowledge (q.1–20); (2) the good and the appetite for good (q.21–29). Aside from the intrinsic interest of the subjects treated, *De ueritate* is particularly interesting for following and understanding the thought of Aquinas. On certain points (providence, Christology, grace, instrumental causality), he had already changed his opinion from those expressed in the commentary on the *Sentences* and he would change his views again in the later works.[15]

Unlike the ordinary daily disputations proper to the school of a determined Master, the public quodlibetal disputations only took place twice a year during Lent and Advent. They took place in two sessions: in the first, and as their name indicates, the assistants, masters, students, or even curious onlookers could raise any sort of question (*de quolibet ad voluntatem cuiuslibet*). The master would normally allow his bachelor to respond and would not intervene unless he ran into problem; he would give his magisterial determination in the second session, which would take place the next day or several days later.[16] Aquinas left two series of such questions: the first (*Quodlibets* VII–XI) date from the first period in Paris; the next set (I–VI and XII) dates from the second period (1268–72). The subjects treated are numerous (260, with more than 20 for each meeting); the questions of high speculation are well represented, but the practical questions are not lacking. The quodlibetal literature is deeply rooted in the life of the university (a quarrel between mendicants and seculars; the unity or plurality of substantial forms), but the subjects of private or public morality and of economics relate also to the pastoral preoccupations of the participants. In the life of the university, then, is reflected that of the entire era and this makes a fascinating subject of study.[17]

Associated with this same era, the *Super Boetium De Trinitate* is one of the few testimonies of his own writing (along with a part of the *Summa contra Gentiles* and the commentary on the *Sentences*); it is also the only commentary of this text of Boethius to be written in the thirteenth century. While the subject matter of the work makes it eminently theological in character, this work provides the most extended Thomistic explanation of the methods of the various sciences.[18] Fruit of personal reflection carried out with pen in hand, the date of this work is uncertain: "somewhere between the middle of *De ueritate* and the beginning of *Contra Gentiles*, either in 1257–58 or at the beginning of 1259".[19] The same is true for the other commentary on Boethius: *Expositio libri Boetii De ebdomadibus* is probably after *Super Boetium*, but it is not possible to say more exactly.[20] Essentially a work on metaphysics, the purpose of this short work is to discover whether beings are good in their essence or by participation; this is why philosophers naturally begin their study of Aquinas's account of participation with this work.[21]

Stay in Italy: Orvieto (end 1259–1265)

At the end of the preceding period (June 1259), Aquinas had to go to Valenciennes to the General Chapter of the Dominicans to participate in a commission charged with the task of promoting studies. It is not clear exactly when he left for Italy, where he went first to Naples (?; 1259–61)[22] and then to Orvieto (1261–65). In this last convent, Aquinas took the role of convent lector and helped his confreres prepare for the ministries of teaching and confession. He also brought with him several major works.

The date of the *Summa contra Gentiles* (*SCG*) has been the object of extended research of specialists.[23] It is certain that the fifty-three first chapters were written before he left Paris, that Book I was finished in Italy between 1259 and 1261, Book II in Orvieto in 1261–62, Book III in 1263–64, Book IV in 1264–65.[24] The work may be characterized as having two purposes: "to display the Catholic faith" and "to reject the contrary errors." The *SCG* has given rise to the most varied interpretations (philosophical, missional, apologetical, ecumenical). It is a theological enterprise, as the use of arguments from authority (Scripture, the Fathers of the Church, the Symbols of faith) clearly show. The work proposes to study all that human reason can discover about God:

I. What is proper to God: His existence and His perfections.
II. The procession of creatures from God; that is to say, the act of creation and its effects.
III. The ordering of creatures to God as their end: providence and divine governance.
IV. The truths inaccessible to reason and known only by faith: God as Trinity, the Incarnation of the Word and redemption, sacraments and the last things.

The order of the first three books clearly echoes the structure Aquinas had already found in the *Sentences* of Lombard, and it prefigures the circular structure that he sets out in the *Summa theologiae*: all things come from God and all things return to God under His guidance. It should be said that this structure also follows Aquinas's own logic, as was shown by G. Emery.[25] Parallel to the *SCG* and moving back and forth between the two works, Aquinas wrote the first part of the *Compendium theologiae* (1–246: *De fide*). This "handbook," written at the request of his friend Raynald, would be taken back up in Naples in 1272–73, but would remain unfinished.[26]

At the same time (1263–65), Aquinas wrote *Super Iob*, which offers a lovely example of literal exegesis that is used in the service of doctrinal reflection on the suffering of the just innocent, which suffering is reconciled with divine goodness: "The entire *intentio* of the book is to show by probable reasons that human affairs are governed by divine providence."[27] This was also the central subject of Book III of *Summa contra Gentiles*, which was written at about the same time; it can be seen that Aquinas knew how to organize his work.

Many other works of more modest size were written at the same time to satisfy friendly requests: *De emptione et uenditione* (1262) is on the morality of lending with interest; *Contra errores Graecorum* (1263–64) is a study of the contested doctrines that were given him by Pope Urban IV. To the very end of this period in Orvieto (unless they belong to the beginning of his stay in Rome), we can also attribute *De rationibus fidei, Expositio super primam et secundam Decretalem*, and *De articulis fidei et ecclesiae sacramentis*, which are brief explications of the Catholic faith written at the request of various correspondents.[28]

From amid these various works, the composition of the Office of *Corpus Christi* (1264), which was also requested by Pope Urban IV, must be brought out. Once contested by the Bollandists, its authenticity is accepted today and it must be noted that this is an important text for understanding its author's Eucharistic doctrine. The authenticity of the hymn *Adoro Te*, also suspected, is no longer in doubt thanks to the work of R. Wielockx.[29] It is, once again, at the request of Urban IV that Aquinas undertook the *Catena aurea*, a commentary on the gospels with the help of excerpts from the Fathers of the Church (*On Matthew* was finished in 1264; *Mark, Luke*, and *John* were completed in Rome from 1265 to 1268). This work reveals Aquinas's stunning erudition in the Patristics: he is the first in the Occident to use the complete corpus of the first ecumenical councils.[30] Well versed in the Greek and Latin Fathers (57 Greeks and 22 Latins), he has an affinity for some authors: Gregory the Great (2,470 uses), John Chrysostom (3,563 uses in the scriptural commentaries), but above all Augustine whose considerable influence (some 10,000 citations in the entire works of Aquinas), which grew over the course of Aquinas's work (*Sentences*: 1,518; *ST*: 2,801), is particularly clear on the subjects of the divine ideas (a transposition of a platonic theme), the Trinity, the fittingness of the Incarnation, the nature of the soul, beatitude, law, grace and sin, and so on.[31] Called a "turning point" by Weisheipl, the *Catena aurea* served as a source of references for Aquinas himself over the course of his career and exerted a great influence on the rest of the history of theology.[32]

Stay in Rome (1265–1268)

In 1265, Aquinas was sent to Rome by his superiors to found an "experimental" *studium* at Santa Sabina for some select students of his Order over whom he would have complete authority.[33] According to Ptolemy of Lucca, Aquinas would have once again commented on Book I of the *Sentences*; Ptolemy said he had seen a copy of this work, but he also said that the manuscript had disappeared. Over the course of the twentieth century, the researchers of the Leonine Commission found anonymous annotations in the margins of a commentary on Lombard in a manuscript at Oxford (Lincoln College, lat. 95). L. Boyle was certain that these were the course notes of a student of Aquinas that reflect the lost commentary on Book I of the *Sentences*. This fragmentary text, which corresponds to Distinctions 1–18 and 23, was recently edited by John F. Boyle who has no doubt regarding its authenticity;[34] other scholars are also of this opinion.[35] It is nevertheless permissible to raise a few doubts: many of the annotations are clearly Thomistic, but others are not. Those that are authentic, far from representing a new work and an intermediary stage in the evolution of Aquinas's thought presuppose rather the prior existence of the works from which they are borrowed. The identification of the marginalia with the lost commentary seems, then, to remain a matter of conjecture.[36]

By all accounts, the three years in Rome (1265–68) were occupied with several major projects of which the principal was the beginning of the *Summa theologiae* (*ST*). The writing of this work seems to have been provoked by the dissatisfaction Aquinas felt after his experience at Orvieto. To compensate for the insufficient formation received by his young confreres, he would have conceived a new work that would treat the entirety of theology, dogmatic and moral, in one organic and ordered whole.

The dates of the writing of the *ST* were long contested by scholars; here is what seems to be the most certain. Written in Rome between 1265 and 1268, the *Prima Pars* (*ST* I) was circulating in Italy by the latter date. The *Prima Secundae* (*ST* I-II) was not begun before the return to Paris (1268); according to an old opinion, its completion was in the summer of 1270,[37] but Gauthier has shown that it was not written until 1271.[38] As to the *Secunda Secundae* (*ST* II-II), begun shortly afterwards, it was finished before December 1272. It was thought until recently that the 20 or 25 first questions of the *Tertia Pars* had been written in Paris at the end of the winter of 1271–72, but it seems more likely that this part of the *Tertia Pars* (*ST* III) was written in Naples by December 6, 1273, the date when Aquinas stopped writing. He had reached the sacrament of penance.[39] The rest, known under the name "*Supplementum*," was written by his disciples and based on his commentary on the *Sentences*. Aquinas would have, thus, carried with him the burden of this work during the last seven years of his life in spite of the other occupations that he undertook at the same time.[40]

The structure of the *ST* has given rise to numerous discussions.[41] Aquinas makes use of a circular structure that leads the reader in a dynamic movement of the "exit" (*exitus*) of creatures from the first Principle, Creator of all things, and their "return" (*reditus*) to Him. If a Neoplatonic influence is not to be excluded, it is not to be overestimated either, as this movement is not a necessary emanation but rather a free creation. Aquinas more likely found his inspiration in contemplation of God of the Bible, the Alpha and Omega of all things. Without having exclusive claim to this circular way of seeing things (it is to be found first in Albert and, to a lesser degree, in Bonaventure), Aquinas uses it in several of his works where he is able to integrate into it the contingency of the history of salvation and, above all, the work of Christ "come from God and [going] to God" (John 13:3).

As to its content, the Thomistic synthesis begins with a sort of preface (*ST* I q.1) in which the author explains the nature and the method of *sacra doctrina* (a concept with more breadth than our "theology"). The *Prima Pars* treats of God in himself in this way: first in the divine essence (q.2–26) and then in the Trinity of Persons (q.27–43). Contrary to what is sometimes said, this is not a purely philosophical treatment of *De Deo uno* followed by *De Deo trino* of the Christians, but rather this is the one and only living God of the Bible known through His works and through revelation that He made of Himself (cf. Exod. 3:14 and Rom. 1:18 ff.) and at whose service Aquinas placed all of the intellectual resources he had at his disposal (Aristotle and his commentators, Boethius and Augustine, among others). This is followed by a consideration of the way in which creatures proceed from God: creation in itself (q.44–46); the distinction of creatures: in general and in particular, according to the good and the bad (q.47–49); spiritual creatures (q.50–64); the work of six days, which is a commentary on the biblical narrative of creation (q.65–74); man, in his rational nature and as the image of God (q.75–102); the government of creation, where secondary causes concur with the work of God (q.103–19).

The study of the return of man to God begins in the *Secunda Pars*. This enormous part is divided into two very unequal parts: first the ultimate *end* of this return movement (*ST* I-II q.1–5: beatitude), then the *ways* by which the human being comes to this end or, to the contrary, turns away from it. This vast category of "ways" stretches out over two volumes. The *Prima Secundae* first takes up human actions in themselves (q.6–89), which is to say voluntary and free actions that are, thus, capable of either good or evil (q.6–21). Then it treats the passions of the soul (q.22–48). Having come through Cicero, Seneca, and Ambrose of Milan, the stoic heritage contributes greatly here. Next comes the interior qualifications of human actions, the virtues and vices generally (q.49–89), then the exterior factors that influence human action: law (q.90–108) and grace (q.109–14).

The *Secunda Secundae* is a detailed reprise of these first things as an analysis of the theological virtues: faith, hope, and love (*ST* II-II q.1–46), the cardinal virtues: prudence, justice, fortitude, and temperance (q.47–170). With each virtue is included its proper acts and contrary vices. This is followed by a study of the charisms and states of life in the Church. This section is completed by the treatise on the contemplative life (q.171–89), which corresponds, by provisional inclusion, with the definition of beatitude at the beginning of the consideration of human action.[42]

The *Tertia Pars* is consecrated to Jesus Christ who, in his humanity, is the way to beatitude. The first section (*ST* III q.1–59) is divided in two major sections in which Aquinas studies: (1) the ontology and the psychology of Christ in the mystery of the Incarnation in itself (q.1–26) and (2) that which the Word did and suffered in his flesh for the salvation of humanity (q.27–59). The second section is constituted by a study of the sacraments: in general (q.60–65), then baptism, Eucharist, penance (q.66–90; the rest is left unfinished). A third section would have given a detailed consideration of the blessed life, which man enters through the resurrection of Christ, but Aquinas died before being able to write this part (the *Supplementum*, which sometimes completes certain editions of the *ST*, was composed by his disciples based on his *Commentary on the Sentences* and thus does not reflect his final thoughts on the matter).

As to its sources, the Thomistic synthesis owes tribute to multiple philosophies from stoicism (through Cicero and St. Ambrose) to Neoplatonism (through Augustine and Pseudo-Dionysius), but Aristotle is the dominant authority along with his Arabian (Avicenna and Averroës) and Jewish (Avicebron and Maimonides) commentators. From a theological point of view, the predominant influence is that of the Bible and the Fathers of the Church.

These elements are, nevertheless, only materials and sometimes even simple instruments for the unified theological project at the service of the subject to be known: God Himself. Everything else is placed in relation to Him. Developed above all in the *Super Boetium De Trinitate* and the *ST* (I q.1), this theological theory is at once speculative and practical. Its contemplative orientation (*speculativa*) remains within the line of the *intellectus fidei* of Augustine and Anselm but, in the service of this end, Aquinas uses two givens from Aristotle.

The notion of "science" is verified as soon as there is "discourse" in which reasoning about two given truths puts them into relation with each other: the first, which is better known, plays the role of the explanatory principle; the second is dependent insofar as it is the explained conclusion. Little by little, the whole of revealed truth is thus organized, according to its internal relations, into a coherent synthesis that reproduces, in a human manner, something of the intelligibility of the divine design of the world and the history of salvation.[43]

The theory of subalternation, also received from Aristotle, is of utmost importance for the status of this *sui generis* science: thanks to subalternation, theology is attached by faith to the knowledge that God has of Himself. It is situated on the trajectory that goes from faith to the beatific vision: the end of this *scientia* (also called *sacra doctrina*) is contemplation of the first Truth.[44] Equally practical, this knowledge is the director of human action, which it must orient properly and clearly toward its final end, God Himself. *ST* is not only a dogmatic reflection centered on the mystery of God; it also develops an important part of moral theology that treats of human action in an ample way unequaled until that time.

Not all was equally new in this vast synthesis that takes up and organizes all that was essential of the theological heritage of the preceding centuries. In particular, the metaphysical views that underpinned the project provoked, in that time, lively reactions. The principal merit of the *ST* was and still is to make intelligible the internal connections of that which is given by faith. If some of its "physical" presuppositions (the celestial bodies) hold no interest today except for historians of thought, most of its elaborations remain part of the common good of Catholic theology. The treatise on God and especially the Five Ways to establish His existence, the divine names and the Trinitarian relations; Creation; the ontology of Christ and the instrumental character of His humanity; the relations of human freedom to the all powerful divinity in light of the theology of grace; these are the most remarkable points of the work.

Two features of the work must be brought out more clearly than is usually done. First, there is the moral theology in its entirety that shows itself to be new on two points.

1. It assembles into a single organically structured work all the material of dogmatic and moral theology. This method stands in sharp contrast to the manuals of the time.[45] Ethics is here torn away from the narrow confines of voluntarism and passes from a morality of duty to a morality of virtue and beatitude of profoundly evangelical inspiration.

2. The unification of the treatment of human action in the light of its ultimate end is an intuition that continues to bear fruit.[46]

In strict correspondence with the contemplative nature of theological knowledge, the moral theology of *ST* opens with a consideration of the beatitude to which the Christian is called. It could not proceed in any other way, "because the first Truth, which is the object of faith, being also the end of all our desires and of all our actions, faith acts through charity in a manner which, according to Aristotle, the speculative intellect becomes practical by 'extension.'"[47] Completely impregnated with the theological virtues, theology is therefore able to grow into a spirituality whose main axes easily stand out: the Trinitarian vocation of man, the image of God, restored to the image of the first born son, thanks to the first gift of the all present and acting Holy Spirit. Grace not destroying nature, it is also possible to envisage a spirituality of creation in which the glorious liberty of the children of God can begin to flourish.

Second, in the treatment of Christology, Aquinas integrates for the first time in the Occident the givens from the major Christological councils. His most original contribution is found in the questions consecrated to the "mysteries" of the life of Christ.[48] Aquinas is the first and only one of the medievals not only to speak of the principal events that, from birth to death, mark the human existence of the incarnate Word (the *acta et passa Christi in carne*) but to treat them as a structured whole, conceived as an element in his speculative theology.[49] Each mystery is considered in the context of soteriology along with its ontological and moral implications. Aside from their theological interest, the pages in which Aquinas examines the role of the humanity of Christ in the work of salvation methodically and with careful attention to Scripture and the Fathers have an evident bearing on spiritual theology. The effects of mysteries of the life of Christ in the one who receives them opens up rare and fruitful vistas on the Christian life. For, not only does grace comes to us through Christ; it is also "Christ-molding."[50]

The work of Aquinas is not reducible to the *ST*, but it offers a good overview of his thought. It must be noted, nevertheless, that even though the author's views are strong enough to be found in several of his works, he did evolve and change on several points. *ST* may be read most profitably by keeping in mind that it is the work of a searching spirit. To ignore this would be to transform it, mistakenly, into a rigid system. For, although it is in fact a coherent synthesis, it remains open.[51]

During his stay in Rome, Aquinas not only completed the writing of the *Catena aurea* (1265–68), but he also disputed or wrote several Disputed Questions. The series of ten Questions *De Potentia* (1265–66) brings into view two main subjects. The first six questions are brought together around the theme *De Potentia*:

1. The power of God in general
2. The generative power of God
3. The creative power
4. The creation of matter
5. The conservation in being of created things
6. Miracles.

The last four questions pertain to Trinitarian theology:

7. The simplicity of the divine essence
8. Relation in God
9. The divine persons
10. The procession of the divine persons.

If not in its volume, at least in its metaphysical profundity, *De Potentia* is comparable to *De ueritate* and it represents a link of the greatest importance in the evolution of the thought of the Master. It is not possible to speak of the Thomistic theology of creation, of divine government, or the Trinity without having recourse to these elucidations. The twenty-one questions of *De anima*, held at Santa Sabina during the school year 1266–67, appear to have been disputed before a public comprised of more than just the students of Aquinas; it was the time when Aquinas was writing the corresponding questions of the *ST*. As to the question *De spiritualibus creaturis*, which was disputed or written the following year (1267–68), it was not published until after his return to Paris.[52]

Although its date has long been uncertain, *De diuinis nominibus*, the commentary on the treatise on the *Divine Names* by Pseudo-Dionysius, is to be situated sometime after March 1266 in Rome.[53] Aside from its own proper interest, this work offers the occasion of recalling the importance of the Platonic elements present in Thomistic doctrine.[54] This influence is notable (1,702 citations, of which 899 are from the *Divine Names*); Dionysius is, with Augustine, one of the means by which Neoplatonism counterbalanced what would otherwise be the dominating influence of Aristotle. His supposed apostolic authority is not imposed in an absolute way on Aquinas. Thus, for the knowledge of God, although Aquinas retains his theory of the three approaches (causality, negation, eminence), the apophatism of the *Divine Names* is only a step in a much longer and more global approach in which the positive knowledge of God is admittedly analogical, but real all the same.[55] The Dionysian influence is also felt in numerous other themes such as angelology and the category of sign in the theology of the sacraments. Dionysius is nevertheless carefully criticized on several key points: for Aquinas, God is not beyond being but is the *Ipsum esse subsistens*; being is prior to goodness, and the axiom *Bonum est diffusivum sui* is interpreted in an Aristotelian sense.[56]

Several responses to theological consultations (*Responsiones de 108, de 43, de 6, de 30 et 36 articulis*) also date from this time in Rome (1265–68), as well as the short work *De regno ad regem Cypri*.[57] But the activity of commenting on Aristotle that Aquinas began around that time with *Sentencia libri De anima* must be mentioned. The three books of this work were finished and spread through Italy before September 1268, but *De sensu et sensato*, which completes it, was not finished until 1269 in Paris. As with all of the commentaries on Aristotle, these books were not taught orally but were written in order to prepare for the *ST*.[58]

Second Assignment to Paris (1268–1272)

Aquinas is to be found back in Paris starting in September 1268; three reasons seem to have motivated recalling him there.

There had been a renewed outbreak in the quarrel between the mendicants and the seculars; against the latter, Aquinas would write *De perfectione spiritualis vitae* (1269–70) and *Contra retrahentes* (1270–71). Many questions from the *Quodlibets* II–V and several sermons bear witness as well to this agitation.[59]

Aquinas also had to combat the conservatives who saw in Aristotle nothing but a threat to the Christian faith. From the outset of the propagation of the *Physics*, the question of the eternity of the world was of concern to theologians, in particular, to Bonaventure and Pecham. They declared this thesis inconceivable and thought themselves to have demonstrated that the world had a beginning. Aquinas held, by contrast, that only faith can show that the world began and that it is not possible to construct a proof to the contrary. This thesis was a constant for Aquinas, and it reappeared with force in *De aeternitate mundi* (1271): not only had the beginning of the world not been demonstrated and could not be demonstrated, but it is possible that the world is eternally created.[60] Aquinas placed himself in opposition to the same Franciscan theologians on the subject of anthropology: in order not to attribute spiritual activities and animal functions to the same soul, they postulated the existence of three different souls according to the different levels of human life: vegetative, sensitive, intellectual. For Aquinas, the very same soul exercises the triple function of animation because the higher power of the substantial form includes and realizes the lower power. The unity of the living being of an intellectual nature that is man is thus more perfectly assured. The disagreement took place also in Christology: for the Franciscans, the existence of a *forma corporeitatis* was necessary for the numerical continuity of the body of Christ during the three days of his death; for Aquinas the permanence of the hypostatic union was sufficient to maintain the numerical identity of the body of Christ between the moment of his death and that of his resurrection.[61]

It was also necessary to oppose the monopsychism (only one soul) of the "Averroist" masters of the faculty of arts (notably, Siger de Brabant and Boethius of Dacia).[62] *De unitate intellectus contra averroistas* (Nov.–Dec. 1270) is the pivotal point in the controversy. Making use of the most recent translations of Aristotle and of his commentators, Aquinas shows his adversaries to what extent their Averroës is opposed both to the doctrine of Aristotle and to Christian faith and he embarrasses these philosophers by defying them to give some account of the common experience that "this particular man thinks" (*Hic homo singularis intelligit*).[63]

Despite these various conflicts, Aquinas continued his regular teaching.[64] This is the era of *Super Matthaeum* (1269–1270); *Super Ioannem* (1270–1272), one of the most finished scriptural commentaries; a second *Lectura in epistolas Pauli* (1271–72; Romans and the beginning of I Corinthians). Aquinas skipped from Matthew to John because he thought that the first took the place of the two other Synoptics, whereas the fourth gospel had something unique to offer: "The other evangelists treat principally the mysteries of the humanity of Christ; John brings his divinity to the forefront."[65]

Aquinas also disputes and writes the first fifteen questions *De malo* (1270–71) finishing Question 16 in 1272. The question *De unione Verbi incarnati* is likely most properly placed at the end of this stay in Paris (Spring 1271), but this date is contested,[66] as well as that of question *De uirtutibus*.[67] *Quodlibets* I–VI and XII also date from this period,[68] as well as the writing of the *Secunda Pars* of the *ST* in its entirety (1271–72). To this several letters and theological consultations written at the request of different correspondents must be added: *De mixtione elementorum, De motu cordis, De operationibus occultis naturae, De iudiciis astrorum, Epistola ad ducissam Brabantiae*, and so on.

Two works stand out from among these, but it is not clear whether they were written in Paris or in Naples (1272–73). Unfinished, *De substantiis separatis* was called "one of the most important metaphysical works of the Aquinian," and its first chapter is seen as the most elaborate Platonic synthesis of Aquinas. As to *Super De Causis*, which compares *Elementatio theologica* of Proclus to the Dionysian corpus, Aquinas was the first to identify its author with an anonymous Arabic philosopher who had borrowed a great deal from Proclus.[69]

The commentaries on Aristotle are worth mentioning separately. The writing of the following works can be set in Paris: *Physica*: 1268–70; *Peryermenias*: 1270–71; *Ethica*: 1271–72; *Politica I–III*: 1272 [?]; *Posteriora Analytica I* 1–26: 1271–72. Begun in Paris, the other works were continued in Naples (1272–73), but left unfinished: *Posteriora Analytica* I 27–II 20; *Metaphysica; De caelo et mundo*; *De generatione et corruptione*; *Super Meteora*. Although Aquinas was once considered a faithful disciple of Aristotle, contemporary researchers are more reserved with regard to the exactness of his commentaries; Aquinas reads the Stagirite in his own way hoping to stretch him in a Christian direction rather than to recover the Aristotle of history. Added to the other works, these writings represent an extraordinary amount of labor; it is likely that Aquinas was aided by several secretaries.[70]

Return to Naples and the Last Years (1272–1274)

In the spring or at the beginning of the summer of 1272, Aquinas was sent back to Italy to found a new Dominican *studium* in Naples. In addition to the commentaries on Aristotle, he continued working on the *Tertia Pars* of the *ST* (*ST* III q.1–90) and probably taught a class on the epistle to the *Hebrews* and on the *Psalms* (1–54).[71] He recommenced work on the *Compendium theologiae* but wrote only a few chapters (II 1–9: *De spe*). He preached also to the faithful on the *Ten Commandments*, the *Credo*, and on the *Pater* (1273).

Thanks to the depositions at the process of canonization in Naples (1319) and at Fossanova (1321), which are precious to the historian, we know this last period of Aquinas's life in greater detail than the rest of his life. His confreres at the convent describe his life and his person: he became more peaceful and receptive; his manner of preaching was simple and concrete. He renewed relations with his family and was designated by his brother-in-law Roger of Aquila as executor of his will. Due to repeated mystical experiences and massive physical and nervous fatigue, Aquinas ceased writing and teaching around December 6, 1273. Called by Gregory X to the council of Lyon and victim of an accident along the way, he fell ill and died on March 7, 1274, at the Cistercian abbey of Fossanova. Canonized by John XXII in 1323, Aquinas would be proclaimed Doctor of the Church by Pius V on April 15, 1567.[72]

NOTES

1. This brief biography presupposes the others done elsewhere, aside from William of Tocco. *Ystoria sancti Thome de Aquino de Guillaume de Tocco (1323)*, ed. Claire le Brun-Gouanvic (Toronto: Pontifical Institute of Mediaeval Studies, 1996); see also Jean-Pierre Torrell, O.P., *Saint Thomas Aquinas*, vol. 1, *The Person and His Work*, rev. ed. (Washington, D.C.: Catholic University of America Press, 2005); Jean-Pierre Torrell, O.P., *Saint Thomas Aquinas*, vol. 2, *Spiritual Master* (Washington, D.C.: Catholic University of America Press, 2003); Simon Tugwell, O.P., *Albert and Thomas: Selected Writings* (New York and Mahwah, N.J.: Paulist Press, 1988); and James A. Weisheipl, O.P., *Friar Thomas d'Aquino: His Life, Thought and Works* (Garden City, N.Y.: Doubleday, 1974; 2d ed. with Corrigenda and Addenda, 1983) for the necessary justifications.

2. Aquinas, *Opera omnia*, iussu Leonis XIII P. M. edita (Roma: Commissio Leonina, 1882–), I* 1 (1989), 67*–68*; hereinafter cited as Leonina.

3. Despite the divergent sources and their apologetical embellishments, the historical reality of this episode cannot be doubted; cf. A. Tilatti, "La cattura di Tommaso d'Aquino da parte dei parenti," in M. C. De Matteis, ed., *Ovidio Capitani: Quaranta anni per la storia medioevale* (Bologna: Patron Editore, 2003), 345–57.

4. Tocco, *Ystoria* 10:110–11.

5. Torrell, *Saint Thomas Aquinas*, 1:1–17.

6. According to A. Oliva, *Les Débuts de l'enseignement de Thomas d'Aquin et sa conception de la* sacra doctrina. *Avec l'édition du prologue de son commentaire des* Sentences. (Paris: Vrin, 2006), 207–24, the first biblical commentaries must be situated in Paris instead of Cologne.

7. Torrell, *Saint Thomas Aquinas*, 1:18–35; Jean-Pierre Torrell, O.P., and D. Bouthillier, "Quand saint Thomas méditait sur le prophète Isaïe," *Revue Thomiste* 90 (1990): 5–47.

8. Torrell, *Saint Thomas Aquinas*, 1:36–53; cf. Alain de Libera and Cyrille Michon, ed. and trans., Thomas Aquinas–Dietrich de Freiberg, *L'Etre et l'essence, Le vocabulaire médiéval de l'ontologie*; commentary by Alain de Libera and Cyrille Michon, "Point: Essais" (Paris: Seuil, 1996).

9. M.-M. Dufeil, *Guillaume de Saint-Amour et la polémique universitaire parisienne, 1250–1259* (Paris: Picard, 1972).

10. Torrell, *Saint Thomas Aquinas*, 1:75–95.

11. Cf. Torrell, *Saint Thomas Aquinas*, 1:54–59, 120–21, 198–201, 250–61.

12. Thomas G. Weinandy, OFM Cap., D. A. Keating, and J. P. Yocum, eds., *Aquinas on Scripture: An Introduction to the Biblical Commentaries* (London and New York: T. & T. Clark International, 2005); Gilles Emery, O.P., "Biblical Exegesis and the Speculative Doctrine of the Trinity in St. Thomas Aquinas's Commentary on St. John," in Gilles Emery, O.P., *Trinity in Aquinas* (Ypsilanti, Mich. and Naples, Fla.: Sapientia Press, 2003; 2d ed., 2006), 271–319; M. Aillet, *Lire la Bible avec S. Thomas: Le Passage de la littera à la res dans la Somme théologique*, Studia friburgensia 80 (Fribourg: Éditions universitaires, 1993).

13. W. G. B. M. Valkenberg, *Words of the Living God: Place and Function of Holy Scripture in the Theology of St. Thomas Aquinas* (Leuven: Peeters, 2000), 211–27.

14. B. C. Bazán, "Les Questions disputées, principalement dans les facultés de théologie," in B. C. Bazán, G. Fransen, J. F. Wippel, D. Jacquart, *Les Questions disputées et les questions quodlibétiques dans les facultés de théologie, de droit et de médecine*, Typologie des sources du moyen âge occidental 44–45 (Turnhout: Brepols, 1985), 12–149.

15. Torrell, *Saint Thomas Aquinas*, 1:59–69; S.-T. Bonino, *Thomas d'Aquin: De la vérité Question 2 (La science en Dieu)*, Introduction, traduction, et commentaire, Vestigia 17 (Paris: Cerf; Fribourg: Éditions universitaires, 1996).

16. J. F. Wippel, "Quodlibetal Questions Chiefly in Theology Faculties," in Bazán et al., *Les Questions disputées*, 151–222; J. Hamesse, "Theological *Quaestiones quodlibetales*," in C. Schabel, ed., *Theological Quodlibeta in the Middle Ages: The Thirteenth Century*, Brill's Companion to the Christian Tradition, I (Leiden-Boston: Brill, 2006), 17–48.

17. Torrell, *Saint Thomas Aquinas*, 1:207–12; cf. Leonard E. Boyle, "The Quodlibets of St. Thomas and Pastoral Care," in Leonard E. Boyle, *Facing History: A Different Thomas Aquinas* (Louvain-La-Neuve: Federation Internationale des Instituts d'Etudes Medievales, 2000), 13–35 (also *The Thomist* 38 [1974]: 232–56); Kevin White, "The *Quodlibeta* of Thomas Aquinas in the Context of His Work," in C. Schabel, ed., *Theological Quodlibeta in the Middle Ages: The Thirteenth Century* (Leiden: Brill, 2006), 49–133.

18. Cf. Jean-Pierre Torrell, O.P., "Philosophie et théologie d'après le Prologue de Thomas d'Aquin au *Super Boetium de Trinitate*. Essai d'une lecture théologique," *Documenti e Studi sulla tradizione filosofica medievale* 10 (1999): 299–353.

19. Leonina 50, 6.

20. Leonina 50, 263–64.

21. Cf. Louis Bertrand Geiger, *La Participation dans la philosophie de S. Thomas d'Aquin*, 2d ed., Bibliothèque thomiste 23 (Paris: Vrin, 1953); Cornelio Fabro, *La Nozione metafisica di partecipazione secondo S. Tommaso d'Aquino* (Turin: Società editrice internazionale, 2d rev. ed. 1950; 3d ed. 1963); G. Casey, "An Explication of the *de Hebdomadibus* of Boethius in the Light of St. Thomas's Commentary," *The Thomist* 51 (1987): 419–34.

22. This is the hypothesis of Weisheipl, *Friar Thomas*, 165–66. Tugwell, *Albert and Thomas*, 221, is in agreement on this point.

23. Cf. R.-A. Gauthier, "*Introduction*" *à Saint Thomas d'Aquin, Somme contre les Gentils* (Paris: Editions universitaires, 1993); this book brings to light and sensibly modifies the first "Introduction historique" by the same author and that was published in a translation of *Contra Gentiles*, by R. Bernier and M. Corvez (Paris: Lethielleux, 1959), 7–123.

24. Leonina 25/2, 486–88.

25. Torrell, *Saint Thomas Aquinas*, 1:101–16, 415; Gilles Emery, O.P., "The Treatise of St. Thomas," in *Trinity in Aquinas*, 71–120; there are excellent introductions and commentaries in the French edition: Thomas Aquinas, *Somme contre les Gentils*.

26. Jean-Pierre Torrell, O.P., *Thomas d'Aquin: Abrégé de théologie (Compendium theologiae)*, Introduction, Texte latin, trad. Française, et annotations (Paris: Cerf, 2007), 7–34.

27. Cf. Denis Chardonnens, *L'Homme sous le regard de la Providence*. Providence de Dieu et condition humaine selon l'*Exposition littérale sur le Livre de Job* de Thomas d'Aquin, Bibliothèque thomiste 50 (Paris: Vrin, 1997).

28. Cf. Gilles Emery, O.P., ed. and trans., Thomas d'Aquin, *Traités. Les Raisons de la foi. Les Articles de la foi et les sacrements de l'Église*, Introduction, traduction, et annotation (Paris: Cerf, 1999).

29. Torrell, *Saint Thomas Aquinas*, 1:129–36; R. Wielockx, "Poetry and Theology in the *Adoro Te deuote*: Thomas Aquinas on the Eucharist and Christ's Uniqueness," in Kent Emery and Joseph Wawrykow, eds., *Christ among the Medieval Dominicans: Representations of Christ in the Texts and Images of the Order of Preachers* (Notre Dame, Ind.: University of Notre Dame Press, 1998), 157–74.

30. Cf. M. Morard, "Thomas d'Aquin lecteur des Conciles," *Archivum Franciscanum Historicum* 98 (2005): 213–365.

31. P.-Y. Maillard, *La Vision de Dieu chez Thomas d'Aquin: Une lecture de l'*In Ioannem *à la lumière de ses sources augustiniennes*, Bibliothèque thomiste 53 (Paris: Vrin, 2001); M. Dauphinais, B. David, and M. Levering, eds., *Aquinas the Augustinian* (Washington, D.C.: Catholic University of America Press, 2007).

32. Torrell, *Saint Thomas Aquinas*, 1:126–38; Weisheipl, *Friar Thomas*, 163–76.

33. Leonard E. Boyle, *The Setting of the Summa theologiae of Saint Thomas*, Etienne Gilson Series 5 (Toronto: P.I.M.S., 1982).

34. Cf. Thomas Aquinas, *Lectura romana*, 1–57.

35. M. M. Mulchahey, *"First the Bow is Bent in Study...." Dominican Education before 1350*, Studies and Texts 132 (Toronto: P.I.M.S., 1998), 278–306.

36. Cf. A. Oliva, "La Questione dell'*alia lectura* di Tommaso d'Aquino," *Quaestio* 6 (2006): 516–21; Jean-Pierre Torrell, O.P., "Lire saint Thomas autrement," in Boyle, *Facing History*, xxi–xxiv; Torrell, *Saint Thomas Aquinas*, 1:45–47 and 413.

37. P. Glorieux, "Pour la chronologie de la Somme," *Mélanges de science religieuse* 2 (1945): 59–98; I. T. Eschmann, "A Catalogue of St. Thomas' Works," in E. Gilson, *The Christian Philosophy of St. Thomas Aquinas*, trans. L. K. Shook (New York: Random House, 1956), 386–88; Weisheipl, *Friar Thomas*, 221–22.

38. Gauthier, *Introduction*, 80; cf. 65–67; cf. R. A. Gauthier, ed., *L'Ethique à Nicomaque*, II, *Introduction* (Louvain: Nauwelaerts, 2d ed., 1970), 128–29, n. 135. The reason for this date is that the *ST* I-II relies heavily on the *Rhetoric* of Aristotle (more than 100 times) according to the translation of Moerbeke, which Aquinas did not have in hand until the end of 1270. Gauthier is in agreement with O. Lottin on this, who placed the *Prima Secundae* after q.6 of *QDM* (end 1270).

39. *ST* III q.90 a.4.

40. With more or less hesitation, many think that Raynald of Piperno could be the author of the *Supplement* but others are more reserved (Leonina 12, p. xvi ff.); Eschmann, *A Catalogue*, 388.

41. Torrell, *Saint Thomas Aquinas*, 1:50–156; Torrell, *Saint Thomas Aquinas*, 2:101–5.

42. For more details on the *Secunda Pars*, see Stephen J. Pope, ed., *The Ethics of Aquinas* (Washington, D.C.: Georgetown University Press, 2002).

43. Cf. Marie-Dominique Chenu, O.P., *Introduction à l'étude de Saint Thomas d'Aquin*, 2d ed. (Montréal and Paris: Institut d'Études Médiévales and Vrin, 1954), 255–76; Marie-Dominique Chenu, O.P., *La Théologie comme science au XIIIe siècle*, 3d ed. (Paris: Vrin, 1957).

44. *Super Sent* I, Prol., q.1, a.3, sol.1; Torrell, *Saint Thomas Aquinas*, 2:1–18.

45. Cf. Leonard E. Boyle, "Notes on the Education of the *Fratres communes* in the Dominican Order in the Thirteenth Century," in R. Creytens and P. Künzle, eds., *Xenia medii aevi historiam illustrantia oblata Th. Käppeli O.P*, t. 1, Storia e Letteratura, Raccolta di Studi e Testi 141 (Edizioni di storia e letteratura, Rome, 1978), 249–67 (reprinted in Leonard E. Boyle, *Pastoral Care, Clerical Education and Canon Law, 1200–1400* [London: Variorum Reprints, 1981], Etude VI); Boyle, *The Setting*.

46. Servais Pinckaers, O.P., *The Sources of Christian Ethics* (Washington, D.C.: Catholic University of America Press, 1995).

47. *ST* I–II q.3 a.2 ad 3.

48. *ST* IIIa q.27–59.

49. L. Scheffczyk, "Die Stellung des Thomas von Aquin in der Entwicklung der Lehre von den Mysteria Vitae Christi," in M. Gerwing and G. Ruppert, eds., *Renovatio et Reformatio*, (Münster: Aschendorff, 1986), 44–70.

50. Torrell, *Saint Thomas Aquinas*, 2:125–52. Cf. also Jean-Pierre Torrell, O.P., *Le Christ en ses mystères: La Vie et l'œuvre de Jésus selon saint Thomas d'Aquin*, Jésus et Jésus-Christ 78–79 (Paris: Desclée, 1999), 1:13–27.

51. For more on the *ST*, see Jean-Pierre Torrell, O.P., *Aquinas's Summa: Background, Structure, & Reception*, trans. Benedict M. Guevin, O.S.B. (Washington, D.C.: Catholic University of America Press, 2005); the *ST* continues to inspire numerous studies: D. Berger, *Thomas von Aquins "Summa Theologiae"* (Darmstadt: Wissenschaftliche Gesellschaft, 2004); Andreas Speer, ed., *Thomas von Aquin, Die Summa theologiae: Werkinterpretationen* (Berlin: Walter de Gruyter, 2005); Rik Van Nieuwenhove and Joseph Wawrykow, eds., *The Theology of Thomas Aquinas* (Notre Dame, Ind.: University of Notre Dame Press, 2005).

52. Leonina 24/1 and 2; Torrell, *Saint Thomas Aquinas*, 1:161–64, 427–28.

53. Torrell, *Saint Thomas Aquinas*, 1:127–29, 434.

54. Amid the numerous works in this area must be recalled at least these few: Vivian Boland, *Ideas in God According to Saint Thomas Aquinas: Sources and Synthesis*, Brill Studies in the History of Christian Thought 69 (Leiden and New York: E. J. Brill, 1996); C. D'Ancona Costa, "La Notion de l'un dans Thomas d'Aquin: Une confrontation des commentaires sur les Noms divins et sur la Métaphysique," *Recherches de théologie et philosophie médiévales* 64 (1997): 315–51.

55. Thierry-Dominique Humbrecht, O.P., *Théologie négative et noms divins chez saint Thomas d'Aquin*, Bibliothèque thomiste 57 (Paris: Vrin, 2005).

56. J. Turbessi, "S. Thomas d'Aquin" in "Denys l'Aréopagite," *Dictionnaire de spiritualité, ascétique et mystique*, ed. Marcel Viller (Paris: Beauchesne, 1954), 3:349–56; G. O'Daly, "Dionysius Areopagita," *Theologische Realenzyklopädie*, ed. Gerhard Müller (Berlin and New York: Walter de Gruyter, 1981), 8:772–80; Fran O'Rourke, *Pseudo-Dionysius and the Metaphysics of Aquinas*, Studien und Texte zur Geistesgeschichte des Mittelalters 32 (Leiden: Brill, 1991).

57. Torrell, *Saint Thomas Aquinas*, 1:167–71.

58. Torrell, *Saint Thomas Aquinas*, 1:171–78.

59. Torrell, *Saint Thomas Aquinas*, 1:182–84; M. M. Dufeil, "Évolution ou fixité des institutions ecclésiales: Une controverse universitaire. L'édition critique de trois oeuvres polémiques de saint Thomas d'Aquin," *Revue des sciences philosophiques et théologiques* 55 (1971): 464–79.

60. Torrell, *Saint Thomas Aquinas*, 1:184–87; Torrell, *Saint Thomas Aquinas*, 2:227–31. Cf. L. Bianchi, *L'Errore di Aristotele: La Polemica contro l'eternità del mondo nel XIII secolo* (Firenze: La nuova Italia, 1984); T. B. Noone, "The Originality of St. Thomas's Position on the Philosophers and Creation," *The Thomist* 60 (1996): 275–300; Cyrille Michon, ed., *Thomas d'Aquin et la controverse sur L'éternité du monde*, Traités sur l'éternité du monde de Bonaventure, Thomas d'Aquin, Peckam, Boèce de Dacie, Henri de Gand et Guillaume d'Ockam, GF Flammarion 1199 (Paris: Flammarion, 2004).

61. Cf. *SCG* II.58; *ST* I q.76 a.3–4; Torrell, *Saint Thomas Aquinas*, 1:187–90; Torrell, *Saint Thomas Aquinas*, 2:252–59.

62. R.-A. Gauthier, "Notes sur les débuts (1225–1240) du premier "averroïsme," *Revue des sciences philosophiques et théologiques* 66 (1982): 327–74; Leonina 45/1, 218*–35*.

63. Torrell, *Saint Thomas Aquinas*, 1:191–96; Alain de Libera, ed., Thomas d'Aquin, *L'Unité de l'intellect contre les averroïstes, suivi des Textes contre Averroès antérieurs à 1270*, Texte latin. Traduction, introduction, bibliographie, chronologie, notes et index, GF 713 (Paris: Flammarion, 1994); C. Luna, "Quelques précisions chronologiques à propos de la controverse sur l'unité de l'intellect," *Revue des sciences philosophiques et théologiques* 83 (1999): 649–84.

64. Torrell, *Saint Thomas Aquinas*, 1:197–223.

65. Torrell, *Saint Thomas Aquinas*, 1:197–201. Cf. M. Dauphinais and M. Levering, eds., *Reading John with St. Thomas Aquinas* (Washington, D.C.: Catholic University of America Press, 2005).

66. Jean-Pierre Torrell, O.P., "L'Unité d'être du Christ: Etat de la question," in *Thomas Aquinas, Le Verbe incarné*, t. III: Summa theologiae IIIa Questions 7–15, New edition with translation and annotations (Paris: Cerf, 2002), 391–402; Mulchahey, "*First the Bow is Bent in Study*," 315–18; M. H. Deloffre, ed. and trans., *Thomas d'Aquin, Question disputée: L'Union du Verbe incarné* (*De unione Verbi incarnati*) (Paris: Vrin, 2000), 13–27.

67. See also our discussion, in Torrell, *Saint Thomas Aquinas*, 1:429–30, on the debated authenticity of two other Disputed Questions, which some have tried to attribute to Thomas (*Utrum anima coniuncta cognoscat seipsam per essentiam*; *De immortalitate animae*).

68. Table of dates: Torrell, *Saint Thomas Aquinas*, 1:211.

69. C. D'Ancona Costa, "Saint Thomas lecteur du *Liber de Causis*: Bilan des recherches contemporaines concernant le *De Causis* et analyse de l'interprétation thomiste," in C. D'Ancona Costa, *Recherches sur le Liber De Causis*, Études de philosophie médiévale 72 (Paris: Vrin, 1995), 229–58.

70. Torrell, *Saint Thomas Aquinas*, 1:224–46.

71. Torrell, *Saint Thomas Aquinas*, 1:250–66.

72. Torrell, *Saint Thomas Aquinas*, 1:267–95.

CHAPTER 2

AQUINAS AND ARISTOTLE

JAMES DOIG

Introduction

Aquinas's relation to Aristotle was that of a theologian to a source of philosophical doctrines and concepts with whose aid he formulated his theological synthesis of Christian revelation. The value for theology that Aquinas saw in Aristotelian thought led him to undertake the composition of "expositions" and *sententiae* respecting individual works of Aristotle. Through these compositions, Aquinas offered his readers the possibility of greater understanding, as well as recognition of the value of that thought for theology.

Aquinas chose Aristotle's *Posterior Analytics* and *On Interpretation* as the subjects of what medieval Masters termed "expositions," that is, studies proceeding through an explanation focusing on the words of the text being examined; however, only the exposition on the *Posterior Analytics* was completed. As concerns what can be considered the principal works of the Aristotelian *corpus*—the *Metaphysics*, the *Physics*, the *De anima* ("On the Soul"), and the *Nicomachean Ethics*—Aquinas completed *sententiae* (singular: *sententia*), that is, presentations in summary fashion of the doctrines he understood Aristotle to propose in each work. While he began five other *sententiae* on works of Aristotle, only one was completed, that treating in succession the two works, "On Sense and the Sensed" and "On Memory and Remembering."[1]

As was true generally of thirteenth-century Masters, Aquinas knew no Greek but read Aristotle in a variety of Latin translations. While some of these were made directly from Greek manuscripts, others were based on Arabic translations several removes from any Greek text. Since the sixth century, Latin Europe had known Aristotle's *Categories* and *On Interpretation* in Boethius's translation, but the remaining parts of the *Organon* became available in Latin only by the middle of the twelfth century. Then too, only in the middle of that same century did Aristotle's strictly philosophical works begin to appear in Latin, and even these were at times only in a partial translation. Moreover, during Aquinas's lifetime one could not have found consensus on the exact number or identity of the works of Aristotle. Nor did Aquinas and his contemporaries have adequate historical information respecting the relation of Plato and Aristotle, not to speak of Neoplatonism and its effects on the numerous philosophical works that were being introduced into the Latin world in the twelfth and thirteenth centuries.[2]

Yet Aquinas's mastery of the Aristotelian corpus available to him is evidenced by the "divisions of text" everywhere proposed in his expositions and *sententiae* on individual works. By these divisions, he not only proposed the unity he saw as constituted by the books that together make up a given Aristotelian work, but he also explained both the flow from chapter to chapter within each book and the fashion in which Aristotle proceeded from point to point within each chapter. In his expositions and *sententiae* on Aristotle, we encounter Aquinas the teacher intent on explaining both the doctrine he understood Aristotle to offer and the procedure by which it was offered. In what follows, it is Aquinas's interest in the four principle works of Aristotle's philosophy and the use of that philosophy in Aquinas's theology that is of concern.

The *Sententia* on the *De anima* and the *Summa theologiae*

In 1268, Aquinas composed the first of his *sententiae*, that concerning the *De anima* (hereinafter, *In DA*). Aristotle's study of the soul is seen to focus on the substantial form or first intrinsic formal cause that explains both the possession of life and, remotely, the motions and activities typical of various types of living beings. The soul is defined as "the first act of a physical, organic body having life in potency," and each type of soul, vegetative, sensitive, and intellective, is examined in terms of the potencies proper to each. The intellective soul, as "first act," is the substantial form whose union with a body proportionate to that soul's vegetative and sensitive powers results in the existence of a human being. While some of its powers are exercised through the organs found in the human body, its intellective power acts in a manner intrinsically independent of anything material and so is "separated."[3] As the first act of a human body, the intellective soul is understood as entailing the individualization in each human being of the intellective power, just as it insures the individualized vegetative and sensitive powers.[4] Sketched thus in broad terms is the philosophy Aquinas found in the *De anima*.

Aquinas's understanding of Aristotle's conception of the intellective soul as the substantial form of a living being differed from what was proposed by authors enjoying some influence at the time. Masters in Arts and in Theology commonly considered the intellective soul as a subsistent spiritual form, complete in itself, that is, a particular reality.[5] Many asserted that this soul was composed of spiritual matter and form.[6] For some, each human being was constituted by several substantial forms, only one of which was the intellective soul.[7] Also proposed was the soul's presence to itself, a presence so immediate that the soul could understand itself independently of any reflection on its activities.[8] For some, the soul's grasp of its nature was indicated by Avicenna's Flying Man image: by imagining oneself as created, suspended in air in such a way that no bodily part experienced sensation of any kind, one realizes that one exists as a reality totally distinct from anything material.[9] For these Masters, when Aristotle considered the intellective soul as "first act" of an organic body, he could only have intended the soul's role as governing the body much as a sailor governs his ship.[10]

Contrary to such interpretations, Aquinas's *In DA* proposes that governance of the body is essential to the intellective soul's nature, for this soul is the form imparting to the human body whatever life it has,[11] a form that will always be incomplete if divided from the body that is its own.[12] According to Aquinas, the soul's "separation" from the body is nonetheless safeguarded; its separation or ability to act with intrinsic independence of anything material[13] accords with Aristotle's doctrine that an intellective soul, although incomplete in itself, has a nature not completely exhausted by its reality as the animating principle of a body.[14] Moreover, precisely because this soul comes into being as the first act of a body, its intellective potency is limited to knowledge whose source is found in sensation; the soul is not in any manner present to itself in such a way that it understands itself independently of reflection on its activity.[15]

These differences between Aquinas's understanding of the intellective soul and other proposals current in the 1260s suggest the goal of the *In DA*.[16] This goal may also be implicated in features characteristic of both *Prima Pars* of the *Summa theologiae* and the *In DA*, each of which was composed in 1268. Both works aim at a complete explication of their subject; both avoid unnecessary detail; both strive for clarity, never offering lengthy digressions arguing against views contrary to their proposals. As Aquinas made explicit, the *Summa*'s simplicity, directness, and completeness were intentional, for he was offering to "beginners" in the study of Christian religion all they needed to know on the subject.[17] Perhaps the *In DA* was intended as a companion piece to the questions of the *Summa* being composed at the time, that is, questions respecting the human being, his intellective soul, the relation of the soul to the human body, and the soul's powers.[18]

The *Sententia* on the *Physics*

When in 1268–69 Aquinas offered his *sententia* on the *Physics* (hereinafter, the *In Phy*), he appears to have been particularly interested in correcting interpretations proposed by Averroës.[19] The *In Phy* finds in Aristotle a general study of natural science focusing on mobile being as its subject. The conception of "mobile being" entails that of "nature," or intrinsic principle of motion.[20] After Aristotle defines motion as the act of what exists in potency to a terminus precisely insofar as it is in potency to that terminus,[21] he notes that, while motion depends on the intrinsic material cause of the existence of mobile being (its prime matter), it is especially the intrinsic formal cause (its substantial form) that is at the root of motion.[22] Place and its opposite, the vacuum, are investigated, for they concern the most basic type of motion. Time too is examined in some detail as the measure of motion.[23] To avoid the impossible consequences of an infinite regress in causality, Aristotle proposes the necessity of including the conception of a first motion that is caused by a first immobile mover.[24] To this point in the *Physics*, Aquinas sees Aristotle discussing *communia*, that is, as showing what is entailed in a coherent view of the conceptions of motion and of mobile being, given their definitions.[25] But now Aquinas notes that Aristotle turns from *communia* to reality in proposing the existence of a first immobile being as the final cause or goal of the eternal circular motion of the first heaven. The latter, in its capacity as the first agent cause, is the first intermediary between the first immobile mover and the temporal motion of the realities of our material world.[26] Such in general is the Aristotle that Aquinas proposes in his *In Phy.*

In addition to criticizing Averroës, the *In Phy* contains a critique of Aristotle's notions of the first final and agent causes. The proof of eternal motion is said to lack efficacy insofar as Aristotle's arguments assume what they conclude, namely, that every mobile being that begins to undergo motion has itself been produced through a previous motion, and that every moment of time marking the beginning of a motion is preceded by a previous moment. Aquinas insists that Aristotle was misled by his imagination; every moment of time, every beginning of motion, was imagined as preceded by, respectively, a previous moment of time and a prior motion. Aquinas notes too that Aristotle's proposal in the *Metaphysics* of a first cause of being as such, when added to Aristotle's distinction between an agent acting by will and an agent acting by nature, should have led the latter to recognize as possible that the eternal immobile first mover could simultaneously be the first agent that, acting by will, brings into being the first motion and so, the first moment of time.[27]

Aquinas offered these criticisms while carefully explaining Aristotle's text. It is as if Aquinas wished to present a completely detailed and brief interpretation of the *Physics*, while simultaneously reducing the danger that some might feel on encountering Aristotle's doctrines of the immobile first mover.

The *Sententia* on the *Nicomachean Ethics* and the *Summa theologiae*

In 1271–72, Aquinas composed both *Secunda Pars* of the *Summa theologiae* and the *sententia* on the *Nicomachean Ethics* (hereinafter, the *In NE*), both treatises on morality. In this *sententia*, Aquinas explains that Aristotle presents the first part of moral science insofar as he discusses only the life of the individual human being as an agent voluntarily acting for an end through the performance of virtuous activity.[28] That ultimate end, termed "happiness," consists in the pleasurable activity of man's supreme power, namely, his contemplative intellect,[29] yet activity exercised within a society governed by the appropriate laws.[30] Moreover, this pleasure must be complete and self-sufficient if it is to satisfy the human person's natural appetite for happiness.[31] Yet as Aristotle remarks, complete happiness sufficient of itself to satisfy human nature's longing is finally unattainable. Hence, Aristotle concludes by asserting that only imperfect happiness is attainable in this life. That is, human beings can only be "blessed as men."[32]

This conclusion, while a necessary element of the moral science Aquinas saw in the *Nicomachean Ethics*, is also an element of Aquinas's theological view where it is incorporated with the Christian notion of an afterlife in which perfect happiness is had through union with God. Yet in the *In NE*, Aquinas leaves unstated any reference to this Christian belief. This silence accords with what appears to be the goal of the work. In this regard, a parallel can be noted between, on the one hand, the relation of Aquinas's *In NE* to *Secunda Pars* of the *Summa theologiae* and, on the other, the relation of his *In DA* to *Prima Pars* of that work. Both *sententiae* present the Aristotelian concepts and doctrines that function fundamentally in the respective sections of the *Summa*. Just as in the *Summa*'s *Prima Pars*, the *De anima* provides the philosophical material so fundamental to Aquinas's theological exposition of the human person, so in *Secunda Pars*, the *Nicomachean Ethics* provides the philosophical foundation of his analysis of the human virtuous activity that, elevated by grace, orients the human person toward the ultimate happiness envisioned in Christian revelation. Just as the *In DA* reveals Aquinas standing almost alone in his understanding of Aristotle's vision of the intellective soul, so the *In NE* presents a view of Aristotle's intent at odds with the other two principal interpretations current at the time. Those interpretations, by Averroës and Albert the Great, considered Aristotle's discussion of virtuous activity as depicting a morality oriented to happiness within human society, rather than morality directed toward the ultimate happiness to which human nature is oriented.[33] Similar to what was noted above regarding Aquinas's presentation of his reading of the *De anima*, one suspects his *In NE* was intended as a companion piece to *Secunda Pars* of the *Summa*, a "handbook," so to speak, justifying his understanding of the Aristotelian concepts and doctrines employed in such a basic manner in the latter.

The *Sententia* on the *Metaphysics*

The *sententia* on the *Metaphysics* (hereinafter, the *In Meta*) was chronologically the last on a work of Aristotle fundamental to Aquinas's theological synthesis.[34] Aristotle is shown to develop "wisdom" or the "cognition of truth" had through knowledge of the first causes and principles of reality.[35] Wisdom clarifies the concepts common to all types of cognition, "substance," say, or "principle," although its subject matter is being as such.[36] In this context, wisdom establishes the existence and the essence of the subjects of all subordinate sciences, while leaving to the latter the study of their subjects on the basis of information gathered through the senses.[37] Substance, the principal type of being,[38] is understood to have as its intrinsic principles prime matter and substantial form.[39] The first agent and final causes of being as such are investigated when the science turns to eternal sensible substances. The doctrines of the latter causes are similar to those proposed in the *Physics*,[40] although Aristotle adds that the first mover is an intellect identical to the intellection of itself, knowing nothing except itself.[41]

In addition to the above, Aquinas announces in the *In Meta* his own doctrine of *esse* (to-be, or being) as the intrinsic principle, which, united to essence, constitutes a substantial being as real.[42] Additionally, Aristotle is said to propose a first cause of being, as well as a first cause of motion.[43] Finally, Aristotle's doctrines of the ultimate final and agent causes are criticized just as they were earlier in the *In Phy*, although much more briefly.[44]

In regard to the doctrine of *esse*, given its role in Aquinas's theological writings, one supposes that the reader of the *In Meta* is being invited to adopt as philosophically valid a transformed Aristotelian position on being. For instance, Aristotle speaks of the intellective soul as giving being to matter, resulting in the existence of a human being.[45] Aquinas would be inviting his readers to consider the human soul as only the formal cause of the specific type of reality had in a human being; only through a principle of *esse*, proportionate to the human soul, would there exist an individual human being.[46]

Aquinas's claim that Aristotle asserts a first cause of being, and not only of motion, points to the importance of consulting both the Latin translations of Aristotle known to Aquinas and his very careful reading of them. In the present case, each of four translations of the *Metaphysics* used by Aquinas appears to justify his interpretation. For instance, one translation reads: "Nor is something the cause whereby they [i.e., the truest and the greatest of beings] exist, but they are the causes whereby others (exist)."[47]

Aristotle's argument that the first mover can know only itself supposed that knowing something other than itself would be an imperfection. Aquinas responded that in knowing himself, God would know all reality as the effect of his causality; however, as long as God does not rest enjoyably in knowledge of creatures, no imperfection is had.[48]

In both the *In Meta* and the *In Phy*, Aquinas presents Aristotle's distinction between prime matter and substantial form. In the *Physics*, Aristotle is said to examine the universal notion of the coming-to-be of material substances. In contrast, in the *Metaphysics* an examination of "the way of predication" is noted as Aristotle's procedure in comparing the diverse contents of knowledge expressed through predicates used "denominatively," that is, when they "name" a subject. In the example offered, "This material thing is a man," the predicate "man" expresses or "names" the totality of the intelligibility proper to an individual such as Socrates. Other possible predicates, such as "white" or "large" express something much less intelligible. Accordingly, Aristotle concludes that a being is constituted by the union of a meaningless subject or matter—signified by "this material thing"—and the human essence signified by "man." As is true of every essence, its intelligibility is traced to its form.[49]

The same "way of predication" is central to Aquinas's understanding of the clarification of "common" concepts that constitutes *Metaphysics* V. Whether the concept is "being" or "principle," "habitus" or "act," or any other of the more than thirty terms studied, Aquinas clarifies its meaning by noting the ways in which it is used to name something.

Also clearly evident in Aquinas's *In Meta* is his intent to oppose interpretations basic to the commentaries on the *Metaphysics* by Averroës and Albert the Great, as well as doctrines found in Avicenna's *First Philosophy*.[50] Given this situation, as well as the evident use throughout Aquinas's theology of the common concepts clarified in the *Metaphysics*, one supposes that Aquinas intended the *In Meta* as a presentation of the science of wisdom that he found so useful in synthesizing Christian revelation.

Aristotle and the *Summa theologiae*

The principal instance of Aquinas's theological synthesis, his *Summa theologiae*, presents in easily recognizable form multiple examples of the presence of Aristotelian doctrines and concepts similar to those just mentioned in regard to the *In Meta*. Then too, this theological synthesis is conceived in accord with what Aquinas saw the *Metaphysics* propose concerning a subordinate science, that is, a study whose legitimacy and principles are established by a superior science, in this case, by divine knowledge and the revelation of the divine intention for humankind.[51] In its second question, the licit character of the proofs of God's existence is guaranteed by their adherence to the requirements of Aristotle's "demonstration of the fact."[52] In the fourth proof for the existence of God, Aristotle's authority is explicitly cited respecting the crucial basis of the argument.[53] One might continue working through the *Summa* in this way. Yet alongside the straightforward use of Aristotelian concepts and doctrines, the *Summa* employs the methodology Aquinas recognized in the *Metaphysics* when Aristotle studied not only the matter–form distinction but, more important, the common concepts.[54]

Are human terms appropriately used in speaking of God? The *Summa*'s response reveals the metaphysician investigating "the way of predication." Human intellectual knowledge, Aquinas explains, is built on terms used to signify things in one of two ways. Some terms signify concretely for they signify complete, subsisting realities, for example, "man" as predicated of an individual human being to signify the specific nature embodied in him. Other terms, however, signify abstractly, since their signification is of a simple form, not as a subsisting reality, but rather as "that by which something is." For example, "whiteness" signifies the form by which some reality is white in color. With this knowledge at hand, Aquinas turns to his question of whether human terms can appropriately be applied to God. Because God is simple and subsistent, abstract terms or names can be attributed to him, thus signifying his subsistent simplicity. As well, since God is complete or perfect in all ways, concrete terms can be predicated of him to signify his subsistent completeness. Accordingly, terms attributable to God are at hand, even though their ultimate origin in human contact with the material world insures that they fall far short of signifying God as he is.[55]

The metaphysician is also evident when the *Summa* asks whether a relation in God is identical to the divine essence. Aquinas notes that the predication of terms falling under the genera of accidents signifies a reality having being in a subject. However, of the terms signifying accidents, only a term of relation refers the subject to something other than itself. Thus, the term "paternity" will signify the divine essence itself as begetting the divine Son. (Although the human mind conceives of the Son as distinct from the divine essence insofar as the Son is the term of the relation signified by "paternity," we recognize in that distinction only one of reason.)[56]

In discussing the possibility of the presence in a human being of a plurality of substantial forms, Aquinas remarks, "This appears impossible from the way of predication." If "animal" signified one form, and "man" another, then they could be predicated of one another in one of the following two ways. First, as a *per accidens* predication, the terms in "Man is an animal" would have no order to one another, in this paralleling the terms in "The white thing is sweet." Second, if the proposition were in the second mode of per se predication, then the subject is the basis for the predicate, after the fashion of "The object's surface is colored"; if this were so, then "man" would fall within the definition of "animal." But because "animal" is part of the definition of "man," the proposition is a strict per se predication; that is, it indicates that the meaning of "animal" is part of what is signified by "man." "Therefore it must be that it is the same form through which some reality is an animal and through which it is a man."[57]

These are but three examples. Yet one finds everywhere in the *Summa* the influence of the way of predication. Whether or not Aquinas makes that use explicit, his conceptualization of Christian revelation includes the constant application of the meanings given concepts as a result of their use in naming things.

Conclusion: Aquinas and Aristotle

The dependence of Aquinas's theology on the philosophy of Aristotle appears then in two forms. One is the evident application of Aristotle's doctrines or concepts; the other, not as noticeable, is the application of the method Aquinas found proper to Aristotle's metaphysician. The presence in Aquinas's theology of such dependence on Aristotle, when set alongside the *sententiae* composed on individual works of Aristotle, point to the former's high regard for the latter. This regard in which Aristotle was held should not be surprising. One of Aquinas's strongest convictions concerned the impossibility that error can arise from the correct use of the human cognitive abilities given by God. That the human mind is made for the world is surely everywhere evident in Aquinas's works. And because he held this basic truth, might he not have wondered what better tool to use in developing a systematic understanding of Christian revelation than the philosophy he saw in Aristotle? For in that philosophy, Aquinas found first, the metaphysician who investigated by "the way of predication" the common human concepts properly used in knowing the world; and second, the knowledge developed through the application in the subordinate sciences of the common concepts and principles whose value is guaranteed by the work of the metaphysician. Truly, for Aquinas, Aristotle was *the* Philosopher.

NOTES

1. The unfinished *sententiae* concerned *Meteorology*, *Politics*, *Heaven* (known to Aquinas as "On Heaven and on the World"), and *Generation and Corruption*. Aquinas's writings on Aristotle are discussed in: Jean-Pierre Torrell, O.P., *Initiation à saint Thomas d'Aquin: Sa personne et son oeuvre* (Fribourg, Suisse/Paris: Éditions universitaire/Cerf, 1993), 498–503. For the notions of medieval "expositions" and *sententiae*, see R. A. Gauthier, "*Praefatio*," *Sententia libri Ethicorum*, in *Sancti Thomae de Aquino Opera Omnia*, 47/1 (Rome: Sancta Sabina, 1969), 244*–45*; R. A. Gauthier, "Le Cours sur l'*Ethica nova* d'un maitres es arts de Paris (1235–1240)," *Archives d'histoire doctrinale et litteraire du moyen age* 43 (1975): 76–77.

2. On the influx of translations of Greek, Jewish, and Arabic works into Latin during the twelfth–thirteenth centuries, see Frederick Copleston, *A History of Philosophy* (Garden City, N.Y.: Doubleday, 1985), 3:205–11; Marie-Therese D'Alverny, *La Transmission des textes philosophiques et scientifiques au Moyen Age*, ed. C. Burnett (Aldershot: Variorum, 1994), chs. 2–3. For the Latin translations of Aristotle's works, see the various volumes of *Aristoteles Latinus*, ed. L. Minio-Paluello (Paris: Brouwer, 1965–1995).

3. Aquinas, *Sententia Libri De Anima*, Leonina, vol. 45-I (Roma: Commissio Leonina, 1984), 72–73, l. 366–92; 88–89, l. 70–131; 207, l. 358–83. Hereinafter cited as *In DA*.

4. *In DA*, 88–89, l. 43–131.

5. The remote source of this view is: Pseudo-Augustinus, *De spiritu et anima*, in *Patrologia Latina* (Paris: J. P. Migne, 1857), 40: col. 781 (hereinafter cited as *PL*). Influential was the assertion that the intellective soul is more properly "perfection" of the body, rather than its form: Avicenna, *Liber de anima seu sixtus de naturalibus*, in S. Van Riet, ed., G. Verbeke, intro., *Avicenna Latinus*, 2 vols. (Vol. I, Louvain/Leiden: Peeters/Brill, 1968; Vol. 2, Louvain/Leiden: Éditions Orientalistes/Brill, 1972), 1:16, l. 87–21, l. 48. Later proponents of the soul as subsistent spiritual form included: Alexander of Hales, *Glossa in quatuor libros Sententiarum Petri Lombardi* (Quaracchi: Collegium S. Bonaventura, 1952), 2:145, l. 16–146, l. 3; Jean de La Rochelle, *Summa de anima*, ed. J. S. Bougerol (Paris: J. Vrin, 1995), 80, l. 1–2; William of

Auvergne, *Tractatus de anima*, in *Guilielmi Alverni Opera Omnia*, Vol. 2 (Paris, 1674); reprinted: Frankfurt am Main: Minerva GMBH, 1963), fol. 67, col. A; Bonaventure, *Commentaria in quatuor libros Sententiarum*, in *Opera omnia* (Quaracchi: Collegium S. Bonaventurae, 1885), 1–4: responsio, 414b–415a; ad 5, 415b; Peter of Spain, *Scientia libri De anima*, ed. M. A. Alonso, 2d ed. (Barcelona: Flors, 1961), 17, l. 18–31; 20, l. 10–16; 304, l. 17–18. A witness to the ideas current at the time Aquinas left Paris (1259) dates from ca. 1260, although probably not known to him: Anonymous, *Questiones in tres libros De anima*, in *Ein anonymer Aristoteleskommentar des XIII. Jarhunderts*, ed. J. Vennebusch (Paderborn: F. Schöningh, 1963), 116, l. 22–117, l. 33.

6. Dominicus Gundisalvus, "The Treatise *De anima* of Dominicus Gundissalinus," ed. J. T. Muchkle, intro. E. Gilson, *Mediaeval Studies* 2 (1940): 58, l. 28–31. Johannes Blund, *Tractatus de anima*, ed. D. A. Callus and R. W. Hunt (London: Oxford University Press, 1970), 90, l. 28–91, l. 5. Alexander of Hales, *Summa theologiae* (Quaracchi: Collegium S. Bonaventurae, 1928), solutio, 399a–b. Pseudo-Peter of Spain, *Expositio libri De anima*, published as: *Pedro Hispano. Obras Filosóficas*, Vol. 3, ed. M. Alonso (Madrid: Instituto Luis Vives, 1954), 328, l. 32–329, l. 6. Jean de La Rochelle, *Summa de anima*, 67, l. 75–82; 70, l. 67–69 and 75–77. Bonaventure, *Opera omnia*, responsio 414b–15a; ad 6, 415b–16a. Anonymous, *Questiones*, 455, l. 262–456, l. 276.

7. The source of this doctrine appears to be had in Avicebron, *Fons vitae*, ed. C. Baeumker, in *Beiträge zur Geschichte der Philosophie des Mittelalters*, Bd. 1, H. 2–4 (Münster, 1892), 211–27. Proponents included the following: Alexander of Hales, *Summa theologiae*, ad 1–7, 422b; Peter of Spain, *Commentarium in De anima*, ed. M. A. Alonso, in *Obras Filosóficas*, n. 2 (Madrid, 1944), 656, l. 9–30; Anonymous, Magister Artium, *Lectura in librum De anima a quodam discipulo reportata* (Ms. Roma Naz. V. E. 828), ed. R. A. Gauthier (Grottoferrata: Collegium S. Bonaventurae, 1985), 155, l. 212–256, l. 233; 214, l. 311–315, l. 326; 219, l. 442–44. Somewhat similar to the doctrine of a plurality of forms is the notion of the intellect as a separated substance whose union with the sensitive soul results in a composed form that as such is the act of the human body: Anonymous, *Questiones*, 142, l. 70–76; 176, l. 118–28.

8. Bonaventure, *Opera omnia*, responsio, 86a; ad 1, 90a. Bonaventure, *Opera omnia*, obj. 3, 122a.

9. Avicenna, *Liber de anima*, 36, l. 49–37, l. 68. Gundisalvus, "The Treatise *De anima*," 37, l. 17–32. Jean de La Rochelle, *Summa de anima*, 51, l. 27–41. William of Auvergne, *Tractatus de anima*, fol. 82, col. B – fol. 83, col. A. Peter of Spain, *Commentarium in De anima*, 650, l. 3–24.

10. Gundisalvus, "The Treatise *De anima*," 42, l. 11–15. Blund, *Tractatus de anima*, 5, l. 23–26, l. 3; 7, l. 1–13. Alexander of Hales, *Summa theologiae*, 385–86. Jean de La Rochelle, *Summa de anima*, 385b–386a. Anonymous, *Questiones*, 163, l. 51–59; 176, l. 131–32, dated ca. 1260, the year following Aquinas's departure from Paris, illustrates the currency of this view of Aristotle's definition of the soul.

11. *In DA*, 79, l. 106–21; 85, l. 155–74.

12. This is implied in these texts: *In DA*, 74, l. 36–75, l. 44; 76, l. 141–50; 86, l. 239–57.

13. *In DA*, 222–23, l. 202–20.

14. *In DA*, 207, l. 372–83.

15. *In DA*, 216, l. 65–86.

16. Although Aquinas devotes a few paragraphs to the rejection of the interpretation of the agent and possible intellects attributed to Averroës, both the failure to mention the latter's name and the brevity of the discussion also indicate that Aquinas's goal is to present Aristotle's views in as straightforward a way as possible. See *In DA*, 220, l. 89–221, l. 166.

17. *ST* I, prologus.

18. *ST* I q.75–88.

19. The twenty-some "corrections" range from the mild: *In octo libros Physicorum Aristotelis expositio*, ed. M. Maggiolo, (Turin: Marietti, 1954), no. 8: "His [i.e., Averroës's] exposition is inappropriate because as a whole it does not have one goal and because the Philosopher does not intend to show" to the harsh: *In Phy*, no. 966: "The argument Averroes has proposed is completely frivolous," and in no. 1083: "What the Commentator says is evidently false." Hereinafter cited as *In Phy*.

20. *In Phy*, no. 145.

21. *In Phy*, no. 285.

22. *In Phy*, nos. 150 and 152–53.

23. Place and the vacuum: *In Phy*, 201–70, lect. 1–14; time: 273–312, lect. 15–23.

24. *In Phy*, nos. 885–86 and 891–94.

25. *In Phy*, nos. 972 and 1083.

26. *In Phy*, nos. 1004–5, 1081–84, and 1168.

27. *In Phy*, nos. 974–90.

28. *Sententia Libri Ethicorum*, Leonina, vol. 47 (Roma: Commissio Leonina, 1969), 4–5, l. 50–54, and 99–109. Hereinafter cited as *In NE*. For moral virtue in general, see: *In NE*, Bk. II, cc. 1–11; for the principles of virtuous activity, such as voluntary action and choice, see: Bk. III, cc. 1–13; for individual moral virtues, see: Bk. IV, c. 14–V, c. 17; for intellectual virtues, see: Bk. VI, cc. 1–11.

29. *In NE*, 582–83, l. 1–15; and 583, l. 71–78.

30. *In NE*, 597, l. 1–29.

31. *In NE*, 14, l. 1–6; 31–32, l. 60–76; and 32–33, l. 136–217.

32. *In NE*, 60, l. 215–22; and 595, l. 141–44.

33. Averroës, *Commentarium in Ethicorum*, in *Moralem totam philosophiam complectentes cum Averrois Cordubensis in Moralia Nicomachia expositione*, Vol. 3 of *Aristotelis Stagiritae Libri* (Venice: Juncta, 1562–1574; reprint Frankfurt am Main: Minerva G.m.b.H., 1962), fol. 8vH-I and fol. 9vG-H. Albertus Magnus, *Super Ethica commentum et quaestiones*, ed. W. Kübel, in *Opera omnia*, T. XIV, P. I–II (Cologne: Aschendorff, 1968–72 and 1987), 75, l. 72–76, l. 4; 714, l. 27–31; 746, l. 5–16. For a more complete statement of interpretations of the *Nicomachean Ethics* current at this time, see James C. Doig, *Aquinas's Philosophical Commentary on the Ethics* (Dordrecht: Kluwer, 2001), 8–24.

34. A detailed study showing the *In Meta* to be Aquinas's proposal of the structure Aristotle intended for the *Metaphysics* is had in: Gabriele Galluzzo, "Aquinas on the Structure of Aristotle's *Metaphysics*," *Documenti e studi sulla tradizione medievale* 15 (2004): 353–86.

35. *In duodecim libros Metaphysicorum Aristotelis expositio*, ed. M. R. Cathala & M. Spiazzi, (Turin: Marietti, 1950), nos. 1, 35, and 51. Hereinafter cited as *In Meta*.

36. *In Meta*, no. 534.

37. *In Meta*, nos. 1147–51.

38. *In Meta*, nos. 1245–47.

39. *In Meta*, nos. 1276–79.

40. *In Meta*, Bk. XII, lect. 5–9.

41. *In Meta*, nos. 2611–14.

42. *In Meta*, nos. 556–58.

43. *In Meta*, nos. 295 and 1164.

44. *In Meta*, nos. 2496–99.

45. *De anima*, II, 1, 412a8–9. The Latin translation used by Aquinas is found in: *In DA*, 67. Aquinas's interpretation is had in: *In DA*, nos. 100–17.

46. e.g., see: *ST* I q.76 a.1 ad 5; a.2 ad 2; *QDP*, q.6 a.6 ad 8.

47. The passage in question is *Meta.*, II, 1, 993b26–30. The translations are found in *Aristoteles latinus* 1970–95: (Vol. 25/1–1a, 37, l. 7–11 *Vetustissima trans.*; 120, l. 3–7 *Vetus trans.*); (Vol. 25/2, 37, l. 6–10 *Media trans.*); (Vol. 3/2, 44, l. 29–34 *Moerbecana trans.*). The Latin text of Aristotle given in *In Meta*, 84, while not a critical edition, is very close to the *Moerbecana*, which makes Aquinas's point more clearly than the other three.

48. *In Meta*, nos. 2614–16. The difference between Aquinas's approach to Aristotle's position in the *In Meta* and the *QDP* illustrates the care with which Aquinas interprets Aristotle when that interpretation is his goal; see *QDP*, q.3 a.16, obj. 23 and ad 23.

49. *In Meta*, nos. 1287–89. That the metaphysical proof is more demonstrative, see *In Phy*, no. 107. A related discussion adding detail is had in *QDP*, q.9 a.1, resp.

50. James C. Doig, *Aquinas on Metaphysics: A historico-doctrinal Study of the Commentary on the Metaphysics* (The Hague: Nijhoff, 1972), chs. 4–5.

51. *ST* I q.1 a.2. See *In Meta*, nos. 391–92, 1147–51, and 2249–51.

52. *ST* I q.2 a.2. See *In libros Posteriorum analyticorum*, in *In Aristotelis libros Peri Hermeneias et Posteriorum analyticorum expositio*, ed. R. M. Spiazzi, (Turin: Marietti, 1955), nos. 195–97. Hereinafter cited as *In PA*.

53. *ST* I q.2 a.3, where Aquinas cites *Metaphysics* II as asserting first, that the most true beings are the greatest beings and then, that the greatest reality included within a genus is the cause of all others within that genus. For his interpretation of the passage at issue, see *In Meta*, nos. 292–98. An additional indication that Aquinas saw the fourth proof as Aristotelian and not Platonic is had in *ST* I, q.6 a.4.—Two or three years prior to *ST* I, Aquinas offered what is essentially the fourth proof; see *QDP*, q.3 a.5, cor.

54. Note, e.g., the investigation of predication in *In Meta*, Bk. V, lect. 1–22.

55. *ST* I q.13 a.1 ad 2.

56. *ST* I q.28 a.2.

57. *ST* I q.76 a.3 ad 2.

CHAPTER 3

AUGUSTINE TO AQUINAS (LATIN-CHRISTIAN AUTHORS)

ALEXANDER FIDORA

One of the most outstanding features of Thomas Aquinas's thought is the way in which he integrated the newly translated philosophical sources, that is Greek, Arabic, and Jewish authors, into a unique synthesis with his own Christian tradition. An adequate appraisal of Aquinas's merits both as a philosopher and as a theologian therefore has to emphasize his interpretation and transformation of these "new" texts and their rich doctrines, which cover a wide range of topics, from ethics to epistemology, from logic to metaphysics, and so on. Yet it is often forgotten that the originality of any synthesis of "new" and "old" material does not only lie in the way in which the former is dealt with:[1] it is equally important to take into account the use and interpretation of what is frequently regarded as the mere historical background against which such innovative developments are displayed.

In the case of Aquinas, this means we need to view him not only as a sharp and original interpreter of Aristotle and the Graeco-Arabic Neoplatonic tradition (e.g., the anonymous *Liber de causis*)[2] but also to acknowledge his role as a lucid commentator and subtle critic of his own Latin-Christian tradition. As a matter of fact, during his years as a student in the *artes liberales* in Naples, and also while working with Albert the Great (ca. 1200–1280) in Cologne or while studying at Paris, Aquinas would not only have become acquainted with ancient and Arabic sources, but his academic training would have consisted above all in a thorough reading of Latin-Christian texts. Thus, the first systematic work he wrote,[3] while teaching at the University of Paris during the years 1253–56, was a commentary on Peter Lombard's *Sentences*, by then the standard textbook for theology. It is no exaggeration to say, therefore, that the authors in this Latin-Christian tradition are at the very basis of Aquinas's intellectual evolution.

Aquinas and Aristotle versus Augustine?

The most prominent, and certainly one of the most influential, among Aquinas's Latin-Christian authors of reference is Augustine of Hippo (354–430).

The influence of the North African bishop on intellectual discussion at the end of the twelfth and during the thirteenth centuries cannot be overstressed: his books constituted the primary stock of any academic library of that time. Both Franciscans and Dominicans, such as Aquinas's contemporaries Bonaventure (1221–1274), on the one hand, and Robert Kilwardby (ca. 1215–1279), on the other, embraced Augustine's authority in theology and philosophy.

In this respect, Thomas Aquinas's relation to the venerated Church Father reveals rather peculiar traits, since his attitude toward Augustine differs quite significantly from that of his contemporaries. For while there can be no doubt that Aquinas acknowledged the authority of Augustine in theological matters, he introduced extremely important differentiations with regard to some of the bishop's philosophical tenets. Aquinas follows Augustine in theological matters such as Trinitarian theology, and the questions of divine providence and grace. In philosophy, however, he is more reluctant: while accepting Augustine's doctrines on causality and exemplarism, he clearly rejects some of his metaphysical teachings, as well as a series of claims concerning theory of knowledge and psychology, namely the role of the "seminal reasons" and of divine illumination.[4]

I shall dwell for a moment on the latter, not only because of the systematic relevance it has in the context of Aquinas's thought but also with regard to the important methodological and historiographical discussions to which it gave rise during the last century. For Aquinas, the human intellect has a natural light that suffices to attain certain truths; therefore, man does not need any special illumination to reach true knowledge, as Augustine held. According to Aquinas, true knowledge comes from experience, which we acquire through our senses rather than from "above"; sensory cognition, in turn, is subject to a process of abstraction, and it is by means of this process that we attain intellectual knowledge of reality. As can easily be seen, this discussion, which is central to Aquinas's theory of knowledge, reprises one of the most controversial questions in the philosophical tradition concerning human knowledge—one that is most often associated with the names of Plato and Aristotle. Indeed, in the passages of his *Summa theologiae*, which discuss the role of divine illumination for human understanding, Aquinas places the issue in the larger setting of different philosophical options, such as Augustine vs. Aristotle, Arabic philosophy vs. the "genuine" peripatetic tradition, and Platonism vs. Aristotelianism.[5]

Now this very setting has led some scholars to present Aquinas's approach toward Augustine as a clear opposition between Thomistic Aristotelianism, on the one hand, and Platonic Neo-Augustinianism, on the other. Thus, in a highly influential study from 1926, Étienne Gilson answered the question of "why St Thomas criticized St Augustine" precisely with reference to the latter's conception of divine illumination and its incompatibility with an adequate interpretation of Aristotle's claims about knowledge as laid out in the latter's *De anima* and elsewhere.[6] In short, Aquinas would have criticized and rejected Augustine—and also Avicenna—because in his own theory of knowledge he wanted to be a pure Aristotelian. In Gilson's eyes, this supposedly irreconcilable alternative was also to have important consequences for the general path philosophy should take over the next decades, becoming the crucial issue for the division into Thomistic Aristotelianism, aiming at an adequate interpretation of the Greek philosopher's doctrine, and Platonic Neo-Augustinianism.

These strong claims and their far-reaching implications for our understanding of the history of medieval philosophy did not remain uncontested. In 1931 Maurice De Wulf took up the question under the label of "augustinisme avicennisant,"[7] an expression coined by Gilson to summarize the psychological positions that Aquinas was confronted with and the school to which these supposedly gave rise. For De Wulf, Gilson's account and its division into two opposing camps was an undue simplification not only of Aquinas's admirable synthesis but also of the conceptual wealth of medieval thought: thought that could hardly be reduced to having a single philosophical tenet as its watershed. Such a simplification, in addition, could easily lead to the misinterpretation of Aquinas as the representative of Aristotelian thought par excellence, overshadowing all of his Neoplatonic legacy and, on the other hand, to eclipsing the important tradition of Aristotelizing Augustinianism.[8]

While this is not the place to discuss this controversy in depth, I shall draw from it at least two observations: on the one hand, both accounts agree on the fact that Aquinas's approach toward Augustine was not simply a dialogue with the philosophical tradition but also a debate with his contemporaries who followed other options, regardless of whether it has to be classified as a polemical issue between different schools or not. On the other hand, the controversy shows how important a correct appraisal of Aquinas's Latin-Christian sources is for our interpretation of his overall thought, and especially for his reception and interpretation of Aristotle, since the different accounts leave us with very different pictures of Thomistic thought.

Putting this controversy to one side, one has to say that at all events Augustine's influence on Aquinas with regard to both theology and philosophy extends much further than the question of divine illumination. For, as I noted above, it also shapes such central subjects of Thomistic metaphysics as causality and the connections between the Creator and creatures in general. Although their relation was a complex one, as we have seen, it is therefore no exaggeration to conclude with Marie-Dominique Chenu's words "that it is impossible to think of Thomas Aquinas without Augustine."[9]

Aquinas, a Belated Reader of Boethius?

No less important is the case of Boethius's (ca. 480–524) influence on Aquinas. Concerning Augustine I have stressed that, in general terms, Aquinas's attitude differs from the thirteenth-century mainstream in that he assumes a more critical position with regard to some of the bishop's philosophical teachings. As far as his interest in Boethius goes, there is, too, a remarkable "anomaly" or, rather, an anachronism that needs to be pointed out: writing commentaries on Boethius's *Opuscula Sacra* (or *Theological Treatises*) is a marked exception among thirteenth-century authors. In fact, with his two commentaries, that is on *De Trinitate* and on *De hebdomadibus*, Aquinas takes up a practice that was extremely popular during the twelfth century, but no longer in the thirteenth. Thus, twelfth-century commentaries on the *Opuscula Sacra* abound, most of them associated with the School of Chartres (namely, those of Gilbert of Poitiers, Thierry of Chartres, and Clarembald of Arras), while there is no strong evidence for the continuity of this genre in Aquinas's time. The fact that he wrote such commentaries, which were completely out of fashion, must be taken as an expression of the enormous systematic interest he found in Boethius.[10]

The first of these two commentaries, on Boethius's tract *De Trinitate*, dates from 1256–59 and was written in Paris. The text, which is incomplete, is preserved in an autograph manuscript. As for its literary form, Thomas chose a combination of literal commentary and question form, namely, he divided his text into three parts, each of which starts with a literary commentary on a passage from Boethius, followed by two questions on the text, which are in turn each subdivided into four articles. In the First Question he addresses the possibility and limits of rational knowledge about God. The Second Question asks whether God can be the subject of a science. The Third Question is concerned with the different meanings of "faith." The Fourth Question deals with the word "plurality" as found in Boethius. The Fifth Question discusses the twofold nature of theology as philosophical theology, on the one hand, and revealed theology, on the other. Finally, the Sixth Question examines the different methods of the theoretical sciences, that is, natural philosophy, mathematics, and metaphysics.[11]

From a systematic point of view, it is Questions 5 and 6 that deserve our particular attention, since here Aquinas develops fundamental epistemic categories that allow for highly differentiated concepts of both philosophy and theology. The starting point for this discussion in Question 5 is Boethius's important distinction between the respective objects and methods of natural science, mathematics, and theology/metaphysics. Thus, according to Boethius, natural philosophy deals with motion and is not abstract (*inabstracta*), mathematics does not deal with motion and is not abstract (*inabstracta*), and theology/metaphysics does not deal with motion and is abstract (*abstracta*). To this, Boethius adds that, with regard to their methods, natural philosophy proceeds according to the mode of reasoning (*rationabiliter*), mathematics to the mode of learning (*disciplinaliter*), and theology/metaphysics to the mode of intellection (*intellectualiter*). While this division seems very clear and lucid at first glance, it involves, in fact, a series of difficulties for its interpretation, such as the qualification of mathematics as dealing with what is not abstract or the precise meaning of the three modes used to describe the respective methods of the sciences.

While in his literary commentary on these passages, which precedes Question 5, Aquinas engages with some of these difficulties, his merit does not lie so much in an *explication de texte*, but rather in his systematic and extremely original reflections which he offers in the following articles. In fact he reinterprets Boethius's text with the help of Aristotelian and Avicennian material (from the *Second Analytics*, the *Metaphysics*, and sections of the *Kitab as-Shifa* or *Book of Healing*) so as to arrive at a comprehensive epistemological account. This account establishes both the different steps in human cognition, that is, the role of the senses, of the *phantasmata*, the intellect, the process of abstraction, as well as the autonomy of the different sciences, assigning to each of them their proper object and method.[12]

With regard to this latter point, Aquinas adds an important precision to Boethius's account in introducing a differentiation into the vague concept of theology/metaphysics as used in *De Trinitate*. Thus, Aquinas distinguishes Christian theology and metaphysics as a philosophical discipline, each in their own right, explaining their specific methods and objects. He argues that even though the two seem to have the same object (or subject matter), that is divine beings, because they both formulate assertions on these, nevertheless this object is not viewed under one and the same respect in both. For, while in theology divine beings are dealt with as principles that are themselves complete natures, in metaphysics they come into the scope of the investigation not insofar as they are complete natures in themselves, but insofar as they are the principles of (other) complete natures. In this way, Aquinas is able to explain that both Christian theology and metaphysics have something to say about God; yet, while the former deals with Him as its proper object, the latter speaks about Him only with a view to his being the principle of its proper object, which is being as being.[13]

Aquinas's second commentary (Paris 1259?)[14] is dedicated to the short tract *De hebdomadibus*, in which Boethius set out to analyze the goodness of substances. In this text, Boethius coined some very influential ontological key notions, in particular the distinction between *id quod est* and *esse*. Aquinas pays a good deal of attention to this distinction, interpreting Boethius's *id quod est* as *ens*, that is that which participates in the act of being (*actus essendi*), whereas being itself (*ipsum esse*) is defined as that which does not participate in anything else. While scholars still argue about whether Aquinas's account is simply a faithful reading of Boethius's words or rather the outcome of a highly innovative personal interpretation of the text,[15] there can be no doubt that these reflections are at the very heart of Aquinas's own ontological doctrines, not only because they help to develop important elements of his real distinction between *esse* and *essentia* but also with regard to his notion of participation.

In general, both commentaries clearly show that Aquinas was a very subtle commentator on Boethius, whose influence would be fundamental for the development of some of the central tenets of Thomistic epistemology and ontology.[16] Or, to put it as Ralph McInerny did: "Perhaps it is only with the help of Thomas's commentaries that Boethius can speak to us today. But it is equally true that Thomas can only be understood by seeing what he learned from Boethius.... It is time we stopped trying to imagine a Thomism unindebted to its sources."[17]

I pointed above to the fact that Aquinas's interest in Boethius could seem somewhat anachronistic, and one may, of course, wonder what reasons urged him to write such commentaries. An answer to this question is certainly not easy to provide, and it is quite possible that there is not just one single reason that explains his choice. Nevertheless, turning back to the discussion from the previous section on Aquinas's criticism of Augustine's theory of knowledge, it seems plausible to suggest that, in Boethius, Aquinas found an account of human cognition and of scientific knowledge that was much more in line with his own philosophical convictions and his reading of Aristotle. In this context it has to be emphasized that, also in a broader perspective, Boethius—and above all his *Opuscula Sacra*—played a major part in the reception of Aristotelian epistemology, especially during the twelfth century, even though Boethius's role within this process has not been sufficiently appreciated thus far.[18]

Seen in the light of Aquinas's criticism of Augustine's account of human knowledge, on the one hand, and Boethius's role for the reception of Aristotelian theory of knowledge and science, on the other, Aquinas's outstanding interest in the Roman philosopher seems to be anything but incidental.

Aquinas and the Scholastic Tradition: Theology as a Science

A comprehensive study of Aquinas's Latin-Christian sources—which is still to be written—will have to do justice to a very long list of prominent thinkers, especially those from the pre-scholastic and scholastic periods, such as Anselm of Canterbury,[19] St. Bernard,[20] Richard of St.-Victor,[21] John of La Rochelle,[22] William of Auvergne,[23] and many others.

Among all the influences on Aquinas from the (pre-)scholastic tradition of the twelfth and thirteenth centuries, I wish to highlight one in particular in this brief survey, namely the concern of Latin-Christian thinkers for building a systematic theology, that is the transformation of the theological corpus into a science. Aquinas shared this same concern, and the intention and relevance of his thought can only be described adequately by placing it in the context of the previous attempts at a systematization of Christian theology.

The earliest of these attempts go back to Peter Abelard (1079–1142) and Hugh of St.-Victor (1096–1141). Abelard's works can be read as the first important step toward a systematic presentation of a *theologia christiana*, structuring the contents of theology according to the pattern *fides-caritas-sacramentum*. Hugh of St.-Victor, in turn, chose another *ordo disciplinae* for his *De sacramentis christianae fidei*—the first veritable *summa*—namely, history of salvation.[24] Yet the most important expression of this striving for the systematization of theology is the *Four Books of Sentences* (around 1150) by Peter Lombard, which I mentioned earlier. It was this text that Aquinas commented on in Paris during the 1250s. Since all bachelors in theology had to offer such a commentary to take their master's degree, this, unlike the commentaries on Boethius, was a quite conventional genre at the time. But even so, the lectures of the young *sententiarius* show that already in this early work, Aquinas did not simply follow the paths of tradition, but explained the text in a very productive manner, combining Lombard's exposition with arguments from his teacher Albert the Great and the Franciscan Bonaventure.[25]

One of Aquinas's most important and far-reaching innovations in this respect precisely concerns the *ordo disciplinae*, which I mentioned above. For, in his commentary Aquinas does not follow the (Augustinian) division proposed by Peter Lombard into things (*res*) and signs (*signa*). Instead, he suggests a different scheme for the systematic presentation and discussion of the contents of theology. Developing ideas from the *Summa aurea* (1215–29) by William of Auxerre, as well as from the *Summa Halensis* (before 1245) by Alexander of Hales (continued by John of Rupella and Bonaventure), Aquinas explains in his *Commentary on the Book of Sentences* that the subjects of theology should be organized according to the procession of all things from God as their source and their return to God as their end. In accordance with this Neoplatonic *exitus-reditus* scheme he lays out the contents from Trinity, to creation and to the nature of creation, on the one hand, and from salvation to atonement, on the other.[26]

This reorganization of the subjects of theology, which depends strongly on Aquinas's use of William of Auxerre, Alexander of Hales, and other authors, would become extremely important for his overall thought, determining the very structure of his major work, the *Summa theologiae*, written more than ten years after his commentary on Peter Lombard. Thus, in this work we again find the basic scheme of procession/God the source (*Prima Pars*), return/God the end (*Secunda Pars*), and the Christian "conditions" of this return (*Tertia Pars*).

It would, of course, be unjust to seek to reduce the influence of scholastic thinkers on Aquinas so far, but the peculiar methodological awareness, as well as the idea of a complex system of Christian theology, which together account for its status as a science, are beyond any doubt among the most decisive influences that Aquinas gathers from twelfth- and thirteenth-century Christian authors: decisive, because without these elements, which establish theology as a science, Aquinas's admirable synthesis of Christian doctrine and Greek and Arabic learning would hardly be imaginable.

Final Remarks

Introductory surveys of Aquinas's thought, if they ever deal with what he inherited from the Latin-Christian tradition, tend to point out that research on this topic is still at its very beginning and that in the near future important results are expected.[27] Curiously enough, even though time has passed by, they keep reiterating this.

In fact the problem one is facing with regard to Aquinas's Latin-Christian sources is not an isolated one, but has very much to do with the general approach to twelfth- and thirteenth-century philosophy. Historiography has characterized this period as an intellectual revolution brought about by the introduction of "new" texts and doctrines, from both Greek and Arabic philosophy, and it is therefore no surprise that these new materials feature large in the accounts of twelfth- and thirteenth-century philosophy. There can be no question that the reception of ancient Greek as well as Arabic philosophy is a distinctive hallmark of this epoch of Latin-Christian thought. Yet, as I have said, it is precisely in order to obtain an adequate interpretation of this phenomenon that one has to draw attention to the way in which the tradition of Latin-Christian philosophy and theology itself is received and transformed during these years, taking, as it does, an active part—and not just being a passive background—in some of the most salient intellectual developments of the time.

Far from being played off against a traditional—and supposedly conservative—background, the *via Thomae* is part of a much broader trend in Latin-Christian thought that has been described as the process of occidental rationalization. As I have tried to show, it is from this tradition that Aquinas takes many of his fundamental philosophical and theological motives and intuitions, which were to assume a leading role in his reception of Greek and Arabic philosophy, and which concern the theories of human knowledge and science, together with some of the key concepts of ontology and metaphysics, as well as the idea of theology as a science.

NOTES

1. Many introductions and presentations of Aquinas, when coming to discuss his sources, start off directly with Aristotelian and Neoplatonic texts. And even more well-balanced accounts tend to put his Latin-Christian bases in second place. Cf., for instance, *Tommaso d'Aquino nella storia del pensiero I: Le fonti del pensiero di S. Tommaso (Atti del congresso internazionale Tommaso d'Aquino nel suo settimo centenario)* (Naples: Edizioni Domenicane Italiane, 1975), where the chapters on Aquinas's Latin-Christian sources are placed right at the end of the volume.

2. For which, see the chapters "Aquinas and Aristotle" by James Doig, "Aquinas, Plato, and Neoplatonism" by Wayne Hankey, and "Aquinas and Jewish and Islamic Authors" by David Burrell in this volume.

3. Before this, as a *baccalaureus biblicus* at Paris, Aquinas had already written a series of Bible commentaries, i.e., on Isaiah (1251/2), Jeremiah (1251/2), Lamentations (1251/2), and the Psalms (1252/3 or later). These biblical commentaries, interesting as they are, still await a thorough appraisal. Recently Eleonore Stump has drawn attention to the (philosophical) significance of some of them: Eleonore Stump, *Aquinas* (New York: Routledge, 2003), especially 455–78 (Chapter 16: "Providence and Suffering"). Cf. also Thomas G. Weinandy et al., *Aquinas on Scripture: An Introduction to the Biblical Commentaries* (London and New York: T. & T. Clark International, 2005).

4. See, among others, the accurate account in Marie-Dominique Chenu, *Introduction à l'étude de Saint Thomas d'Aquin*, 2d ed. (Montréal/Paris: Institut d'Études Médiévales/ Vrin, 1954), 44–51.

5. For Aquinas's gnoseological position and his criticism directed at Augustine, cf. *ST* I-II q.109 a.1. In *ST* I q.79 a.4, the question seems to address both Augustine and Avicenna.

6. See the classical study by Étienne Gilson, "Pourquoi Saint Thomas a critiqué Saint Augustin," *Archives d'histoire doctrinale et littéraire du Moyen Âge* 1 (1926): 1–127.

7. See Maurice De Wulf, "L'Augustinisme 'avicennisant'," *Revue néoscolastique de philosophie* 33 (1931): 11–39.

8. Steven Marrone, *The Light of Thy Countenance: Science and Knowledge of God in the Thirteenth Century*, 2 vols. (Leiden: Brill, 2001), here 1:2.

9. Chenu, *Introduction à l'étude de Saint Thomas d'Aquin*, 47.

10. For Aquinas's place with regard to this twelfth-century tradition, see Gillian R. Evans, "The Discussions of the Scientific Status of Theology in the Second Half of the Twelfth Century," in Matthias Lutz-Bachmann, Alexander Fidora, and Andreas Niederberger, eds., *Metaphysics in the Twelfth Century: On the Relationship among Philosophy, Science and Theology* (Turnhout: Brepols, 2004), 161–83.

11. The work is available in an excellent English translation: Thomas Aquinas, *Faith, Reason and Theology*, trans. by Armand Maurer (Toronto: Pontificial Institute of Mediaeval Studies, 1987) (= *In BDT*, q.1–4) and Thomas Aquinas, *The Division and Methods of the Sciences*, 4th rev. ed., trans. by Armand Maurer (Toronto: Pontificial Institute of Mediaeval Studies, 1986) (= *In BDT*, q.5–6).

12. Cf., for instance, Matthias Lutz-Bachmann, "Die Einteilung der Wissenschaften des Thomas von Aquin. Ein Beitrag zur Rekonstruktion der Epistemologie in Quaestio 5, Artikel 1 des Kommentars von Thomas zum Trinitätstraktat des Boethius," in Rainer Berndt and Matthias Lutz-Bachmann, eds., *"Scientia" und "Disciplina": Wissenstheorie und Wissenschaftspraxis im 12. und 13. Jahrhundert* (Berlin: Akademie Verlag, 2002), 235–47.

13. Cf. *In BDT*, q.5, a.4, resp. On this topic, cf. Pasquale Porro's essay "Metafisica e teologia nella divisione delle scienze speculative del *Super Boetium De Trinitate*" in his edition of Thomas Aquinas, *Commenti a Boezio*, ed. and Italian trans. by Pasquale Porro (Milan: Bompiani, 2007), 467–526. See also the introduction to the Latin-German edition of Thomas Aquinas, *Kommentar zum Trinitätstraktat des Boethius II*, ed. and German trans. by Peter Hoffmann (Freiburg i. Br.: Herder, 2007), 7–42.

14. 1259 is the traditional dating of the work, insofar as it is seen as a follow-up to the commentary on *De Trinitate*. Yet, on the grounds of some formal coincidences with Aquinas's later commentaries on pseudo-Dionysius and Aristotle, the editors of the Leonina suggest dating its redaction to a later period. On the other hand, some scholars have claimed that the work, like the commentary on *De Trinitate*, remained a fragment; but there is hardly any evidence for such a hypothesis.

15. See, for instance, Ralph McInerny, *Boethius and Aquinas* (Washington, D.C.: Catholic University of America Press, 1990), p. xiv: "Boethius taught what Thomas said he

taught." Against this categorical claim, see Andreas Speer, "The Hidden Heritage: Boethian Metaphysics and its Medieval Tradition," in Pasquale Porro, ed., *Metaphysica—sapientia—scientia divina* (= Quaestio 5) (Turnhout: Brepols, 2005), 161–79, here 166f.: "This completely a-historical construction... overlooks the fact that Thomas, in discovering the underlying idea of the Boethian metaphysics, dismissed it fundamentally."

16. It is worth noting that Aquinas was also indebted to Boethius on other subjects, such as divine eternity and knowledge as well as the concept of *persona*.

17. McInerny, *Boethius and Aquinas*, 253.

18. On Boethius and his relevance for the reception of Aristotle in the twelfth century, see Alexander Fidora, *Die Wissenschaftstheorie des Dominicus Gundissalinus: Voraussetzungen und Konsequenzen des zweiten Anfangs der aristotelischen Philosophie im 12. Jahrhundert* (Berlin: Akademie Verlag, 2004), esp. 89–95.

19. See, among others, Matthew R. Cosgrove, "Thomas Aquinas on Anselm's Argument," *The Review of Metaphysics* 27 (1974): 513–30.

20. Cf. Clemens Vansteenkiste, "S. Bernardo nell'opera di San Tommaso," *Rassegna di letteratura tomistica* 10 (1978): 35–47.

21. See Ralph J. Masiello, "Reason and Faith in Richard of St. Victor and St. Thomas," *The New Scholasticism* 48 (1974): 233–42.

22. Cf. Beryl Smalley, "William of Auvergne, John of La Rochelle and St. Thomas Aquinas on the Old Law," in *St. Thomas Aquinas, 1274–1974: Commemorative Studies*, foreword by Étienne Gilson, 2 vols. (Toronto: Pontificial Institute of Mediaeval Studies, 1974), 2:11–71.

23. See the study by Amato Masnovo, *Da Guglielmo d'Auvergne a S. Tommaso d'Aquino*, 3 vols. (Milan: Società Editrice Vita e Pensiero, 1930–45).

24. Both can be considered important prefigurations of some of Aquinas's concerns with regard to theology. See, respectively, Rudolf Thomas, "Die Präfiguration thomistischen Denkens bei Petrus Abaelardus," in *Tommaso d'Aquino nella storia del pensiero I: Le fonti del pensiero di S. Tommaso (Atti del congresso internazionale Tommaso d'Aquino nel suo settimo centenario)* (Naples: Edizioni Domenicane Italiane, 1975), 392–98, and Rainer Berndt, "La Théologie comme système du monde: Sur l'évolution des sommes théologiques de Hugues de Saint-Victor à Saint Thomas d'Aquin," *Revue des sciences philosophiques et théologiques* 78/4 (1994): 555–72.

25. See Ludwig Jeßberger, *Das Abhängigkeitsverhältnis des hl. Thomas von Aquin von Albertus Magnus und Bonaventura im dritten Buche des "Sentenzenkommentars"* (Würzburg: Ph.D. thesis, 1936).

26. Cf. *Super Sent* I.1, d.2, q.1, pr. On this innovative rearrangement and its consequences, see Chenu, *Introduction à l'étude de Saint Thomas d'Aquin*, 226–37 and 258–65. In addition, see Elisabeth Reinhardt and Josep-Ignasi Saranyana, "La configuración de la ciencia teológica: De Hugo de San Víctor a Tomás de Aquino," *Veritas* 43/3 (1998): 549–62.

27. Cf., for instance, Fernand Van Steenberghen, *La Philosophie au XIIIe siècle* (Louvain/Paris: Publ. Univ. Louvain/Béatrice-Nauwelaerts, 1966), 335.

CHAPTER 4

AQUINAS, PLATO, AND NEOPLATONISM

WAYNE J. HANKEY

WHAT AQUINAS KNEW AND HOW HE KNEW IT

The influences of Plato, and of the wide variety of ancient, Arabic, and medieval Platonisms, on Aquinas must be distinguished from what he knows about them. The first are pervasive, persistent, and ever increasing. The second change markedly as he reads more of the commentaries and treatises of the Hellenic Neoplatonists and Peripatetics during the last decade of his work.[1] Exemplary of these is William of Moerbeke's translation of Proclus's *Elements of Theology* finished in 1268. It enabled Aquinas to discern that the *Liber de causis* was not—as had been supposed by medieval Latin Peripatetics, including himself—the cap of the Aristotelian system, describing the emanations from the First Principle. Rather, he learned, it was composed of excerpts from the *Elements*—and, unknown to Aquinas, from Plotinus—modified to conform to the needs of Islamic monotheism, just as the *Dionysian Corpus* had modified its Neoplatonic sources in Christian directions. The *Corpus*, with its quasi-Apostolic origin for Aquinas, was his most authoritative and influential source of Neoplatonism—a character intensified when conveyed in Paris interlarded with unattributed glosses from Eriugena.[2] The *Elements* confirmed what Aquinas discerned to be Dionysius's Platonic style and way of thinking, when he had explicated *The Divine Names* (1265–68); his earliest view had been that the Areopagite "mostly followed Aristotle."[3] Expositing the *Liber* in 1272 involved comparing the *Elements*, the *Dionysian Corpus*, and the *Liber* and reinforced his conviction that the latter agreed on fundamental matters—a similarity partly explained by knowledge of the *Corpus* in the Arabic circles where the *Liber* was confected.[4] In the Arab Peripatetic tradition, where Aquinas's understanding of Aristotle was formed, the philosopher had absorbed Plotinus and Proclus.[5] In judging Aquinas's Platonism, we must remember how Neoplatonic his Aristotle was because Aquinas inherited the reconciliation of Plato and Aristotle at which the Neoplatonists and Arabic Peripatetics aimed. Even what are taken to be his most characteristically Aristotelian positions, for example, intellection by way of abstraction from the sensible, are given their character in that concordance.[6]

Besides the *Dionysian Corpus* and the *Liber*, his most influential early sources of Platonism were Aristotle and Augustine; he probably read almost nothing by Plato except what was quoted by others, for example, fragments of the *Timaeus* in the commentary by the Platonist Calcidius. For Aquinas, Augustine, as well as Dionysius, "followed Plato as far as Catholic faith allowed."[7] Augustine, who shares with Avicenna—as seen by Aquinas[8]—a doctrine of human knowledge through illumination by intelligible forms, and Dionysius, for whom humans know by turning to the sensible—this is probably why Aquinas initially thought that he was an Aristotelian—are Neoplatonists in markedly different ways. Aquinas, however, treated philosophical schools as if they were syllogistic arguments in which the "way" of thinking, or "reason," determined the premises, and thus the conclusions. This framework kept him from reflecting on some of the fundamental differences within the two big groupings—Platonic and Aristotelian—between which he divides most philosophers and their Christian followers. Although, as his many and careful commentaries show, he is a diligent and determined—if sometimes polemical—student of the history of philosophy, this structure is probably the cause of his shifting and somewhat inconsistent categorizations, as well as of his judgments about philosophical thinkers that are often insensitive to important differences.

Aquinas greatly prized the Neoplatonic, as well as the Peripatetic, commentaries and paraphrases he gradually acquired, because they enabled getting to the Hellenic sources. This retrieval assisted in establishing a Neoplatonized Aristotle, in such matters as the individualization of the Agent Intellect, against the Averroism Thomas polemically ascribed to members of the Faculty of Arts in Paris.[9] Thus, for example, his last expositions of Aristotle have great portions lifted from the two commentaries of Simplicius he possessed in Moerbeke's translations.[10] His later works contain structures and conceptions derived from these, and, in his final accounts of the history of philosophy, he looked at Aristotle, as well as Plato, from the inclusive standpoint of this last great pagan Neoplatonic commentator.[11] The Neoplatonic commentaries of Macrobius and Boethius, among the Latins, and Ammonius, among the Greeks, are also important sources and influences.

Placing Platonism in the History of Philosophy

A great part of Aquinas's last writing was devoted to explicating Aristotle's works—including the *Liber de causis* attributed to him. Aquinas wishes to understand the philosophical schools: their characters, the differences between and within them, their memberships, influences, histories, and the extent to which they are complementary and may be brought into concord. For him Platonism belongs within a providentially ordered progressive development of philosophy, enabling it to serve Christian sacred doctrine. Although he distinguishes between the positions of Plato and "other Platonists" within the progress, still what the Platonists teach has been reduced to a fixed way of thinking like that of other philosophical schools and "no text...points to a difference in the via."[12] From the first, he criticizes it from within Aristotle's polemical accounts, although, under the influence of Simplicius, he came to think that at least some of Aristotle's opposition was based on misunderstanding Plato's poetic and storytelling style, a misconstrual that was particularly marked among the Peripatetics.[13] Some of the criticisms are, however, confirmed for him by later Neoplatonists, like Simplicius, who shared with Proclus, Dionysius, and the *Liber* an account of the human soul so completely descended into the realm of becoming that it is forced to turn toward the sensible. Aquinas's most knowledgeable and extensive treatments of Platonism are found in his late *On Spiritual Creatures*, *On Separate Substances*, and his exposition of the *Liber*. All show that he has read the commentary of Simplicius on the *Categories* (translation finished in 1266).

What Aquinas reproduced from that commentary enabled him to establish a complementary characterization of Platonism and Aristotelianism, set up in terms of simple oppositions occurring within the schematized progress of reason:

> The difference between these two positions stems from this, that some, in order to seek the truth about the nature of things, proceeded from intelligible reasons, and this was the particular characteristic of the Platonists. Some, however, proceeded from sensible things, and this was the particular characteristic of the philosophy of Aristotle, as Simplicius says in his commentary *Upon the Categories*.[14]

The procedure "from intelligible reasons" thinks in terms of the inherent independence of the separate substances. Despite its problems, this approach to reality was not only a necessary step on the way to Aristotle but also corrects deficient tendencies in the "Aristotelian way" with its procedure "from sensible things."

In *On Separate Substances* Aquinas gives an extended treatment of the history of philosophy, including lists of differences and agreements between Plato and Aristotle, beginning with "the opinions of the ancients and of Plato." Because of the continuous flux of bodies and the deception of the senses, the early Physicists had thought it impossible for humans "to know the certain truth of things."[15] Plato, agreeing with them "that sensible things are always in flux" and "that the sensitive power does not have certain judgment about reality,"[16] solved the problem of knowledge by positing natures in which the truth would be fixed. These were separated from what fluctuates; by adhering to them our soul knows the truth. "According to this reasoning, because the intellect when knowing the truth apprehends something beyond the matter of sensible things, Plato thought some things existed separately from sensible realities."[17]

In What Plato Erred, What He Got Right, and Where He Corrects Aristotle

Philosophy begins, thus, with two errors that must be overcome. One is the denial that humans can know with certainty. The second is that nothing exists separate from bodies. Theology requires that both errors be overcome because our understanding that God is a separate substance depends upon demonstrating His existence.[18] In fact, "we discover that God exists, by unbreakable reasons proved by the philosophers."[19] Plato solved the two errors together. However, the connection between knowledge of the truth and the existence of separate substances is not what Plato took it to be. In order to save knowledge, Plato simply reversed the Physicists, projecting what belongs to our thinking onto an external reality. In common with the Physicists, Plato held that like was known by like. The Physicists, supposing that only bodies existed, determined the knower from the known: "they thought that the form of the object known should be in the knower in the same way that it is in the thing known." On the contrary: "Plato, having perceived that the intellectual soul is immaterial and knows immaterially, held that the forms of things known exist immaterially."[20]

The Platonic reversal of the Physicists is correct because: "the nature of knowledge is opposite to the nature of materiality."[21] However, by simply changing the direction of the likeness, so that the structure of knowledge is transferred to reality, Plato remained too close to his adversaries. From a Neoplatonist, Thomas had learned very early that cognition should be considered according to a twofold way: "namely, the mode of the thing known and the mode of the knower, the mode of the thing known is not the mode of the knower, as Boethius says."[22]

When much later he compared the *Liber* with the *Elements*, while looking at the *Divine Names* of Dionysius, Aquinas examined Platonism through a work of Proclus and two of its derivatives. He arrived at a very full picture of the many levels of intellectual objects and modes of intellection in the Platonic spiritual cosmos. *On Separate Substances* represents Plato as positing two genera of entities separate from sensible things in accord with two modes of intellectual abstraction, "mathematicals and universals which he called forms or ideas."

For Aquinas, Platonic hierarchy placed mathematicals between the forms and sensibles.[23] At the highest level were entities like the good itself, intellect itself, and life itself—realities like, but, crucially, not identical with those Aquinas rightly regarded as posited in the *Divine Names*. These Dionysian conceptual names are what made Aquinas think of Dionysius as a Platonist, despite his acknowledgement that we know higher things by way of their sensible veils, which made Dionysius seem Aristotelian. Aquinas judged that the Platonic error here involved a false separation of the object from the subject of intellection. The intelligibles were separated from the intellects when the "gods, which is what Plato called the separate intelligible forms," were separated from knowing.[24] The "order of gods, that is of ideal forms, has an internal order corresponding to the order of the universality of forms."[25] This philosophical error has religious consequences. Thus, in this aspect of his teaching on the kinds of separate substances, Aristotle's parsimony is "more consonant with the Christian faith." Aristotle does not need separate forms to explain how we know, and Aquinas agreed with him in not positing forms intermediate between God and knowing beings.[26] According to Aquinas, on this, as well as when he refuses to make the first principle unknowable because it is the one-not-being, Dionysius agrees with Aristotle, the *Liber*, and Christian faith against the Platonists as understood through the *Elements*. The Areopagite abolishes the independent subsistence of the good itself, intellect itself, and life itself "for all these things are essentially the very first cause of all things...and thus we posit not many gods but one."[27] Doubtfully, Aquinas places Dionysius, whom he never contradicts, within the same Neoplatonic tradition where we locate Aquinas, that is within the ontology of pure being, probably originating in Porphyry, rather than within the henological stream, where we put Proclus. Certainly Aquinas's language here is Platonic: the one God "is itself the infinite to be" in which finite beings participate.[28] However, Aquinas is not yet finished with Platonism in his history; crucially, the Platonic tendency to multiply entities also benefits the truth.

When Aquinas treats Aristotle in *On Separate Substances*, he does not leave his Neoplatonic framework behind. Echoing a statement he found in Simplicius *Upon the Categories*, he matches what he wrote of the first of the five ways in the *Summa theologiae*. He judges that Aristotle's way of reasoning, by way of motion, to the existence of separate substances is "more evident and more certain."[29] Simplicius, adhering to the Neoplatonic tradition originating in Iamblichus, to which Proclus and Dionysius also belonged, had judged the Aristotelian way to have a more persuasive necessity in virtue of its relation to sense.[30] It is essential to this "way of motion" that its beginning belongs to the kind of knowing proper to the human place in the hierarchy of cognition. Staying "with what does not depart much from what is evident to sense" gives a greater certainty to our rational knowledge of the existence of separate substances. It shows its limits, however, when determining their kinds and numbers. On this, Aristotle's position seems "less sufficient than the position of Plato."[31] Aristotle wanted only "a dual order of separate substances" and tied their numbers to what is required to move the heavens.[32]

As against these opinions, Thomas asserts that the phenomena associated with demon possession and magic "can in no way be reduced to a corporeal cause." These phenomena require the kind of explanation "through some intellectual substances," which Thomas associates with the Platonists.[33] He is against a reduction of the phenomena to "the power of the heavenly bodies and of other natural things." Against "the Peripatetic followers of Aristotle,"[34] Aquinas makes common cause with Augustine, with Plotinus, and the Platonists generally (as represented by Augustine and many others), in asserting the existence of demons that lie outside Aristotle's two kinds of separate substance. Nonetheless, even here, the Platonists are not entirely right.

Despite the beginning from intelligible reasons, which they supposed themselves to have made, ultimately the Platonists could not escape determining the numbers of the separated intelligible forms from sensible things. For Aquinas, in the tradition of the same post-Plotinian Neoplatonic understanding of the place and orientation of the human individual soul in which Simplicius and Dionysius also stand, human reasoning in fact begins with the sensible. In consequence, the Platonists cannot avoid reproducing the sensible world in the intelligible realm: "For, since they are not able to arrive at knowledge of such substances except from sensible things, they supposed the former to be of the same species as the latter, indeed, better, to be their species."[35] The kinds of sensible things, in fact, determined for them the numbers of the separated universals. That the lower should dictate the kinds or numbers of the higher is always repugnant to Aquinas, whether the culprits are Aristotelians or Platonists. Provided that they do not make the false separation of intellection and its objects, and commit the errors which follow, Plato and his followers are right as against Aristotle. This is because, in principle, the Platonists correctly considered the nature of separated substances and the whole order of intellectual beings according to its own proper reality,[36] and in relation to the First Principle, rather than from below, and thus arrived at more kinds of separate substances, an expansion that served some of the needs of sacred doctrine.

There is much more in *On Separate Substances* concerning their numbers, including an elaborate reasoning that saves verbally opposed positions of both Proclus and Dionysius. Without following this, we can conclude that Thomas writes the history of philosophy by drawing the Platonists and the Aristotelians into a single argument in which they complement and correct each other. The principle of this correction is the Christian faith, which philosophy ultimately serves.

Some Fundamental Neoplatonic Aspects of Aquinas's *Summa theologiae*

Aquinas began the final book of the *Summa contra Gentiles* with this thoroughly Neoplatonic assertion:

> Because the most perfect unity is found in the highest summit of things, God, and because with each reality so much the more it is one, so much the greater is

> its power and dignity, it follows that, to the extent that things be further away from the First Principle, so much greater is the diversity and variety found in them. Therefore it is necessary that the process of emanation from God be united within this Principle itself, and be multiplied according to the lowliness of things, where it comes to its end.[37]

According to his own account, in the *Summa theologiae* Aquinas was finally able to give sacred teaching the order in which its proper structure would be intelligible. Thus, in order to get a glimpse at how pervasive Neoplatonism is in Aquinas, we may suitably conclude with some remarks on how, not only the *Summa theologiae* as a whole, but also particular treatises within it, describe the Neoplatonic structure of remaining, going out, and return by which all things except the One revert upon their principle.[38]

The first circle within the *Prima Pars* (*ST* I q.3–11) is constructed when, beginning with simplicity, we arrive back at unity, by way of the going out of the existence of God into all things. The circles succeeding it return to the principle by way of more and more differentiated processions. We have a unification of the Platonic dialectic of the one and the many with Aristotle's logic of activity as *entelecheia* in a Neoplatonic hierarchy.[39] Moreover, the Neoplatonic figures determine content, as well as form.

For example, a Proclean conception, that incorporeal substances have complete return upon themselves, enables the *Summa*'s progress from the circle described by simple being returning to itself as unity to the questions on the divine activities of knowing, loving, and power. Creation for Aquinas requires three emanations of two kinds. First, there are the internal emanations or processions within the divine essence, which produce real distinctions and relations within the Principle. The two emanations of the eternal Word and Holy Spirit are necessary and natural. Thomas invokes Avicenna on behalf of this necessity in God and has in mind a principle, frequent among the Neoplatonized Arabic Peripatetics, "from a simple one nothing except a unity can come."[40] Equality as a characteristic is especially appropriated to the Word as the first emanation from the Father who is the principle of the Trinitarian processions. Thus, Aquinas writes, once more in a Neoplatonic mode:

> The first thing which proceeds from unity is equality and then multiplicity proceeds. Therefore, from the Father, to whom, according to Augustine, unity is proper, the Son processes, to whom equality is appropriate, and then the creature comes forth to which inequality belongs.[41]

The multiplication of equals is the origin of the other kind of emanation, that of "all being from the universal being."[42] Throughout his writing, the emanations of divine Persons are the cause and reason of all subsequent emanations.[43] The characteristics of the procession of creatures are contrary to those within the divine essence, but determined by them. This procession is voluntary because the divine being is necessarily willing. A figure, by which the Neoplatonists reconciled Plato and Aristotle, the idea of motionless motion as characterizing the activity of the perfect, enables Aquinas to call God "living." A structure, taken from Proclus via Dionysius and the

Liber, provides the framework for the consideration of all spiritual substances from the soul to the divine; they have essence, power, and act.[44]

God is unknown to us in this present life, but not, as with Proclus, in principle. However, reason understands its own ignorance. By a combination of two Neoplatonic structures: (1) the relation between the grade of a substance in the hierarchy and its way of knowing, with (2) the systematic analogy between the ways of knowing and the grades of being, Aquinas develops his doctrine of analogy to prevent all our judgments about God being false. The correction of the mode of our knowing of God, by comparing it to the mode of his being, requires that we are simultaneously looking at reality in a human way, and regarding our place in the cosmos from the divine perspective. This capacity to look at ourselves from beyond ourselves is consequent on our participation in the higher knowing of separate substances, a characteristically Neoplatonic reworking of a reconciled Aristotle and Plato.[45] This participation is as much a fact about the psychological and ontological structure of the cosmos—and thus about the constitution of our nature and how it functions within its hierarchically situated place—as it is something vouchsafed by revelation. In fact, the top-down movement of knowing, which Aquinas reserves for revelation in contradistinction from the upward movement of philosophy, belongs to the Neoplatonic correction of Aristotle.[46]

NOTES

1. See Wayne John Hankey, "Aquinas and the Platonists," in Stephen Gersh and Martin Hoenen, eds., *The Platonic Tradition in the Middle Ages: A Doxographic Approach* (Berlin and New York: de Gruyter, 2002), 279–324.

2. Wayne John Hankey, "*Participatio divini luminis*, Aquinas' Doctrine of the Agent Intellect: Our Capacity for Contemplation," *Dionysius* 22 (2004): 165 and Larry Michael Harrington, ed., *A Thirteenth-Century Textbook of Mystical Theology at the University of Paris* (Paris, Leuven, and Dudley: Peeters, 2004).

3. *Super Sent* I.2, d.14, q.1, a.2 and *Diu. nom.*, proemium. Translations are mine.

4. See on Arabic and earlier translations of the *Corpus*, Alexander Treiger, "The Arabic Version of Pseudo-Dionysius the Areopagite's *Mystical Theology*, Chapter 1: Introduction, Critical Edition, and Translation," *Le Muséon* 120: 3–4 (2007): 365–93.

5. Alain de Libera, *La Querelle des universaux: De Platon à la fin du Moyen Age* (Paris: Des travaux, 1996), 117.

6. See Houston Smit, "Aquinas's Abstractionism," *Medieval Philosophy and Theology* 10 (2001): 85–118 and Hankey, "*Participatio divini luminis*."

7. *QDSC* 10, ad 8.

8. *SCG* 2, 74; *ST* I q.84 a.4; see Dag Nikolaus Hasse, *Avicenna's* De Anima *in the Latin West: The Formation of a Peripatetic Philosophy of the Soul, 1160–1300* (London/Turin: The Warburg Institute/Nino Aragno, 2000), 72.

9. *QDSC* 10, ad 8; *QDV* 16, 3; *ST* I q.79 a.5; see "Simplicius," *On Aristotle on the Soul 3.1–5*, trans. Henry Blumenthal (London: Duckworth, 2000), vii, 8, 220, and Wayne John Hankey, "Why Philosophy Abides for Aquinas," *The Heythrop Journal* 42:3 (2001): 338.

10. e.g. *In DC* 3, 2.

11. See Wayne John Hankey, "Thomas' Neoplatonic Histories: His Following of Simplicius," *Dionysius* 20 (2002): 153–78.

12. Robert John Henle, *Saint Thomas and Platonism: A Study of the* Plato *and* Platonici *Texts in the Writings of Saint Thomas* (The Hague: Martinus Nijhoff, 1956), 447.

13. *In DC* 1, 22; *In DA* 8, 38; *In Meta* 3, 11; *In Phy* 1, 15.

14. *QDSC* 3.

15. *DSS* 1.

16. *QDSC* 10, ad 8.

17. *DSS* 1.

18. *ST* I q.2 a.2 s.c.

19. *QDV* 10, 12; see *QDV* 14, 9 and ad 9.

20. *ST* I q.84 a.2.

21. Ibid.

22. *Super Sent* I.1, d.38, q.1, a.2; see *In BDT*, *Expositio Capituli Secundi* and Wayne John Hankey, "Aquinas, Pseudo-Denys, Proclus and Isaiah VI.6," *Archives d'histoire doctrinale et littéraire du Moyen Âge* 64 (1997): 87–90.

23. *DSS* 1.

24. *DSS* 4.

25. *In CA*, prop. 19.

26. *In CA*, prop. 10 and prop. 13.

27. *In CA*, prop. 3; on the ambiguity of Dionysius, see *Diu. nom.* 5, 1.

28. *In CA*, prop. 6; see Wayne John Hankey, "Self and Cosmos in Becoming Deiform: Neoplatonic Paradigms for Reform by Self-Knowledge from Augustine to Aquinas" in Christopher Bellitto and Louis Hamilton, eds., *Reforming the Church before Modernity: Patterns, Problems and Approaches* (Aldershot: Ashgate, 2005), 49–50 and Jean-Marc Narbonne, *Hénologie, ontologie et Ereignis (Plotin-Proclus-Heidegger)* (Paris: Les Belles Lettres, 2001), 41–70, 222–44.

29. *DSS* 2.

30. Simplicius, *Commentaire sur les Catégories d'Aristote, Traduction de Guillaume de Moerbeke*, ed. Adrien Pattin, vol. 1 (Louvain: Publications universitaires de Louvain, 1971), prologus, 8.

31. *DSS* 2.

32. Ibid.

33. Ibid.

34. *QDM* 16, 1.

35. *SCG* 2, 92.

36. *DSS* 4.

37. *SCG* 4, 1, prooemium.

38. See *ST* I q.2, prologue and Wayne John Hankey, *God in Himself: Aquinas' Doctrine of God as Expounded in the Summa Theologiae* (Oxford: Oxford University Press, 1987), passim.

39. Wayne John Hankey, "*Theoria versus Poesis*: Neoplatonism and Trinitarian Difference in Aquinas," *Modern Theology* 15 (1999): 397–408.

40. *QDP* 2, 4 and *ST* I q.41 a.2; see Wayne John Hankey, "*Ab uno simplici non est nisi unum*: The Place of Natural and Necessary Emanation in Aquinas' Doctrine of Creation," in Michael Treschow, Willemien Otten, and Walter Hannam, eds., *Divine Creation in Ancient, Medieval, and Early Modern Thought* (Leiden: Brill, 2007), 328–31.

41. *ST* I q.47 a.2 ad 2.

42. *ST* I q.45 a.4 ad 1.

43. Gilles Emery, *La Trinité Créatrice: Trinité et création dans les commentaires aux* Sentences *de Thomas d'Aquin et de ses précurseurs Albert le Grand et Bonaventure* (Paris: Vrin, 1995), 280.

44. *ST* I q.75 prologus.

45. *DSS* 4, see Hankey, *God in Himself*, 165.

46. Proclus, *Elements of Theology*, 2d ed., ed. Eric Robertson Dodds (Oxford: Clarendon, 1963), 198–99.

CHAPTER 5

AQUINAS AND JEWISH AND ISLAMIC AUTHORS

DAVID B. BURRELL, C.S.C.

If we wish to gain perspective on the medieval world of reflection, we must replace our Eurocentric image with that of a Mediterranean basin, with the commerce across this interior lake involving warfare and hostilities, yet with scholars profiting from the consequent exchange. We must also remind ourselves that if that basin was partitioned into Muslim and Christian sectors, Christian communities continued to function (and sometimes even thrive) within the Islamic world, while Jews were tolerated in both, often serving as intermediaries. So while the spirit of this basin could hardly be described as "ecumenical" in current terms, for religious differences seemed always to trump commonalities, the convictions they shared become evident to readers today reading the debates which those differences engendered. For Jews, Christians, and Muslims avow the free creation of the universe—that is, all-that-is—by the one God whose action in doing so epitomizes graciousness. That is a startling avowal at any time, yet these traditions had to make it in the early medieval period in the face of a picture of the universe and its origins that was seamless and intellectually satisfying. So the story of Islamic contributions to medieval philosophical theology will recount the ways in which a common Hellenic heritage was challenged to accommodate so startling a faith assertion as that of free creation. The sharp debates within the Muslim context were hardly known to their Christian interlocutors, but the initial recasting of al-Farabi and Avicenna (Ibn Sina) certainly were—as the "Theology of Aristotle" and the "*Liber de causis*," so the ways in which Christian thinkers adapted those schemes make a fascinating tale.

Initial Islamic Forays into Philosophical Theology: "The Philosophers"

When Islam entered the sophisticated world of the Byzantine empire, the works of Plato and of Aristotle were made available to them by virtue of Syriac translators from Greek into Arabic.[1] Of the works of Plato, it was the *Republic* that offered a model for the role of reason in the formation of a new society, and al-Farabi (875–950) articulated that model in his ground-breaking essay on the "ideas of the inhabitants of the virtuous city."[2] In that distinctly Neoplatonic work, the One is deemed to emanate all-that-is according to a perfect order, to be emulated by those responsible for ordering the perfect society. A distinctively Islamic note was struck by insisting that those responsible be prophets, as well as philosophers, since the earthly imitation of divine ordering needs to be communicated to each person in society, few of whom can follow the pattern of deductive reasoning that comprises the original emanation. It is the Qur'an, after all, which offers the paradigm of a text divinely revealed and hence impeccably wise, yet cast in a language accessible to all, replete with images and examples. None but prophets are able to order metaphor and image so as to communicate the results of philosophical reasoning, so Muhammad offers the paradigm for a responsible and wise ruler.

It was Aristotle's *Metaphysics*, however, which offered the paradigm for doing philosophy to al-Farabi's successor, Avicenna (980–1037). His *al-Shifa* adapted the cosmological scheme of al-Farabi, whereby the planetary spheres transmit the primary causal influence of the One successively to the earth.[3] So this One provides far more than Aristotle's prime mover, for in the spirit of Plotinus and of Proclus, the movement from unity to multiplicity is at once one of logic and of vitality: what is communicated is a participation in what the One possesses by nature, existence and all that flows from it. What Avicenna added to al-Farabi was an all-important distinction between this ordering and the activity that suffused it. Things are what they are by virtue of their inherent natures; their actual existence they owe directly to the One as the source of all activity. This distinction between *what something is* and the *fact that it is* had been suggested in Aristotle but never exploited by the Greeks. Its presence in a thinker as preoccupied with essences as Avicenna leads one to ask why he deemed it central to his effort to articulate the movement from the One to the many. The most plausible response is to see it as a philosophical residue of the Qur'anic teaching that the universe was freely created by the one God. It is little more than a residue, however, since the entire process of emanation flows ineluctably from the One; yet the metaphor stands nonetheless and will be exploited by Thomas Aquinas as the keystone in his attempt to articulate "the distinction" of the creator from creation.

The Distinction of *Essence* from *Existing*

God alone, as both al-Farabi and Avicenna had averred, is understood to be One whose very nature is to exist; everything else must have existence bestowed upon it by the One to whom everything that is traces its origination. In this way the distinction of *essence* from *existence* offered Avicenna a handy way of articulating what he had already recognized to be the fundamental division in being: between that One, which exists of itself, and everything else, which may or may not exist. Aristotle had defined contingency in terms of some things being able to be other than they are; Avicenna found a yet deeper understanding: everything other than the One source of all might never have been at all! By focusing in this fashion on *existing* as something that "comes to" an essence, he was able in one formula to distinguish necessary from contingent beings, as well as to limit necessary being to the One, so offering a philosophical analogue to the Qur'an's insistence that all-that-is derives from a single creator. Furthermore, the formula that God is that very one whose essence is to exist provides a formulation of "necessary being," which corresponds to the deeper understanding of contingency just noted. It is this formulation that Aquinas will exploit to offer a way of uniquely characterizing God, as well as signaling "the distinction" of creatures from the creator.[4] So we may signal the distinction that Avicenna identified as the primary contribution of Islamic thought to medieval philosophical theology. His unfortunate articulation of *existing* as an "accident," following the etymology of the Arabic (and Latin) expression of its "*coming to* the essence," however, left him vulnerable to the trenchant critique of Averroës, in his *Tahafut al-Falasifa* [*Incoherence of the Philosophers*]. It also revealed his own predilection for essences, a tendency which Aquinas sought to correct in his early opusculum, *On Being and Essence*.[5] So the distinction of essence from existing, as it came to be known, offers an intellectual reflection of the act of creating by one God, an act which (in Aquinas's terms makes the existence of creatures to be an "existence to" [*esse* ad] the creator[6]), thereby transforming Aristotle's notion of substance as simply "that which is" *tout court*. Creatures can only exist by divine action, so creating and conserving are the same action, though considered from different viewpoints.

So one can fairly say that the distinguishing mark of medieval philosophy, by contrast with its traditional Hellenic parentage, lies in its need to articulate, in properly philosophical terms, the free creation avowed in Jewish and Muslim revelational texts. Here is where the Mediterranean exchange figures prominently. We have noted how Aquinas registered his debt to Avicenna in one of his earliest writings, apparently responding to a request from his Dominican brothers to clarify the confusing terminology muddling their attempts to understand Aristotle's *Metaphysics*, and the study of *being qua being*. Yet in the process, in a characteristically creative move, he radically modified the way Avicenna had expressed the essence/existing distinction. Instead of portraying *existing* as something that "comes to" the *essence*, as an *accident* comes to a *substance*, Aquinas reached for the most profound level of composition that Aristotle had proposed: that of *potency/act*. So as *form* is said to bring *matter* into *act*, so *existing* could be said to bring *essence* into *act*. This would mean that *form*, which had been one of Aristotle's key candidates for *substance*—the very touchstone of *being-as-being* for Aristotle—would now be "reduced" to something in potency. Put otherwise, Aristotle's prime example of *act* had to be said to be in potency to *existing*. This re-iteration of the *potency/act* principle would never have occurred to Aristotle, who simply presumed that things—indeed the universe itself—exist. So it appears that the *essence/existing* distinction, as introduced by Avicenna and recast by Aquinas, is conceptually derivative from the revelation of a creator—an originating activity that Aristotle would have found unnecessary.

Moses Maimonides

Moses Maimonides (1135–1204) lived all of his life in the Islamicate, that is the linguistic and cultural world of Islam, coming eventually to serve as court physician for Saladin in Foster, the modern Cairo. He composed works of philosophy in Judaeo-Arabic (that is, Arabic with Hebrew orthography), the most significant of which is the *Guide of the Perplexed*, addressed to his student, Joseph. It was quickly translated into Hebrew, coming to Aquinas's attention in Latin translation. Aquinas's citations of this work show that he sensed an affinity with "Rabbi Moses," engaging his work in a spirit of shared inquiry, notably around the issue of free creation and that of "naming God," another place where revelation and reason intersect. As for creation, medieval discussions tended to focus on the eternity of the world versus its beginning in time, reflecting a religious concern that divided Jewish, Christian, and Muslim thinkers sharply from their pagan predecessors. Aristotle had maintained the eternity of the world because he had no way of conceiving it as a whole but could only presume it as a given—as the context for whatever else might be said or thought. When Plotinus would take the next step to insist on origination, the presumption of everlasting origination held. Indeed, the contrary assertion—that it had been created in the moment when time thus began—would require access to a perspective beyond the world. Affirming creation required faith in a revelation, and revelation presupposed one revealing. As Maimonides put it: "as for us, the matter is clear...: that all things exist in virtue of a purpose and not of necessity, and that He who purposed them may change them."[7] Necessary emanation from the One (as Maimonides understood Plotinus, refracted through al-Farabi) does not count as creation, for on that picture the First is not clearly distinct from the ensuing series, so the Oneness of God is jeopardized. Aquinas will accept Maimonides' contention that we cannot demonstrate from such a purposeful dependence clearly "in favor of the world's having been produced in time,"[8] yet the presumption in favor of an eternal world had also been shown to be undemonstrable, leaving Torah believers free to accept creation *de novo*, as well as *ex nihilo*.

The philosophical discussion, however, has only begun. Avicenna had tried to reconcile Qur'anic assertions about creation with a pre-existent (and eternal) matter because he could see no other place to locate the possibility that what came to be would come to be. (Aquinas distinguished real possibility from merely conceptual non-repugnance, located within the mind of the maker.) Yet a clear conception of *creatio ex nihilo* would similarly founder on identifying the proper effect of the creator, since analogies with human making inevitably demanded something be presupposed. Maimonides did not even attempt this articulation, though his endorsing practical knowing as a useful way of intimating to ourselves the divine knowing that utterly escapes us[9] offers Aquinas a leading analogy of artisan to artifact. Similarly, Avicenna's distinguishing existence from the essence of created things will allow Aquinas to identify "*esse* as the proper effect of the first cause,"[10] once he had painstakingly refined Avicenna's distinction, as we have seen, as well as carefully distinguished practical from speculative knowing. As Maimonides notes, "a great disparity exists between the knowledge an artificer has of the thing he has made and the knowledge someone else has of the artifact in question."[11] The latter form of knowledge corresponds to our way of knowing "the things from which we acquire the knowledge [we have] of them," whereas "the things in question follow upon [God's] knowledge," as the artifact an artisan. The analogy is hardly a novel one; creating is usually proposed as a making or modeling. Besides Genesis 2, we are also reminded of Jeremiah: "as clay is in the potter's hand, so you are in mine, House of Israel" (Jer. 18:6). What makes it a bold comparison, however, is to think of God so related to all there is as artisan to artifact. For the knowledge involved is too inarticulate to satisfy the philosopher in us, while the relationship of clay to potter is too passive and mute to meet the demands for independent agency that we associate with freedom.

So Aquinas will need to specify what it is that can properly be said to come forth from God, as the shape of the pot does from the potter's hands. Maimonides' context evoked a parallel concern: "to explain to you...that what exists indicates to us of necessity that it does exist in virtue of the purpose of One who purposed it,"[12] yet how can one safeguard the integrity of created natures while acknowledging the creator's sovereignty? Aquinas refines the distinction introduced by Avicenna at the heart of all created being to identify the effect proper to God's creative action: the very existence of things. Avicenna's distinction of essence from existence was well known to Maimonides; he in fact invokes it to characterize God as the One whose "existence is identical with His essence and His true reality"—unlike everything else where "existence is an accident attaching to what exists."[13] But as his literal adherence to the language of Avicenna suggests, Maimonides had not yet seen how one might characterize this "accident" as a constitutive principle of created being.

That was to be Aquinas's signal achievement, elaborated early on and used, as we have seen, to characterize the uniqueness of God (in a passage reminiscent of Maimonides), as well as in his treatment of creation. So for Aquinas, "everything...is potential when compared to existence," so much so that we must acknowledge that "existence is more intimately and profoundly interior to things than anything else."[14]

Indeed, that is how the creator is present to each created thing "according to the manner in which it has its existence"[15] because "*esse* (existence) is the proper effect of the first and most universal cause."[16] Since the fact that something exists is not a feature of a thing—not an *accident*, as Avicenna's unfortunate choice of words suggested—we need not fear to identify it as an effect proper to divinity, for there will be no way for us to pick it out as we can find traces of ordinary causes. The situation is paradoxical, not unlike a Zen *koan*: that which is most actual in each thing—what makes it exist—escapes our notice because it cannot be isolated as a feature of the thing. In that sense, then, we cannot talk about it, for what we call features of things are precisely those things we can say about them. On reflection, however, that should not surprise us, since the fact that something exists is not customarily listed among its characteristics. It must, then, be a special sort of fact, which is exactly Aquinas's point in singling out *esse* as "the actuality of every form or nature" that exists.

By recasting Avicenna's distinction as he has, Aquinas is able to offer a coherent characterization of the act of creation without pretending to have described it. That is appropriate, moreover, since the relation of the One who is source of all to all that originates from it will not be susceptible of description, since it is not a relation within the world. Existence [*esse*], understood as actuality, becomes the vehicle for articulating God's transcendence, as well as what links created things with their creator. It should now be clear how central a role this account of creation plays in the development of Aquinas's thought. We have seen how it offered him a philosophical basis for confidently asserting a transcendent referent for analogous terms: "whatever is said both of God and creatures is said in virtue of the order that creatures have to God as their source and cause."[17] Although such terms will "signify what God is... imperfectly,"[18] that is to be expected, since they are not being used to signify an object in the world but the source of all. What is remarkable, then, is not that we cannot speak adequately of divinity, but that we can use our language to speak truthfully of God at all.[19]

So Maimonides' concern that the demands of philosophical discourse does not undermine the uniqueness and transcendence of God is Aquinas's as well; he has simply discovered a way of enriching that discourse to the point where philosophy can serve our confession of faith in the One while exploiting hidden resources in our ordinary human language to highlight his distinctive way of characterizing that divine activity. For his part, Maimonides was clearly working without a developed notion of analogical discourse, which led to his celebrated "agnosticism" regarding our knowledge of God. Against the background of a Muslim controversy regarding how we might responsibly apply ninety-nine names to the one God, Maimonides had to insist that nothing could be said accidentally of the One without compromising the primary confession of the community's faith: "the Lord, our God, is One."

Aquinas develops his own position in explicit opposition to Maimonides,[20] suggesting some disparity in the thought world each inhabited. For a century or more of preoccupation in the West with the diverse uses of language in the Scriptures had prepared the ground for the fruitful ways in which Aquinas would develop Aristotle's rather cryptic remarks on "analogy," whereas the Islamic philosophers with whom Maimonides (and his friend Joseph) were conversant had been engaged on a more architectonic enterprise, while the rabbis in Moses' own tradition had been content to remind themselves how frequently "the Torah speaks in the language of men." Yet a systematic grappling with religious language demands greater sophistication for the semantics structuring our use of terms attributing perfections to God.

Aquinas called upon and expanded key distinctions already articulated in the "speculative grammar" developed during the century preceding him. Recent studies on analogy in Aquinas have made us attend to the way his treatment follows the contours of our linguistic capacities. So, by way of offering a constructive alternative to Maimonides' radical agnosticism, Aquinas insists:

> Words are used of God and creatures in an analogical way, that is in accordance with a certain order between them.... In this way some words are used neither univocally nor purely equivocally of God and creatures, but analogically, for we cannot speak of God at all except in the language we use of creatures, and so whatever is said both of God and creatures is said in virtue of the order that creatures have to God as their source and cause in which all perfections of things pre-exist transcendently.[21]

So "this way of using words [that] lies somewhere between pure equivocation and simple univocity"[22] will require neither an intermediary between God and the world nor a predication of God that is accidental. Instead, Aquinas focuses on the ordering that relates creature with creator, noting how certain words are especially useful to articulate that order—namely, those that express the perfections accruing to creatures from their source while also orienting rational creatures to that same source as their goal. It is all here, compressed in Aquinas's lapidary prose: the elasticity which ordinary usage demands of certain terms, as well as the way those same terms can invoke spiritual creatures' intentional orientation to the creator as their final end. So the "fact" of creation is presumed as a premise in the argument, allowing us to recognize how normative terms require us to distinguish the "mode of signifying" from the "thing signified"—our characteristic mode of expression from its intended object, thereby pointing to a transcendent dimension in our ordinary usage. For we could never aspire to a more just society, if "just" merely described arrangements we were familiar with. That certain terms possess this transcendent dimension in their ordinary usage manifests a constitutive feature of intentional creatures in their struggle to "go on," so revealing a feature of creation itself.

Aquinas can then insist that such terms can "signify what God is although they do so imperfectly" and show as well how their distinct meanings do not imply a plurality of features in God. Attention to language, coupled with explicit reliance on the order following upon creation, enables him to clarify issues that so vexed Islamic thinkers: "since we know God from creatures, we understand him through concepts appropriate to the perfections creatures receive from him."[23] The language of perfections must outstrip itself, as we have seen, so we are entitled to project it responsibly to its transcendent source while renouncing any claim to thoroughly understanding that use: "such terms signify what God is...imperfectly." One reason we cannot attain an adequate grasp of the transcendent application of these terms is that such perfections must "pre-exist in God in a simple and unified way," since asserting that God is just is not so much to discover that God is characterized by justice, or even to celebrate God as the source of justice, but to encourage us to reflect on how such a source itself might exist, even when its mode of existence will escape our characterization.

Moreover, the other side of that reminder is to return to where we began to note how "what pre-exists in God in a simple and unified way is divided among creatures as many and varied perfections."[24] So it is not the mere "fact" of creation that is presupposed to this argument, but the dynamic orientation of intentional creatures to their source. Normally associated with the fifth-century philosophical theologian, pseudo-Dionysius, who showed Aquinas how to incorporate the power of Neoplatonism without adopting its luxuriant hierarchical schemes, this ordering from and to a creator not only accounts for the very structure of the *Summa theologiae* but also provides the key for Aquinas's remarkable articulation of dependent beings as independent agents. Yet we can see how, in doing just that, he remained beholden to his Jewish and Muslim predecessors, who had helped him articulate conceptual innovations in the Greek philosophy they had all inherited, to articulate the key relational datum of free creation.

NOTES

1. Richard Walzer, *Greek into Arabic: Essays in Islamic Philosophy* (Columbia: University of South Carolina Press, 1962).
2. Richard Walzer, *Al-Farabi on the Perfect State* (Oxford: Clarendon Press, 1985).
3. Avicenna, *The Metaphysics of Healing*, trans. Michael Marmura (Provo, Utah: Brigham Young University Press, 2005); Robert Wisnovsky, *Avicenna's Metaphysics in Context* (London: Duckworth, 2003).
4. *ST* I q.3 a.4: "God is God's own *existing*."
5. David Burrell, *Knowing the Unknowable God: Ibn Sina, Maimonides, Aquinas* (Notre Dame, Ind.: University of Notre Dame Press, 1986).
6. *ST* I q.45 a.3: "creation is in creatures as a *relation*."
7. Maimonides, *The Guide of the Perplexed*, trans. Shlomo Pines (Chicago: University of Chicago Press, 1963), 2.19.
8. Ibid. 2.21.
9. Ibid. 3.21.
10. *ST* I q.45 a.5.
11. *Guide*, 3.21.
12. *Guide*, 2.19.
13. *Guide*, 1.57.
14. *ST* I q.8 a.1.
15. *ST* I q.8 a.1.
16. *ST* I q.45 a.5.

17. *ST* I q.13 a.5.
18. *ST* I q.13 a.4.
19. *ST* I q.13 a.12.
20. *ST* I q.13 a.2.
21. *ST* I q.13 a.5.
22. Ibid.
23. *ST* I q.13 a.4.
24. Ibid.

PART II

METAPHYSICS AND THE EXISTENCE OF GOD

CHAPTER 6

BEING

JOHN F. WIPPEL

According to Aquinas the word "being" (*ens*) signifies "that which is" or "that which exists."[1] This complexity within the notion of being implies that one does not grasp it by the process of abstraction alone—the intellect's first operation whereby it understands what something is without affirming or denying anything of it. While he acknowledges that this intellectual operation suffices for one to grasp the quidditative aspect of being ("that which"), Aquinas appeals to the intellect's second operation (whereby one affirms or denies by composing or dividing), often referred to as judgment, to account for one's grasp of the existential aspect of being and thus to complete one's understanding of being as that which is. As he explains, while the intellect's first operation is directed to the nature (essence) of a thing, its second operation is directed to a thing's existence (*esse*).[2]

The Subject of Metaphysics

Aquinas holds that the subject of metaphysics is being as being, or as he sometimes expresses this, being in general, rather than any restricted part of being such as mobile being (studied by physics) or quantified being (studied by mathematics). Hence, the subject of metaphysics—being as being—does not depend upon sensible matter and motion to exist and to be understood (as does the subject of physics), nor does it depend upon sensible matter to exist although not to be understood (as does the subject of mathematics).[3] But he also distinguishes two ways in which something studied by a theoretical science may not depend upon matter and motion to exist or to be understood, first, in the sense that it can never be found in matter, as is true of God and angels, or second, in the sense that it need not be found in matter and motion although it sometimes is, as is true of substance, quality, being, potency, act, the one and the many, and things like this. It is this second kind of freedom from dependence upon matter and motion that Aquinas assigns to the subject of metaphysics—being as being.[4]

In order to account for one's discovery of being as being, Aquinas appeals to another kind of judgment, a negative judgment, as distinguished from the positive judgment of existence described above, and which in his Commentary on the *De Trinitate* he calls "separation." Through this judgment one recognizes a distinction between that by reason of which something enjoys being as such and that by reason of which it enjoys a given kind of being, and one denies that being as such must be restricted to any particular kind of being. One thereby discovers being taken universally, that is, being as being, the subject of metaphysics, and what one may call a metaphysical notion of being.[5]

In defending being as being as the subject of metaphysics, Aquinas is following Aristotle's thinking as set forth in Book IV, cc. 1–2 of his *Metaphysics*, and in the opening lines of Book VI, c. 1. But because of an approach introduced in the latter part of Book VI, c. 1 (1026a 10–32), according to which first philosophy or divine science studies separate substances, two different lines of interpretation had developed within the Aristotelian tradition. One tradition, well represented by Avicenna, denies that God is the subject of metaphysics and insists that its subject is rather being as being.[6] Another, represented by Averroës, is heavily influenced by Aristotle's text in *Metaphysics*, Book VI, c. 1, and concludes that the subject of this science is separate entity or divine being.[7]

Aquinas offers an interesting solution to this issue. A theoretical science must have a distinctive subject. But it also belongs to a theoretical science as its end or goal to arrive at knowledge of the cause or principle of its subject. Aquinas agrees with Avicenna (and with most of his thirteenth-century contemporaries) that the subject of metaphysics is not God or divine being, but being as being; he holds that it pertains to metaphysics to arrive at knowledge of God as its end or goal and that, because of this, it can also be called divine science. Thus, there is in fact no distinction between metaphysics, the science of being as being, and a philosophical divine science. Even so, Aquinas also maintains not only that God is not the subject of metaphysics, but that he is not included under the notion of being as being that serves as its subject. God is considered by metaphysics only indirectly, as the cause and principle of its subject—being as being.[8]

Division and Multiplication of Being

Given the universal character of the subject of metaphysics—being as being—, Aquinas must account for the multiplication of being itself and therefore, because multiplication presupposes division, for some kind of division within being. He recognizes with Parmenides that being cannot be divided by something completely outside being itself in the way a genus is divided into species by differences; for outside being there is only nonbeing and, as he also holds, being is not a genus.[9]

Against Parmenides, however, Aquinas reasons that being can be divided by certain modes that are realized within being itself. These may be either certain general modes that follow upon every being, or more particularized modes that correspond to diverse modes of existing. The general modes of being (often referred to as transcendentals) are found wherever being itself is realized so that every being is also "one" (undivided from itself), a "thing," "something" (distinct from other things), "good," and "true."[10] Corresponding to the more particularized modes are the ten predicaments, each of which corresponds to a particular mode of existing (*modus essendi*).[11] Going beyond Aristotle, on at least two occasions Aquinas offers a detailed justification of ten predicaments, each time ending up with substance, quantity, quality, relation, condition (*habitus*), time when (*quando*), place where (*ubi*), position (*situs*), action, and passion. While Aquinas recognizes their importance as logical categories, by ultimately grounding them in distinctive modes of existing, he shows that they also fall under the consideration of metaphysics.[12]

Most important for Aquinas, as for Aristotle, is the first of the predicaments—substance, especially when taken as the individual subject (*suppositum*), which he often refers to as a "particular something" (*hoc aliquid*). Aquinas denies that a proper definition can be given for substance or for the other predicaments because each of them is a supreme genus and again because being itself cannot be regarded as a genus. As regards substance, one might attempt to define it as "being which exists in itself (per se)." While Aquinas does at times refer to it this way, he rejects this as a proper definition of substance, but offers a description or "quasi-definition" of it as "a thing to whose quiddity it belongs to exist not in something (else)." Likewise, he rejects the definition of accident as "that which exists in something else" and accepts as a correct description of it "a thing to whose nature it belongs to exist in something else."[13]

Essence and Existence

Aquinas argues for a fundamental composition and distinction within every finite substance of two distinct ontological principles of being: an essence that accounts for the fact that it is a being of a given kind and a distinct act of existing (*esse*) that accounts for the fact that it actually exists. Since he often uses the Latin term *esse* to describe this second principle, the reader should be aware that he also frequently enough uses the same Latin word *esse*, or one of its derivative forms, simply to signify the fact that a given thing exists. For Aquinas, if a substance actually exists, this can only be because an intrinsic act of existing is present within it, which actualizes its essence. These two usages of *esse* must not be identified or confused with one another.[14]

Aquinas regards this act of existing as the most fundamental ontological principle within any existing substance and refers to it as the "actuality of all acts and the perfection of all perfections."[15] It is always realized in a finite substance only to a finite degree. Given Aquinas's view that act is not self-limiting, it follows that within any finite being its act of existing is received and limited by its corresponding essence. Indeed, this is one way in which he argues for the presence of these as two distinct principles within finite entities.[16] He also argues formally for the presence of this distinction and composition in such entities in a number of other ways. Perhaps best known is the long and complex argument presented in his youthful *De ente et essentia*, c. 4. There he is rejecting a theory he attributes to Avicebron, according to which all beings with the exception of God are composed of form and matter—a spiritual matter in the case of created separate substances and human souls. Many of Aquinas's contemporaries maintained that such matter–form composition is necessary in order to avoid attributing the perfect simplicity of God to created spiritual entities. Against this, Aquinas argues that while purely spiritual beings cannot be composed of matter and form, they are nonetheless not perfectly simple; for they are composed of a form (= essence) and a distinct act of existing, which are correlated as potency and act.[17]

To support this, Aquinas reasons in a first stage of his argument that whatever is not included within the understanding of an essence or quiddity comes to it from without and enters into composition with it. This is because no essence or quiddity can be understood without an understanding of its parts. But every essence or quiddity can be understood without anything being understood of its existence *(esse)*; for I can understand what a human being is or what a phoenix is, and not know whether it exists in reality. Therefore, its existence (*esse*) is other than its quiddity or essence.[18] If one were to end this argument here and remove it from its context, it would be open to two serious criticisms. First, while it suffices to show that it is different for us to understand what something is and to understand that it is, this of itself would not justify our concluding immediately to the presence of two distinct ontological principles—essence and an act of existing, within finite beings themselves. Second, in appealing to one's ability to know what something is without knowing that it exists, one is taking the term *esse* as signifying the fact that something exists; but to succeed the argument must conclude to the presence of *esse* taken as an act of existing distinct from the essence of any finite being.

Aquinas, however, does not stop at this point but goes on to consider the possibility that there might be some being that is identical with its act of existing. If there is, perhaps, such a being, he reasons, it can only be unique and first, since it could be multiplied in only one of three ways: (1) by the addition of a difference in the way that a generic nature is multiplied in its species, or (2) in the way a form is received in different instances of matter when a specific nature is multiplied in different individuals, or (3) because in one instance it is absolute and unreceived, and in all other cases it is received in something else. But if there were a being that is nothing but its act of existing (subsisting *esse*), it could not be multiplied in the first way; for then it would be its act of existing plus a differentiating form. Nor could it be multiplied in the second way by being received in different instances of matter, for then it would no longer be pure *esse*, but *esse* plus the particular matter that receives and multiplies it. By process of elimination, therefore, Aquinas concludes that there can at most be one being that is its very act of existing, since, under the third hypothesis which he accepts, in all other entities with only one possible exception, a thing's act of existing is received in a distinct subject, that is, its essence. Given this, he concludes that in all other beings including separate substances, there must be a distinction between a thing's quiddity or nature or form and its act of existing.[19]

In the third stage of this argument, Aquinas uses the distinction he has just established between an essence and an act of existing in all beings, with only one possible exception, to show that such beings depend upon something else for their existence and are therefore efficiently caused. Then, by reasoning from their efficiently caused existence, he concludes to the existence of an uncaused cause of their existence, which is identical with its act of existing, and which is God. In other words, he now proves that the one possible instance of a being that is identical with its act of existing exists in actuality. And since in every other being its essence principle receives its act of existing, in such entities essence is related to existence as potentiality to actuality.[20]

In other contexts Aquinas argues for this same distinction and composition in other ways, frequently in his more mature writings by developing the reasoning he had proposed in stage two of the argument from the *De ente*. In order to account for the division and multiplication of beings and their distinction from God, he reasons that one must posit a composition and distinction of essence and act of existing within them. For instance, in *SCG* II, c. 52, he offers three different versions of this type of argument, each of which maintains that there can be only one instance of self-subsisting existence (*esse*) and hence that in all other beings essence and the act of existing must differ. In this context, since he has already established God's existence in Book I, c. 13, he assumes in these arguments that God actually exists, unlike his approach in *De ente*, c. 4. But the inner logic of these arguments does not require this assumption.[21] He also sometimes reasons from the participated character of finite beings to a distinction and composition within them of a participated act of existing and an essence that receives and participates in the act of existing.[22]

Participation

The last mentioned approach may be used to introduce another important part of Aquinas's metaphysics, his theory of participation.[23] As Aquinas explains in his Commentary on the *De Hebdomadibus*, "To participate is, as it were, to take a part [of something]. And, therefore, when something receives in particular fashion that which belongs to another in universal (or total) fashion, the former is said to participate in the latter."[24] In other words, participation is a way of accounting for the fact that the same kind of perfection can be shared by many different subjects, or of addressing the problem of the One and the Many.

Here Aquinas distinguishes different types of participation. First, human being may be said to participate in animal because it does not possess the nature of animal according to its full universality; and in like fashion an individual such as Socrates may be said to participate in the species human being. In each of these cases, a less universal concept (whether of a species or an individual) shares in but does not exhaust the intelligible content of a more universal concept (whether of a genus or of a species), and hence these are examples of what we may call logical participation. In addition, a subject may be said to participate in an accident, and matter may be said to participate in form because either the accidental form or the substantial form, each of which in itself is common, is restricted to this or that subject. These are examples of real or ontological participation. But Aquinas then lists a third kind of participation, which is also an example of real or ontological participation, whereby an effect may be said to participate in its cause, and especially when it is not equal to the power of its cause.[25]

One may ask where the participation of beings in the act of existing (*esse*) fits into Aquinas's division, since this is of greatest interest to the metaphysician. He argues that the act of existing cannot participate in something else in either of the first two ways he has just distinguished. But he often refers to being, or essence, or nature as participating in the act of existing. For instance, here he writes that because being (*ens*) is expressed concretely, [a] being can be said to participate in existence as something taken concretely participates in something taken abstractly.[26] He also notes that if something is to be the subject of an accident, it must participate in the act of existing, that is to say, it must exist. And so, he continues, if the act of existing and "that which is" differ only intentionally in perfectly simple beings, they differ really in composite entities. But because there is only one perfectly simple being (God), there is only one being which does not participate in the act of existing and which is subsisting existence itself.[27]

Moreover, he distinguishes different ways in which the term existence (*esse*) can be understood when one speaks of a being or nature as participating in it, namely, (1) as participating in self-subsisting *esse* (God), or (2) as participating in the act of existing viewed universally (*esse commune*), or (3) as participating in its own act of existing.[28] A finite or created nature or being participates in self-subsisting *esse* or God by likeness as in its unparticipated source and as in its first efficient cause (and exemplar cause, as Aquinas sometimes adds), and so this kind of participation clearly fits under the third main type distinguished above. By extension, therefore, it seems appropriate to locate the other two ways of participating in *esse* under that same division.

NOTES

1. See *ST* I-II q.26 a.4: "being (*ens*) in the absolute sense is that which has existence (*esse*)." *Sancti Thomae de Aquino Opera Omnia* (Rome: Leon. ed., 1882), v. 6, p. 190 = Leon. 6.190; *Expositio libri Boetii De hebdomadibus* [*In BDH*], lec. 2: "so we can say that being (*ens*), or that which is, is insofar as it participates in the act of existing" (Leon. 50.271:57–59); line 97: "But that which is, or being. . . ." (translations of Aquinas throughout are mine).

2. See *In BDT*, q.5, a.3 (Leon. 50.147:89–105). Also see *Super Sent* I, d.19, q.5, a.1, ad 7 (Mandonnet ed., vol. 1, 489); d.38, q.1, a.3, 903. Étienne Gilson has emphasized Aquinas's appeal to judgment to account for the intellect's grasp of being as existing, especially in his *Being and Some Philosophers* (Toronto: Pontifical Institute of Mediaeval Studies, 1952), c.6. For my interpretation of this and for references to some who reject this reading of Aquinas, see John Wippel, *The Metaphysical Thought of Thomas Aquinas: From Finite Being to Uncreated Being* (Washington, D.C.: Catholic University of America Press, 2000), 24–30.

3. *In BDT*, q.5, a.1 (Leon. 50.138:141–55).

4. Ibid., lines 155–60. Also see q.5, a.4 (Leon. 50.154:186–99), and lines 160–61 on the subject of metaphysics as being insofar as it is being. For reference to this as being in general (*ens commune*), see *In Meta*, Prooemium (Turin and Rome: Marietti, 1950), 2.

5. *In BDT*, q.5, a.3 (Leon. 50.148:161–69; 149:156–258, 270–74, 276–79). A correct understanding of Aquinas's teaching on "séparation" finally became possible when a correct text of the key passages was finally published, beginning with a fundamental article by Louis-B. Geiger, "Abstraction et séparation d'après s. Thomas *In De Trinitate* q.5, a.3," *Revue des sciences philosophiques et théologiques* 31 (1947): 3–40, followed by an excellent critical edition by Bruno Decker, (1955, 2d ed., 1959), and finally the Leonine ed. (1992). On "separation," see Wippel, *Metaphysical Thought of Thomas Aquinas*, 45–51 and 51–62, on the dispute among Thomistic scholars concerning whether it presupposes prior knowledge of the existence of some separate substance.

6. *Liber de philosophia prima sive scientia divina I–IV*, ed. S. Van Riet (Louvain/Leiden: Peeters/Brill, 1977), I, c.1, 4–6; c.2, 9–13.

7. *In Phy* I, com. 83, in his *Opera omnia* (Venice: 1562–74), v. 4, fol. 47rb-vb; *In Meta* VI, com. 2–3, v. 8, fols. 146rb–147ra. For this in Avicenna, Averroës, and many medieval thinkers, see Albert Zimmermann, *Ontologie oder Metaphysik? Die Diskussion über den Gegenstand der Metaphysik im 13. und 14. Jahrhundert* (Leuven: Peeters, 1998).

8. See *In BDT*, q.5, a.4 (Leon. 50.153:80–87, 154:157–201). Also see *In Meta*, Prooemium, 1–2, on *ens commune* as the subject. For his exclusion of God from *esse commune* (which is coextensive with *ens commune*), see *Div. nom.* V, lec. 2, ed. C. Pera (Turin and Rome: Marietti, 1950), 245, n. 660. See Zimmermann, *Ontologie oder Metaphysik*, 216–23.

9. See *QDV*, q.1, a.1 (Leon. 22.1.5:106–111); *In Meta* I, lec. 9, 41, n. 138, and n. 139, where he accuses Parmenides of having viewed being as if it were univocal, like the nature of a genus.

10. *QDV*, q.1, a.1 (Leon. 22.1.5:124–61). On all of these, see Jan A. Aertsen, *Medieval Philosophy and the Transcendentals: The Case of Thomas Aquinas* (Leiden, New York, and Cologne: Brill Academic Publishers, 1996).

11. *QDV*, q.1, a.1 (Leon. 22.1.5:114–23).

12. See *In Meta* V, lec. 9, 238, n. 890: "Wherefore it is necessary that being be restricted to diverse genera in accord with diverse modes of predicating, which modes follow upon diverse modes of existing." See pp. 238–39, nn. 891–92 for his derivation of the ten

predicaments. For a slightly different derivation, see *In Phy* III, ed. P. M. Maggiòlo (Turin and Rome: Marietti, 1953), lec. 5, 158–59, nn. 322–23. On these derivations, see Wippel, *Metaphysical Thought of Thomas Aquinas*, 210–28.

13. For references to substance as existing per se, see *In Meta* IV, lec. 1, 152, n. 539; *In Meta* V, lec. 10, 903; *QDP*, q.9, a.1, ed. M. Pession (Turin and Rome: Marietti, 1953), 226; *QDV* q.1, a.1 (Leon. 22.1.5:119–23). For Aquinas's rejection of being per se as the definition of substance and defense of his alternative, see *Super Sent* IV, d.12, q.1, a.1, ql.1, ad 2 (Moos ed.), v. 4, 499; *SCG* I, c.25 (Ed. Leonina manualis, Rome, 1934), 27; *QDP*, q.9, a.1, ad 4 (194); *ST* I q.3 a.5, ad 1 (Leon. 4.44). On accidents, see *Super Sent* IV (ibid.); *Quodl* 9, q.3, a.1, ad 2 (Leon. 25.1.99:78–90). For discussion, see Wippel, *Metaphysical Thought of Thomas Aquinas*, 228–37.

14. On this distinction, see Wippel, *Metaphysical Thought of Thomas Aquinas*, 31–35.

15. *QDP*, q.7, a.2, ad 9, 192; *ST* I q.3 a.4 (Leon. 4.42).

16. See *Super Sent* I, d.8, q.5, a.1 (Mandonnet ed.), v. 1, 226. For discussion and other texts, see Wippel, *Metaphysical Thought of Thomas Aquinas*, 170–76.

17. *DEE*, c.4 (Leon. 43.375:1–376:93, esp. lines 90–93).

18. Ibid., lines 94–103.

19. Leon. 43.376:103–377:126.

20. Ibid., 377:127–53. The proper interpretation of Aquinas's argumentation in *De ente*, c.4, has been much disputed by various scholars. For the reading offered here, see Wippel, *Metaphysical Thought of Thomas Aquinas*, 137–50. For other interpretations, see there nn. 11 (with references to a series of discussions between Joseph Owens and myself), 13, 14 (esp. the references to Cornelio Fabro and Scott MacDonald), 15. Also now see David Twetten, "Really Distinguishing Essence from Existence," in Peter A. Kwasniewski, ed., *Wisdom's Apprentice: Thomistic Essays in Honor of Lawrence Dewan, O.P.* (Washington, D.C.: Catholic University of America Press, 2007), 40–84.

21. Ed. Leon. man., p. 145, the first three arguments. On these and other arguments of this type, see Wippel, *Metaphysical Thought of Thomas Aquinas*, 151–57.

22. See ibid. 161–70 for texts and discussion.

23. Much credit for the rediscovery of this long neglected doctrine in Aquinas must be given to Cornelio Fabro, *La nozione metafisica di partecipazione secondo S. Tommaso d'Aquino*, 2d rev. ed. (Turin: Società editrice internazionale, 1950); L.-B. Geiger, *La Participation dans la philosophie de S. Thomas d'Aquin*, 2d ed. (Paris: J. Vrin, 1953). Also see more recently Rudi te Velde, *Participation and Substantiality in Thomas Aquinas* (Leiden: E. J. Brill, 1995); Wippel, *Metaphysical Thought of Thomas Aquinas*, 94–131.

24. Leon. 50.271.70–73.

25. Leon. 50.271:77–85.

26. Ibid., lines 85–102.

27. Leon. 50.272:180–85; 272:204–73:205; 273:249–58.

28. See *Quodl* 12, q.4, a.1 (Leon. 25.2.404:16–25), on participating by likeness in the First Act, which is subsisting existence (*esse*); *In BDH*, lec. 2 (Leon. 50:273:240–43), on participating in existence in general (*esse commune*); *Super Sent* I, d.29, q.5, a.2 (Mandonnet ed., v. 1, 491), on a creature's participating in its own created *esse*.

CHAPTER 7

MATTER, FORM, AND INDIVIDUATION

JEFFREY E. BROWER

FEW notions are more central to Aquinas's thought than those of matter and form. Although he invokes these notions in a number of different contexts, and puts them to a number of different uses, he always assumes that in their primary or basic sense they are correlative both with each other and with the notion of a "hylomorphic compound"—that is, a compound of matter (*hyle*) and form (*morphe*). Thus, matter is an entity that can have form, form is an entity that can be had by matter, and a hylomorphic compound is an entity that exists when the potentiality of some matter to have form is actualized.[1] What is more, Aquinas assumes that the matter of a hylomorphic compound explains certain of its general characteristics, whereas its form explains certain of its more specific characteristics. Thus, the matter of a bronze statue explains the fact that it is bronze, whereas its form explains the fact that it is a statue. Again, the matter of a human being explains the fact that it is a material object, whereas its form explains the specific type of material object it is (namely, *human*).

My aim in this chapter is to provide a systematic introduction to Aquinas's primary or basic notions of matter and form. To accomplish this aim, I focus on the two main theoretical contexts in which he deploys them—namely, his theory of change and his theory of individuation. In both contexts, as we shall see, Aquinas appeals to matter and form to account for relations of sameness and difference holding between distinct individuals.

MATTER, FORM, AND CHANGE

Since change is the context in which Aquinas first introduces the notions of matter and form, we can do no better than to begin our discussion with it. And here it will be useful to proceed, as Aquinas himself does, by focusing on particular examples.[2]

Consider, therefore, one of Aquinas's favorite examples of change—namely, one by which a statue is made from a lump of bronze. To fill out this example, let us suppose our lump starts off being spherical but is later melted down and recast as a statue. In that case, we will have a situation that, for the sake of future reference, we can represent as follows (using a circle to stand for our sphere, a square to stand for our statue, and a dotted arrow to represent the direction of time):

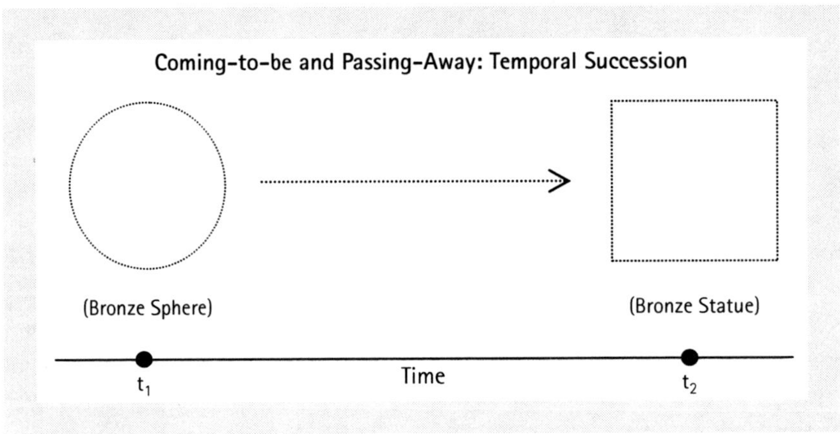

As this diagram is intended to make clear, our example involves a process that begins with an entity that can be characterized in one way (namely, as a sphere) and ends with an entity that can be characterized in another way (namely, as a statue). In this respect, Aquinas thinks, our example is perfectly representative of all change. We might put the point by saying that, for him, change essentially involves the temporal succession of distinct entities—or, in terminology closer to his own, the "coming-to-be" of one thing and the "passing-away" of another.[3]

Although coming-to-be and passing-away is an essential part of change, Aquinas insists that change always involves more than this. After all, God could have caused our statue to come-to-be *out of nothing*; likewise, he could have caused our sphere to pass-away *into nothing*. But in that case, Aquinas thinks, we would have an example of *creation* and *annihilation* rather than change. And this is because, in keeping with common sense, he thinks of change as requiring the existence of some *thing* that is changed—that is, a subject that literally endures the change or remains numerically the same over time.[4] Thus, if we want to represent our statue example, as Aquinas himself is thinking of it, we cannot merely appeal to the temporal succession of distinct entities. On the contrary, we must introduce some complexity into such entities, so as to indicate that they not only (a) involve distinct elements (and hence are distinct) but also (b) share a common constituent (and hence overlap). Since Aquinas himself describes the change in terms of the same bronze having different shapes at different times, we can represent his understanding more accurately as follows:

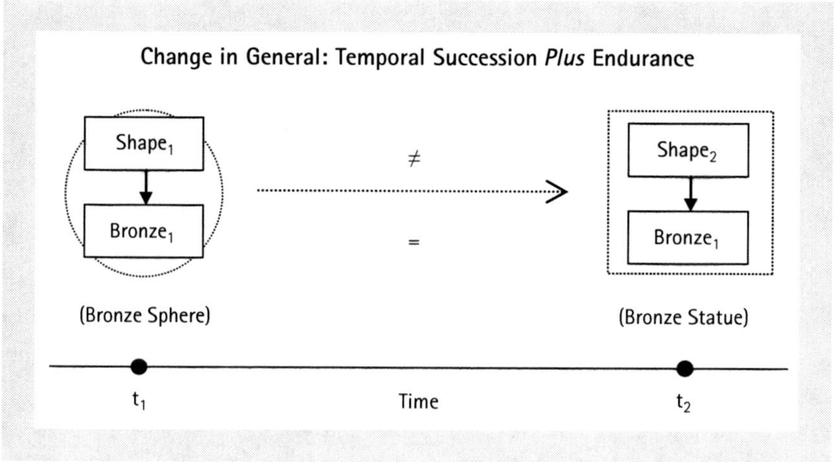

As this diagram helps to illustrate, Aquinas thinks of change not merely in terms of distinct entities coming-to-be and passing-away, but rather in terms of their coming-to-be *from* and passing-away *into one another*. In order to distinguish this special type of coming-to-be and passing-away from other types (such as creation and annihilation), Aquinas speaks of it in terms of "generation" and "corruption"—where, as we can now see, these notions are to be understood in terms of the temporal succession of distinct individuals that overlap with respect to a common constituent that literally endures the change itself.[5]

As it turns out, it is a very short step from this general account of change to Aquinas's hylomorphism. For in this context, Aquinas just introduces the term "matter" (*materia*) to stand for that which remains the same throughout a given change—that is, for the enduring subject of change. He introduces the term "form" (*forma*) to stand for that with respect to which the matter or enduring subject is changed—that is, for the elements of change that do not endure or remain the same. Finally, he introduces the term "compound of matter and form" (*ex materia et forma compositum*) to stand for that which exists in virtue of some matter possessing a form, and hence for the type of entity that can be generated or corrupted. As Aquinas also makes clear, the notions of matter, form, and compound are closely connected to the notions of potentiality and actuality. Indeed, in the context of change he identifies matter with that which is in potentiality to receiving form (*ens in potentia*); he identifies form with that which can actualize the potentiality of matter—namely, actuality (*actus*); and he identifies the compound with that which is actual in some respect (*ens actu*).[6]

As all of this suggests, change for Aquinas just consists in the generation and corruption of hylomorphic compounds (or compounds of potentiality and actuality). For the sake of clarity, we can represent this general account of change as follows:

Change in General

A change C occurs if and only if

(i) there is some matter, *M*, which exists from some time *t1* to some later time *t2*;
(ii) there exist some distinct forms, *F-ness* and *G-ness*;
(iii) *M* has *F-ness* at *t1* (thereby composing a hylomorphic compound, which is *F*) and *M* has *G-ness* at *t2* (thereby composing a distinct hylomorphic compound, which is G).

Although this general account of change does not tell us everything we might like to know about matter and form, it does go some distance toward clarifying Aquinas's understanding of them. Two things in particular are worth noting. First, this account entails a sort of *realism* about matter and form—and compounds. Entities of all three kinds are required, Aquinas thinks, in order to account for any given change. And yet, for obvious reasons, they cannot be identified with one another. Since the matter of any given change can exist without the forms with respect to which it changes, it cannot be identified with form; and since both matter and form are required for the existence of compounds, the latter cannot be identified with either matter or form.

It will be important to keep in mind the sort of realism implicit in this account of change as we go. Commentators sometimes suggest that Aquinas should be understood as an antirealist about the matter involved in at least certain changes (namely, substantial changes).[7] But if the above account is perfectly general, and hence applies to all change, this cannot be correct.

The second thing worth noting about Aquinas's general account of change is that the notions of matter, form, and compound it employs are (at least in the first instance) purely functional in nature. To be matter, on this account, is just to be an entity playing a certain function or role—that of accounting for the sameness involved in change (namely, sameness of subject over time). Likewise, to be form, on this account, is to be an entity playing a distinct function or role—that of accounting for the difference involved in change (namely, difference of characterization over time). Finally, to be a hylomorphic compound, on this account, is just to be an entity that possesses such functional matter and form, and hence one capable of being characterized by the special type of coming-to-be and passing-away associated with change (namely, generation and corruption).

It will also be important to keep in mind the functional nature of Aquinas's hylomorphism as we go. Aquinas often speaks of matter and form as if they were entities belonging to specific ontological types or categories—namely, *concrete individuals* and *properties*. Thus, he identifies the matter of our statue example with a lump of bronze, which he regards as a concrete individual (indeed, a concrete individual *substance*); and he identifies the forms of this same example with different shapes, which he regards as contingent properties or accidents. Even so, there are contexts (as we shall see shortly) in which Aquinas denies that matter and form can be identified with entities of either type. Given his functional understanding of matter and form, this is perfectly intelligible.

Aquinas's functional understanding of matter and form also explains something else that might otherwise seem puzzling—namely, his willingness to speak of "matter" in connection with immaterial objects. Consider an angel who comes to have a new thought or volition. In such a case, Aquinas thinks, we have a change in which an immaterial (or spiritual) substance acquires a new contingent property or accident. Like all changes, this one will involve the generation and corruption of hylomorphic compounds, and hence entities composed of both matter and form. Unlike other changes, however, the "matter" of this change (namely, the angel) will itself be immaterial. Again, this is perfectly intelligible if we keep in mind that the matter here is purely functional. As Aquinas himself says at one point:

> If the term "matter" is used in its proper and common sense, it is impossible for there to be matter in spiritual substances.... But if the terms "matter" and "form" are used for any two things which are related as potentiality to actuality, then there can be no objection (unless it is a mere verbal dispute) to saying that spiritual substances have both matter and form.[8]

As this passage makes clear, Aquinas does have a substantive or metaphysical notion of matter, but to see what it is, and how it is related to his purely functional notion, we must look at his distinction between different types of change.

Types of Matter, Form, and Change

Aquinas thinks that all of the changes we have been focusing on so far belong to a single type—namely, ones involving a substance (which plays the role of matter) changing with respect to one of its contingent properties or accidents (which plays the role of form). For obvious reasons, he calls changes of this type "accidental change," and he calls the compounds thereby generated or corrupted "accidental compounds (or unities)."[9]

Although Aquinas regards many familiar examples of change as accidental, he denies that all of them are. On the contrary, he thinks there are also familiar examples of substantial change—that is, changes by which substances themselves are generated or corrupted. Aquinas's favorite example here is the change by which a human being (such as Socrates) is generated from sperm and menstrual blood (or as we now know better, sperm and ova). In order to highlight the connection between Aquinas's understanding of substantial change and his account of change in general, let us pretend for the moment that he thinks of human beings as being generated not from two things (namely, sperm and menstrual blood or ova), but rather from a single thing (namely, a fertilized egg or zygote).[10] In that case, we can represent Aquinas's example of substantial change as follows:

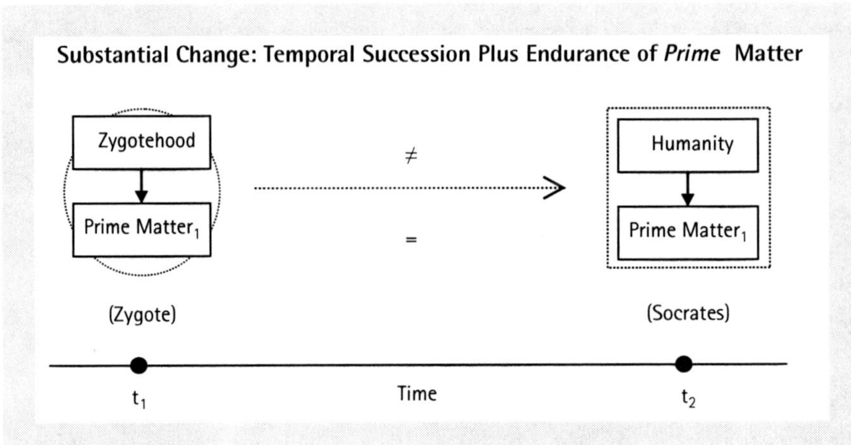

As this diagram is intended to show, substantial change, like change in general, involves the generation and corruption of hylomorphic compounds. Because the compounds generated and corrupted here are substances, however, this type of change is possible only for *composite* substances—that is, substances which are themselves composed of matter and form. As Aquinas sees it, only material substances have the relevant sort of composition; hence only they can be generated or corrupted. (Immaterial substances such as angels, by contrast, lack such composition and hence can only be created or annihilated.) What is more, since the type of matter possessed by material substances is precisely what distinguishes them as material, he refers to it as "matter in the primary sense" or "prime matter" (*materia prima*); again, since the type of form it combines with makes a substance, he refers to it as "substantial form" (*forma substantialis*).

Aquinas's account of substantial change raises a host of difficulties that we cannot fully enter into here. Even so, we must at least touch on some of them—two in particular—if we are to appreciate how this type of change affects his views about matter and form generally.

First, what is prime matter? This is perhaps the most familiar difficulty, and clearly concerns the nature of the entity playing the role of matter in substantial change. What sort of entity could it be? Like other medieval philosophers, Aquinas denies that it can be a full-fledged substance: for no substance can be composed of other substances, whereas all material substances are composed of prime matter. But if prime matter is not a substance, what is it? An individual of some other type—say, *bare particular*? Or something else altogether?[11]

I shall return to this difficulty shortly. But first I need to highlight a second difficulty, this one having to with the precise role that prime matter plays in substantial change. For as will emerge, if we want to understand the type of entity that can play the role of prime matter, we must first be clear about the role itself.

To see what is distinctive about the way prime matter functions, recall what we know about the role of matter in change in general. First, the entity playing this role is always something that goes from having one form or property, *F-ness*, to having another form or property, *G-ness*. Second, when this role is played, the result is the generation and corruption of compounds that are *characterized* by the same forms or properties—that is to say, compounds that are themselves either *F* or *G*. (For sake of clarity, let us say that a subject *a* is *characterized* by a form or property *F-ness* only if *a* is *F*.) Thus, in our statue example what plays the role of matter is a lump that goes from possessing *sphericity* to *statuehood*, which in turn results in the generation of a *statue* and the corruption of a *sphere*. Likewise, in our human example what plays the role of matter is some prime matter that goes from possessing *zygotehood* to *humanity*, which in turn results in the generation of a *human* and corruption of a *zygote*.[12]

So far so good, but here is a crucial difference between the two cases. In the statue example, as in all accidental changes, it is not only the compounds serving as the termini of change, but also their matter that can be said to be characterized by the forms or properties successively possessed. Strictly speaking, our lump goes not only (a) from *possessing sphericity* to *possessing statuehood* but also (b) from *being a sphere* to *being a statue*. That is to say, we can truly describe it as a sphere at one time and a statue at another. Note, however, that the same cannot be said about substantial changes, such as that involved in our human example. For a human to be generated from a zygote, there must be something—namely, some prime matter—that goes from *possessing zygotehood* to *possessing humanity*. Even so, such prime matter cannot itself be said to go from *being a zygote* to *being a human*. That is to say, we cannot truly describe it as a zygote at one time and a human at another. And the reason has to do at least partly with the nature of the substantial forms or properties themselves. Unlike *sphericity* or *statuehood*, *humanity* is not the sort of form or property that can characterize its possessor accidentally. On the contrary, it is a form or property that characterizes its possessor essentially: if something is *human* at any time it exists, it must be *human* at all (possible) times it exists. For the same reason, Aquinas thinks, it makes no sense to speak of something *coming-to-be* human—and likewise for *zygotehood* or any of the other forms involved in substantial change.[13]

What all of this shows is that the role played by matter in substantial change is very different from that played by matter in accidental change. Both types of change will involve something that functions generally as an enduring subject, and hence something that goes from having one form or property to having another. This follows straightforwardly from the account of change in general. But whether this same subject can be *characterized* by the forms or properties it successively takes on is a further issue and will in fact determine the specific type of change (as well as the specific type of matter, form, and compound) involved. Indeed, we can just define the difference between substantial and accidental change in terms of whether the enduring subject of change can be so characterized. More precisely:

Substantial Change

A substantial change C_s occurs if and only if

(i) there is some (prime) matter, *M*, which exists from some time *t1* to some later time *t2*;
(ii) there exist some distinct (substantial) forms, *F-ness* and *G-ness*;
(iii) *M* has *F-ness* at *t1* (thereby composing a substance, which is *F*) and *M* has *G-ness* at *t2* (thereby composing a distinct substance, which is *G*);
(iv) *M* itself does not go from being *F* to being *G* at these times.

Accidental Change

An accidental change C_a occurs if and only if

(i) there is some matter (or substance), *M*, which exists from some time *t1* to some later time *t2*;
(ii) there exist some distinct (accidental) forms, *F-ness* and *G-ness*;
(iii) *M* has *F-ness* at *t1* (thereby composing an accidental compound, which is *F*) and *M* has *G-ness* at *t2* (thereby composing a distinct accidental compound, which is *G*);
(iv*) *M* itself does go from being *F* to being *G* at these times.

As should be clear from this more precise statement, substantial and accidental change differ only with regard to their fourth condition.

There is something deeply puzzling about the role that Aquinas assigns to matter in substantial change. Admittedly, if we accept his account of change in general, as well as the reality of substantial change, we will have no choice but to allow that something can have forms or properties without being characterized by them. Still, we would like to know how such a thing is possible. Intuitively, forms or properties are essentially characterizing (e.g., *F-ness* and *G-ness* are essentially such as to make their possessors *F* or *G*). This is what makes plausible Aquinas's claim that forms always characterize their compounds and, at least in the case of accidental change, also characterize their matter. But if forms always characterize their compounds, and sometimes also characterize their matter, why don't they always characterize both?

It is at this point that we must return to our initial difficulty about the nature of prime matter. For as it turns out, it is precisely the special nature of prime matter that prevents it from being characterized by the forms or properties it possesses. If prime matter were an individual of any sort—even a bare particular—it would be impossible to deny that it is characterized by its forms or properties. Indeed, Aquinas thinks, if prime matter were an individual, we would have no choice but to regard it as a full-fledged substance and all of its forms as contingent or accidental properties.[14] For the same reason, he insists that prime matter is not an individual. This, I take it, is the point of his saying that, unlike all other existing things, prime matter "lacks actuality of itself" and hence is "pure potentiality."[15] But if prime matter is not an individual, what is it? It is, I suggest, a sui generis type of entity best conceived along the lines of what contemporary philosophers sometimes refer to as "stuff"—that is, a type of entity that, though not itself individual, combines with (substantial) forms or properties to make individuals.[16]

If this interpretation is right, we have a straightforward explanation of why prime matter cannot be characterized by the forms or properties it possesses: it is of the wrong ontological type or category. Only an individual can be characterized as a *zygote* or *human*. But if prime matter is stuff, it is nonindividual. Hence, even if it possesses *zygotehood* at one time and *humanity* at another, it cannot *be* a *zygote* at one time and a *human* at another. And likewise for all other substantial forms.[17]

Any interpretation of Aquinas's account of prime matter is bound to be controversial, and mine is no exception.[18] Even so, it is worth noting that, in addition to resolving our two difficulties, the prime-matter-as-stuff interpretation has a number of other things going for it, some of which are more or less implicit in what we have already said. I will briefly highlight four.

First, the prime-matter-as-stuff interpretation fits well with what Aquinas says about the special ontological status of prime matter. Here I am thinking not only of the descriptions of prime matter already mentioned (e.g., "pure potentiality") but also of Aquinas's agreement with Aristotle that prime matter is itself "neither a what—that is, a substance—nor a quality, nor any of the other categories by which being is divided or determined."[19]

Second, this interpretation makes good sense of why Aquinas famously maintains, against most of his contemporaries, that prime matter cannot exist by itself, even by the absolute power of God.[20] For nonindividual stuff, at least as it is ordinarily conceived, can occur only as part of a larger object. Presumably, therefore, not even God could create it all by itself.

Third, this interpretation helps to explain Aquinas's unwavering commitment to the so-called "unicity of substantial forms" doctrine—that is, the view that no substance can have more than one substantial form. For once some prime matter or stuff combines with a form or property, it is natural to think of the result as an individual substance each of whose further forms are accidental.[21]

Finally, the prime-matter-as-stuff interpretation fits well with a further role that Aquinas assigns to prime matter. According to Aquinas, what is distinctive about objects possessing prime matter is their capacity to "fill a place" (*locum replere*) or "possess extension in three dimensions" (*trinam dimensionem habere*).[22] We will have to return to this role in connection with Aquinas's theory of individuation. But for now let us simply note that the assignment of this role makes good sense on the assumption that prime matter is stuff. For stuff, it is natural to suppose, is just that which accounts for an object's extension or capacity to fill a certain region.

One final clarification before we leave Aquinas's account of change. So far I have been speaking as if all changes, whether substantial or accidental, involve the generation of a *single* thing (say, a statue or a human being) from the corruption of another *single* thing (say, a lump of bronze or a zygote). This is, in fact, an oversimplification. In addition to such *one-one* changes, Aquinas also allows for the possibility of more complicated changes. As already noted, he in fact regards the generation of a human being as a type of *many-one* change—since it involves the corruption of both sperm and menstrual blood—and he explicitly allows for various types of *one-many* changes as well.[23] There is no space to explore these more complicated changes further, but it is important to note that they will still involve the endurance of matter (whether prime matter or substance), as well as the replacement of distinct forms over time (whether substantial or accidental). What makes them more complicated is simply that their enduring matter is combined with (or divided from) other matter, with the result that the number of distinct forms involved varies over time.

Matter, Form, and Individuation

By now it should be clear that, in the context of change, Aquinas invokes matter and form as principles to explain certain types of sameness and difference. Thus, he invokes matter (such as a lump of bronze or some prime matter) to explain the type of sameness involved in change—namely, *sameness of subject over time*. And he invokes forms (such as *sphericity* and *statuehood*, or *zygotehood* and *humanity*) to explain the type of difference involved in change—namely, *difference of characterization over time*.

These are not, however, the only types of sameness and difference to which Aquinas's account of change calls our attention. This is especially clear if we consider some of the more complicated changes. Suppose, therefore, our statue had been generated not from a single sphere, but from several smaller spheres. Or again, suppose the corruption of our zygote resulted in the generation not of a single human being, but of twins—say, Romulus and Remus. In either case, note that on the "many" side of the change we have multiple objects belonging to the same kind, and hence relations of sameness and difference holding between distinct individuals. These relations, however, obtain *at a time* rather than *over* time, and hence could obtain even in the absence of change. Moreover, instead of involving *sameness of subject* and *difference of characterization*, these relations involve *difference of subject* and *sameness of characterization*.

Given the connection between matter and subject, on the one hand, and form and characterization, on the other, it should come as no surprise that here, as in the context of change proper, Aquinas appeals to matter and form to explain the relevant relations of sameness and difference—though, of course, this time it is form that explains the sameness and matter that explains the difference.[24] For the sake of clarity, we can contrast the different roles Aquinas assigns to matter and form in different contexts using the following chart:

Context	Principle of Sameness	Principle of Difference
Over Time (In Change)	Matter (Sameness of Subject)	Form (Difference of Characterization)
At a Time (Outside of Change)	Form (Sameness of Characterization)	Matter (Difference of Subject)

In the remainder of this chapter, I want to take a closer look at the roles that Aquinas assigns to matter and form outside the context of change, since these are essentially connected with his theory of individuation.[25] Once again my strategy will be to proceed by way of example.

Let us return, therefore, to Romulus and Remus and consider them at some time at which they both exist.[26] Like all material objects, Aquinas thinks of these twins as ultimately composed of prime matter and substantial form. Insofar as they belong to the same kind, they are material objects sharing a common nature or form; and insofar as they are distinct members of this kind, they differ with respect to their prime matter.

So far I have been speaking as if relations of sameness and difference could always be understood in terms of strict identity. This is useful heuristically because it makes intuitive Aquinas's suggestion that matter must be a principle of individuation in some sense. If Romulus and Remus literally share one and the same substantial form, then they must differ with respect to their prime matter, since Aquinas thinks this is the only other type of entity of which they are ultimately composed. Despite the heuristic value of this way of speaking, we will eventually see that it too involves an oversimplification.

Although Aquinas thinks that prime matter plays an essential role in individuation, he is often at pains to emphasize that it not prime matter as such that plays this role. Nor is it hard to see why. Since Romulus and Remus are alike not only in their possession of a common substantial form (namely, humanity) but also in their possession of prime matter, it cannot be prime matter as such that individuates them.[27] On the contrary, it must be that each possesses his own distinct prime matter—and likewise for any distinct material objects belonging to the same natural kind. Aquinas himself often puts the point by saying that the principle of individuation must be understood as *designated* (rather than *undesignated*) matter. And for reasons I will now try to explain, he identifies designated matter with *matter under determinate dimensions*.[28]

Recall that prime matter is that which explains a material object's capacity to "fill its place" or "have extension in three dimensions"—a type of nonindividual stuff, on my interpretation, which cannot exist apart from some larger compound or other. Even so, Aquinas thinks, if we want to explain the precise dimensions of a material object such as Romulus, or the exact size of the place he fills, we cannot appeal to his prime matter alone. On the contrary, we must also appeal to certain of his accidents or quantities. To put the point another way: although Romulus will fill some region or other solely in virtue of having prime matter, and his distinct prime matter may well put some restrictions on the size of this region, his precise extension cannot be determined apart from certain of his accidental or quantitative properties—what Aquinas calls his "determinate dimensions" (*dimensiones determinatae vel terminatae*) or "dimensive quantities" (*quantitates dimensivae*). And, obviously, since Romulus himself cannot exist without some dimensions or other, the same will be true of his prime matter.[29]

Now if we add to all this that the determinate dimensions of a substance are the only means by which its prime matter can be picked out or designated, we can see why Aquinas would say that the matter associated with a particular substance—that is, its designated matter—is to be understood in terms of matter under determinate dimensions. For the sake of clarity, let us illustrate this as follows for the particular case of Romulus (this time setting matter and form side-by-side, and using a solid line to indicate their relation to one other and a dotted line to indicate their relation to the larger compounds of which they are a part):

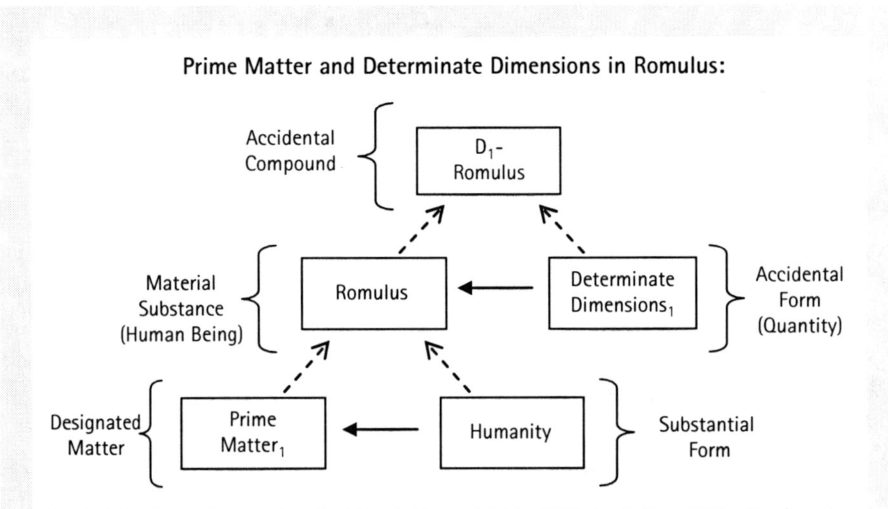

As this diagram is intended to show, in the particular case of Romulus we have some distinct prime matter (namely, prime matter$_1$) combining with a substantial form (namely, humanity) to make Romulus, and then Romulus himself combining with another form (namely, the determinate dimensions by which his prime matter can be designated, which we can abbreviate "D_1") to make what I have called (for lack of a better term) "D_1-Romulus"—that is, an accidental compound consisting of Romulus having a particular extension.

In light of the foregoing, we can see why Aquinas describes prime matter as the primary principle of individuation, even though he reserves a role for a certain type of accident to play here as well. For prime matter, he thinks, is what ultimately explains there being *distinct* material objects belonging to the same kind. Still, prime matter cannot exist without some determinate dimensions or other, and hence the latter are required for prime matter to play its role, even they do not themselves account for the distinction in question.

Quantity, Individuality, and The Individuation of Forms

If individuation, for Aquinas, involved nothing more than explaining the *distinction* of material objects, we could perhaps leave our discussion here. But, in fact, this is not the case. To see why, consider Romulus and Remus again and note that they are not merely distinct entities, but distinct *individuals*. The qualification is important because, as we have seen, there are entities (e.g., Romulus's and Remus's respective prime matter) which are distinct but nonindividual. But, then, how are we to account for the *individuality* (as opposed to distinction) of Romulus and Remus? Obviously, we cannot account for it in terms of their prime matter, since as we have just noted, it is nonindividual. But neither can we account for it in terms of their substantial form, since this is something they share in common. But if we cannot account for Romulus's and Remus's individuality either in terms of their (nonindividual) prime matter or in terms of their (common) substantial form, how can we account for it?

This question highlights a further aspect of Aquinas's views about individuation in which determinate dimensions have a more direct role to play. What accounts for the distinction of material objects, Aquinas thinks, is their prime matter, which can only exist under some determinate dimensions or other. But what accounts for the individuality of material objects is the particular determinate dimensions under which their prime matter exists. For unlike prime matter, Aquinas says, such dimensions are not only individual, but individual in and of themselves.[30]

Now as the discussion of determinate dimensions makes clear, at least some of the forms of material objects are individual. But what about their other forms? As it turns out, Aquinas thinks that all the forms of all material objects, whether substantial or accidental, are individual.[31] Unlike determinate dimensions, however, he thinks these other forms must be individuated. That is to say, instead of being individual in and of themselves, they must get their individuality from their relation to something else. And here, as in the case of material objects themselves, we can distinguish two aspects of their individuation. Thus, compare the substantial form of

Romulus with that of Remus. These are, Aquinas thinks, distinct individuals of the same type, humanity. What accounts for their distinction is the distinct prime matter with which they are associated, whereas what accounts for their individuality is the determinate dimensions with which they are associated. And likewise for each of Romulus's and Remus's other forms, as well as those of material objects generally.

We can now see why I said earlier that, despite the fact that Romulus and Remus "share a common form," this cannot be understood in terms of strict identity. Romulus's humanity is a distinct individual from Remus's humanity. Even so, we can also see why Aquinas wants to insist that Romulus and Remus nonetheless share something in common. For although Romulus's humanity is distinct from Remus's, it is not intrinsically distinct from it (or for that matter, from anyone else's humanity). Nor is it intrinsically individual or unique to Romulus. To make the point vivid, suppose we had a metaphysical microscope that allowed us to see all and only what is intrinsic to a given entity; and suppose that we used this device to inspect Romulus's and Remus's humanities.[32] We would not be able to tell the difference between them. In each case it would be clear that we have a form or property of humanity before us. But if we wanted to see whose it was, or its distinction from others, we would have to "zoom out" in such a way as to include its associated prime matter and determinate dimensions. As this makes clear, when Aquinas speaks of forms as "common" to many, he is calling attention not to their numerical sameness but rather to their *intrinsic* sameness.[33]

From what we've seen so far, it might appear that although all the forms of material objects are individual, only certain of them are individuated by other things—namely, all those besides determinate dimensions. For determinate dimensions, as we've seen, have a kind of individuation in themselves, which just appears to mean that their individuality, and hence their distinction both among themselves and from other things, is intrinsic to them. Even so, Aquinas insists, the forms of material objects are always individuated by their subjects: their substantial forms are individuated by their prime matter, and their accidents are individuated by their substances. Nor does he allow any exceptions for determinate dimensions.[34]

We can, I think, make sense of Aquinas's views here, as well as fill out his account of individuation generally, by noting that there is a further question we can ask about distinct individuals belonging to the same kind—namely, what accounts for their identity?[35] For even though determinate dimensions are intrinsically individual, and hence intrinsically distinct from other things, they cannot exist apart from the particular substances in which they inhere. That is to say, despite their intrinsic individuality and distinctness, there is still a sense in which they must be individuated, since their identity is bound up with other things—namely, the substances of which they are the accidents.

We can illustrate this further type of individuation, as well as contrast it with the other types we have already seen, if we return one last time to our example of Romulus and focus on his relationship to his prime matter and determinate dimensions:

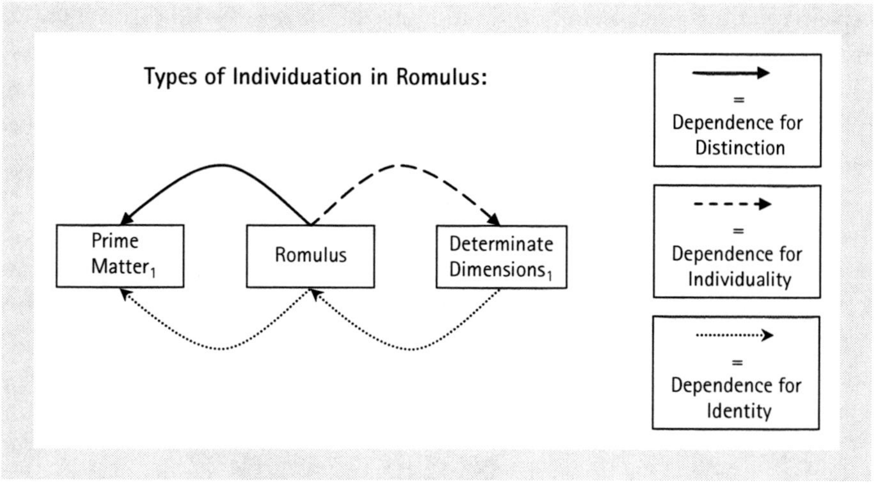

As this diagram makes clear, Romulus depends for his distinction (from other material objects) on his prime matter, whereas he depends for his individuality on his determinate dimensions. But Romulus also depends for his identity on his prime matter, which is just to say he cannot exist apart from it.[36] In the same way, Romulus's determinate dimensions depend on him: since they cannot exist apart from Romulus in particular, their identity is bound up with him.[37] Indeed, given the dependence of Romulus on his prime matter, there is a sense in which the identity of his determinate dimensions is ultimately bound up with his prime matter as well.

In short, we can see that there are really three different aspects of Aquinas's views about individuation, corresponding to three different questions we can ask about individuals belonging to the same kind:

1. What accounts for their distinction?
2. What accounts for their individuality?
3. What accounts for their identity?

In order to answer the first and third questions, Aquinas thinks, we must appeal to prime matter. But in order to answer the second question, we must appeal to one of the things that prime matter cannot exist without: namely, determinate dimensions. In light of Aquinas's answers to these questions, we can see why in certain contexts he speaks of matter as the primary principle of individuation and dimensive quantity as a secondary principle.[38]

Conclusion

This completes our examination of the two main contexts in which Aquinas develops his notions of matter and form—his theory of change and his theory of individuation. In each case, as we have seen, Aquinas invokes matter and form to account for certain relations of sameness and difference holding between distinct individuals. In each case, moreover, he is able to do so because he thinks of matter and form as distinct entities that both serve as constituents of larger wholes (namely, hylomorphic compounds) and explain certain of their general and specific characteristics.

There is much more that could be said about Aquinas's understanding of matter and form, especially in other contexts such as theology or logic. But we have already seen enough, I think, to appreciate the essential aspects of these notions in their primary or basic sense, and hence to have a basis for understanding the further uses to which Aquinas puts them.[39]

NOTES

1. I use the term "entity" throughout to refer to beings in the broadest possible sense—that is, to anything that exists or has being in any sense.

2. Unless otherwise indicated, the discussion below is based primarily on Aquinas's discussion in the first two chapters of *DPN*, though in most cases parallel passages can be found in *In Phy*, his other main discussion of change. All translations are mine.

3. Strictly speaking, these remarks apply only to Aquinas's account of *intrinsic* changes in things. Ultimately, I think Aquinas wants to explain all change in terms of these, but in what follows I shall ignore complications arising from *extrinsic* (or mere *Cambridge*) changes.

4. Cf., e.g., *ST* I q.45 a.2 ad 2: "It is part of the nature of change (*de ratione mutationis*) that it involves the same thing (*idem*) being different now from the way it was before.... By contrast, in the case of creation, where the entire substance of things is produced [*ex nihilo*], it cannot be said that we have the same thing being different now from the way it was before—except according to a certain way of thinking."

5. When Aquinas wants to speak of change in the broadest possible sense (*motus*, *mutatio*), he always does so in terms of generation (*generatio*) and corruption (*corruptio*). Following Aristotle, however, he also uses these latter notions in a narrower sense to apply only to substantial change, and thus to contrast with accidental change (more on the distinction between substantial and accidental change below). But even here, he sees a close connection between the different senses of the terms. As he says in *DPN*, c.1: "In an unqualified sense, generation and corruption are found only in the category of substance. But in the other categories they are found in a qualified sense." For Aquinas's discussion of how these different senses of generation and corruption connect with Aristotle's texts, cf. *In Phy*, bk.3, lec.2 and *In Meta*, bk.1, lec.12.

6. Cf. *In DA*, bk.2, c.1, n.5, for an especially clear example of this identification outside of *DPN*.

7. Cf. Robert Pasnau, *Thomas Aquinas on Human Nature* (Cambridge: Cambridge University Press, 2002), 131–40.

8. *QDSC*, a.1.

9. Cf. the references in note 5.

10. Given the controversy surrounding Aquinas's embryology, it should perhaps be emphasized that this pretense is adopted solely for the sake of simplicity and is not

intended to reflect a stance on any substantive metaphysical or interpretive issues. For introduction to the relevant issues and controversy, cf. the exchange between Robert Pasnau and John Haldane and Patrick Lee in *Philosophy* 78 (2003): 255–78, 521–31, 532–40.

11. For the sake of precision, let us call any individual that is not a property a "particular." It is often taken for granted nowadays that all particulars, whether bare or otherwise, are substances. But during the medieval period, the precise relationship between particularity and substantiality was a disputed question.

12. In what follows, I shall use the term "humanity" to refer to the substantial form of a human being, both because it serves to highlight the parallel between our human and statue examples and because Aquinas says that this is the form that locates human beings within their natural kind (cf. *DEE*, c.4). It should be noted, however, that Aquinas himself often reserves the term "humanity" (*humanitas*) for the natural kind or essence itself (cf. *DEE*, cc.2–3), which as we will see below includes not only substantial form but also prime matter.

13. In the case of *humanity*, Aquinas puts the point this way: "When a human comes to be, we can truly say not only that it was previously not human, but also that it previously was not (full stop)" (*In Phy*, bk.1, lec.12, n.10).

14. Cf., e.g., *DEE*, c.5.

15. In addition to *DPN*, cc.1–2, cf. *ST* I q.7 a.2 ad 3; *QDV*, q.8, a.6; and *SCG* I, c.17. Cf. also *Super Sent* 4, d.12, q.1, a.1, sol. 3, ad 3, where Aquinas insists that part of what it is to be an individual is to be a being in actuality.

16. Cf., e.g., Ned Markosian, "Simples, Stuff, and Simple People," *Monist* 87 (2004): 405–28.

17. This is not to say that prime matter or stuff cannot be characterized at all. Obviously it can be—it is, after all, *prime matter* or *stuff*, *nonindividual*, *existent*, *identical-to-itself*, etc. The point is just that not all characterization is to be explained in terms of forms or properties. On the contrary, Aquinas thinks that in many cases the fact that an entity can be characterized in a certain way is to be explained by the entity itself (rather than by some distinct property the entity possesses). Cf., e.g., the discussion of divine simplicity in *ST* I q.3.

18. For a taxonomy of different possible interpretations of Aquinas's account, as well as references to the literature, see John D. Kronen, Sandra Mennsen, and Thomas D. Sullivan, "The Problem of the Continuant: Aquinas and Suarez on Prime Matter and Substantial Generation," *The Review of Metaphysics* 53 (2000): 863–85. (If I understand these authors correctly, my interpretation is version of the position they label "Gamma.") Cf. also the reference to Pasnau in note 7 for an example of an antirealist interpretation of Aquinas's prime matter.

19. Cf. *In Meta*, bk.7, lec.2.

20. Cf. esp. *Quodl* 3, q.1, a.1. For further passages and discussion of the historical context, cf. John Wippel, *The Metaphysical Thought of Thomas Aquinas: From Finite Being to Uncreated Being* (Washington, D.C.: Catholic University of America Press, 2000), esp. 312–27.

21. Indeed, as the prime-matter-as-stuff interpretation helps us to see, Aquinas's distinction between substance and accidental compound is really distinction between two different types of particulars. Substances are primary or basic particulars (insofar as they do not include within themselves any other particulars playing the role of matter), whereas accidental compounds are secondary or derived particulars (insofar as they do include within themselves particulars playing the role of matter).

22. Cf. *ST* I q.3 a.1 obj.1; q.52, a.1–2; and *In BDT*, q.4, a.3.

23. Cf., e.g., *In Meta*, bk.7, lec.16, where he mentions simple living things (such as certain worms) that can be cut in half to form two new living things.

24. The problem of "explaining sameness of characterization" is, of course, just the traditional problem of universals. Aquinas's appeal to form, therefore, is part of his solution to this problem. More on this below.

25. Indeed, it is because of matter's role here that he speaks of it as "the principle of individuation" (*principium individuationis*) and it is because of form's role here that he speaks of it as belonging to a thing's "essence" (*essentia*) or "common nature" (*natura communis*). Cf., e.g., *ST* I q.3 a.2; q.75 a.4; q.76 a.2.

26. For reasons that will emerge, Aquinas thinks of prime matter (or stuff) as the *primary* principle of individuation. In what follows, therefore, I will focus on the example involving the twin human beings rather than that involving the multiple spheres.

27. As this consideration makes clear, the nature or essence of human beings includes not only substantial form but also prime matter. It is because Aquinas is willing to extend the term "form" to the whole essence of a thing that he famously distinguishes "the form of the whole" (*forma totius*), which is the essence, from the "the form of the part" (*forma partis*), which is the substantial form. Cf. *DEE*, c.2 and *In Meta*, bk.7, lec.9.

28. Aquinas's views about individuation seem to have changed over time. In his earliest writings, he identifies the principle of individuation with matter under determinate dimensions (cf. *Super Sent* 1, d.23, q.1, a.1 and *DEE*, c.2). Later, he suggests that it should be identified with matter under indeterminate (rather than determinate) dimensions (cf. *Super Sent* 4, d.12, q.1, a.1–2 and *In BDT*, q.4, a.2). By the end of his career, however, he appears to have returned once again to the determinate-dimensions view (cf. esp. *QDA*, q.9 and *In DA* 2, c.12). There is considerable controversy over whether these different ways of talking correspond to different stages of development. Since I cannot enter into such controversies here, in what follows I shall simply focus on what I take to be Aquinas's most plausible views. For a helpful introduction to the relevant texts and controversies, cf. Wippel, *Metaphysical Thought of Thomas Aquinas*, 351–75.

29. It is important to emphasize that the type of dependence involved here is a sort of generic existential dependence. For despite the fact that both Romulus and his prime matter depend for their existence on some determinate dimensions or other, there are no particular dimensions on which each either depends for its existence. We might put the point by saying that, although each depends for its existence on determinate dimensions, neither depends for its "identity" on them (since for any such dimensions, they can exist without them).

30. In accordance with this aspect of individuation Aquinas says: "dimensive quantity has in itself a kind of individuation" (*ST* III q.77 a.2). Cf. also *In BDT*, q.4, a.3; *Quodl* 7, q.4, a.3; and *SCG* 4, c.65.

31. Cf., e.g., *DEE*, c.3. With respect to the problem of universals, therefore, Aquinas is what would nowadays be called a "trope theorist."

32. My talk here of inspecting forms "under a metaphysical microscope" is intended to be the contemporary analogue of Aquinas's talk of the "absolute consideration" of forms. Cf. *DEE*, c.3.

33. For further discussion, along with relevant texts, cf. Jeffrey E. Brower and Susan Brower-Toland, "Aquinas on Mental Representation: Concepts and Intentionality," *Philosophical Review* 117 (2008): 193–243, esp. section 2.1.

34. Cf. *In BDT*, q.4, a.2; *ST* I q.29 a.1 and II-II q.24 a.5 ad 1.

35. Cf. note 29 above.

36. Actually, it would be better to speak of the dependence here in terms of origins. Strictly speaking, Aquinas thinks, Romulus depends on his prime matter only for his origin

or initial existence (since the prime matter of which Romulus is composed of can and does change over time). Cf. *In BDT*, q.4, a.2.

37. Here again it would be better to speak of Romulus's determinate dimensions as dependent on Romulus only for their origin or initial existence (since Aquinas thinks that, on analogy with the Eucharist, God can preserve Romulus's determinate dimensions without Romulus, once they have come into existence). Cf. *Quodl* 7, q.4, a.3.

38. Cf. *Super Sent* 4, d.12, q.1, a.1, sol.3, ad 3.

39. An earlier version of this text was presented at the 2008 Cornell Summer Colloquium in Medieval Philosophy. I am grateful to the audience on that occasion, as well as to Michael Bergmann, Susan Brower-Toland, Timothy Pawl, Michael Rea, Michael Rota, Thomas Sullivan, and the editors of this volume, for helpful discussion, comments, and criticism. I am also grateful to the Alexander von Humboldt Foundation for a grant, which supported the initial research for this text.

CHAPTER 8

CAUSATION

MICHAEL ROTA

THE sense of Aquinas's term "*causa*" is broader than the English "cause." Following Aristotle, Aquinas distinguished four types of causes: "Now the genus of 'cause' is fourfold, namely, final, formal, efficient, and material.…"[1] As a general rule, a material cause is that which something is made up of (its matter), and a formal cause of a thing is a form of that thing. This chapter will focus on efficient causation, with some discussion of final causation as well.

Apart from his brief, early work *On the Principles of Nature* and some relatively short sections of his commentaries on Aristotle's *Physics* and *Metaphysics*, Aquinas wrote nothing that could be considered a systematic treatise on causation. His understanding of causation must therefore be gleaned from comments scattered throughout his works. When those scattered comments are brought together and analyzed, we find a complex and multifaceted theory. A good place to begin is with a paradigm instance of ordinary efficient causation: the production of a statue.

On Aquinas's Aristotelian account of change, any change involves (i) something that persists throughout the change (the subject of the change), (ii) something that accounts for the fact that the subject is actually configured or characterized as it in fact is at the end of the change (the form), and (iii) the lack of that form at the beginning of the change (the privation). Any subject of a change can be referred to as "matter," for Aquinas, so we can also refer to the subject of change as the matter of the change.

When, for instance, an irregularly shaped lump of bronze is formed into a statue, the bronze is the matter of the change, the distinctive shape of the finished statue is the form of the change, and the lack of that shape at the beginning is the privation.[2] Now, while distinguishing these three factors can help us specify the nature of this change, they cannot by themselves explain why the change has occurred. As experience tells us, bronze does not make itself into a statue. It is in this context, the explanation of change, that Aquinas introduces the notion of an efficient cause in *On the Principles of Nature*:

> But these [three factors] are not sufficient for generation.[3] For what is in potency is not able to reduce itself to actuality; just as bronze, which is potentially a statue, does not make itself [into] a statue. But there needs to be something operating, which draws forth the form of a statue from potency to actuality.... Therefore, it must be that, besides matter and form, there is some principle which acts, and this is said to be the maker [*efficiens*], or the mover, or the agent, or that from which the beginning of motion comes.[4]

Upon reading this passage, one would be inclined to think that, for Aquinas, the efficient cause of the statue in our example is the sculptor, end of story. Aquinas would indeed say that the sculptor is an efficient cause of the statue,[5] but he also holds that the *art* of the sculptor is an efficient cause of the statue.[6] As it turns out, the notion of an efficient cause is used analogically, in Aquinas, and the term "efficient cause" has a broad, manifold application. To get a full picture of Aquinas's views here, we need to turn to his account of transitive action, which is, roughly, action on something. This will involve a discussion of the following concepts: agent, patient, power, inclination (or tendency), end, action, and passion.

Agents and Patients

When Aquinas uses the term "agent," he is almost always referring to a created substance or to God. Occasionally Aquinas likens a power to an agent,[7] but in the proper sense of the term, an agent is a substance that acts,[8] for example, an angel, a human being, a cat, or even an inanimate substance like fire.

Two points of explanation are in order here, since the contemporary reader might find it strange that fire is an "agent" according to Aquinas, and that two things as disparate as a human being and fire both count as substances. First, Aquinas is comfortable saying that fire can *act* and that fire is an agent (*agens*, literally "an acting thing") because he does not restrict the application of the predicate "act" to subjects that are conscious agents. We sometimes use this predicate in the same broad sense, as in "the pancreatic juice acts on all classes of food."[9]

Second, according to Aquinas's concept of substance, substances are set apart from accidents by the fact that substances are subsistent things, in this sense: they do not exist in another being as in a subject (whereas accidents do). An accident, like the color of Socrates' hair, is the sort of thing that exists *in* something (Socrates' hair), while Socrates himself does not exist in any subject. He exists in his own right, so to speak. Aquinas thinks that each substance belongs to a particular species and has a complete nature common to any other members of that species that there may be. And corresponding to each specific nature is a distinctive set of causal powers. So Aquinas counts both a particular human being and a particular fire as individual substances capable of action because he thinks that each is a subsistent thing with a complete specific nature and a distinctive set of causal powers.[10]

Correlative to the agent (*agens*, "the thing acting") is the patient (*patiens*, "the thing undergoing"). The patient is the substance, or aggregate of substances, upon which the agent acts (e.g., the bronze in our sculpture example).

Aquinas calls the change (or motion) produced by the agent the "passion."[11] More precisely, the passion is the change, recognized as being something that occurs in the patient. That is, "passion" refers to the change and connotes the fact that the change takes place in the patient. Thus, Aquinas can say, "passion is the effect of the agent in the patient."[12]

Powers

Given the view that the agent produces a change in the patient, we can next ask *how* the agent produces that change. While a sculptor has many properties or features, only some of them are called into play when the sculptor makes a statue. The sculptor's power to move his hands is clearly salient here in a way that his ability to sing middle C is not. He performs the action of sculpting through the use of his power to move his hands (among other powers), but not through the use of his power to sing. Aquinas generalizes this way of thinking, and holds that any action of any agent occurs through the use of some particular power: "In any action there are two things to consider, namely the *suppositum* acting, and the power by which it acts, just as fire heats by heat."[13] Why posit the existence of powers? Perhaps the idea is just this: if a thing performs some sort of action, then it is reasonable, at least in many cases,[14] to think that there must be some real, positive feature of the thing that enables it to perform that sort of action. If a species of bird appears to use the earth's magnetic field to navigate, for example, then it is reasonable to think that members of that species have some sort of faculty for detecting magnetic fields. An *active* power is a feature of some thing that we posit to account for the fact that that thing is able to perform some action.[15] Aquinas thinks of active powers as real (though not necessarily physical) components of a thing that enable it to act in certain ways. A *passive* power is something we posit to account for the fact that a thing is capable of being acted upon in a certain way, that is, to account for the fact that a thing is capable of undergoing a certain sort of passion.[16]

As is indicated by the last quotation above, Aquinas thinks of heat as a power. Other examples are the powers of nutrition and growth (in all living things), the powers of sensation and movement (in animals), and the powers of intellect and will (in human beings). Aquinas also thinks of productive arts like the art of building and the art of medicine as powers.[17] Aquinas holds that an art—the art of building, say—is a feature of a person's mind.[18] To say that a person possesses the art of building is to say that that person has a certain cognitive feature. And because the possession of that feature enables him or her to perform a certain sort of action (building), that feature counts as a power.

Ends and Inclinations

On Aquinas's views, the sculptor's powers play an important role in the analysis of the example of efficient causation we are considering—the making of a statue. But while various powers of the sculptor explain his ability to sculpt, they do not by themselves explain why he gets up in the morning, goes to his studio, and sets to work. To explain these things, we need to make reference to the sculptor's desires and choices, to acts of will.[19] A choice to make a statue today, for instance, explains why the sculptor goes to his studio and begins to sculpt. The existence of active powers in a thing grounds facts about the actions that thing can perform, but explaining how it is that an agent *can* perform an action is somewhat different than explaining why it is that it *does* perform an action in a given situation. It is for this reason that Aquinas's discussions of action make reference to *inclinationes* (inclinations or tendencies), as well as powers.

We can grasp what Aquinas means by an "inclination" by examining something he says about ends, that is, final causes. In several places Aquinas claims that every agent (living and nonliving) acts by intending some end.[20] Because of the connotations of the English "intend," and because we sometimes identify ends with the purposes of rational agents, this claim of Aquinas's can sound wildly implausible. In fact, Aquinas did *not* think that inanimate objects do things out of an awareness of some goal.[21] Although a purpose or goal of a rational agent is one sort of end, the general definition of an end is much broader: for Aquinas, an end is merely that to which an agent tends, that is, that to which an agent has an inclination, whether cognized or not.[22]

At *Summa theologiae*, I-II q.1 a.2, Aquinas gives an argument for the claim that every agent acts out of an intention (i.e., an inclination) for an end. A close look at a single line in this argument will shed light on what Aquinas takes inclinations to be, and why he includes them in his ontology. The line in question reads: "For if an agent were not oriented to some effect, it would not do this more than that."[23] Consider that electrons regularly repel other negatively charged particles when in close proximity to them. To state the matter in terms of actions, an electron regularly performs one sort of action (repelling negatively charged particles) and not another (attracting negatively charged particles). That is, an electron does *this* more than *that*. Faced with this fact about the behavior of electrons, it is natural to seek an explanation. It would be absurd to think that the consistent behavior of electrons is merely a coincidence. So it is reasonable to think that the regular behavior in question (that electrons regularly repel other negatively charged particles) has an explanation. A quite natural explanation is provided by positing a feature about the electron itself, by supposing that it itself possesses some feature that leads it to repel negatively charged particles. Call that feature an inclination. The inclination in question here would be the electron's negative charge, conceived of as a property of the electron that makes it regularly repel negatively charged particles.

If we asked Aquinas to justify the inclusion of inclinations in his ontology, his answer, I believe, would focus on the explanatory role they play, and most especially the role they play in explaining the regular behavior of nonrational agents and the purposeful behavior of rational agents. On Aquinas's way of thinking, the best available explanation of the regular behavior of agents involves the positing of inclinations, where an inclination is conceived of as an intrinsic feature of an agent that leads it (inclines it, disposes it) to engage in some action.

Where I have used an electron as the agent in my example, Aquinas would have used an agent familiar to him, like fire, but his reasoning would have been just the same. Fire regularly performs one sort of action (heating) and not another (cooling). This regularity of behavior is not a coincidence; it must have some explanation. The best explanation is that fire has some feature that inclines it to heat things in close proximity. Calling this feature an inclination, Aquinas now has a reason to posit the existence of inclinations (given that the argument was perfectly generalizable to agents other than fire).

Aquinas distinguishes two types of inclinations: natural and voluntary. Examples of natural inclinations are fire's inclination to heat and a stone's inclination to fall.[24] A voluntary inclination is just any act of the will.[25] In both cases, an inclination is the sort of thing whose presence can explain the initiation and occurrence of action or change.[26]

Action and Passion

Aquinas accepts Aristotle's position that an action (like this fire's heating that water) and a passion (the water's being heated) are not two different motions, but are one and the same motion. Consider the phrases "the road from Thebes to Athens" and "the road from Athens to Thebes."[27] In reality, there is just one road. But people can travel on that road in either of two directions. When we are thinking of the road as having Thebes as its starting point, or when we want to advert to the fact that people sometimes start from Thebes and go to Athens, then we speak of the road from Thebes to Athens. When we are instead thinking of the road as having Athens as its starting point, we speak of the road from Athens to Thebes. Similarly, if fire heats water, we can talk about the action (heating) and the passion (being heated). In reality, there is just one motion or change, but when we want to advert to the fact that the motion is caused by the agent, we speak of the action. When, instead, we are calling to mind the fact that the motion occurs in the patient, we speak of the passion.

In explaining this position Aquinas discusses an example of Aristotle's concerning teaching and learning.[28] The initially puzzling view held by both Aristotle and Aquinas is that teaching and learning are not two different motions but are one and the same motion. In the course of explicating this view, Aquinas asserts that the action of teaching and the passion of learning are the same "in subject," but differ "*secundum rationem*," that is, they differ conceptually or in definition.[29] I think we can best understand Aquinas's position here by saying that, for Aquinas, the action of teaching and the passion of learning are the same in reference (they refer to one and the same change, which occurs in the learner), but different in sense ("action" expresses the fact that the change is caused by the teacher, and "passion" expresses the fact that the change occurs in the learner).[30]

Transmutation

To return to our example: the sculptor (the agent), on account of his inclinations and through the use of various powers, brings about a change in the bronze (the patient), so as to give it a new accidental form (its distinctive shape). This is an example of what Aquinas calls "transmutation." In any case of transmutation, an agent,[31] on account of its powers and inclinations, produces a change in some already existing patient. This change might terminate in the patient's possession of a new accidental form, or it might terminate in the existence of a new substance.

Causal *Relata*

Because contemporary philosophers almost always use the word "causation" to refer to a relation,[32] it is natural to ask what the terms of the relation of efficient causation are, according to Aquinas. In our example, what exactly is the efficient cause and what is the effect? As briefly indicated above, Aquinas uses the concepts of efficient cause and effect quite broadly, applying both notions to items from many different ontological categories. Aquinas applies the notion of an efficient cause to substances,[33] to powers,[34] to acts of will (and thus to inclinations),[35] and to processes or activities.[36] When Aquinas says that "passion is the effect of the agent in the patient,"[37] he is applying the notion of an effect to a change, which is an event. (Likewise when he speaks of an action as something that is "produced" by the agent.[38]) And because the change that an agent produces terminates in a new accident (in cases of accidental change) or a new substance (in cases of substantial change), Aquinas sometimes speaks of accidents[39] and substances[40] as the effects of transmuting causes. Further, in cases of transmutation, for a new accident to be produced is just for some substance (or substances) to be given a new accidental form, and for a new substance to be produced is just for some prime matter to be given a new substantial form. Accordingly, Aquinas can speak of forms (whether accidental or substantial) as the effects of transmuting causes.[41] Thus, rather than thinking that, for Aquinas, *the* relation of efficient causation in our example is a relation existing between the sculptor and the bronze, we should keep in mind Aquinas's fuller story: the sculptor brings about a change in the bronze, via his powers and inclinations (and various tools too, no doubt), and by so doing produces a statue and a new accidental form.

The Three Kinds of Efficient Causation and What They Have in Common

In addition to transmutation, Aquinas recognizes two other fundamental kinds of efficient causation: God's creation of a thing out of nothing and the conservation of existing things in existence.[42] What all three have in common is their relation to action.[43] To transmute something is to bring about a change in it. To create something is to produce it, but not out of any pre-existing material. To conserve something is to maintain it in existence. Each involves the action of one thing on or with respect to something. To create, to conserve, to transmute—these are all what Aquinas would have called transitive actions. It is therefore not surprising that Aquinas distinguishes efficient causation from material, formal, and final causation by means of the notion of action or operation: "For an efficient cause is a cause insofar as it acts."[44] For Aquinas, then, something counts as an efficient cause precisely because of its connection to some transitive action.[45] What all three types of efficient causation have in common is this: a metaphysically complete description of any case of efficient causation will be a description of the transitive action of one or more agents.

The Generic Notion of Causation

We can get a clearer understanding of the connection between efficient causation and action by examining something Aquinas says about causation in general. A principle (*principium*) is a source or starting point of some kind, or simply something that is first in some sequence, and a cause is a certain sort of principle, namely, a source of *being*: "Every cause is related as a principle to the being of its effect."[46] This statement is meant to apply to all four causes, as is the similar claim: "The name 'cause' implies some influence with regard to the being of the thing caused."[47] Each of the four causes has an influence on the being of that of which it is a cause, but the kind of influence is different for the different kinds of causes. The matter and form of a thing have an influence on the being of that thing by being constituents of it (more specifically: matter has its influence by being the subject of form, and form has its influence by being that which accounts for the thing's actually being whatever (or however) it is).

Efficient and final causes influence their effects too, but in quite different ways: "Just as influencing for an efficient cause is acting, so for a final cause influencing is being sought and being desired."[48] We might express Aquinas's view by saying that the way in which an efficient cause influences the being of its effect is by acting. But care must be taken to understand this in the correct sense. Aquinas's point is not that an efficient cause does one thing (influencing) by doing something else first (acting). Rather, his idea is that acting *is* influencing—acting consists in either (1) bringing about a change in something, (2) creating something out of nothing, or (3) conserving something in being, and any of these count as a kind of influencing.[49] The sense in which an efficient cause influences the being of its effect is that an efficient cause produces or conserves something (in a word, an efficient cause *acts*).

Given the prevalence of reductive analyses of causation in the contemporary literature on causation, it is worth noting that when Aquinas makes reference to the notion of transitive action in order to distinguish the efficient cause from the other genera of causes, he is not attempting to reductively define or analyze efficient causation in terms of some noncausal concept. On the contrary, action, in the sense at issue here, is already a causal concept.

Contemporary Accounts of Causation

An adequate treatment of Aquinas's views on causation would require discussion of several other topics, including especially the distinctions between *per se* and *per accidens* causation[50] and between primary and secondary causation. But in the very short space remaining, I want to focus instead on ways in which Aquinas's views relate to recent philosophical reflection on causation. Despite a few passages that might mislead an unwary reader, Aquinas clearly rejects a transference theory of causation.[51] And while he does recognize a close relationship between counterfactuals and causation, he never attempts to reductively analyze causation in terms of counterfactuals. Or in terms of anything else, for that matter—Aquinas seems happy to accept at least some causal concepts and some causal facts as basic. For this reason, and because of his focus on powers and inclinations, Aquinas's understanding of causation has most in common with contemporary dispositionalist accounts of causation, which take causal powers as irreducible aspects of reality.[52]

NOTES

1. *ST* II-II q.27 a.3. For the Latin texts of Aquinas I have used S. Thomae de Aquino, *Opera omnia*, ed. Enrique Alarcon, <http://www.corpusthomisticum.org/iopera.html>. Translations are my own.

2. A word about prime matter: Aquinas recognizes several different uses of the term "matter" (*materia*). (See *DPN*, chs. 1–2, and *ST* I-II q.55 a.4.) For my purposes here it is only necessary to distinguish two such uses, corresponding to the two types of change, accidental and substantial. In an accidental change, the matter of the change is a substance (or an aggregate of substances) and the form acquired in the course of the change is an accident. When Socrates loses his tan and becomes pale, Socrates (a substance) acquires paleness (an accident). The example of a lump of bronze being formed into a statue is also an example of an accidental change, since bronze is a substance in its own right that persists through the change, receiving in the process only a new shape (which is an accident).

In case of substantial change, by contrast, the matter of the change is not an independently existing substance (or an aggregate of such substances), but is rather what Aquinas calls *materia prima* ("prime matter" or "primary matter"). Matter such as bronze is a subject of form (e.g., this bronze is the subject of a particular shape), but bronze is itself something that has a matter–form structure. Aquinas holds that any material substance is composed of two metaphysical parts or constituents: substantial form and prime matter. As a first approximation: the substantial form of a material substance *S* is that constituent of *S* that accounts for the fact that *S* is the kind of substance it is, and not a substance of some other kind made out of the same prime matter, while the prime matter of *S* is that constituent of *S* that persists, and begins to be the matter of some new substance, when *S* passes away. Prime matter is matter that is not itself composed of form and matter.

According to Aquinas, prime matter can be separated from form in thought, but it can never be so separated in reality, because prime matter can never exist on its own, without having some form or another. For more on prime matter, see *DPN* 2; *In Phy* I.13.118; *In Meta* VII.2.1285–1296, and VIII.1.1689.

3. Here by "generation" Aquinas intends to include both generation *simpliciter* (substantial change) and generation *secundum quid* (accidental change). See *DPN* 1.4, and *In Meta* I.12.199.

4. *DPN* 3.15.

5. *In Meta* V.2.773.

6. *In Phy* II.5.182.

7. *ST* I q.82 a.4.

8. *ST* II-II q.58 a.2.

9. A sentence from the entry on "act" in *Webster's New Collegiate Dictionary* (Springfield, Mass.: Merriam, 1956).

10. For more on Aquinas's theory of substance, see Brown 2005, ch. 3, and the chapter on Being in this volume.

11. See *In Phy* III.5.

12. *ST* I-II q.26 a.2.

13. *ST* I q.36 a.3 ad 1. Here, the term "*suppositum*" refers to the substance that acts.

14. I say "at least in many cases" because there may be cases where a thing performs an action of a certain sort, such that it would not necessarily be reasonable to infer the existence of a single positive feature that enables the thing to perform actions of that sort. Human beings occasionally hiccup; should we infer that humans possess a power of hiccupping? Not necessarily, because a hiccup might just be the accidental result of several distinct powers functioning (or misfunctioning) together. Be that as it may, what is crucial to Aquinas's view is only the claim that, at least in many cases, it is reasonable to infer the existence of powers.

15. See *ST* I q.25 a.1; *QDP* 7.9c; and *SCG* IV. 77.

16. On the ontology of passive powers, see *In Meta* V.14.963.

17. *In Meta* IX.3.1796 and *In Meta* V.14.955.

18. See *In Meta* VII.6.1407.

19. By "act of will" I mean to translate Aquinas's "*actus voluntatis,*" which is a generic term that covers at least six different acts of which the will is the subject: enjoyment (*fruitio*), intention (*intentio*), volition (*voluntas*), choice (*electio*), consent (*consensus*), and use (*usus*). See *ST* I-II, q.11–16.

20. *ST* I-II q.1 a.2; *DPN* 3.16; *SCG* III.2; *In Phy* II.13–14.

21. *DPN* 3.16 and *QDV*, q.22, a.1, ad 2.

22. See *DPN* 3.16; *SCG* III.16 [3]; and *In Phy* II.10.240.

23. *ST* I-II q.1 a.2.

24. Fire always heats, but a stone does not always fall (e.g., if it is held up by something). Does this mean that a stone sometimes has an inclination to fall, and sometimes lacks such an inclination? No. Aquinas's theory seems to be this: A stone that is located anywhere but at the center of the Earth always has an inclination to fall. (Indeed, maybe it would be best to characterize the stone's inclination as an inclination to move to and rest in its proper place, which is the center of the Earth.) Now, a stone falls only in certain circumstances *not* because it sometimes has the inclination to fall and sometimes does not have that inclination, but rather because its always-present inclination to fall is sometimes impeded, and sometimes not. If something is in the way of the stone and the center of the Earth, then the stone's inclination to fall may not be able to issue forth in actual movement.

25. *ST* I q.87 a.4: "An act of the will is nothing other than a certain inclination following upon an understood form, just as a natural appetite is an inclination following upon a natural form." See also *ST* I-II q.6 a.4; *ST* I-II q.15 a.1; *QDV*, q.22, a.12c; and *QDC*, q.1c.

26. Aquinas customarily speaks as if power and inclination are distinct (see, e.g., *ST* I q.106 a.2 and *ST* I q.80 a.1 ad 3). It is easy enough to see why we should think there is such a distinction in the case of voluntary inclinations, but in cases of natural inclination it is less clear. Why think that the substance fire has two ontologically distinct features, one of which is its active power to heat and one of which is its inclination to heat? Some of Aquinas's comments (e.g. at *ST* II-II q.27 a.4) suggest that he thinks of an inclination as the actualization of an active power. If so, then there is always at least a conceptual distinction between a thing's powers and its inclinations. Perhaps Aquinas could hold, however, that in cases where an active power is always actualized (as with fire, which is always inclined to heat anything in its proximity), there exists just one actual feature, which grounds the truth of both the claims that "this agent has power *P*" and "this agent has inclination *I*."

27. *In Phy* III.5.318.

28. *In Phy* III.5.

29. *In Phy* III.5.318.

30. The reader might be puzzled by the fact that, for Aquinas, "the action of teaching" refers to a change in the learner, and not to a change or process in the teacher. To motivate Aquinas's use of language here, imagine that a teacher is writing at a blackboard and verbally explaining some argument. Now suppose that there is in fact no one else present in the room. There is a sense in which we would deny that the teacher is engaged in the action of teaching. The action of teaching (in this sense) actually occurs only when some learner is undergoing a certain type of cognitive change. This is the sense of "action of teaching" that Aquinas is using when he holds that the action of teaching and the passion of learning are one motion taking place in the learner.

31. Or, a number of agents working together.

32. The word may also be used to refer to an action, as in "The production of one thing by another is one type of causation."

33. *In Meta* V.3.780.

34. *ST* I q.82 a.4; *In Meta* VII.6; *DPN* 5.26.

35. *QDV*, q.28, a.8, ad 7: "Consent is the efficient cause of marriage."

36. See *In Meta* V.2.771, where Aquinas asserts that the (ancient medical) processes of reducing and purging can be called causes from which motion comes, i.e., efficient causes.

37. *ST* I-II q.26 a.2.

38. *SCG* III.70 [5].

39. See *ST* I-II q.75 a.4 (evil dispositions and habits, which are accidents, are efficiently caused by acts of sin).

40. e.g., at *In Meta* V.2.765 Aquinas takes up Aristotle's characterization of the father as "the cause of the child," in which case the child (a substance) is being thought of as an effect.

41. *QDM*, q.5, a.5, ad 16: "the form itself is an effect of the agent." See also *De aeternitate mundi.*

42. *Diu. nom.* 4.5: "For these three things seem to belong to the notion of an efficient cause: to give being, to move, and to conserve." On creation, see *ST* I q.45. On conservation, see *ST* I q.104, a.1–2.

43. The sense of "action" at issue here is that of transitive action, as opposed to immanent action. A transitive action is, roughly, an action on something. This is to be contrasted with an action in the sense of the actualization of a potency of the agent, which actualization remains within the agent. When Feynman understands the fundamental theorem of calculus, for instance, Feynman is the subject of an action of understanding, which is an action remaining within him. Aquinas discusses the distinction between actions passing over into exterior things and actions remaining within the agent in several texts, including *SCG* II.1; *ST* I q.18 a.3 ad 1; *ST* I q.23 a.2 ad 1; *ST* I q.54 a.1 ad 3; *ST* I q.85 a.2; and *In Meta* IX.8.1862–1865. This distinction has been referred to by later thinkers as the distinction between (i) transitive (or transient or transeunt) action and (ii) immanent action.

44. *In Meta* V.2.775. See also *QDV*, q.28, a.8c.

45. Thus, Aquinas uses *agens causa* (acting cause) and *efficiens causa* (efficient cause) as synonyms (compare *ST* II-II q.27 a.3 and *SCG* III.10 [5]).

46. *Super Sent* 1.29.1.1c. See also *Super Sent* 3.11.1.1, ad 5.

47. *In Meta* V.1.751.

48. *QDV*, q.22, a.2c. The meaning of the second clause in this sentence is that a final cause has the influence it has by being the object of some inclination.

49. In this way, the statement that an efficient cause influences by acting is not like the statement that one gets a promotion by doing good work, but is like the statement that a cyclist exercises by cycling. It is not as if the cyclist does one thing (cycle), which in turn allows him to do a second thing (exercise). Rather, his cycling *is* his exercising.

50. See *ST* I-II q.85 a.5; *QDM*, q.1, a.3c; *In Meta* V.3.789.

51. *SCG* III.69 [28].

52. See, e.g., Cartwright 1989, Ellis 2001, Ellis 2002, and Molnar 2003. I am grateful to Jeffrey Brower, Brian Davies, Colleen McCluskey, Kent Staley, and Eleonore Stump for their helpful comments on what I have written here.

CHAPTER 9

THE FIVE WAYS

TIMOTHY PAWL

Introduction

The Five Ways are five proofs or demonstrations that Aquinas offers near the beginning of his *Summa theologiae* to establish the existence of God.[1] Although the Five Ways compose only a miniscule portion of Aquinas's *Summa*—less than 775 words, or nearly one word for every fourth page in a standard edition of the work—one would be hard-pressed to find another part of Aquinas's corpus that has been commented on as much as the Five Ways. Yet despite their minute size and the gigantic secondary literature on them throughout the centuries, whether Aquinas succeeds—and even what it is that Aquinas is attempting to do or how he intends to do it—is still debated.

Some scholars think that Aquinas's Five Ways are meant to demonstrate the existence of the particularly Christian God. But if one considers that Aquinas follows the article containing the Five Ways with an article questioning whether God has a body[2] and then later with articles questioning whether God is perfect, good, infinite, immutable, eternal, and even whether there is just one God, one sees that Aquinas does not take himself to have already shown that the God of the Christian creeds exists.[3] Others treat Aquinas's Five Ways as attempts to demonstrate the existence of something omniscient, omnipotent, and wholly good.[4] The text does not bear this interpretation. In fact, Aquinas explicitly argues that God has each of these attributes at different points later in the Treatise on God (in the case of God's power, over twenty questions later).[5] Aquinas is attempting to demonstrate something much weaker here as a first step in arguing for a being with the traditional divine attributes; namely, that there is something or other that moves things but is unmoved, and that there is something or other that causes but is uncaused, and so on.[6]

One also finds authors treating the Five Ways as if they are the summit of Aquinas's careful thought about demonstrations for the existence of God and intended by Aquinas as the last word when it comes to what can be said when arguing that God exists.[7] But this was not his intent.[8] He had previously written something considerably longer and more detailed on the argument from motion in the *Summa contra Gentiles*, and he had already discussed the other ways, or arguments very similar to them, elsewhere.[9] Had his intent been to produce carefully crafted, full-fledged arguments with the aim of convincing agnostics or atheists of the existence of God, he would have used the arguments he had already worked out in careful detail. Since the Five Ways are not his most in-depth, carefully crafted arguments for God's existence, finding them wanting, if one does find them wanting, does not entail that Aquinas never successfully argued for the existence of God. To judge on that topic, one must look to the *SCG* and elsewhere, as careful commentators, both sympathetic to Aquinas and not, have done.[10] The *Summa* was written as a theological textbook for students just beginning their theological training. In fact, there is a case to be made that it was written for the formation of priests who were not going on into academia, "young and run-of-the-mill Dominicans."[11] If one of our contemporaries had produced a detailed and careful defense of a particular position, we would not judge the merit of her arguments for that position based on what she says about it in an introductory text she has also authored. Rather, we go to the more detailed work. Our policy should be the same when it comes to Aquinas.

Nevertheless, the focus of this chapter is exclusively the Five Ways, which are without a doubt Aquinas's most well-known arguments for the existence of God.[12] Here I will analyze the Five Ways and discuss what I take to be the most important points raised in the secondary literature.[13]

The First Way: The Way from Motion

Aquinas calls his First Way the most manifest of the Five Ways.[14] He argues:[15]

(1) There exist some things that are moved.
(2) For anything that is moved, it is moved by something not identical with it.
(3) A series of movers does not regress infinitely.
(4) Therefore there must be a first unmoved mover.
(5) This first unmoved mover all people understand to be God.[16]

There are multiple debates concerning the exact meaning of "motion" in the First Way. One debate is over whether Aquinas uses "is moved" (*movetur*) in a passive or intransitive sense. Does he mean in (2), for instance, that anything that is in motion (intransitive) is moved by another, or that anything that is moved by something (passive) is moved by another?[17] Following Scott MacDonald and John Wippel,

I read the verb in the passive sense.[18] Another question concerns the scope of motion discussed in the First Way. Aquinas is not discussing solely metaphysical motion because he is talking about changes that are "plain to the senses," such as wood heating up (or of the movement of heavenly bodies, which is his example in *SCG* I.13 where he discusses this argument).[19] Such changes are prime exemplars of physical change.[20] Considering physical motion, Aquinas is not discussing only local motion, since one of his own examples of motion in this text is that of fire heating up wood, and that sort of motion is not local motion.[21] It seems most reasonable then to think that he means the three accidental types of Aristotelian change: local motion, qualitative change, and quantitative change.

Allowing for the scope of "motion" to extend beyond local motion provides an easy response to an objection that the First Way has faced. Some argue that the First Way is unsound due to its dependence on an obsolete Aristotelian physics. For instance, I. M. Bochenski writes, "Since 'movetur' is to be understood as 'is in spatial motion', the claims made in the proof rest substantially on Aristotelian *physics*. But since such views are no longer defensible, the *prima via* is not valid."[22] If the scope of "motion" in the First Way extends beyond local motion, this objection, if apt, would only show that the scope of "motion" would need to be reined in so as not to include local motion; it would not show that the First Way fails.[23]

Concerning justification for the premises of the First Way, Aquinas takes (1) to be "certain, and plain to the senses." Some things are moved locally, qualitatively, or quantitatively: people move about, tan and sunburn, bulk up and thin out.

Aquinas offers arguments for premises (2) and (3). He argues as follows for (2):

(2.1) To move something is to bring it from being potentially some way to being actually that way, say, potentially *F* to actually *F*.
(2.2) Nothing is moved to being actually *F* unless it is first potentially *F*.
(2.3) Nothing brings another thing from being potentially *F* to being actually *F* unless it is in an appropriate state of actuality.[24]
(2.4) It is not possible that something be both potentially *F* and in the appropriate state of actuality to bring something to be actually *F*.
(2.5) Thus, it is not possible that something move itself.
(2) Therefore, for anything such that it is moved, it is moved by something not identical with it.[25]

One thing to note about this argument is that it does not address the epistemic possibility—that is, possibility *for all we know*—of something going from being potentially *F* to being actually *F* without the aid of any mover whatsoever.[26]

Premise (2.4) needs justification. If the appropriate state of actuality were simply *being actually F*, then it would be easy to see why one would think that something could not be both potentially *F* and actually in an appropriate state of actuality to make something else actually *F*. But the appropriate state of actuality need not be *being F*, since God brings things to states of being without sharing those states of being—God makes material things without being material, or hot things without being hot.[27] Here commentators point to *being actually F or virtually F* as the appropriate state of actuality, where something is virtually *F* when that thing is not *F*, but is such that it can cause things to be *F*.[28] But now one wonders why it is that something cannot be virtually *F* and potentially *F*, as (2.4) implies. Perhaps Aquinas would maintain that the only way something can be virtually *F* is if it cannot be potentially *F*. But now we need an argument for that claim.[29]

Aquinas's argument for (3) is as follows:

(3.1) Secondary movers move things in virtue of their being moved by a first mover.
(3.2) Thus, if there is no first mover, then there are no secondary movers.
(3.3) If it is the case that a series of movers regresses infinitely, then there is no first mover.
(3.4) But there are secondary movers.
(3) Thus, it is not the case that a series of movers regresses infinitely.[30]

Premises (3.2) and (3.4) seem to prove, by themselves, the conclusion of the First Way, namely, that there is a first mover. They also seem to prove the existence of an *unmoved* mover, since, if the mover were to be moved, it would not be *first*. It seems as if Aquinas could simply give (3.2) and (3.4) as an argument for a first mover rather than giving the whole First Way.

To elucidate (3.1), Aquinas provides an example of a stick causing something to move in virtue of the stick being moved by a hand. This leads one to think that Aquinas is discussing something more than just a mere series of movers. Instead it seems that the series must be ordered such that the members all move at the same time and the later members in the series move in virtue of the motion of the earlier members. I will take up the issue of such ordered series in the discussion of the Second Way.

One thing to note about the main deduction from (1)–(3) to (4) is that, while Aquinas intends the argument to conclude that there is something wholly unmoved, it seems that at most the argument can conclude that there must be some mover at the beginning of any particular series of movers.[31] It could be that each series has a first mover, but each of those movers is an intermediate member of some other series of movers. If that is possible, then one can affirm (1)–(3) and deny (4), that there is anything wholly unmoved—unmoved in all ways whatsoever.[32]

Peter Geach provides an interpretation of the First Way (and all Five Ways) in which, rather than focusing his argument on individual causal chains, Aquinas is "treating the whole world as a great big object" and then asking what accounts for the motion of this great big object.[33] If Geach were right, pointing out that the first mover of any particular series might also be an intermediate mover of another series, as I have done in the previous paragraph, is irrelevant to the First Way, since Aquinas would be trying to show that all motion, taken together, needs a first, unmoved mover, and not that one can trace a chain of a certain type of motion back to a first, unmoved mover. Thus, if this lumping together interpretation is correct, one could not affirm (1)–(3) and deny (4) in the way I have presented in the preceding paragraph. This strategy is not without costs, however. One major problem with Geach's interpretation of the First Way is that the text does not seem to bear it out. There is no evidence in the First Way that Aquinas meant to lump together the entire world as, for instance, the thing that is moved in (2), or as a secondary mover, as the sub proof for (3) discusses.

The Second Way: The Way from Efficient Causation

Aquinas's Second Way is similar to the First Way, but rather than focusing on motion, it focuses on efficient causation.[34] Aquinas argues as follows:[35]

(6) There is an ordered series of efficient causes among sensible things.
(7) It is impossible that a thing be the efficient cause of itself.
(8) It is not possible for an ordered series of efficient causes to continue infinitely.[36]
(9) Therefore, there is a first efficient cause.
(10) This first efficient cause all people call "God."[37]

An order of efficient causes is more than just a particular series of efficient causes. We know this, in part, because Aquinas claims that there is no conceptual problem with a series of efficient causes continuing infinitely. He says, for instance, that there is nothing impossible about a series of male ancestors having no first member.[38] For a series of efficient causes to count as *ordered*, and hence for it to be the sort of series whose infinite continuation is ruled impossible in premise (8), a chain of efficient causes must be one in which its members exist and perform their causal work simultaneously, and the members downstream in the causal series exercise their causal action in virtue of the causal action of their predecessors in the series.[39] Such a series (also referred to as a per se series) is one where the causal work of the later members in the series depends on the causal work of the earlier members of the series, and not merely that the existence of earlier members in the series at some time or other is a necessary condition for the causal work of the later members of the series. So we see that in a chain of male ancestors the conditions for being ordered are not fulfilled.

Aquinas takes (6) to be clear from the perceptible world. One should note that, given the definition of an "order" of efficient causes, the sort of efficient causation that is ordered and clear from sensible things is not generation and corruption. This is because we are not familiar with any entities that are such that they generate other beings, which generate still other beings in virtue of the simultaneously employed causal power of the previous beings in the series. That is, we do not know of any series of efficient generators that fulfill the requirements of an *ordered* series of efficient causes.[40] Similarly, we do not find an ordered series of conserving efficient causes among sensible things.[41]

For (7), Aquinas argues as follows:

(7.1) If *x* is an efficient cause of *y*, then *x* is prior to *y*.
(7.2) But it is impossible that a thing be prior to itself.
(7) Thus, it is impossible that a thing be the efficient cause of itself.

It is important to notice that Aquinas is talking about explanatory or logical priority here, and not temporal. Aquinas thought that God is the efficient cause of all temporal things and, since eternal, not temporally prior to any of them.[42]

The other premise in the argument for the Second Way that Aquinas defends is premise (8). He argues:

(8.1) In any case of ordered efficient causes, the first is the cause of the intermediate cause or causes, and the intermediate is the cause of the ultimate effect.
(8.2) If a cause is removed, then its effects are removed.
(8.3) Thus, if there were not a first cause with regard to efficient causes, there would be no intermediate causes or ultimate effects.
(8.4) But if efficient causes were to proceed infinitely, then there would not be a first cause with respect to efficient causes.
(8.5) Thus, there would not be any intermediate causes or ultimate effects.
(8.6) But there are intermediate causes and ultimate effects.
(8) Therefore, it is not possible for an ordered series of efficient causes to continue infinitely.

One worry about this argument is that premise (8.2) refers to "removing" (*remota*; *removetur*) a cause. It seems as if the removing in mind is the taking away of what is already there. So if it were the case that you removed what was there, counterfactually plucking away something upstream in the causal ordering, then you would not have what followed from it. But (8.3) and (8.4) make no mention of removing. It may well be that if one were to remove the first cause in an order of efficient causes, then the effects would not follow, but it is less clear that if there just is not a first cause at all, as (8.3) has it, not even one to be removed, then there cannot be any intermediate causes or ultimate effects. The series of causes could be infinite, and such a series would have no first cause. Of course, Aquinas denies the possibility of an infinitely regressing ordered series—that is precisely what he is arguing for here: (8). But he cannot use (8) to support (8.2), a premise in the argument for (8).

As with the First Way, the inference from (6)–(9) to (10) does not seem to yield a particularly impressive being. It is difficult to find among sensible things an order of generative causes or an order of conserving causes. The only pertinent sort of efficient causation remaining is that of the moving cause. But then the Second Way seems to collapse into the First Way, though perhaps as an argument that starts from movers moving things rather than things being moved.

The Third Way: The Way from Possibility and Necessity

Aquinas says that his Third Way is from possibility and necessity (*ex possibili et necessario*), but we must be careful how we understand "necessity" or "possibility," as we shall see. He argues:[43]

(11) Some things are such that they are able to be or not to be.
(12) It is not possible that everything be such that it is able to be or not to be.
(13) Therefore, there must exist something that is necessary.
(14) For anything that is necessary, it either has its necessity from something else or it does not.
(15) It is impossible for the objects that have their necessity from something else to proceed infinitely.
(16) Therefore, one must posit something that has its necessity from itself, which is the cause of the necessity of other things.
(17) This everyone calls God.[44]

Aquinas provides justification in the text for premises (11), (12), and (15).

In defense of (11) he points out that some things are able to be generated or corrupted. This is indicative of his understanding of possible being and necessary being in this argument. Necessary things, at least in this argument, are things that cannot cease to exist by corruption (e.g., decomposition). Non-necessary things are those that can cease to be through corruption. Likewise, necessary beings cannot be generated by composition, while non-necessary beings can be generated through composition.[45] On this understanding of necessity, human souls, since they are incorruptible, are necessary beings.[46] But they are not necessary in the sense that they cannot not be, as the term "necessary" is often used today and as Aquinas himself sometimes used the term.[47]

The proof for premise (12) is where the majority of the secondary literature on the Third Way focuses. In defense of (12), Aquinas argues:

(12.1) Suppose that it is possible that everything be such that it is able to be or not to be.
(12.2) Anything that is able not to be at some time is not.
(12.3) Therefore, if all things are able not to be, then at some time nothing existed in reality.
(12.4) Anything that begins to be, begins only through something that is.
(12.5) Thus, if nothing had existed at some time, then it would be impossible for anything to have begun to be.
(12.6) And thus nothing would exist now.
(12.7) But something does exist now.
(12) Thus, it is not possible that everything be such that it is able to be or not to be.

Premises (12.2), (12.3), and (12.4) each seem doubtable.

Consider (12.2). Could it not be that some thing or things preserve an object that is able not to be throughout the long—perhaps infinite—history of the world? Such an object would still be able to be, since it is, and would also be able not to be, since it *could*—but does not—cease to be through corruption. Or could it not be that something or other created a temporal world for only five minutes, and that there were some corruptible things that existed for the full five minutes?[48] Why think it is true that if something *can* not be then it *must* not be at some time or other?[49]

Premise (12.3) has received the most press in contemporary literature on the Third Way. It seems to be derived by a quantifier shift fallacy, in which Aquinas concludes from (12.2), that for everything that is such that it is able not to be, there is some time when that thing is not, to the claim that there is some time such that nothing exists. But that is an invalid inference.[50]

Commentators have defended this step in multiple ways, though almost all defenses have the same form: while the step envisioned from (12.2) to (12.3) is rightly considered invalid as is, Aquinas had in mind another, tacit premise, which, when combined with (12.2), provides for a licit inference. David Conway, for instance, critically discusses one such commonly held tacit premise: that Aquinas is supposing for argument that the world has an infinite past and that, given an infinite amount of time, all possibilities will have been actualized.[51] Martin De Nys can be understood as saying that the tacit premise is something like the following: if each part of a whole is contingent, then the whole itself must be contingent.[52] This, along with the supposition that all things are contingent, entails that the whole universe is contingent. That, along with (12.2), yields that the whole—the universe—at some time is not.[53]

Premise (12.4) is a modest causal principle: nothing comes from nothing. But even if it is modest, there are still some who doubt it.[54] There are some who may think that it is at least epistemically possible that there are some things which, having no efficient cause, come into existence. And if things can come into existence without a cause, then (12.4) is false (and, I should note, the Second Way would fail as well). There are, however, grave philosophical and scientific difficulties with denying (12.4).[55]

In defense of premise (15), Aquinas claims that "it is not possible for the objects that have their necessity from something else to proceed into infinity, just as it is not possible to have an infinite chain of efficient causes, as was proven." I refer the reader back to the discussion of the Second Way here; in particular, (8), (8.1) to (8.6), and the discussion following. The argument in the Second Way required the notion of an *ordered* series of efficient causes. If that previous argument from the Second Way is to be of use here, the series of causes of necessary existence must be an ordered series as well. But why think that any series in which *A* causes *B* to exist necessarily and *B* causes *C* to exist necessarily must be an ordered series? Could not *A* cause *B* to exist necessarily, and then *B*, by itself and at some later time, cause *C* to exist necessarily? One needs a reason to think that any series of causes of necessity is an ordered series in order for Aquinas's reference to the previous way to support (15). One place to look for such a reason may be an analysis of ungenerated being and the necessary conditions for its coming to be.

THE FOURTH WAY: THE WAY FROM GRADATION

The Fourth Way, and following Fifth Way, go more quickly than the others. In the previous three ways, Aquinas has provided some attempts to justify the controversial premises he employs. But here, and in the next way, we see very few attempts to justify difficult premises. Given the aim of the *Summa* and its intended audience, we should not be too hard on Aquinas for these omissions. Nevertheless, these omissions do make it more difficult to gauge the soundness of the arguments.

Aquinas's Fourth Way is taken from the gradation that we find in the world:[56]

(18) There are things that are more or less good, more or less true, more or less noble, and so on.
(19) But things are called more or less *F* insofar as they are closer or further from that which is maximally *F*.
(20) Thus, there is something maximally good, maximally true, and maximally noble.
(21) That which is maximally true is maximally being (or most fully being).
(22) Therefore, there is something which is maximally being (or most fully being).
(23) Anything that is maximally *F* is the cause of all things that are *F*.
(24) Thus, there is something that is the cause of all beings, their goodness, and each and every of their perfections.
(25) This we call God.

By "maximally *F*," Aquinas means that there is something as *F* as anything could be, something at the very pinnacle of the *F*-ness scale, and not the weaker and obvious claim that if two or more things are related as more or less *F*, then there must be one of those things that is more *F* than the others (or a tie). Premise (23) would make no sense on the weaker reading.

An interpretive difficulty with the Fourth Way has to do with the sort of causation in question in (23) and (24). Some interpreters have argued that it is formal causation, others efficient, still others final, and at least one commentator argues that it is all three of them.[57] As Linwood Urban has shown, it is not decisive to point to the fact that Aquinas writes of fire causing the hotness of hot things, since Aquinas sees fire as not only an efficient cause but also a formal, material, and final cause.[58] The argument seems most intuitive when understood as formal causation, but then it seems to incur the difficulty of showing that, if sound, it demonstrates more than the existence of the Platonic forms.

Aquinas takes (18) to be clear from observation. Premises (19), (21), and (23) are each susceptible to difficulties and to modern ears may sound incredible. While we do not get arguments in support of these premises, we do get two appeals to authority and two examples.

Consider (19) and its scope. Aquinas would not have affirmed it to be true for all predicates. For instance, we call things more or less evil, but Aquinas would not have affirmed that there is a maximally evil entity.[59] The mention of "perfections" (*perfectionis*) in (24) leads the reader to think that one could limit the range of (19) to perfections. This would be a fortunate scope restriction, since it would not require Aquinas to posit a stickiest thing, a smelliest thing, or a sleepiest thing, or, at the other end of the spectrum, the most amucilaginous, most aromatic, and most aware things.[60] But this restriction runs into exegetical problems, since Aquinas's example for (19) is that the hotter something is, the closer it is to what is maximally hot. Being hot, though, is not a perfection.[61] So while there must be some limitation to the scope of (19) to rule out maximally evil or sleepy things, what exactly that limitation would be, for Aquinas, is difficult to know.

Even aside from questions about (19)'s scope, it still seems highly doubtful. Provide whatever narrow scope you want for (19), why think that it is true? As John Wippel rightly points out, "It is unnecessary for us to assume that something enjoys a maximum degree of heat in order to be aware that one kettle is hotter than another."[62] Surely, there is one kettle that is hotter than the others (or a tie for hottest), but that is a far cry from saying that there is something maximally hot, in the strong sense of "maximal" spelt out earlier.

Aquinas points to the authority of Aristotle as justification for premises (21) and (23), in particular, Aristotle's *Metaphysics*, Book II. Aquinas is not talking about the truth that accrues to a thought, sentence, or proposition in virtue of its conforming with reality. He is not saying that the thought (or...) maximally in conformity with reality is maximally existent or that it is the cause of all other things. Rather, he is talking about "ontological truth"—a property that every being has in virtue of its being conformable to intellects.[63] Though an account of Aquinas's theory of transcendentals and levels of being is beyond the scope of this section, an understanding of them is required in order to see why Aquinas would maintain that the most true thing is the most fully in being.

In addition to the appeal to Aristotle, Aquinas provides an example for premise (23)—fire, which is maximally hot, is the cause of all hot things. Aquinas here means that fire is the cause of the *being hot* of hot things, and not the cause of the actually hot *things*—this premise does not require fire to be the cause of the kettles themselves; it just needs to be the cause of the tea kettles being a certain way; namely, *being hot*.

The Fifth Way: The Way from Governance

The Fifth Way, and final way, is from the governance of things:[64]

(26) There are some things that lack cognition yet act for ends.
(27) Anything that lacks cognition does not act for an end unless it is directed by something that is cognizant and intelligent.[65]
(28) Thus, there is something intelligent by which all natural things are ordered to their ends.
(29) This thing we call God.[66]

Aquinas offers an argument and example to support (26) and offers an example for (27). Some corporeal things do not cognize but sometimes act for ends. Tomato plants lack cognition but very frequently act to bring about tomatoes. The argument for (26) is as follows:

(26.1) Some things that lack cognition always or frequently act in the same way to bring about that which is best.[67]

(26.2) If some things that lack cognition always or frequently act in the same way to bring about that which is best, then they act for an end, and this not by chance but by design.

(26) Thus, there are some things that lack cognition yet act for ends.

The example for (27) is that of an archer shooting an arrow. Just as the archer directs the flight of an arrow, so the designer directs the actions of the noncognizant beings that act for an end.

There is one main problem facing both (27) and (26.2). Darwinism provides an account of how it could be that something acts for an end, and does so always or for the most part, but does not act for an end as a result of the design of an intelligent agent. Darwinism grows (evolves?) another horn onto the head of the old dilemma: design or chance. It could be that nonintelligent things act for ends as a result of selective evolution (though that is not to say that there is something, evolution, which selects for the sake of evolving things, as if it were acting for an end).

This may just push the argument back, though. Rather than focusing on things that we see around us, like tomato plants, a proponent of this argument could focus his or her argument on things that did not evolve yet still act always or for the most part for an end. For instance, electrons act always or for the most part to attract positively charged particles. This action, however, was not selected for by means of an evolutionary process. So the objection from Darwinism, while narrowing the scope of the examples Aquinas could give, does not vitiate the argument.

But (27) and (26.2) still stand in need of a positive defense. Even if electrons do not attract positively charged particles because of an evolutionary process, why could it not be that they do so without design and not by chance? It seems epistemically possible that it just be a brute fact that electrons attract positively charged particles. They do so by nature, and that nature was not designed by a designer. If that were the case, then the Fifth Way would be unsound.

Conclusion

In this paper I have presented the Five Ways and discussed some of the most common criticisms of them in the secondary literature. I have provided citations in the notes for readers looking for additional reading on these issues.

NOTES

I thank Gary Atkison, Brian Davies, Matthews Grant, Robert Gressis, Mathew Lu, Rachel Lu, Faith Glavey Pawl, Michael Rota, Jon Stoltz, Eleonore Stump, and Chris Toner for helpful comments on this chapter.

1. *ST* I q.2 a.3.
2. *ST* I q.3 a.1.
3. Aquinas writes that believers ought not try to prove the tenets of Christian belief that are beyond the scope of reason, an example of which is that God is triune, since such proofs will fall short and lead unbelievers to scoff at believers (see *SCG* I 9, para 2). Aquinas writes this shortly before going on to provide a detailed argument that is quite similar to the First Way. It would be absurd for Aquinas to claim that one ought not try to prove the existence of a triune God—the God of the Christian creeds—in one stroke and go on, in the next, to attempt such a proof.
4. See Elliott Sober, *Core Questions in Philosophy* (New York: Macmillan Library Reference, 1991), Lectures 4 and 5, pp. 36–56. To see similar treatment at a popular and polemical level, see Richard Dawkins, *The God Delusion* (New York: Bantam Press, 2006), 77–79. John Wilcox thinks something similar. Wilcox seems to think that each of Aquinas's Five Ways is an attempt to prove the existence of a simple, infinite entity. See John Wilcox, "The Five Ways and the Oneness of God," *The Thomist* 62 (1998): 245–68.
5. Aquinas argues that God is supremely and essentially good in *ST* I q.6, that God is omniscient in *ST* I q.14, and that God is omnipotent in *ST* I q.25.
6. Bochenski writes, for instance, "he is using the word '*deus*' in a very general and vague sense; it designates Pagan gods as well as the one God of the great religions and of philosophers. Hence '*deus*' ought to be interpreted as a general term rather than a description" (Joseph M. Bochenski, "The Five Ways," in Adolfo García de la Sienra, ed., *The Rationality of Theism* [Atlanta, Ga.: Rodopi, 2000], 61–92; 67). See also Herman Reith, *The Metaphysics of St. Thomas Aquinas* (Milwaukee, Wis.: Bruce, 1958), 177–78; Timothy McDermott, *Summa Theologiae*, vol. 2, *Existence and Nature of God:1a. 2–11* (Cambridge: Cambridge University Press, 2006), Appendix 4: The Meaning of the Word "God"; David Twetten, "Clearing a 'Way' for Aquinas: How the Proof from Motion Concludes to God," *Proceedings of the American Catholic Philosophical Association* 70 (1997): 259–78, 264–67; Richard Cartwright, "The Second Way," *Medieval Philosophy and Theology* 5 (1996): 189–204; 190–91 for a discussion of Aquinas's intended conclusion to the Second Way; Brian Davies, "Aquinas's Third Way," *New Blackfriars* 82 (2001): 450–66; 463 for a discussion of Aquinas's demonstrative aim in the Third Way; John Wippel, *The Metaphysical Thought of Thomas Aquinas* (Washington, D.C.: The Catholic University of America Press, 2000), 461.
7. Again, see Dawkins, *God Delusion*, 77–79 and Sober, *Core Questions*, 36–56.
8. See Fergus Kerr, "Theology in Philosophy: Revisiting the Five Ways," *International Journal for Philosophy of Religion* 50 (2001): 115–30; 128 and Bochenski, "The Five Ways," 68.
9. For an excellent discussion of Aquinas's arguments for God's existence, see Jules Baisnee, "St. Thomas Aquinas's Proofs of the Existence of God Presented in Their Chronological Order," in John K. Ryan, ed., *Philosophical Studies in Honor of the Very Reverend Ignatius Smith, O.P.* (Westminster, Md.: The Newman Press, 1952), 29–64.
10. See, for instance, Anthony Kenny, *The Five Ways: Saint Thomas Aquinas' Proofs of God's Existence* (London: Routledge & K. Paul, 1969); Norman Kretzmann, *The Metaphysics*

of Theism: Aquinas's Natural Theology in Summa contra Gentiles *I* (Oxford: Clarendon Press, 1997), ch. 2; Wippel, *Metaphysical Thought of Thomas Aquinas*, Part III.

11. See Leonard Boyle, "The Setting of the *Summa Theologiae*," in Brian Davies, ed., *Aquinas's* Summa Theologiae: *Critical Essays* (Lanham, Md.: Rowan & Littlefield Publishers, 2006), 1–25; the quotation is from page 12.

12. There are many general points about the Five Ways that deserve attention but would push this chapter well beyond its size constraints. So, for instance, questions often asked about why *five* ways, why *these* ways, and why this *ordering* of the ways, are left aside. A reader interested in these questions should consult Bochenski, "The Five Ways," 67–68; Leo Elders, *The Philosophical Theology of St. Thomas Aquinas* (Leiden: E. J. Brill, 1990), 86–89; Kenny, *The Five Ways*, 36–39; Reith, *Metaphysics of St. Thomas Aquinas*, 176–78; William Young, "From Describing to Naming God: Correlating the Five Ways with Aquinas' Doctrine of the Trinity," *New Blackfriars* 85 (2004): 527–41; John Zeis, "The Epistemic Passage of the Five Ways," *Proceedings of the American Catholic Philosophical Association* 68 (1994): 73–84.

13. Considering secondary literature on the whole of the Five Ways, any serious student of the arguments should look to Kenny, *The Five Ways* and Wippel, *Metaphysical Thought of Thomas Aquinas*. Two other useful discussions of the whole of the Five Ways are: Elders, *Philosophical Theology of St. Thomas Aquinas*, and C. F. J. Martin, *Thomas Aquinas: God and Explanations* (Edinburgh: Edinburgh University Press, 1997), the latter being not only helpful but also quite humorous. For an in-depth analysis of the logic of the Five Ways, one could do no better than Bochenski, "The Five Ways." For a thorough list of parallel passages and some discussion, see Baisnee, "St. Thomas Aquinas's Proofs."

14. All translations are my own. I have been aided in my translations by consulting Alfred Freddoso's unpublished translation of the *Summa*, available at <http://www.nd.edu/~afreddos/summa-translation/TOC.htm>.

15. Baisnee, "St. Thomas Aquinas's Proofs," 62–64, provides the following parallel passages to the First Way, noting that it is the second most common argument for the existence of God found in Aquinas's corpus: *SCG* I, 13; *CT*, c.3; *In Phy* VII, l.2; *In Phy* VIII, l.1–3, 7–13, 21–23; *In Meta* XII, l.5–10. Baisnee also cites *Super Johan* Prologue, though I do not find the argument from motion in that text.

16. For a discussion of the logic of the First Way, see Jan Salamucha, "The Proof 'Ex Motu' for the Existence of God: Logical Analysis of St. Thomas' Arguments," *New Scholasticism* 32 (1958): 334–72, as well as Bochenski, "The Five Ways."

17. Some thinkers, like Kenny, accuse Aquinas of moving illicitly from the intransitive use of "move" to the transitive usage. See Kenny, *The Five Ways*, 8–9; 18–19; 24, for the charge, and for a response to the charge, see Scott MacDonald, "Aquinas's Parasitic Cosmological Argument," *Medieval Philosophy and Theology* 1 (1991): 119–55, 121–24, especially footnote 6. See also Wippel, *Metaphysical Thought of Thomas Aquinas*, 414–15.

18. See MacDonald, "Aquinas's Parasitic Cosmological Argument," 121–24, and Wippel, *Metaphysical Thought of Thomas Aquinas*, 414–15. One should note here that a common objection against the passive reading of *movetur* is misguided. The common objection is that if Aquinas meant *movetur* in the passive sense, then his claim that whatever is moved is moved by something is trivially true. However, this is not Aquinas's claim in the First Way. He does not claim that whatever is moved is moved *by something*, he claims that whatever is moved is moved *by something else*. The exclusion of self-motion removes the triviality from Aquinas's claim, as MacDonald and Wippel both note.

19. Kenny raises this point as well, Kenny, *The Five Ways*, 9–11. For a defense of a metaphysical interpretation of the argument and discussion of the existential and physical

readings of the First Way, see Twetten, "Clearing a 'Way' for Aquinas," 260–64; 267–71, and John F. X. Knasas, "Ad Mentem Thomae: Does Natural Philosophy Prove God?" *Proceedings of the American Catholic Philosophical Association* 61 (1987): 209–19.

20. See Wippel, *Metaphysical Thought of Thomas Aquinas*, 446–47. It seems reasonable to hold, along with Wippel, that while Aquinas's examples clearly show that he has physical motion in mind in the argument, the principles he appeals to and arguments he provides for those principles would justify an extension to more than just mere physical motion or change.

21. Contra Bochenski, "The Five Ways," 74.

22. Ibid. See also Kenny, *The Five Ways*, 15–17; 28–31.

23. To see a defense of the compatibility of Aristotelian *physics* with Newtonian mechanics, see William Wallace, "Newtonian Antinomies Against the 'Prima Via'." *Thomist: A Speculative Quarterly Review* 19 (1956): 151–92. This reining in is also suggested by MacDonald, "Aquinas's Parasitic Cosmological Argument," 136–38.

24. The language of being "in an appropriate state of" actuality is not in the *ST*. Rather, there it merely says that the mover must be in actuality, then gives an example of fire, which is actually hot, bringing wood from being potentially hot to being actually hot. But being in actuality *alone* is not enough to bring a being from potentially *F* to being actually *F*. The mover must be in an appropriate state of actuality to do such a thing; hence the addition to the premise.

25. Aquinas provides two additional proofs for (2) in the discussion of arguments from motion in the *SCG* I, 13. For helpful discussions of these arguments, see Kenny, *The Five Ways*, 11–23; Etienne Gilson, *The Christian Philosophy of St. Thomas Aquinas* (Notre Dame, Ind.: University of Notre Dame Press, 1994), 60–61, and Wippel, *Metaphysical Thought of Thomas Aquinas*, 415–21. Macdonald, "Aquinas's Parasitic Cosmological Argument," 129–30, formalizes this argument.

26. MacDonald, "Aquinas's Parasitic Cosmological Argument," 130–33, points out that Aquinas does not address this possibility and suggests that he tacitly assumes a modest principle of sufficient reason.

27. Aquinas calls God an analogical cause. See *ST* I q.13 a.5 ad 1; *SCG* I, 33; *QDV* I, q.4, a.6, resp; *QDV* II, q.11, a.3, ad 4. For more on God and analogical causation, see Timothy McDermott, *Summa Theologiae*, vol. 3, *Knowing and Naming God:1a. 12–13* (Cambridge: Cambridge University Press, 2006), Appendix 2: Causes.

28. Sometimes one finds being virtually *F* referred to as being "eminently" *F*. This sort of causation is sometimes referred to as "equivocal causation."

29. To see discussions of what it is to be virtually *F*, see MacDonald, "Aquinas's Parasitic Cosmological Argument," 133–35, and Linwood Urban, "Understanding St. Thomas's Fourth Way," *History of Philosophy Quarterly* 1:3 (1984): 281–95; esp. 285–87.

30. As with (2), Aquinas provides two additional proofs for (3) in the *SCG* I, 13. Again, see Kenny, *The Five Ways*, 23–27; Gilson, *Christian Philosophy*, 61–63; and Wippel, *Metaphysical Thought of Thomas Aquinas*, 421–25.

31. It might be, as Kenny says, that there is an unmoved mover with respect to qualitative change, and another with respect to local motion. In fact, it could be that the first qualitative changer heats up the first local mover, and the first local mover moves the qualitative changer around. In that case, there is no unqualifiedly unmoved mover, but each series of movers has a mover that is not moved in that series. See Kenny, *The Five Ways*, 23.

32. Cf. Kenny, *The Five Ways*, 33, who provides a poignant quotation from Suarez to the same effect; MacDonald, "Aquinas's Parasitic Cosmological Argument," 148–49.

33. G. E. M. Anscombe, and Peter Geach, *Three Philosophers* (Oxford: Basil Blackwell, 1961), 112. This interpretation is well known in the discussion of the Five Ways.

34. For a helpful discussion of Aquinas on efficient causation, see Michael Rota's contribution to this volume. See also Rosemary Lauer, "The Notion of Efficient Cause in the Secunda Via," *The Thomist* 38 (1974): 754–67.

35. Baisnee, "St. Thomas Aquinas's Proofs," 62–64, provides only one parallel passage to the Second Way: *SCG* I, 13.

36. I have inserted the "an ordered series of" into this premise, though the original text does not include the restriction. I include it because, as the first step in the forthcoming proof for (8) makes clear, as does (6), Aquinas is discussing an ordered series of efficient causes.

37. For a discussion of the logical form of the Second Way, see Bochenski, "The Five Ways," 75–77, and Cartwright, "The Second Way," 92–94. Here and in the following three ways I number the conclusions differently, since the "this" in each conclusion points to the thing named in the proceeding step of the argument in question. For instance, the "this" in the Second Way refers to the first efficient cause and not the first mover of the First Way. Also, it is an open question whether the first mover must be the first efficient cause, the cause of necessity in things, the maximally good thing, and the orderer of the universe.

38. As Aquinas says in this oft-quoted passage *ST* I q.46 a.2 obj. 7 and ad 7. Also see the parallel passage in the *SCG* II, ch. 38, para. 13, and McQueen's discussion of that passage, Donald McQueen, "What is Aquinas' Second Way?" *History of Philosophy Quarterly* 11:1 (1994): 23–35; 28–29.

39. For helpful discussions of Aquinas on ordered series, see Cartwright, "The Second Way," 196–200; Elders, *Philosophical Theology of St. Thomas Aquinas*, 93; and Wippel, *Metaphysical Thought of Thomas Aquinas*, 461. For a seminal work on God and simultaneity, see Eleonore Stump and Norman Kretzmann, "Eternity," *Journal of Philosophy* 78 (1981): 429–58. For a recent discussion of God and simultaneity, see Eleonore Stump, *Aquinas* (London and New York: Routledge, 2003), ch. 4, "God's Eternity." The reader may substitute "perform their causal work at no temporal distance from one another" for "perform their causal work simultaneously" if she finds atemporal simultaneity problematic.

40. Compare this claim with the thought of Gilson, Owens, and Rowe, who think that the Second Way concludes to a bestower of existence. See Gilson, *Christian Philosophy*, 67; Joseph Owens, "Aquinas and the Five Ways," *The Monist* 58 (1974): 16–35, reprinted in *St. Thomas Aquinas on the Existence of God: Collected Papers of Joseph Owens*, ed. John Catan (Albany: State University of New York Press, 1980), 132–42, 135, and William Rowe, *The Philosophy of Religion: An Introduction* (Belmont, Calif.: Wadsworth, 1993), 17.

41. Such a series would require *A* to stand in the conserving relation to *B*, and *B* to conserve *C* in virtue of the causal power of *A*. Compare this with Cartwright, who claims that the Second Way concludes to a conserver of existence. See Cartwright, "The Second Way," 202. Conservation seems to have only two relata for each series: God and the thing being conserved. But an ordered series, as understood by Aquinas (and Cartwright) requires at least three relata. See also Lauer, "The Notion of Efficient Cause."

42. *ST* I q.44 a.1; *ST* I q.10 a.4. Cf. Kenny, *The Five Ways*, 40.

43. Baisnee, "St. Thomas Aquinas's Proofs," 62–64, provides the following parallel passages to the Third Way: *SCG* I, 15–16 and *SCG* II, 15. Baisnee also cites *Diu. nom.* V, l.1 as a parallel text, but I do not find the argument from possibility and necessity in that text.

44. For a discussion of the logic of the Third Way, see Bochenski, "The Five Ways," 77–81; Mauricio Beuchot, "Saint Thomas' Third Way: Possibility and Necessity, Essence and

Existence" in Adolfo García de la Sienra, ed., *The Rationality of Theism* (Atlanta, Ga.: Rodopi, 2000), 93–108; Martin De Nys, "If Everything Can Not-Be There Would Be Nothing: Another Look at the Third Way," *The Review of Metaphysics* 56 (2002): 99–122; 101.

45. One should note that non-necessary things, at least for Aquinas, can begin existing without being generated and cease existing without being corrupted, if God creates them *ex nihilo* or ceases to uphold them in existence.

46. *ST* I q.75 a.6.

47. Aquinas did use the term "necessary" in this way as well. And, in fact, he used the term "possible," in some cases, such that anything that is necessary is also possible. See, for instance, *SCG* 3b, ch. 86. For discussions of Aquinas's different understandings of "necessity," see: Patterson Brown, "St. Thomas' Doctrine of Necessary Being," in Anthony Kenny, ed., *Aquinas: A Collection of Critical Essays* (Notre Dame, Ind.: University of Notre Dame Press, 1976), 157–74; S. Knuuttila, "The 'Statistical' Interpretation of Modality in Averroes and Thomas Aquinas," *Ajatus* 37 (1978): 79–98; S. Knuuttila, *Modalities in Medieval Philosophy* (New York: Routledge, 1993); J. J. MacIntosh, "Aquinas on Necessity," *American Catholic Philosophical Quarterly* 72 (1998): 371–404; Timothy Pawl, "A Thomistic Account of Truthmakers for Modal Truths" (Ph.D. thesis, Saint Louis University, 2008), ch. 4.

48. Cf. Michael Augros, "Aquinas's *Tertia Via*," *Angelicum* 83 (2006): 767–92; 773.

49. For further discussion, including attempts to answer this question, see Augros, "Aquinas's *Tertia Via*," 775–79; Beuchot, "Saint Thomas' Third Way," 101–102; Davies, "Aquinas's Third Way," 456–58.

50. Others have called this dubious step a fallacy of composition, since it appears that Aquinas is arguing that since each thing does not exist at some time, the whole composed of all those things also must not exist at some time. See De Nys, "If Everything Can Not-Be," for a helpful discussion of the considerations here. For one influential presentation of the charge, see Kenny, *The Five Ways*, 56.

51. See David Conway, "Possibility and Infinite Time: A Logical Paradox in St. Thomas' Third Way," *International Philosophical Quarterly* 14:2 (1974): 201–209.

52. The reader should note that De Nys is not making the (false) claim that if each part of a proposition has its truth-value contingently, then the whole proposition does as well. Consider any contingently true proposition, *P*. Both *P* and ~*P* have their truth-values contingently. Their disjunction, however, does not have its truth-value contingently. See De Nys, "If Everything Can Not-Be," 114–18.

53. See De Nys, "If Everything Can Not-Be," Section III. Section II of the same article provides a helpful, critical discussion of the responses of Gilson, Edwards, and Owens to the quantifier shift charge. See also Beuchot, "Saint Thomas' Third Way," 102–4; Davies, "Aquinas's Third Way," 458, and notes 11 and 20; Elders, *Philosophical Theology of St. Thomas Aquinas*, 104; and Anscombe and Geach, *Three Philosophers*, 115.

54. Rowe understands this step as an appeal to a principle of sufficient reason, not a causal principle. Nevertheless, he claims that the principle required for this step of the argument might be false. See Rowe, *The Philosophy of Religion*, 26–28.

55. See G. E. M. Anscombe, "'Whatever Has a Beginning of Existence Must Have a Cause': Hume's Argument Exposed," *Analysis* 34:5 (1974): 145–51 and the excellent debate on this issue between Quentin Smith and Thomas Sullivan: Quentin Smith, "The Uncaused Beginning of the Universe," *Philosophy of Science* 55:1 (1988): 39–57; Thomas D. Sullivan, "Coming to Be Without a Cause," *Philosophy* 65 (1990): 261–70; Quentin Smith, "Can Everything Come to Be Without a Cause?" *Dialogue: Canadian Philosophical Review* 33:2

(1994): 313–23; Thomas D. Sullivan, "On the Alleged Causeless Beginning of the Universe: A Reply to Quentin Smith," *Dialogue: Canadian Philosophical Review* 33:2 (1994): 325–36.

56. Baisnee, "St. Thomas Aquinas's Proofs," 62–64, provides the following parallel passages to the Fourth Way: *Super Sent* D.III Divisio primae partis textus; *Super Sent* D.I, q.1, a.1–2; *SCG* I, 13; *QDP*, q.3, a.5.

57. See Urban, "Understanding St. Thomas's Fourth Way," for a helpful discussion of causation in the Fourth Way. Urban is the commentator who believes that all three types of causation mentioned are at play in the Fourth Way.

58. See Urban, "Understanding St. Thomas's Fourth Way," 283–84, where he points to *DPN* IV 27 and other texts.

59. This is an example of Urban, "Understanding St. Thomas's Fourth Way," 292. Aquinas considered evil a privation and not a thing.

60. The example of a smelliest thing is from Dawkins, *God Delusion*, 79. Some commentators, for instance, Wippel, go further and restrict the argument to *transcendental* perfections. Wippel writes, "I shall restrict the argument to transcendental perfections such as goodness and truth" (*Metaphysical Thought of Thomas Aquinas*, 472). See also Elders, *Philosophical Theology of St. Thomas Aquinas*, 111.

61. One might think that the convertibility of being and goodness allows Aquinas to claim that being hot is a perfection after all. But then limiting the scope of (19) to perfections would not be useful in removing difficult examples from the range of (19), since the convertibility move would also be applicable to being aromatic, for instance. At least one commentator claims that Aquinas did not intend being hot as an instance of (19). Instead, the heating claim "is only a comparison and not an instance" (Elders, *Philosophical Theology of St. Thomas Aquinas*, 111). But, if that were true, and it might be, it surely is a poor example to offer for (19).

62. Wippel, *Metaphysical Thought of Thomas Aquinas*, 472. For a discussion of different ways of understanding the beginning moves of the argument, (18) to (20), especially (19), see Joseph Bobik, "Aquinas's Fourth Way and the Approximating Relation," *Thomist* 51 (1987): 17–36.

63. See Wippel's helpful two part article: John Wippel, "Truth in Thomas Aquinas," *Review of Metaphysics* 43:2 (1989): 295–326; John Wippel, "Truth in Thomas Aquinas," *Review of Metaphysics* 43:3 (1990): 543–67.

64. Baisnee, "St. Thomas Aquinas's Proofs," 62–64, provides the following parallel passages to the Fifth Way, noting that it is the most common argument for the existence of God found in Aquinas's corpus: *Super Sent*, d.I, q.1, a.1; *QDV*, q.5, a.2; *SCG* I, 13; *SCG* I, 44; *QDP*, q.3, a.6; *In Meta* XII, l.12; *Super Johan*, Prologue; *Super Symbolum Apostolorum*, a.1. Baisnee also lists *SCG* II, 43 as a parallel text, but I do not find the argument from the governance of things in that text.

65. Elders, *Philosophical Theology of St. Thomas Aquinas*, 123, discusses a potential justification for this premise.

66. For a discussion of the logic of the Fifth Way, see Bochenski, "The Five Ways," 84–85.

67. For a discussion of this premise, see Elders, *Philosophical Theology of St. Thomas Aquinas*, 121–22.

PART III

THE DIVINE NATURE

CHAPTER 10

GOD'S SIMPLICITY

ELEONORE STUMP

Introduction

The doctrine of divine simplicity is perhaps the most difficult and controversial piece of medieval philosophical theology but also one of the most important.[1] It derives from the conviction that God is a being whose existence is an absolutely perfect being, self-explanatory, completely actual.[2] Aquinas was among the most influential expositors and defenders of this doctrine, and the doctrine is central to his philosophy and theology. It is not possible to do justice to this doctrine in short space; here I will only sketch its basic outlines.[3]

The doctrine of simplicity, as Aquinas understands it, can be summarized in three claims. The first distinguishes God from material objects:[4]

(1) It is impossible that God have any spatial or temporal parts that could be distinguished from one another as here rather than there or as now rather than then.

The second claims that the standard distinction between an entity's essential and intrinsic accidental properties cannot apply to God:[5]

(2) It is impossible that God have any intrinsic accidental properties.

And the third rules out the possibility of components of any kind in the essence that is the divine nature. Even when it has been recognized that all God's intrinsic properties must be essential to him, it must be acknowledged as well that

(3) whatever can be intrinsically attributed to God must in reality just be the unity that is his essence.

For this reason, God is his own essence or nature.[6] For all things other than God, there is a difference between what they are and that they are, between their essence and their existence; but on the doctrine of simplicity the essence that is God is not different from God's existence. Therefore, unlike all other entities, God is his own being.

There is a large literature attempting to explain and evaluate these claims, and it is not possible in this brief essay to explore the controversies at issue in this literature. Here I will just outline the heart of the doctrine by focusing on Aquinas's connection between God's simplicity and the *quid est* or essence of God.

Agnosticism about God's Nature

It is helpful to begin by setting aside one interpretation of Aquinas's position.

Aquinas places a discussion of God's simplicity at the beginning of his treatment of the nature of God in the *Summa theologiae*,[7] and he begins that discussion with a short prologue. In the prologue, he says,

> When we know with regard to something *that* it is, we still need to ask about its mode of being (*quomodo sit*), in order to know with regard to it what it is (*quid sit*). But because we are not able to know with regard to God what he is, but [rather] what he is not, we cannot consider with regard to God what the mode of being is but rather what the mode of being is not....it can be shown with regard to God what the mode of being is not by removing from him those things not appropriate to him, such as composition and motion and other things of this sort.

This passage and others like it have sometimes been cited as evidence for an interpretation of Aquinas as committed to the *via negativa* in a radical way. So, for example, in presenting Aquinas's position on human knowledge of God, David Burrell says,

> That God's nature, otherwise utterly unknown, must be affirmed simply to be, gives a warrant of sorts for taking to-be as an act.[8]

And Leo Elders says,

> The comprehension of God's essence is altogether excluded. This conclusion is presupposed in the Prologue to the Third Question....Even if we say that God is perfect, good or eternal, we must realize that we do not know what these terms mean when predicated of God.[9]

Claims such as this can give the impression that, for Aquinas, because of God's simplicity, it is not possible for human beings to have any positive knowledge of God. On this interpretation of Aquinas's views, Aquinas maintains that because God is simple, human beings can know what God is *not*, but they cannot know anything of what God is.[10]

But caution is warranted here. It is true that Aquinas explains divine simplicity in terms of what God is not—not a body, not composed of matter and form, and so on. On the other hand, however, in the course of showing what God is not, Aquinas relies heavily on positive claims about God. So, for example, he argues that God is not a body on the basis of these claims among others: God is the first mover; God is pure actuality; God is the first being; God is the most noble of beings. In arguing that God is not composed of matter and form, Aquinas in fact makes a huge, substantial, positive metaphysical claim about the nature of God. He says,

> a form which is not able to be received in matter but is subsistent by itself (*per se subsistens*) is individuated in virtue of the fact that it cannot be received in something else. And God is a form of this sort.[11]

In *ST* I q.13, the question about the names of God, Aquinas explicitly repudiates the sort of agnosticism some scholars attribute to him; Aquinas himself associates such a position with Moses Maimonides and attacks it vigorously. In still other texts, Aquinas bluntly rejects the view that human beings can have no positive knowledge of God. In *QDV*, q.7, a.5, for example, he says,

> the understanding of a negation is always based on some affirmation. And this is clear from the fact that every negation is proved by an affirmation. For this reason, unless the human intellect knew something affirmatively about God, it would be unable to deny anything of God.

For all these reasons, it is a mistake to read the prologue to *ST* I q.3 as implying a radical agnosticism with regard to knowledge of God.

The problem in interpreting Aquinas's remarks in the prologue correctly has to do with the expression "*quid est*" in the claim that we do not know of God what he is (*quid est*).[12] The expression *quid est* is a technical term of medieval logic. For example, Peter of Spain, the author of a standard scholastic logic text, gives the traditional medieval formula for a genus as "that which is predicated of many things differing in species in respect of what they are (*in eo quod quid est*)." The same phrase in a slightly different definition captures the notion of species. The *quid est* of something therefore has to do with the genus or species of that thing, or more generally, with the kind of thing it is. So if one cannot know something's *quid est*, one cannot know what *kind* of thing it is.

It is helpful to see in this connection that one can know a great deal about something even if one does not know (or cannot know) what kind of thing it is. According to quantum physics, we do not know what kind of thing light is. The best we can do is sometimes to think of light as a wave and sometimes to think of it as a particle, although we certainly understand that nothing can be at the same time both a wave and a particle. And yet we have a great deal of positive knowledge about light, notwithstanding our inability to know what kind of thing light is.

Esse and id quod est

On the doctrine of simplicity, God is his own *quid est* or essence, and his essence is being or *esse*. It seems to follow from these claims that God is *esse*. (Given the difficulties of the doctrine, in what follows I will use the Latin terms for the concepts crucial to the interpretation defended here.)

In his commentary on Boethius's treatise *De hebdomadibus*, Aquinas makes a careful distinction between *esse* and an entity or *id quod est* (literally, *that which is*).[13] Among the many differences between *esse* and *id quod est* that Aquinas introduces, he calls attention to the fact that "*id quod est*" signifies something concrete whereas "*esse*" does not.[14] He also highlights the fact that *id quod est* is particular,[15] whereas *esse* is not.[16] In these and other ways, Aquinas argues for the metaphysical difference between *esse* and *id quod est*. Since, on the doctrine of simplicity, God is *esse*, and *esse* is distinct from *id quod est* in these ways, some scholars conclude that for Aquinas God is not an entity at all.[17] For such scholars, this is a strength of Aquinas's position, because it emphasizes the transcendence of God, who is not to be numbered as one entity among others.[18]

It is another advantage of this interpretation that it helps to explain the three basic claims of the doctrine of simplicity formulated above. Nothing that is not an *id quod est* has temporal or spatial parts. And nothing that is not an *id quod est* has intrinsic accidents either. For example, *animality* and *whiteness* have no intrinsic accidents. They are the wrong *sort* of thing, we might say, to have intrinsic accidents. If we think of intrinsic accidents as belonging somewhere in the nine Aristotelian categories other than substance, then it is easy to see why nothing that is not an *id quod est* should be thought to have intrinsic accidents. *Whiteness* does not have a certain size or quantity, for example; it does not engage in action or receive the action of anything else—and so on. *Whiteness* is what it is—whiteness—and nothing else at all.

Furthermore, in the case of *esse*, if it is not an *id quod est*, then even existence cannot be attributed to it in any way. If it is not an *id quod est*, then it would be true that there *is esse;* but its being *esse* would be all there is to it. We could not separate *esse* into itself and its existence. If we did, *esse* would become something concrete, an *id quod est* rather than only *esse*.

So thinking in these ways of God as only *esse* helps to make sense of the three claims of simplicity presented at the outset.

The problem is that, so understood, the concept of God as nothing more than *esse* seems religiously pernicious. Alvin Plantinga puts the problem in terms of God's being a property, but his objections remain the same if we transpose his "property" into "*esse*" (where *esse* is taken as something that is not an *id quod est*). Plantinga says,

> This view [that God is identical to *esse*] is subject to a difficulty both obvious and overwhelming. No property could have created the world; no property could be omniscient, or, indeed, know anything at all.[19]

And Plantinga summarizes the problem in a way that is especially apt for my purposes here. He says,

> If God is a property, then he isn't a person . . .[20]

We do not need to worry whether a triune God can be thought of as *a person* in order to see the power of Plantinga's complaint. Even on the doctrine of the Trinity, which takes God to consist in three persons (where "person" has a technical, theological sense), God is characterized by mind and will. Anything with mind and will, however, is an *id quod est*. For this reason, Plantinga is right to say that if God is a property—or only *esse*—then God is not a person, in our sense of the word "person." Nothing that is not an *id quod est* could be a person or enter into personal relationship with human persons. As far as that goes, nothing that is not an *id quod est* can act at all.

Consequently, if the doctrine of simplicity implies that God is *esse* alone, then it seems that many of the standard divine attributes discussed and accepted by Aquinas cannot be applied to God. Those attributes apply only to something that is an *id quod est*. Moreover, many of the biblical stories about God's interactions with human persons, which Aquinas himself takes seriously and literally,[21] cannot be understood as Aquinas understands them if God is only *esse* and not *id quod est*.

So, here is where matters stand. As Aquinas himself is at pains to show in his commentary on Boethius's *De hebdomadibus*, there is all the difference in the world between something that is *esse* and something that is *id quod est*. If the doctrine of simplicity is correctly understood as some defenders of the doctrine, and some detractors of it such as Plantinga, suppose, to mean that God is only *esse*, then it is hard to know how to ward off the dramatic infelicities that Plantinga laments.

Quantum Metaphysics

It is worth noticing, however, that on this interpretation, represented by both defenders and detractors of the doctrine, we do in fact know the *quid est* of God, at least to some limited extent. That is because, on this interpretation, we know that God is *esse*; and we know something about the *quid est* of *esse*, as Aquinas's own discussion of it in his commentary on Boethius's *De hebdomadibus* shows, where he gives a detailed characterization of the nature of *esse*. So, if the doctrine of simplicity has to be interpreted as claiming that God is only *esse* and nothing more, then, on Aquinas's own views, we would actually know a reasonable amount about the *quid est* of God. But, as we saw, Aquinas is insistent that we are unable to know the *quid est* of God because of God's simplicity. And so the implication that we do know a reasonable amount about the *quid est* of God should be a warning sign about this interpretation.

In my view, the problem with this interpretation is not that it identifies God with *esse*. The problem is that it rejects the notion of God as *id quod est*. This rejection looks sensible, especially given Aquinas's care to distinguish *esse* from *id quod est;* but, in fact, it is not true to Aquinas's position.

In his commentary on Boethius's *De hebdomadibus*, Aquinas begins his discussion of *esse* and *id quod est* by saying,

> We signify one thing by "*esse*" and another thing by "'*id quod est*,'" just as we signify one thing by "running" ("*currere*") and another thing by "a runner" ("*currens*"). For "running" and "*esse*" signify in the abstract, just as "whiteness" also does; but "*id quod est*," that is, "an entity," and "a runner," signify in the concrete, just as "a white thing" also does.[22]

And he concludes that discussion this way:

> it is evident on the basis of what has been presented that in composite things *esse* and *id quod est* differ as regards the things themselves (*realiter*).[23] ... And so [Boethius] says that in every composite thing, *esse* is one thing, and the composite thing itself [the thing as *id quod* est] is another.[24]

But, having worked so hard to distinguish between *esse* and *id quod est* in this way, Aquinas then goes on immediately to say something that is on the face of it quite surprising. He says,

> In simple things, [however,] *esse* itself and *id quod est* must be one and the same as regards the things themselves (*realiter*).[25]

And, after giving an argument that there cannot be more than one thing that is both *esse* and also *id quod est*, Aquinas sums up his position by saying,

> This one sublime simple is God himself.[26]

On Aquinas's view, then, the distinction he has been arguing for between *esse* and *id quod est* does not hold in God's case. It is true that God is *esse*, as the doctrine of simplicity makes clear. But this *esse* is also—somehow—an *id quod est*.

We could suppose that in making this claim about God Aquinas is willing to violate the laws of logic as regards God, since he himself has just shown that the characteristics of *esse* and those of *id quod est* are incompatible. But this would be a rash conclusion, since in many other places Aquinas manifestly supposes that even God cannot do what is logically contradictory.[27] But if we remember Aquinas's insistence that we cannot know the *quid est* for God, then another interpretation suggests itself. Another way to think about the doctrine of simplicity, as Aquinas understands it, is as the expression of a kind of quantum metaphysics.

What kind of thing is it that has to be understood both as a wave and as a particle? We do not know. That is, we do not know the *quid est* of light. At the ultimate foundation of all reality, things get weird, we might say. The ultimate foundation of *physical* reality includes light, and our best attempt at understanding the kind of thing light is requires alternately attributing to it incompatible characteristics. Analogously, we can ask: What kind of thing is it that can be both *esse* and *id quod est*? We do not know. The idea of simplicity is that at the ultimate *metaphysical* foundation of reality is something that has to be understood as *esse*—but also as *id quod est*. We do not know what kind of thing this is either. And this conclusion is precisely what we should expect from Aquinas's insistence that we do not know the *quid est* of God.

As Aquinas sees it, however, we can have considerable positive knowledge about God, even so, just as we can have a significant body of knowledge about light, even according to quantum physics. We can begin by recognizing that God's nature is such that there is something false about conceiving of it either as *esse* alone or as *id quod est* alone. That is why Aquinas says of God,

> With regard to what God himself is (*secundum rem*), God himself is neither universal nor particular.[28]

For this reason, we have to exercise care in the way we frame our claims about God. It is acceptable to say that God is *esse*, provided that we understand that this claim does not rule out the equally true claim that God is *id quod est*, an entity, a concrete particular.

Aquinas puts the point this way:

> Those material creatures that are whole and subsistent are composite. But the form in them is not some complete subsisting thing. Rather, the form is that by means of which some thing *is*. For this reason, all the names imposed by us to signify some complete subsisting thing signify in the concrete, as is appropriate for composite things. But those names that are imposed to signify simple forms signify something not as subsisting but rather as that by means of which something is, as for example "whiteness" signifies that by means of which something is white. Therefore because God is both simple and subsistent, we attribute to God both abstract names—to signify God's simplicity—and concrete names—to signify God's completeness and concreteness. Nonetheless, each kind of name falls short of God's mode [of being], just as our intellect does not know God as he is, in this life.[29]

We can gain insight into Aquinas's position here by considering that there are scriptural texts claiming that God is loving and scriptural texts claiming that God is love.[30] It seems, however, that these claims cannot be true together. If they were, it would have to be true that love is loving. But love is abstract and universal. And, as Plantinga objects, an abstract universal is not a person; it is not the sort of thing that can be loving. So it seems just a category mistake to attribute loving to love. On Aquinas's understanding of the doctrine of simplicity, however, we can make sense of both these scriptural claims. Because God is simple and we do not comprehend his *quid est*, the best we can do is to adopt quantum metaphysics. Sometimes we have to characterize God with abstract terms—and so we say that God is love—and sometimes we have to characterize him with concrete terms—and so we say that God is loving.

Consequently, it turns out that, in one sense, Plantinga is after all in agreement with Aquinas. Each of them thinks that God must be characterized as an *id quod est*, a concrete entity. The difference between them lies precisely in the quantum metaphysics mandated by the doctrine of simplicity. For Aquinas, it is right to describe God as an *id quod est*, capable of creating, loving, and acting—but only with the proviso that it is *also* right to think of God as being *esse*.

Conclusion

On the doctrine of eternity, God is outside time.[31] Some scholars have taken that doctrine to imply that God cannot act, since (on their view) all action presupposes temporal duration or temporal location; or they have supposed that God's mode of existence is that of a frozen point, as it were, without duration of any kind, since (on their view) all duration is persistence through time. In effect, such an interpretation takes the doctrine of eternity to imply a metaphysical smallness about an eternal God by comparison with temporal creatures. But, on Aquinas's view, an eternal God is able to act at any and every point in time, and his mode of existence is broad enough to encompass all of time within it.[32] From Aquinas's point of view, the doctrine of eternity implies a metaphysical greatness about God, above the status of any creatures in time.

There is an analogous conceptual move to be made as regards interpretations of the doctrine of simplicity. On the doctrine of simplicity, God is without parts of any kind whatsoever; there is no composition in God. Some scholars have taken the doctrine to imply that God is identical only to *esse*,[33] giving rise to the complaint voiced by Plantinga that a simple God cannot act as persons do, or to the equally worrisome objection that everything about God is absolutely necessary, since there are no accidents in God. In effect, such an interpretation takes the doctrine of simplicity to make God metaphysically more limited than concrete things such as composite human beings, who can act and who can do otherwise than they do.

But this is to get the doctrine upside down. The doctrine of simplicity implies that at the ultimate metaphysical foundation of all reality there is *esse*. But it also implies that this *esse*, without losing any of its characteristics as *esse*, is something subsistent and concrete, with more ability to act and with more freedom in its acts than any concrete composite entity has. Trying to summarize this idea, Aquinas says,

> although God is *esse* only [and not something composite, as material creatures are],... nonetheless God has all the perfections which are in all the genera [of created things]....And this is because all these perfections come together in him in accordance with his simple *esse*. By way of analogy, if someone could bring about the functioning of all qualities by means of one quality, he would have [in effect] all the qualities in that one quality. In just this way, God has all the perfections in his *esse*.[34]

The difficulty of thinking one's way up the ladder of being can leave one with the impression that the immutable, impassible, eternal, simple God of Thomistic philosophical theology is frozen, static, inert, unresponsive, and incapable of action. But Aquinas's notion of God is exactly the opposite. If it were not so subject to misinterpretation, one might well say that for Aquinas God is maximally dynamic, and not static at all. On Aquinas's views, there is more ability to act—one might say, more action—on the part of a God with the classical divine attributes than there could be on the part of a composite entity acting in time.[35] That is why Aquinas can say that in the *esse* that is God there are all the perfections of all the genera of created things—including responsiveness and action, which are perfections of any *id quod est* with mind and will.[36]

On this way of understanding divine simplicity, when the *esse* that is God acts, its action is not an accident in it. This is not because *esse* is an inert universal that is the same in all possible worlds. Rather, it is because this *esse* is more metaphysically one than any composite thing could be. When it acts, it acts just as *esse*, and its acting remains within its character as *esse*. That is, the acts engaged in by the *esse* that is also an *id quod est* are not added on to *esse* as something additional to *esse*. In acting, the *esse* that is God remains *esse;* it does not become *esse* plus the property of acting. The *esse* that is the ultimate foundation of reality can do more than created, composite things without ceasing to be *esse* only. That is why, in the power and the richness that is *esse*, God can also do otherwise than he does without ceasing thereby to be *esse*.

In *our* sense of the term, then, there is contingency in God. As Aquinas himself is at pains to point out, Christians are committed to the claim that God can do otherwise than he does. Creation is a free and not a necessitated act on God's part.[37] But it is still not the case that there are accidents in God. For composite things, contingency (in our sense of the term) comes with composition of subject and accident; but not for God.

For this reason, it is also the case that a simple God can be responsive to things in time. A simple God cannot do anything *after* something happens in time, but a simple God can certainly act *because of* something that happens in time. That is because, if something in time had been otherwise, a simple God might have acted otherwise than he did. To say this is clearly not to say that God decides what to do after something happens in time or that God can change in time. To say this is only to claim that God can do otherwise than he does, as Aquinas explicitly claims.[38] As long as a simple God can do what he does *because of* what happens in time, God can be responsive to things in time.

To try to explain the doctrine of simplicity in this way is not to provide an argument for the truth or even the compatibility of its claims. It is just to try to contribute to insight into this most challenging part of Thomistic philosophical theology. If, *contra* Aquinas, we could grasp the *quid est* of something that is both *esse* and *id quod est*, we might understand exactly how to explain what kind of thing can be described in all these ways. But, as it is, on Aquinas's views, we do not comprehend God's *quid est;* and so we are limited to the kind of quantum metaphysics sketched here.[39]

NOTES

1. This doctrine has also been the subject of a voluminous literature. The most sustained and sophisticated attack on Aquinas's position can be found in Christopher Hughes, *A Complex Theory of a Simple God* (Ithaca, N.Y.: Cornell University Press, 1989). Hughes's attack, however, seems to me based on misunderstandings of crucial elements of Aquinas's metaphysics, as reviewers have pointed out (see, e.g., David B. Burrell, "Review of Christopher Hughes, *On a Complex Theory of a Simple God*," *Journal of Religion*, 72:1 [Jan 1992]: 120–21), and so I will not consider it here.

2. The derivation of divine simplicity from such considerations is apparent in Aquinas's *QDP* 7.1, as Mark D. Jordan has pointed out in his article "The Names of God and the Being of Names" in Alfred J. Freddoso, ed., *The Existence and Nature of God* (Notre Dame, Ind.: University of Notre Dame Press, 1983), 161–90; see esp. 176–79.

3. For more extended discussion, see the chapter on simplicity in my *Aquinas* (London: Routledge, 2003). For sympathetic treatments published since then, see, e.g., Jeffrey Brower, "Making Sense of Divine Simplicity," *Faith and Philosophy* 25 (2008): 3–30: Brian Leftow, "Divine Simplicity," *Faith and Philosophy* 23 (2006): 365–80; and Brian Davies, "Simplicity," in Chad Meister and Charles Taliaferro, eds., *The Cambridge Companion to Christian Philosophical Theology* (Cambridge: Cambridge University Press, 2009). For recent book-length treatment, see Peter Weigel, *Aquinas on Simplicity: An Investigation into the Foundations of His Philosophical Theology* (Frankfurt: Peter Lang, 2008).

4. *ST* I q.3 a.1–2; cf. also *ST* I q.9 a.1 and q. 10 a.1.

5. *ST* I q.3 a.6.

6. *ST* I q.3 a.3.

7. *ST* I q.3.

8. David Burrell, *Aquinas: God and Action* (Notre Dame, Ind.: University of Notre Dame Press, 1979), 139. See also 60–61. "We cannot speak of God at all . . . [on Aquinas's theory of divine simplicity] unless it be under the rubric of 'the first cause of all.' Yet such a cause leaves no proper traces since its *modus operandi* cannot conform to the ordinary patterns whereby effect resembles cause. . . . In the measure, then, that our language embodies a subject/predicate, genus/species grammar . . . no description can succeed in identifying a trace of divinity."

9. Leo Elders, *The Philosophical Theology of St. Thomas Aquinas* (Leiden: E. J. Brill, 1990), 143.

10. For discussion of this position in the secondary literature, see the chapter on simplicity in my *Aquinas* (London: Routledge, 2003).

11. *ST* I q.3 a.3 ad 3.

12. See, in this connection, particularly *SCG* I.14.

13. In this connection, cf. also *De ente et essentia*, c.3. Cf. also the chapter on being by John Wippel in this volume.

14. *In BDH*. II.22.

15. *In BDH*. II.24.

16. There is a complication in this regard that I can only touch on in this brief essay. The *esse* at issue here must be distinguished from *esse* that is common to all things in existence. (In this respect, see especially *De ente et essentia*, c.5.) This common *esse* is a mental abstraction and so is a universal in the sense of the term usual for Aquinas, who takes universals to exist only in the mind. What distinguishes the *esse* that is God from the common *esse* is that the divine *esse* precludes combination with anything else, whereas the common *esse* is open to combination with form and matter. Even with this distinction between common and divine *esse*, however, divine *esse* considered just as *esse* is not concrete or particular. It does not follow that God is a universal for Aquinas, or that for Aquinas there is *one* universal that exists outside the mind, namely, God. As the rest of this essay makes clear, the heart of Aquinas's position is that we cannot know the *quid est* of God. The best we can do is to alternate between language that identifies God with what is universal—"God is love"—and language that identifies God with a concrete particular—"God is loving."

17. Cf., e.g., Leo Elders, *The Philosophical Theology of St. Thomas Aquinas* (Leiden: E. J. Brill, 1990), 22; "For St. Thomas God is never 'an object,' for God is far above our understanding."

18. Cf., e.g., David Burrell, *Knowing the Unknowable God* (Notre Dame, Ind.: University of Notre Dame Press, 1986); and, more recently, "Act of Creation with Its Theological Consequences," in Thomas Weinandy, Daniel Keating, and John Yocum, eds., *Aquinas on Doctrine* (London and New York: T & T Clark, 2004).

19. Alvin Plantinga, *Does God Have a Nature?* (Milwaukee, Wis.: Marquette University Press, 1980), 47.

20. Ibid.

21. As he does, e.g., with regard to God's interactions with Job; see his prologue to his *Expositio super Job*.

22. *In BDH.*, 22.

23. The qualifier "*realiter*" is needed here because in the preceding discussion Aquinas has examined the distinction between *esse* and *id quod est* considered as concepts. Once that conceptual distinction has been established, he moves next to show that the conceptual distinction is exemplified by all composite things, but that it does not apply to the one thing which is entirely simple, namely, God.

24. *In BDH.*, 32.

25. *In BDH.*, 33. Cf. also, e.g., *SCG* I, c.38.

26. *In BDH.*, 35.

27. For an excellent discussion of Aquinas's theory of modality and its connection to God's nature, see Timothy Pawl, "A Thomistic Account of Truthmakers for Modal Truths" (Ph.D. thesis, Saint Louis University, 2008).

28. *ST* I q.13 a.9 ad 2.

29. *ST* I q.13 a.1 ad 2. Cf. also *SCG* I, c.30.

30. For an example of the first, see 1 John 4:10; and for an example of the second, see 1 John 4:8.

31. For defense of this claim, see the chapter on eternity in my *Aquinas*; for a contrasting view, see the chapter on eternity by Brian Leftow in this volume.

32. For explanation and defense of these claims, see the chapter on eternity in my *Aquinas*.

33. That is, not to common *esse* but to the *esse* that is God; for the distinction see note 16.

34. *De ente et essentia*, c.6.

35. God's actuality or act of being is an important implication of the doctrine of divine simplicity, but a detailed exploration of this issue has to be left to one side in this brief essay.

36. In this connection, it is hard to resist calling attention to the case of light again. When Newton first discovered that white light contained within it all the richness of the other colors of light, there was considerable opposition to his finding. The opposition supposed that the simplicity of white light *excluded* the other colors, whose richness was thought to be somehow tarnishing of the pure whiteness of white light. Goethe, who was among the opposition, summed up this sort of attitude by saying that white light is "the simplest most undivided most homogenous being that we know." I am indebted to Andrew Pinsent for the point and the historical information.

37. For a discussion of this point and the relevant Thomistic texts, see the chapter on simplicity in my *Aquinas*.

38. For a more detailed discussion of this point, see the chapter on simplicity in my *Aquinas*.

39. I owe a debt of gratitude to Theodore Vitali, C.P., whose relentless questioning of my previous presentation of the doctrine of simplicity led me to want to examine the topic again. And I have learned a great deal from the seminar presentations on divine simplicity given by John Foley, S.J. His seminar presentations led me to rethink the doctrine in the way I have outlined it here. I am also grateful to him for trenchant criticism of an earlier draft, which caused me to rework one central part of this essay. I am grateful as well to David Burrell, Tim Pawl, Andrew Pinsent, and especially Brian Davies for helpful comments on an earlier draft.

CHAPTER 11

GOD'S GOODNESS

LUDGER HONNEFELDER

Introduction

That "good," "goodness," or "being good" has to be predicated of God has been clear in philosophy and theology at least since Dionysius Pseudo-Areopagita's *De divinis nominibus*.[1] It became a traditional part of medieval philosophical theology because it was demanded in the Jewish and Christian context by several biblical texts. But the mode of this predication is not self-evident: Is God—as the Platonists say[2]—primarily "good" or "goodness itself" and therefore the cause of the "goodness" of all other things? Or can God only be called "good" because "good" is—as Aristotle seems to say[3]—a common predicate that must be predicated of God, as well as of everything else that exists? What does "good" even mean? Is it interchangeable with "being," so that something is "good" insofar as it has "being"? How is "good" related to "being," and what does "good" add to "being"?

Since Philip the Chancellor inaugurated the debate, the medieval doctrine of the transcendentals[4] (i.e., the transcategorical predicates) had developed as a wide-ranging discussion. The following questions, in particular, were hotly disputed: Which predicate deserves epistemological and/or ontological priority? In what sense can "goodness" be predicated of God? And how should the relation of God's goodness to the goodness of all other beings be understood?

The *locus classicus* that requires Aquinas to deal with these questions is the first part of his *Summa theologiae*. Given that "sacred doctrine," as he establishes in *ST* I q.1, must be the science whose subject is God, it must deal first with God's nature. This task can be accomplished only by determining which predicates characterize God: existence/being, simplicity, perfection, goodness, and so on.

The order Aquinas follows in *ST* I q.2–6 is not arbitrary. Because God is not the natural object of any of our cognitive powers, neither God's existence nor essence can be presupposed as naturally known, but must instead be demonstrated. "In this life," as he explains in *ST* I q.13 a.1, "we cannot see God in his essence, but rather we cognize him through creatures under the aspect of a cause, abstracting from creatures the mode of excellence."[5]

If in general God is not naturally known in his essence, God's "goodness" in particular is not self-evident, but must be demonstrated on the basis of a number of premises. Demonstrating God's goodness is possible only if we grant that God is a being (as shown in *ST* I q.2), whose nature is simple and perfect (as shown in q.3 and q.4), and that the predicate "good" is common (as shown in q.5).[6] On this background, it can be argued in *ST* I q.6 that God need not be the precise adequate subject of goodness (a.1), but that God must be the "highest good" (a.2), and this must be in virtue of God's nature (a.3). Thus, no other being can be considered as "good" except by participation in divine goodness (a.4).

The *ST* is not the only and not the first place where Aquinas treats God's goodness. Already in *QDV*, q.21 he deals with God's goodness as the "first goodness" on which goodness in general depends. The approach in *QDV*, q.21 is different than that in *ST* and has as its background the commentaries that Aquinas devoted to Boethius's *De hebdomadibus* and to Dionysius's *De divinis nominibus*. In *SCG* it is the treatment of God's nature in the first book that requires Aquinas to consider God's goodness (ch. 37–41). Since the doctrine of God's goodness in *ST* is the last and the decisive treatment, we should start with a short explanation of this version of Aquinas's position, adding occasional observations on the earlier parallel texts.

Is "Being Good" Appropriate for God? (*ST* I q.6 a.1)

The first article of q.6 of *ST* I (in which Aquinas intends to demonstrate that "goodness" must be attributed to God) begins with Aristotle's definition: something is "good" insofar as it is "desirable" (*appetibile*). In a first step, Aquinas concludes (1) that every being desires its perfection, (2) that this perfection or form is a similitude of the agent that causes perfection by actualizing a thing's form, and (3) that therefore the agent cause itself must be something desirable and therefore good as stated in the previous definition. The second premise follows from the axiom that any agent acts or produces something similar to itself. If God is the first efficient cause of all things (as demonstrated in *ST* I q.2), then the final conclusion follows: God is something desirable, that is, "good." As Aquinas remarks, Dionysius Areopagita demonstrates God's goodness in the same way in his *De divinis nominibus*, ch. 4 on the basis of God's universal causality.

But by contrast with the Neoplatonic position—as represented by Dionysius—Aquinas takes the position that the predicate "good" is not prior to that of "being."

From an Aristotelian perspective the "appetite" (*appetitus*) does not constitute the *appetibile*, but rather the appetite presupposes that there already *is* something (actually or potentially) that can function as an object of desire. As Aquinas remarks in *QDV*, q.12, a.6, "the *ratio* of good implies a relation (sc. to an appetite), not because the name 'good' signifies only a relation, but because it signifies something to which the relation is directed by its relatedness."[7]

Though Aristotle introduced his definition of "good" in *NE* I, 1 as the "desirable" (*appetibile*) only as regards active human desiring agents, Aquinas extends it beyond active agents, claiming that *all beings* have a fundamental desire, namely to reach their perfection.[8] In his answer to the second counterargument of *ST* I q.6 a.1—namely, that the Aristotelian definition of good is too restricted, because only those things can be desired that are known, and not all things can know God—Aquinas argues that even non-rational creatures desire God insofar as God has given them a natural inclination to their ends. Thus, Aquinas presupposes a general ontological teleology. But how does he understand and justify this assumption?

Aquinas provides the answer implicitly in his treatment of the previous question. In *ST* I q.4 a.1, he introduces and defines the predicate of *perfection* in order to demonstrate that God is "perfect" (*perfectus*). Something is *perfect* when it does not lack what belongs to its mode of perfection. To explain what is missing, Aquinas refers to the Aristotelian doctrine of act and potency.[9] Something such as matter, he argues, cannot be considered perfect because it is only something in potency; it lacks something. This supports the general assumption "that something is perfect only insofar as it is actual [*aliquid esse perfectum secundum quod est in actu*]." Since God as the first active principle is the most actual, he therefore has to be considered as something "that is maximally perfect [*maxime esse perfectum*]."

In *QDV*, q.21, a.1, Aquinas distinguishes a twofold way in which something can be perfected with regard to the two predicates "true" (*verum*) and "good" (*bonum*). The intellect is perfected by its object according to its kind (*species*), the will according to its being (*esse*). In the first way of perfection a thing can be called "true" in that it is perfected by its object, and in the second way, a thing can be called "good" by virtue of its perfective object. In the case of the predicate "good," "the being that perfects another thing [*ens perfectivum alterius*]" is called "good" primarily and in principle, while the being that is perfected so "that it achieves its own end [*ductivum in finem*] in virtue of a perfective being is called 'good' in a secondary sense."[10]

In the following a.2 of *QDV*, q.21, Aquinas emphasizes that all things have a tendency to being (*esse*) in virtue of a natural appetite; even matter (*materia*)—according to Aristotle—seeks form. This allows Aquinas to conclude that all beings have the tendency to preserve their being. Thus, he claims that "*esse* itself has the *ratio* of 'good'. For, since it is impossible that something exists without being [*esse*], it is necessary that every thing is 'good', because it has *esse*."[11]

Is God the Highest Good? (*ST* I q.6 a.2)

The approach Aquinas uses in *ST* I q.6 a.1 is quite different than that of *QDV*, q.21. In both texts he defines "good" as something desirable, but the order of explanation is reversed. In *QDV*, q.21 he starts from the primary meaning of "good" (from which a secondary meaning is derived) and explains the general meaning of "good" in relation to the "*bonum perfectivum*." In *ST* I q.6, he starts from the general meaning of "good" (as demonstrated in q.5) and explains it with reference to the perfection that something possesses insofar as it is actual, that is, its *esse*. In the earlier text (*QDV*) the meaning of "good" as the *appetibile* is derived from the *ens perfectivum*, in the later text (*ST*) from the *ens perfectum*. And even the order of causality is different: In *QDV* Aquinas starts with final causality and proceeds to efficient and formal causality, but in *ST* I q.6 and q.4 he follows the inverse order.[12]

The earlier text (*QDV*) implies the problem of how we can presuppose that "good" is the *ens perfectivum*. By contrast, the later text (*ST*) raises a corresponding difficulty: how can God be called "good" in the same manner as other beings without an infringement on his transcendence?[13] Or to put it another way: if goodness is coextensive with perfection, and perfection is related to the specific or generic mode of that which is called perfect, how can God be called "perfect" or "good" without subsuming God under a proper genus?

The answer is given in *ST* I q.6 a.2, where Aquinas explains the way God is the "highest good" (*summum bonum*). The reference to q.5 (where it is explained why "good" has to be understood not in a generic, but in a transcendental sense) does not suffice, because it would not solve the problem. Aquinas starts from what has been said in a.1 about God as the first active cause of the perfections in all other beings. For the efflux (*effluxus*) of these perfections from God, he explains, is not a *univocal* causation. In cases of univocal causation, the cause "agrees" (*convenit*) with the caused insofar as both share a common generic or specific nature. Consequently, a univocal cause can only cause something of its own genus or nature. Or as Aristotle often remarks, "A human being generates a human being (and nothing else)."[14] Therefore, in cases of univocal causation, the similarity between a cause and what it causes is (as already noted in *ST* I q.4 a.3) complete and uniform (*uniformiter*). By contrast, the causality of the first active agent producing perfections in all caused things, Aquinas continues, has to be compared to the causality of the sun, which is not univocal but *equivocal* insofar as the heat in the sun is not of the same generic or specific nature as the heat in fire. Nonetheless, the sun is the cause of the heat in fire, because the sun contains the heat in a "higher mode" (*excellentius*).

Since according to this order of excellence, God as first active cause of all good things contains goodness in its "highest mode" (*excellentissimo modo*), he can be called a "highest good" (*summum bonum*). Since God is not a univocal cause, his excellent goodness does not imply that God belongs to a genus or species of goodness. And since God is "outside of a genus" (*extra genus*), Aquinas can answer the third objection, which claims that comparison presupposes a common genus. It is quite possible to compare God and other beings under the aspect of "goodness" (as is done in the phrase "highest good") without conceding that God and other beings must share a common *genus* with regard to "goodness."

Is Being Good Essentially a Property of God? (*ST* I q.6 a.3)

But this result is not a completely satisfying answer to the aforementioned objection. Although the reference to God's causality (as made in *ST* I q.6 a.2) can safeguard God's transcendent "goodness" and justify calling him the "highest good," it does not explain *in what sense* God can be called the "highest good" without violating his transcendence: Is he only accidentally "good," or finally, or by his essence?

The answer to this objection is contained in *ST* I q.6 a.3, where Aquinas returns again to God's perfection (as demonstrated in q.4) to show that being good by essence is an exclusive property of God. Perfection, Aquinas explains, can be understood in a threefold way: (1) with regard to what constitutes something as a being, (2) with regard to those qualities that are required as necessary conditions of its perfect operation and (3) with regard to what is necessary for something to reach its end. In this view fire is only perfect when it (1) exists by its substantial form, (2) possesses qualities like heat, lightness, dryness, and so on, and (3) is able to remain in its place.

Taken this way, only God possesses perfection "according to his essence" (*secundum essentiam suam*). Because (1) only God's being (*esse*) is his essence (*essentia*), as shown in q.3 a.4, (2) only God possesses *through his essence* such properties as omnipotence, wisdom, and so forth that are added to other beings *only accidentally*, and (3) only God is in his essence the end to which all other beings are ordered (and only God has no end other than his own essence). If God therefore possesses perfection through his essence in all three senses of perfection, we can conclude that only God is good through his essence.

Are All Other Things Good through the Divine Goodness? (*ST* I q.6 a.4)

As Aquinas already remarks in his answer to the first objection of *ST* I q.6 a.3, there remains the question of how creatures can be called "good" at all if they are not good through their essence. If every being is *one* through its essence, why are they not *good* in the same way?

The answer is contained in *ST* I q.6 a.4, where Aquinas discusses the question of whether all beings are good through the divine goodness. His point of departure is the distinction between predicating something *by extrinsic denomination* and predicating something "*in an absolute way*" (*absolute*). And here Aquinas's example of extrinsic predication is location; a thing's location (*locatus*) is predicated of it by extrinsic denomination from its place (*locus*). When Plato argues that Socrates is denominated as a *human being* by the idea of *human being* and understands this idea as something separately existing (calling it the "*per se homo*"), he is wrong because he assumes the separate existence of the idea of *homo*. But, by contrast, he is right when he claims that concepts like *homo* or *ens* or *unum* can be predicated either per se or *per participationem*. Since God has to be called a "per se *ens*," Aquinas argues, insofar as his essence (as shown in q.3 a.4) is nothing other than his being (*esse*), he can also be called a "*per se bonum*." All other beings, which are created beings, must be called "good by participation" (*bona per modum participationis*).

"Participation" means in this use of language, as Aquinas explains, that *A* shares *B* insofar as it is *similar* to *A*, that is, it is a restricted similitude of *A*. Because God is not only the efficient cause but also at the same time the exemplary and final cause of all other beings, these beings can be called "good through the divine goodness" (*bona bonitate divina*).

This "*participation par similitude*" (as L.-B. Geiger has called it[15]) allows Aquinas to say that something is formally good because its goodness, as a similitude of the divine goodness, is *formally inherent* in it. And at the same time, Aquinas can say that calling it "good" is a denomination derived from the divine goodness as its exemplary cause.

Aquinas's Doctrine of God's Goodness: A Comprehensive View of Two Different Approaches or Elements

To evaluate Aquinas's doctrine of God's goodness in *ST* I q.6, it is helpful to look at the structure of his argument. A brief comparison with his approach in *QDV* shows that even in his doctrine of goodness (as well as in his metaphysics in general) Aquinas wants to connect central elements of different traditions to achieve a comprehensive view of goodness. With *Aristotle* he keeps in mind that we do not have a *God's Eye View* (not even by inborn concepts); our epistemological approach is restricted. Nonetheless, with regard to God, it is not completely negative. We can follow the *via causalitatis*; on the basis of transcendental concepts attained by an analysis of our conceptual knowledge, we gain insight into a certain metaphysical structure. With *Plato* Aquinas holds that reality as a nondualistic whole must be understood as "good" and that "goodness" has to be traced back to the first final cause.[16]

To explain "goodness" Aquinas identifies two central approaches in the tradition. The first defines the concept of "goodness" as the concept of an end and understands the end as a perfection that is reached when the potentialities of a thing are completely actualized according to that thing's nature. The second defines "goodness" as something caused by a first cause that is "goodness itself." The first can be called (with reference to Aristotle) the "nature approach"; the second (with reference to Boethius's *De hebdomadibus*), the "participation approach."[17]

In his comprehensive view in *ST* I q.6, Aquinas starts with the "nature approach," instead of the "participation approach" he had employed in *QDV*, q.21, a.1. Nonetheless, he integrates a revised form of the "participation approach" in a second step of the *ST* argument. His point of departure is the Aristotelian analysis of the nature of those things we cognize in empirically based natural knowledge. But while Aristotle analyzes perfection only as the actualization of a form in its corresponding matter, Aquinas extends this analysis to a deeper metaphysical level. In his view, matter-form composition has to be conceived of as only a special case of more general composition. The most general form of metaphysical composition is that of *essentia* and *esse*, a form of composition that can be found not only in material beings but also in immaterial beings.

It is this general metaphysical structure that allows Aquinas to connect the Aristotelian act-potency structure to the Platonic idea of participation in the second step of his *ST* argument.[18] The Aristotelian priority of the act (mediated through the form) can be conceived of as the priority of the "act of being" (*actus essendi*).[19] For it is the "act of being" (*actus essendi*) that constitutes a "being" (*ens*), insofar as the *actus essendi* is the actualizing principle of the *essentia*, conceived of as the receiving potency.

As the act that constitutes any being (*as being*) and actualizes all the inherent perfections of a being, *esse* can be understood as the act of all other acts and perfections. "As such, *esse* is the most perfect of all things, as the act of all things to which it can be compared. For nothing has actuality except insofar as it is. Hence *esse* is the actuality of all things, even of their forms."[20] And in *QDP*, q.7, a.2, ad 9, Aquinas writes, "being is the actuality of all acts, and on that account it is the perfection of all perfections [*esse est actualitas omnium actuum, et propter hoc est perfectio omnium perfectionum*]."

As that which can be predicated as something common to all beings "*esse*" (*commune*) is a general concept; as the act that actualizes the form or essence of a particular being it is a *principium quo*. But in prolongation of the Aristotelian axiom that "whatever is the maximum in a genus is the cause of all other members of that genus,"[21] the first efficient cause of all beings must be conceived of as that whose essence comprehends *esse* as the perfection of all other perfections. It can, therefore, be called a "subsisting act of being" (*esse subsistens*).[22] Aquinas's explication of the statement that "God is good" in the sense that "he is goodness itself" follows from this explication of the concept of God as the first cause, as that which cannot be conceived of except as that whose essence is unrestricted *esse*.

The Order of Elements or Levels

Comparing the two approaches in *QDV* and *ST*, we can conclude that what is the initial step in Aquinas's explication of goodness in *QDV* is the last step in his explication in *ST*. Only if goodness can be explained as perfection through the *ST*'s analysis of being as a composition of *esse* and *essentia* can "goodness" be interpreted in both ways: as the divine goodness, which is the goodness of the *esse subsistens*, and as the goodness of all other beings, since their perfection is identical with their *esse*.

The reference to the "participation approach" gives Aquinas the opportunity to solve a problem that is connected to the application of the distinction between predication per se and *per accidens*. Since it is only God of whom "good" can be predicated per se, because God alone is substantially good, all other beings can only be called "good" accidentally or by extrinsic denomination. But that being the case, the "goodness" of creatures remains something extrinsic, which is not very convincing as compared with the "nature approach."[23] Therefore, in the case of "being" and "good" Aquinas prefers to use the distinction between predication *per essentiam* and predication *per participationem*. But this distinction as introduced by Boethius in his *De hebdomadibus* must be transformed. What is shared by created beings, according to Aquinas, is divine goodness insofar as the inherent perfection of these beings is a similitude of God's goodness. This "*participation par similitude*" is in created beings a result of their "*participation par composition*" and therefore not extrinsic.

This explains why "good" and "being" are predicated of created beings in different ways: something is "'being' absolutely" (*ens simpliciter*) insofar as it exists, but its additional properties, its accidents and operations, are "'being' in a certain respect" (*ens secundum quid*). When something exists, it is "good in a certain respect" (*bonum secundum quid*), that is with respect to the perfection of "being," but it is "absolutely good" (*bonum simpliciter*) only when it has reached its final perfection.[24] Following an approach that can already be found in Albert the Great,[25] Aquinas teaches that "being" and "good" are identical in that "being" and "good" are attributed to a thing in virtue of the same state of reality. But "being" and "good" differ "conceptually" (*secundum rationem*), insofar as "good" connotes a relation to the perfective object[26] or a "relation to the final cause" (*habitudo causae finalis*).[27] This relatedness is not extrinsic because it consists in the similitude of a being to the first efficient and final cause of that being. The priority of "good" in relation to "being" can be reduced to priority "in a causal relation" (*in causando*).[28]

Because God is not composed of *esse* and *essentia*, but absolutely simple, what can be predicated of him is predicated of him in a different way than it can be predicated of created beings. Thus, *esse* can be predicated of God essentially, though in creatures it is only a *principium quo*. "Because God is simple and subsisting, even abstract nouns signify his simplicity."[29] While Aquinas criticizes the Platonic doctrine of separated forms with respect to created beings, in the case of God he agrees (as does Aristotle) that "goodness" subsists as "being" (*esse*).[30] In the first cause of the perfections of all other beings, all perfections must pre-exist "in a more excellent manner" (*secundum eminentiorem modum*).[31] Distinguishing between essential predication and predication by participation at *Quodl* II, q.2, a.2, Aquinas notes that "God is called good essentially, because he *is* goodness itself, but creatures are called good by participation, because they *have* goodness."[32] It is this ontological model of participation that allows us to call "good" both what desires goodness and what confers goodness, the *ens perfectum* and the *ens perfectivum*, good as *quod omnia appetunt* and good as *diffusivum sui*.[33] And it is this model that makes it possible to substitute the concept of causality with regard to creation for the emanation of the Neoplatonic tradition.

Perfection and Goodness: A Circle?

But even the doctrine of God's goodness in *ST* I q.6 is open to question. It supposes that the *actus essendi* (act of being) as the *perfectio omnium perfectionum* (perfection of all perfections) constitutes goodness—in created things *per participationem* (by participation) and in God *per essentiam* (by essence). But, the solution seems circular, since it is goodness as the perfection of the *actus essendi* that causes goodness in God and creatures. And we can also ask how we know that the *actus essendi* is the ultimate perfection.

Aquinas would not only concede but emphasize that there is a circle insofar as "being" and "good" are really identical because both refer to the same reality. But this circle is not vicious, since "good," as Albert the Great emphasizes,[34] is different than being on account of its relation to the appetite of the will, which is not included in the meaning of perfection.

But even if "being" is conceptually distinct from "good," Aquinas's solution is open to objection, since it presupposes an analysis of "being" (*esse*) as perfection that precedes the analysis of "being" (*ens*) as good. Isn't this the hidden priority of value to being that characterizes the Platonists and that Aquinas wants to avoid?

Indeed, Aquinas's understanding of "being" (esse) is not neutral. But he would argue that the positive evaluation of "being" (*esse*) is not arbitrary, since unless we affirm "being" (*esse*), we cannot cognize anything. Being is the first thing we can know, and its affirmation has priority over its negation because being is presupposed even when we deny the "being" (*esse*) of something. As Aristotle emphasizes, the ontological reason for this is that act precedes potency, and even potency is not "real" except in relation to act.

NOTES

1. Cf. Dionysius Pseudo-Areopagita, *De divinis nominibus*, c.4. My thanks to Rega Wood (Stanford) for her help with the above; thanks, too, to Jennifer Ottman for her assistance with matters of English style.

2. Cf. ibid.; Boethius, *De hebdomadibus.*

3. Cf. Aristotle, *Ethica Nicomachea* l.1, c.4 (1096 a 19–29).

4. Cf. Philip the Chancellor, *Summa de bono.*

5. *ST* I q.13 a.1; cf. Eleonore Stump, *Aquinas* (London: Routledge, 2003), 93 ff.

6. Cf. Jan A. Aertsen, *Medieval Philosophy and the Transcendentals: The Case of Thomas Aquinas* (Leiden, New York, and Köln: E. J. Brill, 1996); id., "Good as Transcendental and the Transcendence of the Good," in Scott MacDonald, ed., *Being and Goodness: The Concept of the Good in Metaphysics and Philosophical Theology* (Ithaca, N.Y. and London: Cornell University Press, 1991), 56–73; Rudi te Velde, "The Concept of the Good according to Thomas Aquinas," in Wouter Goris, ed., *Die Metaphysik und das Gute: Aufsätze zu ihrem Verhältnis in Antike und Mittelalter* (Leuven: Peeters, 1999), 81–103; Scott MacDonald, "The Metaphysics of Goodness and the Doctrine of the Transcendentals," in Scott MacDonald, ed., *Being and Goodness: The Concept of the Good in Metaphysics and Philosophical Theology* (Ithaca, N.Y. and London: Cornell University Press, 1991), 31–55.

7. Aertsen, *Medieval Philosophy and the Transcendentals*, 300; te Velde, "The Concept of the Good."

8. Cf. *In NE* I l.1; see Aertsen, *Medieval Philosophy and the Transcendentals*, 299 f.

9. Cf. *ST* I q.5 a.5.

10. *QDV* q.21, a.1.

11. Ibid.

12. Cf. te Velde, "The Concept of the Good."

13. Cf. Aertsen, "Good as Transcendental."

14. Aristotle, *Physics* l.2, c.7 (193 a 26 f.), l.2 (193 b 8 ff.).

15. Cf. Louis-Bertrand Geiger, *La participation dans la philosophie de S. Thomas d'Aquin*, 2d ed. (Paris: Vrin, 1953), 63–73.

16. MacDonald, "The Metaphysics of Goodness," 37, calls it the Agency Account.

17. Scott MacDonald, "The Relation between Being and Goodness," in Scott MacDonald, ed., *Being and Goodness: The Concept of the Good in Metaphysics and Philosophical Theology* (Ithaca, N.Y. and London: Cornell University Press, 1991).

18. Cf. Wolfgang Kluxen, "Thomas von Aquin: Das Seiende und seine Prinzipien," in Josef Speck, ed., *Grundprobleme der großen Philosophen* (Göttingen: Vandenhoeck & Rupprecht, 1972), 174–214.

19. See the contribution of John F. Wippel in this volume.

20. *ST* I q.4 a.1–2; cf. Leo J. Elders, *The Philosophical Theology of St. Thomas Aquinas* (Leiden, New York, København, and Köln: E. J. Brill, 1990), 163.

21. *SCG* l.1, c.41, referring to Aristotle, *Met.* l.2, c.1.

22. Cf., e.g., *ST* I q.44 a.1: *ipsum esse* per se *subsistens.*

23. Cf. Ralph McInerny, "Saint Thomas on *De hebdomadibus*," in Scott MacDonald, ed., *Being and Goodness: The Concept of the Good in Metaphysics and Philosophical Theology* (Ithaca, N.Y. and London: Cornell University Press, 1991), 74–97.

24. Therefore, Aertsen, *Medieval Philosophy and the Transcendentals*, 317, states that according to Aquinas "good" is both in the category of substantial being and in the category of accidental being. Cf. Aertsen, "Good as Transcendental."

25. Cf. Albertus Magnus, *Summa theologiae*, tr.6, q.28, sol. (ed. Siedler, Ed. Colon. t.34, 1 p.214); MacDonald, "The Metaphysics of Goodness."

26. *QDV* q.21 a.1 ad 1.

27. *ST* I q.5 a.2 ad 1.

28. *ST* I q.5 a.2 ad 1.

29. *ST* I q.13 a.1 ad 2.

30. Cf. *ST* I q.6 a.4; *In NE* l.1, c.6.

31. *ST* I q.4 a.3.

32. Cf. Aertsen, "Good as Transcendental."

33. Aertsen, *Medieval Philosophy and the Transcendentals*, 302, speaks of the "attractive and the productive side of goodness"; te Velde, "The Concept of the Good," distinguishes between "good in itself" and "good for itself."

34. See note 25.

CHAPTER 12

GOD'S KNOWLEDGE AND WILL

JAMES BRENT, O.P.

Aquinas divides perfections into two types: entitative and operative. An entitative perfection is something that a thing *is*, an operative perfection is something that a thing *does*. The terms "knowledge" and "will" both signify operative perfections. The terms possess different senses in our own thinking, but when applied to God both terms refer to the absolutely simple divine *esse*. In keeping with our way of thinking, Aquinas has one account of God's knowledge and another account of God's will. In two parts, this article treats both of Aquinas's accounts.

God's Knowledge

Aquinas presents God's knowledge (1) as a divine perfection and (2) as divine ideas. In addition, there is the special question of (3) God's knowledge of future contingent events such as creaturely free choices. Each topic deserves its own consideration.

God's Knowledge as a Divine Perfection

For Aquinas, all creatures imitate God to some degree, but to an extent and in a way far removed from what God is. All creaturely perfections are thus inadequate imitations of God. Given Aquinas's account of the divine perfections and divine names, terms referring to creaturely perfections such as "life," "goodness," and "power" refer to something very different in God than what they refer to in creatures. Knowledge is a case in point.

Let us say that Socrates knows things or has knowledge. The terms "know" or "knowledge" refer to (Aquinas would say "signify") some reality in Socrates. Now, precisely by knowing things or having knowledge, Socrates inadequately imitates God. Because Socrates, as someone who knows things, does indeed *imitate* God to some extent, we can also say that God knows things or God has knowledge. On the basis of how Socrates' knowledge imitates God, the term "knows" or "knowledge" refers to some reality or perfection in God. But because of how *inadequately* Socrates' knowledge imitates God, we must also say that the term "knows" or "knowledge" refers to some reality or perfection in God quite different from and more eminent than what the same term refers to in Socrates.[1] So for God to know things or to have knowledge is something different from and more eminent than what it is for Socrates to know things. Now, what is it to say that God's knowledge is "more eminent" than Socrates?

To say that God's knowledge is more eminent than what we find in Socrates' knowledge is to say something best understood through a series of increasingly stronger claims. First, God's knowledge is not the same kind of knowledge that we find in Socrates or in any creature whatsoever. Second, God's knowledge does not belong to any genus or species at all. Third, God's knowledge is not for these two reasons inferior to the sort of knowledge that we find in Socrates or in other creatures. Rather, God's knowledge is superior to the knowledge that we find in Socrates or in any creature or in any genus or species whatsoever. For, fourth, God's knowledge, together with God's will, is somehow the *source* or *author* of all genera, all species, and all perfections of all individuals. Since God's "knowledge" is so very different from any sort of knowledge that we find in creatures, one hesitates to call this reality in God "knowledge" except that knowledge of the kind found in Socrates and other creatures imitates God to some extent.

So what is knowledge as it is in God? What is knowledge as a divine perfection? For Aquinas, no one in this life can *see* what God's knowledge is either by the light of reason or by the light of grace. By the light of reason, one cannot perceive its genus and differentia (for God's knowledge belongs to no genus).[2] And so no definition of God's knowledge is possible by the light of reason. By the light of grace given to people in this life, one also cannot see what God's knowledge is. For the light of grace given to people in this life does not raise anyone to the vision of God's essence, and to see what God's knowledge is amounts to the same as seeing what God is (for reasons given below).[3] These limits to our knowledge of God's knowledge, limits of which Aquinas is aware, constitute limits to the account of God's knowledge that one can reasonably expect to give or possess in this life. Within these limits, one can still make *some* truthful statements about God's knowledge. And that is the task Aquinas takes up in *ST* I q.14 and elsewhere.[4]

Following the account in the *Summa theologiae*, Aquinas argues first that there is knowledge in God (a.1). Aquinas arrives at this view from his frequently repeated principle that being cognitive comes from being immaterial. Since God is immaterial, it must also be that God is cognitive. Now, *what* does God know? Rather than immediately saying "everything," Aquinas first says that God knows or understands (*intelligit*) himself (a.2).[5] The order in which Aquinas talks about God's knowledge is important to note. First, Aquinas speaks of God's knowing himself. Subsequently, Aquinas speaks about God's knowing creatures. And it is God's knowledge of himself that illuminates for us God's knowledge of creatures. This order of proceeding will be repeated when speaking of God's will.

So, first there is God's knowledge of himself. What does God know about himself? God knows or understands *everything* about himself (a.3). More specifically, God understands everything that could possibly be understood about himself. Aquinas calls the complete understanding of a thing "comprehension." So Aquinas says God comprehends himself. If God did not comprehend himself, then what God understood himself to be would be less than what God is. But Aquinas considers that impossible, since divine simplicity requires that there be no difference between what God is and what God understands himself to be. For Aquinas argues from the divine simplicity that God, his intellect, its activity, and its object, like all divine perfections, are all the one simple *esse* that is God (a.4). That is why to see what God's knowledge is is simply to see what God is.

One difference between creaturely knowledge and God's knowledge is that Socrates knows what he does by performing an act of cognition distinct from his substance, whereas God knows what he does not by such a distinct cognitive act but just by being himself. To be God is to be gazing.[6] Does God also know things other than himself? Aquinas thinks so (a.5). And Aquinas's reason for saying that God knows things other than himself is that God comprehends himself. Since God knows everything about himself, he knows what he does or can cause. But what God does or can cause are things other than himself. So, God knows things other than himself. In other words, God knows creatures. But he knows creatures by knowing himself, that is, by knowing his own creating causality and its actual and possible extent. In other words, for God to know himself is for God to know the extent to which he, as the cause of creatures, can and will cause them. And there is nothing more to creatures than what God can and will cause them to be. So God knows them. And since God knows the cause of creatures completely (i.e., since God knows himself completely), he knows creatures completely (a.6). He knows all their genera, their species, and their particularities (a.6, a.8, a.12). Furthermore, he knows what they themselves do or can cause. Consequently, God knows all things both by knowing himself as their ultimate cause and by knowing one creature as the proximate cause of another. Two potential confusions now need clarification.

First, when a perfection that is found in creatures exists in God, it is in him as one who is wholly knowing. As an imperfect illustration of the way in which creaturely perfections exist in God, Aquinas's preferred analogy is the artist. Just as the artwork is in the artist's mind beforehand, so creaturely perfections are in God. Like an artist contemplating the artwork in his own mind, God knows things not as they are in themselves, but as they are in him.[7] What Aquinas means is that God does not know his artwork by turning his glance away from himself and toward his artwork, but by eternally glancing at himself he beholds his artwork there, that is, for what he eternally comprehends it to be. The artist–artwork analogy is potentially confusing, since it may give the impression that God has a mind populated with multiple concepts or ideas of things. This confusion will be addressed below when discussing the divine ideas.

Second, another potential confusion is that when Aquinas says God knows his creatures by knowing himself as their cause, one may think that God has inferential knowledge. Or one may think at least that Aquinas is committed to saying that God has inferential knowledge. If right now one knows that three miles away there is a flagpole standing in the afternoon sunshine, one knows also that there is a shadow on the ground next to it. One knows there is a shadow there not by seeing the shadow (since it is three miles away), but by inferring so from the premises that whatever stands in the afternoon sunshine casts a shadow and the flagpole is standing in the afternoon sunshine. Aquinas would call this knowing the shadow "*through* its cause." When one reads in Aquinas that God knows creatures by knowing himself as their cause, one may think Aquinas is saying that God knows creatures *through* their cause, that is, by inference. But Aquinas says otherwise.[8] God does not know things *through* their cause or by inference because God's knowledge is not discursive (a.7). God's knowledge is not discursive, since God is immutable in every respect. He does not move from one topic of thought to another and he does not perform inferences. Neither does God possess knowledge in unchanging argumentative form. For God does not form propositions or possess them in his mind, since God would then not be simple (a.14). God's knowledge thus does not consist of a "set of propositions." Rather than knowing creatures *through* their cause, God knows creatures *in* himself, as the artist knows the artwork in himself or in his own mind. But what precisely is it for God to know things *in* himself this way?

Here we reach a limit of our knowledge of God's knowledge. We cannot see what it is for God to gaze upon himself so completely that he also comprehends absolutely every thing other than himself. To gaze upon oneself in such a manner is to be God.

God's knowledge is a simple unchanging *vision* of things – a glance at everything as it is in himself (a.9). Not only does God gaze upon himself so completely that he comprehends absolutely every other thing, but he gazes upon himself so completely that he *at once* comprehends every other thing. He "sees all things together and not successively" (a.7). "The present glance of God extends over all time, and to all things which exist in any time, as to objects present to him."[9] God is thus like "one who sees the whole road from a height" and "sees at once all those traveling on it."[10] God sees everything down the road of time from us (the past and future), but sees it all as present before his vision now (a.14). Some implications of this for creaturely freedom are addressed below.

God's Knowledge as Divine Ideas of Created Things

On Aquinas's account of divine names, perfection terms such as "life," "good," and "power" refer to distinct perfections when predicated of creatures, but co-refer to one and the same simple *esse* when predicated of God. Since these perfections are distinct in creatures, and since we get our sense for terms such as "life" and "good" from our experience of creatures, the senses of the terms remain distinct in our thought even when predicated of God. For Aquinas, we know enough about the simple divine *esse* to be able to say that it is life, that it is good, that it is power, and so on. But we do not know enough to be able to see the reality in God or simple *esse* to which each of these terms refer. What it is to be divine life, divine goodness, and divine power, all in one simple divine *esse*, is hidden from us.

But none of this is hidden from God. Since God comprehends himself, he "knows all the ways in which His own perfection is able to be participated in by others."[11] He knows the various ways in which creatures can possess and imitate, in their limited degrees and diverse forms, what only he himself is essentially and simply. He knows himself as imitable in one way by dogs, another way by cats, another way by zebras (and by individuals of these species). To provide an analogy not found in Aquinas, we can think of a man who is modeling the human form for a studio full of painters. The model stands in the middle of a circle, the painters stand in fixed positions on the perimeter of the circle around him. Each painter portrays what the model is and appears to be given the painter's location on the perimeter. If the model knew everything about himself, he would know himself as portrayable in one way by a painter at this position, as portrayable in another way by a painter at that position, etc. And if the model could know everything about himself in one unchanging glance, he would know all at once all the ways he is portrayable. Aquinas himself uses similar language in his question on divine ideas. God "knows his essence as so imitable by such a creature, and knows it as the particular model and idea of that creature."[12] The divine ideas are God seeing his own simple *esse* as susceptible to participation or imitation in various ways by various creatures. The plurality is in the many creatures that imitate, and in the various ways they imitate, not in the one whom they imitate.

Aquinas also sometimes says that the divine ideas are causes, but he qualifies this by saying that the divine ideas *together with God's will* are causes.[13] The divine ideas are a special sort of cause that has no causality apart from God's willing. The divine ideas are *exemplar* causes.[14] The issue of God's knowledge as causal has received significant attention and debate in recent literature.[15]

God's Knowledge of Future Contingent Events

It can seem that the extensiveness of God's knowledge precludes the possibility of there being contingent events. For "everything known by God must necessarily be...and no future contingent thing must necessarily be. Therefore, no contingent future thing is known by God."[16] In such reasoning, Aquinas finds an equivocation with the term "necessarily be." The equivocation amounts to a shift between necessity *de dicto* and necessity *de re*.[17] The first statement could mean:

(1) For any event *x*, if God knows that *x* will occur in the future, then necessarily (God knows that *x* will occur).
(2) For any event *x*, if God knows *x* will occur in the future, then God knows (*x* will necessarily occur).

Statement (1), Aquinas thinks, is true. Statement (2), Aquinas thinks, is false. Statement (1), however, is not enough to arrive at the conclusion that for any event *x*, God knows (*x* will necessarily be). So much can be understood as a matter of logic alone. But grasping Aquinas's answer to the question of future contingents is more than a matter of seeing through formal fallacies.

A good deal turns on the order in which Aquinas goes about speaking of God's knowledge. First, God knows himself. Second, God knows creatures. But within the second moment, when speaking of God's knowledge of creatures, Aquinas seems to be sensitive to a certain complexity. Creatures are both one and many, but in different respects. Creatures are one whole (the whole of creation), and many individuals (this or that singular creature). When speaking of God's knowledge of creatures, Aquinas first thinks of God as seeing creatures *as a whole* and secondarily thinks of God as seeing creatures as one part or another, one individual or another. All at once, in the eternal glance at himself, God sees the whole of creation.

When God sees in himself the whole of creation, he comprehends it. He knows everything that could be known about it. He sees all the parts and so all the properties of all the parts. So when God comprehends the whole of creation, God sees the actuality, modality, causality, and morality (if applicable) of any and every entity or event within the whole. For example, God sees that Mt. Vesuvius erupts at *t*, that Mt. Vesuvius might not have erupted at *t*, that a certain set of factors caused the eruption, and so on. Similarly, God also sees at once all the free choices rational creatures make and all the properties of those choices. In his comprehension of the whole, God sees concerning any free choice *that* the person will choose something, *what* the person will choose, *why* the person chooses it (i.e., sees the person's *liberum arbitrium* produce the action), *whether* the individual could choose otherwise, and *whether* that ability or inability to choose otherwise is morally relevant in the circumstances. In other words, in one glance at himself God comprehends the whole panoply of individual creaturely free choices and comprehends each choice *as* an essentially free contingent act. Such comprehension of our choices, although it is prior to our choices, does not predetermine our choices. Rather, God's prior comprehension of them is a comprehension of them *as* essentially free contingent acts. God's comprehension of those acts entails no necessity in them except the necessity of being what God comprehends them to be, that is, essentially free contingent acts.[18]

In recent years, there has been new and intense debate amongst philosophers about what views of time, modality, eternity, knowledge, and free will Aquinas is committed to given his views on God's knowledge.[19]

God's Will

Aquinas's account of God's will touches upon four related topics: (1) God's will as a divine perfection, (2) God's willing of creatures, (3) God's love and joy, and (4) God's justice and mercy. Each topic deserves its own treatment.

God's Will as a Divine Perfection

Like knowledge, will is a perfection found in creatures. And similar to the term "knowledge," the term "will" refers to a reality in God that is different from and much more than what the same term refers to in creatures. But in the case of will, matters are slightly more complicated than the case of knowledge. For the term "will" refers to several distinct things in creatures. On the one hand, "will" can refer to the power of appetite. On the other hand, it can refer to the act of that appetite. But in God, given the divine simplicity, there is no real distinction between the power of appetite and its act. God's will is his willing. Furthermore, when referring to creatures, "to will" (i.e., the act of willing) can refer to three different acts.

(1) To will is to *want* something that one perceives as good but which one lacks—as when one wants some water to drink.
(2) To will is to *possess* or rest in something that one perceives as good—as when one has or enjoys the water that one drinks.
(3) To will is to *give* a good to another—as when parents will their wealth to their children.

And so in our own minds we have three different senses of the term "to will." Because of the three senses of "to will," the issue of God's will is really several questions of whether God wills, what God wills, and in what senses God wills which things. In response to these questions, Aquinas makes three main points. First, in God there is no will in the sense that God lacks something and wants it. Second, in God there is will in the sense of possessing or resting in something good, namely, God possessing and resting in himself as highest good. Finally, in God there is will in the sense of giving something, namely, God gives being to creatures. Each of these points deserves individual attention.

(1) God does *not* will things in the sense of hungering for a perceived good that he does not have. For having such a hunger would consist of being in a state of (passive) potentiality with respect to the perceived good, and in God there is no (passive) potentiality. It would also amount, on Aquinas's physics, of needing to be moved by another, and God is not moved by another.[20] So in God there is no will as lacking something. There could only be will as possessing and will as giving.

(2) In God there is will as possessing something that one perceives as good. In God there is will as "loving and delighting in what he possesses."[21] In this sense, God wills himself. Sometimes Aquinas says that God loves and delights in himself, and sometimes Aquinas says God possesses and rests in himself. Stated whichever way, Aquinas has in mind his account of God's goodness and self-knowledge.

On Aquinas's account of God's goodness, God is good, the highest good, essentially good, completely good, pre-containing every actual and possible creaturely perfection, and so lacking in no good whatsoever. Indeed, God is goodness itself.[22] Further, on Aquinas's account of God's knowledge, God knows himself completely and so knows himself as goodness. But for Aquinas, to know goodness as goodness is already to love it.[23] So God loves what he is and is what he loves. He rests and delights in being himself. To be God is what God loves to be or to do as a pure end in itself. Furthermore, God cannot be or do otherwise. It is absolutely necessary for him to love himself and delight in himself just for being God.[24] In that sense, God "wills himself to be"[25] and "necessarily wills himself to be."[26] Furthermore, given the divine simplicity, God's willing of himself is God.[27] Just as when treating God's knowledge, Aquinas begins with the claim that God knows himself, and on that basis accounts for God's knowledge of other things, so when treating of God's will Aquinas begins with the claim that God wills himself and on that basis accounts for God's willing other things. So, after treating of God's willing himself, Aquinas turns to God's willing of creatures.

(3) In God there is will as giving. God wills things other than himself in the sense that he communicates "as far as possible to the others the good possessed."[28] God gives to other things a share in his own goodness, which is being (*esse*). As parents will a share in their wealth to their children, so God wills a share in his wealth (*esse*) to his creatures.[29] To be clear, the share of wealth that children receive from their parents differs in many ways from the share in *esse* that creatures receive from God. But the analogy affords some understanding of the sense in which one can say that God wills created things. God wills them in the sense that God gives them being.

Aquinas often repeats that God wills creatures as a means to an end. What Aquinas means is that God gives *esse* to creatures as his way of being God or as his way of loving and delighting in being himself. For "the things that we love for their own sake we want to be multiplied as much as possible. And God wills and loves his essence for its own sake."[30] Therefore, God wills the multiplication of *esse*, that is, God gives a share in *esse* to other things. And to give a share in *esse* to other things is God's way of being God. Furthermore, God need not have willed (given being to) things other than himself as his way of being God. He could have and would have been God, been goodness itself, known goodness itself, loved goodness itself, possessed goodness itself, and enjoyed goodness itself, and lacked nothing, simply by being himself—even if he had never given being to anything other than himself. So it is not absolutely necessary that God will (give being to) other things.[31] But God in fact wills to be himself in this way: by giving a share in his *esse* to creatures. What is the modal status of that fact? From the point of view of merely logical possibility, that God wills creatures is contingent. But from the point of view of "conditional necessity," that God wills creatures is necessary. For God is immutable in every respect. Therefore, his will toward creatures could not have come into being in God and could not cease to be in God. Rather, God's act of willing creatures simply is God.[32] *Given* that God in fact wills creatures, God cannot do or be otherwise. In that sense, God's willing of creatures is necessary.

God's Willing of Creatures

Several vexatious questions surround God's will with respect to creatures. Does God's willing creatures preclude creaturely free choice? Does a change in a creature willed by God entail a change in God's will? Does God will evil? Does petitionary prayer change the divine will, and if not what is the point of such prayer? The point of this section is to look at Aquinas's big picture of God's will toward creatures and to consider three special questions.

Aquinas's big picture of God's will toward creatures is as follows. God gives being to a *plurality* of things. The plurality is a whole (creation as a whole) and so has parts. The parts are all individual entities and their perfections. Furthermore, for Aquinas, God gives being to the whole of creation as an *end* and gives being to the parts (individual entities and their perfections) as a way of giving being to the whole. In addition, God gives being to an *ordered* whole. The order of creation as a whole requires there to be certain kinds of parts and the same order fittingly contains other kinds of parts. Given with the whole of creation, as a way of giving being to the whole, God gives being to every required and fitting part, that is, to all created entities and their perfections. God wills (gives being to) some things that are actual and does not will other things to be actual. God wills (gives being to) some things that change, and some things that do not change. God wills some things that are necessary and other things that are contingent. God wills some things that result from other things, and some things that provide for other things. God wills some entities that are persons, and others that are not. For Aquinas, God exists prior to the whole matrix of creatures, gives being to the whole, and in doing so gives being to each particular creature and its perfections. In giving being to the whole, God gives being to physical beings and their perfections, and so to time (an accident of physical beings), to the various causal activities amongst the various physical beings, to the various modes of their being and modes of causal connections, and also gives being to persons, some invisible and angelic, others bodily and human, and so gives being to free agency.

Viewed this way, God's will does not exclude the possibility of contingent entities and processes such as free choices, but actually produces them as part of the whole creation. This point is a vexatious one, since talk of free choices being "produced" or "caused" in any way seems to mitigate against the very idea of freedom. God's will, on Aquinas's account, can seem omni-determining in a way that calls into question not only the freedom of created persons, but the innocence of God, given that many choices made by created persons are in fact morally evil. In his various treatments on God's will, Aquinas says little to address such concerns except to say that God's will does not impose necessity but rather produces contingent beings and causes. Rather than finding the answer to such concerns in Aquinas's treatments of God's will, the answers seem rather to be scattered throughout Aquinas's account of God's work of creation and Aquinas's account of human freedom (*liberum arbitrium*). To venture a summary, when God wills (gives being to) created persons God continuously gives them all the principles necessary for them to be free agents and to make free choices. But those same God-given principles do not always exclude the possibility of the created persons' making morally evil free choices.

Turning now to some special questions concerning God's will toward creatures, there are three.

(1) Do changes in creatures entail a change in God? Aquinas says it is one thing to change the will and another to will a change.[33] One can continuously, without changing one's will, will certain things to change, for example, all throughout a rainy day one wills the sky to change from rainy to sunny. No change in a creature causes a change in God's will. Rather, God—without changing his will—wills some things to change.

(2) Does God will the salvation of all? Aquinas distinguishes between antecedent and consequent will.[34] To will a good antecedently is to will it prior to considering all particular circumstances. To will a good consequently is to will it given the consideration of all particular circumstances. Aquinas's example is a judge in court. Prior to considering what crimes a certain human being has committed, a judge wills all human beings to live. The judge antecedently wills all human being to live. But given the consideration that a certain human being has committed a certain crime, say murder, the judge consequently wills him or her to die as punishment. Similarly, God antecedently wills all human beings to be saved. But God does not consequently will the salvation of this or that particular human being. Aquinas is careful to say that "this distinction must not be taken as applying to the divine will itself," as though God's will could change from one moment to the next or as though his knowledge of circumstances could change as his attention turns from one thing to another. Rather than being a distinction between two acts of will in God, Aquinas says, it is a distinction in "the things willed."[35] How precisely to understand Aquinas on this point is a matter of long-standing discussion among Aquinas's interpreters.

(3) Does God will evil? Aquinas answers from within a set of views about the nature of good, evil, being, perfections, and so on. For Aquinas, all being is good. Evil is essentially a privation, that is, the lack of a perfection that a thing should have given its nature. All privation is found in a being. Therefore, all privation is

found in something that is good. And so all evil is found in something that is good. So, any being that is evil in one respect is also good in at least one other respect—good at least insofar as it has being. Nothing is completely evil, for then it would not exist at all. It would be wholly privation and lack every perfection—including being. Because any being that is evil in one respect is also good in at least one other respect, the expression "to will evil" is ambiguous. It could mean to will what is evil because it is evil, and it could mean to will what is good but which happens also to be evil in some respect. God does not will what is evil because it is evil. No one does. But God does will some things that are good in one respect even though evil in another respect. In short, God wills good things that also have some bad features or some bad side effects. For example, God wills (gives being to) plants as food even though a bad side effect of their being food is that they will undergo destruction. To say that God wills the destruction of plants is to say something true *per accidens*.

Morally evil choices, however, present a further complication. In the case of morally evil choices, there is something that is good in one respect and evil in another respect. The created free agent is good as a being, as living, as having the power of free choice, and so on. But he or she is evil in the sense of intending and choosing to lack the rectitude required by the moral order. The agent is good in one respect but evil in another respect *that he or she intends* (due to the mere appearance of goodness). And God in no way shares that intention. God in no ways wills such creaturely intended and creaturely produced privations in created free agents.[36] It cannot truly be said even *per accidens* that God wills persons to make evil choices. It should be said rather that God permits persons to make them.[37]

God's Love and Joy

Aquinas claims that there is love and joy in God.[38] The claim is difficult since in human beings love and joy are passions, and Aquinas wants to say that there are no passions in God.[39] For passions, on Aquinas's view, are essentially changes in the physical organs of animals who are responding to what is perceived through the senses. And no such thing can occur in God who is immutable and immaterial. But Aquinas distinguishes the *passions* of love and joy from the "simple operations" of love and joy, and here he finds a way to say there is love and joy in God.[40] The simple operations of love and joy are acts of intellect and will as spiritual powers. This spiritual love and spiritual joy are found in God, but like all other divine perfections this spiritual love and joy exist in God in a higher and more eminent way than in creatures.

In creatures, to love something is to respond to some preceding goodness found in it. The goodness already present in things, being apprehended, moves our wills to love them. But God's will is not moved in any respect. So God's love is not his response to the preceding goodness found in things. Rather, God's love is the cause of whatever goodness there is to be found in them. This counts as love because "to love anything is nothing else than to will good to that thing"[41] and God wills the good of being (*esse*) to things.[42] In that sense, God loves everything. For God, to will creatures is to give them being, and to give them being is to give them something good, and to give them something good is to love them.

Does God love himself? Aquinas says God wills himself *to* himself and *for* himself.[43] For he is goodness itself. And being what he wills to himself and for himself, he is joyful. For joy is a "certain resting of the will in its object."[44] And "God is at rest in himself, as containing all abundance in himself."[45]

God also rejoices in his creatures. For "each thing takes joy in its like as in something agreeable," and creatures are like God in being and in goodness (albeit as *inadequate* imitations).[46]

God's Justice and Mercy

Aquinas holds that in God there is both justice and mercy, but the justice and mercy of God are different from and much more than the justice and mercy found in human beings.[47] Among human beings, there is commutative and distributive justice. Commutative justice is the disposition or virtue by which one human being renders to another what is his or her due in exchanges between them. Distributive justice is the disposition or virtue by which rulers render what is due to their subjects. Aquinas says that in God there is nothing corresponding to commutative justice in humans, for God has no equal with whom he makes exchanges. But in God there is something corresponding to distributive justice. For God is like a ruler, and creatures are like his subjects, and in a sense God renders to his creatures what is their due. In what sense does God render to his creatures what is their due?

The question is difficult because God does not owe it, either to himself or to creation, to give being to creation as a whole. Creation is always first gratuitous. In that sense, "God is no one's debtor."[48] On account of the gratuitousness of the initial act of giving being to things, any claim that creatures have to good things from God is always a claim qualified by a prior gratuity that has been shown to them—the prior gratuity being that they even exist at all and have a certain nature and purpose under God's plan. On account of this prior gratuity, Aquinas holds two things.

First, God does not owe any good thing to creatures in the strict sense of "owe"—as though a creature could have self-sufficient standing and unqualified rights before God. Any talk of God owing it to himself or to his creatures to give them some good thing is always a qualified talk of owing. To say that God "owes" something to a creature is to say that it is fitting or becoming for God to give it in light of his prior and gratuitous act of willing them (giving being to them) to exist with a certain nature and purpose under his plan. God owes nothing more or less to his creatures than what coheres with or figures in well with his perfectly wise plan for them.

Second, on account of the prior gratuity of creation Aquinas thinks that God's justice always presupposes God's mercy. Mercy, in human beings, is the disposition by which one is "moved with sorrow at the misery of another as though it were one's own."[49] As such, mercy is a passion. Today it might be called "compassion." The effect of mercy or compassion is to dispel the misery of the other or to expel the defects of the other. Mercy cannot be in God as a passion, since God has no passions. But mercy can be predicated of God on the basis that the effects of mercy come forth from God. To say that God is merciful is not to say that the misery of creatures moves God to sorrow for them, but it is to say that God expels the defects of his creatures in accord with his wise plan. Now, if being is a good, and Aquinas thinks it is, then nonbeing is a defect. To expel nonbeing from creatures (that is, to give them being) is thus an act of mercy. So, for creatures to have any being at all, and to have a certain nature and purpose under his plan, and to have on account of that nature certain claims on good things from God, is first of all a mercy God has shown to his creatures.

But since God has in fact shown such mercy to creatures as to give being to creation as a whole according to a plan or order, and given that God has shown such mercy as to give beings, natures, purposes, and perfections to things as part of his plan for creation, God has mercifully bestowed upon creatures various sorts of dueness.[50] Since God has given to his creation these various sorts of dueness, it is only fitting that God should render to creatures what is due to them under His plan. God owes it to himself, not strictly speaking but in the sense that it befits his goodness and wisdom, to render to creatures according to the dueness they have from God under his plan. By so rendering to creatures what is their due, God manifests a perfection like, but much more than, distributive justice. It is like distributive justice insofar as God as superior renders to his subjects what is their due. It is much more than distributive justice, since the subjects have no claim on God giving them anything except whatever claim God has mercifully given them to begin with.

NOTES

1. *ST* I q.13 a.2 and a.16 both speak about perfections being "more eminent" in God than in creatures.
2. *ST* I q.12 a.4.
3. *ST* I q.12 a.13 ad 1.
4. Aquinas treats of God's knowledge elsewhere than the *Summa theologiae*, but I am focusing on the *ST* treatment, since it is the most mature thought of Aquinas.
5. I use "know" and "understand" synonymously throughout this article, for knowledge in God corresponds most to what understanding in Aquinas's sense of the term denotes.
6. But to be God is to be gazing in a higher and more eminent sense of "gazing" than what we find in creaturely gazing.
7. *ST* I q.14 a.5 and a.7 ad 2.
8. *ST* I q.14 a.7 ad 2.

9. *ST* I q.14 a.9.
10. *ST* I q.14 a.13.
11. *ST* I q.14 a.6.
12. *ST* I q.15 a.2.
13. *ST* I q.14 a.8 resp. and ad 1; q.19 a.11 ad 1.
14. Gregory T. Doolan, *Aquinas on the Divine Ideas as Exemplar Causes* (Washington, D.C.: The Catholic University Press of America, 2008); Vivian Boland, *Ideas in God According to Saint Thomas Aquinas* (New York: E. J. Brill, 1996); John Wippel, *Thomas Aquinas on the Divine Ideas*, The Etienne Gilson Series, no.16 (Toronto: Pontifical Institute of Mediaeval Studies, 1993); John Lee Farthing, "The Problem of Divine Exemplarity in St. Thomas," *The Thomist* 49 (1985): 183–222.
15. James Ross, "Aquinas' Exemplarism; Aquinas' Voluntarism," *American Catholic Philosophical Quarterly* 64 (1990): 171–98; Armand A. Maurer, "James Ross on the Divine Ideas: A Reply," *American Catholic Philosophical Quarterly* 65 (1991): 213–20; Lawrence Dewan, "St. Thomas, James Ross, and Exemplarism: A Reply," *American Catholic Philosophical Quarterly* 65 (1991): 221–34; James Ross, "Response to Maurer and Dewan," *American Catholic Philosophical Quarterly* 65 (1991): 235–43; Eleonore Stump and Norman Kretzmann, "God's Knowledge and Its Causal Effects," in Thomas Senor, ed., *The Rationality of Belief and the Plurality of Faith* (Ithaca, N.Y.: Cornell University Press, 1995), 94–124; Brian Shanley, "Divine Causation and Human Freedom in Aquinas," *American Catholic Philosophical Quarterly* 72 (1998): 99–122.
16. *ST* I q.14 a.13 obj.3.
17. For a study of necessity *de dicto* and *de re*, and also a discussion of how the distinction applies to God's knowledge of creaturely properties, see Alvin Plantinga, *The Nature of Necessity* (Oxford: Clarendon Press, 1974), 9 ff.
18. *ST* I q.14 a.13.
19. A. Kenny, "Divine Foreknowledge and Human Freedom," in A. Kenny, ed., *Aquinas: A Collection of Critical Essays* (London: MacMillan, 1969), 255–70; Eleonore Stump and Norman Kretzmann, "Eternity," *Journal of Philosophy* 78 (1981): 429–51; William Lane Craig, *The Problem of Divine Foreknowledge and Future Contingents from Aristotle to Suarez* (Leiden: E. J. Brill, 1988), 99–126; William Lane Craig, "Aquinas on God's Knowledge of Future Contingents," *The Thomist* 54:1 (January 1990): 33–79; Brian Shanley, "Eternal Knowledge of the Temporal in Aquinas," *American Catholic Philosophical Quarterly* 71:2 (Spring 1997): 197–224; "Eternity and God's Knowledge: A Reply to Shanley," *American Catholic Philosophical Quarterly* 72:3 (Summer 1998): 439–45; Theodore J. Kondoleon, "God's Knowledge of Future Contingent Singulars: A Reply," *The Thomist* 56:1 (January 1992): 117–39; David Burrell, "God's Knowledge of Future Contingents: A Reply to William Lane Craig," *The Thomist* 58:2 (April 1994): 317–22; "Eternity, Awareness, and Action" *Faith and Philosophy* 9 (1992): 463–82; Eleonore Stump, "God's Knowledge," in *Aquinas* (London: Routledge, 2003), 159–87; Harm Goris, "Divine Foreknowledge, Providence, Predestination, and Human Freedom," in Rik van Nieuwenhove and Joseph Wawrykow, eds., *The Theology of Thomas Aquinas* (Notre Dame, Ind.: University of Notre Dame Press, 2005), 99–122; Harm Goris, *Free Creatures of An Eternal God* (Nijmegen: Stichting Thomasfonds, 1996).
20. *ST* I q.19 a.1 ad 2 and 3.
21. *ST* I q.19 a.1 ad 2.
22. *SCG* I, c.38.
23. *SCG* I, c.72, n.2: "Since the understood good is the proper object of the will, the understood good is as such willed."

24. *ST* I q.19 a.3; *SCG* I, c.80.
25. *SCG* I, c.75, n.2.
26. *SCG* I, c.80, n.3.
27. *ST* I q.19 a.1.
28. *ST* I q.19 a.2.
29. This analogy is not found in Aquinas.
30. *SCG* I, c.75, n.3.
31. For contemporary discussion of this point, see Norman Kretzmann, *The Metaphysics of Theism* (Oxford: Clarendon Press, 1997), 217–25; John Wippel, "Norman Kretzmann on Aquinas's Attribution of Will and of Freedom to Create to God," *Religious Studies* 39 (2003): 287–98; John Wippel, "Thomas Aquinas on God's Freedom to Create or Not," in *Metaphysical Themes in Thomas Aquinas II* (Washington, D.C.: The Catholic University Press of America, 2007), 218–39.
32. *ST* I q.19 a.1 ad 1.
33. *ST* I q.19 a.7.
34. *ST* I q.19 a.6 ad 1.
35. *ST* I q.19 a.6 ad 1.
36. *ST* I q.19 a.9.
37. *ST* I q.19 a.10 ad 3.
38. On God's love and joy, see Kretzmann, *The Metaphysics of Theism*, 226 ff; Brian Davies, *The Thought of Thomas Aquinas* (Oxford: Clarendon Press, 1992), 149 ff.
39. *SCG* I, c.89.
40. *SCG* I, c.90, n.2.
41. *ST* I q.20 a.2.
42. *ST* I q.5 a.1.
43. *ST* I q.20 a.1 ad 3.
44. *SCG* I, c.90, n.3.
45. *SCG* I, c.90, n.3.
46. *SCG* I, c.90, n.6.
47. On God's justice and mercy, see Davies, *The Thought of Thomas Aquinas*, 152–57.
48. *ST* I q.21 a.1 ad 3.
49. *ST* I q.21 a.3.
50. *SCG* II, c.29.

CHAPTER 13

GOD'S IMPASSIBILITY, IMMUTABILITY, AND ETERNALITY

BRIAN LEFTOW

The claim that God is impassible can assert that God has no passions, no negative emotions or no emotions, or that God is not causally passive—not caused to have any attribute. I discuss these claims in this order, then turn to immutability.

For Aquinas, God has no passions.[1] Having passions, he holds, requires having a body, senses, and more generally "passive potency" (of which more anon); God has none of these.[2] Leaving "passive potency" aside, we might jib at this: if I were a disembodied soul, I might well care passionately about philosophy. But the truth is that "passion" in this context is for Aquinas a technical term, so defined as to apply only to mental states appropriately involved with physical states.[3] We use "passionate" in a loose sense allied to "intense." That God has no passions, in Aquinas's sense, would not rule out his being intellectually passionate in our sense.

God's perfection, Aquinas thinks, rules out his having negative emotions, such as sorrow, fear, envy, or anger.[4] Aquinas's arguments on these scores are likely to leave us unsatisfied. Sorrow, he tells us, is about evil we have; since evil cannot befall God, God cannot sorrow.[5] But what of sorrow over evil befalling creatures God loves? And if we love another sufficiently, evil befalling that other is or entails evil befalling us: it is a tragedy for a husband if his beloved wife is crippled, and not necessarily for self-regarding reasons. Again, surely evil befell God the Son in the Crucifixion, and he seemed in the Garden to sorrow over it in advance, and even to fear it. It is not clear that a Christology should even want to deny this, nor that orthodox Christology can. The fear is a mental state generated in Christ's human nature, but that does not stop the state from belonging to the Son, else there are two mental subjects, two persons, in the incarnate Christ, which is the heresy of Nestorianism.

Again, Aquinas takes it from Aristotle that anger supposes sorrow over injury done and entails an appetite for another's evil for the sake of revenge.[6] On this account, he thinks, God cannot be angry both because he cannot sorrow and because he cannot be injured. But Christ was God and was angry at times, and again, the anger had to belong to the Son. Further, anger can issue in a desire for just punishment. Just punishment is not a form of revenge; further, one who imposes just punishment imposes evil but only because he/she intends a good, for the community and even for the one punished. Again, one can be angry over injuries others suffer. Finally, Aquinas classes envy as a passion in his technical sense, and so ruled out merely by lack of a body, yet he grants that the Devil was envious.[7]

Turning now to emotions more generally, Aquinas is willing to say that God loves.[8] But he so parses this that it is not altogether clear that it counts as what we would call an emotion. As it exists in God, love involves only intellect and will. It is not a passion, or caused by its object, for reasons we see shortly; while love in us involves a response to valued qualities we find in others, God's love causes those valued qualities *ex nihilo*.[9] Aquinas's account of love is entirely in functional terms: it is the first act of the will, wills the good for the beloved and moves the lover toward union with the beloved.[10] One could be pardoned the thought that on Aquinas's account, love is something God does, not something God feels. But surely an emotion, whatever else it involves, is something one feels. Norman Kretzmann suggests that the best term for what Aquinas has in mind here is "attitude," and having an attitude is not a matter of feeling at all.[11] Yet "attitude" is not quite right either because attitudes are dispositions. Aquinas's God has none, and he repeatedly calls joy, delight, and love "operations," things the divine will *does*.[12] If anything like feeling comes into Aquinas's account of God's emotional states, it is when he ascribes joy and delight to God.[13] But here the arguments again leave one worried. Aquinas writes, for instance, that since our understanding is delightful when perfect, God's, which is perfect, will be all the more delightful.[14] Well, maybe. Why should we think that God will resemble us in this way? Nothing else in Aquinas's story about God encourages us to ascribe any particular affective tone to his inner life.

Causal Impassivity

The emotional side of impassibility is for Aquinas a minor detail in the doctrine of God. On the other hand, God's causal impassivity is a consequence of a fundamental, far-reaching claim that Aquinas makes about God: he has no "passive potency."[15] Passive potencies are best thought of as *potentials* to acquire attributes. A passive potency is an ability to "move" (change), or rather be moved,[16] with respect to having an attribute. For Aquinas, "motion" is as such the actualization of a (passive) potency.[17] And any item that passes from potency to act has the potency (i.e., potentially has the attribute) temporally before it has the actuality (i.e., actually has the attribute).[18] This being so, passive potencies are potentials to *become*,[19] to come to have some attribute. So lack of passive potencies is the root of God's intrinsic immutability. We see below that Aquinas thinks that this entails divine timelessness. Aquinas's commitment to immutability and timelessness conditions a great deal else he says about God. So then does his denial of divine passive potencies.

Again, whatever passes from passive potency to actuality is for Aquinas caused to do so.[20] So Thomist passive potencies are also liabilities to be caused. And so something with no passive potencies is causally impassive: nothing can cause it to have any attribute. The claim that God is causally impassive plays a large role in Aquinas's accounts of God's knowledge (God cannot be *caused* to know anything, and so his knowledge cannot literally be observational) and providence (while God responds to us, we do not cause Him to do so). Our first question, then, must be why Aquinas thinks God lacks passive potency. I then pass to immutability and atemporality.

Why No Passive Potencies?

Aquinas's most straightforward argument that God has no passive potencies comes in his *Compendium Theologiae*. One way Aquinas seeks to prove God's existence is with an argument, the "First Way," that there is an unmoved mover of all moving things.[21] Aquinas's belief in God's pure actuality has roots in this argument, for he writes in *CT* that "In the first mover, if it is in all ways incapable of motion, it is impossible for potency to be with act. For whatever is in potency is for this reason able to move."[22]

The key to Aquinas's move is a feature of the First Way that passes almost without notice: it depends on a metaphysical account of motion that applies not just to actual kinds of motion but to all possible kinds, since it explicates the very nature of motion. So while the First Way begins only from actual, observed sorts of motion, if it is sound, it could equally begin from any possible case of motion. Let's grant Aquinas that the First Way is sound—that all its premises are true. Then any possible case of motion traces back ultimately to the same single unmoved mover, God. Then in any possible world, at any time at which there is motion, God does not move. But, of course, in any world at any time at which there is no motion, God does not move. Thus, at no time in any possible world does God move; God is incapable of moving. But "whatever is in potency is for this reason able to move": as we have observed, potencies for Aquinas just are liabilities to move, to become such-and-such. The conclusion then does follow: God has no passive potencies (and can have none).

That the First Way really is sound is (to put it mildly) controversial. But while Aquinas has many other arguments against divine passive potencies,[23] they all make metaphysical commitments at least as substantial as and in most cases harder to motivate than the First Way's. It is no great surprise if it is hard to find a strong argument for the no passive potency claim in Aquinas. For the conclusion has consequences that should give us pause, and if it is not in fact true, there are no sound arguments for it. As already noted, if God has no passive potencies, then on Aquinas's terms, he cannot literally observe us. So he cannot learn what we freely do by watching us do it. For if God observes us, our actions cause Him to have certain cognitive states, and so God has a passive potentiality to have those states, which our actions actualize. But then just how does God learn what we freely do? We think we are free in a sense that implies that we can originate some of our own actions. If we are not, the problem of evil becomes very hard (and perhaps impossible) to handle, for then even our worst actions ultimately originate in God. But if our actions originate in us, either God knows what they are by observing, or he has predetermined in some way that they shall originate with us, and knows what we freely do by knowing what he has predetermined us to do. If this is so, we are the actions' source, but we do not have the ability to do otherwise than we do. Say this, though, and the problem of evil again becomes much harder to handle, for even if God is not literally our actions' origin, he has made them inescapable for us and so bears responsibility for them. The problems of evil and our beliefs about our freedom, then, are strong reason to want to ascribe observational knowledge to God. But for Aquinas, at any rate, at this point in his theology the die is cast.

Aquinas on Immutability

If God has no passive potencies, again, there is nothing he can become. So God cannot change intrinsically.[24] Intrinsic changes are changes like reddening, growing, or forgetting, which (roughly) occur entirely within the changing item. For Aristotelians there is also genuine change from place to place, but this is not intrinsic and (Aquinas thinks) gets ruled out not because God is immutable but because he is omnipresent: wherever God might be said to move to, he is already.[25]

Changes are extrinsic just if they are not intrinsic. Very roughly, for Aquinas, A changes extrinsically just when a new predicate becomes applicable to A owing entirely to an intrinsic change in something wholly distinct from A, as when I become shorter than Joe only because Joe grows. Aquinas is explicit that God can change extrinsically.[26] When Moses comes to exist, God becomes the Lord of Moses. Moses' coming to exist and God's thus becoming his Lord does not involve any intrinsic change in God; all that happens here is that a new title comes to apply to God. Further, even if this did rest on acquiring a new real relational property, this would not realize a potency of God, Aquinas thinks. For the realizing of a potency involves "motion," and Aquinas accepts from Aristotle that there is no "motion" in the category of relation.[27] Rather, new relations arise without having been in process of change, due to motion in another category.[28]

For Aquinas as for most other medieval Aristotelians, intrinsic properties fall into three categories: substance, quality, and quantity.[29] Aristotelians see change with respect to substance—the kind a thing belongs to—as impossible; Aristotelians see kinds as essential properties. Thus, for Aquinas, the doctrine of divine immutability (DDI) rules out only change in quality (e.g., color, intelligence) or quantity (size, shape). For Aquinas, some things acquire real inhering relational properties by being changed in these categories: when I grow, I acquire a real relational property of being equal in height to others of my new height. But because God cannot be changed in these categories, he cannot acquire a new inhering relational property. God can only be spoken of in new ways by relational predicates.

We can distinguish a weak and a strong DDI:

WEAK. In no continuation actual history has or could have had does God change intrinsically.

STRONG. In no possible history does God change intrinsically. There could not have been a past that could have led to a future in which He did so.

God's actually having no passive potencies entails only (WEAK). But for reasons we have seen, the First Way, if sound, would back (STRONG). Aquinas also thinks that (WEAK) entails (STRONG). For general metaphysical reasons, Aquinas thinks that the past, once it has become past, is absolutely necessary.[30] There *could have been* a different past: before *t*, Socrates was able both to drink the hemlock and to refrain. But now that Socrates has in fact drunk it, there cannot have been a different past: it is no longer so much as possible that he not have drunk it. So for Aquinas, every world that still is genuinely possible includes the actual past, in which God never changed. And so (WEAK) guarantees that in no future that remains possible—that is, no future that continues on from the only past there now can have been—does God change. Given Aquinas's modal metaphysics, then, in every world that remains possible, God does not change intrinsically, and so (STRONG) is true.

Immutability and divine emotional impassibility are logically independent. DDI does not entail emotional impassibility. An immutable God could be unchangeably sad about something, if he lacked certain other properties that Aquinas thinks he has. Nor does emotional impassibility entail DDI. A God who cannot have negative affects could grow happier as time passes (again, if he lacked the full panoply of Thomist properties). DDI does not directly rule out beginning and ceasing to exist. Something changes only if it goes from being not-*F* to being *F*, for some *F*. Nothing can be *F* unless it exists to be *F*. So a changing thing exists at both the beginning and the end of the change in question. But something which begins to exist was not there before this event, and something which ceases to be is not there at its end. That something begins or ceases to exist is a change in the world, but not in the strict sense a change in that thing. Aquinas argues that DDI indirectly rules out beginning or ceasing: whatever begins or ceases to be, he suggests, does so through change, and so what cannot change, cannot begin or cease.[31] But Aquinas himself undercuts this argument. He is explicit that creation *ex nihilo* is a non-change that caused the world to begin to exist.[32] Aquinas also thinks that God could simply annihilate something, making it cease entirely to exist, leaving no remnant.[33] But then surely just as God could cause the world to begin at an instant, he could cause it to cease in an instant, at a last point in time, without changing it intrinsically in any way beforehand.

Aquinas thinks that DDI entails that God is eternal. Let us now examine his case.

Eternality

Aquinas adopts Boethius's definition of eternity, "the all-at-once and perfect possession of interminable life."[34] In his *Sentence* commentary,[35] Aquinas says that the definition's basic thought is that to be eternal is to have being without limits.

i. A thing's whole duration (Aquinas passes from talking about limits of "being" to limits of duration with no suggestion that he is changing topic[36]) is limited by a beginning and end. "Interminable life"—life without termini, or endpoints—rules out this sort of limit. This explanation might make it seem that Aquinas thinks of God's eternality as somehow limitlessly enduring or extended. Aquinas adds that Boethius used "possession" rather than "duration" because "duration" by its very meaning entails a kind of "distension" and so "inquietude," which should not be understood of God's being.[37] This rules out *passage* in the divine being, but would not rule out having a duration, a timelike extension, that did not "pass" as time does.[38] "Atemporal duration" is not in Aquinas's view a contradiction: he also speaks of aeviternity, angels' distinctive mode of duration, as non-temporal.[39] So if Aquinas does think of God's eternality as involving duration, it does not follow that he thinks of it as everlasting existence in time. He might instead think of it as a timelike analogue to a true spatial atom: perhaps as a true spatial atom has an extension but has no really distinct parts filling it, an eternal duration might have an extension but have no really distinct event-parts filling it.
ii. Parts of a duration are limited by the parts that precede and follow them. That an eternal thing's existence is "all at once" rules out its containing temporal parts, since these occur one before another, and so rules out eternity's having this sort of (internal) limitation. (*ST* rules out temporal parts by ruling out eternity's *containing* beginnings and endings, e.g., the beginning and ending of an hour, a day, etc.[40]) If having parts preceding and following constitutes a limit, this also rules it out that God's existence

is just for an instant of time. *ST* rules this out by saying that eternity involves permanence.[41]

iii. A thing's being is also limited in a third way if it is received by a "supposit" distinct from the being received. Aquinas suggests, with a bit of strain, that "perfect" rules this out, because only something that does not receive its being in a "supposit" has perfect being. *ST* makes no less a stretch when it takes "perfect" to rule out the "imperfect" temporal now.[42]

As Aquinas explains it, God's life does not stretch through all time. This is ruled out by its containing no temporal parts—any life lived through time is lived through one hour, then another, and so has one hour-long part, then another. Nor does God's life occupy part of time: this is ruled out by its having no beginning or end. Nor does it last just an instant. So Aquinas must see God's existence as atemporal.[43] One might object to this that Aquinas also says eternity "includes all times"[44] and that God "always"[45] exists.[46] The first, though, brings to mind Anselm's thesis that an atemporal God has present to Him in eternity, in an atemporal way, all times insofar as they are present, which Aquinas appears to endorse in *ST* I q.14 a.13.[47] To image the relation of eternity to time, Aquinas adopts from Boethius the simile of an eternal being as a point in the center of a circle, co-existent with every point on the circumference though not located on it.[48] This simile is naturally cashed out in terms of Anselm's picture. "Includes all times" does not, then, have to be read as suggesting existence at all times, and the circle simile in fact points another way, since center-points do not exist at every point on their circumferences. The use of "always exists," moreover, is at best ambiguous: it could mean no more than that if God is atemporal, at every time, it is true that he timelessly exists, just as at every point on a circumference, it is true that the center exists—across from it.

Rory Fox suggests that Aquinas does not hold either that God is timeless or that he is everlasting.[49] Fox points out that Aquinas is willing in the case of angels, which are not temporal, to say that when they have effects in time, their actions are in time,[50] adding "and so they could be said to be existing, in effect, in time."[51] Fox thinks Aquinas should say the same of God, who also has temporal effects.[52] Fox adds that Aquinas is happy to say that God exists in place in virtue of sustaining all things in all places and suggests that Aquinas should concede in parallel that God exists in time (in some way) in virtue of sustaining all things in all times.[53] But Fox's point about the angels takes a step too far. It is a standard part of Aristotelian theories of causation that the action of a cause takes place in its effect: the action of the fire occurs in the water, when the fire causes the water to heat up. It does not follow that the fire exists where the water is; in fact this would be impossible, to an Aristotelian. To say that an angel's action exists in time is to say no more than what we would mean by saying that its effect is in time. Thus, there is for Aquinas just no move to be made from an angel's action occurring in our time to the angel's literally existing in our time. In fact, in discussing angelic motion, Aquinas holds that moving angels exist in their own kind of time, one discrete rather than continuous, rather than claiming that they exist in our time, even though they move through places we share with them.[54] This is in part because their motion just consists in their actions' being at different places at different times.[55]

Fox's other argument, about presence in space and time, should resonate particularly for those who believe we live in a four-dimensional universe, one not of space in time but of spacetime, a single entity of which "space" and "time" denote abstracted aspects. For if this is true, then in any sense in which God is in space, he is also in time. But Aquinas did not think he lived in such a universe. And the sense in which Aquinas says God exists in place is too weak to support a claim that God is in any sense intrinsically other than a-spatial, or literally located in space. For all Aquinas means by this is that all things are subject to God's power and that God directly knows all things and causes all things to be.[56] His knowing them hardly places him literally where they are. His causing effects in them, again, places his action but not God himself in space. Thus, there is no basis here for any jibbing about whether Aquinas's God is atemporal.

Arguments for Timelessness

Aquinas has more than one route to the claim that God is eternal. One begins from the claim that God exists necessarily. This is the Third Way's conclusion, and something like the Third Way occurs in *SCG* in an argument for God's eternity.[57] *CT* suggests that since God cannot have been caused to exist, he must exist by his own nature, per se, and therefore necessarily.[58] This warrants a stronger form of necessity than the Third Way does; that God exists by his very nature entails (so Aquinas thinks) that "God exists" is a truth per se *notum in se*, an analytic truth, one broadly logically necessary. Given divine necessity, God always exists; there can be no time at which a logically necessary truth is false.[59] But if God always exists and is immutable, Aquinas thinks, it follows that he is eternal in Boethius's sense. Since he never changes from being not-*F* to being *F*, there never are two phases of his life distinguished as the phase in which he is not-*F* and that in which he is *F*, and so, Aquinas suggests, there are no phases at all; instead God's life is "all at once."[60]

This last move seems too quick. Having no phases that differ by a change of divine quality does not rule out earlier and later phases in which God is qualitatively identical. One might suggest that if God lasts through time, he changes in quantity—the quantity of life he has had. If that is true, then God cannot be quantitatively changeless if he exists in time. But Aquinas is clear, following Aristotle, that time does not measure a quantity of things in time[61]—a thing's lifespan is a quantity of its existence, not the thing. Passage of time brings with it relational change. Even if I did not change in quantity or quality, in 1999 I co-existed with the earth's 1999th trip round the sun since a particular time, in 2000 with its 2000th. So if change in relation counted as incompatible with divine immutability, immutability would rule out being temporal. But Aquinas accepts that change in extrinsic relational property is compatible with DDI.[62] So he cannot move from immutability to timelessness in this way.

Aquinas's *ST* argument for God's eternality is this:

> The concept (*ratio*) of eternity is a consequence of immutability. Whence because God is maximally immutable, He is maximally eternal . . . the "standing now" makes eternity according to our apprehension. Just as our apprehending the flow of the now causes us to apprehend time, so inasmuch as we apprehend the standing now, this causes in us the apprehension of eternity.[63]

Aquinas takes it without argument that even a God he thinks atemporal has a now. Perhaps this is because God is conscious, and a "now of experience" seems conceptually inseparable from having experience at all. Aquinas says that we apprehend God's "standing now." We do so, I think, by apprehending that God is immutable; it is because immutability leads us to see that God's now "stands" rather than "flows" that it leads us to conclude that God is atemporal. The connection between these things runs via Aquinas's account of time.

Aquinas believes that the temporal now "flows"—that time really, objectively passes.[64] One question we can ask believers in a flowing now is why it flows: what "powers" the passage of time. Some see time's passage as a process unto itself, primitive, not further explained.[65] Aquinas disagrees. For Aquinas, our time is the time of material things, whose time is the number of local motion, change of place.[66] (I explain "the number of" shortly.) For Aquinas, angels have their own sort of time, which is the number of succession—change—in their mental operations.[67] Our time for Aquinas is an accident of the "first motion," the revolution of the outer Aristotelian heavenly sphere.[68] Now for Aquinas, their subjects make accidents exist.[69] So Aquinas's claim is that the motion of the outermost sphere makes our time exist. He is so firm on this, in fact, that he holds that if there were many Aristotelian universes, each with its own outermost sphere, each would therefore have its own time: there would be many distinct temporal series.[70] Since for time to exist is for it to "flow"[71]—time for Aquinas is generated by the flow of the now[72]—for Aquinas, the outermost sphere's motion makes time pass: what makes our time "flow" is the first motion.

To see what's behind this, note that Aquinas accepts Aristotle's definition of time as "the number of motion."[73] As Aquinas understands this, it means that time is the countable or measurable aspect of motion. Aquinas thinks of the day as a natural first unit of time.[74] A day, which is a stretch of time, *just is* the time taken by one revolution of the sun around the earth (as Aquinas thought): a particular motion occurs in its very definition, as that in which the property of being a day long inheres per se. If the day is the *first* unit, we do not measure it: there is no other, prior unit available to measure it with. Instead we just count days, by counting the times the sun reappears at the same point in the sky, having completed one revolution. Given this standard unit, we can measure other lengths of time, and so other time-units are definable as parts or multiples of this one. The first motion provides the day, a natural unit by which all other time-stretches, and so all other motions, are to be measured: it provides the "standard meter" of motion.[75]

Now there are two ways to parse Aquinas's view:

(a) a day is the length of a movement, one revolution of the sun;
(b) a day *just is* one revolution of the sun—it is that movement, taken as a unit for measuring the length of other motions.

On (b) the motion of the outermost sphere makes time pass—in fact *is* time's passing. For on (b), for time to pass is for (say) a new day to begin, and for a day to begin just is for a new cycle of the motion whose duration is a day to begin. Time in a strong sense *reduces to* motion, and as we see shortly, the Aristotelian first motion is causally as well as chronologically basic. On (a), we might wonder whether the sphere's motion really makes time pass. For we might wonder whether, if the sun stopped revolving but other motions continued, time would not after all continue to pass, "powered" by other motion, which might eventually add up to the duration of a day even without the sun. But in the cosmology Aquinas adopted from Aristotle, the outermost sphere's motion is what causes all else to move. If it stopped moving, all else would, and Aquinas is explicit that in this case the time of material things would cease.[76] (There might still be angelic time.) So given Aquinas's Aristotelian cosmology, even on (a), the outermost sphere powers time's passage.

Still, Aquinas is careful to make a distinction. To Aquinas, time is of its nature the number of the first motion, whatever that motion be. Aquinas thinks that time is only accidentally, contingently the number of the motion of the outermost heaven. Aquinas has biblical reasons to take seriously the hypothesis that the outermost heaven did not begin to move at the instant of creation. He notes that if this is so, there was time between Creation and its beginning to move. But he adds that this time would have been the number of whatever "first motion" then existed: "if there were another first motion, that motion would be the measure of time, because everything is measured by the first in its genus."[77] Thus Aquinas's view is in fact detachable from Aristotle's natural science. His basic thoughts are that for nature to contain our sort of time, there must be in the material world a clock-process to provide a natural first unit, and that time's passage depends on and perhaps reduces to some physical process that powers its passage.

Still, in Aquinas's eyes, de facto, Aristotle's natural clock-process also causes all else to move. For Aquinas, time is in other motions in material nature insofar as they are all ultimately caused by the first motion of which time is an accident:[78] there is quite generally a way causes exist "in" their effects. Moreover, Aquinas is willing to say that time is in things at rest[79] insofar as they are *subject* to the causation of the outermost sphere, but just happen then not to be moving. When we see that God cannot move, then, we see that a moving now is not in Him. The outermost sphere cannot cause God to move. Further, there is nothing else to "power" a "flow" of the now in God's case, unlike the angels'—and so we see that his now must stand still.

Aquinas's thought, then, is this. A thing is in time only if it can take part in the flow of a now. Only things that can change can take part in the flow. For things that can change either "power" a time-flow by their changes or get caught up in one in virtue of being able to change. God cannot change. So when we "apprehend" this, we see that God must be atemporal. But Aquinas's condition for taking part in a time-flow is debatable. Why not say instead that just given that time flows, God's life is timed by it—that its passage measures the length of his life even if he cannot change?

This brings us to Aquinas's main *SCG* argument that God is eternal:

> Only things that are moved are measured by time, for time is "the number of motion." But God is wholly without motion... so He is not measured by time. So... He does not have being after non-being, nor... non-being after being, nor can any succession be found in His being, because these cannot be understood without time. Therefore He lacks beginning and end, having His being all at once: in which consists the nature of eternity.[80]

Aquinas's "are moved" must be read with care. Aquinas accepts that things at rest but able to move count as temporal.[81] He adds that what cannot move is therefore not in time.[82] So it is a safe bet that his argument is really

1. If anything is "measured by time," it can "move."
2. God cannot "move." So
3. God is not "measured by time." So
4. God is not temporal.

That the argument moves by way of being *measured* by time suggests that it might address our lingering worry with the *ST* argument. Part of statement (2) is God's inability to move spatially, for Aquinas holds that (our sort of) time follows upon change of place, so much so that only things in some way in place are "measured" by (our sort of) time.[83] (Aquinas considers our time the number of *local* motion.[84]) Statement (2) also asserts Aquinas's DDI: for Aquinas, if God had a succession of mental operations, this would place Him in the angels' sort of time. But we may wonder why time so construed measures only *motions* (and rest periods of movable things). Aquinas takes it from Aristotle[85] (and not implausibly) that standards for measurement must share a kind with the items they measure.[86] To measure, we establish congruence between all or part of the item to be measured and a standard unit. Thus, the standard must be of a sort to be congruent with the item to be measured—it must be of its kind, so that we can lay the standard unit alongside the measured item (literally in the case of some lengths, in other cases figuratively). Thus, lengths can only be measured by lengths, not by hues or pitches. If the standard for measuring time is or necessarily inheres in a motion, Aquinas seems to think, we can only "lay that standard alongside of" another motion: other things are measured by time only insofar as they have motion, or can have it.[87]

This argument rests on sound general points—that measurement depends on standard units and that standard units must be of the right sort to measure what they measure. But things fall into not just kinds, but superkinds. So we might ask why a standard unit, which is a motion, must share with what it measures its most specific kind, *motion*. Why not instead a more general kind, like change (thus bringing angels into ordinary time), event, or state? The last, and perhaps even the next to last, might bring an immutable or even a Boethian-eternal being into time. I suggest, then, that Aquinas has more work to do if he is to produce a convincing argument for divine timelessness.

NOTES

1. *SCG* I, 89.
2. Ibid.
3. *ST* I-II q.23, *passim*.
4. *SCG* I, 89.
5. *ST* I q.20 a.1 ad 2.
6. Ibid. and *SCG* I, 89.
7. *ST* I q.63 a.2.
8. *SCG* I, 90–91.
9. *ST* I q.20 a.2.
10. *SCG* I, 91; *ST* I q.20 a.1.
11. Norman Kretzmann, *The Metaphysics of Theism* (Oxford: Oxford University Press, 1997), 231.
12. *Loci cit.*
13. *SCG* I, 90.
14. Ibid.
15. So, e.g., *QDP* 1, 1.
16. *CT* I, 9.
17. *SCG* I, 16.
18. *ST* I q.3 a.1; *CT* I, 9.
19. Thus given an independent argument for immutability, one can also argue from immutability to lack of passive potency, as Aquinas does in *SCG* I, 16.
20. *ST* I q.2 a.3.
21. E.g. *ST* I q.2 a.3.
22. *CT* I, 9.
23. See, e.g., *SCG* I, 16; *QDP* 7, 1; *ST* I q.3 a.1.
24. *ST* I q.9 a.1.
25. *ST* I q.9 a.2; q.51 a.3 ad 3.
26. See, e.g., *ST* I q.13 a.7.
27. Aristotle, *Physics* V 2, 225b11, and Aquinas, *In Phy*, V, nos. 666–67.
28. Aquinas, *loc. cit.*
29. Many medievals classed relational properties as intrinsic too, but they meant by this only that they involved real inhering "forms." They did not mean to call relations intrinsic in the sense this term bears in contemporary discussion.
30. *ST* q.25 a.4. For a full discussion of this, see my "Aquinas, Divine Simplicity and Divine Freedom," in Kevin Timpe, ed., *Metaphysics and God* (London: Routledge, forthcoming).

31. *SCG* I, 15; *CT* I, 5.
32. *ST* I q.45 a.2 ad 2 and q.46 a.3.
33. *ST* I q.104 a.3.
34. *ST* I q.10 a.1; *CT* I, 8.
35. *Super Sent*, I, d.8, q.2, a.1, *corpus*.
36. Rory Fox would explain this by saying that Aquinas and other thirteenth-century thinkers deployed concepts of "non-extensional, non-temporal types of *duratio*" (Rory Fox, *Time and Eternity in Mid-Thirteenth Century Thought* [Oxford: Oxford University Press, 2006], 37) and sometimes used "*duratio*" simply to express actual existence (ibid. 36). That they thought in terms of non-temporal duration is clear from their treatments of angelic aeviternity, but that they thought in terms of non-*extended* duration is at least in Aquinas's case rather less clear. Fox offers as his main proof-text for this in Aquinas's case *Super Sent* 19, 2, 1, which I translate from the text he provides (37 n. 36) as "duration attends everything according as it is in act; a thing is said to endure for as long as it is in act, and not when it is in potency." The "as long as" (*tamdiu... quamdiu*) undermines the claim that there is nothing extensional here.
37. *Super Sent*, I, d.8, q.2, a.1, ad 6.
38. Even such apparently anti-extensional texts as *In Phy*, VIII, l. 2, no. 990 can be read thus.
39. E.g., *ST* I q.10 a.5.
40. *ST* I q.10 a.4.
41. *ST* I q.10 a.1 ad 6.
42. *ST* I q.10 a.1 ad 5.
43. We see below that Aquinas actually has more than one kind of time in play in his thinking, but this does not affect the present conclusion.
44. *ST* I q.10 a.2 ad 4.
45. e.g., *CT* I, 7.
46. For which reasons Brian Davies holds that Aquinas's God is temporal (*The Thought of Thomas Aquinas* [Oxford: Oxford University Press, 1992], 108).
47. Obviously much would have to be said to make sense of this. For one account, see my *Time and Eternity* (Ithaca, N.Y.: Cornell University Press, 1991), 183–245.
48. *SCG* I, 66.
49. Fox, *Time and Eternity*, 328.
50. *SCG* III, 61.
51. Fox, *Time and Eternity*, 320.
52. Ibid. 324.
53. Ibid.
54. *ST* I q.63 a.7 ad 4.
55. *ST* I q.53 a.1.
56. *ST* I q.8 a.3.
57. *SCG* I, 15.
58. *CT* I, 7.
59. Ibid.
60. *CT* I, 8. This bit of the reasoning recurs in *SCG* I, 15.
61. *In Phy*, IV, l. 20, no. 609.
62. *ST* I q.13 a.7.
63. *ST* I q.10 a.2, resp. and ad 2.
64. He is also a presentist: he believes that in time, only the present exists (*ST* I q.47 a.1 ad 3; *In Phy*, IV, l. 32, no. 629).

65. So, prominently, Richard Taylor on "absolute becoming" (see, e.g., his *Metaphysics*, 4th ed. [Englewood Cliffs, N.J.: Prentice Hall, 1992], 82–83).

66. *In Phy*, IV, l. 18, no. 587.

67. For texts and discussion, see J. MacIntosh, "St. Thomas on Angelic Time and Motion," *The Thomist* 59 (1995): 547–75.

68. *ST* I q.10 a.6; *Super Sent* II, d.2, q.1, a.2.

69. So, e.g., *De ente et essentia*, c.6.

70. *Super Sent*, I, d.37, q.4, a.3.

71. *SCG* III, 61.

72. *In Phy*, IV, l. 18, nos. 585–86; *Super Sent*, I, d.37, q.4, a.3.

73. e.g., *SCG* I, 15.

74. *In Phy*, IV, l. 23, no. 634.

75. *Super Sent*, II, d.2, q.1, a.2, ad 1.

76. *QDP* 5, 5, ad 11.

77. *ST* I q.66 a.4 ad 3.

78. *In Phy*, IV, l. 17, no. 574.

79. *QDP* 5, 5, ad 10; *In Phy*, IV, l. 20, no. 608.

80. S. Thomae Aquinatis *Summa Contra Gentiles* (Turin: Marietti, 1909), 1:15, p. 15, my translation. *SCG* is a bit puzzling; along with this occur two arguments that seem to conclude that God is everlasting and two whose conclusions seem indifferent between being everlasting and being atemporal.

81. *QDP* 5, 5, ad 10. For Aristotle, see *Physics* IV, 11, 221b7–14.

82. *QDP* 5, 5, ad 10.

83. *SCG* II, 96.

84. *In Phy*, IV, l. 18, no. 587.

85. *Metaphysics*, bk. 10, 1053a24 ff.

86. *In Phy*, IV, l. 20, no. 601. This implies that items of different genus must have different measures, a point Aquinas applies in a related context in *Super Sent*, II, d. 2, q. 2, a. 1c.

87. *QDP* 5, 5, ad 10; *In Phy*, IV, l. 20, no. 602. I am unsure that Aquinas and Aristotle are really entitled to the claim that time measures the duration of rest, but I cannot pursue this here.

CHAPTER 14

GOD'S OMNIPOTENCE

BRIAN LEFTOW

THE doctrine that God is omnipotent takes its rise from scriptural texts:

> Lord... nothing is too hard for you. (Jer. 32:17)
> Our God is in heaven; He does whatever pleases Him. (Pss. 115:3, 135:6)
> the Lord... can do all things. (Job 42:2)
> nothing is impossible with God. (Luke 1:37)
> with God all things are possible. (Matt. 19:26)

These texts concern two linked topics. One is how much power God has to put behind actions: enough that nothing is too hard, enough to do whatever he pleases. Let us call this "how strong God is." The other is the range of action in which he can use this power, that is, how much God can do: "all things." Christian accounts of omnipotence prior to Aquinas focused mainly on how much power God has.[1] In contemporaries like Bonaventure, talk of range became a bit more prominent but was still only one note among many. Aquinas offers a pure range definition of omnipotence, in which the strength notion is absent. Scotus and Ockham followed Aquinas. So has almost every account of omnipotence since. The move can fairly be called one of Aquinas's most enduring contributions to philosophical theology.

Aquinas on God's Strength

As Aquinas saw it, God's power is infinite (unlimited) because

a. God needs no help from anything else to produce his effects—it is not limited by dependence on another;
b. nor does what might receive his effects limit his power, as no recipient is necessary;

c. nor does any intrinsic limitation in his being limit his effects;
d. the number of his effects is unlimited—no matter how many he has had, there can always be more; and
e. its intensity is unlimited—no matter how intense his action, it can always be more intense.[2]

Statement (a) implies a strength point, since one way something can need help is by being not strong enough to produce what it tries to. Statement (b) implies the same one, since one way something can help in producing an effect is by being what receives an agent's power. Aquinas's thought about (c) seems to be this: as I have the being of a man, I can produce only a man's effects. God has no such limitation because his being is not received into a particular nature distinct from itself, but is instead identical with his nature and himself. Statement (d) involves range, but also strength, since we measure strength by what it can effect. Statement (e) is clearly a strength notion.

The infinity of God's strength, Aquinas suggests, is the cause, not the very nature, of his omnipotence.[3] Since Aquinas's doctrine of divine simplicity rules out taking him to mean that infinite strength is one attribute and omnipotence is a second distinct attribute that supervenes on it, his point is that we can explain the range of God's power by its infinity. His *ST* explanation focuses on (c):

> To every active power corresponds a possible being as its proper object, according to the nature of that act in which the active power is founded, as the power to heat is referred to the being able to be heated as its proper object. The divine being, on which the nature of the divine power is founded, is unlimited being, not limited to some genus of being...whence whatever can be is contained under those possible beings in respect of which God is called omnipotent.[4]

Hot things, *qua* hot, can heat heatable things; by analogy unreceived, unlimited being, being-itself, can cause to be be-able things—absolutely possible things.

More than an argument by analogy can be had by way of (d). Strength could be limited in its effect by needing help, a receiver, and so on, or by lack of knowledge and other intrinsic restrictions. If none of these apply, whatever one is strong enough to bring about, one can bring about, given only suitable opportunity. How much is God strong enough to bring about? Consider the field of all that is in any way possible. No matter what of this we begin by saying God is strong enough to bring about, if there is more left of it, then per (d), God is able to bring about still more, given opportunity. The infinity of (d) thus pushes the range of God's power outward till it finally coincides with the range of the possible.

To a Definition

That this is God's range of effects hardly implies that being omnipotent consists solely of having this range of effects. But neither Scripture nor Creed define omnipotence, and so Aquinas, like all others, is free to offer what account he will. Aquinas gives his account this way:

> whatever things...do not imply a contradiction are contained among those possible things with respect to which God is called omnipotent...God is called omnipotent because He can do all absolutely possible things.[5]

For Aquinas, God is "all-powerful," but "power is said in reference to possible things"—that I can do *x* implies that *x* can be done, which implies that the result of doing *x* can be produced, and so can be. Because this is true, any doctrine of God's power could at most say that he can do anything possible, in some sense of "possible." The only way to argue that Aquinas has not pushed God's power far enough would be to say, against Aquinas, that at least some contradictions are possibly true—as some think Descartes believed. As Aquinas does not want to say this—we see why below—the only remaining question for him is how to explicate "possible." Aquinas says there are just two options: (1) that being possible = being producible by the relevant power ("whatever is subject to human power is said to be possible to man") or (2) that the possibility in question is absolute, that is, without reference to anything's power. If the relevant power is God's, the first would yield just that omnipotence is just the power to do whatever God can do, so that "God is omnipotent" would make the vacuous claim that God can do whatever God can do. If the relevant power is any other being's, the first would entail that God's being omnipotent is just his being able to do what is possible to some/all other powers. Thus, God's omnipotence would limit him to producing what created things can produce. Aquinas rejects this because God can do miracles. So he opts for absolute possibility.[6]

What is the Definition?

Aquinas's definition can easily be misread. Given the last line of the quoted text ("God is called omnipotent because He can do all absolutely possible things"), it can seem that Aquinas holds that

1. God is omnipotent $=_{\text{df.}}$ God can do all absolutely possible things.[7]

But this is not right. *SCG* II, 25 lists many things we can do but God cannot—alter his own being, move, change, fail, tire, forget, be defeated, repent, be angry, sorrow. God cannot do these because God by his nature cannot have "passive potencies," abilities to be changed. For Aquinas, God necessarily wills himself to be, be good, be happy, and so cannot produce the contrary volitions, though we can. Again, God cannot will evil.[8] So the "can do" formulation, in terms of tasks or powers, is not perspicuous for what Aquinas has in mind. Perhaps Aquinas would say that for God to do these things would be to bring about a contradiction, that a being with no passive potencies acts in ways that entail having passive potencies, or a necessarily good being does evil, or a necessarily happy being is not happy.

The first part of the quoted text ("God is omnipotent") might suggest that for Aquinas,

2. God is omnipotent $=_{\text{df.}}$ God can bring about all states of affairs not involving contradictions.

But this is not quite right either. *SCG* II, 25 adds that God cannot act contrary to the nature of being or of made being: his power is to make beings, and any power can produce only what its nature encodes—the power to heat produces heat, and the power to produce beings produces made beings. So what cannot be a made being, or a being, cannot be produced, and so God cannot produce it. Contrary to being made are making God (who is uncreated), making something equal to God (since it is better to be underived than derived), or making a thing God did not make and preserve. The "being made" addition suggests that Aquinas's definition of omnipotence is really:

3. God is omnipotent $=_{\text{df.}}$ God can bring about all states of affairs producible without a contradiction following.

His examples also suggest that Aquinas is really concerned with what we would call broad metaphysical impossibility, which he *takes* to be coextensive with that whose contradictory implies a contradiction. The twentieth century has made this claim of coextension controversial. Statement (3) does not say *by whom* these states of affairs are producible; it commits Aquinas to God's being able to produce anything anyone else can produce. This creates at least one obvious worry: I can produce my free actions, but how can God? What is necessarily so is possibly so. And it is not obvious that the necessary cannot be produced without a contradiction following. So it might seem that Aquinas's definition implies that God can produce necessary states of affairs, that is, that 2 + 2 = 4. But Aquinas does not mean this. "Possible" was sometimes used for "contingent" in Aquinas's day, and he undoubtedly means to restrict omnipotence to range over the contingent: for him, God himself is the truthmaker for all necessary truths, and so God could produce the necessary just if he could produce himself.[9] Thus, for Aquinas, the necessary falls under the nonproducible. Aquinas does not need a separate clause to rule it out.

Still, even (3) does not quite capture Aquinas's intent. Surprisingly, though he thinks God is outside time, Aquinas wants to relativize omnipotence to times, and hold that what an omnipotent being can bring about varies with what time it is. There are things God is too late to bring about, for example, that the Germans won World War II. It is absolutely possible that they have done so. But for Aquinas, it is now impossible that anyone, even God, bring it about. Aquinas thinks that what is producible without a contradiction following changes as time passes, as I will explain shortly. This does not imply that God's power changes intrinsically. Rather, at some times certain things are absolutely possible, and later they are not because their contradictories are past.[10] With this in view, Aquinas's real account of omnipotence is that

4. God is omnipotent at $t =_{df.}$ God can bring about all states of affairs producible at t without a contradiction following.

WHY NONCONTRADICTION?

Statement (4) prompts us to ask why Aquinas "limits" omnipotence to what does not entail a contradiction. Descartes, after all, is at least reputed to have seen this as not power enough for God. One argument in Aquinas takes its rise from the claim that contradictory states of affairs are literally inconceivable, even by God.[11] If God cannot conceive them, God cannot will to make them obtain: what cannot be grasped by the intellect cannot be willed, since the will is of the understood good.[12] And what God cannot will, he cannot produce, since he can do nothing save by willing it.

Let us ask, then, why Aquinas thinks contradictions cannot be conceived to be true. Aquinas writes in his *Sentence* commentary that "what is being and not-being, neither is being nor not-being."[13] He expands the thought a bit in *de Potentia*: a contradiction not only cannot have the nature of being, but cannot even have the nature of nonbeing, because "being removes non-being and non-being removes being."[14] If this is true, it is impossible to picture what would be so were a contradiction true. Picturing that P or that $\neg P$ is the case does not picture both being true at once. Superimposing a mental picture of a P-world on one of a $\neg P$-world would not give one a grip on a P and $\neg P$ world either, as Aquinas sees it. For in his eyes, a P and $\neg P$ world could not be even determinately both. We now distinguish negation and denial. Negation is a feature of the content of a proposition—the feature which makes the difference between P and $\neg P$. Denial is something we *do* with or to propositions, removing what they say from our picture of the world. Aquinas seems to run the two together. He seems to think of someone who says "not P" not as asserting that $\neg P$ but as denying that P, expressing a mental operation of removal. So in Aquinas's eyes, to conceive a contradiction, one would have not to superimpose a mental picture of a P-world on one of a $\neg P$-world, but simultaneously to add P to and subtract P from one's world picture. What it is to add and subtract makes it the case that there is no such thing as the product of such an intellectual operation. So we can see why Aquinas writes in *ST* that a contradiction does not count as a "word"—a possible product of intellectual conception.[15] As he sees it, a contradictory sentence just does not express anything definite for an intellect to grasp.

But this leads to a deeper line of thought. For if this is so, a contradictory sentence does not really express any state of affairs, even a contradictory one. To Aquinas, this is not because of some limitation of language or mind. It is because to construct a contradictory state of affairs, one would have to at once posit and remove the same state of affairs. There is no state of affairs that is the being posited *and* removed of some state of affairs. And so a contradiction cannot be true because there is no state of affairs whose being actual would make it true. A contradictory state of affairs cannot be possible because there is no state of affairs there to bear the modality of possibility. Of course, given this line of reasoning, Aquinas could as easily say that a contradictory state of affairs cannot be *im*possible: that too is a modality. But what is straightforwardly impossible is that a contradictory sentence standardly interpreted express something true, there being nothing there for it to express when so interpreted, or something the mind can grasp.[16]

On this line of thought, God cannot will that a contradiction be true, in the end, because contradictory sentences are just a sort of nonsense: they express no proposition to will to be true. But the suggestion that this somehow limits God is worth resisting. If there just is not such a thing as a contradictory state of affairs, a God who cannot bring about contradictory states of affairs may nonetheless literally be able to bring about every state of affairs there is. This will be so if every absolute impossibility involves a contradiction. Aquinas asserts this in *QDP* 1, 3: they all "imply affirmation and negation to be at once."[17] If this is right, then for Aquinas, again, there is nothing beyond God's power, to be the place it cannot go.

Aquinas's line of thought generates a subordinate metaphysical account of why God can produce only noncontradictory states of affairs. It is a fact about causation, Aquinas thinks, that every agent produces effects that are somehow like itself.[18] God's nature is his existence, and existence itself: God is *esse-ipsum*. Thus, all of God's possible effects must resemble him at least in being beings. Contradictory states of affairs cannot be beings, for reasons we have seen. So they cannot be like God in even this way. So they cannot be divine products.[19] This account depends on the fact about causation and Aquinas's distinctive understanding of negation. I do not recall a text in which Aquinas explains either further. The fact about causation *could* have its roots in God's own nature. Perhaps it is a primitive fact about God's nature that he can produce only his like. And perhaps it is another that nothing other than himself can exist unless he produces it. Perhaps this determines what other agents can be. For God can only produce his like, and while this is obviously compatible with producing things unlike him in many ways, perhaps this is one way in which his effects must be *very* like him: perhaps it is a primitive fact about God's power that he can produce only things that (like him) can produce only their like. So as there cannot be anything God has not produced, there cannot be an agent not thus constrained, and so what "began" as a fact about God's nature ends up a general theorem about the nature of causality.

Changing the Past

Whether an omnipotent being can alter the past was a standard topic in medieval theology, inherited ultimately from Augustine. Aquinas's argument on the subject is this. Suppose Socrates sat. Then for God to bring it about that he did not sit would entail that Socrates sat and did not sit—a contradiction. So for God to alter the past would entail his bringing about a contradiction.[20] Now this argument can seem to beg the question. Granted, if God does not remove Socrates' sitting from the past, we get a contradiction. But why couldn't God remove this? That is, why could he not make it the case simply that Socrates never sat—that it has never been the case that Socrates did anything other than not sit? Aquinas does not say in *ST*.

In *SCG* II, 25, Aquinas may say why he thinks God cannot just remove the past. He states that the past, once past, is necessary, that is, that it is no longer possible that it have been other than it is. If the necessity involved is strong enough, it then follows that what can be produced without a contradiction following changes as more past is "laid down." But which modality "necessary" imports is unclear. If Aquinas is claiming only that the past has "necessity of inevitability"—that is, is something one cannot now do anything about—this would be equivalent to the claim that the past is fixed. But the past is fixed just if God cannot alter it, and so to invoke this here would beg the question. Suppose, on the other hand, that Aquinas's claim is that the past, once past, is *absolutely* necessary per accidens (i.e., contingently). One question that would then arise is whether Aquinas thinks this is a consequence of his contradiction argument. If he does, he cannot appeal to this necessity to explain God's inability to just remove the past. But without some such support, the claim is too strong to be plausible: the most we might grant is that the past is fixed. For it just does seem possible, and still possible today, that I have had eggs instead of cereal for breakfast yesterday. Further, if the past is only contingently necessary, why would not a God able to effect all that is contingent retain his power to have something else have been necessary?

Omnipotence and Impeccability

As we have seen, Aquinas thinks that God cannot do evil. It is not immediately clear that someone could be both impeccable and omnipotent. If God can bring about only morally permissible states of affairs, then it seems that there could be a being able to effect every permissible state of affairs that God can bring about, plus the evil ones he cannot. But nothing can be more powerful than someone omnipotent; if such a being is possible, it is impossible to be both omnipotent and impeccable.

Aquinas makes just two moves on this problem. One claims that "God can do evil if he will" is a true conditional whose antecedent and consequent are impossible.[21] This seems to contain a slip: surely what Aquinas means is that if God wills to do evil, he does evil, not that if God wills to do it, he acquires the power to do it. With this revision, Aquinas's claim is overall that if God willed to do evil, he would succeed—that is, he has the power to—but impossible that he will to do evil, so impossible that he do evil. The intent is clearly to suggest that the conditional is true due to God's underlying possession of power enough, rather as it is true of a glass never actually scratched that were a diamond to scratch across it, it would leave a mark. But Aquinas's move does not clearly entail that God in any real sense actually has the power to do evil. It might be equally true that if a rock willed to do evil (and it were not impeded), it would do it; we do not infer that the rock is able to do evil.

Aquinas's other move runs this way: to sin is to fall short of a perfect action. So to be able to sin is to be able to fall short. So God cannot sin precisely because he is omnipotent.[22] This argument is hard to evaluate because what "perfect" means is not explained. If it expresses *moral* perfection, the argument begs the question, or at any rate leaves us none the wiser as to why omnipotence generates the supposed inability. What other sense might be meant is not obvious. Perhaps the most favorable gloss is this: to fall short of a *complete* action is to fail to attain the end for which one acts. Rational agents all act ultimately to be happy (a standard Aristotelian thesis). Every evil action falls short of attaining that, given the universe we live in (with Hell), or suitably strong natural-law assumptions and claims about rational nature. But God cannot fail to attain the end for which he acts: God cannot fail to be happy, or to possess himself (which makes him happy). He cannot because he is perfectly knowledgeable (and so knows what will make him happy), perfectly rational (and so wills it), and omnipotent (and so must obtain what he wills). So God's omnipotence is *part* of the reason he cannot sin. This does not entail that Aquinas is restricting the range of omnipotence to less than all that is possible, for as we have seen, Aquinas thinks that God's doing evil is metaphysically impossible.[23] However, if this is Aquinas's intent, it does seem a rather strained route to the goal. The real reason God cannot sin is surely simply that he possesses himself, hence could not have a motivation to do so and is powerful and knowledgeable enough to avoid less-than-fully voluntary sin. Omnipotence does not really seem involved in the explanation.

NOTES

1. For a survey, see my "Omnipotence," in Thomas Flint and Michael Rea, eds., *The Oxford Handbook of Philosophical Theology* (Oxford: Oxford University Press, forthcoming).
2. *QDP* 1, 2.
3. *QDP* 1, 7.
4. *ST* I q.25 a.3, 174a21–34.
5. *ST* I q.25 a.3, 174a12–20, 42–45. Cf. *QDP* 1, 7.
6. *ST* I q.25 a.3.
7. Among others, Daniel Hill so reads him (Daniel Hill, *Divinity and Maximal Greatness* [London: Routledge, 2005], 131).
8. *SCG* I, 95.
9. For an account of this, see my "Aquinas on God and Modal Truth," *Modern Schoolman* 82:3 (2005): 171–200.

10. *ST* I q.25 a.4 ad 2. Geach suggests that the account of q.25 a.3 is inconsistent with allowing that God's power varies over time (Peter Geach, *Providence and Evil* [Cambridge: Cambridge University Press, 1977], 19). In Aquinas's eyes, at least, it is not, because what is producible changes with time.

11. *QDP* 1, 3, ad 1 opp.; *ST* I q.25 a.3; *Quodl* V, q.2, a.3.

12. *SCG* I, 84.

13. *Super Sent* I, d.42, q.2, a.2, p. 991.

14. *QDP* 1, 3, p. 9. So also *SCG* II, 25. Yet he also says in *SCG* II, 22 that things which imply a contradiction include nonbeing in their *ratio*. Perhaps Aquinas has one account of things that *are* contradictions and another of things that are not themselves self-contradictory but imply contradictions.

15. *ST* I q.25 a.3.

16. The qualification "standardly interpreted" allows for this sort of silly counterexample: if I decided to use the sentence "*P* and not *P*" to express the claim that I am a philosopher, it would express something true.

17. *QDP* 1, 3, p. 9.

18. Ibid.

19. *QDP* 1, 3; *SCG* I, 84.

20. *QDP* 1, 3, ad 9; *ST* I q.25 a.4.

21. *QDP* 1, 6, ad 1 and *ST* I q.25 a.3 ad 2.

22. *ST* I q.25 a.3 ad 2.

23. *Contra* Eric Funkhouser, "On Privileging God's Moral Goodness," *Faith and Philosophy* 23 (2006): 412.

PART IV

ETHICS AND ACTION THEORY

CHAPTER 15

HUMAN FREEDOM AND AGENCY

THOMAS WILLIAMS

The End of Human Action

Aquinas opens the second part of the *ST* by arguing, in a series of careful steps, that there is one and only one ultimate end for all human actions. The placement of this argument is no accident, since the notion of an end is of fundamental importance not only in Aquinas's theory of human action but in his accounts of practical reasoning, law, and the virtues. Yet the interpretation of Aquinas's argument in *ST* I-II q.1, is a matter of considerable controversy. I shall first follow the argument through its successive steps and then briefly consider three possible ways of understanding Aquinas's claim that all human actions have exactly one ultimate end.

Aquinas first argues that every human action is for the sake of some end. That is, every human action is purposive in some way; it is done for the sake of attaining some goal or realizing some desired state of affairs. To the obvious objection that we do things all the time without any purpose at all, Aquinas replies by distinguishing between a human action (*actus humanus*) and an action of a human being (*actio hominis*). Human actions, properly so called, are those that proceed from human beings in virtue of their distinguishing power, which is to be in control of their own actions (*dominus suorum actuum*) through reason and will. Anything else that a human being does can be called the action of a human being, but not (in the proper sense) a human action. Human actions, then, are those that are willed on the basis of rational deliberation. And since "the object of the will is an end and a good, it follows that all human actions are for the sake of an end."[1]

What, precisely, is meant by the "end" of a human action? Aquinas tells us in a.2 that an end is something cognized as good. It must be something *cognized* because otherwise we just have "natural appetite," the sort of built-in directedness by which heavy objects are moved toward the center of the earth. And an end must be cognized *as good* because the will is moved only by what is good. As Eleonore Stump emphasizes, the will is not a neutral steering wheel; it is "an inclination for what is good, where the phrase 'what is good' is used attributively and not referentially."[2] And because only beings with the capacity for abstract thought can cognize what is good *qua* good (as opposed to merely cognizing something that is in fact good), only they can have will, the appetite that follows upon intellectual cognition of something as good. "The object of the will," Aquinas says, "is the end and good universally." But the end of any particular action will not be good-in-general, but some particular thing cognized as good. This end is what gives each particular action its species (a.3), what makes the action the kind of action it is.

In a.4 Aquinas argues further that every human action has an ultimate end: that is, an end that, with respect to that particular action, is not itself for the sake of some further end. It is impossible for there to be an infinite series of ends, each of which moves the appetite only instrumentally, as a means to some more ultimate end. There has to be some mover that moves the appetite on its own account. This non-instrumental mover of the appetite is the ultimate end for the sake of which a particular action is performed.

And it is not merely that every action must have at least one ultimate end. Aquinas argues further that, at any given time, a human being can have only one such ultimate end. The most persuasive of his three arguments for this claim runs as follows:

> Since every thing desires (*appetat*) its own perfection, what someone desires as an ultimate end is what he desires *qua* perfecting and completing him.... For that reason, an ultimate end must so fulfill a person's whole desire that nothing more is left for him to desire; and that cannot be so if something additional is required for him to be perfect. And that is why desire cannot aim at two [distinct] things as if each were its perfect good.[3]

This single ultimate end can be an aggregate of goods that the agent regards as collectively constituting his perfection; the arguments of a.5 do not commit Aquinas to understanding the ultimate end as a unitary good.

This ultimate end, whether unitary or aggregate, must be (Aquinas argues) the ultimate explanation for all of a given person's actions. For whatever the agent desires, she desires *sub ratione boni*: under the notion or aspect of the good. Now if something is not desired as the complete, all-inclusive good (that is, the ultimate good), it must be desired as aiming at or leading to the complete, all-inclusive good. The "as" does not mean that an agent will always be thinking of the ultimate end in every action she performs, any more than someone on a journey must be consciously thinking about her destination in order to be truly said to be aiming at that destination. But the desire for the ultimate end is what explains every other desire.

The ultimate end is the first mover of desire, and secondary movers—that is, any desirable objects other than the ultimate end—move desire only in virtue of their relation to the ultimate end, whether the agent is thinking explicitly about that relation or not. As Aquinas puts it, "the power of the first intention, which is of the ultimate end, remains in any desire of any object whatever, even if one is not actually thinking of the ultimate end."[4]

Finally, Aquinas argues that this ultimate explanation for all actions is the same for every human being. All human beings have the same ultimate end, for all human beings desire their own perfection, though different people will have different ideas about what perfection consists in. So Aquinas says that all human beings have the same ultimate end as far as the intelligible formula for the ultimate end goes (*secundum rationem ultimi finis*), but not in terms of the object that people think is aptly described by that formula (*secundum id in quo finis ultimi ratio invenitur*).

To summarize: Aquinas argues in the first question of *ST* I-II that (a) all human actions are performed for the sake of an end; (b) any given human action has one and only one ultimate end; (c) this one ultimate end is the same for all of a given human being's actions; and indeed (d) all human beings have the same ultimate end. Interpreters of Aquinas have disagreed about how to construe each of these claims, but the most widely divergent readings concern (b) and (c). The most obvious way of taking (b) and (c) is as descriptive claims about the psychology of human actions. But when taken as descriptive claims, (b) and (c) strike many interpreters as flatly indefensible. We may take Jean Porter's objection as representative:

> Not many of us have the self-possession, or the fanaticism, to shape our whole lives around devotion to some one object, cause, or ideal. And even those few of us who do cannot be said literally to direct all our actions toward one end. Even the most dedicated individuals indulge in an ice-cream cone or a joke once in a while.... Let me say at once that if Aquinas does indeed claim that each person *always* directs *all* her actions and activities toward some one goal or idea, then I do not see how that claim could be defended.[5]

In light of such reservations about (b) and (c) taken as descriptive claims, some interpreters argue that what Aquinas sets forth in the opening question of I-II is normative rather than descriptive: his claims "state criteria of fully rational action, and the arguments for them draw attention to what is required by the concept of rational action,"[6] as Scott MacDonald puts it. On this interpretation Aquinas is not denying that human beings sometimes act without having a single ultimate end in view, but instead saying that such actions are not fully rational and therefore not fully human. As Porter, another defender of the normative reading, says, this analysis "leaves room to admit that some behaviors which do not meet this ideal can still be said to be rational, and hence truly human actions, albeit in a derivative sense."[7]

A third interpretation is possible, according to which Aquinas's claims in the opening question of I-II are neither descriptive nor normative, but explanatory. That is, Aquinas is analyzing the metaphysical preconditions for human action. His arguments for a single ultimate end are akin to his arguments for a single unmoved mover or uncaused cause; they are at bottom neither psychological descriptions nor conceptual analysis, but *quia* arguments intended to trace the phenomena of human action to their ultimate explanation in a good that awakens desire, and thereby initiates action, in its own right and not in the power of any other good. The natural desire for perfection explains why we desire anything at all. Since every human being has this desire, every human action is ultimately to be explained with reference to one and the same ultimate end—though, owing to the variabilities of human reason, different people will seek their fulfillment in different objects or states.

The Structure of Human Action

A human action, as we have seen, is one over which the agent has control in virtue of possessing reason and will. Since the object of will is an end—something cognized as good—every human action will begin with cognition: an intellectual apprehension of some object or state of affairs as good in the agent's circumstances. (The cognition of the circumstances is also the work of the intellect, which means that even before there is any act of will, there are two ways in which human agents can go astray: by taking something to be good that is not in fact good, and by misconstruing their circumstances.) As a consequence of this intellectual apprehension, there is an act of will called simply *voluntas* (will) in which the agent desires the end as such.[8] In order for action to result, however, there must be a further act of the will in which one desires the end not merely as a good in itself but as a good that can be attained by means of action. This act, called *intentio*, presupposes an intellectual apprehension of the end as attainable. It also sets in motion the work of the intellect in *consilium* or deliberation. *Consilium* is an investigation of the means by which the intended end may be attained or realized. As the intellect turns up various means, the will can endorse them as desirable, or at least tolerable, means to the desired end; this endorsement is called *consensus* or consent. *Consilium* terminates with an act of *iudicium*, the intellect's judgment that one of the means that have received the will's consent is the best, all things considered. The will then selects the means that the intellect has judged best; this act of will is called *electio*, commonly (if somewhat misleadingly) translated "choice."[9] After *electio*, the intellect orders that the elected means be carried out in action, and the will carries out the intellect's command (*imperium*) by making use (*usus*) of the external bodily powers in the way that the intellect has prescribed, until the intellect apprehends that the end has been attained; only then is the will at rest in the enjoyment (*fruitio*) of that end.[10]

The previous paragraph lays out the basic structure of a fully articulated and complete human action.[11] In practice, as Aquinas recognizes, human actions may not involve all of these steps. For example, if *consilium* turns up only one acceptable means, *consensus* will collapse into *electio*.[12] If the means to the desired end is perfectly obvious, there will be no need for *consilium* to begin with, and the agent can proceed directly from *intentio* to *iudicium*.[13] And the intellect's failure to stick to its command—a manifestation of what Aquinas calls inconstancy—can interrupt *usus* before it comes to completion in the external act by which the agent means to accomplish her end, thereby forestalling *fruitio*.[14] Moreover, the individual acts of will and intellect that go into making up a complete human action need not be separated by any perceptible time. Nor should we think that all these acts will be apparent to the agent's consciousness: as Alan Donagan observes, "the components of simple human acts are ascertained, not by introspecting what happens when we perform them, but by examining cases in which an act is begun but not completed."[15]

Intellectualism and Voluntarism

Note that in Aquinas's account of the structure of human acts, every act of will is preceded by an act of intellect. This is exactly what we would expect, given Aquinas's understanding of will as intellectual appetite. To recur to Eleonore Stump's point, the will is not, on Aquinas's view, a neutral steering wheel; it is "an inclination for what is good, where the phrase 'what is good' is used attributively and not referentially."[16] Hence, the content of any act of will—*what* is willed—has to depend on some intellectual apprehension of something as good in some way and under some description. Aquinas expresses this claim by saying that the intellect is the *formal* cause of the will's acts.

So stated, Aquinas's view appears straightforwardly intellectualist: the ultimate explanation for every human act rests in the intellect, for the will has no independent capacity to shape the exercise of human agency. Yet Aquinas also speaks of ways in which the will controls the intellect: by directing it to consider alternatives, to stop deliberating, to attend to different features of a possible object of will. In doing these things, the will moves the intellect as an *efficient* cause. Many interpreters of Aquinas have appealed to the will's efficient-causal control over the intellect as evidence that Aquinas is not a thoroughgoing intellectualist after all: the ultimate explanation for at least some human acts, they argue, will rest in the will's direction of the intellect in shaping the exercise of human agency.[17]

The fundamental dispute between intellectualist and voluntarist interpretations of Aquinas's action theory is whether the will's efficient-causal control over the will must always be preceded by an act of intellect in which the agent judges that exercising such efficient-causal control is all-things-considered best in the circumstances. For example, Aquinas notes that the will can direct the intellect to consider a proposed course of action under different descriptions. I may be leaning toward spending the day at the beach because it would be pleasant and relaxing, but my will can command my intellect to think of it instead as a shameful retreat from pressing obligations. Must such an act of will itself be preceded by an intellectual judgment that the good thing to do, all things considered, is to attend to the ways in which a day at the beach is not good? Or can the will of its own power direct the intellect to reconsider?

Space does not permit a careful examination of all the relevant texts, so I will simply express my own judgment that Aquinas is an intellectualist. As Jeff Hause explains,

> On Aquinas's view, the will cannot, by any innate capacity, direct the intellect's attention, keep the intellect from issuing judgments about what one ought to do, or keep itself from willing what the intellect has determined one ought to will. Nor can it select one from among a variety of alternatives unless the intellect has first settled on that one as the alternative to be pursued. Which, if any, of a set of objects the will wills, and whether it wills anything at all, depends not on any voluntaristic capacity of the will, but on how the intellect judges the object in question.[18]

In the process that leads to action, the intellect is not in the business of making judgments of the form "Here's an ice-cream cone: take it or leave it—or look around for something else" and then leaving it up to the will to make the choice. The intellect offers a verdict: a *iudicium* or *sententia*. And the will, being nothing more than the appetitive arm of the intellectual soul, elects in accordance with the intellect's judgment. As in a one-party totalitarian state, by the time there's an election, there's only one name on the ballot.

Necessitation, Causation, and Freedom

One reason that many scholars have resisted interpreting Aquinas's account as intellectualist is that they believe an intellectualist account must be deterministic.[19] And since (the argument continues) Aquinas holds that causal determinism is incompatible with freedom and moral responsibility, he must reject intellectualism. This argument fails for at least two reasons. First, an intellectualist account need not be deterministic; if the intellect itself operates indeterministically, Aquinas's theory as a whole will be indeterministic even if it is also intellectualist.[20] Second, and more important, it is not at all clear that Aquinas affirms the incompatibility of freedom and causal determinism. There is, to be sure, a trivial sense in which it is obvious that Aquinas never affirms the incompatibility of freedom and determinism: for determinism in its contemporary acceptation is "the thesis that only one continuation of the state of things at a given moment is consistent with the laws of nature,"[21] and Aquinas does not speak in terms of laws of nature. Aquinas speaks instead of the active and passive causal powers of created things. This point is certainly worth making, because interpreters have been much too quick to speak of determinism as though Aquinas's metaphysics of causation and necessitation can be mapped unproblematically on our own. But the claim that Aquinas never affirms the incompatibility of freedom and determinism is not terribly interesting if we mean it only in this trivial sense, so from here on out I shall use "determinism" as the name of an analogous thesis: that only one continuation of the state of things at a given moment is consistent with the ordinary, non-miraculous working of the active and passive causal powers of created things.

Equipped with a more suitable understanding of determinism, we can now ask what Aquinas has to say about the compatibility or incompatibility of freedom and determinism. And the answer, surprisingly, is nothing. What Aquinas addresses instead is the compatibility or incompatibility of freedom and *necessitation*. Aquinas identifies several distinct senses in which an act might be described as necessary. Not all of them are inconsistent with freedom, and none of them (or so I shall argue) is equivalent or even roughly analogous to determinism. Consider first Aquinas's arguments in *QDM* 6, where the question is whether human beings have free choice (*libera electio*) of their acts or instead choose from necessity. Aquinas says that human beings are *never* necessitated with respect to exercise (that is, with respect to whether we will or do not will), and that we are necessitated with respect to specification (that is, with respect to willing this or that particular object) only in the case of happiness itself. But everything Aquinas says in reaching these conclusions is perfectly compatible with determinism. For example, he argues that the will is not necessitated with respect to specification by anything other than happiness on the grounds that one can think of any such thing either under a description under which it is suitable or under a description under which it is not. This can come about, he says, (1) because one description outweighs the other, (2) because some interior or exterior prompting causes one to attend to the object under one description rather than under the other, or (3) because one is in a state of mind that makes the object salient under one description rather than another. If the will's not being necessitated with respect to specification is explained entirely in terms of these three possibilities, as the text strongly suggests, then non-necessitation is perfectly compatible with determinism. What Aquinas denies is that the intellect, the will, and their objects are such that *in the abstract* only one choice is possible; he does not deny, and indeed seems to lack the metaphysical resources necessary to deny, the nature of the intellect and the will and their objects are such that *in every particular, concrete instance* only one choice is possible.[22]

Nor does Aquinas's denial that the will can be subject to necessity of coercion have any tendency to show that Aquinas rejects the compatibility of freedom and determinism, despite the fact that many interpreters appeal to that denial to establish precisely that conclusion. Aquinas argues in *QDV* 22, a.5 and *ST* I q.82 a.1 that the will cannot be subject to necessity of coercion (*necessitas coactionis*), the kind of necessity that would obtain if the will were compelled by some external agent in such a way that it could not act otherwise. But (contrary to what some interpreters suggest) Aquinas does not argue in these passages that necessity of coercion is incompatible with freedom. Instead, he argues that it is conceptually impossible for the will to be subject to necessity of coercion, because something that is coerced is moved in a way that is entirely against its natural inclination; since the will is itself an inclination, it is impossible for it to will something unless there is in the will some inclination to that very thing. Moreover, it is quite clear that necessity of coercion is not coextensive with determinism. Although every instance of necessity of coercion is a case in which determinism holds true, the converse does not hold: there can be cases of determinism in which there is no necessity of coercion. Necessity of coercion obtains only when a thing is moved in a way that is contrary to its natural inclination. If I open my hands to allow the baseball I am holding to fall toward the earth, the ball falls in accordance with its natural inclination, not by necessity of coercion; yet clearly its downward path is also in accordance with determinism. So Aquinas's denial that the will can be subject to necessity of coercion is not equivalent to, and does not entail, the claim that freedom is incompatible with determinism.

Now it might be objected here that I have stolen a base against libertarian readings of Aquinas (that is, readings according to which Aquinas affirms both that human beings sometimes act freely and that freedom is incompatible with determinism). By defining determinism in the way I have done, I have, it appears, committed libertarians to accepting the Principle of Alternative Possibilities (PAP): *S* does *A* freely at *t* only if it is possible that *S* not do *A* at *t*. Some libertarians deny PAP, and one might argue that Aquinas is just that sort of libertarian.[23] But a PAP-denying libertarian who might wish to enlist Aquinas as an ally would first have to show that Aquinas denies the compatibility of freedom and determinism, or something sufficiently like determinism, in order to count as a libertarian at all. And since (as I have argued) the usual arguments for Aquinas's incompatibilism fail, there is no good reason to think that Aquinas is a libertarian of any kind. Moreover, the PAP-denying libertarian will typically say that on Aquinas's view, it is sufficient for an act's being free that the act proceeds from the agent's own intellect and will, whether the agent has alternative possibilities or not. If that is the case, however, it is perfectly possible for there to be free acts of will even if, given the nature of the will, the intellect, and the external world, no intellectual agent *ever* has alternative possibilities. I cannot myself see how such a view can be accounted a version of libertarianism, but I will not quibble over words.

The passages I have considered, and others like them, do not of course show that Aquinas affirms that freedom and determinism are compatible, just that he fails to give us any reason to think they are incompatible. In the present state of scholarship, it is difficult to say anything more definitive on this subject; Aquinas's modal theory and his theory of causation remain woefully understudied.

One might worry that even if Aquinas can secure for human acts a sufficient independence from other creaturely causes for them to count as free in some meaningful sense, he cannot defend their independence from God as First Cause. For Aquinas holds a strong doctrine of the pervasiveness of God's causal activity. It is not merely that God providentially superintends the whole of creation, but that God is immediately active in every creaturely action, whether the creature acts by nature or by will.[24] Since no creature can thwart God's activity—on the contrary, creatures can act only "in the power of" the First Cause—and God's will cannot be inefficacious, it would seem that God causally necessitates every human action, leaving no room for human freedom.

Aquinas, however, insists that no such conclusion follows. In fact, the supremacy of God's causal activity is precisely what guarantees genuine contingency:

> for those effects that he willed to be necessary, he provided necessary causes; and for those effects that he willed to be contingent, he ordained causes that act contingently, which is to say, causes that can fall short [of producing an effect]. It is in accordance with this characteristic of their causes that effects are called either necessary or contingent, even though they are all dependent on the divine will as their first cause.... God's will cannot fail, but nevertheless not all its effects are necessary; some are contingent.[25]

God's activity as first cause does not override the characteristic manner of acting that belongs to the natures he created. He moves natural causes in such a way that their effects are natural, and he moves voluntary causes in such a way that their effects are voluntary: "He acts in each thing in accordance with its distinctive character."[26]

NOTES

1. *ST* I-II q.1 a.1. All translations are my own.
2. Eleonore Stump, *Aquinas* (London and New York: Routledge, 2003), 278.
3. *ST* I-II q.1 a.5. One might well think that the argument as a whole is question-begging, since the claim that "what one desires as an ultimate end is what he desires *qua* perfecting and completing him" follows from the claim that "every thing desires its own perfection" only if we interpret the latter as meaning something like "every thing desires *only* its own perfection"—but on that interpretation, the argument already presupposes the very unity of desire that it purports to establish. For further analysis of Aquinas's arguments in the opening questions of *ST* I-II, see Peter F. Ryan, "Must the Acting Person Have a Single Ultimate End?" *Gregorianum* 82 (2001): 325–56.
4. *ST* I-II q.1 a.6 ad 3.
5. Jean Porter, *The Recovery of Virtue: The Relevance of Aquinas for Christian Ethics* (Louisville: Westminster/John Knox Press, 1990), 72–73.
6. Scott MacDonald, "Ultimate Ends in Practical Reasoning: Aquinas's Aristotelian Moral Psychology and Anscombe's Fallacy," *Philosophical Review* 100 (1991): 31–66, at 40. Peter F. Ryan, "A Single Ultimate End Only for 'Fully Rational' Agents? A Critique of Scott MacDonald's Interpretation of Aquinas," *American Catholic Philosophical Quarterly* 75 (2001): 433–38, argues that Aquinas is neither making empirical claims nor analyzing the concept of fully rational action, but "trying to articulate a necessary condition for human action as such, a condition that he thinks follows from just what a human act is" (438). Ryan emphasizes, however, that Aquinas's view is empirically falsified if there are any cases of human action that do not meet the necessary condition, and he argues in "Must the Acting Person Have a Single Ultimate End?" that there are such cases.
7. Porter, *Recovery of Virtue*, 73.

8. Aquinas denies that *voluntas* is in general a *necessary* consequence of the intellectual apprehension of something as an end. I take up the issue of necessity and contingency in human action in the last section.

9. For an incisive explanation of the problems with translating *electio* as "choice," see Stump, *Aquinas*, 288–89.

10. This is what Aquinas calls "perfect *fruitio*," as opposed to the "imperfect *fruitio*" that one can have regarding an end that is "possessed only in intention." See *ST* I-II q.11 a.4.

11. Or rather, it sets out one possible, and fairly mainstream, reading of the Treatise on Human Acts. For a sampling of the variety of interpretations in recent scholarship, see Thomas Gilby, trans. and ed., *Summa theologiae*, vol. 17 (Cambridge: Blackfriars, 1970), Appendix 1; Alan Donagan, "Thomas Aquinas on Human Action," in Norman Kretzmann, Anthony Kenny, and Jan Pinborg, eds., *The Cambridge History of Later Medieval Philosophy* (Cambridge: Cambridge University Press, 1982), 642–54; Ralph McInerny, *Aquinas on Human Action: A Theory of Practice* (Washington, D.C.: The Catholic University of America Press, 1992), ch. 3; Daniel Westberg, *Right Practical Reason: Aristotle, Action, and Prudence in Aquinas* (Oxford: Clarendon Press, 1994), Part III; Stephen L. Brock, *Action and Conduct: Thomas Aquinas and the Theory of Action* (Edinburgh: T & T Clark, 1998); Stump, *Aquinas*, 287–94.

12. *ST* I-II q.15 a.3 ad 3.

13. *ST* I-II q.14 a.4, especially ad 1.

14. *ST* II-II q.156 a.1.

15. Donagan, "Thomas Aquinas on Human Action," 654.

16. Stump, *Aquinas*, 278.

17. For interpretations that find some degree of voluntarism in Aquinas, see, e.g., David Gallagher, "Free Choice and Free Judgment in Thomas Aquinas," *Archiv für Geschichte der Philosophie* 76 (1994): 247–77; Eleonore Stump and Norman Kretzmann, "Absolute Simplicity," *Faith and Philosophy* 2 (1985): 353–82; John Finnis, "Object and Intention in Moral Judgments according to Aquinas," *The Thomist* 55 (1991): 1–27; Bonnie Kent, *Virtues of the Will: The Transformation of Ethics in the Late Thirteenth Century* (Washington, D.C.: The Catholic University of America Press, 1995).

18. Jeffrey Hause, "Thomas Aquinas and the Voluntarists," *Medieval Philosophy and Theology* 6 (1997): 167–82, at 168. See also Scott MacDonald, "Aquinas's Libertarian Account of Free Choice," *Revue Internationale de Philosophie* 2 (1998): 309–28.

19. See Gallagher, "Free Choice and Free Judgment in Thomas Aquinas," for an argument of this kind, and Hause, "Thomas Aquinas and the Voluntarists," for a rebuttal.

20. Scott MacDonald, "Aquinas's Libertarian Account of Free Choice," *Revue Internationale de Philosophie* 2 (1998): 309–28 defends this sort of reading of Aquinas.

21. Peter van Inwagen, *Metaphysics*, 2d ed. (Boulder, Colo.: Westview Press, 2002), 203.

22. Note that in *QDM* 6, ad 10, Aquinas says that the will's not being necessitated with respect to specification by any incomplete good is just like the intellect's not being necessitated with respect to specification by any contingent truth. No one takes it that Aquinas is denying determinism with respect to any particular intellectual act in which someone affirms a contingent truth. Why then should any take it that Aquinas is denying determinism with respect to any particular volitional act in which someone elects a partial good?

23. Eleonore Stump, "Aquinas's Account of Freedom: Intellect and Will," *The Monist* 80 (1997): 591–94 and *Aquinas*, 299–306, argues for this understanding of Aquinas's views.

24. *QDP*, q.3, a.7. Cf. *SCG* 3, c.66–67, 70.

25. *In Peri herm.* 1, lec. 14.

26. *ST* I q.83 a.1 ad 3.

CHAPTER 16

EMOTIONS

PETER KING

AQUINAS's theory of the emotions (*passiones animae*) is cognitivist, somatic, and taxonomical: cognitivist because he holds that cognition is essential to emotion; somatic because he holds that their physiological manifestations are partially constitutive of emotions; taxonomical because he holds that emotions fall into distinct natural kinds that are hierarchically ordered. Aquinas supports these claims with a wealth of argument, presented in his three extended treatments of emotion: *Super Sent* 3 d.15 q.2, d.26 q.1 and d.27 q.1, dating from ca. 1252–56; *QDV* q.25–26, dating from ca. 1256–59, and his masterly *ST* I-II q.22–48 (the "treatise on the emotions"), dating from 1271.[1] His presentation and defense proved so effective that later medieval thinkers took Aquinas's theory as their starting point, whether they agreed with it or not, and it remained a contender in affective psychology up to the end of scholasticism.

Aquinas identifies eleven essentially distinct types of emotion, which he sorts into two kinds, and which for the most part occur in conjugate pairs of contraries: the six concupiscible emotions of love and hate, desire and aversion, delight and distress; the five irascible emotions of hope and despair, confidence and fear, and anger (which has no contrary).[2] The concupiscible emotions are directed at objects insofar as they appear to be good or evil, whereas the irascible emotions are directed at objects insofar as they present something good or evil that might be hard to achieve or to avoid. But these are not perspicuous or evident claims; we need to begin with more fundamental issues about emotion in general to appreciate Aquinas's theory.

I will begin with Aquinas's account of the nature of emotion as a psychological phenomenon, as a feature of what he calls "sensitive appetite," after which I will turn to how emotion is related to other psychological faculties, namely cognition and volition. After situating the emotions in Aquinas's psychological system, I will then look at his analysis of their internal structure, which provides a taxonomy of emotional experience. I will conclude with some brief reflections on Aquinas's theory vis-à-vis contemporary theories of emotion.

The Nature of Emotion

Emotion, according to Aquinas, is an objectual nonvolitional affective psychological state. Or, in medieval terms, emotion is an actualization of the sensitive appetite, which is a semiautonomous faculty of the soul. To see what these definitions mean and why they are equivalent, more than a little unpacking is needed.

Psychology, in the Aristotelian tradition, is a subordinate branch of natural philosophy. It studies the activity of living beings *qua* living, and on this score identifies three kinds of clustered activities that living beings exemplify, stemming from three distinct principles, that is, from three types of soul: (a) nutrition, growth, and reproduction, typical of plants and trees, whose principle is the vegetative soul; (b) self-movement and perception of the world, typical of animals, whose principle is the sensitive soul; (c) thought and reasoning, typical of human beings, whose principle is the intellective soul. These kinds of soul are arranged in a hierarchy such that the latter include the former: anything capable of (b) is capable of (a), anything capable of (c) is capable of (b) and (a). Aquinas famously held that these clusters of principles were not really distinct when combined in the same subject—his controversial stand on the unicity, as opposed to the plurality, of substantial form—but this metaphysical disagreement can be set aside in psychology, since all parties to the dispute agree that human beings, for instance, have intellective and sensitive capacities, whether they stem from a single unique principle or a pair of related principles; horses and cats do not have the same cognitive powers as humans, however these powers be related when found together. One question to ask, then, is whether the emotions are features of the sensitive soul (and so common to all animals) or of the intellective soul (and so particular to human beings).

Yet there is another question that is equally pressing. The cluster of powers associated with the sensitive and the intellective souls are not limited to cognition. Animals and human beings do not merely acquire and process information about the world; they engage the world directly, being drawn to some things and driven away by others. Therefore, side-by-side with cognitive powers to acquire and assimilate information, there are appetitive powers to move the subject. Another question to ask, then, is whether the emotions are cognitive (and so dealing with information about things) or appetitive (and so dealing with the things themselves).

Aquinas starts his answer to both questions by considering the nature of emotion.[3] For an emotion is a *passio animae*, literally something that the soul "undergoes" or "experiences"—a capacity for being in a given psychological state—rather than something the soul "does" (the way it reasons, for instance). In medieval philosophical jargon, an emotion is a potency whose principle of actualization is external to its subject; in contemporary terms, an emotion is a *reaction*.

First, if an emotion is a reaction, it is therefore passive as regards whatever brings it about, that is, whatever prompts the reaction. Yet the passivity of an emotion in itself does not entail that the subject is thereby passive with respect to that emotion. Sight is likewise a passive potency—we can see only what is there to be seen—but we can exercise a measure of control over what we see nonetheless: we may close our eyes, avert our gaze, turn our head, and so on. So too we have some degree of control over the emotions. (More will be said about this point below.) Moreover, an emotion is a reaction that may well have causal efficacy: fear of the wolf moves the sheep to flee, a perceived insult causes the proud man to lash out in anger, the hope of winning motivates the runner to put on a final burst of speed at the end of the race. Reactions can cause or motivate subjects to act; their doing so depends on how they are related to other elements in the subject's psychology. That is, being in a given state can be the cause of further events, regardless of how the subject comes to be in that state. Hence, the intrinsic passivity of emotion is of no real importance.

Second, while emotions may be reactions, they are more fundamentally types of *motion*.[4] The subject of an emotion is *moved* by it—drawn toward the object, as in the case of desire; or driven from it, as in the case of hatred. This is more than mere metaphor; in the Aristotelian tradition, "movement" includes more than just change of place. For in living animals the soul plays two roles: on the one hand, it is the substantial form of the body, which vivifies the body and unifies the composite; on the other hand, it exercises its operations through the body, which it informs, causing it to change ("move") from one state to another. Emotions, Aquinas maintains, are psychophysical phenomena: the apprehension of an insult leads to (a) the desire for revenge, which is the formal aspect of anger, and (b) the boiling of blood around the heart—or as we should say the increase in heart rate, blood circulation, the flow of adrenaline, and so on—which is the material aspect of anger.[5] The desire (a) is the formal cause of the physiological changes described in (b), set in motion by the soul.[6] By the same token, the physiological changes in (b) are what make the associated psychological state an emotion: a desire is only a desire if its motivational force is felt in the proper way, and *mutatis mutandis* for the other emotions.[7]

These considerations about the nature of emotion suggest a single reply to the two questions posed above, namely that the emotions properly belong to the sensitive appetite. Aquinas puts this reply concisely in *QDV*, q.26, a.3:

> Since the body is altered due to an operation of the soul in the case of emotion, it must be the sort of power that is joined to a bodily organ and whose function it is to alter the body. Hence emotion is not in the intellective part [of the soul], which does not pertain to the actualization of some bodily organ. Nor again is it in sensitive apprehension, since from sense-apprehension there follows movement in the body only through the mediation of the appetitive power, which is the immediate moving cause.[8]

Emotions are sensitive rather than intellective because they essentially involve physiological changes, unlike the operations of the intellective faculties of intellect and will;[9] they are appetitive rather than cognitive because they "move" the body, that is, because they engender changes in the subject's bodily states—even the psychological movement involved in emotion is typical of the appetitive rather than the cognitive powers, since the appetitive powers engage the subject directly with things in the world.[10] More generally, Aquinas argues that emotions motivate action, as they unquestionably do, only if representations of their objects occur in a context in which they move the agent (as in the appetite) rather than one in which such representations are merely assessed for the information they convey (as in cognition). Thus, the emotions must belong to the appetitive part of the soul.

Hence, there are four distinct types of psychological activity: (1) sensitive cognition also known as perception, the domain of the external and internal senses; (2) sensitive appetite, the domain of the emotions; (3) intellective cognition, the domain of thought and reasoning; (4) intellective appetite, the domain of free will. The first pair is common to all animals and their exercise is bound up with the body; the latter pair is specific to human beings and their exercise is carried out independently of the body. In particular, as features of the sensitive soul, the emotions are common to animals and to human beings. Aquinas's account of emotion must therefore be general enough to apply to nonhuman animals, as well as to human beings.

A final point before turning to examine how the emotions are related to the other types of psychological activity listed above. For Aquinas, emotion has both a formal (psychological) and a material (somatic) component, as we have seen; hence, an emotion is primarily a state of the entire unified soul–body composite.[11] It is the bereft mother who grieves for her lost son, not merely or primarily her soul that grieves, or for that matter her body. Grief is not a mere mental phenomenon, though it of course does involve mental states. As we would put Aquinas's point today, emotions are states of persons.

Cognition, Volition, and Emotion

The preceding section glossed over the details of how Aquinas takes emotion to be related to other psychological faculties, in particular to cognition (both sensitive and intellective), and volition. With regard to cognition, there are two topics to be considered: whether cognition is an essential part of an emotion, and the extent to which cognition can influence or control emotion.

The issue whether cognition might be essential to emotion arises from reflecting on Aquinas's conclusion that an emotion is a power of the sensitive appetite, and hence categorically distinct from any cognitive act—a consideration that might seem to warrant the inference that Aquinas is a "feeling-theorist" about the emotions, holding the position that emotions are essentially (pure) feelings that are known entirely through their phenomenological and qualitative properties.[12]

Now this inference might be warranted if Aquinas were to hold that the intentional aspect of emotion could be separated (at least by divine power) from the actualization of the sensitive appetite, which would thereby lack any cognitive element. This is not his position, however. Aquinas holds that the sensitive appetite "inherits" its intentional character from cognition, which must therefore figure in the account of emotion. Consider, for example, the case of fear—the emotion consequent upon the perception of some thing as a (sensible) imminent evil that is hard to avoid, which is associated with heightened respiration and heart rate, the sudden flow of adrenaline, and the like, where fright is the cause of flight. This is not specifically human; a sheep experiences fear when confronted with a wolf, in the well-worn example. Analyzing the stages of the process sketched here will make Aquinas's position clear.

First, the sheep has a cognitive act, more specifically an act of sensitive cognition: it sees the approaching wolf. This act, properly speaking, is an actualization of the sheep's passive power of vision. As such, like the actualization of any passive power, it takes place due to an external principle, in this instance the wolf. The wolf, as the external principle of the sheep's cognitive act, thereby becomes its object; the sheep has a seeing-of-a-*wolf*, after all. The point holds generally: the external principles that reduce passive potencies to acts are their objects.

Sensitive cognition is the paradigm case, but Aquinas does note that the same analysis can be applied when the object is derived not from occurrent sensing but rather from memory via the imagination. The cognitive act alone, however, whether derived from sense or from memory, is not sufficient for an emotion; a camera linked to image-analysis software could just as well register the (sudden) presence of a wolf without feeling a thing. In addition to the simple cognitive act of seeing a wolf, an act of another type takes place, one that links the cognitive to the appetitive faculties. Aquinas describes it as follows:

> An animal must seek out or avoid some things not merely because they are suitable or unsuitable to the senses, but according to certain other uses and advantages or disadvantages. For example, a sheep seeing an approaching wolf runs away—not due to its unsightly colour or shape, but as if it were a natural enemy. Likewise, a bird collects straw not because it is pleasing to sense but because it is useful for building a nest. Thus it is necessary for an animal to perceive *intentiones* of this sort, which the exterior senses do not perceive. There must be some distinct principle... the proper sense and the common sense are appointed for the reception of sensible forms, but the estimative power (*uis aestimatiua*) is appointed for apprehending *intentiones*, which are not received through sensing.[13]

The object of the animal's cognitive act, be it the wolf for the sheep or the straw for the bird, is also perceived under some *intentio* or other: the sheep perceives the wolf as a natural enemy, the bird perceives the straw as useful in the construction of a nest.[14] These are not perceptible properties. The wolf's dangerousness is not perceived the way its "unsightly color" is. Yet the emphasis Aquinas puts on *intentiones* not being perceptible properties—to the extent of postulating a distinct psychological faculty to perceive them at all—is misleading. After all, no dispositional property is strictly speaking perceptible: rationality, ferociousness, fragility, and the like are not apparent to the exterior senses alone. (Neither is the wolfhood of the wolf, or in general the substance of anything.) No wonder that friendliness or hatred are not perceptible.[15] Yet far more important for Aquinas's purposes is his recognition that *intentiones* are what we should call today evaluative response-dependent concepts. The sheep regards the wolf as a threat, and the bird regards straw as useful, because of the kind of thing each is. The sheep does not regard straw as useful, since it does not build nests of straw; the bird does not regard the wolf as a threat (or as much of one), since it can easily fly away. At bottom this is a built-in capacity: "animals perceive these sorts of *intentiones* only through a kind of natural instinct,"[16] though it may be modified through conditioning and habituation, as when the family watchdog learns that strangers are the only proper targets of its anger, or, in the case of human beings, through the exercise of higher faculties (as we shall see shortly). For now let us take the point that such evaluative response-dependent concepts occur after acts of simple cognition.

Aquinas offers a few examples of *intentiones*: the sheep perceives the wolf as inimical, the bird perceives the straw as useful, or vaguely "advantages and disadvantages." Now it might be thought that these are a motley collection as varied as the nature of evaluation itself ("evaluation" being the root meaning of *aestimatio*). But there is a general way to describe *intentiones* as such, that is, a way to characterize anything that is to count as an *intentio* at all, much the way that for anything to count as visible it must have color.[17] It is *sensible good or evil*, where "sensible" refers to the subject's perception of its object as good or as evil.[18] Hence, an *intentio* must present some thing to its subject as a good or as an evil in some fashion. When the sheep perceives the approaching wolf, it may evaluate the wolf as a danger—that is, as an imminent evil—which is hard to avoid.[19] The initial simple cognition of the wolf is augmented with this evaluative response-dependent cognition, each cognition arguably caused by the wolf, or more exactly by the wolf given the natures of the wolf and the sheep.

So much for the cognitive side of things. At this point there is a hand-off to the sensitive appetite: "the lower appetitive power does not naturally tend to anything until after that thing has been presented to it under the aspect of its proper object,"[20] since in the case of animals "the sensitive appetite is apt to be moved by the estimative power, as when a sheep esteems a wolf as inimical and is then afraid."[21] The sensitive appetite, as a passive power, is reduced from potency to act when it "inherits" objectual content from the evaluative response-dependent concept (which is the actualization of the estimative power). That is to say, the sheep has an act of the sensitive appetite directed at the wolf, which is presented to the sensitive appetite as a hard-to-avoid imminent evil. This "proper object" therefore has a double causal role. On the one hand, it reduces the sensitive appetite from potency to act and is thereby an efficient cause of the resulting act. On the other hand, it makes the resulting act be the kind of act it is and is thereby its formal cause. For the resulting act of the sensitive appetite is the emotion of *fear* when it is caused by the formal object *the wolf as a hard-to-avoid imminent evil*, with the appropriate associated somatic responses. If an object were presented as a hard-to-attain imminent good, say, the way the sheep might appear to the wolf, the act of the wolf's sensitive appetite would be *hope*.

Emotions are therefore objectual, since the sensitive appetite is the passive recipient of the causal and formal agency of the external principle, the wolf in the case of the fearful sheep.

Aquinas is therefore a cognitivist about emotion, since cognitive acts are not only causal preconditions of emotion, but contribute their formal causes as well. The emotion is not the feeling alone: it literally would not be the emotion it is without the formal object it has, and there would be no emotion at all in the absence of a formal object. This is not to say that there cannot be "objectless" states of the sort that are so important to contemporary philosophy, such as angst, dread, or boredom, but that they are not to be understood as emotions: they are rather akin to moods, somatic states that influence psychological states.[22] Despite being a cognitivist, however, Aquinas is also an externalist. For the pair of cognitive acts do not in themselves have motivational force: they act as efficient and final causes of the acts of the sensitive appetite, which do motivate the agent, but even the evaluative judgment implicit in the response-dependent conception of something as a good or an evil does not cause responsive action directly.

The point is important, because the causal link between cognition and appetite is more complicated in the case of human beings. Even in the case of animals such as sheep, the "natural tendency" or "instinct" to respond emotionally in a certain way can be tempered and perhaps even changed by conditioning and habituation. The extent to which this is possible depends on the type of animal, and perhaps even on the particular animal. Kittens and puppies raised together often remain quite friendly with one another as cats and dogs, though they respond in more traditional ways to unknown dogs and cats; sheep, on the other hand, might never learn to be tolerant of wolves, no matter how tame. The strength of the causal linkage in each animal, and its susceptibility to conditioning and to habituation, make all the difference, and these are matters for empirical investigation.

Human beings have higher cognitive faculties, and, in consequence, a more complex and sophisticated emotional life. For one thing, instead of an estimative power, humans have a general "cogitative power," which is sometimes called "particular reason" on the grounds that it combines individual or particular *intentiones*.[23] Aquinas says little about human cogitative power, and nothing about what it is to "combine" *intentiones*. Nor do the details really matter. What does matter to Aquinas is that thinking and reasoning affect the evaluative response-dependent concepts that trigger the sensitive appetite, and that human "cogitative power" is involved in the process.

We can now turn to the second of the two questions posed at the start of this section, namely the extent to which cognition can influence and control emotions.[24] We have already seen that some nonhuman animals are susceptible to conditioning. And, like other animals, humans have some instinctual emotional responses (fear of falling) and some habituated responses (pleasure at the sight of a loved one). But human beings, unlike animals, have an extensive and rich set of conceptual resources that can be deployed even at the level of mere conditioning: the botanist's instant delight at recognizing an unknown species; the anger that follows upon a perceived slight in a complex but thoroughly assimilated code of honor; and so on.[25] Nor is it merely a matter of human beings having a larger conceptual apparatus; human beings are much less tied to their present circumstances, being better able to imagine things in other places and at other times, and in addition are able to conceptualize the world in a universal, rather than merely a particular, way. They can hope for a happier afterlife, become angry at the memory of a rebuke, love wisdom, hate spiders, be saddened at the loss of the sculptures of Phidias—all beyond the capacity of animals.

Aquinas mentions two ways in which human emotion is "cognitively penetrable," that is, capable of being consciously affected by changes in belief or thought after the quasi-instinctual initial response of the sensitive appetite.[26] For although an emotional response "is not completely in our power since it precedes the judgment of reason, it is in our power to some extent."[27] First, we can imaginatively present one and the same thing in different lights, via the imagination, and thereby trigger different emotional responses.[28] The divorced spouse can think of the former partner with love or hatred, depending on which past situations and events are recalled or imagined. Likewise, the imagination can provoke emotional responses by the force of what it imagines. Aquinas offers the example of a believer who reflects on punishment in the afterlife: "imagining the fire burning and the worm gnawing and the like, there follows the emotion of fear in his sensitive appetite."[29] Since deliberate imagination of this sort is in the agent's conscious control, it is clear that some emotions are indirectly subject to the control of reason—though it is a bit like controlling digestion by being able to pick and choose what one eats.

Second, Aquinas notes that the intellect can influence emotion: "anyone can experience for himself that by applying some universal considerations, anger or fear or the like can then be mitigated or even stirred up."[30] Reminding oneself of general truths can affect the understanding of a particular situation. Grief over the death of a friend can be mitigated by thinking of the general truth that we all die; confidence can increase by the thought that only the brave deserve the fair; and so on. Here Aquinas is somewhat hamstrung by his view that the intellect is the realm of the universal, whereas sense is the realm of the particular; if we allow him to relax his strict insistence on this dividing principle, then there are all sorts of ways in which intellectual cognition can (attempt to) influence one's emotions: thinking about the stringent air-safety regulations in place in order to curb one's fear of flying, for example, or thinking about how even lesser lights have been awarded the Nobel

Prize in order to boost one's hopes. The factor in common in all these cases is that the emotional responses seem to follow (when they follow at all) merely upon having the thoughts.

Such techniques do not always lead to success. For the emotions do not always submit to the dictates of reason or imagination; they are unruly and may resist their commands.[31] Yet strictly speaking, it is not the role of reason to "command" at all. That is the province not of cognition, but of the intellective appetite, that is, the will.

Aquinas argues that emotion is the province of the sensitive rather than the intellective appetite on the grounds that the latter, like the intellect itself, has a purely nonphysical operation.[32] Yet just as in the case of cognition, the presence of higher intellective faculties allows human beings to influence their emotions in ways that are not open to animals, though not to dictate them; we cannot simply choose not to have an emotional response, though we can have some effect on what that response might be. Aquinas describes three ways in which this can happen.

First, the sensitive appetite is subordinate to the will, and this subordination affects the kinds of emotions that accompany volition:

> In the case of powers that are connected and ordered to one another, it happens that an intense movement in one of them (and especially in the higher one) overflows into the other. Accordingly, when the movement of the will is directed to something through choice, even the [emotions] follow this movement of the will.[33]

If someone makes a choice that wholeheartedly commits him to a course of action, say, he may thereupon feel delight and hope in its pursuit. Such an "overflow" from the will is an emotion whose inception is in the very choice of the will. In general, the process of habituating emotional responses to choice is part of acquiring practical wisdom, which includes satisfaction with the choices one has made.[34]

Second, the will is not only the principle of choice; it also governs consent. We may consent to our emotions, or withhold consent from them, thereby strengthening or weakening the emotional response. (The latter is usually described as "resisting" the emotion.) In the ordinary course of events an emotion follows upon sensitive cognition, as described above, and so "precedes the judgment of reason" in such a way that there is no issue of consent, whether explicit or implicit.[35] Once the emotional response occurs, the will may then endorse or reject it.

Third, the will can directly affect what Aquinas calls the "motive" or "executive" power, so as to prevent or facilitate the emotion from being causally efficacious.[36] When a human being perceives the sudden approach of a wolf, he experiences fear as a natural reaction, but unlike the sheep he may exercise his free will and choose to stand his ground in the face of his fear, blocking his natural impulse to flee. He would have no success in the face of his more immediate somatic responses; however, he may tremble, grow pale, break into a sweat; his teeth may chatter, his knees knock, his heart race (the physiological expressions of fear that Aquinas catalogues in *ST* I-II q.44).

The Taxonomy of Emotion

Aquinas adopts the traditional distinction of emotions into two fundamental types, namely concupiscible and irascible, and sets out to establish the distinction on a firm philosophical basis.[37] He sketches three arguments that the concupiscible emotions and the irascible emotions genuinely differ and "are not reducible to a single principle":

- *The Interference Argument.* The two types of emotions must be different in kind because they are able to interfere with one another: stirring up anger can lessen desire, and conversely stirring up desire can lessen anger.
- *The Submission Argument.* Sometimes the soul "submits" to distress, against the inclination of desire, so that it may fight against things opposed to it.
- *The Champion Argument.* The irascible emotions arise from the concupiscible emotions, to help them succeed, whereupon they terminate in them. Anger, for example, may be born from distress and, in taking revenge, thereby relieve the distress and end in delight.

A few comments about each are in order.

The Interference Argument, which is ultimately derived from Plato's *Republic*, turns on the fact that the distinct kinds of emotions can be directed at one and the same real thing while nevertheless differing in their formal (intensional) objects. One and the same person can be simultaneously alluring and annoying, for example; these contrary characterizations of the same person conflict with one another. Hence, the emotions must be different in kind, not merely in degree. For while it is true that we speak of the relative strength of the concupiscible and the irascible emotions, as when we say that anger finally won out over desire, this is not to be understood literally. It is quite different, Aquinas maintains, from the case in which two emotions of the same sort compete with one another when I am presented with a choice between chocolate ice cream and vanilla ice cream, for instance, where I have only to consult the relative strength of each desire to make the choice. But when the emotions are of different kinds, their strength does not accurately predict the agent's behavior. Even a tempting bone will not deflect a dog, once angered, from attacking someone.

The Submission Argument takes a different tack. Sometimes the sensible good that is hard to attain is such that the difficulty is an intrinsic feature of the good in question: we want to win the race, become fluent in Icelandic, learn quantum physics. But sometimes the difficulty is in the surrounding circumstances, not inherent in the object itself. It is no challenge to make tea, unless one is stranded on a desert island with tea but no kettle. In cases such as the latter, Aquinas declares, the end can be unproblematically desired, independent of the difficulties associated with it; drinking tea is not an intrinsically difficult or challenging enterprise, even if it is so in certain circumstances. In such cases, though, where the difficulties are not intrinsic to the good sought, one must "submit" to them to reach the desired goal.

The implications of the Submission Argument should be clear. Aquinas holds that we cannot understand all behavior in terms of simple "push/pull" desires, in particular instances of submission to present pain, which involve not merely weighing the relative strength of the desires but at least rudimentary means–ends calculation.

The Champion Argument turns on the fact that the concupiscible emotions are comprehensible in their own terms, whereas the irascible emotions make sense only against the background of the concupiscible emotions. Aquinas presents this as partly a logical claim and partly a causal claim. Overcoming the difficulties means attaining the sensible good, which prompts the emotional response of delight; so much is simple logic. But other connections among the emotions, such as distress, anger, and revenge, are causal rather than logical in nature. Aquinas's point is that in such causal connections, the irascible emotions "come to the aid" of the concupiscible emotions, the former being "champions" of the latter. They can do so in virtue of being a different kind of emotion, for otherwise they would be a constitutive part of the initial (concupiscible) emotional response to the object, not something further.

Having established by these three arguments that there are two basic kinds of emotions, Aquinas then turns to isolating and specifying the distinct varieties of each. Before we turn to the details of his account, however, it is worth remarking on his method. Although Aquinas will be offering a taxonomic theory of emotion, identifying distinct kinds of emotions and their interrelations, his procedure is quite unlike the standard sorts of taxonomies found in ordinary genus/species accounts, or even the less rigid taxonomies found in botany and biology. The fundamental divide between the concupiscible and the irascible emotions is not due to a differentiating feature, but to a distinction of their formal objects: *sensible good/evil taken absolutely* and *sensible good/evil that is difficult.* (If anything, the latter looks like a candidate for a species of the former.) Once we accept this distinction, however, we might think that we could identify the subordinate kinds of each type by proper differentiae—presumably differentiating the formal objects of each, the irascible emotions distinguished by different kinds of difficulty, for instance. But this is not how Aquinas proceeds. Instead, he uses some technical apparatus from Aristotle's natural philosophy to generate a set of principles so as to arrange the six concupiscible and the five irascible emotions into rational groups of coordinate pairs,[38] on the grounds that emotions are, literally, "motions" of the sensitive appetite.

In brief, his account is as follows. Physics teaches us that there are two types of motion: (a) movement either toward or away from a given terminus, in which case it is the "direction" of the movements that are contrarily opposed; (b) movement between two contrary opposed termini. Concupiscible emotions are directed at their object solely as (sensible) good or evil. If the terminus in question is the good, then, Aquinas maintains that the sensitive appetite cannot fail to move toward it; if evil, it cannot fail to move away from it. Hence (a) does not apply. The concupiscible emotions are therefore properly understood as types of movement between contrary termini, that is, of type (b), between the contrary opposites of good and evil: love, desire, and delight toward the good; hatred, aversion, and distress toward evil. The grouping of concupiscible emotions into three conjugate pairs has to do with the flavor of the movement each exemplifies: love and hate are simple tendencies of the sensitive appetite with respect to their objects; they are "emotional attitudes" toward the object, pure and simple—an affective stance to it. The second conjugate pair, desire and aversion, involve moving toward or away from their objects, being drawn to or driven from it. The third conjugate pair, delight and distress, has to do with the affective stance one is in when attaining the object.

Irascible emotions, on the other hand, are directed at (sensible) good and evil not in themselves but *qua* difficult, and so are capable of both directions of movement implicit in (a), as well as movement between contrary termini as in (b). They are properly categorized according to (a), however. Aquinas insists that the irascible emotions do not characterize approach and withdrawal in terms of good or evil but in terms of the surmountability or insurmountability of the difficulties associated with the (good or evil) object. Hope is the irascible emotion that sees its object as a surmountable (attainable) difficult good, so that the difficult good "approaches" the agent's possession; despair, with which hope is paired, sees its object as an insurmountable (unattainable) difficult good, so that the difficult good "withdraws" from the agent's possession. Likewise, confidence is the irascible emotion that regards its object as a surmountable (avoidable) difficult evil, and fear, with which confidence is paired, regards its object as an insurmountable (unavoidable) difficult evil. Finally, there is the irascible emotion *par excellence*, anger, which is unique in not having a contrary; here the sensitive appetite has achieved the evil that was difficult to avoid and "rests" in it, taking in the full measure of its difficulty. Each conjugate pair represents a flavor of motion, as with the corresponding concupiscible emotion: the simple tendency with respect to the object, surmountable obstacle to something good (hope) or insurmountable escape from something evil (despair); movement with respect to the possession of the object, either toward an attainable good (confidence) or away from an unavoidable evil (fear); and finally anger, which dwells on a present evil in its possession that is hard to overcome, and so is a form of "rest."

As noted, irascible emotions also involve movement of type (b), namely between contrary opposites, although in a more complicated way than the concupiscible emotions. Moreover, the irascible emotions are grouped somewhat differently in respect of (b). Hope and fear are paired together in that they each regard their (difficult) objects as likely to be possessed by the agent, hope directed at something good and fear directed at something evil. The same reasoning presumably applies to confidence and despair, each regarding its (difficult) object as likely to not be possessed by the agent, confidence at the prospect of being without something evil and despair at the prospect of being without something good. Anger, as before, obeys a slightly different logic, since it has for its object a present evil that is already possessed and difficult to overcome; there is no contrary irascible emotion of overcoming directed at the possession of a present good; indeed the only proper response to the possession of a present good is delight, a concupiscible emotion.[39]

Aquinas thus takes the overall taxonomic structure of the eleven kinds of emotion to be as follows:

Concupiscible Passions		*Irascible Passions*
Love-Hate	[simple tendency]	Hope-Despair
Desire-Aversion	[movement]	Confidence-Fear
Joy-Sorrow	[repose]	Anger

Given the complexity of the underlying division (not all of which is represented here), it is not clear how to extend the taxonomy to bring into its scope further species of each kind of emotion. In the event, Aquinas does not do this, preferring instead to discuss each emotion one-by-one and to describe the subtypes and varieties of each, as required.

Two examples will give the flavor of Aquinas's discussion of the subspecies of emotions, each the paradigm of its type: love for the concupiscible emotions, anger for the irascible emotions.

In *ST* I-II q.26 a.4, Aquinas puts forward his basic division of love into friendly (*amor amicitiae*) and covetous (*amor concupiscentiae*). This division follows upon his observation that love, strictly speaking, has two targets: the item, seen as a good thing, and the subject who receives the item. Covetous love is love that gives precedence to the good thing, which is typically wanted for oneself; friendly love is love that gives precedence to the recipient, typically someone other than oneself, for whom the good thing is wanted. The two kinds of love are not entirely on a par. The object of friendly love is loved simply and *per se*, whereas the object of covetous love is not loved for itself but for something else. Friendly love is also known as "benevolence" (in q.27 a.3) because of this concern for the other for its own sake, which gives it priority over covetous love. Friendly love is even found among animals, the best instance being the friendly love a mother has for her offspring. The two kinds of love, then, seem quite close to being species of the genus *love* in the traditional sense.

In *ST* I-II q.46 a.8, Aquinas turns to the types of anger (given traditional expression by John of Damascus): wrath, ill-will, and rancor. He proposes that each increases anger: wrath, which might better be termed irascibility (as Aquinas remarks in *ad* 2), denotes the facility of the movement to anger; ill-will the rehearsal of what caused the anger; and rancor the vindictiveness or unquenchable impulse for revenge. But none of these is in any clear sense a "division" of the formal object of anger, namely the desire to overcome a difficult present evil that poses an obstacle. Aquinas seems to recognize the justice of this point, since in his answer to the first objection, which charged that Damascene's enumeration was an accidental division, he declares that "those things that help to complete anger in some fashion are not altogether accidental to it; as a result, nothing prevents them from providing it with a specific differentia" (*ad* 1). Perhaps not, but that is hardly the same as saying that they do provide specific differentiae, which Aquinas carefully does not say. Nor is there any discussion of what we might think of as better candidates for species of anger: annoyance, irritation, rage, and the like. Aquinas seems interested only in finding some way to accommodate tradition, rather than exploring the question in its own right. Later commentators such as Cajetan took note of Aquinas's understated conclusion; in his commentary *ad loc.*, Cajetan concluded that wrath, ill-will, and rancor are not genuine species of anger for Aquinas.

The upshot is that Aquinas leaves us with a careful taxonomy of the emotions at the generic level, along with a variety of observations about some of their species, with no attempt to systematize them. His work on this score remains incomplete. Yet there is good reason to think that this is not what he meant to do. In the remainder of his "treatise on the emotions,"[40] Aquinas takes up each of the eleven kinds of emotions in detail. His analysis of each conforms to a rough pattern: he discusses the causes of the emotion, its nature and formal object, and its effects. Sometimes issues specific to a given emotion are taken up, for example, whether it is possible to hate oneself, given the nature of hatred;[41] sometimes causal connections are explored, for example, whether sympathy from friends can help to alleviate distress.[42] Identifying distinct species of emotion does not seem to be one of his main concerns. In many ways, that is just as well, since taxonomic theories have lost the luster they once possessed, but Aquinas's particular discussions of individual emotions are still psychologically acute and philosophically rewarding.[43]

Conclusion

The last section might well lead one to wonder about Aquinas's theoretical aims, if he is neither giving us quite an empirical theory founded on observation nor a taxonomic genera-species classificatory scheme. There is much to say about the sense in which Aquinas offers us a theory of emotion, but perhaps the best way to approach the issue is to see how his theory is related to contemporary theories of emotion.

We have already seen that Aquinas is a cognitivist (of sorts) about emotion, a finding that puts him with the majority of philosophical treatments of emotion in the last fifty years. But the discussion in the first section gives us an even closer comparison. Given the role played in the psychological economy by sensitive cognition, on the one side, and by sensitive appetite, on the other side, it is clear that Aquinas's account of the emotions is in many ways like contemporary "perception theories" of emotion.[44] Such perception-theories diverge from standard cognitivist accounts in taking the evaluative element crucial to emotion to be not a judgment, with all the cognitive apparatus judgments draw in their train, but rather a perception, or something very like a perception. From the safety of the sidewalk, I might perceive the onrushing traffic as a threat even though I know that I am quite safe where I am; if the evaluative judgment that I am in danger were a requisite part of the emotion of fear, then it seems hard to explain my fear in the face of my knowledge of my safety. Perceptions, however, need not be reasoned, though perhaps permeable to reason; they can be had by nonintellectual subjects, such as babies and dogs, who we want to say experience genuine if primitive emotions; and they can deploy concepts without requiring their articulation—the sheep may regard the wolf as dangerous without having the concept of danger at all.

Aquinas's account of the emotions is in many ways close to such perception theories. Indeed, Aquinas exploits the structural parallel between perception and emotion frequently, and, as with perceptions, he holds that the most fundamental way to understand emotions is to see them as modes of engagement with the world. Again, Aquinas holds that the cognitive penetrability of emotion derives from the susceptibility of perception to being affected by changes in beliefs and thoughts. The rich array of psychological faculties that Aquinas sketches, with the complex interplay among cognitive and affective components, offers a congenial background for the contemporary cognitive scientist accustomed to working with mental modules and their transference of information via representations. If Aquinas draws a sharper line between perceptual and intellectual cognition than most theorists are comfortable with today, that is a small drawback for being centuries ahead of his time. The taxonomic structure he proposes might then be taken as a first attempt to isolate the natural kinds of emotion as an affective phenomenon. In short, we could preserve his insights and his general approach to the emotions, and perhaps even the general taxonomy, but leave behind some of its more medieval features, such as the appeal to the Aristotelian theory of motion, or the necessarily immaterial character of intellectual functions. But a remarkable amount of Aquinas's analysis bears worthwhile comparison to contemporary theories, as well as being a stunning intellectual accomplishment in its own right.

NOTES

1. I adopt the dating of these works given in Jean-Pierre Torrell, O.P., ed. and trans., *Thomas Aquinas, Le Verbe incarné*, vol. 3, *Summa theologiae* IIIa Questions 7–15 (Paris: Cerf, 2002).

2. Respectively, *amor* and *odium*, *desiderium* and *fuga*, *gaudium* and *tristitia*; *spes* and *desperatio*, *audacia* and *timor*, and *ira*. Aquinas adopts this list and much of the structure that supports it from Jean de la Rochelle (*Summa de anima*), by way of his mentor Albert the Great: see Simo Knuutila, *Emotions in Ancient and Medieval Philosophy* (Oxford: Oxford University Press, 2004) and Peter King, "Emotions in Medieval Thought," in Peter Goldie, ed., *The Oxford Handbook of Philosophy of Emotion* (Oxford: Oxford University Press, 2010), 167–87.

3. *QDV*, q.26, a.2 and *ST* I-II q.22 a.1.

4. See Peter King, "Aquinas on the Passions," in Scott MacDonald and Eleonore Stump, eds., *Aquinas's Moral Theory* (Ithaca, N.Y.: Cornell University Press, 1998), 101–132; Robert Miner, *Thomas Aquinas on the Passions* (Cambridge: Cambridge University Press, 2009), ch. 2.3, and the discussion in §4.

5. See *ST* I-II q.44 a.1: "In the case of the emotions, the formal aspect is the motion of the appetitive potency and the material element is a physiological change, where the one is proportionate to the other."

6. Aquinas takes this direction of influence from the soul to the body as a mark of emotion, which he calls by the name of "animal emotion" (*passio animalis*) in *QDV*, q.26, a.2.

7. A corollary of Aquinas's insistence that physiological changes are essential to emotion is that nonphysical beings, such as angels and God, strictly speaking do not have emotions. See Miner, *Thomas Aquinas on the Passions*, ch. 2.2 and the references therein, as well as Peter King, "Dispassionate Passions," in Martin Pickave and Lisa Shapiro, eds., *Reason and Emotion in Medieval and Early Modern Philosophy* (Oxford: Oxford University Press, 2011).

8. All translations are my own. Latin texts are cited from their respective editions, with the punctuation as given (not always respected in the translations).

9. *ST* I-II q.22 a.3. Aquinas offers two further arguments for the view that emotions do not belong to the will: the will is a free active power whereas emotions are not, and the will tends to a universal object whereas the emotions tend to a particular object (*QDV*, q.25, a.1).

10. *ST* I-II q.22 a.2. This is Aquinas's preferred proof when he has to give a brief account of why the emotions are appetitive: see, e.g., *Diu. nom.* 2.4 §191 or *In NE*, 2.5 §291.

11. See Diana Cates, *Aquinas on the Emotions: A Religious-Ethical Inquiry* (Washington, D.C.: Georgetown University Press, 2009), ch. 4.

12. See Shawn Floyd, "Aquinas on Emotion: A Response to Some Recent Interpretations," *History of Philosophy Quarterly* 15 (1998): 161–75; Patrick Gorevan, "Aquinas and Emotional Theory Today: Mind–Body, Cognitivism, and Connaturality," *Acta Philosophica* 9 (2000): 141–51; and Thomas Ryan, "Revisiting Affective Knowledge and Connaturality in Aquinas," *Theological Studies* 66 (2005): 49–68.

13. *ST* I q.78 a.4. See also *Super Sent* 3 d.26, q.1, a.2, §25, where much the same account is given. Miner, *Thomas Aquinas on the Passions*, ch. 3.3, discusses the estimative and memorative powers in Aquinas with regard to the emotions.

14. It is unclear whether this cognitive act is distinct from the initial perception of the wolf—perhaps the sheep's "concept" of a wolf has dangerousness built into it—but it is enough for our purposes that it is logically distinct.

15. These are the examples that Aquinas mentions in *Super Sent* 3, d.26, q.1, a.2, §25.

16. *Ibid.* The "natural instinct" may be nothing more complicated than the way the animal is wetwired: whenever a wolf-form occurs in sensitive cognition, the adrenal glands begin pumping, heart rate increases, and so on.

17. This is the medieval notion of the "proper object" or the "primary object"—the terminology was fluid—of a cognitive potency, in this case of the estimative power.

18. The terminology is not perspicuous, since the *intentio*, which must be a form of sensible good or evil, is, as Aquinas has remarked, not a perceptible feature of the object. The key point to keep in mind is that "sensible" here refers to the particular that is grasped in its presentation as a good or an evil.

19. As we shall see in more detail in §3, the formal object of the irascible emotions is *sensible good or evil that is difficult*.

20. *QDV*, q.25, a.4, *ad* 4.

21. *ST* I q.81 a.3.

22. Moods were often thought to be completely explained in purely physiological terms, having to do with the relative balance among the four bodily humors. Acts of the

vegetative soul in the higher animals, such as sexual arousal or hunger, were also thought to be objectless and hence not emotions—a view in keeping with their contemporary classification as drives or urges. Aquinas points out that male impotence effectively demonstrates the difference between mere bodily arousal and sexual desire, a form of the emotion of desire (*concupiscentia*) and an altogether different thing.

23. *ST* I q.78 a.4 and q.81 a.3.

24. See Claudia Murphy, "Aquinas on Our Responsibility for Our Emotions," *Medieval Philosophy and Theology* 8 (1999): 163–205; and Elisabeth Uffenheimer-Lippens, "Rationalized Passions and Passionate Rationality: Thomas Aquinas on the Relation between Reason and the Passions," *Review of Metaphysics* 56 (2003): 525–58.

25. Aquinas notes that the irascible emotions, in virtue of having a more complex formal object, are thereby "closer to reason" and more susceptible to its influence. He takes this point from Aristotle, *In NE* 7.6 (1149a25–b3): see for instance *Super Sent* 3, d.26, q.1, a.2, §28 and *QDV*, q.25, a.6.

26. Of course, humans can condition themselves over time through a variety of techniques: training, education, brainwashing, self-hypnosis, repetitive practice, and so on. But here we are concerned with Aquinas's focus on the ways in which someone can attempt to affect his or her emotional responses directly.

27. *QDV*, q.25, a.5.

28. *QDV*, q.25, a.4.

29. *QDV*, q.26, a.3, ad 13. See Umberto Galeazzi, "Le passioni secondo Tommaso d'Aquino: *De veritate* q. 26," *Aquinas* 47 (2004): 547–70.

30. *ST* I q.81 a.3.

31. *ST* I-II q.17 a.7. See also *ST* I q.81 a.3 ad 2. The allusion is to Aristotle, *Pol.* 1.2 (1254b2–5), in which the rational part of the soul is said to control the irrational part "with a political and royal rule" rather than a tyrannical rule.

32. *QDV*, q.26, a.3 and *ST* I-II q.22 a.3.

33. *QDV*, q.25, a.4. See also *ST* I-II q.24 a.4 ad 1.

34. Aquinas takes this point from Aristotle, *In NE* 2.5 (1105b25–29).

35. *QDV*, q.25, a.5, ad 5.

36. *QDV*, q.25, a.4.

37. The following discussion is derived from *Super Sent* 3, d.26, q.1, a.2; *QDV*, q.25, a.2; and *ST* I-II q.81 a.2.

38. There seems to have been some development in Aquinas's conception of how the emotions are structured and organized. The account given here mostly follows the mature analysis given in *ST* I-II q.23 a.2–4. This is Aquinas's major advance over Jean de la Rochelle, who had organized emotions into their conjugate pairs, but who did not offer any principles underlying their organization.

39. This last point illustrates a logical and causal truth for Aquinas, namely that the irascible emotions begin from and finally terminate in the concupiscible emotions (*ST* I-II q.25 a.1–2).

40. *ST* I-II q.26–48.

41. *ST* I-II q.29 a.4.

42. *ST* I-II q.38 a.3.

43. There have recently been several studies of Aquinas's views about particular emotions: Marcos Manzanedo, "El deseo y la aversión según Santo Tomás," *Studium* 27 (1987): 189–233; Marcos Manzanedo, "Efectos y propriedades de la delectación," *Studium* 29 (1989): 107–39; Marcos Manzanedo, "El dolor y sus causas," *Studium* 31 (1991): 63–97; Marcos Manzanedo, "La audacia según Santo Tomás," *Studium* 34 (1994): 437–53; Mark

Drost, "In the Realm of the Senses: St. Thomas Aquinas on Sensory Love, Desire, and Delight," *The Thomist* 59 (1995): 47–58; Stephen Loughlin, "*Tristitia et dolor*: Does Aquinas Have a Robust Understanding of Depression?" *Nova et Vetera* 3 (2005): 761–83; Keith Green, "Aquinas on Attachment, Envy, and Hatred in the *Summa theologiae*," *Journal of Religious Ethics* 35 (2007): 403–28; the need for such careful studies of particular emotions is the central theme of Miner, *Thomas Aquinas on the Passions*.

44. See, e.g., Robert C. Roberts, *Emotions: An Essay in Aid of Moral Psychology* (Cambridge: Cambridge University Press, 2003).

CHAPTER 17

HAPPINESS

BRIAN DAVIES

The word "happiness" means different things to different people. Nobody with a modicum of education disagrees when it comes to answering questions like "What is a caterpillar?" Yet plenty of people have varying answers to give to the question "What is happiness?" Thus, for example, some will say that happiness is what people have achieved as soon as they have obtained what very much appeals to them at a material level, such as an expensive house or a new car. Others, however, will declare that happiness lasts over time and need not necessarily have anything to do with possessions, even the possession of health. Some have even concluded that happiness is compatible with (or even sometimes dependent on) what we might normally think of as its opposite (pain or struggle, for instance).[1]

Does happiness depend on being morally good? Here again we find different responses. For some people the morally good life is a happy life and happiness depends on being morally good. For others, though, even the most wicked of people (some of them, anyway) can be thought of as happy. "Happiness," we might say, is a weasel word, like "liberal" or "conservative." No uncontroversial definition of it seems to be forthcoming. And even those who think that they have a pretty good idea of what happiness amounts to raise many different questions about it. Is it a state? Is it an activity? Is it episodic, or is it prolonged? Is it something single, or does it come in a variety of species? Does it admit of quantity or degrees? Does everyone seek happiness, or are some unconcerned with it? Is happiness purely subjective and infallibly known as had by those who claim to be happy, or can we be wrong when thinking that we are happy? Is happiness a matter of self-interest, or is there more to it than that? Is it confined to life before death? Can it be fully achieved before death? Can it be had by nonhuman animals, as well as by ourselves? Can it be ascribed to God? Can people be happy if there is no God? All of these are familiar questions raised by thinkers (especially moral philosophers) who have turned their minds to the topic of happiness. Not surprisingly, therefore, there is a large amount of literature that offers hugely different perspectives.[2]

An interesting feature of Aquinas's treatment of happiness is that much of it consists in trying to explain what happiness is not. He certainly has a definite and positive view about happiness, and we shall presently be seeing what this positive view amounts to. But we shall not understand it, or his reasons for saying what happiness is not, unless we are first of all prepared to try to understand him when he is talking about issues that might not initially strike one as directly bearing on happiness in its own right. As has often been noted (and as readers of the present volume will quickly discover), Aquinas is a systematic thinker whose views on one subject frequently depend on what he has to say on other matters. His explicit discussions of happiness illustrate this point very well. In order to present what Aquinas says about happiness, therefore, I shall have to begin with a brief account of his theory of human action and desire.

In the first place, it helps to note that Aquinas distinguishes between what he calls *actus hominis* (an act of a human being) and *actus humanus* (a human action).[3] Actions are often bodily processes through which people go, but some of them occur without us thinking about them at all while others involve reflection.[4] Deeply engrossed in a conversation with you, I might inadvertently scratch my chin or stroke my hair. Ask me why I did so and I might not even remember that I had done so. Bits of basically unthinking behavior like these are things we indulge in constantly, and here we have Aquinas's notion of an act of a human being (*actus hominis*). Suppose, however, that I end my conversation with you by giving you a birthday present, and assume that I am here acting freely and not under the influence of hypnosis or whatever. Now, thinks Aquinas, we are dealing with a human action (*actus humanus*), not merely an act of a human being.

For Aquinas, human action in what we might call its highest form is something *thought out*. It is deliberative and goal-directed. And it typically results from a process of what Aquinas calls "practical reasoning," a working out (though not necessarily a long-winded one) of how best to get that for which we are aiming. Suppose that I want to travel to Paris from New York in less than ten hours. Unless I am a complete idiot, I shall consult plane schedules and, all things being equal, plan a trip accordingly.[5] In terms of this account, human action is intentional, purposive, and desire-driven. We identify what we are attracted to, and we consciously take steps to obtain it. In fact, thinks Aquinas, this is always the case with human action. In his view, we do not aim for what we do not want, and when aiming for what we want we make use of our reason. He is, of course, perfectly aware that we sometimes willingly act while our minds are on other matters (as when I cook a stew while planning my summer holiday). He is also aware that we sometimes act in ways that conflict with what normally entices us: that, for example, we pay visits to the dentist or read books that bore or bemuse us. But he does not take any of this as refuting his claim that we act (as in *actus humanus*) so as to get what we think that we want. He would say, for example, that we go to the dentist in order to get rid of a toothache, or that we might read something that displeases us because we are anxious to pass a literature exam, and so on.[6]

For Aquinas, then, human action is essentially directed to what people take to be good, attractive, satisfying, and fulfilling. He thinks of it as always happiness-oriented. Just as cats delight in chasing mice, so, Aquinas thinks, people naturally (indeed, inevitably) seek to be happy.[7] They can, he frequently notes, be completely wrong when it comes to what will actually make them happy (so he does not think of happiness as a sensation like having a pain in the neck; he does not think of it as something about which one cannot be mistaken). But (dentists, unlovable books, and even martyrdom notwithstanding) he finds it inconceivable that we should ever act without aiming for what we think will somehow make for our happiness, a matter of what we *want*. By parity of reasoning, he also concludes that people do not act so as to make misery for themselves the end for which they are aiming in what they do. The desire for happiness, we might say, is central to Aquinas's theory of human action. To think otherwise would be a bit like supposing that Wall Street could continue to function without any interest in money.

But does Aquinas have anything that might be thought of as a definition of "happiness"? And how does he think that we can achieve happiness? Like almost every human being who has ever existed, he certainly believes that happiness is possible and that its occurrence is as real as any actual thing you might care to mention.[8] But what does he take it to be? And how does he suppose us to obtain it? To answer these questions we need to be aware of even more of his thinking on human beings in general. And the point to stress at this stage is that he takes them to be first and foremost thinking animals.

Some philosophers have believed that people are essentially nonmaterial objects (minds, souls, selves, or egos), which are somehow attached to bodies but are really distinct from them. For Plato, Descartes, and many other authors the real me (what I call "I") is an incorporeal substance, and for at least some of these thinkers this implies that happiness is rather beyond what the body has to offer. It is "inward" or "mental" or "intellectual" or "spiritual." On the other hand, of course, there have been (and still are) philosophers who take people to be nothing but bodies in motion. So, though without necessarily doubting that there may be more happiness to be gained from reading Shakespeare than playing golf, these thinkers naturally gravitate toward talking of happiness in which material, physical, or even emotional notions feature very prominently. So as prime and typical examples of happiness, which they often call "pleasure," they will cite dining well, having a night on the town, being in excellent health, having a marvelous sex life, owning lots of money, and so on.

Now Aquinas's view of people and his corresponding approaches to happiness fall somewhere between the two positions that I have just very summarily sketched.

Unlike authors such as Descartes and Plato, he certainly does not think that we are "ghosts in machines."[9] His view (sometimes referred to as *hylomorphic*) is that we are *essentially* physical objects. As bodies, he holds, we are a biological species, just like dogs or camels. And, so he thinks, it is only because we are bodily that we manage to learn about or get a grasp on the world. We learn what things are, where they are, and what they can do because we engage with them at a physical level. Rather in line with the legal expression "offences against the person," Aquinas takes (human) persons to be spatio-temporal individuals. He would, for example, never try to defend a rapist by saying that the offender was not raping a person but rather that he was doing something to a bit of anatomy mysteriously connected to something essentially distinct from what is bodily (a mind, soul, ego, or whatever).

On the other hand, however (and it is important also to remember this when trying to understand him on happiness), Aquinas believes that when people know or understand it is not just a physical process that is at work. He is, to be sure, happy to admit that physical processes can indicate what we think, know, or understand. And he is equally happy to agree that physical processes can strongly affect our ability to think, know, or understand. He is well aware that my behavior can tell you much about my state of mind. He is also aware that my chances of following and getting a grasp of Newton's thoughts on motion are likely to be much impaired by my first drinking ten glasses of whiskey or suffering from brain damage. But thinking, knowing, and understanding (when they occur) are not, for Aquinas, physical processes in me (albeit that they can be truly ascribed to me). Sensations, of course, are just that. When I burn my hand, I feel pain in *my* hand. When I blush, I feel warm in *my* face. But Aquinas holds that thinking, knowing, and understanding are categorically different from sensations.[10] For him, sensations are *private* property (the pain in *my* hand or the warmth in *my* cheeks). He does not deny that you and I can have similar sensations. But he takes them to be private in something like the sense that your bank balance is private to you even though you may have exactly the same amount of money in it as I have in mine. Yet this kind of privacy is not, Aquinas thinks, involved when it comes to thinking, knowing, and understanding (albeit that he does not, of course, deny that my act of understanding such and such can be truly attributed to me and not to you). For example, in his view, when you and I think that Rome is the capital of Italy, we can have (indeed, must have) exactly the same thought, knowledge, or understanding (albeit nonnumerically). Very much as Ludwig Wittgenstein did, Aquinas thinks of meaning (and, therefore, thought and understanding) as public, not as an event in someone's body (let alone something felt as one feels a toothache or an itch). So he takes thinking, knowing, and understanding to be immaterial. Or as Herbert McCabe succinctly puts it: "Both Wittgenstein and Aquinas would agree that I can say, 'This is what it *feels like for me*'; and both would agree that you cannot say, 'This is what the word 'hallucinatory' *means for me*'. A word has its meaning not in any material individual but in the language which transcends individuality and thus transcends matter."[11]

But, yet again, Aquinas is not someone who wants to downplay bodily factors when it comes to human happiness. Anyone who reads him seriously will continue to find him noting how we may often find happiness in what even some of the most hedonistic of thinkers have extolled: food, sex, money, leisure, fine weather, and so on. These are all things that Aquinas can take to be good and, therefore, as sources of human happiness. He is anything but puritanical when it comes to what we might think of as "earthly goods." In fact, and again with a debt to Aristotle, he encourages us to pursue almost all of them, albeit with moderation and on the understanding both that one can have too much of (be damaged by) a good thing and that it matters from where one obtains one's good things. Casting matters in contemporary terms, Aquinas would certainly applaud my enjoying a glass of wine and a good movie after a hard day at work (assuming that I have not stolen these items). And without even trying to put his clerical hat on, he would advise against my drinking two bottles of gin at a sitting (his reasons here being more or less those that my doctor would give me). He is also, we might note, generally against the principle that too little is intrinsically good. He thinks, for example, that there is a place for self-denial when it comes to material things and so favors fasting on certain occasions.[12] But he cannot be remotely grouped with those who think that the more physical damage we do to ourselves the better we are. He would not, for example, say that (except, perhaps, in exceptional circumstances) people ought to be trying to starve themselves to death, work until they drop, and so on. Or, to put the matter even more simply, Aquinas (who actually thinks that all created things are good) is keen on "earthly goods" and the happiness we might gain from them. His whole approach to philosophical ethics, we might add, is written with an eye on earthly happiness.[13] Aquinas (again following Aristotle) takes a good and happy human life to be a life exhibiting virtues. What does Aquinas take a human virtue to be? At its best, he takes it to be a permanent, acquired habit, which is a certain readiness to act in certain ways that are perfective and fulfilling of people *qua* people—something that makes for happiness, therefore. He is, indeed, fully aware that we can be stymied by circumstances and that virtuous people may end up in a sorry state (think of the many who have suffered at the hands of those to whom they have been trying to bring education and health care). At the same time, though, he relentlessly insists that people (considered as people and not just as people finding themselves stuck in unfortunate contexts) need certain virtues in order to be happy. Notwithstanding the ills that can afflict the virtuous, a book on Aquinas on human virtue could quite properly be titled "How to be Happy."[14]

Again, though, does Aquinas have a general or defining notion of happiness? As I noted above, the answer is that he does. He takes happiness to be the perfection of the totality of a well-lived human life. But we shall not understand quite what he means by this until we are clear on what he thinks happiness *not* to be. So we need now to follow him down what we might call his "negative" route. Even before doing that, however, I need to flag a crucial linguistic point concerning Aquinas on happiness, one of which readers of Aquinas on happiness need to be constantly aware.

The English word "happiness" can be used to translate at least two different Latin terms: *felicitas* and *beatitudo*. Aquinas makes copious use of both of these words, and there are times when he writes as though they are equivalent or synonymous. Primarily, however, he speaks of *felicitas* when he means happiness enjoyed by people before death (earthly happiness, so we might say): the delights that food can provide, the pleasure of looking at a beautiful painting, the enjoyment of good health, freedom from pain and worry, and so on. For Aquinas, *felicitas*, we might say, is what your average television commercial is trying to sell us. Yet such is not the case when it comes to his notion of *beatitudo* (which is the kind of happiness in which he seems to be most interested). This, for him, is complete fulfillment to which nothing can be added by way of improvement or variation.[15] Nor can it ever be lost. And that is because he takes it to be the *ultimate* good for people: union with God after death (something he calls the "beatific vision"). For Aquinas, therefore, *felicitas*, good though it may often be, is happiness in an imperfect or restricted sense while *beatitudo* is not (rather as a pleasant acquaintance with someone is nice but dramatically different from what was supposed to be going on between Romeo and Juliet).

To cut a long story short, here is the gist of Aquinas's take on happiness as *beatitudo*:

1. People by nature desire to be happy.
2. So in day-to-day life they aim, all things being equal, for what attracts them.
3. But they differ from nonhuman animals (who, thinks Aquinas, also strive to be happy or content) in that they are intellectual agents whose happiness, therefore, crucially or intrinsically includes an intellectual dimension (i.e., the ability to understand and not just be "turned on" by or to be physically affected by things). A purring cat may be thought of as a happy individual. But, thinks Aquinas, it is disadvantaged in its range of happiness by comparison with a properly functioning human being. Cats and the like (the lucky ones anyway) are content at a sensory level, but their behavior is instinctual, and they do not know or understand as we do. They have no scientific abilities. They cannot arrange a college education for themselves. They cannot work with or grasp concepts (like "cat," "purr," "sensation," or "veterinary surgeon").[16] Following Aristotle, however, Aquinas believes that people can form concepts and display (or play out) their nature as people as they come to know what things are, were, or might be, and as they plan, aim, and act with such concepts in mind.
4. Pursuing this line of thought, Aquinas holds that understanding is essential to and perfective of human beings (rather like breathing, eating, or sleeping). As it happens, he thinks that human understanding is a low grade kind of thing when compared with the understanding of some individuals (here he has angels and God in mind). But he still rates it highly as something that belongs to us by nature and, therefore, as utterly necessary when it comes to us being happy. "Since happiness," he observes, "is the proper good of an intellectual nature, happiness must pertain to an intellectual nature by reason of what is proper to that nature."[17] For Aquinas, happiness for people (whatever forms it may take) lies in what critically distinguishes them from other things in the world: knowing or understanding.

5. Yet, in what might our *ultimate* happiness consist? Unlike many who have written about happiness (and here I think of authors like David Hume, Jeremy Bentham, John Stuart Mill, Friedrich Nietzsche, and Jean-Paul Sartre), Aquinas is adamant that it can consist only in a post-mortem knowledge and understanding of God, whom he takes to be the source of everything creaturely that makes for human happiness in this life (in this sense, *beatitudo*, for Aquinas, goes way beyond *felicitas*). According to Aquinas, God, the beginning and end of all things, contains in himself the goodness and perfection of all creatures, not to mention the goodness and perfections proper to him alone. Knowing himself to be what he is, God, for Aquinas, is completely happy (he enjoys *beatitudo* without qualification). And, following the lead of the New Testament, Aquinas holds that people (holy people, those who persevere in loving God in word and deed) will share in the happiness that is God's. In 1 John 3:2 we find the lines: "Beloved, we are God's children now; what we will be has not yet been revealed. What we do know is this: when he is revealed, we will be like him, for we will see him as he is."[18] Then again, 2 Peter 1:4 speaks of us escaping from "the corruption that is in the world" so as to "become partakers in the divine nature." Strongly influenced by texts such as these, Aquinas's conclusion is that our final and *complete* happiness (something in a much higher league than *felicitas*) lies in union with God in the life to come (the "beatific vision," should we achieve it).[19] In this sense we may say that Aquinas on ultimate happiness is decidedly theocentric.[20] We may also note that Aquinas is perfectly willing to allow that pursuit of *beatitudo* might rightly involve us in an avoidance of *felicitas* (as, for example, when we dedicate ourselves to union with God in a way that prevents us from aiming at certain worldly goods: for example, refusing to deny the reality of God when offered money or sexual gratification to do so).

So happiness in the fullest sense turns out, for Aquinas, to be a theological notion (indeed, a *Christian* theological notion) with an eschatological focus (as is not the case with, for example, Aristotle, whose views on happiness still, as I have said, have very much in common with those of Aquinas). But this, of course, brings us back to ways in which Aquinas travels down his negative route, the one in which he tries to explain why he thinks what *beatitudo* (ultimate or complete happiness) *cannot* amount to. A good place to see him doing so is *ST* I-II q.2.[21] This consists of six articles (all in the form of questions). For a quick sense of Aquinas's thinking in this text, I shall simply list some of its questions in order and paraphrase each of his answers to them together with some points he makes when elaborating on these answers.[22] Thus:

1. *Does Ultimate Happiness lie in riches?* Riches can be natural in that they can satisfy our natural or basic needs (food, drink, and shelter would be "natural riches"). Riches can also be artificial (as, for example, is money). Ultimate happiness lies in neither kind of riches, since both are merely

means to ends. We seek food and the like because we aim at keeping ourselves alive. We desire money and the like, since they help us to obtain what we need to live. Also, riches can be had by both good and bad people while perfect happiness is incompatible with evil of any sort.

2. *Does Ultimate Happiness lie in honors?* No, because honors, even if they make us happy, go to those who have achieved something and therefore cannot be the cause or aim of these achievements (i.e., we cannot think of ultimate happiness as consisting in present achievements for which we are already honored). And, like riches, honors can be had by people who are bad.
3. *Does Ultimate Happiness lie in fame or glory?* No, since fame and glory can be illusory.
4. *Does Ultimate Happiness lie in power?* No, since power is what enables activity while ultimate happiness is an achievement. Also, power can be used well or badly while ultimate happiness involves no possible badness. Furthermore, power (like riches, honors, fame, and glory) can all be had by people who lack other sources of happiness, which is not the case with those who enjoy ultimate happiness. Note also that riches, honors, fame, glory, and power can all sometimes lead to the harm of those who have them. Also note that riches, honors, fame, glory, and power come from sources outside ourselves (and do so often by luck or chance), whereas ultimate happiness lies within us and fulfills what is intrinsic to us.
5. *Does Ultimate Happiness lie in bodily well-being?* Human bodily qualities cannot make for people's ultimate happiness for such qualities are often found to a greater degree in nonhuman animals (for example, elephants live longer than we do, and lions are stronger than we are). Also, since we are essentially intellectual beings, our ultimate happiness cannot lie in physical (or sensory) well-being alone (nice though that can often be).
6. *Does Ultimate Happiness lie in bodily (sensory) pleasures?* No, for these are not the only sources of enjoyment. They are also temporary and individual physical states while ultimate human happiness depends on our sustained intellectual grasp of what goes well beyond these.

In short, Aquinas finds it hard to believe that ultimate happiness (*beatitudo*) can lie in anything creaturely. Or, in his own words:

> For man to rest content with any created good is not possible, for he can be happy only with complete good which satisfies his desire altogether: he would not have reached his ultimate end were there something still remaining to be desired. The object of the will, that is the human appetite, is the Good without reserve, just as the object of the mind is the True without reserve. Clearly, then, nothing can satisfy man's will except such goodness, which is found, not in anything created, but in God alone. Everything created is a derivative good.[23]

This conclusion obviously raises a number of questions. Does God exist? Do people act for ends? Do people naturally seek to be happy? Can sense be made of a beatific vision? If so, how is it that the beatific vision satisfies the human desire for happiness? No doubt, a full justification of Aquinas's account of happiness will depend on answers to these and other questions, which I cannot try to deal with here.[24]

NOTES

1. We all know the athlete's slogan "No pain, no gain." But think also of people who would speak of themselves as finding happiness in living lives that many would find distasteful in the extreme (members of certain rather austere religious orders: Carthusians or Cistercians, for example).

2. For a useful introduction to theories of happiness, see Steven M. Cahn and Christine Vitrano, eds., *Happiness: Classic and Contemporary Readings in Philosophy* (New York and Oxford: Oxford University Press, 2008). See also Elizabeth Telfer, *Happiness* (London and Basingstoke: Macmillan Press, 1980).

3. Cf. *ST* I-II q.1 a.1.

4. I say "not always" in this sentence since, I presume, we can talk about mental activity (such as following an argument or envying someone) without thinking of overtly physical processes (like going for a walk or mending a washing machine). Aquinas in various places distinguishes between "immanent" and "transient" action. Here he is (surely rightly) thinking that there is a big difference between, for example, my admiring you and my trying to kiss you.

5. I say "all things being equal" since, of course, practical reasoning, unlike theoretical reasoning, can be affected by the addition of extra premises. A formally valid argument is not vitiated by the addition of extra premises. But a piece of practical reason might be. Thus, for example, the reasonableness of my getting on a certain plane from Paris to New York might be deeply affected by learning that this particular plane has certain critical parts missing from it. Cf. Anthony Kenny, *Will, Freedom, and Power* (Oxford: Basil Blackwell, 1975), ch. 5.

6. My impression is that Aquinas thinks that we could be aiming for happiness even should it be the case that what appeals to us is masochism.

7. I have heard it said that Aquinas denies that nonhuman animals enjoy happiness. In fact, though, he often ascribes pleasure to nonhuman animals. Cf. *ST* I-II q.31 a.1 or I-II q.4 a.2. He knows very well that animals can be thought of as happy in some sense. What he denies is that their happiness, when they have it, is something gained by them as an intellectual goal pursued and understood by them as such. And he thinks that this is so because he takes nonhuman animals not to have what he means by "intellect".

8. It might be said that Arthur Schopenhauer was someone who disbelieved in the existence of happiness. In *The World as Will and Representation* (1818), he pessimistically seems to claim that, given the nature of our will or desire, it is impossible for anyone to be genuinely happy.

9. The phrase "ghost in a machine" is, perhaps, best known from Gilbert Ryle's use of it in his highly influential anti-Cartesian book *The Concept of Mind* (London: Hutchinson, 1949).

10. In "Analytical Philosophy and the Spirituality of Man," Elizabeth Anscombe interestingly observes how Descartes (a "ghost in the machine" thinker when it comes to

people) internalizes sensations so as to make them nonbodily occurrences on the dubious ground that he can doubt that he has a body but not that he hears, sees, and so on. See Elizabeth Anscombe, *Human Life, Action and Ethics* (Exeter: Imprint Academic, 2005), 5. By contrast, Aquinas (surely with more sense on his side than Descartes) takes hearing, seeing, and so on (understood, of course, in nonmetaphorical senses) as inextricably bodily. The "darkness" of the Middle Ages did not seem to prevent Aquinas from recognizing that, speaking literally, you need ears to hear, eyes to see, and a nose to smell. I presume that he would think along the same lines today were he to know of rare nonhuman animals (of the kind who amaze us as we view the numerous television programs about them) whose engagement with the world does not depend on them having human organs or anything that look remotely like them.

11. Herbert McCabe, *On Aquinas* (London and New York: Continuum, 2008). One might rightly accuse me (and McCabe) of here presenting a conclusion of Aquinas in somewhat anachronistic terms (ones which take Aquinas to be thinking of understanding chiefly on the model of talking). But I think that this is actually a helpful way of getting his main point about understanding across to contemporary readers especially since both Aquinas and Wittgenstein are concerned that we should not misread linguistic life by assimilating it to sensations or to events in the brain. For an example of Aquinas precisely speaking in his own voice and terminology, see *ST* I q.75 a.2. Here his argument for human understanding being immaterial runs: "It is obvious that man's understanding enables him to know the nature of all bodily things. But what can in this way take in things must have nothing of their natures of their own, for the form that was in it by nature would obstruct the knowledge of anything else.... Accordingly, if the intellectual principle had in it the physical nature of any bodily thing, it would be unable to know all bodies. Each of them has its own determinate nature. Impossible, therefore, that the principle of understanding be something bodily." I quote from vol. 11 of the Blackfriars edition of *ST* (London and New York: Eyre and Spottiswoode, 1970).

12. Cf. *ST* II-II q.146 a.1.

13. I should note that, speaking purely as a philosopher, Aquinas concentrates on the classical cardinal virtues, the possession of which he takes (as did Aristotle) to be vital when it comes to human happiness in this life. But, speaking more theologically, Aquinas believes in what he calls "theological virtues," which he believes to be critically important when it comes to ultimate human happiness. More on this matter (as on other issues on which I touch above) can be found in some other contributions to the present volume.

14. With this thought in mind, readers might be interested in consulting Herbert McCabe, *The Good Life: Ethics and the Pursuit of Happiness* (London and New York: Continuum, 2005).

15. Aquinas thinks that everyone naturally desires beatitude whether they realize it or not. That is because he holds that whatever enjoyment I might achieve by *X*, *Y*, or *Z*, such enjoyment is but a getting hold of something good, not of being in a state in which nothing is left for me to want. As long as there remains something we lack but can add to our happiness then, thinks Aquinas (reasonably as it seems to me, though not, perhaps, to some non-theistic millionaires), we have not achieved perfect happiness (*beatitudo*) and are always looking for more.

16. See note 5 above.

17. *SCG* III, 26.

18. I quote from the New Revised Standard Version of the New Testament.

19. Aquinas's account of the beatific vision is a complicated one and I do not think that this is the place to try to explain what it amounts to in detail. Perhaps, though, I ought

at least to note (a) that he obviously does not equate it with looking at God as one might look at a physical object, and (b) that he basically thinks that it involves us sharing, at least to a limited degree, in the life and being of God. For a general study of the concept of the vision of God, see Kenneth Kirk, *The Vision of God: The Christian Doctrine of the Summum Bonum* (New York: Harper Torchbooks, 1966). For a discussion of Aquinas on the beatific vision written with an eye on what St Albert the Great says on the topic, see Jeffrey Hergan, *St. Albert the Great's Theory of the Beatific Vision* (New York: Peter Lang, 2002). Kirk deals with Aquinas on pp. 379–94 of his volume. Hergan does so in his ch. 5.

20. I should note that ultimate human happiness (however much they might desire it) is not, for Aquinas, something that people can achieve by their natural human abilities or powers. For him, *beatitude* (the "beatific vision") is a gift of God. Cf. *ST* I-II q.5 a.5. But then, of course, one also has to remember that, for Aquinas, everything created is a gift of God.

21. See also *SCG* III, chapters 26–33.

22. I should note that in his discussion of what happiness does not consist in Aquinas's questions and answers very much resemble what we find in bk 3 of Boethius's *The Consolation of Philosophy*. Aquinas's discussion of happiness is surely heavily indebted to that of Boethius.

23. *ST* I-II q.2 a.8. I quote from vol. 16 of the Blackfriars edition of the *ST* (London and New York: Eyre and Spottiswoode, 1969).

24. For two recent, detailed, and interesting books on Aquinas and happiness, see (1) Denis Bradley, *Aquinas on the Twofold Human Good: Reason and Happiness in Aquinas's Moral Science* (Washington, D.C.: Catholic University of America Press, 1997), and (2) Stephen Wang, *Aquinas and Sartre on Freedom, Personal Identity, and the Possibility of Happiness* (Washington, D.C.: Catholic University of America Press, 2009). See also the entry on "Happiness" by Georg Wielad in Stephen Pope, ed., *The Ethics of Aquinas* (Washington, D.C.: Georgetown University Press, 2002). I should add that for critical comments on earlier versions of this contribution to the present volume I am much indebted to Christopher Arroyo, Michael Baur, Gyula Klima, Turner Nevitt, and Giorgio Pini.

CHAPTER 18

LAW AND NATURAL LAW

MICHAEL BAUR

In his often-quoted definition, Aquinas tells us that law is "nothing other than an ordering of reason for the common good from one who has care of the community, and promulgated."[1] For Aquinas, law is essentially an ordering of reason, and not of will, since law is a rule and measure of acts; the first principle of action is the end; and it belongs to reason to direct things to an end.[2] Aquinas acknowledges that law would have no motive force, and thus no power to cause or prohibit action, if it were not for the will.[3] But without the ordering of reason, the will's motive force would be without aim or direction. For "to command is essentially an act of reason"[4] and "to order is the proper act of reason."[5] Aquinas's account of law as an ordering of reason for the common good of a community depends on his mereology (i.e., his theory of parthood relations, including the relations of parts to parts and parts to wholes), and so a fuller exploration of his account of law might well begin with an examination of parts, wholes, and the common good in his thought.

Parts, Wholes, and the Common Good

Aquinas tells us that "all who are included in a community stand in relation to that community as parts to a whole,"[6] and "every individual person is compared to the whole community as part to whole."[7] Now for Aquinas, it is possible for things to constitute a plurality of separate, unified wholes in one respect, while being parts of another unified whole in some other respect. Thus, individual human beings are separate, unified wholes insofar as they are individuated living substances capable of performing their own biological and psychological functions and undertaking action on their own behalf; but they may also be parts of some other unified whole insofar as they belong to a community such as a political order. Aquinas notes that any multitude whatsoever can be regarded as a unified whole in some respect. But he goes on to observe that only substances (such as living organisms) can be regarded as unified wholes absolutely speaking, or without qualification; by contrast, things that are a plurality of substances absolutely speaking, but unified wholes in a certain respect, are not said to be unified through any substantial unity but rather through a "unity of composition or order."[8]

Significantly, Aquinas holds that the perfection of wholes through the proper ordering of their parts does not entail the elimination of diversity, but in many cases requires diversity. Thus, "the order and perfection of a whole" is not possible if there is not a "disparity among its parts."[9] In a whole where each part is essentially the same as every other part (such as in a homogeneous body of water), the parts are interchangeable and the whole can remain what it is, no matter how the parts might be rearranged. This is clearly not the case in a more perfect whole (such as in the body of a living organism), where the whole could not remain what it is if the parts (like eyes and legs) could be switched around indiscriminately. For Aquinas, it is precisely the presence of diverse parts within a whole that accounts for a whole's greater degree of excellence and perfection. Thus, even if a particular part within some whole were to become more excellent by becoming more like some other, nobler part (e.g., if the foot were to become more like the eye), the whole itself would have less perfection and dignity as the whole that it is.[10] Also, Aquinas asserts that the existence of a genuine ordering among diverse parts does not render the parts merely passive or acquiescent, but in fact requires that the parts be capable of action in their own right: "If we take away the actions of things we take away the order of things to one another, for there is no tying together of things that are diverse according to their natures into the unity of order except by the fact that some are active and some are passive."[11] For Aquinas, a community of merely passive, noninteracting beings would not be a genuinely ordered community, but a mere aggregation of things that had nothing to do with one another and that could not be ordered with respect to one another.[12]

For Aquinas, there are two ways in which we can talk about the ordering of parts within a whole: first, insofar as the parts are ordered with respect to one another; and secondly, insofar as the parts are ordered toward an end.[13] Corresponding to this twofold ordering of parts within a whole, we can also talk about a twofold good of any whole. First, there is the intrinsic good; this is the form of the whole, which arises through the unity and ordering of the parts within the whole and is the end of generation or alteration. Second, there is the extrinsic good; this is an end that is external to the whole as such and for the sake of which the whole as a whole exists.[14] Aquinas illustrates this twofold good by talking about the form of an army (its intrinsic good), which is the ordering of its parts to one another, and that for the sake of which the army and its internal ordering exists (its extrinsic good), which is military victory.[15] Aquinas also notes that "whenever we find a multitude whose members are ordered to each other, that multitude must necessarily be ordered to some external principle."[16] Thus, the ordering of a whole's parts to one another (the whole's formal cause or intrinsic good) is always for the sake of the ordering of the whole to its extrinsic end (its final cause). As Aquinas says (following Aristotle), the final cause and not the formal cause is properly called "the cause of causes."[17]

On Aquinas's account, the good toward which the law directs a community is called the "common good" of that community. Now that which is said to be "common" can be understood in two different ways: on the one hand, something that is "common after the manner of an effect or predication" is found in many things according to one intelligible character, as the intelligible character of "animal" is common to all human beings; on the other hand, something that is "common after the manner of a cause" remains numerically one but extends to many effects.[18] It is in this latter sense that the "common good" toward which law orders a community is said to be "common." In fact, Aquinas says that what is common by way of predication—such as "the unity or community of human nature"—is nothing in reality, but only in the consideration of the mind.[19] While the law directs individuals in their actions, and actions are always particular, it remains the case that law is not directed to the particular good of any individual but rather to the common good of a community. The particular actions of individuals are referable to the common good of a community, not as to a common genus or species, but as to a common final cause or end.[20] It is in this sense that Aquinas can use the term, "common good," to refer to: God (as the common end of all creatures[21]), victory in battle (as the common end of an army's soldiers[22]), justice (as the common end of citizens[23]), and children (as the common end of two parents[24]).

Notice that, for Aquinas, the common good or common end toward which members of a community are ordered can be the sort of end that the agents bring into existence through their own actions (e.g., justice within a community), or the sort of end (like God) that can exist apart from the actions of the agents whose end it is.[25] Furthermore, the common good or end toward which a community is ordered can be an extrinsic common good (e.g., God, victory in battle, or children) or an intrinsic common good (e.g., justice or order within a particular community). In any case, since the final cause (and not the formal cause) is the "cause of all causes," the primary sense in which the law orders a community to a common good is in the sense of an extrinsic and not intrinsic good; this is because a community can be ordered to an intrinsic common good only on account of its being ordered to an extrinsic common good.[26] What remains "common" (i.e., "common by way of predication") to any common good is that the common good is the common or shared end or goal (or, in the case of rational creatures, the object of a common or shared willing) at which the community's members aim precisely insofar as they are members of that community.

On Aquinas's account, the common good of a community is not reducible to the particular goods of any of its parts. Furthermore, what is fundamentally good about the common good of a community is not that the common good serves as a means for securing the particular goods, or for coordinating the particular ends, of its various parts. Just as a community has its own kind of being that is distinct from the being of any of its parts, so too the common good of a community is a distinctive kind of good, not ultimately explainable in terms of the goods of its parts. What is fundamentally good about the common good of a community is that the common good is perfective of the community as a whole, precisely in connection with the kind of unity and being that the community has. For Aquinas, to speak of a whole is to speak "of those things in which something one and perfect emerges from all the parts taken together, and this perfection pertains to none of the parts, as in a house or an animal."[27] Just as we can talk about actions that are attributable to a group taken as a whole but not attributable to any of the individual parts (e.g., "the team won," "the company issued stock," "the nation declared war"), so too we can talk about goods that are goods of the whole as such, but not of any of the parts: "For the good that results from the composition of parts, through which the whole is good, is not in any of the parts. Hence the parts are not good by that goodness which is proper to the whole."[28]

In virtue of being common ("by way of causation"), a common good on Aquinas's account remains numerically one and undivided while simultaneously being desired by and perfective of many different parts, precisely insofar as they are parts. In other words, a good that is common by way of causation is essentially a shareable good. When one member of a community enjoys the goodness of a common good, this enjoyment by one part does not in itself entail subtraction from or detriment to the similar enjoyment of the same common good by another part or parts. When Lily and Grace discuss philosophy over a bottle of wine, the particular sips of wine that they imbibe and enjoy while conversing are particular goods. The very same sip of wine (the numerically one and undivided portion of wine) that Lily imbibes and enjoys simply cannot be imbibed and enjoyed by Grace, so when Lily imbibes and enjoys more of the wine, there is less of the wine to be imbibed and enjoyed by Grace. By contrast, the philosophical conversation that Lily and Grace are having (while imbibing the wine) is a common good; it can remain numerically one and undivided while both are enjoying the conversation. In itself, Lily's enjoyment of the conversation does not entail any subtraction from or detriment to Grace's enjoyment of the conversation. When Lily enjoys the conversation more, it does not follow that Grace has to enjoy the conversation less. The important point here is that the common good enjoyed by members of a group or community is formally different, and not just quantitatively different, from the particular goods enjoyed by those members: "The common good of the realm and the particular good of the individual differ not only in respect of the *many* and the *few*, but also under a formal aspect."[29] It is on account of this formal difference that a good that is common by way of causation can be enjoyed by many without division or subtraction, while a particular good cannot.

Aquinas also holds that, strictly speaking, the end of some given whole (the common end or good that is a common good for its parts) does not stand in opposition to or in conflict with the end or ends of its particular parts as such; for "the part is not divided in opposition to the whole, but in opposition to another part."[30] But it is certainly possible for there to be opposition or conflict between the end or ends of the whole and the end or ends that a part may have insofar as the part is regarded as the part of some other whole or as a distinct whole in its own right. To explain this further, we need to recall, as Aquinas observes, that reason may consider a single thing under many different aspects:

> therefore, if a man's will wills a thing to be, according as it appears to be good, his will is good: and the will of another man, who wills that thing not to be, according as it appears evil, is also good. Thus a judge has a good will, in willing a thief to be put to death, because this is just: while the will of another—e.g., the thief's wife or son, who wishes him not to be put to death, inasmuch as killing is a natural evil—is also good.[31]

Now insofar as a judge is authorized to act on behalf of an entire community, anything that he or she wills as a judge will be willed under the aspect of the common or universal good (under the aspect of what is a proper end for the community as a whole); and what a wife wills regarding her husband or a son wills regarding his father is something willed under the aspect of its being some particular good, suited to the kind of relationships that exist between wives and husbands, and sons and fathers. Now the very same thing may happen to be good under a universal aspect, and yet not good under a particular aspect. Thus, the will of the judge (in favor of killing the man) and the wills of the wife and son (opposed to the killing of the man) can both be good, even though they seem to will opposite things. For as Aquinas points out, they will opposite things only accidentally, and not under the same formal aspect. It is not the case that the wife and son will that justice be violated; nor is it the case that the judge wills the death of a man precisely as a death. Rather, the judge wills that justice be done, and the wife and son will that the husband and father should live. There is no conflict between these ends as such; the conflict is incidental to what the parties will, formally and properly understood. Or to make the same general point in a different way, when regarded as parts of the whole political community, the wife and son are able to will (along with the judge) that justice be done. It is only when they are regarded as parts of some other whole (e.g., a family) or as distinct wholes in their own right (e.g., as individuals in some respect) that the wife and son can be seen as having ends that stand opposed to the community's end of seeing that justice be done.

Aquinas observes that the wife and son may act in accordance with their proper inclinations as parts of the political whole (that is, they can will that justice be done) while simultaneously acting in accordance with their proper inclinations as wife and son (that is, they can also will that the life of their loved one be spared) if they will the common good (justice) *formally* and the particular good (the preservation of a man's life) *materially*. Here, to will a common good *formally* is to be attracted to a single final cause or goal precisely under its aspect of having many effects, though these many effects remain unspecified or unenumerated; and to will a particular good *materially* is to be attracted to a single final cause or goal precisely under its aspect of having some particular effect on some specific individual or individuals. For Aquinas, the wife and son ought to will formally the common good (that justice be done) and will materially the particular good (that a particular man's life be preserved), all the while subordinating their material willing of the particular good to their formal willing of the common good. Notice that this does not require the wife and son to engage in any self-contradictory willing; that is, they are not required to will both in favor of some particular action and against the same action in the same respect. However, it does require that they subordinate their material willing of the particular good to their formal willing of the common good, and thus that they be willing to risk losing some particular good that they cherish (e.g., the life of a loved one, their wealth and possessions, or even their own lives) for the sake of the common good, in the event that it becomes impossible in some particular situation for both the common good and the particular good to be preserved.

For Aquinas, a good citizen is one who is willing to subordinate his or her willing of particular goods to his or her willing of the political community's common good. Indeed, Aquinas holds that it is a natural tendency of every part, as such, to subordinate the love that it has for its own particular good to the greater love that it has for the common good of the whole:

> each part naturally loves the common good of the whole more than it loves its own particular good. This is evidenced by its operation, since the principle inclination of each part is towards common action conducive to the good of the whole. It may also be seen in civic virtues whereby sometimes the citizens suffer damage even to their own property and persons for the sake of the common good.[32]

On Aquinas's account, citizens are generally willing to bear their fair share of a political community's tax burden, since for the most part they recognize that their shared shouldering of the tax burden is essential for the achievement of a common good or goods that could not otherwise be attained.

Of course, it might be objected that: (a) individual citizens would not pay their taxes if they were not reasonably confident that others would do so as well; (b) individual citizens are confident that others will pay their taxes, since the law has established certain mechanisms to punish those who do not pay their taxes; and therefore (c) individual citizens are induced to pay their taxes only because of a generalized threat of punishment and not because they love the common good more than they love their own particular goods. Aquinas would be able to acknowledge that (a) and (b) may both be true, while nevertheless denying that (c) follows. Indeed, on Aquinas's account, the attempt to argue from (a) and (b) to (c) commits the error of mistaking the effect (the establishment of some mechanism for punishment) for the cause (lawfulness). That is to say, (a) and (b) can be taken to support not (c), but rather the conclusion that (d) individual citizens generally recognize that as citizens they share a common end whose importance is sufficiently weighty to justify the establishment of certain mechanisms for coercing those who do not willingly contribute their fair share toward the attainment of this common end. If individual citizens did not willingly and for the most part shoulder their fair share of the overall tax burden, then the very notion of lawfulness would cease to apply. For if tax monies essential to sustaining the common good had to be coercively wrested from a majority of the citizens, then the community would have to expend large sums of its wealth simply in order to enforce the tax code. But there is a point at which the costs of enforcing the tax code would exceed the gains to be had through such enforcement, in which case the very effort at enforcement would cannibalize itself. Just as an excessive amount of cancer will eventually destroy the body (and thus destroy the cancer itself), and an excessive amount of counterfeit will eventually destroy a currency (and thus destroy the counterfeit itself), so too excessive costs in enforcement will eventually destroy the common good for which such enforcement exists, and thus undermine the whole point of enforcement itself. On Aquinas's account, lawfulness is compatible with the need to compel compliance in some instances, but incompatible with the need to compel compliance in most instances.[33]

Law Establishes a Principle of Action that is Internal to the Beings that are Subject to the Law

The preceding considerations point us toward an aspect of Aquinas's account of law that is frequently overlooked, even by his most sympathetic commentators. For Aquinas, the term "law" does not denote an externally imposed command or ordinance, but rather a rule or ordering whose effective force in directing individuals to act for the sake of the common good is present within the individual beings thus directed. Of course, law does involve the direction of one thing by another, for—strictly speaking—one does not make law for oneself, but only for another. But in making law for another, the lawmaker establishes a principle or rule of action that is *internal* to the beings subject to the law.[34] It is for this reason, Aquinas asserts, that human beings—notwithstanding their ability to exercise control over nonrational creatures—are unable to make law for nonrational creatures. For when human beings exercise control over nonrational creatures (e.g., when a farmer plows a field by controlling the actions of oxen), the actions taking place are not the actions of the nonrational creatures, but rather the actions of the human beings who are using the nonrational beings as instruments (e.g., thus it is the farmer who plows the field by using the oxen as instruments, and not the oxen who plow the field). The reason why we cannot make law for nonrational creatures is that the principles by means of which we control nonrational creatures are the principles of our actions alone, and not the (internalized) principles of the actions of the nonrational creatures under our control.[35]

For Aquinas, to be subject to law in its broadest sense is to be a member of a community, and to be a member of a community is to be attracted to the common good of the community in such a way that in acting in accordance with one's own nature and inclinations (and not merely as an externally controlled instrument of another), the individual also acts for the benefit of the common good. Thus, actions of an individual that might otherwise seem puzzling may become intelligible, when regarded as the actions of an individual that is also a member of a community. Consider the African wild dog (*Lycaon pictus*) whose behavior is typical of many canids. After a successful hunt, the mother dog is greeted in the den by her pups, whose licking of her face elicits from her an instinctive regurgitation reaction: the mother dog instinctively disgorges portions of the flesh that she had just devoured.[36] If one regards the mother dog simply as an isolated individual, one might think that this spontaneous regurgitation reaction is a sign of some illness or disease. But if one regards her as a member of a community, such behavior becomes perfectly intelligible: the regurgitated bolus provides partially digested flesh for the pups to eat, and thus contributes to the care of the young and the survival of the species. This natural behavior of the mother dog illustrates what, for Aquinas, is meant by law: law is in the mother dog in the sense that her own actions, emerging from her own natural instincts and inclinations, are directed toward the common good of the community (in this case, toward the survival of the species). As Aquinas observes, even sensuous inclinations in animals have the character of law, insofar as they are ordained to the common good, which consists in "the preservation of nature in the species or the individual."[37]

On Aquinas's account, there are different ways in which law may be said to be in individual beings. If the community under consideration is a biological species, then the source of law is the species as a whole, and—as we have seen—the individual organism is directed to the common good of the species by means of the instinctual makeup that the individual has, thanks to its species membership. If the community under consideration is the entire community of created beings, then the lawgiver is God as creator of the whole universe, and law is in every created being in the sense that every inclination and every action of every created being is an effect of God's creative and legislative action, and is thereby directed to the common good of the whole universe. For Aquinas, there is nothing in the created universe (whether contingent or necessary) that falls outside the scope of "eternal law," which is the name that Aquinas gives to God's creative act of legislation for all things.[38] Nothing that pertains to God's essence, however, is subject to eternal law, since God's essence is not different from the eternal law itself,[39] and to be subject to law, strictly speaking, is to be subject to the governance of another.[40] Along with eternal law, says Aquinas, we can also talk about "divine law," but divine law is nothing other than eternal law itself, only apprehended under the aspect of its being made known by God to human beings through revelation, primarily through the Old and the New Testaments.[41]

Eternal law is present in, and directive of, every created being, even when one created being is harmed as a result of the activity of some other created being (e.g., when the zebra is preyed upon by the African wild dog); for, according to Aquinas, although it is not something good for the zebra when it is preyed upon by the African wild dog, nevertheless, it is good for the perfection of the universe as a whole that there should exist many different kinds of beings, some of which might thrive and perfect themselves at the expense of others.[42] On Aquinas's account, eternal law is the cause of all created beings and all their acts, and it is by virtue of such creative, legislative causality (not by virtue of any legislative act that supervenes upon already existent beings or acts) that eternal law directs all things to the common good of the universe.[43] For Aquinas, this common good of the universe is an extrinsic good, God himself,[44] insofar as every created being is attracted to God and manifests its desire for God in its very act of seeking its own perfection, for in attaining its own perfection, each created being—in its own way—attains some likeness to God's perfection.[45] But in seeking God, each created being also seeks—again, in its own way—the perfection of the created universe as a whole. This perfection consists in the ordered coming together of the many diverse beings in the created universe which—by being thus ordered to one another and to God—constitute an imperfect likeness of the perfect, fully nondiverse, and undivided goodness of God.[46] Thus, in being attracted to the extrinsic common good of the universe (God himself), all created beings are also attracted to the intrinsic common good of the universe (the order and perfection of the created universe as a whole[47]).

For Aquinas, there are two ways in which we can talk about the presence of eternal law in a created being: in one way, eternal law is said to be in a created being as in that which is ruled and measured; in a second way, eternal law is said to be in a created being as in that which rules and measures.[48] Now eternal law is in all created beings in the first way, since all created beings are directed to the common good of the universe and are thus ruled and measured in accordance with such direction. But in addition to this first way, there is also a second way in which eternal law is in some (but not all) created beings: it is in us rational beings as in that which rules or measures. The presence in us of eternal law, in this unique, twofold way, is what Aquinas calls "natural law." It is important to note that, for Aquinas, natural law is not something separate from eternal law.[49] Rather, for Aquinas, the natural law is the eternal law itself, but regarded under the aspect of its being in us (rational beings) in this unique, twofold way: it is in us as in created beings that are ruled, measured, and directed by means of it, but also in us as in created (rational) beings that rule, measure, and direct (both ourselves and other things) by means of it.[50]

Aquinas identifies yet another way in which we can talk about law, which he calls "human law." Recall that for Aquinas, "natural law" denotes the unique way in which we, as rational beings, are subject to eternal law in a twofold way: as both directed and directive, as both ordered and ordering. As Aquinas notes, it is by virtue of the natural law that we are providential both for ourselves and other beings,[51] which is to say that we rationally direct both ourselves and others to the ends that we apprehend as ends. But when we thus direct both ourselves and others to the ends that we apprehend as ends, it is not necessarily the case that the principles operative in our directive, ordering acts should become the internal principles of the actions of those things that are subject to our acts of ordering and direction. Thus, we can exercise control over nonrational beings and direct them to the ends that we apprehend as ends, but we do not prescribe for them any principles that become the internal principles of their own actions; as we have seen, we do not make law for nonrational beings. But for Aquinas, there may be instances in which our acts of giving order and direction do include the establishment of principles of action that are the internal principles of the actions of those beings that are subject to our acts of ordering and direction. When, for the sake of some common good, we prescribe principles of action that become the internal principles of action of the beings subject to our direction, we are engaged in acts of lawmaking. While we cannot make law for nonrational beings, we can make law for other human beings. This is because human beings, by virtue of their ability to communicate rationally with one another and persuade one another by means of rational discourse, are able to "imprint" on the minds of others a rule or principle that becomes in these others an internal principle of action.[52]

For Aquinas, just as natural law is not something separate from eternal law, so too human law is not something separate from natural law. Rather, human law is the special way in which natural law is in us when we not only provide rational direction for ourselves and other beings subject to our control, but do so in such a way that the principles of our directive, ordering activity become the *internal* principles of action in those other (human) beings that are directed by us for the sake of some common good. It is against this backdrop that one must understand Aquinas's famous statement to the effect that "unjust law is no law at all."[53] The point of Aquinas's statement is not that individuals have license to disobey legal directives that are unjust or morally defective in some respect, on the grounds that such directives are not really laws at all. The point, rather, is that legal directives have the character of law—properly speaking—only insofar as they are the sort of directives which, for the most part, serve as the internalized principles of the actions of the (rational) human beings subject to them. If legal directives are not, for the most part, internalized, then they must as a rule be externally imposed on individuals, which is to say that they are "violent" and not internally motivating (they are "not binding in conscience"). For Aquinas, legal directives that have to be externally imposed in this way, simply fail to satisfy what it *means* to be law. But even if certain legal directives are, for the most part, externally imposed on individuals and thus lack the character of lawfulness, it may still be the case, so Aquinas argues, that individuals may nevertheless be morally obligated to obey such directives; for individual acts of disobedience may ultimately be more harmful than beneficial to the common good (which, after all, is that for the sake of which law exists).

Eternal Law, Natural Law, and Human Freedom

To say that natural law is in us, is to say that eternal law is in us (and thus that we are attracted and directed to God and the perfection of the created universe) in a twofold way: eternal law is in us as in beings that are ruled, measured, and ordered, and it is in us as in beings that are also capable of ruling, measuring, and ordering. Now it is tempting to think that the two ways in which eternal law is in us correspond to two different kinds of inclinations in us: (a) inclinations in us by virtue of our "pre-rational" nature, which are inclinations that we share with nonrational beings (including our inclinations toward self-preservation, self-reproduction, the rearing of the young, etc.[54]) and which correspond to the way that eternal law is in us as in beings that are ruled, measured, and ordered; and (b) inclinations in us by virtue of our "rational" nature, which are inclinations that are absent in nonrational beings (such as the inclination to know the truth about God[55]) and which correspond to the way that eternal law is in us as in beings that are capable of ruling, measuring, and ordering. But Aquinas himself would reject any theory that entailed this sort of twofold correspondence. For Aquinas, *all* of our inclinations are in us as a result of the eternal law in us, which is to say that *all* of our inclinations are in us as in beings that are ruled, measured, and ordered by the eternal law. Indeed, for Aquinas, there cannot be any single inclination or action in us at all, except insofar as it is brought into being through the creative, legislative causality of the eternal law (which is nothing other than God's own essence). For Aquinas, none of our acts can be acts of ruling, measuring, ordering, and causing, without at the same time also being acts that are ruled, measured, ordered, and caused by God through eternal law. Indeed, on Aquinas's account, all of our acts (whether freely chosen by us or not, whether sinful or not) are caused and directed by God, insofar as they are acts at all. Yet according to Aquinas, we remain solely responsible for our sins, for sin denotes a being or action that is lacking in some due actuality or goodness. While God is the cause of our sinful acts insofar as they are acts, he is not the cause of the privation or lack of due goodness that makes these acts sinful.[56]

For Aquinas, those acts of ours that are identifiable as acts of ruling, measuring, ordering, and causing by us, do not belong to a set of beings and acts that is separate from the set of beings and acts that is ruled, measured, ordered, and caused by the eternal law. Rather, our acts of ruling, measuring, ordering, and causing represent a *unique way* of being ruled, measured, ordered, and caused by the eternal law. Our acts, which are always acts of being ruled, measured, ordered, and caused by the eternal law, can in some cases take on the character of being acts of ruling, measuring, ordering, and causing as well, insofar as they are accompanied by—or perhaps better, they are defined by—a kind of rational knowing that makes them the special kind of acts that they are. This rational knowing does not allow us to evade the all-encompassing, inescapable causality and direction of the eternal law, but rather allows us to continue being caused and directed by the eternal law in such a way that we can at the same time apprehend the appetible objects toward which we are inclined (by the eternal law) under their intelligible or universal aspects.

For Aquinas, when we apprehend a particular appetible object under some intelligible or universal aspect, we are able to apprehend multiple possibilities regarding that object and thus able to make free choices with respect to it. When Daniel imagines a house that he might build, any image that he entertains will be of some particular house, with some particular shape (for imagination, according to Aquinas, is a sensuous faculty). But the particular image that Daniel entertains need not attract him and move him ineluctably to build the house as imagined. For if Daniel understands what he is imagining and thus (for example) apprehends the image under its formal or intelligible aspect of being an image of a "house," he thereby apprehends something universal, which remains open to many different possible instantiations (e.g., many different possible shapes). Since the proper object of Daniel's rational appetite (or will) is not just some particular appetible object, but rather an appetible object as understood,[57] Daniel may be attracted to and moved by the appetible object as understood by him, and yet nevertheless remain free to build a house that is circular, square, or rectangular. For Aquinas, our actions always have to do with particulars; however, what attracts us about particular objects—to the extent that we have an understanding of what we are doing—is not the particular object that we imagine or experience, but rather some intelligible or universal aspect of the object as understood.[58] On Aquinas's account, no particular object as merely imagined or experienced can by itself attract or move our will, any more than a particular object as imagined or experienced can by itself cause the act of understanding in us.[59]

In addition, Aquinas holds that it is within our power as rational beings to think or refrain from thinking about the various intelligible aspects under which we comprehend objects; and so it is within our power to think of the objects that we imagine and experience under one intelligible aspect or another. For example, Daniel can think of the house that he might build under the aspect of its being a possible dwelling for himself, or a marketable piece of property that he can sell, or something that obstructs his neighbor's view and thus might draw him into a civil lawsuit. For Aquinas, then, the very same object might be apprehended by us as attractive and good in one respect, and yet unattractive and not good in some other respect. Now the human will by nature seeks universal and perfect goodness, and cannot ultimately be lulled by anything other than that which is universally, infinitely, and perfectly good, namely God himself. Every created being is good only by participation, and thus falls short of universal, infinite, and perfect goodness. Thus, every finite appetible object or action, no matter how attractive and good in certain respects, can always be regarded by us as not attractive and not good in some other respect.[60] Because of this, our will can never be moved of necessity to pursue any finite appetible object or action. Even when being attracted by this or that intelligible aspect of some finite object or action that we are contemplating, it remains within our power as rational beings to consider whether the object or action is unattractive and thus not good in some other respect; and thus it remains within our power to refrain from acting, or to pursue alternative courses of action. Our will can be made to act out of necessity, only if it is "offered an object which is good universally and from every point of view," and such an object is none other than God himself.[61] For Aquinas, then, our freedom consists in the ability to pursue alternative courses of action with respect to the finite goods that we find attractive, but not with respect to the infinite and perfect good, God, who—if seen by us, as in the

Beatific Vision—will move us toward him of necessity. If, however, our will is thus moved by God, its being moved will not be coercive or violent, since God's action in moving us is not the transitive action of one being in relation to another, but rather the creative action of God who gives us being in the first place and thus who can never act upon us externally or violently.[62]

From the foregoing, it follows that none of the finite goods at which we aim on account of the natural law in us—including even the good of self-preservation—is good in every respect. Correspondingly, none of our natural, God-given inclinations—insofar as they direct us toward finite goods—dictates straightforwardly what we ought to do in any particular situation. Of course, Aquinas does hold that every inclination that is in us by virtue of the natural law is an inclination toward what is good and perfective of us as human beings.[63] More broadly, he holds that every natural inclination or tendency in creatures (whether accompanied by knowledge or not) is an inclination toward what is good and perfective for the kind of creatures that have such inclinations.[64] Nevertheless, it would be wrong to think that, on Aquinas's account, the naturalness of certain inclinations in us can by itself dictate which actions are choiceworthy for us.[65] After all, the securing of one finite good, which is the proper object of a natural inclination in us, may well impede or prevent the securing of some other good. Thus, while I have a natural inclination to pursue the good of self-preservation,[66] there may be circumstances under which it would be wrong for me to act with the intention of preserving my own life, for example: if I had a duty to risk my life for the sake of defending the commonwealth,[67] or if I have been justly condemned to death.[68] For Aquinas, "reason was given to man that he might ensue those things to which his nature inclines, not in all cases, but in accordance with the order of reason." [69]

On Aquinas's account, the rightness or wrongness of our actions is ultimately determined not by the naturalness of the inclinations that incline us toward certain goods, but rather by the rational ordering of the goods toward which we are inclined. For what is natural to us as human beings, above all, is that we act in accordance with reason, and what is proper to reason is to make comparisons of things[70] and to put things into their right order.[71] But what is the right order? Recall Aquinas's remark that "whenever we find a multitude whose members are ordered to each other, that multitude must necessarily be ordered to some external principle."[72] What this implies, in the present context, is that it is not possible to determine the relative choiceworthiness of two or more goods toward which we are inclined, except by reference to some larger context or whole that allows us to prioritize different and potentially competing goods. While all of our desires and inclinations are aimed at some good, there may be evil in our desires and inclinations to the extent that there is lack of due order or proportionality among them. Thus, human beings perform evil actions, not because they directly intend what is evil, but rather because their actions involve the sacrificing of some greater good for the sake of some lesser good (for "it is impossible that any evil, as such, should be sought for by the appetite, either natural, or animal, or by the intellectual appetite which is will"[73]). On Aquinas's account, this "greater" and "lesser" can be measured only by reference to some larger context or whole, such as a whole life or a whole community. Consider the fact that human beings naturally desire to have friends and to know the truth. Each of these desires, in itself, is aimed at what is perfectly good and choiceworthy; but if considered in isolation and not within the context of some larger whole, it is not possible to determine which of these goods is to be preferred, if the securing of one impedes or prevents the securing of the other. On the face of it, the good of having friends and the good of knowing the truth seem to be altogether "basic" and incommensurable with one another. But as Aquinas notes, it is possible to show that the good of having friends ought to be sacrificed to the good of knowing and honoring the truth, if it is not possible to secure both goods at the same time, since both goods ought to be understood within the context of our overarching vocation as human beings, which is to live a life of virtue. If someone were to prefer the having of friends to the knowing and honoring of the truth, then he or she would also be willing to "make false judgment and bear false witness in their defense," and that would be contrary to a life of virtue.[74]

For Aquinas, just as the naturalness of certain inclinations does not automatically dictate the choiceworthiness of particular actions, so too the choiceworthiness of certain actions does not automatically dictate the desirability of particular acts of legislation. One can think of a large number of possible actions that would be evil and thus not choiceworthy; but it does not follow from this that the law always ought to prohibit such actions. The reason for this is that, for Aquinas, law exists for the sake of the common good of a community, and not for the sake of the individual goods of the community's members.[75] While the legal prohibition of certain evil actions might be a good thing for some individuals, such prohibitions might cause greater harm to the common good than the evil actions themselves would. Thus, Aquinas approvingly cites Augustine to the effect that it would be a mistake to pass laws prohibiting prostitution; for if prostitution were made illegal, then the behaviors to which people would resort in order to satisfy their inordinate sexual desires would cause even greater harm to the common good.[76] It is worth emphasizing here that Aquinas's (and Augustine's) argument against the legal prohibition of prostitution does not depend on any doubts about whether or not prostitution is really evil; and it does not depend on the notion that the law ought to be "value neutral" regarding certain activities. For Aquinas (as for Augustine), prostitution is doubtlessly an evil, and the law is never "value neutral." But it remains the case that legal commands and prohibitions ought to be contemplated with a view to the common good and not just individual goods. Aquinas further observes that human law, by refraining from prohibiting certain evils and vices, emulates the eternal law of God himself. For as Aquinas notes, God allows certain evils to take place in the universe, since his preventing of them would require the forfeiture of greater goods or the admission of greater evils. Whether one is talking about a political community, or the community of the created universe as a whole, the perfection of a whole community, so Aquinas holds, requires that particular goods are sometimes lost and particular evils sometimes not prevented.[77]

NOTES

1. *ST* I–II q.90 a.4.
2. *ST* I–II q.90 a.1.
3. *ST* I–II q.17 a.1.
4. Ibid.
5. *ST* I–II q.17 a.2; see also *SCG* III, 78; *In NE* I, lec.1.
6. *ST* II–II q.58 a.5.
7. *ST* II–II q.64 a.2.
8. *ST* I–II q.17 a.4.
9. *SCG* III, 94; *SCG* II, 39; *QDP*, q.3, a.16, ad 1; *In Meta* XII, lec.12, n.2637.
10. *SCG* III, 94; see also *SCG* II, 44–45; and *Super Sent*, bk.1, d.44, q.1, a.2, ad 6.
11. *SCG* III, 69.
12. See also *QDV*, q.11, a.1; *QDV*, q.5, a.8, ad 12; *Super Sent*, bk.2, d.1, q.1, a.5.
13. *In NE* I, lec.1, n.1.
14. *In Meta* XII, lec.12, n.2627.
15. Ibid.
16. *QDV*, q.5, a.3; see also *In Meta* XII, lec.12, n.2630.
17. *In Meta* V, lec.3, n.782; *ST* I q.5, a.2, ad 1.
18. *QDV*, q.7, a.6, ad 7.
19. *ST* I q.39 a.4 ad 3; also *In Meta* VII, lect.13, n.6; *QDP*, q.7, a.4, ad 1.
20. *ST* I–II q.90 a.2 ad 2.
21. *ST* I–II q.19 a.10; *ST* I–II q.109 a.3; *ST* II–II q.26 a.3; *SCG* III, 17.
22. *In Meta* XII, lec.12, n.1303.
23. *In NE* IX, lec.6, n.1839.
24. *In NE* VIII, lec.12, n.1724.
25. *SCG* III, 18.
26. *QDV*, q.5, a.3.
27. *In Meta* V, lec.21, n.1108.
28. *QDP*, q.7, a.1.
29. *ST* II–II q.58 a.7 ad 2.
30. *ST* I q.93 a.2 ad 3.
31. *ST* I–II q.19 a.10.
32. *ST* II–II q.26 a.3; see also *ST* I q.60 a.5.
33. I am indebted to the work of Herbert McCabe for this insight, and for the examples used in illustrating it. See Herbert McCabe, *Faith Within Reason*, ed. Brian Davies (New York: Continuum, 2007), 52–53; and Herbert McCabe, *God and Evil in the Theology of St. Thomas Aquinas*, ed. Brian Davies (New York: Continuum, 2010), 36–39. See also Aristotle, *Physics*, II, 199a34–b33; and Aquinas, *Commentary on Aristotle's Physics*, II, lec.12–14.
34. This dimension of Aquinas's account should make clear that his understanding of law does not stand in tension with, but is in fact closely allied with, a deep appreciation of the role of the virtues in human action.
35. *ST* I–II q.93 a.5; see also *ST* I q.103 a.1 ad 3.
36. See Michael Bright, *Intelligence in Animals* (New York: Reader's Digest Association, Ltd., 1997), 74–75.
37. *ST* I–II q.91 a.6.
38. *ST* I–II q.91 a.1; see also *ST* I–II q.93 a.3; *ST* I–II q.93 a.4–6.

39. *ST* I–II q.93 a.4.

40. *ST* I–II q.93 a.5.

41. *ST* I–II q.91 a.4–5.

42. *ST* I q.22 a.2 ad 2; *ST* I q.48 a.2; *ST* I q.49 a.1–2; *SCG* III, 71.

43. Thus for Aquinas, not only is it the case that eternal law (like every other instance of law) is incompatible with the existence of coerced compliance in most instances. Eternal law is incompatible with any kind of coerced compliance whatsoever; for apart from the creative, legislative causality of God (which is the same as his eternal law), there simply is no created being or created act that is there to be coerced (*ST* I q.103 a.1 ad 3; *ST* I q.105 a.4; *ST* I q.105 a.4).

44. *ST* I q.103 a.1.

45. *ST* I q.44 a.4.

46. *ST* I q.47 a.1.

47. See also *In Meta* XII, lec.12, n.2627–2629.

48. *ST* I–II q.90 a.1 ad 1; *ST* I–II q.91 a.2; see also *ST* I–II q.93 a.6; and *ST* I q.103 a.1 ad 1.

49. *ST* I–II q.91 a.2 ad 1.

50. *ST* I–II q.91 a.2.

51. Ibid.

52. *ST* I–II q.93 a.5; see also *SCG* III, 114.

53. *ST* I–II q.96 a.4; see also Augustine, *De Libero Arbitrio*, I, 5. Literally translated, the statement reads: "What will not have been just, does not appear to be law" ("*Non videtur esse lex, quae justa non fuerit*").

54. See *ST* I–II q.94 a.2.

55. Ibid.

56. *ST* I–II q.79 a.2.

57. *ST* I q.82 a.4.

58. See *QDM*, q.6.

59. See *ST* I q.79 a.3; *ST* I q.86 a.1.

60. *ST* I–II q.2 a.8; *ST* I–II q.17 a.1 ad 2; *ST* I q.105 a.4; *SCG* III, 10.

61. *ST* I–II q.10 a.2.

62. Along these lines, Aquinas observes that it belongs to the perfection of the liberty of the will to be able to choose between opposite things while keeping the order of the end in view; but it is a defect of the liberty of the will for it to choose anything while turning away from the order of the end. Thus, speaking of the beatified angels, Aquinas tells us: "there is greater liberty of will in the angels who cannot sin, than there is in ourselves who can sin." (*ST* I q.62 a.8 ad 3.)

63. See *ST* I–II q.94 a.2.

64. See *ST* I q.59 a.1; *ST* I q.63 a.4; *QDV*, q.21, a.1–2 and q.22, a.1.

65. Holding that the naturalness of certain inclinations dictates the choiceworthiness of certain actions is, as Josiah Royce suggests, similar to holding that our being subject to the law of gravitation dictates "that we all ought to sit down." See Josiah Royce, *The Religious Aspect of Philosophy: A Critique of the Basis of Conduct and of Faith* (Boston: Houghton, Mifflin, and Co., 1885), 80.

66. *ST* I–II q.94 a.2.

67. *ST* I q.60 a.5.

68. *ST* II–II q.69 a.4.

69. *ST* II–II q.69 a.4 ad 1; see also *ST* I–II q.94 a.2 ad 2.

70. *ST* II–II q.110 a.1.

71. *ST* I–II q.17 a.2.

72. *QDV,* q.5, a.3; see also *QDV,* q.5, a.1, ad 9; *ST* I q.11 a.3; *In Meta* XII, lec.12, n.2630.
73. *ST* I q.19 a.9; see also *QDM*, q.1, a.3.
74. *In NE* I, lec.6, n.76.
75. *ST* I–II q.90 a.2.
76. *ST* II–II q.10 a.11; see Augustine's *De Ordine*, II, 4.
77. See *ST* I q.22 a.2 ad 2; *ST* I q.48 a.2; *ST* I q.49 a.1–2; *SCG* III, 71. In a similar vein, Aquinas holds that a judge may sometimes be obligated to pronounce a sentence that he personally knows to be an unjust one. The reason for this is that the judge, insofar as he exercises public authority, is obligated to render judgments on behalf of the community and for the sake of the community's common good; accordingly, the judge may legitimately render judgments based only on knowledge acquired by him as a public authority, and not based on knowledge acquired by him as a private individual (i.e., outside the scope of an appropriate public, judicial process). If the judge in a capital case privately knows that a defendant is innocent, but is unable to remove himself from the case and is unable to bring his privately acquired knowledge to light through some appropriate judicial proceeding, then the judge does no wrong in sentencing the innocent defendant to death (see *ST* II–II q.64 a.6 ad 3; *ST* II–II q.67 a.2; *ST* II–II q.96 a.6).

CHAPTER 19

CONSCIENCE AND *SYNDERESIS*

TOBIAS HOFFMANN

AQUINAS played a major role in clarifying the concept of conscience and theoretical problems connected with it. Like earlier scholastics, he discussed conscience in connection with *synderesis* (a notion received from the Patristic tradition), inquiring how they should be defined and whether they are fallible. His most innovative contribution is his discussion of moral obligation in the case of an erring conscience.[1]

AN INFALLIBLE MORAL AWARENESS: SYNDERESIS

Medieval discussions of *synderesis* and conscience have as their canonical point of reference a passage from Jerome's commentary on Ezekiel. The text is important for two reasons. First, there Jerome introduces the term *synderesis* (presumably a corruption of the Greek word for conscience, *syneidēsis*) to medieval theologians. Second, the scholastics treated some of the observations in the text regarding *synderesis* and conscience as having axiomatic value, on account of Jerome's authority. Ironically, he is only reporting someone else's view—probably Origen's—a view from which Jerome is distancing himself.[2] Despite this misunderstanding, the passage inspired philosophically fruitful debates about the nature and function of *synderesis* and of conscience. The problems raised by Jerome's text, as formulated by scholastic thinkers, are the following: Is *synderesis* a faculty or a habit? Is it cognitive or affective? Is it infallible? What is its relation to conscience?

In Aquinas's early writings, his discussion of *synderesis* and conscience is still organized according to questions similar to these. Yet although he takes the authority of Jerome seriously, his main concern is not exegetical but philosophical. Unlike Bonaventure, who understands *synderesis* as the fundamental desire for the moral good, but in agreement with his teacher Albert the Great, Aquinas assigns to *synderesis* principally a cognitive role.[3] He argues that human beings have a fundamental grasp of right and wrong, which is infallible. According to Aquinas, this fundamental moral awareness is what Jerome and the theologians after him called *synderesis*. In essence, Aquinas argues teleologically; nature endowed human beings with infallible *synderesis* in order to allow for the certitude of all ethical considerations:

> There could not be any stability and certainty in the things that depend on principles, if the principles were not firmly established.... Accordingly, so that rectitude in human actions may be possible, there must be a permanent principle that has an unchanging rectitude, and by which criterion all human deeds are examined. This permanent principle must resist all evil and assent to every good. And this is *synderesis*, the task of which is to rebuke evil, and to incline to the good. Therefore we concede that there cannot be any sin in it.[4]

The role of first practical principles is analogous to that of first theoretical principles, such as the principle of noncontradiction. Both theoretical reason and practical reason rely as a foundation for all reasoning on first principles that are known through themselves (*per se nota*). If the terms of first principles are properly grasped, the principles are understood and error about them is not possible. Among Aquinas's examples of such principles of *synderesis* are these: "evil is to be avoided," "nothing illicit is to be done," "God is to be obeyed," "one must live according to reason."[5] *Synderesis* is the "natural habit" of reason containing these first practical principles, which means that by nature each human being has a fundamental awareness of these principles and that they can be used promptly when needed.[6] By positing first practical principles as the foundation for all moral thinking, Aquinas does not suggest that they are explicitly used as the starting points of all moral reasonings. They are rather tacitly presupposed and made explicit only upon reflection.

Aquinas connects *synderesis* to natural law, identifying the first practical principles, of which *synderesis* is the habit, with the general principles of natural law.[7] In the *Summa theologiae*, he occasionally replaces the word *synderesis* by the term understanding (*intellectus*), the intellectual virtue of grasping the first principles of reason.[8]

Aquinas's optimism about the infallibility of the principles of *synderesis* or of natural law may give rise to doubt. If *synderesis* is infallible, then all human beings—good or bad, Western and Eastern, modern and ancient—must share the same fundamental moral awareness. In this regard, we must consider two features of Aquinas's account of *synderesis*. First, he holds that the ethical principles of *synderesis* operate at an extremely general level. Albert the Great had given them some specific content: "one must not fornicate," "one must not kill," "one must be compassionate with those who suffer."[9] But unlike his teacher, Aquinas understands the directives of *synderesis* as formal principles, not as concrete moral norms. As such, they are merely the condition of possibility for particular directives. A statement like "one must live according to reason" does not endorse any particular ethical theory, but means only that one should conceive of one's actions in ethical terms. Aquinas acknowledges that when we are dealing with more particular directives of the natural law, it is not the case that all people agree.[10]

Second, Aquinas conceives of *synderesis* as habitual knowledge. This means that although we have it, it is not always in our actual consideration. In concrete situations we may be governed by fear or desire, and thus we may fail to apply a principle of *synderesis* to the particular case.[11]

Conscience and Its Fallibility

Aquinas seeks a definition of conscience that is congruent to the etymology of the word and that accounts for the activities commonly attributed to it. He follows Albert the Great in understanding conscience as the act of applying ethical knowledge to a specific case. In other words, conscience is the consideration of a specific case in light of one's moral knowledge. Moral knowledge comprises the first principles of *synderesis*, as well as more particular moral directives. Conceiving conscience as an act, Aquinas denies that it is a special habit or a power, against the claims of the *Summa Halensis* and Bonaventure.[12]

Within conscience, one can distinguish three kinds of consideration. One type of consideration lacks moral assessment; conscience is merely said to witness (*testificari*) concerning the action, as when I say that I am not conscious of having done a certain deed. Another consideration of conscience consists in evaluating an action that I am about to perform. My moral knowledge guides me in finding the appropriate dictate of conscience, and conscience is said to provoke, urge, or bind me to act (*instigare, inducere, ligare*). A third is the judgment of an action I have done. For this, my moral knowledge gives the criteria of examining the action after it is done. Conscience may accuse me or cause me to have remorse (*accusare, remordere*), or it may defend or excuse me (*defendere, excusare*), depending on whether the action under examination is seen to be in disagreement or in accord with my moral knowledge.[13] Of all these, Aquinas only discusses conscience's activity of "binding" in any detail, presumably because it governs the other acts as well. Notice that Aquinas's examples of acts of conscience are all in the first person. Conscience is not a consideration of someone else's obligations, but of what I should do or should have done.

While *synderesis* is infallible, conscience can be mistaken.[14] As we have seen, conscience is the application of moral knowledge to a specific situation. This application has a syllogistic structure. The major of the practical syllogism is obtained from *synderesis*, the minor is administered by practical reason, and the conclusion is the dictate of conscience. Aquinas's most frequently used example for dictates of conscience is about sexual intercourse, such as "I should abstain from intercourse with this woman," or its opposite, "I should have intercourse with this woman." The practical reasoning that leads to these dictates of conscience may be described as follows:

(1) Nothing prohibited by God's law is to be done.
Intercourse with this woman is against God's law.
....
I should abstain from intercourse with this woman.[15]

(2) The good is to be done.
It is my marital duty to have intercourse with this woman.
....
I should have intercourse with this woman.[16]

(3) God's law must not be disdained.
To abstain from fornication (sex out of wedlock) with this woman is to disdain God's law.
....
I should fornicate with this woman.[17]

These examples characteristically differ with respect to their minor premise. In the first and third case, it is obtained through "superior reason," and in the second case through "inferior reason." Aquinas and his contemporaries frequently use this vocabulary in their discussions of conscience, although for Aquinas this distinction is relatively unimportant from the theoretical point of view. Practical deliberations that incorporate considerations concerning God (whether obtained by faith or from natural reason) are attributed to superior reason, whereas deliberations from a merely "secular" point of view (whether from considerations of natural reason or from positive law) are attributed to inferior reason.[18] The dictates of conscience in the first two practical syllogisms may be right or wrong, mainly depending on whether or not "this woman" under consideration is my wife. For Aquinas, the third conclusion is definitely a case of erring conscience, because in his view the minor premise is essentially incorrect. Notice that in practice, the major premise of our moral reasoning is typically not made explicit. The reasoning of the first example would normally be like this: "I should not have intercourse with this woman because it is against God's law."

For correct judgments of conscience, the main difficulty consists in assessing the particular situation and in understanding which premises one should use in order to judge the case at hand. The virtue that is most relevant for conscience is prudence, which is the virtue of applying right reason to a specific action.[19] Yet in Aquinas's account, prudence encompasses more than conscience. Whereas considerations of conscience may well remain at a merely theoretical level, the prudent person takes them to heart and acts accordingly. In contrast, it is quite possible to have a correct conscience and to act against it, as in the case of incontinence. Then the mistake lies in the choice, but not in conscience.[20] In the prudent, conversely, the affection is ordered thanks to the support of the moral virtues (such as temperance, fortitude, justice, and related virtues). Thanks to the affective support of the virtues, the prudent have internalized their practical judgments to the point that they do not abandon them.[21]

Moral Obligation and Erring Conscience

The most intriguing problem concerns moral obligation in the case of erring conscience. Throughout his discussions of the problem, Aquinas aims at integrating objective and subjective criteria that constitute the morality of human actions. In the *Summa theologiae*, he adds considerations about ignorance in order to resolve the tension between objective and subjective factors.

In his discussions of erring conscience, Aquinas discusses the position of an anonymous author who focuses unilaterally on objective criteria for moral goodness. Accounts similar to this anonymous view are found among Franciscan authors of the time.[22] According to Thomas, this author holds that erring conscience binds only in certain situations, depending on what type of action it is concerned with. In the *Summa theologiae*, Aquinas presents this writer as distinguishing three kinds of action: generically good (e.g., believing in Christ), indifferent (e.g., pulling up a blade of grass), and generically evil (e.g., fornicating). According to this view, erring conscience binds only in the case of indifferent acts, as when I think it is forbidden to pull up some grass. But it does not bind when I think that believing in Christ is prohibited, or when I think that fornication is commanded. In these cases, diverging from erring conscience is not evil.[23] Table 1 illustrates the view as Aquinas presents it.

Repeatedly, it has been assumed that that Aquinas's anonymous author was Bonaventure. But Bonaventure sets up the problem somewhat differently. More importantly, he comes to a different conclusion, as seen in table 2.

Like the other view, Bonaventure admits that there are situations in which conscience does not bind one to act or not to act on what it decrees. But unlike that view, he thinks that acting against erring conscience is necessarily a sin, for by doing so, I would be doing some deed that I think is contrary to God's law, and thus I would hold God's law in contempt. Hence erring conscience binds one to revise it.[24]

There is some plausibility to the anonymous author's view that I am not bound by my conscience if it tells me to do something that is in fact contrary to God's law.

Table 1 Erring conscience according to the view expounded in *ST* I–II, q.19, a.5

Moral quality of the act	My conscience decrees I must	Does my conscience err?	Does it bind?	Do I sin if I act against it?
Generically good (e.g., believing in Christ)	Do it	No	[Yes]	[Yes]
	Not do it	Yes	No	No
Indifferent (pulling up some grass)	Do it / Not do it	Yes	Yes	Yes
Generically evil (fornicating)	Do it	Yes	No	No
	Not do it	No	[Yes]	[Yes]

Table 2 Erring conscience according to Bonaventure (*Super Sent* 2, d.39, a.1, q.3)

Conscience decrees an act as obligatory that is	Does my conscience err?	Does it bind?	Do I sin if I act against it?	Do I sin if I act according to it?
In accordance with God's law	No	Yes	Yes	No
Not defined by God's law	Yes	Yes	Yes	No
Contrary to God's law	Yes	Yes, but only to revise it	Yes	Yes

Augustine defines sin precisely as what is done, said, or desired contrary to God's law.[25] Yet if I act against erring conscience, then I do what in fact accords with God's law and I avoid sin. Versions of this argument are frequently used in arguments pro or con (depending on the writer's own view) that introduce questions about binding conscience.[26]

Aquinas rejects the view of the anonymous author, and he would in part contradict Bonaventure as well. For Aquinas, the distinction of generally good, evil, and indifferent acts does not have any bearing on when erring conscience binds and when it does not. Regardless of whether my action is objectively good, evil, or indifferent, conscience binds, for it is by means of conscience that an action is proposed to me as good, bad, or indifferent. Aquinas gives two examples: if on account of erring conscience I consider it evil to abstain from fornication, and I want to abstain from it, then I want something evil, although in truth it is not evil, but only misapprehended as evil. Likewise, if because of erring conscience I think that believing in Christ is evil, then choosing to believe in Christ, I choose it as something evil, although for Aquinas, believing in Christ is really something good. Since conscience presents the action to me as good or bad, Aquinas considers it immoral to act contrary to erring conscience.[27] Conscience should in fact not be seen as a rival to God's law, but rather as the herald of God's law. It binds not on its own account, but on account of the divine precept. Aquinas provides an apt illustration of this point:

> Suppose that a ruling by a king would reach the people only through some inferior leader, and suppose that he says that this ruling comes from the king, although this is not true. What this leader says would then be obligatory qua ruling by the king, and those who disrespect it would deserve punishment.[28]

For Aquinas, the binding character of conscience, whether erring or not, means that acting against conscience is always evil. It does not mean, however, that acting according to conscience is always good. Those who killed the apostles, thinking to please God, are not necessarily excused. Everything depends on whether I am responsible for the fact that my conscience is erring. I may have been negligent in forming my conscience, or I may even have wanted to be ignorant about right and wrong. Ignorance of basic moral rules, such as that adultery is evil, is no excuse.

A man who thinks he is bound to commit adultery could have known better; he errs by vincible ignorance. Yet someone might be ignorant of a particular circumstance without fault. Aquinas gives the example of someone who has intercourse with a woman who, unbeknownst to him, is not his wife.[29]

Aquinas's view of one's obligation to follow one's conscience can be summarized as shown in table 3.

In sum, Aquinas would not say that one must always follow one's conscience. It is true that one must never act against it, but following it might likewise be sinful. This seems paradoxical, for in such situations sin appears unavoidable. Such a dilemma does not occur for the anonymous author's view that Aquinas describes in the *Summa theologiae*, but it constitutes a real problem for both Bonaventure and Aquinas. Like Bonaventure, Aquinas holds that to resolve the dilemma, I must revise (*deponere*) my erring conscience.[30]

The advice to revise my erring conscience is puzzling. Typically, I am unaware of a mistake of conscience, otherwise it would not be completely erring, as Aquinas admits. Understandably, Aquinas argues that a doubtful conscience must be reevaluated. But does it make sense to require the revision of erring conscience?[31] It should be noted, however, that as discussed above, for Aquinas the dilemma occurs only in case of voluntary ignorance, for it is no sin to act in accord with conscience that errs from involuntary ignorance. In Aquinas's eyes, apart from the situation of madness, all instances of ignorance of the moral law (*ignorantia iuris*) are due to voluntary ignorance.[32] It is thus implicit in Aquinas's account that being unaware that my conscience is erring, in other words, failing to notice the conflict between my conscience and the moral law, results from negligence: I could have avoided such obtusion by taking greater care in forming my conscience. But at any time it is possible to stop being negligent, and to raise doubts about my conscience. And once my erring conscience has become a doubtful conscience, I am in a position to revise it. Yet more important than conscience formation is moral education in the practice of the virtues, especially prudence, for the prudent not only make correct moral judgments more easily but also act willingly according to the dictates of right reason.

Table 3 Erring conscience according to Aquinas (*ST* I–II, q.19, a.5–6)

Moral quality of the act	My conscience says it is	Does my conscience err?	Does it bind?	Do I sin if I act against it?	Do I sin if I act according to it?
Good	Good	No	Yes	Yes	[No]
Bad	Bad				
Good	Bad	Yes	Yes	Yes	*If ignorance is...* - *involuntary*: no - *voluntary*: yes
Bad	Good				

Conscience, for Aquinas, has a decidedly cognitive dimension. It is an act of practical reason, not an affection of the will or a feeling. Metaphorically, one might call it the voice of reason, but Aquinas does not view it as an "inner voice" in the sense of a God-given instinctive impulse toward the right decision. Instead, Aquinas's emphasis on reason points in the direction of secular accounts, such as Immanuel Kant's conception of conscience as an "inner judge" that applies the "moral law" to specific circumstances.[33]

NOTES

I wish to thank the Alexander von Humboldt Foundation for supporting me during my work on this text.

1. Aquinas's discussions of *synderesis* and conscience are found in *Super Sent* 2, d.24, q.2, a.3–4; *Super Sent* 2, d.39, q.3; *QDV*, q.16–17; *ST* I, q.79, a.12–13; *ST* I-II, q.19, a.5–6; *ST* I-II, q.96, a.4; *Quodl* 8, q.6, a.3; *Quodl* 9, q.7, a.2; *Quodl* 3, q.12; *In Rom* 2, lec.3; *In Rom* 14, lec.3. His most detailed treatment is that of *QDV*, q.16–17. There is a certain evolution of Aquinas's thought leading up to the view he holds in the *Summa theologiae*, but the developments concern refinements or shifts in emphasis, not doctrinal revisions.

The most useful studies of Aquinas's account of *synderesis* and conscience in their historical contexts are by Odon Lottin, "Syndérèse et conscience aux XIIe et XIIIe siècles," in *Psychologie et morale aux XIIe et XIIIe siècles*, vol. 2/1 (Leuven: Abbaye du Mont César; Gembloux: J. Duculot, 1948), 103–349; "Problèmes moraux relatifs à la conscience," ibid., 353–417. Some of the texts discussed by Lottin are translated in Timothy C. Potts, *Conscience in Medieval Philosophy* (Cambridge: Cambridge University Press, 1980).

2. Jerome, *In Hiezechielem* I, i, 6–8, CCL 75:10–12. For an English translation, see Potts, *Conscience in Medieval Philosophy*, 79–80. For a discussion of this passage in its own right, see Douglas Kries, "Origen, Plato, and Conscience (*Synderesis*) in Jerome's Ezekiel Commentary," *Traditio* 57 (2002): 67–83. The text-critical question of reading *syneidēsis* (conscience) or *syntērēsis* (conservation) in Jerome's original text is not yet settled. For a recent discussion, see Alain Le Boulluec, "Recherches sur les origines du thème de la syndérèse dans la tradition patristique," in Christian Trottmann, ed., *Vers la contemplation: Études sur la syndérèse et les modalités de la contemplation de l'Antiquité à la Renaissance* (Paris: Librairie Honoré Champion, 2007), 61–77.

3. Bonaventure, *Super Sent* 2, d.39, a.2, q.1. Albert the Great, *De homine*, De viribus animae motivis 4: De synderesi, q.1, Editio Coloniensis 27/2 (Münster: Aschendorff, 1951ff.), 527–31; *Quaestio de synderesi* a.1, Editio Coloniensis 25/2:232–35.

4. *QDV*, q.16, a.2 (all translations are my own). Teleological considerations about *synderesis* are also found in *Super Sent* 2, d.24, q.2, a.3 and *QDV*, q.16 a.1; an echo of such teleological reasoning is still perceivable in *ST* I q.79 a.12.

5. e.g., *Super Sent* 2, d.24, q.2, a.3–4; *Super Sent* 2, d.39, q.3, a.2; *QDV*, q.16, a.1, ad 9.

6. *Super Sent* 2, d.24, q.2, a.3; *Super Sent* 2, d.39, q.3, a.1–2; *QDV*, q.16, a.1–2; more briefly in *ST* I q.79 a.12. Aquinas's discussion of the first practical principles as propositions that are known through themselves tends to be sketchy. The most detailed discussion is found in his treatment of natural law, *ST* I-II q.94 a.2. For the philosophical and biblical background of the principle "the good is to be done, and evil is to be avoided," see Vernon J. Bourke,

"The Background of Aquinas' Synderesis Principle," in Lloyd P. Gerson, ed., *Graceful Reason* (Toronto: Pontifical Institute of Mediaeval Studies, 1983), 345–60.

7. *Super Sent* 2, d.24, q.2, a.4; *QDV*, q.16, a.1; *ST* I-II q.94 a.1 ad 2.

8. In *ST* I-II q.58 a.4, which is in a specifically Aristotelian context, Aquinas uses the term understanding (*intellectus*) to express the same concept that in II-II q.47 a.6 ad 1 and ad 3 he refers to as *synderesis*.

9. Albert the Great, *De homine*, De viribus animae motivis 4: De synderesi, q.1, Editio Coloniensis 27/2:530.

10. *ST* I-II q.94 a.4.

11. *QDV*, q.16, a.3; cf. *Super Sent* 2, d.39, q.3, a.1, ad 4.

12. *Super Sent* 2, d.24, q.2, a.4; *QDV*, q.17, a.1; *ST* I q.79 a.13. Cf. *Summa Halensis* I-II n.421, Editio Quaracchi (Quaracchi: Typographia Collegii S. Bonaventurae, 1924–48), 3:496; Bonaventure, *Super Sent* 2, d.39, a.1, q.1; Albert the Great, *De homine*, De viribus animae motivis 5: De conscientia, q.1, Editio Coloniensis 27/2:535–36.

13. *QDV*, q.17, a.1, summarized in *ST* I q.79 a.13.

14. For Aquinas's discussions of the fallibility of conscience, see *Super Sent* 2, d.39, q.3, a.1–2; *QDV*, q.16, a.2; *QDV*, q.17, a.2; *Quodl* 3, q.12, a.1.

15. Cf. *Super Sent* 2, d.24, q.2, a.4; *QDV*, q.17, a.2.

16. Cf. *ST* I-II q.19 a.5.

17. Cf. *Super Sent* 2, d.39, q.3, a.3, arg.5; *ST* I-II q.19 a.5–6.

18. *QDV*, q.15, a.3. For Aquinas, superior and inferior reason are not distinct in essence, but only incidentally, depending on whether the object under consideration concerns "higher natures" (God or angels) or "lower things" (earthly matters); see *QDV*, q.15, a.2. For conscience as bound by positive law, see *ST* I-II q.96 a.4.

19. *ST* II-II q.47 a.8; *ST* I-II q.57 a.6. For an insightful account of the relationship between prudence and conscience, see Thomas Deman, "Appendice II: Renseignements techniques," in Thomas d'Aquin, *La prudence: 2ª–2ªᵉ, Questions 47–56*, 3d ed. (Paris: Cerf, 2006), 496–523.

20. *QDV*, q.17, a.1, ad 4.

21. *ST* I-II q.58 a.5; see also *ST* I-II q.57 a.4.

22. E.G., Alexander of Hales, John de la Rochelle, and the *Summa Halensis*, see Lottin, "Problèmes moraux relatifs à la conscience," 354–74.

23. *ST* I-II q.19 a.5. Lottin, "Problèmes moraux relatifs à la conscience," 388, surmises that Aquinas's discussion of the anonymous opinion is based upon the text of Vat. lat. 781, ff. 4va–7rb. For a transcription of the text, see ibid. 368–72.

24. Bonaventure, *Super Sent* 2, d.39, a.1, q.3. The rival view that Aquinas expounds in the *Sentences* commentary agrees with Bonaventure that acting against one's conscience is sinful because of contempt for God, see *Super Sent* 2, d.39, q.3, a.3.

25. *Contra Faustum Manicheum* 22.27, CSEL 25/1:621.

26. E.G., *Summa Halensis* I-II n.421, arg.3 in opp., Editio Quaracchi 3:388; Bonaventure, *Super Sent* 2, d.39, a.1, q.3, arg.3 in opp.; Aquinas, *Super Sent* 2, d.39, q.3, a.3, arg.1; *QDV*, q.17, a.4, arg.1.

27. *ST* I-II q.19 a.5.

28. *Super Sent* 2, d.39, q.3, a.3, ad 3; see also *QDV*, q.17, a.3; and *QDV*, q.17, a.5.

29. *ST* I-II q.19 a.6; see also *QDV*, q.17, a.3. Though this example seems rather unlikely, Aquinas might have in mind an individual who does not realize that his marriage is invalid. For Aquinas on voluntary ignorance, see *ST* I-II q.6 a.8 and *ST* I-II q.76 a.3.

30. *Super Sent* 2, d.39, q.3, a.3, ad 5; *QDV*, q.17, a.4, ad 8; *Quodl* 3, q.12, a.2, ad 2; *ST* I-II q.19 a.6 ad 3. Cf. Bonaventure, *Super Sent* 2, d.39, a.1, q.3, *ad* quaestiones connexas. See also Richard Schenk, "Perplexus supposito quodam: Notizen zu einem vergessenen

Schlüsselbegriff thomasischer Gewissenslehre," *Recherches de Théologie ancienne et médiévale* 57 (1990): 62–95.

31. *QDV*, q.17, a.4; *ST* I-II q.19 a.5 ad 2. For the revision of doubtful conscience, see *QDV*, q.17, a.4, ad 4.

32. *Quodl* 3, q.12, a.2, ad 2.

33. For a useful overview of modern and contemporary conceptions of conscience, see Thomas E. Hill, Jr., "Four Conceptions of Conscience," in Ian Shapiro and Robert Adams, eds., *Integrity and Conscience* (New York and London: New York University Press, 1998), 13–52.

CHAPTER 20

VIRTUES AND VICES

JEAN PORTER

THE concept of virtue plays a central role in Aquinas's thought. Indeed, it plays more than one such role, as is most clearly apparent in his final theological synthesis, the *Summa theologiae*. Recall that this *Summa* is divided into three parts, the second of which is devoted to a analysis of human action, considered as the means through which we attain (or deviate from) our final end of happiness through union with God.[1] The *secunda pars* is further divided into two sections, the first proposing an analysis of the human act as such, its normative structure and its constitutive principles, and the second, analyzing the specific normative ideals governing human life generally, as well as those which pertain to particular roles and states of life (*secunda secundae* prologue). In each of these subparts, the concept of virtue serves as a central organizing principle. In the *prima secundae*, virtue considered as a kind of *habitus* is identified as one of the intrinsic principles of human acts, that is to say, one of the constitutive principles of a properly human kind of causality.[2] As such, it is considered in tandem with the rational and affective faculties, which it disposes toward certain kinds of actions, and contrasted (but not opposed to) the extrinsic principles of human acts, namely Satan and God, the former of whom tempts us toward sin, and the latter who "instructs us through law and aids us through grace."[3] In the *secunda secundae*, Aquinas organizes his material by reference to the virtues considered as normative ideals, in terms of which diverse elements of Christian moral reflection can be perspicuously analyzed and brought together in a coherent way (*secunda secundae* prologue).

Thus, Aquinas's moral theology incorporates both a general theory of virtue, and extensive consideration of the ideals and precepts proper to particular virtues. In what follows, I will consider each of these, although the scope of this chapter will not permit more than a brief look at the specifics of Aquinas's normative analysis. Nonetheless, I hope to say enough to indicate the way in which concepts of virtue and the virtues function as organizing principles for him.

Virtue As A Principle Of Action

A number of scholars approach Aquinas's theory of the virtues as if it were essentially an appropriation of Aristotle's theory that places it in a theological context but adds nothing of substance to it.[4] But when we place Aquinas's theory of virtue within its immediate context, that is to say, scholastic debates over virtue during the twelfth and thirteenth centuries, it is apparent that he takes much of substance, and even more, key questions, from these debates.[5] Going back as far as Abelard, the general contours of an Aristotelian theory of virtue, including the claim that a virtue is a stable disposition of the soul and the identification of the ideal of virtue with a mean, were familiar and widely accepted among scholastic theologians.[6] At the same time, however, some theologians, including most importantly Peter Lombard, preferred an alternative, more Augustinian construal according to which the virtues are dependent on (or equivalent to) the direct bestowal of divine aid through grace; from this perspective, Aristotelian theories appeared inadequate or wrongheaded.

It is noteworthy that Aquinas's preferred definition of a virtue, around which he structures his own systematic analysis, is taken from Peter Lombard's definition, drawn from elements of Augustine's writings: "Virtue is a good quality of the mind, by which we live righteously, of which no one can make bad use, which God brings about in us, without us."[7] However, he immediately qualifies this definition in one critical respect, adding that the last clause applies only to the infused virtues, which God bestows on us without action on our part, in contrast to the acquired virtues, which as the name suggests can be attained through human effort without grace—in contrast to Lombard, who denies the possibility of attaining virtue without grace. What is more, Aquinas interprets this definition in decidedly Aristotelian terms, grounded in analysis of virtue as a *habitus*, that is to say, a stable disposition of the intellect, will, or passions inclining the person to act in one kind of way rather than another.[8] Such dispositions are necessary if we are to be capable of action at all; for example, the child's innate capacities for speech must be developed through the *habitus* of a particular language before the child can actually talk.[9] So understood, the virtues include intellectual capabilities such as knowledge. These are, of course, morally neutral, although they are good in the sense of perfecting the agent in some respect.[10] However, those virtues that shape the passions and the will, and the intellect insofar as it is oriented to action, are necessarily morally significant because they incline toward actions of a kind that is good without qualification.[11]

So far, it might seem that Aquinas has, so to speak, split the difference between the two dominant scholastic approaches to the theory of virtue. The distinctiveness of his theory lies in the way in which he synthesizes these approaches by means of a systematic development of the claim that the virtues are perfections—singly, perfections of the faculties of the soul that comprise the subject of the particular virtues, and taken together, a perfection of the human agent.[12] At the same time, he integrates his analysis of virtue, and by implication his overall account of human agency and the acts expressing it, into his overarching metaphysical and theological system. Within that structure, the idea of perfection serves to integrate the accounts of intelligibility, goodness, and causality in a perspicuous way.[13] According to Aquinas, actuality is the fundamental characteristic of any kind of existence—every actually existing thing is in act and can be said to be perfect insofar as it is fully in act. Perfection is understood, correlatively, as the fullest possible development and expression of the creature's dispositions and capacities, in accordance with the ensemble of intelligible causal powers and inclinations, that is to say, the proper form of the specific kind of thing that it is. To the extent that a creature approximates this ideal, it can be said to be good without qualification. Thus, Aquinas interprets the claim that every creature tends toward, or seeks the good to mean that every creature is naturally disposed toward the attainment of its specific form through the operations proper to that form. For living creatures, including ourselves, perfection consists in operations through which the creature sustains in itself, and generates in others, an orderly way of life in accordance with the ordered capacities constituting its form. The complexity of the human creature implies that we, unlike other animals, can attain perfection in diverse ways and at disparate levels, including some which go beyond our natural capacities. But no matter how perfection is understood, it will necessarily involve some modality of proper development and exercise of the capacities distinctive to us as creatures of a specific kind.

Aquinas acknowledges that we can legitimately regard the traditional cardinal virtues as general qualities of every praiseworthy action, but he prefers a second construal, according to which these are distinct virtues, corresponding to the distinct faculties of the soul.[14] Thus understood, the virtues are perfections, which is to say, the full and appropriate development of the faculties that they inform, actualized in distinctive kinds of good actions. Because the faculties of the intellect, the will, and the desiring and irascible passions are all distinct, each has its proper virtue, identified with one of the four traditional cardinal virtues: prudence or practical wisdom, strictly speaking an intellectual virtue, enables the agent to choose in accordance with rightly ordered desires for one's final end, as these are expressed in particular actions; justice orients the will toward the good of others or the common good, as discerned by reason; and temperance and fortitude shape the passions in such a way that the agent desires what is truly in accordance with reason and is prepared to resist obstacles to attaining it.[15]

Aquinas interprets the kinds of actions traditionally associated with particular virtues in such a way as to display these as perfections of specific faculties, as well as exemplifications of general ideals of praiseworthy behavior. The passions, which are naturally oriented toward what is perceived as desirable and away from what is perceived as noxious through the senses, are shaped through reason in such a way as to aim towards the overall good of the person through virtues of temperance and fortitude.[16] Shaped, but not suppressed—otherwise, the virtues of the sensitive part of the soul would render their subject otiose, rather than perfecting it.[17] Thus, the kinds of actions characterizing temperance and fortitude are irreducibly identified with the passions and the external behaviors typically expressing these, for example, the characteristic exterior acts of chastity always take the form of some kind of sexual behavior or abstinence, reflecting a rational and appropriate disposition of the faculty for sexual desire itself. Similarly, the will, which is intrinsically oriented toward self-love, is shaped by the virtues of justice and ultimately charity to move beyond natural self-love to wider loves, toward the community, one's neighbors, and ultimately toward God himself.[18] At the same time, again, the proper disposition of the will toward a wider range of loves does not do away with, or much less destroy, a properly informed self-love—otherwise, as Aquinas remarks, charity would represent the corruption, rather than the perfection of human (or angelic) nature.[19]

Because the particular virtues represent dispositions of distinctive faculties, Aquinas does not endorse the classical and Augustinian thesis of the unity of the virtues, according to which diverse virtues, properly understood, are all expressions of some one virtue or ideal of goodness, rationality, or charity.[20] Rather, particular virtues represent perfections of the distinct faculties of the soul, as these are informed by rational reflection and judgment and (in the case of the infused virtues) coordinated and directed by charity to one's true final end. Yet the acts of the virtues will always be good without qualification, and for that reason, they must be coordinated—through the rational judgments of prudence, (perhaps) directed by charity—toward action in accordance with the agent's overall good and with right relations with others and God.[21] Thus, Aquinas affirms the connection, rather than the unity of the virtues—the thesis that the operations of the virtues are necessarily interconnected, in such a way that it is necessary to possess all the central virtues in order genuinely to have any particular virtue.[22] It should be noted, however, that this does not imply that the virtues are only possible through charity. While only the infused virtues can be described as such without qualification, the acquired virtues, fully formed through rational reflection and connected through prudence, are also genuine virtues seen in relation to the connatural end of the human person.[23]

This brings us to a further point. Not only do the virtues consist in perfections of the constitutive faculties of the human soul, they operate in tandem to direct the individual toward his or her overall perfection as a rational creature, that is to say, toward beatitude or happiness. At the same time, happiness can be understood in a twofold way. There is a kind of happiness proportioned to our natural capacities, to which the virtues that we acquire by our own efforts are oriented. Indeed, Aquinas frequently identifies this kind of happiness with the practice of the cardinal virtues themselves, regarded as jointly constituting the full development of the principles of action characteristic of the rational creature.[24] But in addition, we have been called to a higher form of happiness, namely, direct personal union with God in the Beatific Vision. This form of fulfillment completely exceeds the natural capabilities, not only of the human soul, but of any creature; thus, it must receive new principles of action in order to attain such an end.[25] Correlatively, these new principles of action are only brought about through God's immediate action on the soul.[26] This transformation is brought about by grace, and the operative dispositions through which grace is rendered active are the infused virtues, including infused versions of the cardinal virtues, as well as the theological virtues of faith, hope, and charity, and the gifts of the Holy Spirit.[27]

Aquinas's analysis of the gifts of the Holy Spirit, traditionally identified as wisdom, understanding, knowledge, counsel, fortitude, piety, and fear, takes its starting points from the complex interpretative tradition generated by the relevant scriptural texts, especially Isa. 11:2–3 and 1 Cor. 12:8–13. This tradition posed a challenge for scholastic theories of virtue, Aquinas's included, because it is not immediately apparent how the gifts are to be distinguished from the virtues. After all, the gifts are dispositions perfecting the human agent in such a way as to lead to good actions, as are the virtues; and while they are bestowed directly by God rather than being acquired through human efforts, the same is true of the infused virtues.[28] Yet the suggested conclusion, that the gifts simply are virtues, implies what Aquinas describes as "no small difficulties," since the accepted lists of the virtues and the gifts do not match, that is to say, not all the gifts are included among the accepted list of cardinal and theological virtues, nor are all these virtues included among the seven gifts.[29] The challenge, therefore, is to find a way to integrate the gifts into the overall theory of virtue, in such a way as to preserve the distinction between the two categories, while also explaining how they operate in tandem to produce good human actions.

After surveying what he regards as inadequate attempts to address this challenge, Aquinas remarks that if we are to arrive at an adequate account of the gifts, we should be guided by the way in which Scripture itself speaks of them, observing that they are described not only as gifts, but more as spirits, for example, "the spirit of wisdom and understanding."[30] A spirit, in this context, implies a divine inspiration, prompting the agent to a particular course of action. (As Aquinas goes on to explain, these inspirations are typically expressed in and through the operations of the agent's intellectual and appetitive faculties, prompting appropriate judgments and desires in such a way as to guide the agent's concrete choices.[31]) Because these divinely infused inclinations come from outside the agent, they fall under the broad category of external principles of human action, but for that very reason, the agent stands in need of a distinctive kind of *habitus* in order to receive and respond to them in an appropriate way. These *habitus* are the gifts properly so called, that is to say, dispositions of the intellect and will which render the agent responsive to the "spirits" to which Scripture refers. As such, they represent a further development of the agent's habitual dispositions toward action, and Aquinas explicitly describes them as "perfections," and indeed, as a necessary further level of perfection which goes beyond the infused cardinal virtues, although not beyond the theological virtues.[32] In this way, he integrates the gifts firmly into his overall analysis of the virtues as perfections of the active powers of the human person, which work in tandem in such a way as to promote the overall perfection of the individual as a rational agent.[33]

But why are the gifts necessary at all? The corresponding acquired cardinal virtues stand in need of no such further dispositions, in order to yield actions appropriate to their constitutive norm of right reason. The fact that the gifts are necessary to salvation—as Aquinas insists[34]—implies that the infused cardinal virtues are in some way less complete, less fully perfections, than their acquired counterparts. As he goes on to explain in this article, there is indeed a sense in which this is the case. Certainly, the infused virtues represent a higher level of perfection than do their acquired counterparts, insofar as they stem from a supernaturally bestowed principle of action, through which the agent is directed toward a kind of perfection altogether outside the scope of its connatural powers. And yet, precisely because the acquired virtues represent perfections of the agent's connatural powers, they can be attained more fully and completely—more perfectly—than the infused virtues. Thus, there is indeed a sense in which the infused virtues are less perfect, seen in comparison to the acquired virtues—not in themselves, of course, but considered as dispositions of the agent, who attains and exercises them in a less perfect way. That is why the infused cardinal virtues, unlike their acquired counterparts, stand in need of distinctive *habitus*, over and above the dispositions bestowed by the virtues themselves, if they are to operate appropriately and effectively. Thus, not only are the gifts perfections, but Aquinas accounts for them in terms of the twofold criterion of connatural and supernatural perfection that informs his overall theory of the virtues.

We need to consider one further distinction between the infused and acquired virtues. That is, the infused cardinal virtues are specifically different from their acquired counterparts because they are directed toward a different end, and therefore observe a different mean.[35] Acquired temperance takes its standards from the overall well-being and health of the body and leads to an appropriate moderation in food and drink. Infused temperance, in contrast, takes its ultimate criterion from the person's desire for salvation and incorporates forms of restraint and discipline, fasting, for example, which will promote the individual's spiritual, as well as her physical health. Note, however, that ascetical exercises that damage one's bodily well-being are vicious, rather than virtuous.[36] The ends of the acquired virtues, namely, the overall well-being of the organism and the community, is thus transformed by the infused virtue, rather than being obviated or undermined by it;[37] again, grace perfects, rather than destroys nature, as we are frequently reminded.[38]

At this point, we come to one of the most interesting and original aspects of Aquinas's analysis of the virtues. Up until Aquinas's time, scholastic accounts of the virtues were organized around a straightforward dichotomy between political and theological virtues. The political virtues are said to serve as a preparation for the theological virtues, and they provide a medium through which the theological virtues are expressed in external acts. Nonetheless, the theological and the political virtues remain in an external relation, with the former directing the latter—there is no need, within this schema, to postulate infused political or cardinal virtues. Aquinas is clearly familiar with this approach,[39] but in the *ST* he replaces it with a more complex set of distinctions between the theological and the cardinal virtues, on the one hand, and between infused and acquired virtues on the other. At first glance, this would seem to introduce unnecessary complications. Why should he have done so?

At least part of the answer to this question lies in the specifics of Aquinas's concept of grace, as developed in terms of his overall analysis of the virtues as perfections of the agent. Recall that for Aquinas, the infused virtues are the operative principles through which grace can be expressed through one's acts.[40] Correlatively, in order for an action to be meritorious, it must stem from grace in some way.[41] What this implies is that the earlier view, according to which the theological virtues direct the political or cardinal virtues, is inadequate. In order for grace to be fully operative and efficacious in every dimension of human life, it must transform all the faculties of the human soul involved in the processes of deliberation and action.[42] Thus, it is not enough that the theological virtues should command the acts of the other virtues; rather, grace must be expressed directly through virtues appropriate to every faculty of the soul, which is to say, through infused versions of all the cardinal virtues.

This still does not explain why Aquinas prefers to speak of the cardinal, rather than the (infused) political virtues. The reason for this shift only becomes apparent when we turn to the detailed moral analyses of the *secunda secundae.* We find that the division between virtues oriented toward beatitude, and those oriented toward social life, is too simple for Aquinas's purposes. Only one of the cardinal virtues, justice, has a direct and defining relation to the good of the community as a whole; indeed, strictly speaking this is the case only for legal justice.[43] Both fortitude and temperance are primarily oriented toward maintaining the individual's equilibrium between passions and reasoned judgments about the overall good, and in that sense, they both have the good of the individual as their primary focus.[44] Similarly, particular justice, which is further divided into commutative and distributive justice, is concerned with right relations toward individuals.[45] Prudence ranges over both sets of considerations and integrates them, and for that very reason Aquinas distinguishes between individual and political prudence.[46]

Where do the vices fit into this analysis? It would seem that the moral virtues, in contrast to some intellectual virtues, are not strictly necessary to the agent's functioning, although arguably, without them the agent cannot function well over an extended period of time. The affective faculties must be disposed through *habitus* in one way or another, if the agent is to be capable of rational action, but they need not be well-disposed—otherwise, there could be no such thing as vices, that is to say, disordered dispositions of the faculties corresponding to the virtues.[47] More specifically, the vices are dispositions to act in ways contrary to nature—human nature in all its dimensions,[48] or more specifically against reason, considered as the defining characteristic of human nature.[49] At the same time, vice does not necessitate the agent to sin, any more than the virtues render their acts necessary.[50]

The Virtues as Normative Ideals

Aquinas analyzes the specific ideals of cardinal virtue in terms of the Aristotelian doctrine of the mean, according to which the virtues are expressed through passions and actions in accordance with a mean as determined by reason.[51] The rational criterion, that is to say, the mean of the virtues of the passions is determined by the overall good of the organism, which places sensual goods in their correct relation to that overall good; hence, these virtues are said to observe a rational mean only.[52] The mean of justice, in contrast, is set by the good of the neighbor or the community as a whole (depending on which form of justice is in question), in such a way as to reflect objective criteria of equity and fairness. For this reason, the mean of justice is said to be a real, as well as a rational, mean.[53] As already noted, the infused cardinal virtues observe a different mean than do the acquired virtues, and the theological virtues are not defined by reference to a mean at all (because there can be no question of moderation with respect to believing, hoping in, and loving God[54]).

Over the past several years, a number of scholars have attempted to appropriate Aquinas's account of the virtues as a basis for a contemporary virtue ethic, which would provide an alternative to a more legalistic ethic based on concepts of law or rules.[55] It should be noted, however, that Aquinas consistently holds the ideas of virtue and law together in his moral thought. In his general analysis of *habitus*, Aquinas argues that these receive their species from their objects, which are further distinguished in accordance with a distinction between good and bad.[56] This language, reminiscent of Aquinas's general analysis of human actions, implies that the virtues are conceptually linked to the kinds of actions that instantiate them.[57] At the same time, these concepts of kinds of actions, which comprise what Aquinas calls the object or the moral species of particular actions, are also correlated with moral rules. This, in turn, implies that the virtues can be correlated with precepts of the natural or divine law, and when we turn to the *secunda secundae*, we find that each of the seven major virtues that Aquinas discusses is indeed correlated with one or more precepts.[58] By the same token, Aquinas argues in the *De malo* that every sin represents a deviation from the mean, thus expanding a concept proper to virtue theory into a general analysis of moral norms.[59]

This is why Aquinas uses the traditional schema of the cardinal and theological virtues as the organizing principle for the detailed discussion of normative ideals and precepts in the *secunda pars*. The diverse elements of the Christian moral tradition—not only normative ideals and precepts of law, but the traditional schema of the beatitudes and the gifts of the Holy Spirit—can all be related to the virtues in some way: as the object of a given virtue, as a precept enjoining the realization of this object or the avoidance of contrary vicious acts, as an expression of what it means to enjoy the exercise of the virtues, or as a disposition through which the human spirit is made responsive to the Holy Spirit in the application of the virtues to specific acts. None of this implies that the precepts of law, or much less the beatitudes and the gifts, are inessential to the Christian moral life—quite the contrary!

But this approach does reflect Aquinas's overall approach, signaled at the beginning of the *prima secundae*, of analyzing human activity in terms of its internal principles of operation, and the external principles shaping and expressing those principles—themselves ultimately expressions of God, the supreme external principle of human acts.

NOTES

1. *ST* I-II q.6 *intro.*
2. *ST* I-II q.49 *intro*. The translation of *habitus* as "habit," while common, is misleading, because the English word implies mindless or stereotypical behavior, whereas for Aquinas a true virtue is precisely not mindless. On the contrary, it is a disposition formed through, and continually informed by, rational reflection. Nor would it be quite accurate to translate the term as "disposition," since a *habitus* is only one example of such. I have therefore simply left the term untranslated throughout.
3. *ST* I-II q.90 a.1. This and all subsequent translations are my own.
4. Most notably, see Ralph McInerny, *Ethica Thomistica: The Moral Philosophy of Thomas Aquinas* (Washington, D.C.: Catholic University of America Press, 1982/1997).
5. The best account of the development of virtue ethics in the medieval period remains the essays collected in Odon Lottin, *Psychologie et morale aux XII et XIII siecles*, vol. 3, parts 1 and 2 (Paris: Louvain, 1949). On Abelard and Peter Lombard, see Lottin, *Psychologie et morale*, 3/1:100–104; for a more detailed account of Abelard's theory of virtue, see John Marenbon, *The Philosophy of Peter Abelard* (Cambridge: Cambridge University Press, 1997), 282–87.
6. As Cary Nederman points out, key ideas from Aristotelian ethics were in general circulation for at least 150 years before the full text of the *Nicomachean Ethics* became available in Latin; see "Aristotelianism and the Origins of 'Political Science' in the Twelfth Century," *Journal of the History of Ideas* 52 (1991): 179–94, 180–81. This does not mean, however, that scholastic theories of virtue were identical to Aristotle's own theory. They were not—the scholastics, including Aquinas himself, do not follow the outline of Aristotle's account of the virtues in the *Nicomachean Ethics* (as Andrew Pinsent rightly points out in his chapter in this volume), and by the same token, they press beyond what Aristotle himself explicitly says about the metaphysical underpinnings of virtue theory. We may fairly regard Aquinas's theory of the virtues as Aristotelian, therefore, without claiming that it simply repeats Aristotle's own view, or denying that it incorporates many other classical and theological voices, as well as Aristotle's own.
7. *ST* I-II q.55 a.4, quoting *Super Sent* II 27.5.
8. *ST* I-II q.55 a.1.
9. *ST* I-II q.49 a.4.
10. *ST* I-II q.56 a.3; I-II q.57 a.1; I-II q.58 a.3.
11. *ST* I-II q.58 a.1.
12. On virtues as perfections of faculties, see, e.g., *ST* I-II q.55 a.3 and I-II q.56 a.1; on virtue as a perfection of the agent, see *ST* I-II q.4 a.7 in tandem with I-II q.3 a.2. I argue for this interpretation in more detail in *Nature as Reason: A Thomistic Theory of the Natural Law* (Grand Rapids, Mich.: Eerdmans, 2005), 163–203.

13. For further details, including further textual references, see Robert Pasnau's illuminating discussion of the metaphysics of actuality in *Thomas Aquinas on Human Nature: A Philosophical Study of Summa theologiae Ia 75–89* (Cambridge: Cambridge University Press, 2002), 143–51; in addition, see Porter, *Nature as Reason*, 158–63.

14. *ST* I-II q.61 a.4.

15. *ST* I-II q.59 a.2; I-II q.60 a.3–5; cf. *De virtutibus in communi*, a.12, which sets forth the relation of the virtues to the different faculties of the soul in more detail.

16. *ST* I-II q.58 a.2.

17. *ST* I-II q.59 a.5.

18. *ST* I-II q.56 a.6; I-II q.60 a.2; II-II q.24 a.1; II-II q.58 a.4.

19. *ST* I q.60 a.5; cf. *ST* I-II q.109 a.3.

20. *ST* I-II q.60 a.1.

21. *ST* I-II q.65 a.1.

22. *ST* I-II q.65 a.1.

23. *ST* I-II q.65 a.2.

24. *ST* I-II q.4 a.7 and I-II q.5 a.5; cf. *QDVCom* a.10.

25. *ST* I-II q.62 a.1 and I-II q.110 a.3.

26. *ST* I-II q.62 a.1.

27. *ST* I-II q.110 a.3; with reference to the gifts in particular, I-II q.68 a.1, 2.

28. *ST* I-II q.68 a.1.

29. *ST* I-II q.68 a.1.

30. Isa. 11:2–3; in this paragraph, I follow *ST* I-II q.68 a.1 except where otherwise noted.

31. See *ST* I-II q.68 a.4

32. *ST* I-II q.68 a.8.

33. For this reason, I would not say (as Andrew Pinsent suggests in his chapter) that Aquinas's account of the gifts of the Holy Spirit reflects a fundamental break with the Aristotelian orientation of his overall theory of virtue, that is to say, with his analysis of the virtues as perfections directed toward the ultimate flourishing of the rational creature. It should also be noted that in this question, Aquinas once again affirms that the acquired virtues are adequate to attain the connatural end of the human person, and that at least some individuals throughout history have in fact fully attained and practiced the (acquired) cardinal virtues without the aid of supernatural grace (*ST* I-II q.68 a.2). At the same time, I would agree with Pinsent that Aquinas's incorporation of the Gifts and Fruits of the Holy Spirit takes him well beyond the parameters of Aristotle's own outline and extends the scope of an Aristotelian construal of the virtues as perfections beyond anything that Aristotle's classical followers would have been likely to envision.

34. *ST* I-II q.68 a.2.

35. *ST* I-II q.63 a.3, 4.

36. *ST* II-II q.147 a.1 ad 2.

37. *ST* II-II q.104 a.6; II-II q.141 a.6 ad 1.

38. e.g., see *ST* I q.60 a.5.

39. *QDVCom* a.9; *ST* I-II q.61 a.5.

40. *ST* I-II q.110 a.3.

41. *ST* I-II q.114 a.2.

42. *ST* I-II q.63 a.3, especially ad 2; I-II q.65 a.3.

43. *ST* II-II q.58 a.7, 8.

44. Ibid.

45. Ibid.; II-II q.61 a.1.

46. *ST* II-II q.47 a.11.

47. *ST* I-II q.71 a.1, 3.
48. *ST* I-II q.71 a.1.
49. *ST* I-II q.71 a.3.
50. *ST* I-II q.71 a.4.
51. *ST* I-II q.64 a.1.
52. *ST* I-II q.64 a.2.
53. Ibid.; also see *ST* I-II q.56 a.6; II-II q.58 a.10.
54. *ST* I-II q.64 a.4
55. See, for e.g., Daniel Mark Nelson, *The Priority of Prudence: Virtue and Natural Law in Aquinas and Its Implications for Modern Ethics* (University Park: Pennsylvania State University Press, 1992), and more recently, John Bowlin, *Contingency and Fortune in Aquinas' Ethics* (Cambridge: Cambridge University Press, 1999), 97–137.
56. *ST* I-II q.54 a.2, 3.
57. See, e.g., *ST* II-II q.27 a.1.
58. The relevant texts are *ST* II-II q.16, 22, 44, 56, 122, 140, and 170; cf. *ST* II-II q.108 a.2.
59. *De malo*, q.2, a.1; sins are said specifically to be opposed to one or more virtues at q.2, a.6.

CHAPTER 21

PRACTICAL REASONING

THOMAS M. OSBORNE, JR.

AQUINAS thinks that practical reason is distinct but not entirely insulated from speculative reason. Although his description of practical reasoning applies to a variety of human activities, his greatest focus is on the practical reasoning that is involved in human action. Although practical reasoning resembles the speculative in its use of a kind of syllogism, its connection with particular affairs precisely as contingent gives it a special character.

PRACTICAL AND SPECULATIVE REASON

Practical reason is distinct from speculative reason because it is ordered to some work or end. These two kinds of reason can also be called kinds of "intellect."[1] Reason denominates investigation whereas "intellect" does not. At least in his later work, Aquinas is clear that practical and speculative intellects are not distinct powers.

Since powers are distinguished by their objects or what they are about, and the practical and speculative intellects have different objects, it might seem that they are distinct powers. But Aquinas argues that the distinction of objects is only accidental and consequently does not indicate distinct powers.[2] The intellect has truth as its object. The difference between the practical and speculative intellects is that the speculative is concerned only with the truth, whereas the practical apprehends the truth for the sake of some further end. In this context Aquinas and his contemporaries attribute to Aristotle's *De anima* the following dictum: "The speculative intellect through extension becomes practical."[3]

Absolutely considered, the thing (*res*) is the measure of the intellect. The rectitude of the speculative intellect consists solely in conformity to things. Although the practical intellect too must conform to the world, its rectitude consists further in an end or operation.[4] It is not only measured by the world but also itself measures the world. Elizabeth Anscombe used the example of a shopping list to illustrate this difference.[5] A man who goes to the store with a shopping list might be followed by a detective. We can assume that the man has been ordered by a legitimate authority to buy everything on the list and nothing else. If the list includes butter but the man buys margarine, then the man makes a mistake. His behavior is judged by the list. The mistake is not in the list but in the man's end or operation. In contrast, if the detective puts down that the man has bought margarine when he has in fact bought butter, the mistake is in the detective's list. Speculative reason is measured only by the thing, whereas practical reason is also measured by the end. This connection to a goal or action implies that practical reason takes its goal from desire or appetite.

The conjunction of practical reason with the appetite makes it possible for practical reason to be causal. Aquinas states, "Now practical and speculative reason differ in this, that speculative reason is only apprehensive of things, but practical reason is not only apprehensive, but also causative."[6] Reason without appetite cannot cause action. For instance, a physician may now know to heal himself and yet not have the desire to be so healed. His knowledge would not heal him even though it could if he were to have the appropriate appetite. Similarly, someone who knows that fornication is wrong may still fornicate if he does not have a well-ordered appetite.

Although both kinds of reason involve both universals and particulars, practical reason considers the contingent and particular precisely as contingent and particular.[7] Whereas, a naturalist's speculative reason might be concerned about what whales are, a whale hunter's practical reason is concerned with how to capture particular whales. The naturalist and the whale hunter both need to understand some universal truths about whales and have knowledge of particular whales. The difference is in the way that the particulars and contingents are considered.[8] The naturalist considers the individual whale insofar as it instantiates universal and unchanging properties of whales. But the whale hunter considers the whale as this whale that can be pursued and even destroyed.

Degrees and Kinds of Practical Knowledge

There are different degrees and kinds of practical knowledge. For instance, the knowledge of a builder is more practical in degree than that of the architecture student. Moreover, the practical knowledge of a just builder as a just person is different from his practical knowledge of building. This latter difference follows the distinction between prudence and art or skill.

Aquinas distinguishes differently between the degrees of practical knowledge throughout his career.[9] The basic problem is that practical knowledge is about something that can be done (*operabile*), but not everyone knows such a work with the purpose of doing it. His consistent point is that there is a kind of practical knowledge that is not fully practical. Perhaps the latest complete division is in the *Prima pars* (1269), q.14, a.16, in which a discussion of God's speculative knowledge leads to a discussion of the degrees of speculative knowledge in general. The degrees among the kinds of speculative knowledge correspond to degrees of practical knowledge.[10]

Aquinas uses the work of building a house to illustrate his point that knowledge can be divided according to the thing known, the way it is known, and the end for which it is known. Knowledge of a house would seem to be practical, since houses are made by human beings. In contrast, the knowledge of mathematical truths is clearly speculative, since it is about something that cannot be changed by human action. But knowledge of a house's structure and parts without any practical consideration is also speculative knowledge, since such knowledge consists in an analysis of its principles. In this case the speculative knowledge is about something that can be made but not as something that can be made. However, in contrast to the knowledge of unchangeable objects, such knowledge remains practical in some respect (*secundum quid*).

Speculative knowledge can also be made practical through the manner of knowing or the end. For instance, an architectural student might also have speculative knowledge of a house as something that can be built. In such a case the knowledge is practical in one respect and speculative in another (*secundum quid speculative et secundum quid practica*). It is possible to know how to build but without the desire or plan to build. There is practical knowledge simply speaking only when the knower orders this knowledge to the end of building. For such completely practical knowledge, there must be a direct connection with action.

The degrees of practical knowledge can be applied to the two kinds of practical knowledge, namely art and prudence.[11] Aquinas takes this division from Aristotle.[12] While knowledge of an art or technical skill is about that which can be made, it is not about the good life as a whole. For instance, the good carpenter knows how to make a table. Prudence is the knowledge of human action, which is evaluated according to the good life as a whole. The carpenter who is a good person has the knowledge of how to work in an orderly fashion and charge a just price for his labor. Whereas art is concerned with the perfection of the product, prudence is concerned with the agent's perfection.

Unlike art, perfectly developed prudence requires the presence of the major moral virtues.[13] A good carpenter may be a bad human being. Moreover, a skillful carpenter may voluntarily make a bad product such as a fragile chair for a heavy person whom he dislikes.[14] Art is subordinated to the agent's further ends. In contrast, an act which ignores the commands of prudence is a sin. Prudence requires that the agent have rectitude toward his ultimate end, which is human flourishing. Such rectitude is impossible without the moral virtues. The prudent person does not need in each case to think explicitly about his ultimate end, but with prudence he performs actions that lead to or are constitutive of this end.[15]

The distinction between the degrees of practical knowledge applies to moral truths. Prudence orders action and therefore is completely practical, in contrast to art and moral philosophy, which can be to some extent speculative.[16] Nevertheless, moral science can be some help to prudence.[17] But virtue is learned more by laws and action than by teaching.[18]

What is the order between art and prudence? Properly speaking, art is subordinated to prudence.[19] Art is concerned with merely particular goods, whereas prudence is concerned with the good life as the whole. For instance, someone who is a good carpenter but unjust may have practical knowledge about making tables but he lacks it with respect to the purpose of his making tables, which is living a good human life. Nevertheless, Aquinas does accept that "art" can be used in a wider sense as right reason: "Augustine commonly takes 'art' to be any sort of right reason. And thus under art even prudence is included, which thus is right reason about what actions can be done, just as art is right reason about what can be made."[20] But in the strictest sense, the term "art" is about making and consequently is not only distinct from prudence but also directed to the ends of prudence.

Principles, Precepts, and the Structure of Practical Reasoning

Aquinas's most detailed discussions of practical reasoning's role in the act's structure are in his *Secunda secundae* and his *Commentary on Aristotle's Ethics*. Although the outline is broadly Aristotelian, his terminology also comes from Stoic sources and the Church Fathers, especially John Damascene.[21] In the *Secunda secundae*, he follows the role of reasoning in the structure of an act in conjunction with the role of the will. Although the discussion is divided according to the will's stages, his intent is to indicate the different ways in which the intellect and will are involved in one and the same act.

The intellect's role in the production of the act involves: (1) the apprehension of and judgment about an end, (2) the deliberation (*consilium*) about the means to the end, (3) a judgment that corresponds to the choice about the end, and (4) a command (*imperium*).[22] In order to act or will the intellect must first recognize some end, which is a good. This end does not need to be a real good, but it must appear to the agent as such. For instance, theft is bad, but it seems good to the thief. The agent's apprehension or misapprehension of the good to large extent depends on his character.[23] There has been some recent controversy over whether for Aquinas the will has some sort of precognitive movement toward the good.[24] But Aquinas frequently reiterates Augustine's statement that "nothing is loved unless it is known."[25] At this stage knowledge precedes volition.

After the willing and recognition of the good, the agent sometimes must deliberate about the means. For instance, if I wish to steal a car I might deliberate about whether to steal the keys or attempt to start the car without the keys. Deliberation occurs when there are multiple means to an end.[26] If I do not know how to start a car without keys and the keys are right in front of me, there is no need to deliberate. Nevertheless, every act requires a judgment of choice about the means. After choosing to steal the car, my intellect then commands the will to carry out the activity. This general account is not meant to describe a temporal sequence among distinct acts but rather to show the stages at which an act can fail.[27] For instance, if I were a just person, then I would not apprehend stealing as good. Or, if I were unjust, perhaps I might want to steal but be unable to discover any means to do so. The act would end in deliberation.

Command is the intellect's counterpart to the will's use of the other faculties in the execution of an action.[28] Aquinas thinks that command is what the intellect does once the agent has chosen to act. For instance, after choosing to steal a car, I should be able to know where the keys are, how to put them in the ignition, and how to evade detection. Daniel Westberg states that for Aquinas "the intellect has command in the sense of 'oversight' or 'seeing something through.'"[29]

What role do principles play in this process of practical reasoning? Aquinas does not think that practical reasoning consists in the demonstrative application of universal principles to particular events, and his ethical thought at times seems remote from the modern concern with recognizably moral principles.[30] Nevertheless, he does think that principles and precepts are necessary for practical reasoning, and he discusses them at some length in the relatively brief discussion of natural law in the *Prima secundae*. The first principle of speculative reason is that of noncontradiction, since we first recognize being and nonbeing.[31] Since practical reason is concerned with the good, the first principle is "Do good and avoid evil." Neither the practical nor the speculative principle need to be explicitly recognized in order to be used. These principles are presupposed in all speculative and practical reasonings, respectively.

Some contemporary scholars suggest that Aquinas's first principle of practical reason is not a moral principle, since it is used in every action, including acts that are sins and those which are simply the exercise of a skill.[32] This reading neglects central features of his theory.[33] The case of sin is relatively straightforward, since for Aquinas sin involves a voluntary mistake in reasoning or the use of incorrect premises.[34] The sinner uses the first practical principle but misapprehends what is good or is negligent in the application of his knowledge. The case with art is more complicated. Some acts such as building a table are not intrinsically good or evil, but as individual human acts they are morally good or bad. As we have seen, art is subordinated to prudence. Building a table considered as such is an exercise of art, but considered as a human action it involves a relation to the human good. The practical reasoning about making particular things involves a wider recognition of what it is good to make. This wider view is moral.

The precepts of practical reason follow an order that exists in nature. Aquinas makes wide use of Aristotle's statement that "art imitates nature."[35] He thinks that this imitation occurs not only in the case of art in its proper sense, as when a builder imitates a tree's roots by making a foundation, but also in the case of practical reasoning in the moral context, as when someone chooses to love God more than himself.[36] The precepts of the natural law are based on human nature.

How are principles involved in human practical reasoning? Some principles or precepts, such as the first practical principle, are implicitly used. *Synderesis* is the ability to recognize the primary ends of deliberation.[37] Some precepts may play an explicit role in deliberation.[38] It is impossible to give some one account of moral principles as there are different kinds of moral precepts, namely affirmative and negative, primary and secondary.[39] Affirmative precepts may always bind but usually require action only in a particular situation.[40] For example, the command to love God explicitly must be fulfilled at some point, but at times the agent may be involved in other activities. But the command binds always because at any time it can be violated. For instance, when an agent at any time sins mortally he violates the command to love God. Negative precepts can similarly bind at all times even though they need not play an explicit role in practical reasoning. For instance, the precept "Do not commit adultery" binds all the time but comes into play only when adultery is an option. Primary precepts such as those listed in the Decalogue are seemingly known through their terms.[41] Some precepts are secondary in that they are not easily known or in that they are good rules of thumb but have exceptions.[42] For instance, the precept "return borrowed goods" usually holds. But I may know that my neighbor asks me to return his gun so that he can harm my country or rob a store. In such a case, it would be imprudent for me to return the gun.[43]

Although principles can be used in deliberation, they do not completely determine what to do in a particular situation. Many affirmative precepts are too general to indicate what to do under particular circumstances. Negative precepts indicate only what one should not do. Secondary precepts have exceptions. The prudent agent knows which precepts to apply in particular situations. Moreover, the application of the precepts is fully practical only if it concludes in the judgment of choice. The judgment of conscience is about particular actions but is only cognitive and does not by itself lead to action.[44]

The Practical Syllogism and Error

Both practical and speculative reason proceed from principles to conclusions.[45] The basic model for this procedure is the syllogism. Speculative reason tries to proceed from the form or "that which is." According to Aquinas's metaphysics, these forms are necessary and unchanging. For instance, the following premises are necessary and unchanging: "All mammals have lungs" and "All humans are mammals." In a speculative syllogism, this conclusion necessarily follows: "All humans have lungs." In contrast, practical reason does not always assent to necessary premises. For instance, everyone wants happiness, but not everyone wants a particular means to happiness, such as building a house. Moreover, the conclusion or operation does not necessarily follow from the same principles. Someone who wills a house may choose different kinds of wood. There can be an indefinite number of reasons for choosing some wood rather than another, such as cost and availability.

Aquinas to some extent follows Aristotle on the practical syllogism.[46] Practical reasoning resembles the speculative syllogism in that there is a universal major, but it differs in the particularity of the minor premise and the connection between its conclusion and action. Aquinas seems to use the practical syllogism in the context of both deliberation and choice.[47] This practical syllogism is only quasi-syllogistic (*quasi sillogistica*).[48] Its conclusion is a "judgment, or [*seu*] choice or [*vel*] operation."[49] In his later treatments, he emphasizes the connection to action and carefully distinguishes the practical syllogism from the syllogisms that are employed in moral science.[50]

In his discussion of the vices that are opposed to prudence, Aquinas lists many ways in which practical reasoning can fail.[51] All of these failures either involve a mistake in the reasoning itself, a mistake in the premises of a practical syllogism, or in the act's execution. The mistaken premises are most important for understanding erroneous practical syllogisms. An error about the major premise is most clearly seen in the difference between the syllogisms employed by the virtuous and the vicious.[52] For example, the temperate and intemperate both use syllogisms with two premises and a conclusion. The temperate agent reasons as follows: "No fornication should be committed; this act is fornication; this act should not be done." The intemperate agent employs an alternative syllogism: "Every pleasurable thing should be enjoyed; this act [of fornication] is pleasurable; therefore this act should be done." The vicious person on account of his vice is blinded to the virtuous agent's major premise, which states that no fornication should be committed. His own major premise is false and in this case it leads to the vicious action.

But error is possible even for someone who knows the correct universal premise.[53] For example, both the continent and the incontinent know that "no fornication should be committed," but their disordered appetites lead them to consider that "every pleasurable thing should be enjoyed." The difference between the two is in which universal premise they use in conjunction with a minor premise. The continent agent reasons by combining the first universal premise with the minor premise that "this act is fornication." The continent agent is drawn by his passion to think that fornication is pleasurable, but he focuses on the fact that fornication is a sin. He is aware of both universal principles but uses only that which is used by the virtuous. In contrast, the incontinent reasons by joining the second universal premise to the minor premise that "this act is pleasurable." Although the incontinent is aware of both universal principles, he only employs that universal premise that is used by the vicious.

Both the incontinent and the vicious err, but they seem to employ valid syllogisms. The error of the incontinent is that out of weakness he shifts to the bad syllogism. He knows but does not use the correct universal premise. The error of the vicious is that he has only a false universal premise. Aquinas regards both errors as culpable. Neither the incontinent nor the vicious have the fully developed intellectual virtue of prudence or the other moral virtues. The incontinent may in general be able to recognize the wrongness of an act, but they are not commanded to the act by prudence. The vicious do not recognize the act's very badness.

The prudent person knows how to reason practically about those goods that concern human life as a whole. The preceding practical syllogisms were fairly straightforward because the virtuous agent's major syllogism has an exceptionless precept as its universal premise. Unlike demonstrative syllogisms, practical syllogisms that are normally sound can sometimes lead to bad conclusions.[54] For instance, even though usually the premise "borrowed items should be returned" leads to a correct conclusion, in exceptional circumstances it does not. Most often the following syllogism would be correct: "Borrowed items ought to be returned; this gun is a borrowed item; this gun ought to be returned." But if a killer asks for the gun's return, the practical syllogism can yield a false conclusion.

Prudence is important not only for reasoning about particular acts by themselves and for commanding acts but also because it considers the good life as a whole. Although prudence is an intellectual virtue, it is not limited to one kind of matter in the way that sciences and arts are.[55] Its concern is with the moral life as a whole. Someone might be more or less prudent with respect to justice but imprudent with respect to temperance. Intemperance often leads to unjust acts. The matter of the different virtues is connected in such a way that fully developed prudence with respect to one of the major virtues requires a fully developed prudence with respect to the others.

In his discussion of infused virtue and the gift of counsel, Aquinas emphasizes the limits of merely acquired prudence for moral reasoning. Since humans are called to a supernatural end that exceeds natural powers, fully developed practical reasoning about life as a whole requires the infused virtue of prudence, which is given by God.[56] Aquinas also emphasizes that not even infused prudence can completely take into account all the particulars. He writes, "human reason is not able to understand the singular and contingent things which are able to happen.... And therefore man needs in the inquiry of deliberation [*consilium*] to be directed by God, who understands everything."[57] Ultimately, correct practical reasoning about human action requires counsel, which is one of the seven gifts of the Holy Spirit. This gift perfects and helps prudence in its judgments.[58] Like Aristotle, Aquinas emphasizes the contingency of human affairs and its importance for practical reasoning. But in what for many might seem to be an unexpected move, Aquinas argues that the uncertainty of human affairs shows that practical reasoning about the good life requires not only the infused virtue of prudence but also a special gift of God.

NOTES

1. *ST* II-II q.49 a.5 ad 3; *In DA*, lib.3, cap.8; *QDVCom* a.7. John Naus, *The Nature of the Practical Intellect* (Rome: Libreria Editrice dell' Universita Gregoriana, 1959), 28. For possible development and many texts, see 17–34.

2. *ST* I q.79 a.11.

3. "intellectus speculativus per extensionem fit practicus." *Super Sent*, lib.3, d.23, q.2, a.3, qc.2; *ST* I q.70 a.11 s.c.; *ST* II-II q.4 a.2 ad 3. For the widespread usage and source of this adage, see Naus, *Nature of the Practical Intellect*, 23–26. For its use in contemporary controversies, see Ralph McInerny, *Aquinas on Human Action: A Theory of Practice* (Washington, D.C.: Catholic University of America Press, 1992), 184–92.

4. *Super Sent*, lib.3, d.33, q.1, a.1, sol.2; *ST* I-II q.64 a.3; *In NE*, lib.6, lect.2.

5. G. E. M. Anscombe, *Intention* (Cambridge: Harvard University Press, 2000), 56. For a contrast of her approach with that of Aquinas, see Steven L. Brock, *Action and Conduct: Thomas Aquinas and the Theory of Action* (Edinburgh: T & T Clark, 1998), 161–71.

6. "Ratio autem speculativa et practica in hoc differunt quod ration speculativa est apprehensiva solum rerum; ratio vero practica est non solum apprehensiva, sed etiam causativa." *ST* II-II q.83 a.1. See also *In DA*, lib.3, cap.8. For reasons and explanations, see Scott MacDonald, "Practical Reasoning and Reasons-Explanations: Aquinas's Account of Reason's Role in Action," in Scott MacDonald and Eleonore Stump, eds., *Aquinas's Moral Theory: Essays in Honor of Norman Kretzmann* (Ithaca, N.Y.: Cornell University Press, 1998), 133–60.

7. *ST* I-II q.57 a.6 ad 3; *In NE*, lib.6, lect.3.

8. *Super Sent*, lib.2, q.2, a.4, ad 6; *Super Sent*, lib.4, d.50, q.1, a.3, ad 3; *QDV*, q.14, a.12, ad 1; *ST* I q.86 a.3; *In PA*, lib.1, cap.8, lect.16; *In NE*, lib.6, lect.1.

9. *QDV*, q.2, a.8, resp.; *QDV*, q.3, a.3; *In BDT*, q.5, a.1, ad 4; *ST* I q.14 a.16. See Naus, *Nature of the Practical Intellect*, 151–69.

10. Ralph McInerny, *Ethica Thomistica*, rev. ed. (Washington, D.C.: Catholic University of America Press, 1997), 38–40.

11. *ST* I-II q.57 a.4; *ST* II-II q.47 a.4 ad 2; *QDVCom* a.12.

12. *In NE*, lib.6, lect.4.

13. *QDV*, q.5, a.1; *ST* II-II q.47 a.13; *In NE*, lib.6, lect.10; *De virtutibus cardinalibus*, q. un., a.2. See Thomas M. Osborne, Jr., "Perfect and Imperfect Virtues in Aquinas," *The Thomist* 71 (2007): 57–62; Daniel Westberg, *Right Practical Reason: Aristotle, Action and Prudence in Aquinas* (Oxford: Clarendon, 1994), 216–21; Naus, *Nature of the Practical Intellect*, 113–17.

14. *In NE*, lib.6, lect.4.

15. Thomas M. Osborne, Jr., "The Threefold Referral of Acts to the Ultimate End in Thomas Aquinas and His Commentators," *Angelicum* 85 (2008): 715–36.

16. *ST* II-II q.47 a.1 ad 3; *ST* II-II q.47 a.2 ad 2, ad 3. See Kevin L. Flannery, *Acts amid Precepts: The Aristotelian Logical Structure of Thomas Aquinas's Moral* Theory (Washington, D.C.: Catholic University of America Press, 2001), 3–24; Naus, *Nature of the Practical Intellect*, 60–68; M-Michel Labourdette, "Connaissance practique et savoir moral," *Revue Thomiste* 48 (1948): 142–79. For the general historical context, see Georg Wieland, *Ethica—Scientia Practica: Die Anfänge der philosophischen Ethik im 13. Jahrhundert* (Münster: Ashendorff, 1981).

17. *In NE*, lib.2, lect.2; *ST* I q.1 a.6 ad 3.

18. *In NE*, lib.10, lect.14.

19. *ST* I-II q.21 a.2 ad 2. See Guiseppe Butera, "The Moral Status of the First Principle of Practical Reason in Thomas's Natural Law Theory," *The Thomist* 71 (2007): 622–23.

20. "Augustinus communiter accipit artem, pro qualibet recta ratione. Et sic sub arte includitur etiam prudentia, quae ita est recta ratio agibilium, sicut ars est recta ratio factibilium." *ST* I-II q.58 a.2 ad 1. See, for instance, *In NE*, lib.3, lect.7. Naus, *Nature of the Practical Intellect*, 62–63.

21. Terence Irwin, "Will, Responsibility and Ignorance: Aristotelian Accounts of Incontinence," in Tobias Hoffmann, Jörn Müller, and Matthias Perkams, eds., *The Problem of Weakness of Will in Medieval Philosophy* (Leuven: Peeters, 2006), 40–58; Westberg, *Right Practical Reason*, 126–35; Vernon Bourke, *St. Thomas and the Greek Moralists* (Milwaukee: Marquette University Press, 1947).

22. *ST* I-II q.9–17. For different schema, see Michael S. Sherwin, *By Knowledge and by Love: Charity and Knowledge in the Moral Theology of St. Thomas Aquinas* (Washington, D.C.: Catholic University of America Press, 2005), 84–94; Eleonore Stump, *Aquinas* (New York: Routledge, 2003), 287–94; John Finnis, *Aquinas: Moral, Political and Legal Theory* (Oxford; Oxford University Press, 1998), 62–71; Westberg, *Right Practical Reason*, 130–35; McInerny, *Aquinas on Human Action*, 51–74.

23. *ST* I-II q.9 a.2; *ST* I-II q.58 a.5.

24. Sherwin, *By Knowledge and by Love*; James F. Keenan, *Goodness and Rightness in Thomas Aquinas's Summa Theologiae* (Washington, D.C.: Catholic University of America Press, 1992).

25. *Super Sent*, lib.3, d.23, q.2, a.5, sc 1; *QDV*, q.2, a.3, sc 7; *QDV*, q.8, a.11, sc 2; *QDV*, q.10, a.9, sc 5; *In BDT*, q.1, a.2, sc 3; *ST* Ia, q.60, a.1, sc; *ST* I-II q.3. a.4 ad 4; *De caritate*, q. un., a.10, sc 2.

26. *ST* I-II q.14 a. 4.

27. *ST* I-II q.8 a.3.

28. Brock, *Action and Conduct*, 175–83; Westberg, *Right Practical Reason*.

29. Westberg, *Right Practical Reason*, 181.

30. Daniel Mark Nelson, *The Priority of Prudence: Virtue and Natural Law in Thomas Aquinas and the Implications for Modern Ethics* (University Park: Pennsylvania State University Press, 1992).

31. *ST* I-II q.94 a.2.

32. John Finnis and Germain Grisez, "The Basic Principles of Natural Law: A Reply to Ralph McInerny," *American Journal of Jurisprudence* 26 (1981): 21–31; Germain Grisez, "The Structures of Practical Reason: Some Comments and Clarifications," *The Thomist* 52 (1988): 269–91; Finnis, *Aquinas: Moral, Political and Legal Theory*, 123–29.

33. Ralph McInerny, "The Principles of Natural Law," *American Journal of Jurisprudence* 25 (1980): 1–15; Russell Hittinger, *A Critique of the New Natural Law Theory* (Notre Dame, Ind.: University of Notre Dame Press, 1987), 10–92; Flannery, *Acts amid Precepts*, 25–49; Butera, "The Moral Status of the First Principle."

34. *ST* I-II q.94 a.6; *ST* I-II q.99 a.2 ad 2.

35. *In Phy*, lib.2, c.8, lect.13, n.4. See Thomas M. Osborne, Jr., *The Love of Self and Love of God in Thirteenth-Century Ethics* (Notre Dame, Ind.: University of Notre Dame Press, 2005), 100–101; McInerny, *Aquinas on Human Action*, 193–206. For a contrary view, see Martin Rhonheimer, *Natural Law and Practical Reason*, trans. Gerald Malsbary (New York: Fordham University Press, 2000), 3–57; Georg Wieland, "Secundum naturam vivere: Über den Wandel des Verhältnisses von Natur und Sittlichkeit," in Bernhard Fraling, ed., *Natur im ethischen Argument* (Herder: Freiburg, 1990), 20–26. For the difference between Rhonheimer and Wieland, see Rhonheimer, *Natural Law and Practical Reason*, 562–70.

36. *ST* I q.60 a.5.

37. *ST* I q.79 a.12; *QDV*, q.16, a.1–3.

38. *ST* I-II q.14 a.3 ad 2. Westberg, *Right Practical Reason*, 239–40.

39. McInerny, *Ethica Thomistica*, 40–59; Westberg, *Right Practical Reason*, 172–74; Flannery, *Acts amid Precepts*, 50–83.

40. *ST* I-II q.71 a.5 ad 3; *ST* II-II q.3 a.2; *ST* II-II q.140 a.2 ad 2.

41. *ST* I-II q.100 a.1; ST II-II q.170 a.2 ad 1.

42. *ST* I-II q.94 a.4–5.

43. *ST* II-II q.51 a.4.

44. *QDV*, q.17, a.1, ad 4; *ST* I-II q.13 a.3. McInerny, *Aquinas on Human Action*, 220–39; Leo Elders, "La Doctrine de la conscience de Saint Thomas d'Aquin," *Revue Thomiste* 83 (1983): 533–57.

45. *SCG*, lib.3, cap.97.

46. Flannery, *Acts amid Precepts*, 8–15.

47. Westberg, *Right Practical Reason*, 149–64, 200–213, makes an unusual distinction between the practical syllogism of deliberation and the "operative syllogism" that results in choice.

48. *QDM*, q.3, a.9, ad 7.

49. "iudicium seu electio vel operatio." *ST* I-II q.76 a.1.

50. Westberg, *Right Practical Reason*, 153–55.

51. *ST* II-II q.53–55.

52. This discussion follows *QDM*, q.3, a.9, ad 7. But see also *ST* I-II q.77 a.2; *In NE*, lib.7, lect.3. See Westberg, *Right Practical Reason*, 204–13.

53. In addition to the texts cited in the previous note, see also Irwin, "Will, Responsibility and Ignorance"; Tobias Hoffmann, "Aquinas on the Moral Progress of the Weak Willed," in Hoffmann, Müller, and Perkams, eds., *Problem of Weakness of Will*, 230–36.

54. Flannery, *Acts amid Precepts*, 195–223.

55. *ST* I-II q.65 a.1 ad 3, ad 4; Cf. *De virtutibus cardinalibus*, q. un., a.2, ad 4.

56. *ST* II-II q.23 a.7; *De virtutibus cardinalibus*, q. un., a.2, resp.

57. "humana ratio non potest comprehendere singularia et contingentia quae ratio comprehendere potest. . . . Et ideo indiget homo in inquisitione consilii dirigi a Deo, qui omnia comprehendit." *ST* II-II q.52 a.1 ad 1.

58. *ST* II-II q.52 a.2. In *ST* II-II q.8 a.3; *ST* II-II q.45 a.3, Aquinas argues that the gifts of understanding and wisdom are to some extent practical.

CHAPTER 22

THE THEOLOGICAL VIRTUES

JOSEPH WAWRYKOW

Aquinas locates the theological virtues in the account of the movement of human beings to the transcendent end set for them by God, knowing and loving God directly in the next life.[1] These virtues orient their possessor to God as the beatifying end of human beings, as made by and for God as their end. In assessing these virtues, Aquinas shows their conformity to the basic pattern of divine–human saving interaction, in which divine initiative and causing take the precedence, but not to the exclusion of genuine human causing. In God's causal love, God ordains eternal life, in God's immediate presence, as the end of human existence; in love, God provides human beings with what they need to reach this end. This includes the theological virtues, which are infused in a person along with habitual grace in conversion, by which a person is moved by God from sin and toward God as end. These virtues, testimony to God's causal love, are something created in the soul,[2] elevating the person to the supernatural order and making possible acts that are pleasing to God and conducive to eternal life. It is by the acts made possible by habitual grace and the theological virtues that a person is readied for eternal life, which is rendered as the reward for these acts. In his analysis of the theological virtues—faith, hope, charity—Aquinas invokes the moral and intellectual virtues to display the theological virtues in their distinctiveness.

Why "Theological" Virtues?

The designation of certain virtues as "theological" suggests their threefold connection to God: the theological virtues are infused by God; they direct a person to God as beatifying end; they become known by God's revelation in Scripture.[3] That God infuses the theological virtues marks a principal difference from the moral and intellectual virtues. Those virtues are acquired through acts of a kind. Acts of a kind lead to a habit of that kind, an inclination to act in that way, which disposes a person endowed with that good habit to further acts of that kind. The theological virtues are not acquired; since they are supernatural, above the natural capacities of the person, one cannot prepare for them or develop them through one's prior acts. Rather, they are, simply, the gift of God, given by God to those who are called to eternal life. Once received, they can be increased, as can the acquired virtues, through acts. By acts of charity, with God's aid, one becomes more rooted in charity, and so more inclined to love God and neighbor.[4] But the reception of the theological virtues is not dependent on human acting, and people can do nothing to occasion their giving. God simply gives them, in accordance with God's will for the elect. God calls these humans to life with God in heaven. In beatitude they will attain a fulfillment that transcends the natural capacities of humans qua human. God seeks to bring human beings to that transcendent end through characteristic human operations, of knowing and willing. But, the natural capacities of the human are not proportioned to God as beatifying end.

The theological virtues, then, enhance human capacity, elevating the person to the supernatural order and making their possessor capable of the acts (of faith, hope, and charity) that bring that person to the end to which grace and these virtues direct him. Each of these virtues in its particular manner relates the person to the God who beatifies. By faith, one believes, on the basis of God revealing, what is needed for salvation: what the end of human existence, in God, is, and the way to that end, as arranged by God. By hope, one aspires to the God who beatifies, trusting in God's aid. And, by charity, one has a friendship with God, made possible by God's outpouring of love for humans; and by willing in charity one comes into union with God, imperfectly in this life, but perfectly in the next. All of this lies beyond the natural principles of the human person, even as perfected by the acquired virtues. Such have to do only with an end that is proportioned to human nature, not with God as beatifying.

It is through Scripture, the locus of the revelation of God's saving will for people and provision for them, that the theological virtues come to be known. Again this marks a difference between these and the acquired virtues. It is not that the acquired virtues are left completely out of the scriptural account. But there are other sources by which they are also known, and known in their full extent. Apart from divine revelation, however, humans would be unaware of that faith that grasps God's saving teaching, or of that hope that expresses the desire for the God who saves and is confident on the basis of the aid of that God in reaching God as end, or of that charity that is marked by true friendship between God and those whom God loves in a special way. In the *Summa theologiae*, Aquinas considers the theological virtues in the order of generation;[5] thus, on the basis of faith, one can come to have hope, which in turn engenders charity, love for the one about whom there is faith and hope. But, that is also, and more fundamentally, the order suggested by Scripture, as shown by a fundamental verse, I Corinthians 13:13, to which Aquinas has frequent recourse.[6]

Thus, in the *Secunda Secundae*, Aquinas treats faith first (q.1–16), then hope (q.17–22), and then brings the consideration of the theological virtues to term by looking at charity (q.23–46). And those treatments have repeated recourse to the scriptural witness in presenting faith, hope, charity, as well as to the precepts for each.[7]

Faith

In discussing each of the theological virtues, Aquinas will consider the act or acts made possible by the virtue, the gift or gifts that perfect the possessor of that virtue and so make her more open to the promptings of the Holy Spirit to act out of that virtue and so in a way pleasing to God, the vices opposed to the virtue, and the pertinent precepts.[8] In what follows on each of the theological virtues, I concentrate on the virtue with its act(s), with some attention to the opposing vices.

Believing, the internal act of faith, is to think with assent.[9] It is an act of the intellect, commanded by the will. By faith, one is related to God as First Truth. The First Truth is both the formal object and, in an extended sense, the material object of faith. God reveals the truths held by theological faith, and it is on God's authority that one assents to these truths. And, these truths involve beatitude: God reveals that God is the beatifying end of human beings, and what God has done, in Christ, to make possible reaching that end. With the tradition, in defining the virtue of faith, Aquinas is content with the words of Hebrews 11:1: "faith is the substance of things to be hoped for, the certainty of things that appear not."[10] One does not see God in this life and so the object of faith does not of itself bring a person to affirm it; faith, not knowledge, is characteristic of the journey, in this life. But, on God's authority, one can believe that God is the beatifying end of the person and that the way to this end is through Jesus Christ; and since God does not lie, there is a certainty to faith (the "assurance" of things that appear not). The word "substance" in the definition is taken in a distinctive sense, to indicate that, by faith, there is an anticipation of heaven. There is, to be sure, a distance between now and what lies in the future. But, by faith, there is a first taste of heaven and an ordering to heaven, a thinking appropriate to life in this world by which the "substance" of heaven is possessed and which promotes the attaining of heaven. To reach an end, one must be aware of the end and the means to it; and this is provided in faith.

With the tradition, Aquinas thinks there are three aspects of the internal act of faith.[11] He adopts a formulation that nuances the relation of the person to God by faith: *credere Deo*; *credere Deum*; *credere in Deum*. By the first part of the formula is indicated God as the formal object of the act of faith. By the second is indicated the material object of faith. On the basis of God revealing and the authority of God (*credere Deo*), one affirms basic truths involved in salvation, that God is the beatifying end of the human journey, that God is triune, and the like (*credere Deum*). The first two parts of the formula deal with the intellect, which is perfected by the habit of faith. The final part of the formula turns to will, which commands the act of the intellect. In the faith that justifies, that puts one right before God, *credere in Deum* bespeaks the virtue of charity, which directs human acts to God as the ultimate end. Charity quickens the act of faith, and makes it worthy before God.

In his fullest depiction of the act of faith, Aquinas will also note the place of grace. The object of faith lies beyond reason, and the object is not known directly. Since it is unseen, the object of faith is not sufficient to move the intellect to affirm it. The act of the intellect must be commanded by the will, and the will need not command the act of faith. That the will commands this act is due to grace, to God moving the will to command the act of faith.[12] Faith, then, has a twofold dependence on God's gracious will: for the infusion of the virtue in the first place, and for the act of the virtue.[13]

What Faith Affirms

What is the content of the faith? Have all believers, whenever they have lived, been bound to hold, explicitly, the same truths? Aquinas's position, in brief, is that in essence the truth of the faith has always been the same, but that it has come to finer expression over time. What was virtually contained in the faith, objectively taken, has been made explicit, been more finely articulated.[14] Aquinas here is invoking his notion of the articles of faith (the truths necessary for salvation, which are revealed by God, cannot be demonstrated by human reason and are to be held by faith),[15] as well as his basic epistemology. The act of faith terminates in a reality;[16] by faith one is related to God as First Truth. This is confirmed by the wording of the creed, which contains the articles ("I believe in God almighty," for example, not "I believe that God is almighty," etc.).[17] But, what is known is in the knower according to the mode of the knower;[18] and so although God is simple, since humans know by analysis and synthesis, certain propositions are formed about the God affirmed in faith, as well as about things in relation to God as these are ordered to human salvation. An article corresponds to the way in which God is unseen; and an article can cover much. There is one sort of difficulty posed by the dying of God. Another sort of difficulty is posed by the resurrection of the dead Word incarnate. And so these fall under different articles of the faith. But, that the Word incarnate suffered and was buried evinces the same difficulty as his dying; and so they are summarized under that same article.[19]

The articles have increased over time; the faith of believers, in terms of the content, has become nuanced, although virtually identical with that held by their predecessors. Aquinas finds in Scripture an apt statement of the faith that all believers have held, whenever they have lived. As Hebrews 11:6 states, "He that comes to God must believe that He is, and that He rewards those that seek God."[20] By the first part is meant all that pertains to the God who is the beatifying end of human existence; by the second, addressing God's providence, is indicated that God saves and does so in keeping with human constitution and need. Over time, as God reveals more about God and the way to God, what was virtual has become explicit; and at present all believers are required to hold, explicitly, a series of truths about God and about Christ, the way to God as end.

These beliefs, now in their fully articulated form, are stated in the creed, which falls into articles of two sorts: those that have to do with the mystery of the triune God who is end, and those that have to do with the mystery of Christ, with what God has dispensed in time to make the attainment of God as end possible.[21] There are seven articles, by Aquinas's counting, under each of these main categories. With regards to the majesty of God, three things are proposed for belief: the unity of the Godhead, the trinity of persons, and the works proper to the Godhead. There are three articles on the trinity of persons, one for each of the persons. There are three articles too for the works of God, one dealing with the order of nature (God as creator), another on the order of grace, affirming the sanctification of people, the third on the order of glory, affirming the resurrection of the dead and life everlasting. As for Christ's human nature, its seven articles treat of his conception, his virginal birth, his passion, death and burial, his descent into hell, his resurrection, his ascension, and his coming to judge.[22]

Again, revelation has been progressive, as has articulation. Earlier believers had a less articulated faith. In describing earlier faith, Aquinas makes use of a fundamental division of the history of the race, theologically construed.[23] Thus, prior to the Fall, humans did affirm God as beatifying end, and affirmed Christ; but, lacking a foreknowledge of their own sin, they did not believe that the Christ to come would have to meet the problem of sin, through his suffering and dying and being raised. They believed only with a view to the coming of beatitude, and so believed in Incarnation, as tailored to making available the elevating grace needed to attain God as end. After the Fall, the need for the suffering, dying, and raising of the incarnate Word came to expression, and so believers affirmed not only Incarnation, but the Passion and Resurrection as well. With the coming of Christ, and the performance of his saving work, what was believed as future has occurred and is held, now, in faith as accomplished. Faith holds that, in Jesus Christ, God has taken decisive action to overcome sin and make possible the attainment of eternal life as intended by God.

Aquinas nuances this "historical" account of the making explicit of the content of faith by working in some reflections on degrees of explicitness, especially in terms of the believers who lived under the Old Law, rendered in the Old Testament. Aquinas distinguishes between the learned and the rest of the people of God.[24] The faith of the leaders was more explicit: they explicitly believed in the Christ to come, who would suffer and die for sins. They knew that their ritual and sacrificial actions, while valuable in themselves for expressing right relation to God, also foretold Christ, and so would find their completion in Christ. The simple, however, lacked this further understanding of ritual and practice. And so their faith in the Christ to come was more implicit, expressed under the figure of these rituals and practices. As for the present time—that is, after Christ—Aquinas too knows of a kind of distinction between explicit and implicit faith among believers, although this plays out differently now. All, whatever their state, are held to explicit faith about God and Christ as expressed in the creed, which summarizes the articles of faith. But, the faith of the leaders must be more advanced, more nuanced, more acquainted with the surrounding details; the faith of the people in the articles as stated in the creed suffices, although they are to be prone to accept whatever else attends belief in, say, the death of Christ as reported in Scripture.

Human beings are involved in God's revealing and the process of articulation. The truths needed for salvation are revealed in Scripture, and God reveals these truths to the human authors of Scripture and does so in such a way that they cannot be mistaken. They pass on these truths to others as God intends.[25] And church leaders articulate the faith through their participation in councils. It pertains to a council to determine, in the face of heretical challenge, on a matter of importance to the faith, that is, to further articulate the faith. This the council does in dependence on Scripture, determining the correct interpretation, in terms of major matters of faith, of Scripture. A council, according to Aquinas, is called by the pope, to whom it also belongs to confirm and publish conciliar articulations. These articulations of the faith constitute the rule of faith, itself reflective of God's revelation, which is the measure of true faith.[26] In both revelation and articulation, the human role is real, albeit secondary. It is God who reveals the truths necessary for salvation; and the Holy Spirit guides the deliberations and determinations of the councils. Humans act instrumentally. In his discussion of faith, Aquinas can mention one other human, whose contribution, however, is the most important: Christ, the Word incarnate. What is to be held by faith, on the basis of God's authority, might also be designated the "doctrine of Christ,"[27] for it is Christ, the God become human, the one to whom the Old Testament has been pointing, who provides the definitive and final revelation of God's saving truth. There is a considerable gap between this human and the others involved in revelation and articulation. Christ is the Word of God become human, and the second divine person is the bearer, the subject, of the human nature of Christ; the human nature stands to the divinity as a conjoined instrument. The others involved in revelation and articulation are not, obviously, God, and act as separated animated instruments of God. Their authority then can only be participated, derived from the God who acts through them. In referring to Christ's doctrine, Aquinas is anticipating the fuller, much more expansive treatment of Christ as teacher in the third part of the *Summa*;[28] that later treatment itself builds on, as does the discussion of faith in the *Secunda Secundae*, the opening question of the *Summa*, on sacred doctrine.[29]

Formed And Unformed Faith; Unbelief

Aquinas distinguishes between formed and unformed faith.[30] What unites them is that both are habits perfective of the intellect; they are also both gifts of God, infused by God in their recipient. They differ in terms of charity, which is perfective of the will. When charity is infused with the habit of faith, there is formed faith; when the habit of faith is infused without charity, that is unformed faith. Charity orders acts, including the act of faith, to God as beatifying end; and acts done under the influence of charity bring the actor closer to that end and are meritorious of that end. When charity is present, the habit of faith is truly good, and the habit is deemed a virtue. Unformed faith, where charity is lacking, is not a virtue.[31] Formed faith can become unformed: this occurs when one sins mortally, destroying charity, the form of faith. Unformed faith can become formed; this occurs when God infuses the virtue of charity, perfective of faith and its act.[32] The move from formed to unformed is due to the human person, who opts for mortal sin. The move from unformed to formed is due to God, in accordance with God's saving will for that person. The person can do nothing to necessitate the giving of charity. And it may be that the person never receives the charity that would form faith to God as beatifying end. That person will simply believe and do so on the basis of God's authority, but to no good, saving effect.

What destroys the habit of faith is unbelief. This is the vice opposed to the internal act of faith.[33] Unbelief is more than the simple absence of faith. It involves a hostility to faith, a rejection of faith. The act of faith is to think with assent; unbelief involves dissent, and a malice in the will, which commands the act of the intellect.[34] To the internal act of faith, Aquinas adds an external act, confession,[35] the public profession of the faith to which one assents, when circumstances require. Blasphemy is the vice opposed to the public profession: this is the overt rejection of what God teaches, through the church, for human salvation.[36]

Heresy is a class of unbelief.[37] Heresy is the obstinate holding of a belief in opposition to the faith. It is to reject one of the articles of faith. With regards to the other articles of faith to which the heretic assents, the heretic has neither formed nor unformed faith. The heretic does not hold those articles as does the person who has received, by God's gift, the habit of faith. In rejecting one of the articles of faith, the heretic has rejected the authority of the Church, which, on the basis of God's revelation in Scripture that is articulated in the rule of faith, proclaims God's saving truth. The heretic will affirm those other articles, not on the basis of God's revealing, conveyed by the Church, but due to his own will. They appeal to his sensibilities and so are affirmed by him.[38]

Hope

To hope is to desire a future good that is difficult yet possible to attain.[39] Perfective of the rational appetite, the will, the theological virtue of hope has God as its principal object. Theological hope aspires to God as beatifying end; God as beatifying is the future good to which hope aspires. Reaching that end is difficult, and certainly lies beyond the natural capacities of any human. But, reaching that end is possible; otherwise there would be no hope; one would simply despair of reaching that end. The possibility affirmed in hope rests in God. God through God's grace makes possible reaching the end that is God. Thomas thus posits two objects of the theological virtue of hope.[40] The principal object is God as beatifying end. The secondary object is the aid of God, on which the person of hope relies in order to reach God as end. By trusting in the aid of God, one can have an assurance of attaining eternal life. Grace, then, can be said to be involved in this theological virtue in two ways. The virtue is infused in the person as a grace, accompanying habitual grace and the other theological virtues. And, God's gracious aid, on which the person relies, moves the graced and virtuous person to the end set for humans by God, God.

Hope finds the mean between two vices that oppose it—despair and presumption.[41] To despair is to deny to oneself the possibility of attaining God as end. Despair is compatible with correct belief.[42] One might hold, correctly, that God does offer salvation to those who repent and who pursue a moral life in keeping with God's salvific will; but one denies that this extends to oneself. There is something in oneself, the one who despairs thinks, that places an obstacle to the working out of salvation in her own case. In hope, by contrast, one does not fixate on one's own limitations, on what makes one unworthy of eternal life. One turns, rather, to God. By God's power and mercy, what is impossible of oneself, is acknowledged as possible and applicable to oneself; one here trusts in God to help in reaching the end set by God for humans.

Presumption can take different forms. One might presume too much about oneself. Such a person would be insufficiently attentive to the difficulty involved in reaching a future good and think that the individual's powers (without the benefit of grace) would suffice for reaching the future good that is God. It is another form of presumption, however, that might be the more likely, according to Aquinas, when thinking of theological hope. One might presume too much on another.[43] In relying on the help of a friend, the one who presumes will leave it all to the friend. Here, then, grace is not denied. But God's expectations of the person who is the recipient of grace are set to the side, and all is left to God and God's grace. For Aquinas, people participate in the working out of their own salvation; that is what God desires. Thus, they must move away from sin and toward God; and once in grace and the infused virtues, they will do what God seeks of humans who are true to themselves, as made by and for God, doing so by the aid of additional graces. God's initiative is throughout maintained; and that initiative is viewed differently, at different points in the saving process. God simply works conversion; God works with the converted and is involved in their merit, and so they progress, in accordance with God's plan for the working out of salvation, to the end set for them by God. But, God does not work out a person's salvation despite that person, but through and with that person. The person, by God's aid, contributes to that person's salvation.[44] Now, by charity people are made friends of God; God is their Friend. And by hope God's friend trusts in God's aid. One presumes too much in that Friend when one is intent on leaving it all to the Friend, ignoring what the Friend seeks of those whom God brings to their God-established end.

It has been suggested that in his talk of the secondary object of hope and reliance on God's grace, Aquinas anticipates the position of Luther about justification by faith.[45] For Luther, the heart of faith is trust, a trust that brings assurance. What is impossible for a human is quite possible for God; and so by faith one renounces one's attempt to save oneself and accepts, in the faith that is trust, God's saving grace. Too much, however, should not be made of the overlap between Aquinas's hope as trust, with the assurance that brings, and Luther's faith as trust, with its confidence, rooted in God's grace. There is considerable distance between the two positions. For Luther, all that is required for being right before God is faith, by which one renounces one's attempts to save oneself and trusts in God's grace. And, that grace is conceived principally as the offer of forgiveness. For Aquinas, however, grace involves forgiveness of sin but is also construed as transformational. The infusion of habitual grace and of the theological virtues, including hope, brings new capacity. The graced and virtuous person is by divine initiative capable of acts that lie beyond the person's merely natural capacity, acts that bring that person to eternal life. And those acts, made possible by God, do make a difference, do contribute to the working out of the person's salvation. God asks them of the beneficiaries of God's grace and other gifts, and will reward them, as done by the human with the aid of further grace. In Luther, trust will exclude merit; in Aquinas, hope and merit are quite compatible.

Charity

The treatise on charity is the lengthiest of those in the *Summa* on the theological virtues, consisting of two more questions (24) than the other two treatises combined (16 questions on faith, 6 on hope).[46] The treatise on charity is divided into four main segments: a consideration of the virtue itself, including an in-depth analysis of its object; the principal act of the virtue, love, accompanied by its effects; the vice opposed to love, hatred, as well as the vices opposed to the effects of charity; and, questions on the precepts, gift of the Holy Spirit, wisdom, that perfects charity, and the vice opposed to wisdom, folly.

That Aquinas offers an analysis of charity in such detail and complexity is most fitting for more than one reason. Scripture makes much of charity, as does the subsequent Christian tradition, and the treatise aims at gathering up and synthesizing these various comments. Charity stands at the heart of the medieval Christian version of the journey to God as end and will be manifested in all acts that lead to the God who beatifies. And, as Aquinas puts it in one of the articles of the treatise,[47] charity, simply put, is the greatest of all the virtues, standing first, in terms of perfection, not only in comparison with the acquired virtues but also in terms of the other theological virtues. The acquired virtues have their particular goods, proportioned to the human as human. The other theological virtues relate the person to God, as to one who offers what the person needs to attain God as end, whether knowledge of the end and the way to the end, or the help required to reach eternal life. Charity unites in will the lover and the beloved: God is loved as God should be, for God's own sake and as God is.

Charity is friendship.[48] For friendship, several criteria must be met: that one wills the good of another, the well-being of that other; that the willing of good be mutual; that there be a community between the two on which charity is based. All of this holds for friendship between God and those endowed with the virtue of charity. The community is that of beatitude. Beatitude pertains to God as God; God wills to share this beatitude with human beings and wills that in love; God's love is causal, and so the virtue of charity is infused in the soul as the created effect of God's love. On the basis of that causal love, human beings have the possibility of attaining to God as beatifying end. The love is mutual. First God loves, and on the basis of that love, with the further aid of grace, the recipient of God's love loves in return, out of the virtue of charity; and this person shows that love in acts of love, elicited by the will, and of acts of will, shaped by charity, that command other acts of the person (see, e.g., on faith, above, and on charity as form, below). God in love wills the person to share in beatitude, and the person loves God, and loves God as God deserves to be loved, as truly and fully good. The friendship, then, is that that pertains to the virtuous:[49] it holds between God, who is fully good, and those whom God makes good, by God's loving gifts.

Objects of Charity

God is the principal object of the love of charity. Aquinas asserts other objects of charity, all ordered to God as principal object. He adopts the list of four objects of charity offered by Augustine, in the first book of the *De doctrina*, in parsing the twofold command, to love God above all things, and the neighbor as oneself.[50] Thus, the person who has received the virtue of charity will love by that charity God, the neighbor, oneself, and one's body. God is loved as the absolute good, who is the beatifying end of the human person. God is loved for God's own sake. One loves the neighbor, and oneself, in charity, as participating in beatitude. One loves the neighbor as made by and for God as end; so too one loves oneself. In this sense, one loves the neighbor and oneself as in God, as ordered to God as beatifying end. The body is loved in charity also in terms of beatitude. In the beatific vision, the soul will be fulfilled in knowing and loving God directly. There will be an overflow to the body, which in this life had been involved in the actions sought by God of those who will attain God as end, from soul: and so in the vision, through this overflow, the body will be clarified, made subtle and agile.

With the tradition, Aquinas thinks of the possibility of progress in charity, of degrees of charity that can be plotted along the journey of a life, which, if successful, finds its term in heaven.[51] There are different pursuits that characterize the three degrees of charity: beginning, progress, and perfection. At first a person will be chiefly occupied with avoiding sin and resisting his concupiscence, which works against charity. In beginners, charity has to be fostered and fed, so as not to be destroyed. Eventually, as one increases in proficiency, the person's chief pursuit is to aim at progress in good. And, finally, the perfect will aim at union with and enjoyment of God; these desire to be dissolved and to be with Christ. Can, however, charity be truly perfect in this life?[52] There is a perfection in charity that is reserved to the next life, when the person who is in God's presence is in act ever and wholly borne toward God. Such an unfailing actual loving of God is not possible in the present life; because of human weakness it is not possible actually to think always of God and so be moved actually at all times to love of God. But, there is a kind of perfection that is possible in the present life, when the person makes an earnest endeavor to give his time to divine things, while scorning other things except as the needs of life in the world demand. Such however is not common to all who have charity. What will be found in others, who fall short of that perfection (as in the members of religious orders who have given themselves wholly over to the single-minded pursuit of God), is a giving of the heart over wholly to God habitually, that is, by neither thinking nor desiring anything contrary to the love of God.

Does the love of charity extend to others, to, say, the sinner, or to the enemy? Jesus, after all, tells his followers to love the enemy,[53] who, however, seems missing from the list of objects of charity adopted by Aquinas from Augustine. That a person is a sinner means that she is at odds with God; and so at first glance would not appear to belong to God and so be subject to the love of charity. And, the enemy can similarly be viewed as at odds with God, having done something that is destructive of community with God and with those who belong to God. Sin, of course, is an impediment to the attaining of God; and charity is incompatible with mortal sin. But, even in terms of the sinner and the enemy, one can posit a connection to God, which is the basis for a community of them with God and with those called to love in charity. For, while not now in correct relationship to God, a human being is potentially in that relationship, and will be in that relationship if sin is rejected and the person turns to God. And, given that potentiality, the sinner and the enemy can be said to belong to God, and so too are subject to charity. One will, as Jesus asks, love the enemy, although not as enemy, and will love the sinner, but not the sin; one loves the sinner or the enemy, for God's sake.

Aquinas thinks of an order among the objects of charity.[54] God is the principal object and is to be loved above all things and for God's sake. The neighbor and oneself are to be loved as called to beatitude, as belonging to a fellowship that God has initiated and sustains. But, another human will be loved more, in accordance with a greater reason, or better, more reasons, to love that one in comparison to another object of love. The basic idea is that community or fellowship with some is deeper than with others. In addition to the fellowship established with all other humans, as made by and for God, who have been the recipients of God's special love, which is causal of their own charity, a person can have additional bonds with others and so be related to them more closely. Aquinas can mention in this regard the bonds of country or city, as well as those of family, all of which can strengthen the links among people. A person will love a relative more than someone to whom he is not related. And, the union with relatives is more stable than those with others, which may come into existence or pass away (e.g., as civic needs and responsibilities come to be but might find an end; the union of kinship abides).[55]

Even among relatives, Aquinas can posit a greater or lesser love. Should a parent be loved more than a child?[56] The better something is and the more akin to God it is, the more it is to be loved; and so in this sense, a parent, who is one's principle (and so like God, the principle of all), should be loved more than one's child. From another perspective, however, one can say that the child is to be loved the more, for the parent is more closely connected to the child, and so the child is better known and so more loved, than the other way around. Aquinas will offer various observations to support this contention. Thus, for example, parents love their children as being part of themselves; so the child is loved as the parent loves himself. And, parents know better that this one is their child; there can be, it appears, some doubt about one's own parents. And, parents love their children right from the start and so longer than a child loves a parent; apparently there is a lag, in coming to love a parent, for a child (who must mature to be capable of expressing love). Aquinas can also inquire about a child loving her parents: whom should be loved more, the mother or the father?[57] Both are principles, and so both have a likeness to God. Should they then be loved equally? Here, trading on his Aristotelian biology, Aquinas opts for the father: the father is the active, the mother, the passive, principle of the child; and so the father, as more alike to God, deserves more love. (This is an argument in need of revision, in light of a more updated account of conception.) And, finally along these lines, who is to be loved more by a man, his wife or his parents?[58] Again, Aquinas will show why each are deserving of love: the parents, as the principle, and so the affinity with God; the wife, to whom the man is united as one, for she is closer to him and is loved by him as he loves himself, in relation to God. Depending on the perspective from which one is answering the question, then, one will answer that one or the other is to be loved the more.

Vices Opposed to Charity

Love is the principal act of charity, elicited by the will informed by this virtue.[59] Thomas asserts other acts or effects of charity. Three are internal: joy,[60] peace,[61] and mercy.[62] Three are external: beneficence,[63] almsgiving,[64] and fraternal correction.[65]

And, each has a vice opposed to it. Thus, the vice opposed to love is hatred: one hates God and that hate destroys the community expressed by charity.[66] Two vices are opposed to joy: sloth is destructive of the joy that one has as joined correctly in will to God and to those who belong to the God who beatifies; envy is destructive of the joy that one has in the good of another.[67] A series of vices are opposed to the peace that charity brings: discord, contention, schism, war, strife, and sedition.[68] And, finally, in terms of vice, there is that of scandal, which is opposed to beneficence.[69] The consideration of acts of charity and the vices opposed to love and joy and the others is nuanced, and certainly suggestive of what would fall under the truly Christian life, and what outside of it. As united in will to God by charity, one will seek God and order all relationships to others in light of that unity with God, and seek the good not only of oneself but of others, and strive to be of service to the other. And, those who reject God as end, will themselves be disordered and contribute to disorder, in various contexts, in the world. But, while the enumeration of acts and effects, with their opposed vices, adds texture to the analysis, the basic point remains: every mortal sin, whatever its sort of vice, destroys charity, disclosing an aversion to God and faulty relation with others.

Charity, Form of the Virtues

Aquinas returns repeatedly to a favorite designation of charity. Whether discussing the virtues in general (in the *Prima Secundae*) or the theological virtues individually (in the *Secunda Secundae*), he refers to charity as the "form of the virtues."[70] Here he is referring to charity not as a formal but as an efficient cause. There are acts particular to the various virtues. These virtues each have their distinctive good, to which the act is ordered. The will commands these other acts; and, when the will is perfected by the virtue of charity, by the charitable will, these acts are ordered to the ultimate end, to the God who beatifies. They are put, as it were, in a larger context, and they are made conducive of attaining the supernatural end to which human beings are called by God.

Aquinas has other designations to make the same point. Charity is too the "root of the virtues" as directing them to the beatifying God; in the same way, it is their "mother."[71] Aquinas can also convey the teaching in a more negative way. Every habit that gives rise to a good act that attains the good of that habit is a virtue. The acquired virtues are virtues, with regards to the end that is connatural to a human being as human. The theological virtues of faith and hope order the person to the supernatural end. But, without charity, all of these, including faith and hope, are only imperfect virtues, not virtues in the full, perfect sense.[72] Charity perfects them, makes them complete, by directing them to God as supernatural end. In performing these acts, as under charity, these acts will be meritorious of eternal life.

Connection

Aquinas asserts the connection of the virtues, with an eye to underscoring the importance of charity.[73] In terms of the theological virtues, asserting their connection is to repeat the claim about charity as the form of the virtues. Faith and hope find their completion in charity, for charity relates them to God as beatifying end. Without charity so orienting, the other theological virtues are imperfect and not conducive to eternal life. Charity in this sense employs these other virtues, in exercising its role as form of the virtues, and disposes them well. These other virtues with their acts provide the matter for the activity of charity. It perfects these virtues and makes their acts better: by charity, one believes well, hopes well, for this believing and hoping leads to God as beatifying end. The connection goes, as well, in the other direction. Here, Aquinas echoes his teaching about the order of generation of these virtues: first faith, then hope, then charity. One loves only on the basis of knowing what is to be loved and having a confidence that what is to be loved can be attained. Remove faith and hope, and there is no charity.

Aquinas asserts an additional connection of virtues, of charity with the infused moral virtues, which are infused with the theological virtues at the term of the process of conversion.[74] The infused moral virtues make possible moral acts that are pleasing to God and lead to eternal life; they are not to be reduced to the acquired moral virtues, gained through acts of a kind and ordered to the person's natural end. The infused moral virtues are, as are the theological virtues, simply infused, given by God as gift, in accordance with God's will for a person. As with that with the other theological virtues, the connection of charity with the infused moral virtues can be thought of as going in both directions. Charity is their form, moving and directing them to God as beatifying end, making them better, well done. And, charity too is dependent on them: the infused moral virtues are the principles of good moral acts that lead to God as end; charity works through them to bring a person to God; take them away and charity has nothing to act on.

Loss of Virtue

In describing increase in the theological virtues, Aquinas can gesture in a relatively straightforward way to what is the case for the acquired virtues. Those increase by acts of that kind; those acts incline the possessor of the acquired virtue the more to acts of that kind. So too for the virtues of faith, hope, charity, which increase by acts of faith, hope, charity, as aided by God. There is no parallel, however, in the losing of the virtues. Language of "decrease" is appropriate to an analysis of the acquired virtues. That decrease will be due to lack of use of that virtue or infrequent use of it. By inactivity, there can be an erosion of that inclination to such act, to the point that the habit disappears. A single act will not destroy such virtue, which had been acquired and built up by acts of that kind. In his lengthy discussion of the loss of charity, however, Aquinas disallows talk of "decrease." Failing to act out of that virtue, or acting only infrequently out of it, may be inadvisable, as rendering the will prone to fall from charity. But such inactivity does not forfeit charity. Rather, the virtue of charity is lost only by sin, mortal sin, and is destroyed by a single mortal sin.[75]

Charity involves fellowship between humans and God, due to the divine initiative. On the basis of God's loving, there is a mutual love between humans and God. One loves God above all things and loves others in relation to God. A mortal sin destroys this community. In sinning mortally, one acts against the love of God and of neighbor; in this there is a loss of the virtue that makes charitable acting possible. It may be that charity will be restored, but that will not be due to the efforts of a person to regain it. The restoration of charity, as in its first giving, is due to God's initiative, in accordance with God's saving will for that person. It may be that there will be no return of that person who has lost charity to fellowship with God.

Aquinas can adopt a different image to account for the destructive effect of mortal sinning. God always offers God's love to the possessor of the virtue of charity. The appropriate response is that person's own loving. Sometimes, however, a person will refuse that response, instead opting to put an obstacle to God's offered love. No longer in relationship to the source of spiritual life, the virtue of charity thus dies.[76] That mortal sin is possible is due to the human will. The virtue of charity inclines its possessor to the act of charity. It does not necessitate such acting. By the will, the one endowed with charity may decide to act in a way that is counter to charity; the virtue then is lost.

Mortal sin also destroys the infused moral virtues that accompany charity in its initial infusion. Those virtues are dependent on charity for their proper ordering and for their good expression. Once charity is destroyed, so too are the infused moral virtues.[77] They will be regained, if they are, only when and if God restores, by God's free giving, charity to a person. But, the loss of charity does not mean the loss of the habit of faith or of that of hope.[78] The mortal sin that destroys charity does not destroy either of the others. What is removed by that sin is the form that perfects them. Aquinas refers frequently to "formed faith" and "unformed faith"; and there is a formed and an unformed hope as well.[79] The form of charity disposes well the believer, the one who hopes, to the God who is the beatifying end; the loss of charity means that belief and hope are no longer related to that God in a way that is savingly conducive. Whether formed or unformed, however, the habit of faith remains; it is no longer virtuous, a full virtue. But, it is still faith. The same is true of hope, whether formed or unformed. Both are, and remain (with or without charity), a gift of God. There can, then, be a move from formed faith to unformed faith; that is due to mortal sin, to the instability of the will and the failure to act out of the charity that binds one to God as beatifying end. There may be a move from unformed faith to formed. But, that is up to God, to the God who gives God's gifts to whom God wills. As long as charity is absent, the act of faith will not justify before God. In terms of the threefold *credere*: when the act of faith issues from the virtue of faith, as shaped by charity, all three aspects are found. One believes God, believes correctly about God, believes in a way that expresses love of God and so brings one closer to that God as end. When charity no longer forms faith, one will still believe God and on the basis of God as first truth; one will not believe unto God, believe in a way that expresses love, bespeaks a correct orientation to God. As for hope, since charity is missing, the one who hopes will not do the moral good that is meritorious before God, and so will not hope in a way that facilitates the end to which one aspires. To destroy the habit of faith, or of hope, a vicious act is required, an act of a vice that is proportioned to that habit. Hence, faith is destroyed by unbelief, hope by acts of despair or of presumption.

Duration

Will the theological virtues remain in heaven?[80] Guided by the Apostle Paul (1 Corinthians 13:8, 10–12), Aquinas denies the virtues of faith and of hope to the beatified. These virtues, suited to the present life, will not be needed in heaven. At the core of each of these virtues is a fundamental imperfection, when viewed in comparison with the heavenly state. "Now we see in a glass darkly, then we will see face to face." In the entry into heaven, belief will yield to vision, which is a superior form of knowing. And, hope has to do with a future good. When that good is no longer future, but present, the need for hope is removed. The one who had hoped, which sustained her in the journey to God in the confidence of God's aid, now comprehends, clings, directly, to the God who is her end. Of the theological virtues, only charity will remain in heaven. By charity, people are united in will to God. In heaven, that union is consummated; charity remains, but in its fullest form, as the person wills God in the immediate presence of God, who loves in return.

In his Christology, Aquinas adds nuance to this account of duration. Did Christ have the theological virtues during his earthly sojourn?[81] On initial reflection, one might think that he did; for, he had the fullness of grace, and the theological virtues are infused with habitual grace. However, Aquinas believed that Christ enjoyed the beatific vision from the first moment of his conception. And so, what holds of those in heaven, holds of Christ. He had the virtue of charity, and in its fullness (and so in his every human action related his acts to God as end), but lacked the virtues of faith, of hope, as unnecessary, to one who is blessed. Yet in that same question on the grace and virtues of Christ, Aquinas adds that while Jesus did not need these virtues, he still had what was perfect or complete in them.[82] What Aquinas means becomes clearer from the parallel discussion in the disputed question on hope. As in the *ST*, Aquinas thinks there of a twofold object of hope: God as future good, and God in God's aiding, by which the one who hopes can attain to God as end. Aquinas then links language of imperfection, and, of completion or perfection, to the two objects of hope. With regards to the principal object of hope, there is imperfection, because that object is in the future, not presently held. But, with regards to divine help, hope is a tendency of someone perfect, for human perfection consists in holding on to God.[83] And so, Aquinas explicitly states later in the same article, with regards to the completeness of the virtue of hope, Christ possessed hope utterly in this sense, since he held utterly on to God's help.[84] Aquinas adds that the same is true of the virtue of faith, which too has a completion or perfection in addition to its fundamental imperfection. Faith is imperfect in that one does not yet see what one believes, but perfect in that it holds on to the witness of the first truth.[85] Through this discussion of Christ, Aquinas has nicely indicated for both hope and faith a fundamental continuity between the present state and heaven, while remaining faithful to Paul's point.

Sources

That the discussion of the theological virtues takes as its point of departure what Scripture proclaims about faith, hope, and charity, and that the scriptural witness frames the analysis, is patent enough. Without Scripture, Aquinas would be unable to discuss these properly Christian things. In reflecting on these virtues, Aquinas has been aided by the intervening Christian theological tradition. He is not, obviously, the first theologian to write about faith and the others, or to think of these virtues as theological; there is the weighty precedent of such as Augustine and Gregory the Great, themselves following after the Apostle Paul on these virtues. Post-scriptural Christian theologians can also provide stimulus to fruitful interpretation in particular ways. Aquinas's understanding of faith as intellectual assent stands in close dependence on Augustine;[86] he owes Augustine as well for the parsing of the act of faith in terms of the threefold *credere*;[87] and, Augustine too had defined virtue in a useful way, emphasizing in that definition what is pertinent to these particular virtues (that is, the grace of God, working these virtues in their recipient).[88] That definition was conveyed to Aquinas through its quotation in the Lombard's *Sentences*. The Lombard could in his own way further Aquinas's analysis of the theological virtues. The Lombard's identification of charity with the Holy Spirit lies behind Aquinas's insistence, to the contrary, that charity is something created in the soul, infused by God to make possible acts pleasing to God.[89] The person is not, as the Lombard's straightforward identification would suggest, simply moved by the Spirit; that person has an endowment, itself owed to God's initiative, that makes the person capable of acts on the supernatural order. It is the person who loves, with the help of the Holy Spirit. The Lombard too helped Aquinas to clarify an important point when it comes to hope. Does one hope on the basis of grace and merits?[90] Rather, Aquinas insists, one hopes for God and in God, not in one's own accomplishments. And yet hope does not exclude merit. God seeks the graced behavior of those who will reach God as end. And so, if that is what the Lombard meant, one can allow a place to merits in the realization of one's hope. And, Aquinas is the beneficiary of what he has read in non-Christian sources, not least in Aristotle. The questions on these virtues are replete with references to the *Ethics*, whether for a definition of habit and virtue, or for an account of the faith, of the hope, of the love, with which Aristotle was familiar. Christian faith is like, but unlike, the faith that the philosopher knew; so too for Christian hope and for Christian charity. Those comments could be useful, then, to put these virtues, unknown to Aristotle, in their proper relief.

NOTES

1. In the *Summa theologiae*, Aquinas discusses the theological virtues at I-II q.62, and in some of the articles in questions that closely follow (q.64 a.4; q.65 a.2–5; q.66 a.6; q.67 a.3–6). The discrete discussions of the theological virtues are found at the beginning of the *Secunda Secundae*: II-II q.1–16, for faith; q.17–22, for hope; and, q.23–46, for charity. Aquinas returns to the theological virtues in his Christology: III q.7 a.3–4, 9. Some of his *Quaestiones disputatae* are devoted to theological virtues: *de caritate* (in thirteen articles), *de correctione fraterna* (in two articles), and *de spe* (in four articles). For all of the disputed questions on the virtues in English translation, see *Thomas Aquinas Disputed Questions on the Virtues*, ed. E. M. Atkins and Thomas Williams, trans. E. M. Atkins (Cambridge: Cambridge University Press, 2005).

2. This is argued at length of charity at *ST* II-II q.23 a.2.

3. For the following paragraphs in the text, see *ST* I-II q.62 a.1.

4. On the increase of charity, see *ST* II-II q.24 a.4–7.

5. See *ST* I-II q.62 a.4; there, reference is made as well to the order of perfection, examined later in the text.

6. See, e.g., *ST* I-II q.62 a.3 s.c.

7. For the precepts of faith, see *ST* II-II q.16; for hope, II-II q.22; for charity, II-II q.44.

8. In treating each of the theological virtues, Aquinas is flexible in the actual order of discussion. Thus, in discussing faith, in looking at faith itself, he considers its object, act, and only then the virtue, and then turns to the gifts, the vices, and the precepts. In discussing hope, he considers hope itself and its subject, then its gift, and then the opposing vices, and finally the precepts. For the order of the discussion of charity, see below in the text, under "Charity."

9. *ST* II-II q.2 a.1. For scholarly discussions of Aquinas on faith: Benoit Duroux, *La Psychologie de la foi chez S. Thomas d'Aquin* (Tournai: Desclée de Brouwer, 1963); Tad W. Guzie, "The Act of Faith according to St. Thomas: A Study in Theological Methodology," *The Thomist* 29 (1965): 239–80; Daniel Bourgeois, "'Inchoatio vitae eternae': La Dimension eschatologique de la vertu théologale de foi chez saint Thomas d'Aquin," *Sapienza* 27 (1974): 272–314; Stephen F. Brown, "The Theological Virtue of Faith (IIa IIae, qq.1–16)," in Stephen J. Pope, ed., *The Ethics of Aquinas* (Washington, D.C.: Georgetown University Press, 2002), 221–31.

10. *ST* II-II q.4 a.1.

11. *ST* II-II q.2 a.2.
12. *ST* II-II q.6 a.1.
13. James 2:19 refers to the believing of the demons. For Aquinas, that belief is not due to a gift of God. And, it does not involve assenting to the actual truths revealed by God and conveyed through the church. Rather, it is based on evident signs: in seeing those signs, the demons recognize that what is taught is from God. That is the basis, and extent, of their believing. That is how they have read the signs, and so they have opted for a faith. But, that faith is vague, and certainly is not salvific. They are not thereby correctly related to God, nor less hostile to God and those who love God. See *ST* II-II q.5 a.2. For the denial that such faith is even unformed faith (discussed later in the text), see ad 2.
14. *ST* II-II q.1 a.7, 16.
15. *ST* I q.1 a.1.
16. *ST* II-II q.1 a.2 ad 2.
17. *ST* II-II q.1 a.2 obj. 2 and ad 2.
18. *ST* II-II q.1 a.2.
19. *ST* II-II q.1 a.6.
20. The verse from Hebrews is quoted at *ST* II-II q.1 a.7.
21. *ST* II-II q.1 a.8.
22. In that same article, Aquinas notes that others think that six, not seven, articles fall under each main heading, the Godhead, and, the humanity of Christ.
23. *ST* II-II q.2 a.7.
24. Ibid.
25. See *ST* I q.1 a.8 ad 2, and in the same question, a.9 ad 2. For Scripture as the locus of God's revealing of saving truth, see too *ST* II-II q.1 a.9 ad 2.
26. On this work of the council and the pope, see *ST* II-II q.1 a.9–10. For the guiding work of the Holy Spirit, see II-II q.1 a.9, s.c.
27. See *ST* II-II q.11 a.1.
28. *ST* III q.42.
29. *ST* I q.1.
30. See *ST* II-II q.4 a.3–5.
31. For the denial that unformed faith is a "virtue," see *ST* II-II q.4 a.5, and I-II q.65 a.4.
32. *ST* II-II q.4 a.4.
33. *ST* II-II q.10.
34. *ST* II-II q.10 a.1–2.
35. *ST* II-II q.3.
36. *ST* II-II q.13.
37. *ST* II-II q.11.
38. *ST* II-II q.5 a.3.
39. For this description of the object of hope, see, e.g., *ST* II-II q.17 a.1. For scholarly discussions of hope in Aquinas: C.-A. Bernard, *Théologie de l'espérance selon Saint Thomas d'Aquin* (Paris: Vrin, 1961); G. M. Conlon, "The Certitude of Hope," *The Thomist* 10 (1947): 76–119, 226–52; V. De Couesnongle, "Le 'Dieu de l'espérance' de saint Thomas Aquinas," *Studia Theologica Varsaviensis* 12 (1974): 103–20; Romanus Cessario, "The Theological Virtue of Hope (IIa IIae, qq. 17–22)," in Stephen J. Pope, ed., *The Ethics of Aquinas* (Washington, D.C.: Georgetown University Press, 2002), 232–43.
40. For the language of principal and secondary, see *ST* II-II q.17 a.4.
41. For despair, see *ST* II-II q.20; for presumption, II-II q.21.
42. *ST* II-II q.20 a.2.
43. *ST* II-II q.21 a.1.

44. See too *ST* II-II q.21 a.2.

45. See S. Pfürtner, *Luther and Aquinas on Salvation*, trans. E. Quinn (New York: Sheed and Ward, 1964); see as well Joseph Wawrykow, *God's Grace and Human Action: "Merit" in the Theology of Thomas Aquinas* (Notre Dame, Ind.: University of Notre Dame Press, 1995), 247–59.

46. For scholarly discussions of charity in Aquinas: A. J. Falanga, *Charity: The Form of the Virtues according to Saint Thomas* (Washington, D.C.: Catholic University of America Press, 1948); J. Aumann, "Thomistic Evaluation of Love and Charity," *Angelicum* 55 (1978): 534–56; P. Wadell, *The Primacy of Love: An Introduction to the Ethics of Thomas Aquinas* (New York: Paulist Press, 1992); G. Mansini, "Similitudo, Communicatio, and the Friendship of Charity in Aquinas," in *Thomistica, Recherches de théologie ancienne et médiévale*, Supplement 1 (Leuven, 1995), 1–26; E. Schockenhoff, "The Theological Virtue of Charity (IIa IIae, qq.23–46)," in Stephen J. Pope, ed., *The Ethics of Aquinas* (Washington, D.C.: Georgetown University Press, 2002), 244–58; M. Sherwin, *By Knowledge and by Love: Charity and Knowledge in the Moral Theology of St. Thomas Aquinas* (Washington, D.C.: Catholic University of America Press, 2004).

47. *ST* II-II q.23 a.6; see too I-II q.66 a.6. In this assessment, Aquinas is echoing Paul, I Corinthians 13:13.

48. *ST* II-II q.23 a.1.

49. On the kinds of friendship, see *ST* II-II q.23 1 obj. 3 and ad 3.

50. *ST* II-II q.25 a.12.

51. *ST* II-II q.24 a.9.

52. *ST* II-II q.24 a.8.

53. Matthew 5:44 is quoted at *ST* II-II q.25 a.8 s.c.

54. *ST* II-II q.26.

55. *ST* II-II q.26 a.8.

56. *ST* II-II q.26 a.9.

57. *ST* II-II q.26 a.10.

58. *ST* II-II q.26 a.11.

59. *ST* II-II q.27.

60. *ST* II-II q.28.

61. *ST* II-II q.29.

62. *ST* II-II q.30.

63. *ST* II-II q.31.

64. *ST* II-II q.32.

65. *ST* II-II q.33.

66. *ST* II-II q.34.

67. *ST* II-II q.35 for sloth; q.36 for envy.

68. *ST* II-II q.37–42.

69. *ST* II-II q.43.

70. See, e.g., *ST* I-II q.62 a.4; II-II q.4 a.3; II-II q.23 a.8.

71. For charity as form, mother, and root, see, e.g., *ST* I-II q.62 a.4, as well as II-II q.23 a.8.

72. On the need for charity for perfect virtue, see, e.g., *ST* II-II q.23 a.7, and I-II q.65 a.4.

73. *ST* I-II q.65.

74. For the following, see *ST* I-II q.65 a.2–3.

75. See *ST* II-II q.24 a.10–12.

76. *ST* II-II q.24 a.12.

77. *ST* I-II q.65 a.2.

78. *ST* I-II q.65 a.4.

79. For a reference to a "formed hope," see, e.g., *ST* II-II q.17 a.8 ad 3; in the background here is the understanding of the order of perfection that holds for the theological virtues, as discussed in *ST* I-II q.62 a.4.

80. *ST* I-II q.67 a.3–6.

81. *ST* III q.7 a.3, did Christ have faith; a.4, did he have hope?

82. *ST* III q.7 a.9 ad 1.

83. *QD de spe*, a.1, ad 4; trans. Atkins, p.222.

84. *QD de spe*, a.1, ad 12; trans. Atkins, p.225.

85. *QD de spe*, a.1, ad 4; trans. Atkins, p.222. See as well *de spe*, a.4, ad 14; Atkins, p.239.

86. See *ST* II-II q.2 a.1 s.c., where Aquinas notes that this is Augustine's definition in *de praedestinatione sanctorum*.

87. See *ST* II-II q.2 a.2 s.c.

88. See *ST* I-II q.55 a.4.

89. For the Lombard's identification, see *Super Sent* Bk. I, d.XVII. For Aquinas's discussion, see *ST* II-II q.23 a.2. On this and other points on which thirteenth-century scholastics questioned the Lombard, see E. Synan, "Brother Thomas, the Master, and the Masters," in *St Thomas Aquinas 1274–1974 Commemorative Studies*, vol. 2 (Toronto: PIMS, 1974), 219–42.

90. Aquinas refers at *ST* II-II q.17 a.1 obj. 2 to a saying in the third book of the *Sentences* (d.26) that appears to make merits, as well as grace, the object of hope.

PART V

EPISTEMOLOGY AND PHILOSOPHY OF MIND

CHAPTER 23

HUMAN KNOWLEDGE

MARTIN PICKAVÉ

WHAT is knowledge and how do we acquire knowledge? These are core philosophical questions, and one can expect any major figure in the history of philosophy to deal with them in one way or other. Naturally, this expectation also applies to Aquinas. It is, however, surprisingly difficult to get a clear picture of his epistemological views. On the one hand, epistemology is not really a central and well-defined topic for Aquinas. He did not write a separate treatise on epistemology, and when he talks about epistemological issues, for instance in the first part of his *Summa theologiae*, he does so mostly from a psychological perspective. On the other hand, it is simply not clear which term in Aquinas's philosophical vocabulary—or in that of medieval philosophers in general—corresponds to what we today call knowledge. As is often noted, Aquinas's fundamental epistemic category is cognition (*cognitio, notitia*); but clearly not everything to which Aquinas refers as cognition is knowledge.[1] For, according to Aquinas, it is possible for cognitions to be false; but false knowledge is clearly a contradiction in terms.[2] However, if we look in Aquinas for knowledge as a mental state directed at truth, we discover that he holds that there is more than just one such state; following Aristotle, he names five: art, *scientia*, wisdom, prudence, and understanding.[3] Commentators regularly turn to Aquinas's account of *scientia* as his account of knowledge; and they therefore regard Aquinas's commentary on Aristotle's *Posterior Analytics* as the key text for his epistemology. But it is not clear that this is legitimate either. When Aquinas talks about *scientia*, he closely follows Aristotle's views about *epistēmē*; in fact the Latin term *scientia* translates the Greek term *epistēmē*. Many scholars, however, believe that Aristotle's theory in the *Posterior Analytics* should be read as a theory of what it means to have (scientific) understanding rather than as a theory of knowledge.[4] So one has to wonder whether the same might not be true of Aquinas's account of *scientia*. Moreover, *scientia* (as *epistēmē*) is said to be only of what is necessary; for

Aquinas, *scientia* is not of contingent facts. But there is nothing wrong with saying, for instance, that I know that a cup and a computer screen are here in front of me. *Scientia* seems to be much too restricted to cover what we consider as instances of knowledge.

Despite the apparent differences between *scientia* and knowledge, I shall attempt in the following to defend a "naïve" interpretation according to which Aquinas's account of *scientia* is his account of knowledge. Since Aquinas's epistemological views cannot be understood without the psychological and metaphysical views on which they are founded, I shall first give a brief summary of Aquinas's cognitive psychology and his views about how we come to cognize something. Unfortunately, I will not have space to say much about Aquinas's general views about cognition. In particular, I will not deal with what exactly cognition is for Aquinas, since my focus is rather on how knowledge is different from other forms of cognitive access to the world. But the most immediate question we have to address is why Aquinas believes that we can know something in the first place. How can Aquinas be sure that human beings are capable of knowledge? The last part of this chapter will deal with what, according to Aquinas, we cannot know, that is, with the limits of human knowledge.

Can We Know Something?

Commentators on Aquinas's epistemological views often emphasize his epistemological optimism and the fact that skeptical worries seem completely absent from his writings. We should not take his attitude for granted. Many Latin philosophers of the thirteenth century were familiar with skeptical arguments from the discussion of ancient skepticism in Augustine's *Against the Academicians* and *On the Trinity*; some were even familiar with Cicero's *Academica*. Henry of Ghent, writing a couple of years after Aquinas's death, begins his own theological Summa with the question whether human beings can know something. Unsatisfied with Henry's treatment of the issue, John Duns Scotus later advances his own refutation of skepticism. These two authors are presumably the best-known examples of medieval philosophers engaging with skepticism. But even during Aquinas's lifetime philosophers found it necessary to examine skeptical challenges. Let me just mention two examples: the Franciscan Thomas of York, who was active in Oxford around the middle of the thirteenth century, and Siger of Brabant, Aquinas's notorious colleague at the University of Paris.[5]

Aquinas's silence with regard to skepticism is indeed striking. The closest he gets to engaging with skeptical worries is when he chastises the Presocratic philosophers for their materialism, which seems to him to rule out knowledge of the material world, or when he insists against Protagorean relativism that natural objects are the measure of our intellectual capacities and our knowledge and not the other way round.[6] But from the fact that Aquinas never discusses the question of whether we can know or cognize things in the first place it does not follow that his epistemological optimism is unfounded. On the one hand, it is founded on some basic theological doctrines such as the view that God is supremely good and that God's creatures are likenesses of God's goodness.[7] Is it really imaginable that a good God brings about a creature endowed with cognitive capacities and that such a creature is systematically led astray by the same capacities? On the other hand, Aquinas's optimism also has a philosophical foundation. The latter becomes clear if we remind ourselves of Aquinas's commitment to two broadly Aristotelian principles. According to the first principle, nature makes nothing in vain.[8] As Aquinas frequently emphasizes, referring to the opening statement of Aristotle's *Metaphysics*, "all men by nature desire to know."[9] If it were impossible for us to know anything, then our natural desire for knowledge would indeed be in vain, because it could never be fulfilled.[10] According to the second principle, which is somewhat related to the first one, everything has its own proper function to which it is directed. But the proper function or operation of human beings is to understand and to reason; in this human beings surpass all other animals.[11] Human beings must therefore be capable of cognition, for otherwise they would not be able to achieve the very operation that is proper to them; and this would be deeply odd.

So, according to Aquinas, we are in principle capable of cognition and knowledge. There is no reason to deny that our cognitive capacities might occasionally go wrong; every one of us experiences this all too often. But in general we can expect them to lead us to cognition and knowledge. For why would we have cognitive capacities such as the senses and the intellect if they did not convey to us cognition about the world around us?[12] For Aquinas, as for many other medieval philosophers, the more serious philosophical problem is rather how falsity and error are possible.

How Do We Acquire Knowledge?

Aquinas's account of cognition and the acquisition of knowledge is grounded on two fundamental principles: (1) that sensory perception is the starting point of human cognition and (2) that there is a huge difference between our sensory powers and our intellect and thus between sensation and acts of intellectual understanding. Let me begin with the latter claim, for it is the least obvious from a modern perspective.[13]

According to Aquinas, human beings are equipped with a variety of sensory powers, which can be divided into two groups: the external senses (sight, hearing, smell, taste, touch) and the internal senses (the common sense, imagination, the estimative power, memory).[14] We share most of these sensory powers with other animals, and although it might be true that as a whole they are more developed in human beings, there is, with the exception of the so-called estimative power, no real qualitative difference between these powers as they can be found in human beings and as they can be found in nonrational animals. On the contrary, we have to acknowledge that nonrational animals often outclass human beings with respect to certain sensory powers. For this reason we employ, for instance, dogs and other animals to sniff out truffles or explosives.

Each of our sensory powers is essentially connected with a specific corporeal organ. When the organ is damaged or destroyed, the sensory power is damaged or destroyed too. Moreover, from the fact that they are tied to specific corporeal organs and thus to material conditions, sensory powers are limited to their specific sensory objects; because of the material conditions of the eye, our visual powers are limited to colors and only colors, because of the material conditions of the ear, our hearing receives information only about sounds and so on. According to Aquinas, we can notice the limitations material conditions impose on sensation when we are sick. A sick person's tongue, for instance, "infected with a jaundiced and bitter humor, cannot perceive anything sweet."[15] However, all of us are also aware that we have a mental capacity that is not restricted to a certain class of objects, for we can think about everything; we can even think about things that do not exist or are completely impossible. Hence, Aquinas concludes that human beings have a cognitive power, the intellect, which transcends the sensory powers. And because of its universal scope Aquinas concludes that the intellect must be incorporeal and cannot be tied up with a corporeal organ.[16] The human intellect is not a highly sophisticated sensory power that uses a corporeal part (the brain) as its organ; it is a cognitive power of an entirely different kind. Thanks to their intellects, human beings are not only open to all kinds of thoughts; the intellect is also the power that enables us to form propositions, engage in deliberation, make arguments, come up with definitions, and so on. Higher-level nonrational animals may exhibit behavior that appears somewhat similar to the behavior of rational creatures, but strictly speaking, nonrational animals do not think.

Despite the qualitative difference between the senses and the intellect, the various cognitive powers of a human being are closely connected. Our intellect simply cannot operate under normal conditions without receiving input from the senses and without cooperation of the sensory powers.[17] Even when we are engaged in the most abstract thoughts, for instance, when we try to prove a mathematical theorem, we need sensory images (such as graphs and signs) to fix our attention. Aquinas describes the intellect's reliance on sensation in general and the images provided by the imagination in particular with the talk of a "connaturality" (*connaturalitas*) between the intellect and the input provided by the sensory powers.[18] In this respect the human intellect is different from the intellective powers of higher-level creatures, like angels, who lack sensory input but also do not require it.

Commentators have frequently noted that Aquinas explicitly endorses the famous empiricist principle according to which "nothing is in the intellect that has not previously been in the senses."[19] So far as I know there is only one passage in his work where he mentions the principle in its classical form, but there are many passages where he expresses the same idea in different terms, for instance, when he claims that "the whole of our intellect's cognition derives from the senses."[20] Of course, this does not mean that the intellect can only understand objects with which we are acquainted through the senses, for then it would be impossible to know anything about God or abstract objects like numbers or truth. What Aquinas means is rather that the senses provide the intellect with the basic "raw material" for higher-level cognitive activity. The intellect's dependence on sensation becomes especially clear if one looks at how Aquinas describes the psychological activity underlying cognitive acts. Cognitive acts require the reception of representational devices or "species" (*species*). The eye sees the color of the wall because it receives a species of the color, conveyed to the eye through the species of the color in the medium (i.e., air). Acts of higher-level sensory powers involve species they receive from lower-level sensory powers. And to be able to think of, say, a tree, the intellect similarly requires a species of the tree. This latter species, an intelligible species (as opposed to a sensible species), cannot be directly transferred from the sensory powers into the intellect. Because of the materiality of the sensory powers, sensible species or other representations produced in the senses are themselves material and thus of no use for an immaterial power such as the intellect. Hence, human beings possess a second intellective power, the so-called agent intellect, the function of which consists in nothing other than to make the sensory content provided by the sensible species available to the intellect by producing an intelligible species from it.[21] The intelligible species is finally able to inform the intellect and provides the basis for the first act of the intellect, the formation of concepts, on the basis of which the intellect can then form propositions and engage in complex acts of reasoning. Only on the level of the operations of the intellect can we expect to find something like knowledge.

Aquinas considers his own account of the acquisition of cognition as opposed to accounts positing innate cognition, in particular innate cognition on the intellectual level. To express his discontent with innativist views, Aquinas appeals to the traditional image of the intellect as a blank slate (*tabula rasa*). In addition, he advances three main arguments against innateness.[22] According to the first argument, innativists fail to explain how the allegedly innate cognition is hidden from us until we first become aware of it. Suppose that we have innate cognition of certain objects. In this case we need an explanation for why we are not aware of such knowledge right away and before we "remember" it. The only real explanation for our initial forgetfulness seems to be the one provided by the Platonists, according to whom the body is to be blamed. But that is odd: our body is part of our human nature, so why would it be natural for human beings to have a body if that body impedes the operation that is most proper to human beings, namely to know? For Aquinas, innateness ultimately involves a mistaken understanding of human nature and of the body's relationship to the soul and its cognitive capacities.[23]

Aquinas's second argument focuses on the role sensory perception would have to play if (some or all) cognition were already innate in the intellect. In the innativist picture, it looks as if the role of sensory perception will be restricted to merely providing occasions to retrieve the concepts and principles innate in the intellect, and it seems that sensation does so by removing an impediment to the intellect's exercise. But this sort of connection between sensation and intellectual understanding seems too loose. For if we lack a certain sensory power, it is impossible for us to have full cognition of the objects related to this power. A blind person, for instance, cannot have full intellectual cognition of colors. But if sensation only removes an impediment to our awareness of what is innate, then it should at least in principle be possible to have intellectual cognition of sensory objects without having the corresponding sensations.[24]

Moreover, Aquinas frequently contrasts the assumption of innate cognition with Avicenna's view, according to which intellectual cognition is acquired by way of emanation from a higher intellectual nature.[25] Whereas for Aquinas innativists such as Plato are mistaken in believing that knowledge derives entirely from within the mind, Avicenna is mistaken in holding that knowledge comes entirely from outside the intellect. So what is at stake, for Aquinas, is the right balance between the spontaneity and the receptivity involved in cognition, a balance that he sees captured best in Aristotle's account of intellectual cognition, an account that takes seriously both the contribution of sensory perception and the activity of the intellect.

Proponents of innateness often restrict the innateness hypothesis to certain nonempirical concepts or first principles, such as the principle of noncontradiction. Aquinas highlights the special role of first principles by calling them the "seeds of knowledge" (*semina scientiarum*); for without such principles no further *scientia* can be attained. Our intellect grasps these first principles immediately and intuitively whenever it is provided with the right sort of sensory input. Because this process is so immediate and natural to our intellect, Aquinas will occasionally say that cognition of first principles is innate in us.[26] However, this should not be taken too literally, for in the light of the arguments above Aquinas clearly does not hold that we have an innate possession of first principles (*habitus principiorum*).[27] What is innate is rather the "light of reason" (*rationis lumen*), that is, the intellective power, through which we have a natural grasp of these principles.[28]

What I have described so far is how Aquinas conceives of the normal processes through which a human being acquires cognition. On the basis of sensory input, the human being is capable of higher-level cognitive acts, for example, acts through which we form propositions such as "this thing in front of me is a tree." The human mind can arrive at holding this proposition and related acts through sensory input and its own spontaneous activity. Nothing further is required for the mind and its "natural light" (*lumen naturale*) to perform such acts; in particular, the human mind does not require special divine assistance. Since God, as the first cause, moves and directs all other things, it is indeed possible to say that God illuminates the mind in all of its acts. But, according to Aquinas, it is not necessary to assume the existence of an additional divine support, a further special illumination, to explain normal cognitive processes. In this respect, Aquinas disagrees with some of his contemporaries who insisted on the necessity of a special divine illumination even for what Aquinas refers to as "natural cognition" (*cognitio naturalis*).[29]

Scientia as Knowledge

As I noted earlier, it is far from clear which expression in Aquinas's philosophical vocabulary corresponds to what we would usually refer to as knowledge. But despite the reservations mentioned above, it can be argued that Aquinas's *scientia* is equivalent to what we call knowledge. When we describe knowledge in the broadest possible terms, we usually compare it to belief or opinion and say that knowledge possesses something that sets it apart from mere belief or opinion. The task of the epistemologist is to capture what exactly knowledge has that belief lacks. Aquinas similarly compares *scientia* with belief (and faith) with the aim of determining how they differ from one another. What would be the point of such a comparison, if *scientia* were for Aquinas right from the start only a very restricted and highly special sort of cognition, such as a specific scientific understanding? It is obvious that belief and faith are different from that in many ways. But isn't there space in between for another cognitive attitude, the comparison with which is more elucidating for the case of belief and faith than the comparison with a strange and highly specific form of cognition?

One way to distinguish *scientia* from belief or opinion (*opinio*) and faith (*fides*) is presumably with respect to the objects to which these different cognitive attitudes are directed. However, Aquinas frequently opts for another way. In his commentary on the *Posterior Analytics*, for example, he distinguishes them by focusing on the subject that has such attitudes. From the subject's point of view, *scientia* and belief and faith are similar insofar as they all incline their subjects to only one of a pair of contrary propositions, as opposed to, for instance, mere suspicion (*suspicio*), where reason is not completely inclined to one or the other. But they differ insofar as belief and faith are "with fear of the opposite" (*cum formidine alterius*).[30] In other texts, Aquinas puts the comparison somewhat differently. There mere belief is characterized by the fear of the opposite, whereas in both *scientia* and faith such fear is absent.[31] The apparent contradiction disappears if we keep in mind that in the first text, Aquinas talks about belief and fear merely insofar as these are cognitive states brought about by the intellect itself. It is true that faith involves a firm commitment to what is believed, but such a commitment "without fear of the opposite" is not brought about by the intellect itself, but by other factors such as the will and grace.[32] If, however, we simply focus on the overall degree of conviction involved in the three states, not regarding the source of the conviction, *scientia* and faith are more similar to each other than to belief.

All this shows that for Aquinas *scientia* is inseparably linked with certainty (*certitudo*).[33] According to Aquinas, I cannot be said to have *scientia* of something if I am in doubt about it. The notion of certainty also explains why Aquinas is so prone to restrict *scientia* to a clearly defined class of objects. In another passage in his commentary on the *Posterior Analytics*, he provides some sort of definition of what it means to know (*scire*). The definition also explains why *scientia* is necessarily about what is true and involves a grasp of the causes of that which is known:

> To know something [*scire aliquid*] is to cognize it perfectly [*perfecte cognoscere*], but this is to apprehend its truth perfectly. For the principles of a thing's being are identical with the principles of its truth, as is clear from book II of the *Metaphysics*. It is therefore necessary that the knower, if she is to cognize perfectly, cognizes the cause of the thing known.... But because *scientia* is also a certain [*certa*] cognition of a thing, yet no one can know with certainty something that could be otherwise, it is also necessary that what is known [*id quod scitur*] could not be otherwise.[34]

One might wonder whether this definition is complete; to give just one example, it does not mention, as Aquinas insists elsewhere, that *scientia* is always of something universal. But however this may be, together with Aquinas's remarks on certainty and the absence of "fear of the opposite," the definition illustrates that, for Aquinas, a series of conditions, both internal and external from the point of view of the knowing person, have to be met for there to be *scientia*. In this way Aquinas combines elements of externalist and internalist epistemologies. If knowing is supposed to be a perfect form of cognizing, it cannot consist simply in a mental state that is founded on more basic beliefs and characterized by a high degree of conviction; people in such a state could, at least in principle, be entirely wrong. *Scientia* also requires that the reasons on the basis of which we are convinced of the truth of something be adequate. Aquinas's remarks on certainty make it especially clear that he takes the certainty involved in *scientia* not only to be subjective certainty, but a certainty which precludes the very possibility of *scientia* being objectively uncertain. This leads Aquinas to restrict knowledge or *scientia* to necessary objects. On the other hand, it is not enough for *scientia* that someone have a true belief, including a grasp of the causes of what he believes to be the case, and that the true belief be about something that could not be otherwise. If such a person lacks subjective certainty and is "with fear of the opposite," one cannot, according to Aquinas, attribute *scientia* to her either. Moreover, due to it being a perfect form of cognizing, *scientia* also involves for Aquinas what Jaakko Hintikka has called the KK-thesis: a knower in the sense of someone having *scientia* also knows that she knows.[35]

Aquinas's definition of *scire* and *scientia* looks like a definition of knowing and knowledge. From a modern perspective his definition is admittedly strange. But there is no reason to assume that Aquinas talks about something other than knowledge rather than that his views on knowledge differ from ours in interesting ways. If we start with the idea that Aquinas's *scientia* is something completely different from our idea of knowledge, we deprive ourselves of the possibility of recognizing how different Aquinas's take on (what we call) knowledge is. It is true that ultimately Aquinas's characterization of knowledge does not apply to many instances of what we would call knowledge, for instance, knowledge of contingent facts. This, however, is not because Aquinas restricts his understanding of knowledge right away to necessary facts, but because only in grasping necessary facts can we finally attain real and absolute certainty and thus perfect cognition. When Aquinas insists, for example, that we do not have knowledge of contingent facts, this does not mean he is denying that we can cognize contingent facts or that we can have true cognition of contingent facts.

It just means that Aquinas does not think that our cognition of contingent facts qualifies as knowledge in the strict sense because such cognition lacks the high degree of certainty that he considers as required for knowledge.

But where there is perfection, there are things that fall short of perfection. By insisting that knowledge is perfect cognition, Aquinas turns knowledge in the strict sense into an ideal. Yet the various cognitive states that fall short of that ideal are not necessarily discounted as mere beliefs. In the passage quoted above, Aquinas insists that perfect cognition requires cognition of the causes; in other words, knowledge as perfect cognition is explanatory. But Aquinas admits that we sometimes know that something is the case not because we know its immediate causes, but because we know certain other facts from which the truth of what we know follows; for instance, when we know about the existence of a cause through the existence of its effects. In those cases we can be said to have knowledge in an extended and qualified sense, and we possess more than just belief. This is just one example; there are many other ways in which true cognition can fall short of knowledge proper, but where Aquinas is happy to talk about knowledge (*scientia*) in a qualified sense.[36]

In different contexts, Aquinas emphasizes different aspects of what I take to be his overall account of what it means to know. The absence of "fear of the opposite" was, as we have seen, a key criterion for distinguishing knowledge from faith and mere belief. When Aquinas explains what causes the cognizing agent not to be uncertain and in "fear of the opposite," he usually points to the grasp of principles, "for knowledge [*scientia*] possesses certainty, which results from the understanding of principles."[37] This leads to the question of how understanding of principles leads to certainty, a question Aquinas usually answers by providing a foundationalist account of knowledge. Foundationalism distinguishes between basic and nonbasic beliefs, where nonbasic beliefs are accepted (and known), directly or indirectly, on the basis of basic beliefs. Aquinas undeniably endorses foundationalism when he declares that *scientia* "proceeds from propositions which are true, first, and immediate, i.e., from propositions which are not demonstrated by something intermediate but which are evident by themselves."[38] Such basic beliefs are for Aquinas either self-evident principles, such as the principle of noncontradiction, or beliefs that we immediately accept on the basis of sense perception. The point of the theory of demonstrative syllogisms, as we find it in Aristotle's *Posterior Analytics* (and in Aquinas's commentary), is thus to explain how nonbasic beliefs are accepted on the basis of basic beliefs.[39]

It is very common among interpreters to classify Aquinas's epistemological views as a whole as a sort of foundationalism.[40] This tendency is understandable in light of what he says about how we acquire certainty in knowledge and if we turn to his commentary on Aristotle's *Posterior Analytics* as a point of reference for his epistemology. Recently, however, some commentators have argued that the picture of Aquinas as a foundationalist is flawed and that he should rather be thought of as defending "an externalism with reliabilist elements."[41] From what has been said above, it should be clear that I do not consider Aquinas an epistemological internalist committed to a purely foundationalist view of knowledge, but I also do not want to downplay the undeniably foundationalist aspects of his epistemology. If what has been said is correct, foundationalism only describes some elements of Aquinas's account of knowledge, namely how we acquire (subjective) certainty and also how we understand something through its causes; these are the elements that he examines in his commentary on the *Posterior Analytics*.[42] But there are other elements, of a more externalist sort, that also have to be in place for something to count as knowledge. A fair appreciation of Aquinas's epistemology will have to do justice to both tendencies.[43]

It is easy to imagine someone resisting my reading of Aquinas's account of *scientia* as an account of knowledge. Take the example of the principles of *scientia:* given Aquinas's definition it would follow from my identification of *scientia* with knowledge not only that we have no *scientia* of those principles but also that we do not know them; a very strange result indeed. But the objection is less problematic than it seems. Although we do not have proper *scientia* or knowledge of these principles, we can still be said to know them in some qualified sense,[44] for our cognitive grasp of the principles is somewhat similar to knowledge proper. Consider as an example the self-evident principle that the whole is greater than its part. We grasp this principle presumably without "fear of the opposite" and although we do not grasp it by means of an inference, that is, by means of an inferential justification, we still perceive its truth by perceiving the self-evident relationship between the various terms making up the principle, that is, we accept it by means of a noninferential justification.

This response, however, invites a new problem: it now seems as if Aquinas ranks *scientia* higher than the simple acts of understanding on which *scientia* is based, for *scientia* is the paradigmatic case of knowledge and knowledge of principles is knowledge only in a qualified sense. And why after all is only *scientia* perfect cognition and not the much simpler intuitive act by which we grasp the principles? An answer to these problems will have to point to some facts about the nature of the human mind. Human beings are rational beings and this means that the typical mode of operation of our intellective capacities is discursive reasoning. Unlike higher-level intellectual creatures (i.e., angels), we do not understand everything intuitively; in understanding we typically move "from one thing to another" (*ab uno in aliud*).[45] From this perspective, *scientia* seems to be the mode of understanding most appropriate to human beings, because in *scientia* too we move from one thing to another, from the understanding of the causes and principles to the understanding of the conclusion.

The Limits of Human Knowledge

From what has been said, it follows that we cannot know everything. The strict requirements of *scientia* or knowledge proper can only be met by a very restricted class of objects, a class that notably contains nonbasic mathematical and logical truths, of which true demonstrative proof from prior causes and principles is possible. But to ask about the limits of human knowledge in this restricted sense is not very illuminating. What can we say about the limits of knowledge in the broader sense, that is, about the limits to what we can have true cognition of without fear of the opposite, and not merely belief? In other words: how far do paradigmatic and nonparadigmatic knowledge extend?

That according to Aquinas all human cognition is either sensory cognition or derived from sensory cognition does not mean that we can only know objects that we can also sense. It is also possible for us to have knowledge of objects that never fall within the scope of the senses, because these objects are immaterial. Presumably the most important question is how we can have knowledge of God. In this respect, Aquinas notoriously holds that "we can know [*scire*] of God that God exists, but we cannot know what God is," a view that gained some additional prominence by the fact that it was included in the list of 219 articles censured by Stephen Tempier, the bishop of Paris, in 1277.[46] Aquinas arrives at his seemingly radical conclusion by arguing that we know the essence or quiddity of something either because our intellect has immediate access to it or because it has access to it by means of something else. The first possibility is ruled out in the case of God, for that way of knowing an essence or quiddity of an object requires sensory information about the object, which is impossible in the case of God. But indirect grasp of the divine essence is also impossible for our intellect, because that would require a close resemblance between the medium and that which is understood by means of the medium. I can, for instance, understand the essence of Socrates as a human being by understanding the essence of another human being, since both individuals fall under a common species. But we cannot understand the essence of God in this way. God is so different from creatures that God and creatures do not have anything real in common.[47] We therefore cannot know what God is, although the proofs for the existence of God, which argue from perceivable effects to the existence of a first cause, provide us with ample evidence that God exists.[48] Aquinas arrives at the same conclusion regarding our capacity to know other immaterial substances: we can at most know about their existence, but because of their entirely different nature, we cannot know anything about their quiddities or essences.

Two questions arise at this point: (1) If in this life we cannot know even through revelation what God is, why does Aquinas engage in theology? Don't we know something about God when we know that God is immaterial, infinite, omniscient, and so on? (2) How can we know of something that it exists if we do not know what it is? The latter question indicates that it is necessary to distinguish between different ways of knowing what something is: perfect quidditative knowledge and imperfect quidditative knowledge. I do not have to know what exactly water is in order to find out whether there is water in my cup; a confused knowledge of what is meant by the term "water" together with some criteria for how to apply the term is presumably enough; in the same way, I do not have to know what exactly God is in order to prove God's existence.[49] It is enough to know that the name "God" stands for "first cause" or "highest being" to go looking whether there is a first cause or highest being. Yet I do not know what this first cause is that I am looking for.

To the first question we can reply in a similar way: yes, in a way we get to know something about God when we manage to show by philosophical (or theological) arguments that God is immaterial, infinite, and the like. By this process we advance our very imperfect knowledge of God, but we never get to a real and perfect understanding of the divine quiddity itself, an understanding Aquinas characterizes as "comprehensive" (*comprehendens*), "defining" (*definiens*), and "adequating" (*adaequans*).[50] All the knowledge we acquire about God in this life is of what God is not: God is not material, does not lack knowledge, is not limited, and so on. This is very different from a positive understanding of God's immateriality, omniscience, infinity, and so on.

Knowing what God is not provides us with at least some knowledge of God. Yet there are certain things about God we cannot know at all (at least in this life), for instance, that God is three persons. The reason for this is simple. Only from God's effects can we derive knowledge about God, but since the persons of the Trinity do not act as separate causes, we have no way of demonstrating—and thus knowing of—their distinctness.[51] For Aquinas, the proposition that God is triune is an article of faith, and articles of faith are in principle not knowable, at least not by natural reason. Aquinas sees, however, an important parallelism between what we know and the principles on the basis of which we are said to know, on the one hand, and theological beliefs and the articles of faith on the basis of which we accept these beliefs as true, on the other hand. This leads Aquinas to the conclusion that there is theological knowledge, which is a nonparadigmatic form of knowledge (*scientia*). The most important distinction between theological knowledge and naturally acquired knowledge is that the principles of naturally acquired knowledge are self-evident for the knowing subject, whereas the principles of theological knowledge, the articles of faith, are accepted on the basis of the light of faith, which is a gift of divine grace.[52]

If human knowledge of nonmaterial things is somewhat restricted, Aquinas's epistemological optimism seems to dictate that we can, at least in principle and often only with nonparadigmatic knowledge, know all aspects of material reality. But here two final questions arise: (1) Given Aquinas's emphasis on the importance of sensory perception one might wonder whether we can really know the substances to which the sensible qualities perceived by the senses belong. Isn't this case similar to the knowledge of immaterial substances? Aren't the sensible qualities just the effects on the basis of which we know the existence of the underlying substances without knowing what they are? (2) In a famous and often quoted passage from his sermon on the Apostle's Creed, Aquinas remarks that "our cognition is so weak that no philosopher was ever able to inquire perfectly into the nature of a single fly."[53] Does Aquinas in the end deny that we can know any nature or quiddity, even that of material things?

To the extent that Aquinas addresses these questions, he seems to address them together. He clearly thinks that we do know material substances and that to provide us with this knowledge is one of the main roles of our intellect.[54] The intellect even has its name from the fact that it is the faculty through which we cognize the inner constitution of an object, whereas the senses only detect an object's external accidental properties.[55] How exactly the intellect understands substances on the basis of a sensory grasp of sensible qualities is less clear in Aquinas, and the whole question turned into an extensive debate a couple of years after Aquinas's death.[56] Related to the view that the intellect understands substances is the further view that the essence or quiddity is the proper object of the intellect. In fact, in most of the passages where Aquinas addresses the cognition of substances, he simply says that the intellect understands the essence of the thing underlying the sensible qualities,[57] the idea being that there is for the intellect nothing else to understand concerning a substance than its essence. This leads us to Aquinas's well-known thesis of the veracity of the intellect, according to which the intellect is, under normal circumstances, never deceived with respect to its natural object, that is, the essence or quiddity of a material object, in the same way as the sensory powers are, under normal circumstances, never deceived with respect to their primary objects. For Aquinas, falsity and error only occur on the level of the second act of the intellect, the act of composition or division through which we form judgments.[58] What exactly the doctrine of the veracity of the intellect amounts to need not detain us here; clearly it does not entail the claim that everyone has a perfect understanding of the natures and essences of the objects around us, for that is obviously not the case. But insofar as the doctrine presupposes the possibility of quidditative knowledge of material objects, it confirms the impression we get from Aquinas's explanation of how we understand substances: human beings not only are capable of understanding essences or quiddities of material objects in a certain way, they also actually attain such knowledge whenever the intellect grasps an object. The best way to make sense of Aquinas's pessimistic remark from his sermon on the Apostle's Creed is thus to distinguish between two ways in which natures and essences are understood: in an imperfect way, when we grasp the nature or essence of the fly as something to be understood further, and in a perfect way, which comes with real knowledge of its nature or essence. The imperfect grasp takes place whenever our intellect's gaze focuses on a material object, but the perfect understanding of a thing's essence is something requiring much effort and time, and sometimes even more than a lifetime. If Aquinas is an epistemological optimist, and I have no reason to doubt this, his optimism is obviously also accompanied by a profound epistemological modesty.

NOTES

1. For the problems in mapping Aquinas's epistemic categories onto ours, see Eleonore Stump, *Aquinas* (London: Routledge, 2003), 217–43; John I. Jenkins, *Knowledge and Faith in Thomas Aquinas* (Cambridge: Cambridge University Press, 1997), 15–17; Scott MacDonald,

"Theory of Knowledge," in Norman Kretzmann and Eleonore Stump, eds., *The Cambridge Companion to Aquinas* (Cambridge: Cambridge University Press, 1993), 160–95.

2. Aquinas talks about false cognition (*cognitio falsa*) in *ST* I q.17 a.3; *ST* I-II q.2 a.3 ad 3; and *In DA*, lib.3, lect.12.

3. *In PA*, lib.1, lect.44; *ST* I-II q.57; *QDVCom* a.7. For Aristotle's account of the five so-called intellectual virtues, see *Nicomachean Ethics*, bk VI.

4. See, for instance, Myles F. Burnyeat, "Aristotle on Understanding Knowledge," in Enrico Berti, ed., *Aristotle on Science: The "Posterior Analytics,"* Proceedings of the Eighth Symposium Aristotelicum (Padua: Editrice Antenore, 1981), 97–139.

5. Thomas of York engages with skeptical arguments in his *Sapientiale*, bk VI, c.24; for an edition of this text, see John P. E. Scully, *Reality and Truth in Thomas of York* (Ph.D. diss., University of Toronto, 1960), vol. 2, 338–60. Siger's discussion of skepticism is examined in Antoine Côté, "Siger and the Skeptic," *Review of Metaphysics* 60 (2006): 305–25. For more on medieval discussions of skepticism, see Dominik Perler, *Zweifel und Gewissheit: Skeptische Debatten im Mittelalter* (Frankfurt a.M.: Klostermann, 2006); Henrik Lagerlund, ed., *Rethinking the History of Skepticism: The Missing Medieval Background* (Leiden: Brill, 2010).

6. For the first, see *ST* I q.84 a.1; for the second, see, for instance, *QDP*, q.7, q.10, ad 5; *QDV*, q.1, a.2. Parts of bk IV of Aristotle's *Metaphysics*, namely the discussion of the principle of noncontradiction, were often read by medieval authors as Aristotle's response to skepticism. In this sense it is possible to read the relevant parts of Aquinas's commentary on the *Metaphysics* as also engaging in such a response.

7. See, for instance, *ST* I q.91 a.3; *ST* I q.93 a.2, a.4, and a.6.

8. See Aristotle, *Politics*, 1253a9; *Parts of Animals*, 658a8; *Progression of Animals*, 704b15.

9. *Metaphysics*, 980a21. For the importance this statement has for Aquinas, see Jan A. Aertsen, "Aquinas and the Human Desire for Knowledge," *American Catholic Philosophical Quarterly* 79 (2005): 411–30.

10. See, for instance, *SCG*, lib.3, cap.48: "Impossibile est naturale desiderium esse inane; natura enim nihil facit frustra. Esset autem inane desiderium naturae si nunquam posset impleri."

11. See, for instance, *SCG*, lib.2, cap.60: "Sed homo habet propriam operationem supra alia animalia, scilicet intelligere et ratiocinari, quae est operatio hominis inquantum est homo, ut Aristoteles dicit in I Ethicorum." See Aristotle, *Nicomachean Ethics*, I 7.

12. A more exhaustive examination of Aquinas's account of the reliability of our cognitive capacities can be found in Norman Kretzmann, "Infallibility, Error, and Ignorance," in Richard Bosley and Martin Tweedale, eds., *Aristotle and His Medieval Interpreters* (Calgary: University of Calgary Press, 1991), 159–94.

13. For more details on Aquinas's cognitive psychology, see Stump, *Aquinas*, 244–76; Robert Pasnau, *Thomas Aquinas on Human Nature* (Cambridge: Cambridge University Press, 2002).

14. For Aquinas's account of sensory cognition and the sensory powers, see *ST* I q.78 a.3 and a.4; *In DA*, lib.2, lect.13–24 and lib.3, lect.1–6; *QDA*, a.13.

15. *ST* I q.75 a.2; translation by Robert Pasnau, *Thomas Aquinas: The Treatise on Human Nature: Summa Theologiae 1a 75–89* (Indianapolis: Hackett, 2002), 5.

16. *ST* I q.75 a.2; *QDA*, a.1 and a.2; *In DA*, lib.3, lect.7; *ST* I q.84 a.2; *ST* I q.86 a.2 ad 4.

17. *ST* I q.84 a.7.

18. *In BDT*, q.1, a.2.

19. *QDV*, q.2, a.3, obj.19 and ad 19.

20. See, for instance, *In BDT*, q.1, a.3.

21. *ST* I q.79 a.3; *ST* I q.54 a.4; *QDA*, a.4; *SCG*, lib.2, cap.77; *In DA*, lib.3, lect.10. Despite its name, the agent intellect is not the power in and by which thinking actually takes place in human beings. Aquinas calls the thinking power the possible intellect, but for sake of brevity I will refer to this power simply as the intellect.

22. Not surprisingly, Aquinas associates innate cognition with Plato. In addition to the two arguments mentioned in the following, Aquinas sometimes also argues against a specific aspect of Plato's version of innate cognition, namely the idea that the soul exists (and understands) before it is joined with the body: see, for instance, *QDV*, q.10, a.6; *QDV*, q.18, a.7.

23. *QDV*, q.10, a.6; *QDV*, q.19, a.1; *ST* I q.84 a.3; *QDA*, q.15.

24. *QDV*, q.10, a.6; *QDV*, q.19, a.1; *ST* I q.84 a.3; *QDA*, q.15.

25. *QDV*, q.10, a.6; *QDV*, q.11, a.1; *QDA*, q.15.

26. See, for instance, *QDV*, q.10, a.6, ad 6; *QDV*, q.11, a.1, ad 5.

27. He also says so explicitly in *In PA*, lib.2, lect.20. See also Horst Seidl, "Über die Erkenntnis erster, allgemeiner Prinzipien nach Thomas von Aquin," in Albert Zimmermann, ed., *Thomas von Aquin: Werk und Wirkung im Licht neuerer Forschungen*, Miscellanea Mediaevalia 19 (Berlin: De Gruyter, 1988), 103–16.

28. *QDV*, q.11, a.1. Some interpreters, however, interpret Aquinas's account of cognition in more innativist terms. For a recent example of this tendency, see Houston Smit, "Aquinas's Abstractionism," *Medieval Philosophy and Theology* 10 (2001): 85–118.

29. *ST* I-II q.109 a.1; *In BDT*, q.1, a.1. See also Etienne Gilson, "Pourquoi saint Thomas a critiqué saint Augustin," *Archives d'histoire doctrinale et littéraire du Moyen Age* 1 (1926/27): 5–127.

30. *In PA*, lib.1, lect.1. Aquinas takes the expression *cum formidine alterius* from Avicenna and uses it frequently in his writings: see, for instance, *In BDT*, q.3, a.1; *Super Sent* III, d.17, q. un., a.2, qc.1; *Super Sent* III, d.23, q.2, a.2, qc.1; *QDV*, q.14, a.1; *In DA*, lib.1, lect.4; *ST* II-II q.2 a.1. Where the Latin translation has *cum formidine*, the Arabic text rather suggests a translation as *cum possibilitate*; see Avicenna, *Liber de anima*, tract. V, cap. 1, ed. S. Van Riet (Louvain/Leiden: Editions Orientalistes/Brill, 1968), 79, including the editor's note. I thank Deborah Black for pointing this out to me. A rendering as "with the possibility of the opposite" (*cum possibilitate alterius*) suggests a less subjective understanding of the cognitive states in question.

31. For instance, in *ST* I-II q.67 a.3.

32. See *ST* II-II q.1 a.4 and q.2 a.1.

33. See also *SCG*, lib.3, cap.39.

34. *In PA*, lib.1, lect.4; see Aristotle, *Metaphysics*, 993b28–31. Aquinas's definition is based on *Posterior Analytics*, 71b9–12, but it is interesting to see what Aquinas adds to Aristotle's words: by saying that knowing is perfectly cognizing Aquinas explains why knowing involves grasp of the causes, and by bringing certainty into the picture he explains why we only know what is necessary. The notion of certainty is in general absent from Aristotle's epistemology and was introduced into medieval epistemology via the Arabic philosophers. For more on this see Robert Pasnau, "Science and Certainty," in Robert Pasnau and Christina Van Dyke, eds., *The Cambridge History of Medieval Philosophy* (Cambridge: Cambridge University Press, 2010), 357–68.

35. *QDV*, q.10, a.10 ad 5. For Aquinas and the KK-thesis see Christopher J. Martin, "Self-Knowledge and Cognitive Ascent: Thomas Aquinas and Peter Olivi on the KK-Thesis," in Henrik Lagerlund, ed., *Forming the Mind: Essays on the Internal Senses and the Mind/Body Problem from Avicenna to the Medical Enlightenment* (Dordrecht: Springer, 2007), 93–108.

36. For a very good discussion of some of these points, see MacDonald, "Theory of Knowledge," 174–80. Aquinas mentions some of the "improper" modes of knowing in *In PA*, lib.1, lect.4.

37. *ST* I-II q.67 a.3.

38. *In PA*, lib.1, lect.4.

39. For a very detailed account of Aquinas's foundationalism, see MacDonald, "Theory of Knowledge."

40. See, for instance, MacDonald, "Theory of Knowledge."

41. Stump, *Aquinas*, 235. Jenkins, *Knowledge and Faith*, and Kretzmann, "Infallibility, Error, and Ignorance," endorse a similar view.

42. In the prologue to his commentary on the *Posterior Analytics* (*In PA*, lib.1, lect.1), Aquinas remarks on the title of Aristotle's work. He notes that the expression "Analytics" means the same as "resolution" (*resolutio*) and explains that both the *Prior* and *Posterior Analytics* have to do with the analysis or resolution of judgments; for only in this way can we achieve certainty in our judgments. From this it is clear that Aquinas considers the *Posterior Analytics* as dealing with how the knowing subject acquires certainty.

43. For a very different attempt to harmonize the externalist and internalist elements of Aquinas's epistemology, see Thomas S. Hibbs, "Aquinas, Virtue, and Recent Epistemology," *Review of Metaphysics* 52 (1999): 573–94. Hibbs sees similarities between Aquinas and modern proponents of virtue epistemology.

Since I have emphasized the notion of certainty (*certitudo*) for Aquinas's account of knowledge, I should add a note of caution. For it is not entirely clear what Aquinas means by *certitudo*. It obviously means more than what we normally call certainty, for it captures more than just, say, the total absence of doubt. *Certitudo* also requires that something cannot be otherwise. And when Aquinas compares different areas of knowledge, he remarks that some, like arithmetic, are more certain than others (see, for instance, *In PA*, lib.1, lect.41). What I have said about Aquinas's account of knowledge as a whole seems also to apply to one of the key notions of this account: in order for something to be certain (*certum*), a series of conditions have to be met, some of which are internal to the knower, and some of which are external.

44. *In PA*, lib.1, lect.4.

45. *QDV*, q.15, a.1; *ST* I q.79 a.8; *In PA*, lib.1, lect.1.

46. *ST* I q.3; *In BDT*, q.1, a.2; *In BDT*, q.6, a.3. For a discussion of the corresponding article of the condemnation, i.e., article 215, see Roland Hissette, *Enquête sur les 219 articles condamnés à Paris le 7 mars 1277* (Louvain: Publications universitaires, 1977), 32–34.

47. *In BDT*, q.6, a.3. For a thorough discussion of the various texts in which Aquinas develops his view of the impossibility of quidditative knowledge of God (in this life), see John F. Wippel, *The Metaphysical Thought of Thomas Aquinas* (Washington, D.C.: Catholic University of America Press, 2000), 501–75.

48. Our knowledge of the existence of God is, of course, knowledge only in a qualified sense. For we have such knowledge not through the causes of God's existence (there are none), but only a posteriori, from God's effects.

49. See *In BDT*, q.6, a.3.

50. *QDP*, q.7, a.5, ad 6.

51. *Super Sent* I, d.3, q.1, a.4; *In BDT*, q.1, a.4; *QDV*, q.10, a.13; *ST* I q.32 a.1.

52. For theology as a non-paradigmatic *scientia*, see Jenkins, *Knowledge and Faith*.

53. *Expositio in Symbolum Apostolorum*, proem.

54. *Quodl* VIII, q.2, a.2: "Intellectus cognoscit ipsam naturam et substantiam rei." See also *ST* I q.17 a.3; *ST* I q.58 a.5; *ST* I q.85 a.6; *Super Sent* III, d.35, q.2, a.2, qc. 1.

55. *QDV*, q.1, a.12: "Dicendum quod nomen intellectus sumitur ex hoc quod intima rei cognoscit; est enim intelligere quasi intus legere: sensus enim et imaginatio sola accidentia exteriora cognoscunt; solus autem intellectus ad interiora et essentiam rei pertingit." For the following see also Philip Reynolds, "Properties, Causality, and Epistemic Optimism in Thomas Aquinas," *Recherches de théologie et philosophie médiévales* 68 (2010): 270–309.

56. See Aurélien Robert, *Penser la substance: étude d'une question médiévale (XIIIe–XIVe siècles)* (Paris: Vrin, forthcoming).

57. See the passages in nn. 54 and 55 above.

58. See, for instance, *ST* I q.85 a.6; *In DA*, lib.3, lect.11. For more discussion of this theory see Jenkins, *Knowledge and Faith*, 101–17, and Kretzmann, "Infallibility, Error, and Ignorance," 181–94.

CHAPTER 24

THE INTELLECTUAL VIRTUES

TOBIAS HOFFMANN

Aquinas's account of the intellectual virtues is highly indebted to the *Nicomachean Ethics*, where Aristotle discusses them mainly with the goal of clarifying *phronēsis* (prudence), which is at the crossroads of practical knowledge, desire, and action. For Socrates, every human virtue is a kind of wisdom because correct practical knowledge entails good moral action, and moral failure is due to ignorance alone. Aristotle, on the other hand, qualifies the importance of knowledge for virtuous action. According to Aristotle, it is not enough to have right knowledge in order to live temperately and justly; rather, temperance and justice are virtues of character, that is, moral virtues, which are not the fruit of teaching but have to be acquired by repeated practice. In his view, most intellectual qualities contribute little or nothing to the practice of the moral virtues; thus someone might be tremendously learned and yet lead a foolish life. Only prudence, which includes the ability to evaluate what contributes to the good life as a whole and the convinced willingness to act accordingly, effectively allows one to put the moral virtues into practice. Conversely, the moral virtues make prudence possible by enabling one to judge correctly in concrete situations. A successful response to Socrates' intellectualism, in fact, turns on an adequate account of prudence. Book 6 of the *Nicomachean Ethics* precisely aims at offering such an account of prudence by distinguishing it from other intellectual virtues. Aquinas's treatment of the intellectual virtues likewise emphasizes prudence. Yet while prudence is pivotal in both Aristotle's and Aquinas's ethics, they also consider theoretical wisdom of utter importance for an accomplished human life.

After brief remarks about Aquinas's conception of intellectual virtue, the present chapter will consider his account of the individual intellectual virtues, with special focus on prudence.[1]

What Is an Intellectual Virtue?

The intellect proceeds differently when understanding a mathematical theorem, making a geometrical demonstration, fixing a car, and choosing a career. We may be better at some kinds of intellectual activities than at others, for example, thanks to natural talent and learning, we may be well disposed to solve difficult mathematical problems, but because of lack of experience, we may not be good at evaluating alternative professional paths in light of all the factors involved, professional and nonprofessional. All of these activities can be perfected by habits (that is, stable dispositions), namely, by intellectual virtues. Aristotle and Aquinas distinguish five principal intellectual virtues: wisdom (knowledge of the highest causes of reality), understanding (the capacity to grasp the first principles of demonstration), science (systematic demonstrative knowledge of a certain subject matter), art (craft knowledge or professional competence), and prudence.

Yet for Aquinas, intellectual virtues are virtues only in a qualified sense. Only moral virtues, that is, habits that are in the appetitive part of the soul or depend for their existence on the appetitive part, are virtues in the full sense. Moral virtues not only make one able to act well, but they also ensure that one make good use of this ability; they are good habits not only materially (insofar as they are ordered to the good) but also formally (insofar as they are ordered to the good under the aspect of good). For example, justice not only disposes a person to just deeds but also effectively makes him or her act justly. In contrast, intellectual virtues are only materially good habits; they make an individual capable of a good activity, such as speaking correct Latin or making good swords, without ensuring that he or she make good use of that activity (e.g., speaking the truth and doing so at the appropriate time; fabricating a reliable sword for an honorable purpose). Accordingly, a bad will is compatible with science or art but not with justice or temperance.[2] This explains why Aquinas regards the virtues of truthfulness and studiousness as moral rather than intellectual virtues. Truthfulness concerns not the ability to know the truth but the willingness to speak the truth; therefore, Aquinas connects it to the virtue of justice. Studiousness likewise does not concern knowledge as such but rather a well-ordered desire for knowledge; hence, it is connected to temperance.[3] Prudence is the only intellectual virtue that is essentially connected with good desire and that is therefore essentially ordered to a good use of the intellectual capacity. Thus, Aquinas considers prudence both an intellectual and a moral virtue.[4]

Although for Aquinas the intellectual virtues (apart from prudence) are virtues only in a qualified sense, he considers them superior to the moral virtues. Qua virtues, the moral virtues excel over intellectual virtues; yet qua habits, the intellectual virtues are nobler, for while the moral virtues perfect the appetitive powers, the intellectual virtues perfect reason, which is superior to the appetitive powers.[5]

The Different Intellectual Virtues

Apart from Aquinas's commentary on book 6 of the *Nicomachean Ethics* (the place where Aristotle discusses the intellectual virtues) and quaestio 57 of the *Prima Secundae* of the *Summa theologiae*, which is like an extension of this commentary, his discussion of the intellectual virtues is scattered throughout his oeuvre. In his *Secunda Secundae*, where he examines the virtues in detail, Aquinas's treatment of the intellectual virtues is much more independent from Aristotle, both as regards the manner of presentation and the substance of his account. The only intellectual virtue that receives extensive treatment in the *Secunda Secundae* is prudence, a cardinal virtue. The reason is that the four cardinal virtues, together with the three theological virtues of faith, hope, and charity, constitute the major organizing principle of the *Secunda Secundae*. Since Aquinas considers art to be morally irrelevant, he does not discuss it in the *Secunda Secundae*. Wisdom, understanding, and science are briefly discussed in connection with the so-called gifts of the Holy Spirit (that is, habits that result not from human reason but from a divine impulse and that dispose one to respond to divine inspiration).[6]

Aquinas uses fundamentally the same criteria as Aristotle to distinguish between the intellectual virtues. Thus, the succinct summary of Aristotle's account in his commentary on the *Metaphysics* expresses both his understanding of Aristotle and his own view:

> [Aristotle] refers to his work on morals, that is *Ethics* 6, where he discusses the way science and art and wisdom and prudence and understanding differ. To put it briefly, wisdom and science and understanding are in the speculative part of the soul, which he here calls the scientific part of the soul. They differ in that understanding is the habit of the first principles of demonstration; science concerns conclusions about lesser things, whereas wisdom considers the first causes, so in the same place it is called the chief of the sciences. Prudence and art are in the practical part of the soul, which reasons about contingent things that can be done by us. But they differ, for prudence directs actions which do not pass into exterior matter but are perfections of the agent; hence prudence is called there right reason about things to be done [*recta ratio agibilium*]. But art directs in making, which passes into exterior matter, such as to build and to saw; hence art is called right reason about things to be made [*recta ratio factibilium*].[7]

Considering the intellectual virtues individually will bring out more clearly how Aquinas understands the distinctive characteristics of the five intellectual virtues, and in particular of prudence, which is the intellectual virtue that is most easily misconstrued.

Wisdom

Aquinas's understanding of wisdom is rooted mainly in Aristotle's *Metaphysics*, where Aristotle provides a more elaborate account of wisdom than in his *Nicomachean Ethics*. For Aristotle, wisdom concerns knowledge of the highest causes and the ability to judge and order subordinate things by these standards.[8] Aquinas understands this idea both in a comparative and in an absolute sense. Comparatively, those are called wiser who are more knowledgeable about things of a higher order, by which knowledge they can evaluate things of a lower order; thus, the architect is wiser than the bricklayer. In the absolute sense, those are wise who have knowledge of the highest cause of the entire universe, which is God. Wisdom as an intellectual virtue concerns God as he is knowable by natural human reason, that is, as he is investigated in the science of metaphysics. In the supernatural order, wisdom can be either identified with "sacred doctrine" (that is, with theology as the science of God that is based upon divine revelation) or with wisdom as a gift of the Holy Spirit (that is, a connatural familiarity with divine matters, by which one is able to evaluate and order things according to a divine standard).[9]

Because of the eminence of the object of wisdom, that is, God, Aquinas considers wisdom the highest intellectual virtue. Wisdom provides one with the criteria by which to judge and order all the other intellectual virtues. Wisdom moreover has an ethical dimension in that it contemplates God, the object of "felicity" (*felicitas*, Aquinas's word for philosophical happiness, as opposed to *beatitudo*, which is supernatural happiness). Thus, Aquinas says that wisdom is even more closely related to happiness than prudence. This reflects his view that the "contemplative life" (that is, living a concern for knowledge of the truth) is superior to the "active life" (that is, the practice of the moral virtues).[10]

Science

Aristotle's and Aquinas's understanding of science is quite different from today's use of the term. As an intellectual virtue, science is a "demonstrative habit,"[11] namely, a habit whereby one possesses knowledge acquired by means of demonstration. Aquinas's most developed account of science is found in his commentary on the *Posterior Analytics*, where he follows Aristotle closely. Since he uses this same account in his theological works as the basis for his discussion of theology as a science, we should assume that his comments on Aristotle's text here reflect his own view and not only his understanding of Aristotle. According to this account, the domain of a specific science is defined by its "subject," which is confined to a single genus. For example, the subject of arithmetic is number, and the subject of geometry is spatial magnitude. Certain derivative facts about the subject of a science are demonstrated; for example, it is demonstrated in geometry that the interior angles of any triangle are equal to two right angles. According to the *Posterior Analytics*, there are a number of conditions for demonstrative scientific knowledge, which Aristotle for the most part does not address in his brief account in the *Nicomachean Ethics*.[12] There he emphasizes merely that science concerns necessary things, that is, things which cannot be otherwise than they are. Thus, science is distinguished by its object from prudence and art, which concern contingent matters that are done through human agency.

Understanding

Whereas science is knowledge obtained through demonstration, understanding is knowledge that is obtained nondiscursively of a proposition which is "known through itself" (*per se notum*), that is, knowable thanks to the terms of the proposition.[13] It may seem that knowledge of what is known through itself is no accomplishment, and thus one may wonder why it has the character of an intellectual virtue. Yet such propositions are not necessarily known instantly and without effort. According to Aquinas, not all that is *per se notum* is clear *to everyone*. Aquinas distinguishes between that which is "*per se notum* to all," because everybody easily grasps the terms of the proposition (such as "whole" and "part" in "the whole is larger than its part"), and what is "*per se notum* only to the knowledgeable," that is, to those who understand a proposition consisting of less obvious terms (as in the statement that an angel does not occupy a specific space). The common English translation of "*per se notum*" as "self-evident" does not take this important nuance into account.[14]

Art

The intellectual virtue of art refers to what the medievals called the mechanical arts. It is distinct from the so-called liberal arts (Grammar, Rhetoric, Logic, Arithmetic, Geometry, Music, and Astronomy). For Aquinas, the liberal arts are speculative habits like the theoretical sciences; they merely have a resemblance to the mechanical arts in that they involve such activities as counting and measuring.[15] Art as an intellectual virtue is what we would call the knowledge or the professional competence of a craftsman. Thus, a cabinetmaker uses his or her art to produce a good piece of furniture. Using Aristotle's formula, Aquinas defines art as right reason about things to be made.[16] Thus, at first sight, art is very similar to prudence, which Aquinas and (less explicitly) Aristotle define as right reason about things to be done.[17] What art and prudence have in common is that they are habits of practical reason, whereas wisdom, science, and understanding are habits of speculative reason. Yet from the ethical perspective, art and prudence differ significantly, even as production and action differ in a crucial respect. As Aquinas explains with reference to Aristotle's *Metaphysics*, production is an activity that passes into a thing outside of the individual, such as to build or to saw. Action, in contrast, is an activity that remains within the individual, such as to see, to think, and to wish.[18] In other words, products are distinct from their producers, while actions are inseparable from their agents. This implies that the work of art is judged solely according to the quality of the product and not according to the good will of the craftsman. The work of prudence, by contrast, is not merely assessed according to the results of action, but above all, whether it is done for the right reason and with the appropriate disposition of the will.[19] Art thus exemplifies what is characteristic of all the intellectual virtues apart from prudence: they provide the ability to carry on intellectual activities, but they do not affect the will of the individual. In order for craftsmen to make good use of their competence, they need the moral virtue of justice that inclines them to work in the fitting manner.[20]

Aristotle's and Aquinas's emphasis on the difference between action and production, or between art and prudence, indicates how far removed their ethics is from utilitarianism, for which this distinction is morally irrelevant. In utilitarianism, what counts are the results of an activity, not the mindset with which it was done.

Prudence

To lead a good life and thus to attain the properly human good means to act in an excellent and thoughtful manner in the various domains and the particular circumstances of life: in other words, it means to act virtuously. None of the previously discussed intellectual virtues can sufficiently provide the knowledge that would effectively allow us to live virtuously. For one thing, the knowledge obtained through understanding of the first practical principles and through moral science is too abstract to guide us in particular situations. Moreover, such general knowledge is often too weak to withstand the interference by desires or fears that make it ineffective. Socrates' claim that it is sufficient to know what is best in order to act accordingly is contradicted by the facts: weakness of will, that is, acting contrary to one's better judgment, is a common human phenomenon. Not just any knowledge, but only prudence guarantees that we judge correctly what specific situations require and that we act accordingly.

For a better understanding of Aquinas's notion of prudence, we must first see what it is not. In English and in the Romance languages, prudence connotes above all the ability to avoid dangers; in German, *Klugheit* evokes astuteness, which is why Kant qualifies shrewd selfish behavior as prudent and dissociates prudence from virtue.[21] In contrast, for Aquinas, who follows Aristotle on this point, a prudent person experiences perfect harmony between correct practical knowledge, upright desire, and action. Furthermore, for Aquinas as for Aristotle, prudence does not concern limited purposes, but rather what is relevant for the good life as a whole.[22] For this reason, Aquinas in one place calls it "wisdom in human affairs."[23] Yet prudence is not only practical wisdom, for it is not mainly about practical *considerations*. Rather, the main task of prudence is to apply general practical knowledge to a specific deed.[24] The passage from correct general practical considerations to a concrete action that embodies these considerations, which is the work of prudence, is anything but trivial. It requires experience, acumen, foresight, circumspection, caution, and other characteristics that enhance the cognitive capacity of prudence.[25] Moreover, it requires the support of well-ordered desire. In prudence, cognitive and appetitive qualities are unified in such a way that the practical knowledge of what is best is fully internalized. No one can replace us in our decision-making. Even when we consult the advice of other prudent persons, or when we act in accordance with a good law, we must appropriate the criteria that prudent people or good legislators are offering us.[26]

In order to appreciate the nature of prudence and its preconditions, we must briefly look at Aquinas's account of the stages of human action. When a sick person is serious about wanting to become healthy, he intends to take specific measures. Unless these measures are immediately apparent, he deliberates about them, such as whether he needs to see a doctor and which doctor would be best. Having concluded that the first step toward health is to visit a particular doctor, he actually goes to see her. Thus, the basic steps in the process of his action are *intention* of an end to be attained by some means, *deliberation* about which means are suitable and which are not, *decision* to employ the most suitable means, and *execution* of the required action(s). In Aquinas's account, each of these stages has a cognitive and a volitional dimension, which interpenetrate each other and which are inseparable.[27]

The practice of the moral virtues involves analogous considerations about means and end. A soldier who intends to act bravely has to deliberate whether a given situation requires him to move toward the enemy or away from him. What in one situation might be considered as brave could on a different occasion turn out to be reckless or cowardly. No routine and no general policy can replace the brave soldier's reflection about which steps are concretely involved in acting bravely and in avoiding cowardice and recklessness. It is the task of prudence to establish the mean of virtue in the ever-changing circumstances of human life, by employing the appropriate means to a virtuous end.[28]

Prudence guides the stages of human action from the good intention to the actual performance of the deed in concert with three subordinate intellectual virtues. The ability to make good practical deliberations is due to *euboulia*, while the aptitude to make the correct practical judgment is owing to *synesis* (in ordinary matters) and *gnome* (in matters where ordinary guidelines must be overruled). Even more crucial than these steps, which as such could even remain theoretical considerations about action, is the application of the decision to a concrete action. Thus, the proper act of prudence, according to Aquinas, is to "command" (*praecipere, imperare*) oneself to put the decision into practice.[29]

Failure is possible at each of the stages of human action. For example, one can fail with regard to the end by seeking an evil end (cunning) or by seeking a good end in a selfish manner without concern for the common good.[30] Or one may fail with respect to deliberation, or the practical judgment that informs the decision or execution; each of these deficiencies constitutes a special kind of imprudence.[31] The moral virtues are crucial to avoid these shortcomings. Above all, the pursuit of good ends is the work of moral virtues, for they make it "connatural" to judge correctly about which specific ends are truly worth pursuing; thus for a just person, the idea of stealing or cheating has no appeal. The moral virtues furthermore temper the passions (such as excessive fear or intemperate desire) that might interfere with practical deliberation, the attainment of the practical judgment, or the "command" by which the decision is carried out.[32]

For Aquinas (as for Aristotle), the interconnection between prudence and the moral virtues implies that all genuine virtues are connected in such a way that one can only possess all moral virtues together with prudence, or none. This claim is not as implausible as it might appear at first sight. If one possesses a "virtue" independently of other virtues, it is only an approximation of virtue, not a true virtue. Moreover, prudence is a single intellectual habit that is required for each genuine moral virtue. For Aquinas, it is not the case that each moral virtue is perfected by its own prudence. Nothing could better illustrate the peculiaritiy of Aquinas's notion of prudence: as an indivisible principle of moral virtue, prudence informs all human action in view of the comprehensive human good. Any specific vice corrupts right reason in general, thereby destroying prudence not only with regard to the virtue in question, but also all the others. Thus, intemperance would sooner or later lead to injustice, as is clear in the case of adultery. In contrast, the other intellectual virtues can be instantiated separately, for they do not originate in a single principle. Thus, a good geometrician might be bad at metaphysics, or a good cabinetmaker might be a bad car mechanic.[33] Later authors, such as Duns Scotus and William of Ockham, rejected Aquinas's view, arguing that each moral virtue has its own distinct prudence.[34] Thus, prudence lost its eminent character as the intellectual virtue that concerns life as a whole. It became a habit that is instrumental to limited goals.

Aquinas admits, however, that prudence has some important limitations with respect to the moral life. For instance, while prudence allows one to find the means by which the moral virtues are implemented, it does not discover the ends to which these are ordered. Aquinas attributes this task to understanding, by which we grasp the first principles not only of speculative reason, but also of practical reason, such as "no evil is to be done" or "no one is to be harmed." Aquinas treats understanding of the first practical principles as synonymous with *synderesis*, the habit of the first principles of practical reason, which belong to the natural law. Like judgments of conscience, so also prudential decisions presuppose insight into the principles of natural law. In a manner that is foreign to Aristotle, Aquinas thus links prudence to the natural law.[35]

A further limitation of prudence, for Aquinas, lies in the fact that the ultimate end of human life consists in friendship with God. Charity, a supernatural habit infused by God, makes it possible to attain this supernatural end. Together with charity, other virtues are divinely infused, including infused prudence, which essentially differs from naturally acquired prudence. Infused prudence informs the infused moral virtues that in turn order the various aspects of life to God.[36] Yet even infused prudence is insufficient to guide decision-making in view of the ultimate end, for infused prudence or infused *euboulia* is limited to deliberations about things one can understand. In order to make the right decisions regarding things that are beyond human understanding, one needs the gift of counsel.[37]

NOTES

I wish to thank the Alexander von Humboldt Foundation for supporting me during my work on this article.

1. While there is abundant secondary literature on Aquinas's account of prudence, the other intellectual virtues have been given significantly less attention. For a general account, see Gregory M. Reichberg, "The Intellectual Virtues (Ia IIae, qq. 57–58)," in Stephen Pope, ed., *The Ethics of Aquinas* (Washington, D.C.: Georgetown University Press, 2002), 131–50.

2. *QDVCom* a.7, c. and ad 5; *ST* I-II, q.56, a.3; *ST* I-II, q.57, a.1.

3. *ST* II-II q.109 a.3; *ST* II-II q.166 a.2, resp. and ad 2; *ST* II-II q.167 a.1.

4. *ST* II-II q.47 a.4. See also *ST* I-II q.57 a.4; *ST* I-II q.58. a.3 ad 1; *ST* II-II q.181 a.2 ad 3; *QDVCard* a.1, ad 3.

5. *ST* I-II q.66 a.3; cf. *ST* I-II q.61 a.1 ad 3.

6. Cf. *ST* II-II prol. For Aquinas's understanding of the gifts of the Holy Spirit, see *ST* I-II q.68 a.1–2.

7. *In Meta* 1, lect.1, n.34, Thomas Aquinas, *Selected Writings*, trans. Ralph McInerny (London and New York: Penguin Books, 1998), 732 (emended translation). See also *QDVCom* a.12.

8. *Met.* 1.1–2.

9. *SCG* 1, cap.1; *ST* I q.1 a.6; *ST* I-II q.57 a.2; *ST* I-II q.62 a.2 ad 2; *ST* I-II q.68 a.1 ad 4; *ST* II-II q.45 a.1–2.

10. *ST* I-II q.66 a.5 resp. and ad 2; *In Meta* prol.; *ST* II-II q.182 a.1. For the eminent role of wisdom in Aquinas's ethics, see Thomas S. Hibbs, *Virtue's Splendor: Wisdom, Prudence and the Human Good* (New York: Fordham University Press, 2001).

11. *NE* 6.3.1139b31–32.

12. For Aquinas's appropriation of Aristotle's account of science, see John I. Jenkins, *Knowledge and Faith in Thomas Aquinas* (Cambridge: Cambridge University Press, 1997), 11–50. Jenkins summarizes the most important traits on pp. 37–39. Aquinas's discussions of the intellectual virtue of science in the *Summa theologiae* are brief; see *ST* I-II q.57 a.2 for the distinction between science, understanding, and wisdom; *ST* II-II q.9 a.1 ad 1 for the distinction between science as an intellectual virtue and as a gift of the Holy Spirit.

13. *In PA* 1, lect.44, n.397. See also *ST* I-II q.57 a.2; *ST* II-II q.8 a.1; *In NE* 6, lect.5, n.1179.

14. See, e.g., *ST* I q.2 a.1; *ST* I-II q.94 a.2. The most comprehensive treatment is found in Luca Tuninetti, *"Per se notum": Die logische Beschaffenheit des Selbstverständlichen im Denken des Thomas von Aquin* (Leiden: Brill, 1996).

15. *Super Sent* 3, d.23, q.1, a.4, qc.1, ad 4; *ST* I-II q.57 a.3 ad 3. See also *In BDT* 3, q.5, a.1, ad 3.

16. *NE* 6.4.1140a10.

17. Cf. *NE* 6.13.1144b27–28.

18. *ST* I-II q.57 a.4; see also n. 7 above. Cf. Aristotle, *Met.* 9.8.1050a30–b2.

19. *ST* I-II q.57 a.3; *ST* I-II q.57 a.5 ad 1; *In NE* 6, lect.4, n.1167.

20. *ST* I-II q.57 a.3 ad 2; *ST* I-II q.57 a.4; *In NE* 6, lect.4, n.1172.

21. See, e.g., *Grundlegung zur Metaphysik der Sitten*, Akademie Ausgabe, vol. 4, 402 and 442.

22. An excellent commentary on Aquinas's account of prudence, originally published in the late 1940s, can be found in Saint Thomas d'Aquin, *La Prudence: 2^{a}–2^{ae}, Questions 47–56*, trans., notes, and appendices by Thomas Deman, 3d ed. (Paris: Cerf, 2006). A perceptive more recent study is Daniel Westberg, *Right Practical Reason: Aristotle, Action, and Prudence in Aquinas* (Oxford: Clarendon Press, 1994).

23. *ST* II-II q.47 a.2.

24. *ST* II-II q.47 a.1 ad 3; *ST* II-II q.47 a.3.

25. *ST* II-II q.49. Aquinas appropriates these traits of prudence from Stoic and Neoplatonic authors.

26. For the inadequacy of substituting someone else's advice for one's own prudent reflection, see *ST* I-II q.57 a.5 ad 2 and *In NE* 6, lect.11, n.1284. For teachableness in a good sense (*docilitas*), see *ST* II-II q.49 a.3. For the need of prudence in following the laws, see *ST* II-II q.47 a.12 and *ST* II-II q.50 a.2.

27. *ST* I-II q.12–17. For Aquinas's explanation of the process of human action, see Westberg, *Right Practical Reason*, 119–83.

28. *ST* II-II q.47 a.6–7.

29. *ST* I-II q.57 a.6; *ST* II-II q.47 a.8; *ST* II-II q.51.

30. *ST* I-II q.57 a.4; *ST* II-II q.55 a.3; *ST* II-II q.47 a.10.

31. *ST* II-II q.53–54; for a schematic overview of the different vices of imprudence, see *ST* II-II q.53 a.2.

32. *ST* I-II q.58 a.5 resp. and ad 3.

33. *ST* I-II q.65 a.1; *QDVCard* a.2, especially ad 4 and ad 8; *In NE* 6, lect.11, nn.1286–88. See also *ST* I-II q.60 a.1 ad 1. For the plausibility of Aquinas's account, see Jean Porter, "The Unity of the Virtues and the Ambiguity of Goodness: A Reappraisal of Aquinas's Theory of the Virtuous," *Journal of Religious Ethics* 21 (1993): 137–63.

34. See Duns Scotus, *Ordinatio* 3, d.36, nn.72–100, Vatican Edition, vol. 10 (Vatican City: Typis Vaticanis, 2007), 249–61; William of Ockham, *Quaestiones variae*, q.7, a.3, Opera Theologica, vol. 8 (St. Bonaventure, N.Y.: St. Bonaventure University, 1984), 362–74.

35. *ST* I-II q.58 a.4–5; *ST* II-II q.47 a.6 resp., ad 1, and ad 3; *ST* II-II q.49 a.2 ad 1. For the relation between prudence and the natural law, see Hibbs, *Virtue's Splendor*, 88–119.

36. *ST* I-II q.65 a.2; *QDVCard* a.2.

37. *ST* II-II q.52 a.1 resp. and ad 1.

CHAPTER 25

THE RELATION OF REASON TO FAITH

BRUNO NIEDERBACHER, S.J.

How does Aquinas conceive of the relation between reason and faith? In order to answer this question I will first briefly summarize Aquinas's account of faith. Then I will identify and assess the different ways in which Aquinas believes that faith and reason are related.

Aquinas's Conception of Faith

By "faith" (*fides*), Aquinas usually means Christian faith. He is aware that "Christian faith" can be used to mean several different albeit related things: the object of faith, the interior and the exterior act of assenting to the object of faith, and the virtue of faith that enables one to assent properly to the object of faith.[1]

The Object of Faith

In Aquinas's view the object of faith is God as the first truth[2] and the last end of human longing.[3] Thus, the object of faith is related to both, intellect (truth) and rational appetite (last end). How intellect and rational appetite (will) are related can be made understandable in the following way. In order to pursue an end one needs some cognition[4] of the end. One needs to grasp what the end consists in, that it is available and how one can attain it.[5] Human beings naturally long for happiness as their last end. But they do not naturally know what happiness consists in and whether it is available. True cognition of this is offered by God's revealing himself to human beings as the fulfillment of their life.

Aquinas sharpens this characterization of the proper object of faith in two ways: first, by taking into account the special conditions of the human cognizer in this life. Human beings cognize things, even simple things like God, in a propositional way.[6] *Via* the propositions believed, they get into contact with the things.[7] Second, Aquinas sharpens the account of the object of faith from an epistemological point of view. What can be demonstrated about God does not—strictly speaking—belong to the object of faith. Only those truths belong to the object of faith that are believed on God's authority.[8] Aquinas calls such truths "*credibles*." Putting the things said together, I suggest the following definition of a credible proposition:

A proposition p is a credible proposition (short: p_c) if and only if

(i) p is true;
(ii) p is revealed by God;
(iii) p is assented to because p is revealed by God;
(iv) p presents truths about God and created things insofar as they are necessary and sufficient for orienting the life of human beings toward their last end.

The Interior and the Exterior Act of Assenting to the Object of Faith

The interior act of faith is a human person's act of assenting to p_c. Aquinas explores the kind of the act involved by doing two things: first, he tries to situate the kind of assent involved in the act of faith by comparing it to other acts of assent to propositions.[9] Regarding the firmness of assent, the act of faith is similar to insight and science. Regarding the way the assent is brought about, the act of faith is rather similar to opinion and conjecture. Their objects do not by themselves sufficiently move the intellect to assent to them. One does not see that they are true. An act of will is required. In Aquinas's words: "The act of believing [*credere*] itself is an act of the intellect assenting to the divine truth at the command of the will that is moved by God through grace."[10] Thus, the act of faith is a cognition action.[11] Second, Aquinas distinguishes three aspects of the *one* interior act of faith with the aid of the traditional formula *to believe that God* (*credere Deum*), *to believe God* (*credere Deo*), *to believe in God* (*credere in Deum*).[12]

(i) The first part of the formula focuses on what is believed, on the content of faith; in short: S assents that p_c.
(ii) The second part focuses on the reason for assenting. A person assents that p_c on God's say-so: because God reveals—directly or mediated through other persons—that p_c. This part of the formula captures the trust aspect

of the act of faith. Putting (i) and (ii) together, one could say: *S* believes God that p_c.[13]

(iii) The third part of the formula focuses on the relation of the object of faith to the will, the rational appetite of the believer. The propositions of faith represent the good believers are lovingly longing for as the fulfillment of their life. This part of the formula captures the existential aspect of the act of faith. What one believes matters heavily for the orientation of one's life as a whole.

With "faith" can be meant the *exterior act* of faith, that is: the speech act of confessing to believe the Christian content.

The Virtue of Faith

Primarily, however, Aquinas means with "faith" the *virtue* of faith, which he defines as "a habit of the mind whereby eternal life is begun in us, making the intellect assent to what is not apparent."[14] Faith belongs with hope and charity to the theological virtues. They are called theological virtues because they have God as their object, because they are infused in us all at once by God alone, and because they are made known only by divine revelation in the Holy Scripture.[15] On the one hand, faith is the first of the theological virtues insofar as one is able to hope for and to love something only if one has some cognition of it. Faith is the cognitive element in Christian life. On the other hand, virtuous acts of faith require that they are motivated—"formed"—by charity.[16] Formless faith leads, like formed faith, to acts of the structure: *S* believes God that p_c. However, acts of formless faith are not virtuous because the assent is not brought about by a will that loves and trusts God but by some other motive.[17] Virtuous faith, then, is an infused habit that enables human beings to believe God out of love that p_c.[18]

The Relations of Reason to Faith

With this sketchy exposition of Aquinas's account of faith, I can now turn to the question of how reason relates to faith.

What Human Beings Cognize by the Virtue of Faith is Above but not Against Reason

In the context of epistemology Aquinas usually means with "reason"—*ratio*—in its wide sense capacities and acts of *natural* human cognition. Natural human cognition starts by sense perception and, through processes of abstraction, ends up by grasping the essences of things. In a narrower sense, "reason" means cognitive acts of drawing conclusions from premises or finding premises for conclusions.

Aquinas claims that human beings are not able to cognize p_c by such acts of reason. Nevertheless, he insists that what human beings cognize by natural reason and what they cognize by faith is consistent with each other. He says: "Although the truth of Christian faith exceeds the capacity of human reason, nevertheless what reason is naturally endowed with cannot be contrary to that truth."[19] This optimistic claim follows from the conviction that God is the origin of both human nature and revelation.

There can be a Science that Deals with Faith

With many other theologians of the thirteenth century, Aquinas claims that sacred doctrine is a science (*scientia*). Thus, he thinks that the content of faith can fulfill the highest rationality conditions as Aristotle developed them in the *Posterior Analytics*. The main obstacle for treating the content of faith within science is the problem of the principles. Sciences proceed from principles that are self-evident. The propositions of faith, however, are not self-evident and cannot be inferred from principles that are self-evident. In order to deal with this problem, Aquinas utilizes the distinction between propositions that are self-evident in themselves and as such known to all cognizers and propositions that are self-evident in themselves and as such not known to all cognizers. He uses this distinction in two different solutions. In a first solution Aquinas bites the bullet and claims that the propositions of faith are self-evident, but only for those who have the infused *virtue* of faith. Thus, he claims that for virtuous Christian believers the propositions of faith have the same epistemic status as the principles that are naturally known.[20] This solution however is problematic. If the propositions of faith were self-evident for those having the virtue of faith, no act of will would be required for assent. This contradicts Aquinas's analysis of faith. Moreover, even Christian believers will not say that the proposition that God is triune in nature is self-evident for them. Aquinas does not mention this solution in his later writings.[21] His famous second solution draws on the model of two related sciences that are hierarchically ordered. The one science has among its starting points what is proved by the other. Applied to our topic: the propositions of faith are self-evident only for God and the blessed. God sees the truth, and through revelation humans on earth come to believe what God sees. In Aquinas's words:

> And in this way sacred doctrine is a science because it proceeds from principles known by the light of a higher science, namely, the science of God and the blessed. Hence, just as music believes the principles taught it by the arithmetician, so sacred doctrine believes the principles revealed to it by God.[22]

This is a congenial solution. For now Aquinas has both: theology is a science in the Aristotelian sense, and nevertheless, the principles of this science are the articles that Christians accept in faith. These principles cannot be demonstrated by human beings. But they can be defended. Thus, Aquinas claims, that one should be able to show that these principles of faith are not impossible, that they do not contradict what is self-evident or demonstrable, that defeaters can be defeated, that one can draw conclusions from the principles in a deductive way.[23]

These are rationality requirements that Aquinas thinks theologians should be able to fulfill. But surely he did not think that normal Christians have to do all this theological work in order to be rational believers. Thus, the question arises as to the rationality of faith itself.

The Deliverances of Faith are Rational

It is rational to believe on the basis of divine testimony

The first and most obvious aspect of reason in Aquinas's account of faith is that one believes on the basis of divine testimony. Aquinas writes:

> The reason why the will is inclined to assent to what it does not see is because God says it, just as a human being concerning things he does not see believes the testimony of a good man who sees what he himself does not see.[24]

Aquinas alludes to dialectics where the epistemic source from authority (*locus ab auctoritate*) is assumed.[25] He says that although the argument from human authority is the weakest, the argument from divine authority is the most efficient.[26] This is understandable. For the human authority might err or lie, and the believer might be mistaken in taking somebody to be an authority. But, in the case of divine authority, deficiencies of the first kind are excluded. The omniscient and supreme good God cannot err or lie.[27] Thus, we have the claim: if God communicates to *S* that p_c, then S is in the highest degree justified in believing that p_c. However, believing God that p_c presupposes at least believing that

(i) God exists;
(ii) what God communicates is p_c.

These two beliefs cannot themselves be part of p_c. There must be independent sources of belief formation and justification for these two beliefs.

Aquinas thinks that (i) can be demonstrated by a demonstration *that*. The Five Ways are instances of such demonstrative proofs. But many will not be able to produce such demonstrative proofs. An alternative to strict demonstrations is Aquinas's idea that human beings produce by natural reason simple cosmological-style arguments. They observe order in the universe and form the belief that there must be an orderer.[28] Moreover, Aquinas thinks that there is evidence for (ii). Some speak of "credibility arguments," a collection of which is contained in the *Summa contra Gentiles*. Aquinas argues that believers of the Christian content do not believe lightly, for God confirms the things that exceed natural cognition by showing "visible works which surpass the power of the whole of nature."[29] Among these works, Aquinas quotes: wondrous healing of the sick, raising of the dead, alteration of movable celestial bodies, inspiration of human minds, such that uneducated people attain in an instant highest wisdom and eloquence, the conversion of many, simple and wise, to Christian faith, not by violence of arms, not through the promise of sensual delights but amid the tyranny of persecutions, and the fulfillment of the oracles of the prophets.

No doubt, Aquinas thinks that arguments for the existence of God and credibility arguments are available. But does he think that such arguments are necessary for rational assent to the propositions of faith? His writings hint in two directions. Some passages suggest the answer "yes."

> That God exists and other like things, that can be known about God by natural reason, as it is said, are not articles of faith, but preambles to the articles. For faith presupposes natural cognition, just as grace nature, and perfection something that can be perfected.[30]

In another passage Aquinas gives the impression that the act of faith includes having credibility arguments. To the objection that accuses believers of being gullible he responds:

> The believer has sufficient evidence for believing, for he is induced by the authority of the divine doctrine confirmed by miracles, and, what is more, by the inward instinct of the inviting God: hence he does not believe lightly. He has not, however, sufficient evidence for scientific knowledge, hence the ground for the merit is not lost.[31]

To be sure, Aquinas does not think that the evidence by miracles is sufficient for assenting, "for of those who see the same miracle, or who hear the same sermon, some believe, and some do not."[32] Nevertheless, miracles confirming the authority of divine doctrine seem to play an evidential role.

On the other hand, there are also passages indicating that Aquinas holds that arguments for the existence of God and credibility are not necessary for rational assent to the propositions of faith. First, he insists that it is possible and safer to believe on faith even the propositions about God that can naturally be known.[33] Second, he comments on the passage of the gospel according to John 4, where the woman comes to believe in Jesus as the Messiah. The woman tells the people of her village about Jesus. At the end the people of the village come to believe in Jesus and they say to the woman:[34] "We no longer believe because of your word; for we have heard for ourselves, and we know that this is truly the saviour of the world." Aquinas comments:

> Faith is proper if one obeys the truth not because of something else but because of the truth itself. And thus [the evangelist] says that they say to the women, that "we now believe" the truth [veritati] "not because of your speech" but because of the truth itself. For three things lead us to the faith of Christ: first, natural reason [...]; second the testimonies of the Law and the Prophets [...]; third, the sermon of the Apostles and others. But when somebody, who is

> guided by this, believes, then one can say that he does believe because of none of them: not because of natural reason, not because of the testimonies of the Law, not because of the sermon of others, but alone because of the truth itself; Gen 15.6: Abraham believed God, and this was credited to him as righteousness.[35]

The first question that arises is whether this passage can be reconciled with the others. I think the passages can be reconciled by interpreting the presuppositions as *preparatory* for faith. But they would not themselves be part of faith. They would be neither necessary nor sufficient for the rationality of the assent to the propositions of faith. Some believers could quote such arguments when asked. But they would not believe *because* of these arguments.

The second question is whether faith that is independent of such arguments or reasons can be rational. For Aquinas, faith is a habit of belief formation, which is together with hope and charity infused by God, designed to get the truth in order to find orientation in one's life toward the last end one is longing for: beatitude. Faith is a cognitive habit *sui generis* that cannot be reduced to other habits of belief formation like intellect, science, or wisdom. This view of faith can be and has been interpreted as a version of epistemological externalism.[36] One's assent to the propositions of faith is epistemically justified by being the outcome of the cognitive habit called faith. Moreover, there are passages that suggest that such beliefs are basic: first, Aquinas compares them with principles. Principles are basic, not inferred, not believed on the evidential basis of other beliefs. Second, when Aquinas deals with the gifts of the Holy Spirit that belong to faith, namely *insight* and *science*, he stresses the nondiscursive character of both these gifts.[37]

However, I said above that believing God that p_c presupposes some other beliefs that cannot themselves be part of p_c, for example, God exists, what God communicates is p_c. These propositions can be inferentially justified. But if Aquinas thinks that even such propositions can be believed on faith, he must have in mind a different, wider, meaning of "faith," perhaps in the sense of taking something to be true without arguments. One suggestion to understand this would be the following: if my mother tells me something I do, of course, not believe her that she exists and that she is communicating something to me. But I do not believe these propositions on evidential grounds either. I just believe them in the basic way. Similarly, if somebody experiences that God speaks to him, he does not believe God that God exists and that God is communicating something to him. But he need not believe these propositions on evidential grounds either. They could be believed in the basic way.

It is rational to believe in the existence of the complete good that attracts the will

The second aspect of reason can be found in the role the will plays in assenting to the propositions of faith. Aquinas writes:

> Sometimes the intellect can be determined to one side of a pair of contradictory propositions neither immediately through the definition of the terms, as is the

> case with principles, nor in virtue of principles, as is the case with demonstrative conclusions; it is rather determined by the will, that elects to assent to one side in a determinate and precise way because of something that is sufficient to move the will but not to move the intellect, namely, since it seems good or convenient to assent to this side. And this is the disposition of the believer, as when somebody believes what another says because it seems fitting or useful to do so. And in the same way also we are moved to believe to what is said insofar the prize of eternal life is promised to us, if we believe. And this prize moves the will to assent to the things said although the intellect is not moved by something that is seen.[38]

This sounds like Pascal's wager. Assent on epistemic considerations alone cannot be brought about. But on practical considerations it can. One is *practically* rational and justified if one assents to the propositions of faith. I doubt, however, that Aquinas understood the passage this way. He would probably deny that such calculated belief is meritorious.

The question is whether the role that the will plays in assent entails also aspects of *epistemic* rationality. I know of two interpretations that suggest this. A first approach can be developed from Aquinas's moral philosophy. In a virtuous human being there is a sort of connaturality between the appetite and real goods. Because of this connaturality the will is attracted by real goods.[39] A judgment that follows such attraction is justified. Similarly, the believer's will is formed by the virtue of charity that is infused by God. Thus, there is a connaturality between the will and the supreme good. Because of this connaturality, the will is attracted by the supreme good presented in the propositions of faith.[40] And assent to the propositions of faith that follows such attraction would be justified. A second approach can be developed from Aquinas's metaphysics according to which the terms "being" and "goodness" are extensionally equivalent: where there is being there is also goodness and where there is goodness there is also being. Limited goodness has some kind of being, but it does not necessarily exist. Thus, if somebody is attracted by the imagination of some limited good one would not be justified to believe that the good actually exists. This is different in the case of perfect being. For what is perfect in being exists necessarily. If somebody is attracted by a perfect good, then one is justified to believe in the existence of this good.[41] From the point of view of contemporary epistemology, both approaches are externalist.

Conclusion

Thomas Aquinas thinks that faith is a virtue. Anthony Kenny, however, writes

> that faith is not, as theologians have claimed, a virtue, but a vice, unless a number of conditions can be fulfilled. One of them is that the existence of God can be rationally justified outside faith. Secondly, whatever are the historical events which are pointed to as constituting the divine revelation must be independently

> established as historically certain with the degree of commitment which one can have in the pieces of historical knowledge of the kind I have mentioned.[42]

Aquinas does not deny that both kinds of arguments can be produced. He seems however to deny that a Christian must have such arguments in order to believe rationally and meritoriously. The virtue of faith alone is necessary and sufficient. Is he right? If faith is a God-given habit, designed to get the truth in matters of God, our last end and the way to achieve it, then the belief resulting from such a habit is justified indeed. If a person's will is heightened by the grace of God and, through being attracted by the supreme good presented in the propositions of faith, influences the intellect to assent, then such assent is justified indeed. The question is: Does the Christian need some justification for the belief that the antecedents are true? In a world without doubts regarding the reliability of faith and without irritations regarding the truth of its output, I think, the answer is: probably not. But we do not live in such a world. In our world where people have very different religious beliefs, I think, some arguments are required: not only in order to defeat the defeaters of one's belief but also in order to sustain belief in the antecedent. Thus, I think that pure epistemological externalism concerning the justification of religious beliefs is not satisfying. This, however, does not mean that every Christian must be intellectually trained. I would like to bring in the old idea of the division of epistemic labor. In other areas, for example, in physics, biology, astronomy, lay people are justified in holding particular beliefs without being in a position to understand the details and to know what speaks in favor of them. They are justified by relying on the experts who are in a position to know the details and the evidence. Similarly, simple religious believers are justified in holding their religious belief without being in a position to understand the details and to have arguments and defeaters against defeaters. They are justified by relying on the experts who do have some arguments. Thus, Aquinas might be right when he claims at the beginning of the *Summa Theologiae* that sacred doctrine in the sense of theology is necessary—even if he intends his argument there to answer a quite different problem.[43]

NOTES

1. Aquinas mentions this distinction in *ST* I–II q.55 a.1 ad 1. Moreover, he construes his treatise on the virtue of faith according to this distinction.

2. *ST* II-II q.1 a.1.

3. *ST* II-II q.1 a.8: "Those things belong per se to faith the vision of which we shall enjoy in eternal life and by which we are lead to eternal life"; *ST* II-II q.2 a.2: "For the first truth refers to will insofar as it has the aspect of an end"; *ST* II-II q.2 a.5: "One must therefore say that the object of faith per se is that by which a human being is made happy."

4. "Cognition" is the translation of the Latin word *cognitio*, which is the broadest concept under which all cognitive acts (understanding, knowledge, opinion, conjecture,

etc.) can be subsumed. In this sense I will also use the rather unfamiliar words "cognizer" and "to cognize."

5. *ST* I q.1 a.1: "But the end must first be cognized by human beings who are to direct their intentions and actions to the end." See also *ST* I-II q.6 a.2.

6. *ST* II-II q.1 a.2: Aquinas here says that on the part of the believer the object of faith is "aliquid complexum per modum enuntiabilis," something complex by way of a proposition. Note that "enuntiatio" is the translation of the Greek "apophansis," Aristotle's central term in *Peri hermeneias*. What is meant by this term is that kind of speech that has the property of being either true or false.

7. In *ST* II-II q.1 a.2 ad 2, Aquinas deals with the problem that in the creed we say "I believe in God almighty" and not "I believe that God is almighty." Thus, the objection runs, the object of faith is the thing itself—God—not a proposition. Aquinas solves the objection by saying that the act of the believer does not terminate in a proposition but in the thing. By forming propositions, we cognize the things.

8. *ST* II-II q.1 a.1: "For the faith of which we are speaking does not assent to anything, except because it is revealed by God. Hence faith proceeds from the divine truth itself like a middle term."

9. *ST* II-II q.1 a.4; *ST* II-II q.2 a.1; *ST* II-II q.4 a.1; *QDV*, q.14, a.1; *In Heb*, c.12, l.1.

10. *ST* II-II q.2 a.9. See also *ST* II-II q.1 a.4 and *ST* II-II q.2 a.1 ad 3. This translation, as well as all the other translations from Aquinas in this article, is my own.

11. Thus, Aquinas is committed to a version of cognitive voluntarism. Whether cognitive voluntarism is tenable is a much disputed issue that I cannot deal with here properly. In my view Aquinas does not hold an extreme cognitive voluntarism but a modest form of it. In Aquinas's view, first, one has voluntary control over belief formation only *vis à vis* some classes of cognitive objects. Second, having voluntary control over belief formation does not require that one has no evidence whatsoever for the truth of the target proposition. Who forms an opinion or a suspicion is not without evidence. Third, habits that we acquire voluntarily over a long period of time play a role. They influence the way we choose and ponder arguments pro and con; they influence how compelling arguments appear to us. For a detailed discussion, see Claudia Eisen Murphy, "Aquinas on Voluntary Belief," *American Philosophical Quarterly* 74:4 (2000): 569–97; Bruno Niederbacher, *Glaube als Tugend bei Thomas von Aquin: Erkenntistheoretische und religionsphilosophische Interpretationen* (Stuttgart: Kohlhammer, 2003), 60–66; Eleonore Stump, *Aquinas* (London and New York: Routledge, 2003), 342–49.

12. *ST* II-II q.2 a.2.

13. Aquinas is aware that revelation comes to most people via mediators such as parents, preachers of faith, etc. Nevertheless, he thinks that the true believer believes human beings insofar as God is speaking through them. See *Super Sent* III, d.23, q.2, a.2, qc.2, ad 3: "The believer believes a human being not insofar he is a human being but insofar as God speaks in him."

14. *ST* II-II q.4 a.1.

15. *ST* I-II q.62 a.1.

16. *ST* II-II q.4 a.3.

17. Cf. *QDV*, q.14, a.2, ad 10; *QDV*, q.14, a.7; *ST* I-II q.65 a.4.

18. *Super Sent* III, d.23, q.2, a.2, qc.2, ad 4.

19. *SCG* 1, 7.

20. *Super Sent* I, Prologus, q.1, a.3, qc.2, ad 2.

21. In *ST* II-II q.1 a.4 ad 2 and ad 3, Aquinas mentions ways in which the believer can be said to "see." But these ways are not meant in the strict sense of insight into the truth of

the propositions of faith but rather in the sense of seeing that the propositions of faith ought to be believed.

22. *ST* I q.1 a.2. The subalternation-idea is also to be found in some editions of *Super Sent* I, Prologus, q.1, a.3, qc.2. For text-critical details, see Johannes Beumer, "Ein nicht-authentischer Text im Prolog zum Sentenzenkommentar des hl. Thomas von Aquin (q.1.a.3.sol.2)," *Scholastik* 33 (1958): 247–52; Marie-Dominique Chenu, *La Théologie comme science au XIIIe siècle*, 3d ed. (Paris: Vrin, 1957); Bruno Niederbacher, "Erläuterungen des Prologs zum Sentenzenkommentar des Thomas von Aquin," in Bruno Niederbacher and Gerhard Leibold, eds., *Theologie als Wissenschaft im Mittelalter: Texte, Übersetzungen, Kommentare* (Münster: Aschendorff, 2006), 277.

23. I collect these rationality-requirements from: *Super Sent* I, Prologus, q.1, a.3, qc.2, ad 2; *ST* I q.1 a.8.

24. *Super Sent* III, d.23, q.2, a.2, qc.2. Cf. *ST* II-II q.2 a.2.

25. *QDV*, q.14, a.2, ad 9.

26. See *ST* I q.1 a.8 ad 2. For a precise analysis, see Niederbacher, *Glaube als Tugend bei Thomas von Aquin*, 67–81.

27. *ST* II-II q.2 a.4; *ST* II-II q.4 a.8 ad 2.

28. See *SCG* 3, 38.

29. *SCG* 1, 6.

30. *ST* I q.2 a.2 ad 1.

31. *ST* II-II q.2 a.9 ad 3; see also *ST* II-II q.2 a.1 ad 1; *ST* II-II q.1 a.4 ad 2.

32. *ST* II-II q.6 a.1.

33. *ST* II-II q.2 a.4; *ST* I q.2 a.2 ad 1.

34. In Aquinas's view, and according to the tradition, the woman symbolizes human reason. See *ST* II-II q.2 a.10. Cf. William of Auxerre, *Summa aurea*, liber 1, prologus.

35. *In John*, c.4, l.5. Cf. *ST* II-II q.27 a.3 ad 2.

36. John I. Jenkins, *Knowledge and Faith in Thomas Aquinas* (Cambridge: Cambridge University Press, 1997) has developed an interpretation along externalist lines, as well as Alvin Plantinga, "Warranted Christian Belief: The Aquinas/Calvin Model," in Godehard Brüntrup and Ronald C. Tacelli, eds., *The Rationality of Theism* (Dordrecht: Kluwer Academic Publishers, 1999), 125–43; and Alvin Plantinga, *Warranted Christian Belief* (New York: Oxford University Press, 2000). See also James R. Brent, "The Epistemic Status of Christian Beliefs in Thomas Aquinas" (Ph.D. diss., Saint Louis University, 2008).

37. See *ST* II-II q.8 a.1; *ST* II-II q.8 a.5 ad 3; *ST* II-II q.9 a.1 ad 1. These gifts of the Holy Spirit are not to be confused with the intellectual virtues of the same name.

38. *QDV*, q.14, a.1.

39. See *ST* I-II q.62 a.3.

40. Cf. *ST* II-II q.45 a.2. For details of this interpretation, see Niederbacher, *Glaube als Tugend bei Thomas von Aquin*, 137–41, and Brent, "The Epistemic Status of Christian Beliefs in Thomas Aquinas," ch. 5.

41. This line of argument is developed in detail by Eleonore Stump, "Faith and Goodness," in Godfrey Vesey, ed., *The Philosophy in Christianity* (Cambridge: Cambridge University Press, 1989), 167–91.

42. Anthony Kenny, *What is Faith? Essays in the Philosophy of Religion* (Oxford: Oxford University Press, 1992), 57.

43. *ST* I q.1 a.1.

CHAPTER 26

PHILOSOPHY OF MIND AND HUMAN NATURE

ROBERT PASNAU

Biological or Theological

A theory of human nature must consider from the start whether it sees human beings in fundamentally biological terms, as animals like other animals, or else in fundamentally supernatural terms, as creatures of God who are like God in some special way, and so importantly unlike other animals. Many of the perennial philosophical disputes have proved so intractable in part because their adherents divide along these lines. The friends of materialism, seeing human beings as just a particularly complex example of the sort of complex organic structure found everywhere on Earth, suppose that we are ultimately constituted out of just the same material from which squirrels and rabbits are made. The friends of dualism, instead, think that such a story can hardly do justice to what is special about human nature. Likewise, the friends of a libertarian, robustly nondeterministic conception of free will see something special in human spontaneity and moral responsibility. To their opponents, human beings operate on the same principles, albeit more complex, as do squid and plankton.

These and other such disputes need not divide along religious lines. One may oppose naturalism without embracing a supernatural theistic perspective; one might, for instance, think it simply a matter of fact that human beings are fundamentally unlike other biological organisms, but yet not suppose we are made that way by any higher power. Conversely, the theist may think it part of the divine plan to have made human beings as nothing more than the most complex of biological organisms, constituted out of the same stuff and constrained by the same laws. So although the choice I have described between two perspectives—biological and naturalistic versus theological and supernatural—captures an important fault line that runs through the debate over human nature, it by no means determines all of one's subsequent philosophical choices.

The philosophy of Thomas Aquinas exemplifies the sorts of tensions that arise from these two perspectives. For while the overall orientation of Aquinas's work is, of course, profoundly theistic, he nevertheless harbors a certain sympathy for a naturalistic, biological understanding of human nature. In some cases, as in his account of the human intellect, the supernaturalist slant clearly wins out. In other cases, as in his conception of human beings as a soul–body union, it is equally clear that biological considerations are paramount. In still other cases, as for instance his views on free will, it is very difficult to say which line of thought holds sway, and the preference of interpreters for one reading or another seems largely governed by their own predilections.

The traditional way of making this point about Aquinas is to describe him as mediating between the theological teachings of the Church and the philosophical writings of Aristotle. Historically, this is an apt place to begin thinking about Aquinas's philosophy, because there is no doubt that the central philosophical challenge Aquinas faced over the course of his career was to find a place for the newly recovered work of Aristotle within the overriding framework of Christian belief.[1] To find a place for Aristotle, however, means finding a place for a conception of human nature that is decidedly biological in its overall orientation. This is clear from the fundamental Aristotelian text on human nature, the *De anima*, which as it happens was the subject of the first and most careful of Aquinas's many Aristotelian commentaries. For us, the notion of a soul (*anima*) has become firmly associated with a supernatural perspective on human nature. But for Aristotle the term "soul" has not the slightest of nonnaturalistic implications. On the contrary, a soul is something that all living things possess, from human beings down to the simplest of life forms, and indeed the *De anima* is not so much a study of human nature as it is the foundational treatise in Aristotle's long sequence of biological works.

The project of reconciling Aristotle and Christianity, however, important as it is to understanding Aquinas's historical situation, does not fit the natural–supernatural distinction as neatly as one might expect. For even if the Aristotelian notion of soul is fundamentally biological, the *De anima* nevertheless seems to treat the capacity for thought—the intellect—as quite a special feature of human nature and, indeed, as "immortal and eternal."[2] As we will see, these few brief, notoriously obscure remarks supply a bridgehead from Aristotle's naturalistic biology to Christian soteriology. There is movement in the other direction as well. For even while there are tendencies in Christian thought toward treating the body in Platonic fashion, as a temporary prison of the soul, there is also the doctrine of the resurrection, according to which the separation of body and soul at death is a temporary state of affairs, to be remedied by the body's ultimate restoration, for all of eternity, at the time of the Final Judgment. As we will see, Aquinas understands the resurrection as pointing toward the fundamentally biological character of human nature, in the sense that human beings are, essentially, not just souls but incarnate souls. Although it is certainly the case that Aquinas regards the most important human attributes—our intellectual and volitional powers—as arising from the side of the soul rather than body, he is nevertheless adamant that a full understanding of human nature requires understanding our bodily nature as well. God did create purely spiritual beings, the angels, who are nothing more than disembodied minds, but that is not what we are. We are, essentially, mind–body composites. So to understand human nature, one must study not just our mental capacities, intellect and will, but also the human body. Hence, the task is partly biological, but not wholly so.

The Human Soul

The most concise and authoritative statement of Aquinas's theory of human nature comes in questions 75–89 of the first part of the *Summa theologiae*, known as the *Treatise on Human Nature.*[3] That discussion begins with a very quick argument for the twin theses that human beings have a soul, and that this soul is not a body. These look like giant, contentious claims to come so quickly at the start, but Aquinas is quick here for a reason: one of the claims is simply a matter of terminological stipulation, and the other is such a large question that it can scarcely be adjudicated within the context of a discussion of human nature. What is supposed to be true by stipulation is that human beings have a soul. Following Aristotle, Aquinas holds that "the soul is said to be the first principle of life in the things that are alive around us."[4] This means that "soul" is simply a convenient catchphrase for the sort of thing that biologists investigate to this day—the fundamental ("first") explanation ("principle") of life in the natural world. If Aquinas were here assuming that there is just one kind of explanation shared by all living things, or even that within a single thing there is just one fundamental explanatory principle, then he would be saying something controversial. But these are further issues that, as we will see, he takes up later. For now we have just the stipulation that "soul" will be used not in any sort of speculative, supernatural sense, but in the down-to-earth biological sense recommended by Aristotle.

Too large to be treated adequately within a theory of human nature is the further thesis that the human soul is not a body. This is not the claim it is likely to seem at first glance. Aquinas is not supposing from the start the truth of dualism in its popular, bastardized form—the idea that the soul is not made of material, corporeal stuff, and so must be made of some other, more ethereal stuff. This is a thesis that medieval authors entertained, but they did so with regard to the celestial realm. Like all of his contemporaries, Aquinas took the heavens to be made of an imperishable sort of stuff utterly unlike the stuff in our familiar material realm—not composed of any of the four elements, then, but of some kind of quintessence. This is an idea that has tempted cosmologists ever since Aristotle, holding sway until

Galileo in the seventeenth century, then going out of fashion, and now coming back into fashion with our modern talk of dark matter. As far as our own natures are concerned, however, it has never seemed very credible on serious reflection to suppose that we are composed of some sort of dark stuff of our own, imperceptible but yet constituting our essence. This way of understanding dualism, indeed, is one that only an opponent of the theory is likely to find very appealing. Historically, the advocate of dualism has generally wanted to say that what makes human beings special is not that we contain some special, ghostly stuff, but that our nature is partially constituted by something that is not stuff at all, but is an entirely different kind of explanatory principle. In the Aristotelian tradition, this principle is known as a *form*.

Aquinas's fundamental thesis about human nature, then, is that we are not just bodies, but bodies animated by a certain kind of form, a soul. This is, however, not a result that is specific to human beings; it is instead an instance of Aquinas's general embrace of Aristotle's hylomorphic metaphysics—that is, the thesis that corporeal substances in general are form–matter composites. Matter by itself—"prime matter"—cannot exist at all without form: "in itself it can never exist, because given that by its nature it has no form, it has no actual existence, since actual existence comes only through form, whereas it is solely in potentiality."[5] On this understanding of the hylomorphic framework, everything that exists has form. So the fact that human nature consists not just of a body, but of an *informed* body, is just an application of a broader metaphysical thesis. And, as we have seen, to call this form a soul is simply an application of the stipulative point that, in the case of living things, that which fundamentally makes them be alive is what will get called their soul. Hence, all things have forms. And all living things have souls.

Nothing could be more important to an overall evaluation of Aquinas's theory of human nature than a just appraisal of its background hylomorphism. Considered most broadly, the appeal to form represents a rejection of the reductive approach of much of early ancient philosophy. The main line of pre-Socratic thought, culminating in the atomism of Democritus, approached philosophical explanation as an exercise in finding the right sort of material stuff to serve as the building blocks of nature. According to Aquinas, "the first of those who philosophized about the natures of things held that only bodies exist. They claimed that the first principles of things are certain corporeal elements, either one or many."[6] On the more refined line of thought pursued by Plato and then, in a different way, by Aristotle, explanation requires appeal not just to matter but to form. This idea, in one shape or another, would hold sway throughout late antiquity and the Middle Ages, first dominating Islamic philosophy and then Christian, all the way until the seventeenth century, when Descartes and others suddenly shook it off and turned back to the reductive approaches of old. Famously, Descartes drew a line between the human case and others, treating the rest of the natural world as simply bodies in motion, while ascribing to human beings alone an explanatory principle of another kind, an immortal soul. This is an instance—indeed the exemplary instance—of the supernatural approach that Aquinas only partly embraces. On his view, instead, human beings have a form just as all things have a form and have a soul just as all living things have a soul. Descartes, however, sees things quite differently. From his perspective, Aquinas and others are best seen not as applying their overarching naturalism to the human case, but as overgeneralizing from the human case to the rest of nature. That is, Descartes regards the appeal to form as inherently supernatural in character, and so treats talk of forms and souls throughout nature as a sort of misguided obscurantism that makes it impossible to give a naturalistic explanation of anything.[7]

However much we may regard hylomorphic explanation as appropriate for the natural world in general, Aquinas thinks that its application to human beings must be handled carefully, inasmuch as we are indeed a special case. For even while he begins the Treatise on Human Nature by situating human beings within the rest of nature, as creatures composed of matter and form, he immediately turns to show that human beings are special, in virtue of having a form that can exist apart from matter. Here is where, as he sees it, the naturalistic approach runs out. Obviously, this is a result that Aquinas needs as a Christian, since if human beings are to survive death it is minimally required that their souls survive death, which means that these souls must survive the destruction of their bodies. Over the course of his career, Aquinas makes various attempts to prove that the human soul can exist apart from its body, and something should be said about these arguments. The first thing to consider, however, is whether it is even *coherent* to treat the human soul both as a form and as independent from matter.

One bad reason for suspicion is an overly crude conception of what a form is. To be sure, if one thinks of a form on the model of a shape, then it will look just preposterous to suppose that the human soul can exist apart from its body. It is indeed hard to see how anyone could think that a shape can exist apart from some sort of stuff that has that shape. Aquinas, however, as will become progressively more clear, does not think of souls as anything like shapes. A moment's reflection will make this obvious. For even if it is natural to motivate the hylomorphic framework by appealing to a case like a statue, where the matter is the bronze and the form is the shape, the human case must clearly be quite different. A statue, perhaps, can be roughly understood as nothing more than a certain sort of stuff having a certain sort of shape—though even here the clever student will see the potential for difficulties. But a human being is more than a certain sort of stuff so shaped. That will not take account, most obviously, of what distinguishes a living body from a corpse. The reductive materialist must disagree. If human beings are just so many molecules organized in such and such a way, then the difference between a living human being and a corpse just will consist in either a difference in molecules or a difference in how those molecules are arranged. But from Aquinas's perspective one can have all the right material and still not have a human being, not because the materials have the wrong spatial alignment—the wrong shape—but because they are lacking some further explanatory principle, a soul. Forms, for Aquinas, are not mere shapes, but are causal principles in the natural world. They are indeed the primary causal principles in nature, actualizing matter that would otherwise be characterless and inert, if it could exist at all.[8] A soul without a body is therefore not to be conceived on the model of a free-floating shape. Souls are causal agents, powers.

A soul is a form of a special kind, a substantial rather than an accidental form, which is to say that it is the kind of form that defines a substance as what it is. Setting aside until later the precise role of a substantial form, and considering forms in general as causal powers in nature, it may look as if all such forms should be able to exist apart from matter. This is precisely the sort of result one finds mocked in Descartes and other seventeenth-century critics of scholasticism. Aquinas, however, thinks the human soul is a special case—the only case where it is naturally possible for a form to exist without the matter it informs.[9] Only our substantial forms are such that "they do not exist in matter in such a way that their existence depends on matter."[10] This is certainly a good reason to be suspicious about the human soul's alleged separability. Why should it be a special case, in a way so nicely calibrated to accommodate the Church's teachings on human immortality? The key idea, for Aquinas, is that the human soul is the sort of causal agent that can operate independently of the matter it inheres in. Whereas every other form in the natural world can act only in virtue of informing a body of the proper sort, the human soul does not require a body. More specifically, the human soul can think without a body. This is the fundamental premise on which the whole of Aquinas's theory of human nature rests. Let us call it the Independent Operation Premise (IOP) and state it in Aquinas's own words:

> IOP: "The intellectual principle, which we call mind or intellect, has an operation of its own, in which the body has no share."[11]

Before turning to the arguments for IOP, we should be clear about what it entails. By itself, clearly, IOP does not show that the "intellectual principle" (the soul that is ultimately responsible for intellectual cognition) is immortal. Moreover, IOP does not even show that the soul has the possibility of existing apart from the body. To get those further results, Aquinas argues, first, that a thing's manner of operation tracks its manner of existence, so that whether or not a thing can operate apart from other things shows whether or not it can exist apart from other things. This shows, as Aquinas thinks of it, that the human soul is a substance, because to be a substance just is to be the sort of thing that can exist without inhering in something else.[12] Of course, not all substances are incorruptible, so to get the further result that the human soul will naturally continue to exist even apart from its body, Aquinas further argues that whereas form–matter composites are always corruptible, substances that are pure forms are by nature such that, once created, it is impossible for them naturally to cease to exist.[13]

The supplementary principles just mentioned are perhaps just as doubtful as is IOP itself, but even so it seems right to keep our focus on that fundamental premise. For if Aquinas can establish that the human soul has an operation of its own, independent of the body, then he will have dealt a fatal blow to the sort of reductive materialism that, then as now, looms as the main adversary to a view like Aquinas's. For we would then know that "human soul" is not just a convenient catchphrase for whatever it is that explains human life, but that it in fact picks out an independent causal principle within us, irreducible to any material description. Admittedly, that alone does not show that the soul can exist apart from the body, but it takes the decisive first step.

The Soul's Independence from Body

When historians of philosophy attend to the arguments of their heroes—if in fact they ever do attend to the arguments themselves, rather than simply gaze in admiration at the unfolding tapestry of doctrines—they often do so with a certain sinking feeling, because the arguments invariably fail. What? Has no one ever proved anything in the history of philosophy? Well, perhaps Newton did in his *Principia*, or Lavoisier in his *Traité élémentaire de chimie*. But precisely because these works were so successful, we no longer read them as part of the history of philosophy. Successful philosophical proofs, as a general rule, form the foundation of a new science. So far, the efforts of the psychologists notwithstanding, we have no science of the soul. Accordingly, when we turn our attention to the arguments that Aquinas gives for one or another of his more substantive conclusions regarding the human soul, we should expect these arguments to fail. If Aquinas had really *proved* anything in this all-important domain, we might expect the world to have noticed, and to have commenced to build upon those foundations.

Even so, an argument may fail to count as a genuine proof and yet still be worthy of attention, either because it strikes many readers as being persuasive to some degree or another, even if not decisive, or because it seems to point, however elusively, in the direction of an argument that might really be decisive. I am not sure whether either of these scenarios obtains in the present case, but here I will simply make the best case I can for several of Aquinas's arguments, and let the reader judge. *The Treatise on Human Nature* makes two distinct arguments for IOP, each of which focuses on a different aspect of the intellectual operation—thought—that is crucially at issue. The first of these arguments runs as follows, with numbers supplied to mark the main premises and conclusions.

> It is necessary to say that the principle of intellectual operation, which we call the soul of a human being, is a nonbodily and subsistent principle. [1] For it is clear that through the intellect a human being can cognize the natures of all bodies. [2a] But that which can cognize certain things must have none of those things in its own nature, because that which exists in it naturally would impede its cognition of other things. In this way we see that a sick person's tongue, infected with a jaundiced and bitter humor, cannot perceive anything sweet; rather, all things seem bitter to that person. Therefore if the intellectual principle were to contain within itself the nature of any body, it could not cognize all bodies. But every body has some determinate nature. Therefore [3a] it is impossible for the intellectual

> principle to be a body. [3b] It is likewise impossible for it to operate *through* a bodily organ, because [2b] the determinate nature even of that bodily organ would prevent the cognition of all bodies. Analogously, a determinate color not just in the pupil, but even in a glass vase, makes liquid poured into that vase seem to be of the same color. [IOP] Therefore this intellectual principle, which is called mind or intellect, has an operation of its own that the body does not share in.[14]

What drives this argument is the idea that the intellect displays a startling plasticity in its cognitive range. Our other cognitive capacities—sight, hearing, and so on—are each rigidly limited to a certain domain, that of color, sound, and so forth. But the intellect, according to the first premise of the argument, can think about anything (or at any rate anything in the material realm, which is as strong a claim as Aquinas takes himself to need). The second premise of the argument then asserts that such plasticity would be impossible if the intellect either (a) were a body or (b) were to operate through a body. From these two premises, the subconclusions of (3a) and (3b) immediately follow, and they together yield IOP.

It hardly needs saying that this falls short of being a demonstrative proof. Although the logical form of the argument is valid, none of the premises are self-evident in the way they would have to be to carry complete conviction. It is not perfectly clear, for instance, that the intellect *can* "cognize the natures of all bodies." Even more doubtful is the second premise (2a, 2b). Although the comparisons to taste and sight point toward the kind of point Aquinas wishes to make, these are merely illustrative examples, and hardly show that the intellect, if it relied on the brain, would similarly be limited in the scope of what it could grasp.

Still, there is undoubtedly something suggestive about the argument. For it really is a remarkable feature of the mind that it can range so widely—in a seemingly unlimited fashion—over the whole of the world around us, readily grasping entirely new concepts of all kinds. Such plasticity is strikingly different, Aquinas thinks, not just from what one finds in the case of the senses, which are so obviously tied down to a single sort of object, but also from what we observe of the higher-level cognitive abilities of other animals, which Aquinas regards as similarly bound to a certain predetermined range of objects. Swallows make judgments of a certain sort about nests, and bees about honeycombs,[15] but they have no capacity to expand beyond their limited horizons. The bee could not form the idea of opening a retail outlet to market its product. And once one gets squarely in focus this remarkable feature of the human mind, it can begin to seem at least worth taking seriously the idea that our soul is not just a larger, more complex version of what swallows and bees have, but that it is something qualitatively different. What exactly that difference might be is again not a claim that Aquinas can establish decisively, but his suggestion is that the soul acts independently of the material conditions that lock other souls into a narrow framework of operation.

A second line of argument for IOP rests on the intellect's capacity to form universal concepts. Aquinas's overarching cognitive theory rests on the empiricist principle that all information arises from the senses.[16] At the sensory level, however, that information is always represented as here and now—a particular sensible quality in the world at a particular place and time. The intellect represents information differently, in abstraction from any such particular conditions, and Aquinas takes such facts to form the basis of an argument for IOP:

> [1] It is clear that everything received in something is received in it according to the mode of the recipient. [2] But any given thing is cognized in keeping with how its form exists in the one cognizing. [3] Now the intellective soul cognizes a thing in that thing's unconditioned (*absoluta*) nature—for instance, it cognizes a stone as it is a stone, without [material] conditions. [4] Therefore the form of the stone exists in the intellective soul without conditions, in terms of the stone's own formal character. [5] Therefore the intellective soul is an unconditioned form, not something composed of form and matter.[17]

The conclusion of (5) is equivalent to (3a) from the previous argument—that is, it is tantamount to the claim that the human soul is not a body. This is a claim that, in some sense, holds of every soul, and every form, as we saw in the previous section. But here Aquinas means to assert the stronger thesis, distinctive of the human soul, that it operates independently of the body. That is, he means to assert IOP. Thus, he immediately goes on to contrast the operations of intellect with the operations of the senses: "For if the intellective soul were composed of matter and form, then the forms of things would be received in it as individuals; then it would cognize only singular things. This is what happens in the sensory capacities, which receive the forms of things in a corporeal organ."

Beyond the fundamental datum of the argument, that the intellect grasps the universal, and the senses the particular, Aquinas is relying on a metaphysical principle that he immediately goes on to make explicit: that "matter is the principle of individuation for forms." So the idea is that the senses, inasmuch as they represent particulars, represent the material conditions of those individuals. If they did not, they would not be representing particulars at all. The intellect, in order to grasp the universal, must strip away the material, to get at the thing's "unconditioned" or "absolute" nature (as premise 3 puts it). This already requires us to embrace a rather robust set of metaphysical assumptions, which would themselves take extended argument to establish, and almost certainly could not themselves be proved.[18] But supposing we do embrace that metaphysics, as well as the fundamental datum that drives the argument, we still need to accept a further and very large claim: that an inference can be made from the representational content of the mind to the mind's intrinsic character. It is the burden of the first two premises of the argument to license this move. Aquinas seeks to show that for the intellect to *represent* the nature of a stone, apart from the individuating material conditions, the intellect must *itself* lack matter. On his picture, that immaterial "mode of the recipient" (premise 1) is what will account for how "the thing is cognized" (premise 2), and so ultimately for the fact that "the form of the stone exists in the intellective soul without [material, individuating] conditions" (premise 4). It is far from clear that this pattern of inference is valid. One might instead think that there is no straightforward connection to be drawn from the content of what a cognitive system represents to the intrinsic character of that system. One can represent visual images using numbers, and represent numbers using visual images; one can use shapes to represent sounds, and use sounds to represent abstract ideas. The sort of argument Aquinas wants to make depends, minimally, on a more elaborate theory of mental representation than he here offers us.[19]

Again, however, one may feel this argument to have a sort of elusive power to it. For there can easily seem to be something quite special and distinctive about the human capacity to think abstractly and universally. What distinguishes us from swallows and bees, it seems, is not just the scope of our cognitive abilities, but our ability to think abstractly. Swallows and bees seem limited to the here and now, whereas we can think not only about the past and future, but more generally about food and shelter in the abstract. This in turn gives rise to the complex linguistic and economic systems that distinguish our species from every other. Are these simply more complex manifestations of the same sorts of biological processes found throughout the rest of nature, or are they evidence of cognitive capacities of a fundamentally different kind?

This second argument displays the same general pattern as the previous one. In each case, there is an initial datum, a cognitive capacity allegedly distinctive of human beings that allegedly points toward the mind's immateriality. Many modern arguments in this domain have a similar sort of structure, but with a different emphasis. What strikes philosophers today about the mind tends to be the phenomenon of consciousness—the way in which to have a thought or a perception involves a certain experience, a vivid "what it is like" that is presumably absent from, say, a computer's representation of reality. Aquinas is strikingly silent about this aspect of the mind, attending instead to features that seem more distinctively characteristic of human beings. In all of these cases, however, what drives the argument is a phenomenon of our cognitive capacities for which we have—to this day—no clear explanation in terms of physical mechanisms. In such cases, it must remain an open question whether or not a thoroughly naturalistic model of explanation will capture what is characteristic of human nature.

The Soul's Powers

The arguments of the previous section seek to open up a divide between human beings and other animals. One way to express this divide is by saying that, among all the souls of all the animals, only the human soul is immaterial. This, however, is liable to mislead. For it is not the case that Aquinas thinks the souls of nonrational animals are corporeal, as if he were resorting to the pre-Socratic notion that the soul of a camel might be some subtle blend of fire, air, or some other kind of stuff. As stressed already, souls are always forms. They are, accordingly, never bodies, and so never material, even in part. The special sense in which the human soul is immaterial is articulated by IOP: the human soul, unlike other souls, has an operation of its own, independent of the body it informs. Other souls are material just insofar as they *need* matter in order to operate, and so in order to exist. This shows that, in a sense, the human soul is not a special kind of entity—it is a form just like other forms, up and down the great chain of being. And although it is unusual, in the context of other animals, for the human soul to have an independent operation, this too, in the greater scheme of things, is by no means unprecedented. The created order, as Aquinas thinks of it, contains many animal species, each bound to a certain kind of body. But, says Aquinas, this world contains an even greater number of angelic species. Indeed, the number of angels "exceeds every material multitude,"[20] which seems to mean that there are more angels than there are physical particles in the universe. (And why not? Angels are God's greatest creation. Does it not stand to reason that God would have created more of what is greater than of what is lesser?) Each angel is an immaterial form of the same general kind as the human soul—an intellectual substance, which is to say a causal power capable of a certain sort of abstract cognition and volition, requiring no body in order to operate. From this point of view, the place of human beings is quite natural and intuitive. We are the animals with minds so advanced as to be like the angels. Or, looked at from the other end round, we are the intellectual creatures with minds so crude that we benefit from union with an animal body.[21]

This sort of big-picture perspective helps one escape the sense that there is something unhappily ad hoc about Aquinas's theory of human nature. Viewed in another way, however, it highlights our unique position. Like other animals, our animating principle is a form, naturally suited to actualize matter. Yet, like other intellectual creatures, that form is capable of operating apart from matter, and so capable of existing apart from matter. We are, then, uniquely positioned between angels and animals, sharing metaphysical principles with each. This raises various hard questions about human nature. One question concerns why human beings have this sort of oddly hybrid status. Why we have immaterial souls, according to Aquinas, has been explained already, by the arguments for IOP. But why then do we, unlike the angels, have bodies at all? Why is this part of our nature? A second sort of question concerns the character of the soul–body union. Granted that there is some sort of advantage to our soul's being joined to matter, what sort of conjunction is this? Given our soul's independence, can we really count as organic unities in the way that other animals are? A third sort of question concerns whether it is even coherent to suppose that our souls are, at the same time, both bodily forms and independently operating minds. Granted that Aquinas has reasons to *want* to say both of these things, how *can* he say both of these things at once?

I will begin by answering the first two questions very briefly, then answering the third in more detail, and finally circling back for the remainder of this chapter to the first two questions. To the first question, then, of why the human soul is joined to a body at all, the quick answer is that our soul benefits from such a body because our mind works best when united to an animal sensory system. Even though, as IOP insists, the mind does not *need* the senses to operate, still the mind does work best that way, for reasons we will consider in more detail in the section on "The Essential Bodily Component." That leads to the second question, of how the soul and body are united. Aquinas's answer is that they are united in the same way that any hylomorphic composite—that is, any material substance—is united. The soul stands to the body as substantial form to prime matter. The details of this union will occupy the section on "The Human Substance." But even this short answer helps to make vivid the problem raised by the final question above: how can the soul be both an independently operating power and the form of the body?

One kind of difficulty here concerns whether the soul can both be a form and be subsistent—that is, be a genuine substance. Aquinas's response is that there is no obstacle to a substance's being itself composed of further substances. The human body, for instance, is composed of integral parts—hands, arms, and so on—each of which is itself an incomplete substance making up the whole. The human soul is, to be sure, not an integral part, inasmuch as it is not a body at all, but it is a kind of substantial constituent of the complete substance that is a human being.[22] Another kind of problem concerns how the soul can be said both to operate independently of the body (IOP) and to be the form of the body. Aquinas acknowledges that these are quite different characterizations of the soul, but he thinks both can be true inasmuch as the soul is multifaceted. Rather than treat the soul as something simple, Aquinas postulates a real distinction between the soul itself and its powers. Considered in its own right, the soul essentially is the form of a body. As such, the soul is the ultimate intrinsic explanatory principle for the existence of the composite substance that is a human being. To make a human being exist, however, is not to be understood as bestowing on a heap of matter some sort of generic property of *existing*. Rather, for a human being to exist is for that matter to become capable of the various operations that characterize human beings, including nutritive, sensory, and intellectual operations. This is to say, however, that the human soul, as the first internal principle of life for a human being, is the source for the various *powers* that a human being requires in order to carry out the operations distinctive of such life. Thus "all the soul's capacities, whether their subject is the soul alone or the composite, flow from the essence of the soul as their source."[23]

Aquinas distinguishes among these powers in various ways. Most fundamental is a distinction between (a) the nutritive or vegetative powers, (b) the sensory powers, and (c) the intellectual or rational powers. The last two categories further divide into those powers that are cognitive and those that are appetitive. The cognitive sensory powers divide into the familiar five external senses and the four internal senses, which is Aquinas's term for those cognitive powers that are lodged in the brain: common sense, imagination (also known as *phantasia*), the estimative or cogitative power, and memory. The appetitive sensory powers divide into the irascible and concupiscible. At the intellectual level there is just one appetitive power, the will, and two cognitive powers, the agent intellect and the possible intellect.[24]

An investigation of these powers would take us into a much wider domain of issues concerning perception, desire, free will, and rationality, all of which are discussed elsewhere in this volume. For present purposes, the point that needs stressing is the way a distinction between the soul and its powers makes it easier for Aquinas to treat the human soul as the form of the body even while he stresses that it operates independently of the body. In discussing these issues, he is always very careful to distinguish between what holds of soul itself, essentially, and what holds of it insofar as it contains one or another power. The soul, considered in its own right, is the form of the body, and its defining function is to actualize that body. But this is consistent with that soul's having powers—intellectual powers—that are not the actuality of the body, and do not even require the body for their operation. Thus, "we do not say that the human soul is the form of the body with respect to its intellective power, which ... is not the actuality of any organ."[25] The great appeal of this strategy is that it lets Aquinas have it both ways. Viewed from one angle, Aquinas treats the human soul in broadly naturalistic terms, as a soul like other souls, inhering in a body and giving rise to the various powers—nutritive and sensory—that other animals possess. But some of those powers that the human soul gives rise to are intellectual, and although these are just some of its powers among many, they make a fundamental difference. For because we have a mind that operates apart from the body, it is possible for our soul to exist apart from the body. Thus we are, ultimately, quite different from other animals.

The Human Substance

In wanting to have it both ways—a biologically grounded account of human nature that leaves room for our distinctively immaterial character—Aquinas wants above all to preserve the organic unity of the human being, as a soul–body composite. This is not something that theories of human nature have always made much effort to accommodate. Plato seems, at least in some dialogues, to have thought that our bodies are not a part of us at all, and Descartes tends in that direction as well. Aquinas's contemporaries generally rejected this Platonic line, supposing instead that human beings are the union of body and soul, but they were hard pressed to explain what that unity consists in. Aquinas, by contrast, has an impressive theory to offer. It is, indeed, the most impressive—and influential and contentious—aspect of his whole theory of human nature.

To understand Aquinas's view, it is helpful to begin with some foundational metaphysical distinctions. Most fundamentally, there is the distinction between genuine beings and mere aggregates. Heaps, for instance, are aggregates, as are artificial constructions like houses.[26] Living things, and substances of all kinds (water, stones, etc.) are beings, as are the accidental properties of substances, which get divided along the lines of Aristotle's category scheme into qualities, quantities, relations, and so on. The problem of accounting for the unity of the soul–body composite, for Aquinas, just is the problem of how to ensure the place of human beings among substances, as genuine entities, rather than as mere heaps, which do not themselves have any proper existence beyond the existence of their parts. Aquinas's solution is to insist on treating the human soul naturalistically, as simply a form like the forms of other living things. That this soul has intellectual powers that are independent of the body does not matter, because Aquinas distinguishes the soul from its powers. It also does not matter that this soul is itself subsistent, since as we saw it is normal for substances to be composed of other substances. All that does matter, then, is that the human soul functions within the human being in the same sort of way that other forms function within other substances.

The theory that Aquinas has to offer at this juncture is his theory of substantial form. Aquinas, like other medieval Aristotelians, distinguishes between two kinds of form, substantial and accidental. Accidental forms are those forms that can come and go while a substance remains; they are the entities that populate the nine accidental Aristotelian categories. The substantial form of a substance defines the substance as the kind of thing it is, which is to say that the substantial form comprises the essence of a thing.[27] Essences, however, at least for the medieval Aristotelian, are not abstract descriptions, but rather a particular sort of causal power within a substance. This, of course, must be so for Aquinas, since we have seen already that souls are causally efficacious in various ways. But what exactly does the soul do as the substantial form? One way in which Aquinas likes to answer this question is by saying that whereas an accidental form makes a thing be thus and so, a substantial form makes a thing be *simpliciter*.[28] But this is liable to suggest a misleadingly obscurantist notion of what a substantial form does, as if there is some sort of abstract property of being, *simpliciter*, for which the rational soul is responsible. Instead, the substantial form is the most basic internal causal explanation for the substance's various intrinsic features. As we have seen already, for instance, a soul gives rise to the various powers associated with life: nutritive, sensory, and rational. More generally, the substantial form organizes the matter of a substance into one chemical structure or another, and consequently is responsible for whether a substance will be hard or soft, shiny or dull, red or green. Of course, whether or not the sun shines on a given day on a given leaf is not something a plant's substantial form controls. In general the substantial form is responsible only for the intrinsic features of a substance—not whether it is well illuminated, or well nourished, or well loved. Still, in general, a certain substantial form, inhering in prime matter, will give rise to a certain kind of substance with certain kinds of properties: "Every natural body has some determinate substantial form. Therefore, since the accidents follow from the substantial form, it is necessary that determinate accidents follow from a determinate form."[29]

The principal advantage of this conception of substantial form is that it yields a highly unified conception of substance. The complex chunk of matter that we think of as a single thing, displaying a consistent pattern of properties over time, but sometimes changing in those properties, can be understood to derive its unity—both at a time and over time—from the substantial form that explains those properties. As long as the same substantial form continues to structure a suitable chunk of matter, we have the same substance, and the chunk itself is unified by being so structured.

Critical to Aquinas's theory, however, and the most contentious part of it, is his claim that each substance has just a single substantial form. This is not the view that most of Aquinas's contemporaries held. They took the distinctively immaterial character of the intellect to require a distinction between it and the substantial form of the body—not a distinction between the soul and a power, as Aquinas has it, but a distinction between the body's substantial form and a further substantial form, the rational soul, that inheres in the prior body–form composite.[30] Such a view, however, wrecks Aquinas's account of substantial unity, and so he complains:

> Everything that gets added to something after its complete existence gets added to it accidentally, since it lies outside its essence. But every substantial form yields a complete being in the genus of substance, since it yields an actual, particular being. Therefore whatever gets added to a thing after its first substantial form gets added to it accidentally. So, since a nutritive soul is a substantial form, inasmuch as *living* is predicated substantially both of human beings and of other animals, it would follow that a [further] sensory soul would get added accidentally, and likewise for a [further] intellective soul. And thus neither "animal" nor "human being" would signify a thing that is unconditionally one, nor would these terms signify any genus or species in the category of substance.[31]

The advocate of a plurality of substantial forms thus loses any ability to treat human beings and other animals as substances. The body would be a substance, in virtue of the first substantial form that inheres in it, but any further form added after that point could not possibly perform the role of a *substantial* form, because that role is already taken. Accordingly, for a living thing to possess a rational soul would be like a tree's taking on a new color—the additional feature would be a mere accidental addition, and rational animal would no more pick out a distinct category of substance than does maple-tree-with-orange-leaves. The cost of failing to explain the substantial unity of a human being, then, is quite dire: human beings fail to be substances at all, which is to say that they fail to count as entities in any proper sense.

The key to the argument is Aquinas's robust conception of substantial forms as causal principles. In effect, Aquinas is advancing a physical, proto-scientific hypothesis about what distinguishes substances from nonsubstances. This is exactly what one should expect from Aquinas's commitment to a biological approach to human nature. Human beings are material substances like other substances, which is to say that we have a unifying intrinsic principle like other substances, explained not by a priori metaphysical considerations, but by the substantial form's concrete causal role within substances. If we were to decide that human beings, and perhaps living things in general, lack any such organizing principle, then we would have to conclude that human beings, viewed as mind–body composites, are not substances at all. Either that, or we would have to formulate an entirely new theory of substance.

The Essential Bodily Component

We have now considered two of the three questions raised earlier: how the human soul can be at the same time a form and an immaterial intellect, and how it can forge a genuine substantial unity with its body. That leaves one final question: why is it so important for the human soul to be united to a body at all?

That such union is important—indeed, that it is essential—Aquinas leaves no room to doubt. As noted already, he regards the body as part of the essence of a human being. We do not need to have any particular corpuscles, of course, since these are constantly changing, but we need to have the kind of body that is distinctively human. Aquinas even relies on this fact in attempting to provide some philosophical justification for the theological doctrine of the resurrection. For it is obvious that, at death, the human body is corrupted. The human soul remains, for reasons that we have seen, but according to Aquinas the survival of the human soul is not sufficient for the survival of the human being: "The soul, since it is part of the human body, is not the whole human being. My soul is not I. So even if the soul were to achieve salvation in another life, it would not be I or any human being."[32] Accordingly, Aquinas's argument for the human soul's subsistence, via IOP, shows less than one would naturally suppose. It shows that some part of me will survive, but it does not show that I myself will survive. In fact, Aquinas thinks that no philosophical argument can establish human immortality—yours or mine—because that is possible only if our souls are reunited with bodies of the right sort to be informed by our souls. Although Aquinas offers various considerations for why God might perform this sort of miracle, the fact that he will do it can be accepted only on faith.[33]

This is a remarkable doctrine. It is one thing to reject the Platonizing denigration of the human body as some kind of punishment imposed on the soul. It takes only a modicum of sympathy for biological naturalism to think that our bodies are not *all* bad. But Aquinas goes much farther than that, insisting not only that our bodies play a positive role in our lives, but that they are in fact essential to our continued existence. This is perhaps the most impressive manifestation of the biological side of Aquinas's theory of human nature. Even in the midst of his commitment to the supernatural doctrine of the resurrection, he insists that what God will preserve is an *animal*—an animal with a mind.

In part, Aquinas holds this view because he regards the order of life in our current state as the natural order. True, it is of only finite duration, dwarfed on either side by the eternity that came prior to creation and the eternity to come after the Final Judgment. Still, our present state is our natural state, one in which there is hope of supernatural aid in the form of grace, but which nevertheless shows us as we essentially are, as created by God.[34] Our having a body, then, for Aquinas, is not a temporary aberration; rather, it defines what we are. And given the hylomorphic conception of unity described in the previous section, according to which our soul is responsible for the kind of body that we have, it is not surprising that Aquinas thinks we not only essentially have a body, but that we essentially have a body of just this familiar sort.

These remarks still leave open the question, however, of why we were created this way—of why a mind such as ours, immaterial and therefore incorruptible, should be attached to a body such as ours, weak and perishable. Aquinas has a good deal of interest to say about this question, much of which turns on the details of how our minds and bodies interact. In referring to mind–body interaction, I do not mean to invoke the much-discussed "problem" of mind–body interaction. That we still think of this as a problem is rather curious, since it is a historical artifact of a few decades in the seventeenth century when philosophers like Descartes formed the conviction that all causation at the material level occurs through mechanical impact, and at the same time wanted to treat the mind as immaterial and still interacting with bodies. Once Cartesian mechanism was abandoned in favor of a broader conception of forces as the causal agents in nature, the mind can be seen as just one among many forces in the natural world. And this is the older Aristotelian perspective as well, inasmuch as our intellectual powers are just forms—powers of the soul—that can act in nature just as other forms, accidental and substantial, act in nature.

Aquinas sees so little difficulty in mind–body interaction that he puts their interlocking roles at the center of his theories of our cognitive and volitional systems. If we focus on the cognitive side, the bodily role is most obvious right at the start of the process, in the mind's need to acquire information through the senses:

> Inasmuch as the human soul has an operation transcending matter, its existence is elevated above the body and does not depend on it. But inasmuch as it is naturally suited to acquire its immaterial cognition from a material cognition, it is clear that the fulfillment of its species can occur only when united to a body.[35]

The senses, relying on the familiar bodily organs of the eyes, ears, and so on, acquire information about the world, and the mind works on that information, abstracting it to form the sorts of universal concepts described earlier. Aquinas does not think that the intellect *must* have such sensory information in order to operate, but this, as he puts it here, is how the intellect is "naturally suited" (*nata*) to operate.

More interesting than this familiar empiricism is Aquinas's insistence on the intellect's need to "turn toward phantasms" every time we think. The term "phantasm" is Aquinas's general label for sensory information as it gets processed in the four inner senses listed earlier. For other animals, this is where the highest level of cognitive processing occurs. The inner senses are important in human beings, too, not just in their own right but also because these images (visual, auditory, etc.) get put at the service of intellectual cognition. They are not just the data by which we initially form abstract thoughts; beyond that, they crucially accompany all of our ongoing thoughts, so that when the intellect is thinking about, for instance, the nature of a triangle, or the nature of a camel, the inner senses are at the same time framing sensory images of triangles or camels. (When one tries to think about things one has never perceived, one may form images that are likely to be a close approximation. When one tries to think about imperceptible things, like the human soul or an angel, still one forms images, but to little advantage, which is precisely why it is so hard for us to think about such things.) Thus, as with the initial gathering of information through the senses, "turning toward phantasms is, for the soul, its natural mode of thinking."[36] In this process, the intellect and the senses run in tandem, with the result that what does the thinking is not the intellect alone or the senses alone, but the human being as a whole, using all of its cognitive faculties.[37]

These remarks threaten to bring us around in a circle, back to the idea that using the senses is simply the soul's nature. What we sought, instead, was an account of *why* it is its nature. Aquinas's view is that the mind not only naturally does work in tandem with the senses, but that it works best that way. This point is made with particular vividness in his discussions of how the soul will operate for the period of time between its death and the resurrection of the body, at the Final Judgment. Apart from the body, the soul will operate as the angels do, by directly grasping intelligible truths conveyed to it by other intellectual substances. (The idea seems to be that our souls will, during this time, communicate telepathically with the angels, and perhaps with other separated souls.) One might suppose that this mode of thought will be better than our earthly mode, thereby making the eventual resurrection of the body undesirable. Not so, according to Aquinas, because although this mode of cognition is better for the angels, it is not better for us. Just as people who are less intelligent need many concrete examples to bring them to an understanding of something abstract, so our minds are such that we work best through the senses: "in order for human souls to be able to have a complete and distinctive cognition of things, they are constituted by nature so as to be united to bodies; in this way they acquire a distinct cognition of sensible things from the things themselves."[38]

Again, and now at a deeper level, we can see the essentially biological orientation of Aquinas's thinking about human nature, even in a highly theological context. The soul will exist apart from the body and will during this time communicate with the angels. But it is not our nature to exist that way, and reflection on our cognitive processes shows why it is not. Even though the mind itself does not use the body when it thinks, nevertheless our minds work best when attached to a body. We are, essentially, rational animals.

NOTES

1. See James Doig's contribution to this volume.

2. Aristotle, *De anima*. III.5, 430a23.

3. The *Treatise on Human Nature* was written ca. 1267. At roughly the same time, Aquinas composed his more detailed *Disputed Question on the Soul* (*QDA*), and his commentary on Aristotle's *De anima* (*In DA*). Readers interested in exploring Aquinas's views should begin with the *Treatise*, which contains the most concise and elementary account, and then look to *QDA* for a more developed statement, and to *In DA* for a fuller

understanding of the Aristotelian background. Also particularly important is the treatment in *SCG* II.56–90 dating from the early 1260s. My translation of the *Treatise* (Hackett, 2002) contains extensive notes intended for non-experts.

4. *ST* I q.75 a.1; cf. *De anima* II.1, 412a28.

5. *DPN* 2 (Leonine lines 112–18; Marietti §349).

6. *De substantiis separatis* 1 (Leonine lines 1–5; Marietti §43).

7. This debate over the status of Aristotelian hylomorphism obviously runs too deep and wide to be pursued here. The main task of my *Metaphysical Themes 1274–1671* (Oxford: Clarendon Press, 2011) is to assess the rise and fall of hylomorphic metaphysics in the years from Aquinas to Descartes and Locke.

8. The paradox of a stuff, matter, that is intrinsically characterless is one of the principal difficulties of the hylomorphic approach, and is handled very differently by different scholastic authors. For Aquinas's approach, see Jeffrey Brower's contribution to this volume and also, for an extensive textual analysis, John F. Wippel, *The Metaphysical Thought of Thomas Aquinas: From Finite Being to Uncreated Being* (Washington, D.C.: Catholic University of America Press, 2000).

9. Supernaturally, Aquinas thinks it is possible for any form to exist apart from matter, a doctrine that looms largest in discussions of the Eucharist. Hereafter, however, I will generally ignore such absolute, supernatural possibilities. When I speak without qualification of what is possible or necessary, the modality at issue will generally be natural or physical, rather than metaphysical or logical.

10. *SCG* II.51.

11. *ST* I q.75 a.2.

12. Aquinas often couches this thesis regarding the human soul as the thesis that the human soul is "subsistent" (e.g., *ST* I q.75 a.2; *QDA* 1). This is his label for the precise characteristic of substances that they are the sorts of beings that can exist without inhering in other things (see my discussion in *Thomas Aquinas on Human Nature* §2.2). To understand scholastic theories of substance, such as Aquinas's, it is important to frame the theory more precisely than is usually done. The theory does not require that substances be (naturally) capable of existing apart from everything else. That criterion immediately admits of obvious counterexamples. Rather, the theory requires that substances be able to exist without *inhering* in any subject. This rules out all accidental forms, which (naturally) require a subject, and rules out all substantial forms other than the human soul, since they require matter for their operation, and so cannot exist apart from matter. (This last inference again presupposes a connection between operating and existing. For that principle, see, e.g., *ST* I q.75 a.3: "all things have existence and operation in a similar way.") The subsistence criterion does not rule out accidental unities such as a heap of stones. A heap is not a substance, however, because it is not a being at all, and so is not even a candidate for the subsistence criterion, which applies only to things or beings. A heap is not a being because it lacks a substantial form, for reasons that will be clearer below.

13. For this stage of the argument, going from IOP to immortality, see, e.g., *ST* I q.75 a.6 and *QDA* 14.

14. *ST* I q.75 a.2. For another version of this argument, see *In DA* III.7 (Leonine lines 131–59; Marietti §680), which elaborates on a sketch along these lines that Aristotle had put forth at *De anima* III.4, 429a18–24.

15. For these examples, see *QDV* 24.1c. The focus there is on free will, but Aquinas takes the distinctive character of human freedom to be the direct result of our greater cognitive capacities. For discussion of this issue, see Thomas Williams's chapter in this volume.

16. Aquinas only once utters the famous principle often associated with his name—"nihil est in intellectu quod non sit prius in sensu"—and he does so only as an initial objection to his position (*QDV* 2.3 obj. 19). In his response to that objection he signals, however, that he accepts the principle, reworded as the thesis that "what exists in our intellect must first have existed in the senses" (*QDV* 2.3 ad 19). Does this make Aquinas an empiricist? As the later history of philosophy demonstrates, one's commitment to empiricism must be judged not so much by abstract principles such as this, but by the rigor with which they are applied.

17. *ST* I q.75 a.5.

18. For Aquinas's theory of individuation, see again Jeffrey Brower's contribution to this volume.

19. On Aquinas's theory of mental representation, see Claude Panaccio, "Aquinas on Intellectual Representation," in D. Perler, ed., *Ancient and Medieval Theories of Intentionality* (Leiden: Brill, 2001), 185–201, as well as Jeffrey Brower and Susan Brower-Toland, "Aquinas on Mental Representation," *Philosophical Review* 117 (2008): 193–243.

20. *ST* I q.50 a.3.

21. For the place of human beings in the larger context of intellectual substances, including the angels, see *SCG* II.46–55, as well as *Disputed Question on Spiritual Creatures* and the treatise *De substantiis separatis*.

22. The first article of Aquinas's *Disputed Question on the Soul* takes up this issue in careful detail, asking whether the human soul can be both a form and a *hoc aliquid*, a particular thing, which he goes on to explain as tantamount to the soul's being a subsistent entity. For a thorough discussion of Aquinas's views in this area, see Bernardo Carlos Bazán, "The Human Soul: Form *and* Substance? Thomas Aquinas' Critique of Eclectic Aristotelianism," *Archives d'histoire doctrinale et littéraire du Moyen Age* 64 (1997): 95–126. For a more general evaluation of Aquinas's position as a version of dualism, see Eleonore Stump, *Aquinas* (London: Routledge, 2003), ch. 6.

23. *ST* I q.77 a.6.

24. For a brief overview of this division, see *ST* I q.78 a.1. For a fuller account of many of the details, see *In DA*. I discuss all of these powers at some length in *Thomas Aquinas on Human Nature*, chs. 5–10. For a recent summary of the broader medieval background regarding the soul's powers, see Dag Nikolaus Hasse, "The Soul's Faculties," in R. Pasnau, ed., *The Cambridge History of Medieval Philosophy* (Cambridge: Cambridge University Press, 2010), 305–19.

25. *DUI* ch. 3 (Leonine lines 378–81; Marietti §233).

26. On the status of artifacts for Aquinas, see, recently, Michael Rota, "Substance and Artifact in Thomas Aquinas," *History of Philosophy Quarterly* 21 (2004): 241–59. It is unclear whether Aquinas wants to recognize aggregates of nonliving substances—e.g., a pool of water or a stone—as a substance over and above the minimal-sized water and stone particles that make up the aggregate. I argue that he does not in *Thomas Aquinas on Human Nature*, ch. 3.

27. This is "essence" in the strict Aristotelian sense of what defines the thing, rather than in the weaker modern sense of merely being necessary. A thing has many necessary properties, but one defining essence. Strictly speaking, for Aquinas, the essence is not simply the substantial form, but rather the substantial form together with the common matter (see *ST* I q.29 a.2 ad 3; I q.75 a.4), a detail that helps safeguard the essentially bodily aspect of human beings.

28. E.g., *ST* I q.76 a.4.

29. *ST* I q.7 a.3. I discuss Aquinas's theory of substantial form in more detail, in its broader historical context into the seventeenth century, in "Form, Substance, and Mechanism," *Philosophical Review* 113 (2004): 31–88. For a still broader and more detailed look at scholastic views in this domain, focusing on the later Middle Ages, see my *Metaphysical Themes*, chs. 24–26.

30. For views prior to Aquinas, see Anton C. Pegis, *St. Thomas and the Problem of the Soul in the Thirteenth Century* (Toronto: Pontifical Institute of Mediaeval Studies, 1934), and Richard Dales, *The Problem of the Rational Soul in the Thirteenth Century* (Leiden: E. J. Brill, 1995). For the later debate, see Marilyn Adams, *William Ockham* (Notre Dame, Ind.: University of Notre Dame Press, 1987), ch. 15; Richard Cross, *The Physics of Duns Scotus: The Scientific Context of a Theological Vision* (Oxford: Clarendon Press, 1998), ch. 4; Pasnau, *Metaphysical Themes*, ch. 25.

31. *SCG* II.58.6.

32. *In I Cor* 15.2.924.

33. An important further detail here is that, for Aquinas, a particular soul can be joined only to a body of exactly the right sort—my soul needs my body, or at any rate a body just exactly like it, and could not be joined to anyone else's body. "Just as specifically the same matter is needed for specifically the same form, so numerically the same matter is needed for numerically the same form. For just as a cow's soul cannot be the soul of a horse's body, so one cow's soul cannot be another cow's soul. Therefore, since numerically the same rational soul remains, it must be united again at the resurrection with numerically the same body" (*CT* I.153 [Marietti §305]). For further discussion of these issues, from a somewhat different perspective, see Eleonore Stump's chapter in this volume on "Resurrection and the Separated Soul." I myself discuss these issues further in *Thomas Aquinas on Human Nature*, ch. 12.

34. Even the punishment of Original Sin is simply the abrogation of a gift given to Adam and Eve; our punishment is having to live in our natural state, infirm and unwise (see *ST* I q.100 a.1). On grace, see the chapter in the present volume by Andrew Pinsent.

35. *QDA* 1c.

36. *ST* I q.89 a.1.

37. On the need for phantasms, see *ST* I q.84 a.7 and *In DMR* 2. I discuss this doctrine in detail in *Thomas Aquinas on Human Nature*, §9.4.

38. *ST* I q.89 a.1.

PART VI

THEORY OF LANGUAGE

CHAPTER 27

THEORY OF LANGUAGE

GYULA KLIMA

AQUINAS does not have a "philosophy of language."[1] He does have, however, some important and interesting ideas on how language (any human language) is related to the world through the mediation of human thought, without the proper understanding of which much of what he has to say in his metaphysics and epistemology will not be properly understood.

Perhaps, the best way to introduce Aquinas's relevant ideas is through the analysis of an example. Take the sentence "Socrates is wise." In contemporary analytic philosophy, the truth conditions of this sentence are usually stated either in terms of set membership or in terms of property possession: this sentence is true just in case Socrates is a member of the set of wise things (this set being "the extension" of the term "wise") or just in case Socrates has the property of wisdom (this property being some abstract, "Platonic entity," sometimes thought of as the "intension" of the term). But in Aquinas's ontology, given his rejection of Platonic abstract entities, there are neither sets nor properties in the modern sense. There are, however, substances, and their individualized forms, whether those forms are substantial or accidental.[2] Thus, on his analysis, what makes this sentence true is the actuality of Socrates' wisdom (as opposed, say, to the non-actuality of his stupid and malevolent accuser's, Meletus's wisdom).

This brief comparison, however, so far only provides us with an indication of the differences of *different ontologies* involving different types of entities (sets, properties, individualized forms, besides individual substances, such as Socrates or Meletus). The fundamental differences in the corresponding conceptions of how language is related to reality will emerge if we focus on the relations themselves that relate items of language to items in these ontologies, that is, *semantic relations*. On the modern conceptions, the semantic function of the predicate of "Socrates is wise," or for that matter of any sentence of this type, would be to *denote* a set or to *express* a property. On Aquinas's conception, however, the corresponding function of the predicate is to *signify* the individualized forms of individuals, whether these forms are actual or not (for, of course, if it signified only actual forms, then no sentence could be false, since for Aquinas, as I have just noted, it is the *actuality* of the form that makes the predicate signifying it true of the subject).

Signification and Imposition

But putting the matter in this way immediately gives rise to some questions. In the first place, what is it that establishes this signification relation? How can a term come to signify these so-called "individualized forms"? Indeed, what are these "individualized forms," if there are any? And what is their actuality or non-actuality, on which, for Aquinas, the truth of our propositions should ultimately depend?

In accordance with the common logical doctrine of the time, Aquinas holds that what establishes signification is an act of *imposition*, a sort of "name-giving." A human language primarily consists of utterances, that is, articulate sounds (and secondarily of written marks or any other forms of conventional symbols that can "stand in" for spoken words or expressions, say, hand gestures, smoke signals, Morse code, etc.), which in themselves may or may not be meaningful (or *significative*, to use an Anglicized version of the Latin technical term). For instance, if I utter the articulate sound "biltrix," an ordinary speaker of English or Latin literally has no idea what I mean. But, of course, we, the users of these languages, can make this utterance meaningful, if we agree what we want to use it for, somehow making clear what we are supposed to have in mind when we are using it in our conversation. This can be done in a number of different ways, for example, by ceremonially naming something or someone by it, as in a baptism, or by providing its definition, or by simply starting to use it in contexts when what we mean is made clear in the situation itself (say, from behavioral clues, the circumstances, etc.; just think of how the utterance "to google" only relatively recently became meaningful in English, for example). What any of these procedures establishes is a connection between this utterance and a cognitive act whereby we conceive of the same thing or things in the same way. Once this connection is established, medieval logicians would say that the utterance *is imposed to signify* precisely the *thing* or *things we conceive of*, and precisely in the ways we conceive of it or them. Thus, the utterance becomes a *significative utterance*, that is to say, a *word* of our language. For medieval logicians, a mere articulate sound, such as "biltrix," is not a word, precisely because it has no connection with a cognitive act, it "brings nothing to mind," or in other words, it constitutes no understanding in the mind of someone who hears it.[3] The cognitive act whereby we conceive of the thing or things signified by the word is called a *concept*. So, an act of imposition is the act establishing the connection between an utterance and a concept, thereby rendering the utterance significative of the thing or things conceived by means of the concept precisely in the way conceived by means of the concept.

But why does Aquinas (and other medieval authors, for that matter) need to complicate the explanation of meaningfulness by bringing in such an obscure item into this explanation, a "spooky mental entity," a concept? Are not words meaningful simply on account of being the signs of things? And are not the meanings of words simply constituted by the ways we use them as such signs?

Addressing these questions very briefly on Aquinas's behalf, one may say that words are meaningful, since they are signs, namely, meaningful symbols of a certain sort, but the doctrine of imposition is supposed to explain how an utterance (or written mark, etc.) can become a conventional sign, a meaningful artificial symbol in the first place. And even if we normally learn the meaning of these symbols through acquiring the ability to use them intelligently, in the way competent users use them, nevertheless, this *competence* and *intelligence* in use clearly rides on our *understanding* of what these symbols can be used for, and it is this act of understanding, which is called a *concept*, to which an act of imposition is supposed to relate an otherwise meaningless entity. This is because we can intelligently use these utterances to talk about things only if we *understand* what things they are supposed to signify and how. For words are not simple labels attached to singular things we can point to; the relationships between words and things in a human language are much more complicated, as medieval authors were keenly aware.

In fact, Aquinas provides an interesting reason for the need to refer to concepts in explaining meaning, in terms of the different ways the same things can be *signified* on account of the different ways in which we *conceive* of them. Commenting on Aristotle's "semantic triangle" of words, concepts, and things, Aquinas provides the following explanation:[4]

> Now the discussion concerns utterances that are meaningful on account of human agreement. Thus, by the phrase "affections of the soul" [*passiones animae*] we must understand the concepts of understanding [*intellectus conceptiones*], which nouns, verbs and expressions immediately signify, according to Aristotle's position. They cannot immediately signify things, as is clear from their mode of signification; for the noun "man" signifies human nature in abstraction from the singulars. Therefore, it cannot immediately signify a singular human, whence the Platonics posited that it should signify the separate Idea of Man. However, since this does not subsist in the abstract in reality according to Aristotle's position, but is only in the intellect, it was necessary for him to say that utterances immediately signify the concepts of the intellect and by their mediation the things.[5]

Since for Aquinas there are no universal entities as Plato imagined, we cannot explain the universality of our universal words by claiming that they signify universal things. The universality of our words, on account of which they are related not just to *one peculiar sort of thing*, a universal, but rather to a multitude, indeed, a potential *infinity* of ordinary things, is the result of our ability to *conceive* of these things in a *peculiar manner*, namely, universally, and to use the word to express this universal conception, or as Aquinas often refers to it, the universal *ratio* of these ordinary things.

Aquinas's notion of *ratio* is what we can justifiably identify as Aquinas's idea of *mental content*, the information encoded by our mental concepts about the things we conceive. Aquinas provides a rather detailed description of what he means by the term *ratio* in the following passage:

> The *ratio* of every single thing is what its name signifies, as the *ratio* of a stone is what its name signifies. But names are the signs of intellectual conceptions, whence the *ratio* of any single thing signified by a name is the conception of the intellect that the name signifies. And this conception of the intellect is in the intellect as in its subject, but it is in the thing thought of as in that which is represented: for the conceptions of the intellect are certain similitudes of the things thought of. But if the conception of the intellect were not assimilated to the thing, then the conception would be false of that thing; for example, if the intellect would think something that is not a stone to be a stone. So the *ratio* of the stone is in the intellect as in its subject, but it is in the stone as in that which causes truth in the conception of the intellect thinking the stone to be such and such.[6]

Thus, the *ratio*, indeed, the same *ratio*, is both in the intellect, as the conception of the intellect, and in the object, as in what is conceived by that conception. This conception is said to be *similar* to the object precisely on account of embodying (or should I say, encoding?), the same *ratio* that is in the object. And it is precisely the presence of the same *ratio* in the object that renders the conception of the intellect true of the object.

In another passage, in connection with the question of how the attributes we predicate of God may apply to Him, Aquinas explains in more detail in what sense we can say that the *ratio* is in the thing:

> we should know that a *ratio*, as taken here, is nothing else, but what the intellect apprehends from the signification of some name, and this in the case of those things that have definition is the definition of the thing itself, in accordance with what the Philosopher says: "the *ratio* signified by the name is the definition."[7] But some things that are not defined are [also] said to have a *ratio* in this way, e.g., things such as quantity or quality, which are not defined because they are most general genera. Nevertheless, the *ratio* of quality is what is signified by the name of quality; and it is that from which quality has it that it is quality. Thus, it makes no difference whether those things that are said to have a *ratio* have a definition. And so it is clear that the *ratio* of wisdom predicated of God is what is conceived of in the signification of this name, even if divine wisdom itself cannot be defined. Nevertheless, the name "*ratio*" does not signify this conception itself, because that is signified by the name of wisdom, or by some other name of the thing, but it signifies the intention of this conception, just as the name "definition" and other names of second imposition do. And thus the second point, namely, the one concerning how the *ratio* is said to be in the thing, is also clear. For this does not mean that the intention itself which is signified by the name "*ratio*" would be in the thing, nor even that the conception to which this intention applies would be in the thing outside the soul, for it is in the soul as in its subject; but it is said to be in the thing insofar as there is something in the thing outside the soul that corresponds to the conception of the soul, as what is signified [corresponds] to the sign.[8]

So, the *ratio* that is immediately signified by the name of some sort of thing is an inherent act of the human mind considered precisely with regard to its information content,[9] that is, a concept, whereby the mind conceives of the sort of thing in question. This relation of *immediate signification*, as we have seen, is established by an act of *imposition*. But when we impose words to signify, we normally do not impose them to talk about our concepts, but to talk about the things we conceive, unless of course we are imposing names on concepts by which we conceive of concepts. The utterance imposed on our concept by which we conceive of human beings, say, "man" in English or "homo" in Latin, is not used to talk about this concept, but rather to talk about what we conceive by this concept. But, of course, we can form concepts by which we conceive of concepts, and thus the name imposed on such a concept is used to talk about these concepts. Such a name, in fact, is the name "ratio," which, as Aquinas indicates in the passage above, (immediately) signifies an intention, namely a concept whereby we conceive of other concepts (by which, in turn, we may conceive external things). An intention or concept of this sort, therefore, is usually referred to in the medieval logical literature as a *second intention* (i.e., an intention by which we conceive first intentions), and its name a *name of second imposition*. But, again, just as a name of first imposition is not used to talk about the concept on which it is imposed, but about the things conceived by that concept, so a name of second imposition is not used to talk about the second intention on which it is imposed, but about the first intentions conceived by this second intention. Thus, although imposition (of any order) primarily establishes the relation of *immediate signification* between an utterance and a concept, because of the *naturally* representative nature of the concept itself, this also establishes the relation of conventional *ultimate signification*, on account of which the word signifies not the concept, but rather the *object* of the concept, namely, whatever it is that is conceived by this concept.

Therefore, Aquinas's conception is by no means susceptible to Wittgensteinian objections to a "private language." On Aquinas's and his contemporaries' conception, our concepts are in fact very public entities. Our concepts form the natural representational system of the human mind, which is therefore common to all human beings, and which we express by each and every meaningful utterance we make, using these utterances to refer, not to some hidden, private mental events, but whatever we conceive by these "mental events," the commonly accessible *objects* of our thought.[10]

Now what is such an *object of thought*, what is it that is conceived by a concept? Clearly, the answer depends on the kind of concept we are talking about. So far, we have only considered concepts that provide the signification of so-called *categorematic* terms, i.e., terms that can be the subject or predicate of a proposition.[11] And even among these, we have only considered simple, universal terms, as opposed to complex terms and singular terms, respectively. Aquinas and his contemporaries were, of course, very much aware of the variety of semantic functions of various parts of speech, which, in line with the common doctrine of imposition and signification, they would all primarily attribute to the different semantic functions of the concepts on which these parts of speech are imposed.

Aquinas wrote at a time when influential textbooks on logic devoted thoroughgoing, subtle discussions to the issue of the signification of *syncategorematic* terms, that is, parts of speech we nowadays would refer to as those expressing *logical connectives*. Of course, none of these authors held that by these concepts we conceive of, and so by the corresponding terms we signify, things in the way we do by categorematic concepts. (Just what would be the thing we conceive by the concepts expressed by the words "no," "and," or "every"?) Therefore, they rather analyzed the ways in which constructing these terms together with categorematic terms modifies the semantic functions of the latter.[12] Aquinas, not being a logician but a theologian, did not devote separate attention to syncategorematic terms per se. However, he did deal in great detail with one syncategorematic term in particular, or rather a term that has both syncategorematic and categorematic functions, namely, the verb "est" ["is"] and its cognates, such as its infinitive form "esse" ["to be"] or its participle "ens" ["being"].

Aquinas on the Copula

For Aquinas, the verb functioning as a copula (as is "est" in Latin, "is" in English, etc.), besides its obvious syntactical function of linking subject and predicate to form a new syntactical unit, a proposition (as opposed to a mere list of terms), also retains the function that it has when it is attached to a subject as an absolute predicate, namely, to signify actual existence. For as an absolute predicate, as in "Socrates est" ["Socrates is"] the verb signifies the existence of the thing referred to by the subject *absolutely*. But when then verb joins a predicate to the subject, as in "Socrates est sapiens" ["Socrates is wise"], it signifies the existence of the *ultimate significate* of the predicate in the subject, that is, it signifies the existence or actuality of the subject not absolutely, but *with qualification*, with respect to this ultimate significate (that is to say, it signifies not the existence of Socrates, but the existence of Socrates' wisdom, i.e., Socrates' actuality, not absolutely, but *with regard to his wisdom*). As Aquinas explains in his commentary on Aristotle's *On Interpretation*, this is why the copulative function of linking predicate to subject is exerted by the verb that primarily signifies existence (as opposed to any other word that might exercise the mere linking of subject and predicate):[13]

> The reason why [Aristotle] says that the verb "is" co-signifies composition is that it does not principally signify composition, but secondarily; for it primarily signifies what occurs to the mind in the way of actuality absolutely: for "is," uttered absolutely, signifies being in act, and hence it signifies as a verb. But since actuality, which the verb "is" principally signifies, is in general the actuality of every form, whether it is a substantial or an accidental actuality, this is why when we want to signify any form or act to actually inhere [*inesse*] in a subject, we signify this by means of the verb "is," either absolutely [*simpliciter*] or with some qualification [*secundum quid*].[14]

This theory of predication (often referred to in the secondary literature as "the inherence theory" on account of the central idea of the *actual inherence* of forms in their subjects) has a number of important, both logically and metaphysically, relevant implications.

(1) According to this theory, for every true singular affirmative predication, there has to be some individualized form signified by the predicate in the subject. However, the forms signified by these predicates cannot all be regarded as beings in the same sense (indeed, they cannot all be regarded as *forms* in the strict metaphysical sense, let alone beings in the same sense as the substances they inform).[15] Consider the predication "Homer is blind." According to the inherence theory, this predication is true if and only if Homer's blindness exists. But for Homer's blindness to exist is nothing but for him not to be able to see, that is, for his sight not to exist. So the existence of Homer's blindness is nothing but the nonexistence of his sight, and so, since nothing can be existence and nonexistence in the same sense, this blindness cannot exist in the same sense as the opposite sight; therefore, this blindness cannot be an existent or being in the same sense as the opposite sight is.

(2) The inherence theory clearly establishes a close connection between the notions of existence and truth, insofar as it grounds the truth of a singular predication in the actual existence of the significate of the predicate in the referent of the subject.

However, these two points immediately give rise to a strictly logical problem (as opposed to the host of metaphysical problems) concerning Aquinas's theory. For Aquinas does indeed claim that the *significata* of various predicates exist in different senses of existence determined by the nature of the significate in question, and yet he also claims that the copula of affirmative predications signifies existence always in the same sense; in the sense in which it signifies the truth of a proposition.[16] How can we reconcile these two claims? Does the copula express various senses of existence, depending on the signification of the predicate it joins to the subject, or does it express uniformly the same sense in all predications? As we shall see, the simple answer is: both. But how is that possible?

The Multiplicity of the Semantic Functions of the Copula

A consistent solution to this problem can easily be provided if we consider the multiple semantic functions of the verb "est" as a copula. As we have seen, the copula signifies the actuality of its subject with respect to what is signified in it by the predicate. However, it also signifies the actuality of what is signified by the proposition that results from its joining the subject to the predicate as a whole, the so-called *enuntiabile*. By talking about an *enuntiabile* as what is signified by a proposition as a whole, Aquinas joins a long tradition (going back at least to Aristotle) of theorizing about the significata of propositions.[17] To be sure, Aquinas's scattered remarks do not provide us with anything like a systematic doctrine found in the logical treatises of his contemporaries and predecessors. However, it is clear even from these scattered remarks that he consciously and deliberately uses this logical tradition, which would regard the total significata of propositions as the "truth-makers" of propositions, in accordance with Aristotle's *dictum* in the *Categories*: "a sentence is true according as the thing is or is not," where "the thing" in question is the significate of the proposition as a whole.[18] Now, whatever such an *enuntiabile* is (nowadays we would probably refer to it as a "state of affairs"), it clearly is in an ontological category that is very different from "ordinary" things. Thus, such things, if they exist, must exist in a sense that is different from the sense in which these "ordinary" things exist. But then, setting the *metaphysical* issue of what these alleged entities are aside, we immediately have a solution to the *logical* problem concerning the signification of the copula raised above.

For positing these *enuntiabilia*, whatever they are, the simple solution is that in any given predication the copula signifies the existence of the ultimate significate of the predicate in the subject in the sense of existence determined by the nature of this significate, and yet it uniformly signifies the existence of the *enuntiabile* in the same sense in all predications. That is to say, it signifies existence in various senses with respect to the *significata* of various predicates, yet it signifies existence in one sense with respect to the *enuntiabile* signified by any proposition. So, it signifies multiply in some respect (i.e., with respect to the significata of various predicates) and uniformly in some other respect (i.e., with respect to the significate of the whole proposition involving any predication). By way of an illustration, consider the following two propositions: "Tom is a cat" and "Jerry is a mouse." For Aquinas, the predicates of these propositions signify cat nature and mouse nature, respectively, and the propositions are true just in case these natures actually exist in their respective subjects. It is precisely the actual existence of these natures, namely, Tom's cat nature and Jerry's mouse nature that the copula signifies in these respective subjects. The existence of cat nature in Tom, however, is nothing but Tom's existence, existence determined, as it were, "catwise," that is, cat life, whereas the existence of mouse nature is existence determined "mousewise," that is, a mouse life. But mouse life and cat life, or existing mousewise or catwise, are certainly radically different (just as much as are cats and mice), and it is this difference that Aquinas is talking about when he says that the significata of different predicates determine different senses and modes of being. So, with regard to these significata of different predicates, signifying different forms or natures, the copula signifies the existence of these natures in different, yet analogically related senses. However, with regard to the states of affairs or *enuntiabilia* signified by these propositions, since they are in the same ontological category, the copula states their existence in the same sense: the state of affairs *that Tom is a cat* obtains or exists (in case Tom does in fact exist catwise) in exactly the same sense as the state of affairs *that Jerry is a mouse* obtains (just in case Jerry does exist mousewise). So the copula signifies existence with regard to the different natures signified by the predicates of these propositions in different senses (determined by the different natures signified by these predicates) and yet with regard to the significata of the whole propositions themselves, the respective *enuntiabilia*, it signifies existence in the same sense (in the sense in which such *enuntiabilia* can exist at all). But this is quite possible, whence there is clearly no inconsistency involved in this position.

Yet, this solution still leaves a number of *logical* questions open (again, disregarding the swarm of *metaphysical* questions it raises). For even if it may provide a consistent interpretation for Aquinas's claims about the multiplicity of the senses of existence expressed in various predications and the uniform signification of the copula with regard to the *enuntiabilia* in all predications, it is still quite unclear how any of the senses of existence expressed by the copula is related to the senses of existence expressed by "est" as an absolute predicate. Furthermore, it is quite unclear how any of these senses is related to the sense of identity Aquinas also attributes to the copula,[19] and in general, how the various senses of existence expressed by any absolute or copulative uses of the verb are supposed to be related to each other in Aquinas's celebrated doctrine of *the analogy of being*.[20]

Predication and the Analogy of Being

For Aquinas, the primary sense of "est," or its English equivalent "is," is expressed by its use as an absolute predicate of primary beings, that is, primary substances, signifying their actuality absolutely, namely, the actuality of their substantial act of being, as in "Socrates est" or "Socrates is." In fact, at one point, he would analyze the semantics of "Socrates est" ["Socrates is"] on a par with "Socrates currit" ["Socrates runs"], insofar as they are both supposed to signify an act, indeed, an activity of the subject. For just as the predicate of the latter sentence signifies an accidental activity of Socrates, namely his running [*currere*], so does the predicate of the former signify the substantial activity of Socrates, namely, his act of being [*esse*], which is nothing but his actual existence, his actuality, absolutely speaking, namely, his substantial activity of living. As Aquinas puts it:

> Existence itself [*ipsum esse*] is not signified as the subject of existence, just as [the act of] running [*currere*] is not signified as the subject of running, therefore, just as we cannot say that [the act of] running itself runs, so we cannot say that existence itself *is*. But just as that-which-is is signified as the subject of existence, so that-which-runs is signified as the subject of running. Therefore, just as we can say of that which runs, or the runner, that it runs, insofar as it is subjected to running, so we can say of a being [*ens*], or that which is, that it *is*, insofar as it participates in the act of existing [*inquantum participat actum essendi*].[21]

So, "est" as an absolute predicate of Socrates, signifies his substantial act of being, his life, as determined by his essence, namely, a human life, although this determination is not expressed in the predication itself. But the predication is true only if Socrates does have his life actually, and since Socrates is essentially human, he can only have a human life, if he exists at all. This determination is expressed, however, when "est" is not used as an absolute predicate, but as a copula linking an *essential predicate* to the subject, as in "Socrates est homo" ["Socrates is a man"]. In this case "est" still signifies the same substantial act of being, namely, Socrates' life, but this time the predicate explicitly imposes the determination of human essence upon the act of existence that Socrates has, explicating that the act of existence on account of which Socrates actually exists is a *human life*. By contrast, in its function as the copula of the predication of an accident of such a substance, signified by an *accidental predicate*, as in "Socrates est videns" ["Socrates is sighted"], the copula has the function of signifying the actuality of the subject not absolutely, but with respect to the accident signified by the predicate, namely, the accidental act of being of Socrates' sight.

In these two cases, therefore, the verb has the function of signifying real acts of being of primary substances, namely, their substantial and accidental acts of being, respectively. However, in the case of the predication of a privation, the verb cannot have the function of signifying any real act of being, for the being of a privation is precisely the nonbeing of the opposite positive quality that would have real being if it existed. Therefore, in the predication "Socrates est caecus," that is, "Socrates is blind" the copula can only signify the actuality of the *lack* of a real act of being: for the presence of blindness is the absence of sight. Still, this absence itself is present; this lack of real being is really actual, so it *is* there in *some further sense* of "is." But obviously the presence of this absence can only be expressed or conceived by means of conceiving the nonpresence of the opposite real being. So, the presence of a privation is conditioned not only on the lack of real being but also on the human mind's ability to conceive of the situation by applying its concept of negation necessarily involved in the concept of any privation. This is the reason why Aquinas would identify the being of privations as a sort of being of reason, *esse rationis*: not that he regarded their being as somehow fictional, or made up by reason, but as something the presence of which is conditioned both on the ways things are in reality and on the ways this reality is conceived by human reason. The same type of consideration applies to the being of the *enuntiabile* signified by the whole proposition: when a proposition is true, then, of course, it signifies a situation that is really actual; but what the proposition as a whole signifies, and what can be referred to by a corresponding sentential nominalization, is also a being of reason, insofar as its presence is conditioned not only on the ways real beings are but also on the activity of human reason capable of conceiving of this real situation by means of forming the proposition in question.[22]

As can be seen from the foregoing, on this conception there is a systematic connection between the various absolute and copulative uses of the verb "est" and its equivalents, which clearly accounts for the analogical relationship between the primary and secondary senses of the verb and the corresponding participle "ens" or "being." The primary sense of the verb is expressed by its use as it is truly predicated of primary substances. Its various secondary senses are expressed by its use in variously qualified predications, where the qualification may be expressed either (1) by a predicate added to the verb functioning as a copula, or (2) as an explicit determination added to the verb used as an absolute predicate, or (3) by the nature of the subject of which the verb is predicated without any explicit qualification, as illustrated by the following three equivalent propositional forms, respectively:

(1) x is F
(2) x is-with-respect-to-its-F-ness
(3) The F-ness of x is

Here x is some primary substance, and F is some *nonessential* predicate of x, signifying in it a real accident or a privation or even a relation of reason as in "Socrates is admired by Plato." What is important to realize about these propositional schemata is that the occurrence of "is" in each signifies the same act of being determined by the significate of the term "F" (referred to by the corresponding abstract term "F-ness" in the last two).[23] If F is an *essential* predicate of x, then the same schemata are further equivalent to a fourth schema, in which "is" is predicated absolutely. For example, if x is "Socrates" and F is "wise," then the first three propositions resulting from their substitution are clearly equivalent. However, in this case "Socrates is" would not entail any of these, since clearly, just because Socrates is, it does not follow that he is wise: for Socrates to be is not for him to be wise. On the other hand, since for Socrates to be is for him to be a man, that is, "man" is Socrates' essential predicate, using "man" in the place of F would render all three resulting propositions equivalent to "Socrates is."

Now where does identity fit into this scheme? It should be noticed here that in the foregoing schemata what provided the qualification on the sense of "is" was the *significate* of the predicate in the thing referred to by the subject. The predicate, however, according to many medieval logicians (actually, a notable exception would be Peter of Spain)[24] functions there also with another one of its semantic values, namely, its (personal) *suppositum*,[25] that is, a thing that actually has its significate. Therefore, the sense of the copula in which it expresses the sense of identity may be regarded as the result of simply adding another qualification to its absolute form, namely, one that refers to the *suppositum*, rather than the significate of the predicate, as in

(4) x is-(actual)-with-respect-to-a-thing-that-is-F,

which is true just in case x is an F, that is, if x is identical with a thing that is F, namely, itself, provided it is F (for if the thing is *not* F, then it is clearly not identical with *any* thing that *is* an F). So, in this sense the qualified sense of "is" clearly expresses the actual identity of x with itself under the designation of being an F.[26]

Indeed, we can also explain along the same lines why the *enuntiabile* signified by the whole proposition has to be signified to be a being by the copula in the same sense, as Aquinas claims, in which it would signify the being of a privation or any other being of reason. For the primary semantic value of the predicate *F* is neither its *suppositum* (a thing that is actually *F*), nor its ultimate significate (the thing's individualized *F*-ness), but its immediate significate, namely, *F*-ness in general, as it is conceived by the abstractive mind forming the abstract concept expressed by the term *F*.[27] So, what the proposition as a whole signifies, namely, that *x* is *F*, is actual in the same sense in which we can say that

(5) *x* is-(actual)-with-respect-to-*F*-ness-(in-general).

Here the qualified predicate obviously has to express the actuality of the subject with respect to a being of reason, given that the qualification itself refers to something that is the direct object of reason, namely, the nature of the thing conceived in abstraction from its individuating conditions.

To be sure, Aquinas never spells out the idea expressed in the propositional schemata listed here in exactly such terms. However, his several remarks made in various contexts about the primary and secondary senses of being relating to each other as unqualified (*simpliciter*) and qualified (*secundum quid*), as well as his remarks about how the different semantic values of the same term added to the copula may provide different qualifications on its primary sense (thereby determining different secondary senses of the verb), may well justify the connections expressed by the foregoing propositional schemata.

Indeed, further justification may be gleaned from the fact that once we realize these connections, it is easy to see how Aquinas's claims about the analogical predication of being of substances, especially of God and His creatures can also receive a consistent interpretation in the same framework.

The Analogy of Being between God and Creatures

Consider the absolute predication of being of some primary substance *x*, as in

(6) *x* is (or exists),

the predication of a substantial predicate *S* of the same, as in

(7) *x* is *S*

and the predication of being explicitly qualified by the significate of this predicate, namely, the essence of *x*, as in

(8) *x* is-with-respect-to-its-*S*-ness.

According to Aquinas's doctrine of the real distinction between essence and existence in creatures and the real identity of the same in God, if the variable "*x*" in these schemata stands for a creature, then the significate of this qualified predicate and the significate of the predicate "S" in x are distinct items of reality. However, if the variable "x" stands for God, then these significates are the same, namely, the absolutely simple, indivisible divine nature, which is nothing but divine existence.

In accordance with the foregoing, the predicates of the two equivalent claims in (6) and in (8) signify the same act of being of x. However, if x is God, then, and according to Aquinas *only* then, the determination referred to in the qualified predicate in (8), namely, divine essence is not distinct from what is signified by the absolute predicate in (6), namely, divine existence. Therefore, in this case and *only* in this case, the qualification does not impose any determination or limitation on the sense of the absolute predicate: God is the only entity that absolutely IS without any limitation whatsoever. By contrast, if x is a creature, then the determination referred to in the qualified predicate in (8), a creaturely essence, is distinct from the significate of the absolute predicate in (6), some creaturely existence. In this case, therefore, the determination does impose some limitation on the mode of being signified by the qualified predicate, in the sense that the nature of the creature delimits what the creature can or cannot be, have, do, or suffer. Thus, since the qualified predicate (8) signifies the same act of being that is signified by the absolute predicate in (6), the qualification imposes a determination also *on the sense* of the absolute predicate: a creature can only exist in the way determined by its limited nature, and so that *it is* can only be true of it in the *sense of being* that expresses this *way of being*. Clearly, a mouse cannot be or exist (that is, live) precisely in the way a cat does (for then it would have to hunt mice, for example), and so it can truly be said to exist only in the precise sense of being that expresses this mode of being: existing mousewise, living a mouse life. That is to say, the nature of a creature, being distinct from its existence, imposes an implicit determination on the sense in which the creature can be. Since for a mouse to be is for it to be a mouse, a mouse can only be in the way a mouse can be, which is an essentially limited form of existence; it certainly does not involve the power of reason and the freedom it yields in human existence, which in turn is still limited relative to angelic existence, but which, again, is still limited, no matter how much more power, freedom, and perfection it involves than human existence.

By contrast, even if also for God to be is for Him to be God, for God to be is not a limited form of existence, since for God to-be-with-respect-to-his-divinity is the same as for God to-be-with-respect-to-his-existence, and an act of existence does not delimit itself.[28] So, it is only God whose existence is absolute BEING, whereas any creaturely existence is only being somehow, in a creaturely way. As Aquinas says:

> A created spiritual substance has to contain two [principles], one of which is related to the other as potency to act. And this is clear from the following. It is obvious that the first being, which is God, is infinite act, namely, having in Himself the whole plenitude of being not contracted to the nature of some genus or species. Therefore, it is necessary that His being itself should not be an act of being that is, as it were, put into a nature which is not its own being, for in this way it would be confined to that nature. Hence, we say that God is His own being.

> But this cannot be said about anything else; just as it is impossible to think that there should be several separate whitenesses, but if whiteness were separate from any subject and recipient, then it would be only one, so it is impossible that there should be a subsistent act of being, except only one. Therefore, everything else after the first being, since it is not its own being, has being received in something, by which its being is contracted; and thus in any created being the nature of the thing that participates being is other than the act of being itself that is participated.[29]

The analogical character of the predication of being in this case is obvious, if we consider the following: just as the predication of being of an accident is diminished relative to the predication of being of a substance, so the predication of being of a created substance is diminished relative to the predication of being of God.[30] To be sure, this does not render the absolute predication of being of created substances diminished in and of itself; it is diminished merely relative to the "absolutely absolute" predication of being of God.

In fact, for Aquinas, the predication of being of created substances is *epistemologically* prior to the predication of being of God. But in the process of forming our concept of the being of God, we have to realize that even if creaturely being is better known, and thus epistemologically *prior to us*, creaturely being cannot be what is primarily signified by "being" absolutely speaking, since creaturely being is, of course, ontologically secondary to divine being. According to Aquinas, it is precisely this disparity between the ontological order and the epistemological order that is reflected in the disparity between the *signification* and *mode of signifying* of the names we can properly apply to God on account of *what* they signify, although not according to *how* they signify:

> We should consider, therefore, that because names are imposed by us, and we do not know God except from creatures, [the names of God] are always defective in their representation with respect to their mode of signifying [*quantum ad modum significandi*], for they signify divine perfections in the way in which they are participated by the creatures. But if we consider the thing signified [*res significata*] by the name, which is that which the name is imposed to signify, we find that some names are imposed to signify primarily the perfection itself exemplified by God absolutely, without implying a certain mode in their signification, while others [are imposed] to signify a perfection in accordance with a certain mode of participation. For example, all cognition is exemplified by divine cognition, and all knowledge by divine knowledge. The name "sense," however, is imposed to signify cognition in the manner in which it is received materially by a power of an organ. But the name "cognition" does not signify a mode of participation in its principal signification. Therefore, we have to say that all those names which are imposed to signify some perfection absolutely are properly said of God, and they apply to Him primarily as far as the thing signified is concerned, although not as far as the mode of signifying is concerned, such as "wisdom," "goodness," "essence," and the like.[31]

Thus, since according to Aquinas we gain our primary concept of being from created substances, we need to understand divine being by analogically "stretching" our mundane concept. We first need to grasp the analogy between the being of created substances and accidents, thereby understanding that accidents exist in a diminished sense relative to substance. Then we can grasp the analogy between the being of created substances and God, whereby we understand that just as accidental being is diminished relative to substantial being on account of the limitation imposed on the accident's act of being by its nature, so creaturely being is diminished relative to divine being on account of the limitation imposed on a creaturely act of being by a creaturely nature. Thus, the primary significate of the term "being" in the ontological order has to be divine being. But this is cognized by us only secondarily, on the basis of a primary concept we first acquire from creaturely being.[32] To be sure, if we gained our primary concept of being directly from God, that is, if the *primum cognitum* of our minds were divine being, and not created being in general, then we could understand created being directly as a sort of diminished being, delimited and specified by the limited nature it realizes, and then the cognitive order would match the ontological order. However, since our mind is first confronted with the being of created substances, it has to arrive at the cognition of divine being in this more circuitous way, at least in accordance with Aquinas's doctrine. But pursuing the implications of this observation would already lead our discussion into the *arcana* of late-medieval disputes concerning the *primum cognitum*, which would be certainly beyond the scope of this chapter.[33]

Aquinas and the "Philosophy of Language"

So, returning in conclusion to the mundane issue of Aquinas's "philosophy of language," I think even this rather sketchy survey of his relevant ideas shows that while, on the one hand, Aquinas does show a keen interest in issues concerning how language actually works in reflecting reality, on the other hand, this keen interest is always subordinated to the overriding interest in putting language to work in finding out about that reality, and even stretching it to its limits to express what is beyond our more directly accessible reality. This is precisely what accounts for the peculiarities of Aquinas's doctrine on language. This is why his doctrine has to be pieced together from cursory observations made in the course of other discussions in the first place. And this is also why the doctrine itself is shot through and through with metaphysical and theological concerns, holding the entire doctrine together. So, Aquinas is definitely not the empirical linguist who just wants to describe how language actually works in its actual use in human reasoning and communication. And he is not even the logician or linguistic philosopher who is theorizing about these empirical phenomena, trying to tease out a theoretical, not merely descriptive, but also normative model for them (establishing, for instance, the theoretical rationale for the rules of grammaticality, logical validity, etc.). Aquinas does have all these mundane interests to a certain extent. However, he always has them subordinated to his primary interest in truth, indeed, not just any mundane truth, but the First Truth.

NOTES

1. In fact, in medieval philosophy in general, there was no philosophical discipline identifiable as "philosophy of language." This is not to say, however, that medieval thinkers had no philosophical reflections on language as the conventional medium of human thought and communication. But these reflections can be found mostly in works on grammar and logic, or scattered all over in works in other disciplines, putting these reflections to work in handling other philosophical, theological, or scientific problems. Aquinas, being a theologian, never produced a major systematic work on grammar or logic. He did produce commentaries on Aristotle's *On Interpretation* and *Posterior Analytics* (Aristotle's logical works dealing with propositions and with demonstrations, respectively), and there are some short logical treatises dubiously attributed to him (on such topics as modal propositions and fallacies). But one has to piece together his views on language mostly from scattered remarks in his other, philosophical and theological works, and from contemporary logical doctrines he knew and used, as something presupposed in his philosophical and theological discussions.

2. By way of a preliminary description, one may say that a form in general is a determination of the way something is. Thus, a form of a thing is what makes the thing actual (i.e., actually existing) either absolutely speaking, if the form is a substantial form, or in some respect, if the form in question is an accidental form. See, e.g., *De Principiis Naturae*, c.1.

3. The allusion in the last clause is to Aristotle's description of signification in his *On Interpretation* (1.6b21–22), which functioned pretty much as "the standard definition" of meaning for medieval logicians. See Aquinas, *In Peri hermeneias*, lib.1, l.5, n.16: "it is a property of a significative utterance that it generates some understanding in the soul of the listener" (*proprium vocis significativae est quod generet aliquem intellectum in animo audientis*).

4. Translations, unless otherwise indicated, are mine.

5. *In Peri hermeneias*, lib.1, l.2, n.5.

6. *Resp. ad lect. Vercell. de art.* 108, q.1. Cf. "The *ratio* that a name signifies is the conception of the intellect about the thing signified by the name" (*Ratio enim quam significat nomen, est conceptio intellectus de re significata per nomen.*) *ST* I q.13 a.4.

7. See, *In Meta*, lb.4, lc.16, n.733.

8. *Super Sent*, lib.1, ds.2, q.1, a.3. *in corpore*.

9. That is to say, a *ratio* is a mental act considered only insofar as it is a carrier of some specific sort of information, regardless of just what sort of entity this carrier of information is, namely, whether it is some brain function or some purely spiritual modification of an immaterial mind. That is a completely separate issue. But then, based on this understanding of what a concept or *ratio* is, Aquinas *will* argue that our universal concepts, carrying just the type of information they do, cannot be the acts of a material organ. See G. Klima, "Aquinas on the Materiality of the Human Soul and the Immateriality of the Human Intellect," *Philosophical Investigations* 32 (2009): 163–82.

10. For a brief discussion of the medieval conception of a naturally common, and in this sense "public" mental language, as opposed to the post-Cartesian conception of "a private" language of ideas, see G. Klima, "Review of C. Panaccio: *Le Discours intérieur de Platon à Guillaume d'Ockham*," *History and Philosophy of Logic* 23 (2002): 71–73. Of course, for an excellent survey and detailed discussion of premodern conceptions of mental language, one should consult Panaccio's book reviewed there.

11. For further niceties of the medieval (and later) distinction between categorematic and syncategorematic terms, see G. Klima, "Syncategoremata," in Keith Brown, ed., *Elsevier's Encyclopedia of Language and Linguistics*, 2d ed. (Oxford: Elsevier, 2006), 12:353–56.

12. This is not to say, however, that some of them did not attribute *any* representative function to such concepts. In fact, Peter of Spain argued that syncategorematic concepts exercise their function of modifying the representative function of categorematic concepts *as a result* of their own representative function, representing as they do certain *modes* of the things represented by categorematic concepts, as conceived by these categorematic concepts. Cf. Peter of Spain, *Tractatus, called afterwards Summule Logicales*, ed. L. M. De Rijk (Assen: Van Gorcum, 1972), 195 and 212; Peter of Spain, *Syncategoreumata*, ed. L. M. De Rijk and trans. J. Spruyt (Leiden: E. J. Brill, 1992), 106–9.

13. After all, we might introduce just any old symbol to do this linking, say, the "=" sign, uttered, for instance, as "equals." So, out of a mere list of names, such as "Socrates," "a man," "Plato," "a philosopher," instead of forming propositions by using the copula (as in "Socrates is a man" or "Plato is a philosopher"), we might form propositions, such as "Socrates = a man," "Plato = a philosopher," in which there would be not a hint of the idea of being or existence.

14. *In Peri hermeneias*, 1.5, n.22.

15. As St. Thomas wrote: "we should say that the thing from which something is denominated does not always have to be a form according to the nature of the thing; it is enough if it is signified in the way a form would be signified, grammatically speaking. For a man is denominated from his actions or from his clothes, which are not forms in reality" (*dicendum est quod illud a quo aliquid denominatur non oportet quod sit semper forma secundum rei naturam, sed sufficit quod significetur per modum formae, grammatice loquendo. Denominatur enim homo ab actione et ab indumento, et ab aliis huiusmodi, quae realiter non sunt formae*) (*QDP*, q.7, a.10, ad 8). Cf. also, e.g., Cajetan: "Don't be misled when you hear that a denominative comes from a denominating form, and don't believe on account of the word 'form' that the denominating thing has to be a form of the thing that is denominated; you have to know that by the name 'form' in this context we understand anything from which something is said to be such, whether in reality it is an accident, or a substance, or matter or form" (*Verum ne fallaris cum audis denominativum a forma denominante oriri, et credas propter formae vocabulum quod res denominans debet esse forma eius quod denominatur, scito quod formae nomine in hac materia intelligimus omne illud a quo aliquid dicitur tale, sive illud sit secundum rem accidens, sive substantia, sive materia, sive forma*) (Cajetan [Thomas de Vio], *Scripta Philosophica: Commentaria in Praedicamenta Aristotelis*, ed. M. H. Laurent [Rome: Angelicum, 1939], 18).

16. Cf. *In Meta*, lb.6, lc.4; *In Meta*, lb.5, lc.9, n.895.

17. Cf. G. Nuchelmans, *Late Scholastic and Humanist Theories of the Proposition* (Amsterdam: North Holland Publishing Co., 1980), and *Theories of the Proposition: Ancient and Medieval Conceptions of the Bearers of Truth and Falsity* (Amsterdam: North Holland Publishing Co., 1973). D. Perler, "Late Medieval Ontologies of Facts," *The Monist* 77 (1994): 149–69.

18. For this interpretation, clearly reflecting Aquinas's doctrine, see Cajetan, *Scripta Philosophica*, 87.

19. Cf. *Super Sent*, lib.3, d.5, q.3, a.3; *In Meta*, lb.9, lc.11; *ST* I q.13 a.12; *ST* I q.85 a.5 ad 3-um; *ST* III q.16 a.7 ad 4-um; a.9, ad 3-um.

20. The literature on this doctrine is simply staggering. For an up-to-date survey of the literature, as well as an eminently accessible account of Aquinas's great commentator's, Cajetan's interpretation, and further articulation of Aquinas's doctrine, see Joshua P. Hochschild, *The Semantics of Analogy: Rereading Cajetan's* De Nominum Analogia (Notre Dame, Ind.: University of Notre Dame Press, 2010).

21. *In De Hebdomadibus*, lc.2, n.22.

22. For a more comprehensive treatment of Aquinas's conception of beings of reason along these lines, see G. Klima, "The Changing Role of *Entia Rationis* in Medieval Philosophy: A Comparative Study with a Reconstruction," *Synthese* 96 (1993): 25–59.

23. For a technical, model-theoretical account of exactly how this secondary signification of "is" can be compositionally obtained from its primary signification, see G. Klima, "Aquinas' Theory of the Copula and the Analogy of Being," *Logical Analysis and History of Philosophy* 5 (2002): 159–76.

24. See G. Klima, "Peter of Spain, the author of the *Summulae*," in J. Gracia and T. Noone, eds., *Blackwell's Companion to Philosophy in the Middle Ages* (Oxford: Blackwell, 2003), 526–31, esp. 529–30.

25. For a brief, up-to-date survey of the medieval theories of supposition, see Stephen Read, "Medieval Theories: Properties of Terms," *Stanford Encyclopedia of Philosophy* (Spring 2006 edition), ed. Edward N. Zalta, forthcoming <http://plato.stanford.edu/archives/spr2006/entries/medieval-terms/>.

26. Cf. *Super Sent*, lib.3, d.5, q.3, a.3 expos. "We have to say that there is a difference between substantive and adjective names. For substantives signify not only a form but also the suppositum of a form and can be predicated on account of both. And when they are predicated on account of the suppositum, then the predication is said to be *predication by identity*; and when on account of the form, then it is said to be *predication by denomination* or *by information*. And the latter is a more appropriate predication, because terms as predicates are taken formally. Adjectives, however, only signify a form, and so they can be predicated only by information. Therefore, this is false: 'the essence is generating', although this is true: 'the essence is the Father'. Thus, when it is said that the Son of God is a man, then the predication is by information and identity; but when it is said that the divine essence is a man, then it is by identity, for [the divine essence] is really identical with a suppositum of *man*, but not by information, for divine nature is not signified as a suppositum subsisting in human nature" (*Dicendum, quod differentia est inter nomina substantiva et adjectiva. Substantiva enim significant non tantum formam, sed etiam suppositum formae, unde possunt praedicari ratione utriusque; et quando praedicantur ratione suppositi, dicitur praedicatio per identitatem; quando autem ratione formae, dicitur per denominationem, sive informationem: et haec est magis propria praedicatio, quia termini in praedicato tenentur formaliter. Adjectiva autem tantum significant formam; et ideo non possunt praedicari, nisi per informationem: unde haec est falsa: essentia est generans; quamvis haec sit vera: essentia est pater. Cum igitur dicitur, filius Dei est homo, est praedicatio per informationem et identitatem; cum vero dicitur: essentia divina est homo, est praedicatio per identitatem, quia est idem secundum rem cum supposito hominis; non autem per informationem, quia natura divina non significatur ut suppositum subsistens in humana natura*). See also *Super Sent.*, lib.3, d.7, q.1, a.1, co; *ST* I q.39 a.6 ad 2; *ST* I q.13 a.12; *Contra errores Graecorum*, pars 1, cap.18 co.

27. See Cajetan's astute discussion of this issue in Thomas de Vio Caietani *In De Ente et Essentia D. Thomae Aquinatis*, Marietti, 1934, *Quaestio 7: Utrum natura absolute sumpta sit illa quae praedicetur de individuis*, 100–101.

28. That an act of existence (a significate of the verb "is" or "exists") does not delimit itself is not some arcane metaphysical principle that only "the initiated" could grasp: in general, a qualification added to a predicate referring to the significate of the predicate itself is non-diminishing, and so it can be dropped *salva veritate*. For example, saying "This sheet of paper is white with respect to its whiteness (or with respect to its color)" amounts to the same as saying absolutely "This sheet of paper is white." By contrast, if the qualification refers to something else, say, the quantity informed by this whiteness, as in "This sheet is white with respect to its one side," then it is diminishing, for this claim can be true of a sheet that is not totally white but only on one side, and in that case the qualification cannot be dropped *salva veritate*, for of *that* sheet the absolute predication "This sheet is white" is not true. For more about the issue of diminishing vs. non-diminishing qualifications and their relation to analogical predication and the related issue of the medieval treatment of the fallacy *secundum quid et simpliciter*, see G. Klima, "The Semantic Principles Underlying Saint Thomas Aquinas's Metaphysics of Being," *Medieval Philosophy and Theology* 5 (1996): 87–141.

29. *QDSC*, q. un., a.1.

30. It should be noted here, however, that this is not "the criterion" on account of which "being" ought to be regarded as predicated analogically of God and creatures. Throughout this chapter, a predicate is regarded as analogical if and only if it has a primary sense and some secondary sense(s) somehow related to, and therefore derivable from, the primary sense by means of some diminishing qualification. This "semantic derivability" need not reflect at all the actual process of the formation of an analogical concept. For the finer details of this issue in the context of thirteenth-century logic, see E. J. Ashworth, "Analogy and Equivocation in Thirteenth-Century Logic: Aquinas in Context," *Mediaeval Studies*, 54 (1991): 94–135, and E. J. Ashworth, "Medieval Theories of Analogy," *Stanford Encyclopedia of Philosophy* (Winter 2004 edition), ed. Edward N. Zalta <http://plato.stanford.edu/archives/win2004/entries/analogy-medieval/>.

31. *Super Sent*, lib.1, d.22, q.1, a.2 co.

32. Cf. "Although in the natural order of cognition God is the first thing to know, nevertheless, as far as we are concerned, his sensible effects are known by us earlier" (*Quamvis enim secundum naturalem ordinem cognoscendi Deus sit primum cognitum, tamen quoad nos prius sunt cogniti effectus sensibiles eius*). *In De Hebdomadibus*, lc.4. Cf. *ST* I q.88 a.3 resp. and ad 1.

33. A difficult, but very illuminating discussion of the problem can be found in the first question of Cajetan's commentary on Aquinas's *De Ente et Essentia*. See op. cit. *Quaestio 1: Utrum ens sit primum cognitum ordine et via originis*, 2–19.

CHAPTER 28

THE LIMITS OF LANGUAGE AND THE NOTION OF ANALOGY

BRIAN DAVIES

The Limits of Language

Why should anyone think that language is limited? Does it not serve us very well and do just what we want it to? Language succeeds in allowing us to communicate with each other. By means of language we describe the world and even tell each other how we feel about it. And we surely have no thoughts that cannot be conveyed by means of language, for our thinking is tied to language just as the color red is tied to a physical manifestation of redness. To think that redness exists is just to think what is said by claims to the effect that this, that, or the other thing is red. Similarly, to think that Paris is the capital of France is just to think what "Paris is the capital of France" says. How, we might ask, can language be limited since it gives us so much? What might we want to do that we cannot achieve by means of language? Obviously, language cannot help us win a lottery or get us from London to New York in ten seconds. But that does not mean that it is limited considered as what it is. My cat Smokey cannot cook a curry, but that does not mean that he is limited as a cat. Considered as such, he lacks limitation, since (be assured) he is in perfect health and is able to do all that one might expect a cat to do. Similarly, language seems to be in good order and not in any way lacking. For it allows us to do just what we expect it to: to communicate, to report, to express feelings and desires, to make jokes, and so on.

Yet might there not be something with respect to which language falls short? We sometimes say things like "I cannot tell you how much I love you," and many people would sympathize with such a statement and believe it to be true. Yet we are not dealing with a limitedness when it comes to language here. Mary may express her love for John in any number of ways that is not captured by the simple sentence "Mary loves John." It remains, though, that what she does (and is) as loving John is perfectly reported by saying that she loves him. In cases like this, we are not dealing with language being limited. We are only dealing with a lack of descriptions. Mary's most accurate biographer shall, in time, be able to tell us how much she loved John even though she may not have been able to do so.

What, though, if we are trying to talk about what does not seem to fit our grammatical and syntactical norms? To say that Smokey is agile is to pick out an individual (a particular cat) and to describe it. "Smokey is agile" is a well-formed sentence, one with a subject term (Smokey) and a predicative term (is agile). And to say that Smokey is agile is to attribute a property or attribute to him, one that can be distinguished from him, since he might cease to be agile without ceasing to exist. Yet what if we want to try to talk about something not distinguishable from its attributes? Here, so one might think, language indeed does fail us. For it does not seem to have the resources to talk about what cannot be distinguished from what it is. Its subject/predicate structure seems to prevent it from doing so (as the shape of a glove prevents it from fitting onto a shower head).

Again, consider the fact that we always speak in language that is tensed. We say that Hannibal *crossed* the Alps, that you *are* reading, and that France's foreign policy *shall* go in such and such a direction in the future. When we single out things to talk about we regularly seem to locate them temporally. Yet what if we want to try to talk about something that has no spatio-temporal location? Here, so one might again think, language fails us. For it does not seem to have the resources to talk about what is not a spatio-temporal individual. Its commitment to tense seems to prevent it from doing so (as a drill is incapable of painting a wall).

Aquinas on God: Some Basics

Aquinas seems to be sensitive to all that I have just said. He recognizes that the ways in which we usually talk pose problems if we are trying to speak about what is not distinct from what can be attributed to it, or about something that has no spatio-temporal location. At the same time, however, he also believes that there *is* something that is not distinct from what can be attributed to it, something that also lacks spatio-temporal location—the something in question here being God, the "beginning and end of all things," as Aquinas likes to say. So, unsurprisingly, Aquinas thinks it worth asking how we can manage to say anything true about God at all.

To understand how he tries to answer this question we need to remember some of his fundamental teachings when it comes to what we can know of God when reflecting philosophically. These are all excellently documented by other contributors to this volume, so I shall be very brief when reporting them for present purposes. Indeed, I shall simply provide a bald list of them. Thus, according to Aquinas: (1) God accounts for the existence (*esse*) of all substances for as long as they exist (and whether or not they began to exist); (2) God is nothing bodily; nor is he something with attributes distinguishable from himself; God is identical with what can be truly affirmed of him; and God is immutable; (3) There is no distinction in God of essence (*essentia*) and existence (*esse*); so God is *ipsum esse existens* ("subsistent being itself").[1]

Many theistic authors do not subscribe to these teachings. All theists agree that God is not material, but lots of them would deny that God and God's attributes are one and the same reality, or that God is subsistent being itself. Many would say that God is an incorporeal "person" with distinct attributes, something that undergoes change as time goes on, something, even, able to be causally altered by the activity of creatures. And theists such as these clearly have few problems when it comes to the question "How can we talk sensibly about God?" If God is an incorporeal person (as, for example, Descartes took himself to be), then the language we use when talking of ourselves is straightforwardly applicable to God. The argument might go like this: I think. So we can say that God thinks. I have knowledge, so we can say that God has knowledge. I am (in certain respects) good, so we can say that God is good. And by "thinks," "knows" and "good" here we can take ourselves to be saying of God exactly what we might say of me.

But what if we do *not* take God to be a temporal person alongside us? What if we agree with Aquinas that God and his nature are not distinct (that God *is* what God *has*)? What if we agree that God's nature is simply to be (and to be simply)? Then, of course, we might worry when it comes to talking of God by speaking of him as we speak of what is not divine. We might ask whether we can speak of God intelligibly. We might, as does Aquinas, wonder whether our language is up to the job of saying what God is. Aquinas believes that God and created things are seriously different from each other. In his view, therefore, there is a real question when it comes to making sense of talk about God. For that borrows from talk of creatures. When we speak of God we do so as if God really were an individual in the world, something to be described by terms that we use when talking of what is not divine, as if God were just another thing that could come under our ordinary categories without further ado. If God is not such an individual, however, then how can our talk of him make sense, or capture what he is?

Rejected Answers

When turning to this question, Aquinas notes two responses to it both of which he takes to be mistaken.

The first holds that all that we say of God should be construed in negative terms—that, for example, "God is good" should be taken to mean "God is not bad," or that "God is living" should be taken to mean "God is not inanimate." Aquinas rejects these construals, since, so he argues, people who say that God is good just do not mean that God is not bad. They mean that God is actually good in and of himself. And people who say that God is living are not just saying that God is not inanimate; they are telling us what God really is (living as opposed to inanimate).

The second response tries to construe talk of God in causal terms and argues that to say that God is *X, Y*, or *Z* is just to say that God causes things to be *X, Y*, or *Z*. In terms of this response, to say, for example, that God is good is just to say that God causes or accounts for there being good things. Turning to this response, however, Aquinas argues that it seems to license us to say what we cannot possibly say when it comes to God. God may cause what is good, but, as Creator of the universe, as the cause of the *esse* of things, God also causes (makes to be) what is bodily. Yet we surely cannot conclude from this that God is something bodily. And should we suppose that God is only good because he brings it about that good things exist? If that were so, then God's being good would depend on him creating good things. Yet, Aquinas argues, God does not have to create and, therefore, we cannot take statements like "God is good" only to mean that God produces something good in the created universe. In Aquinas's view, God is good, and is whatever he is by nature, regardless of what he has brought about (created/caused to be).

Moving Forward

As he seeks to present his account of what is going on as we talk sensibly of God, Aquinas notes two ways in which we use words, and he then asks whether we can think of ourselves as using them in either of these ways as we start to talk about God. His key terms here are "univocal/univocally" and "equivocal/equivocally."

One employs a word univocally, thinks Aquinas, when one uses it to talk of two or more things and when the word means exactly the same each time it is used. Suppose I say that Julius Caesar was a man and that Alexander the Great was a man. According to Aquinas, I would be using "man" here univocally. Again, suppose that I say that Paris is a city and that London is a city, or that Paris is highly populated and that London is highly populated. Aquinas would hold that I am here using "city" and "highly populated" univocally.

By contrast, however, think of someone saying that they have money in the bank and that their boat has just run into a bank (i.e., a river bank). "Bank" used to speak about places in which we keep money, and "bank" used to refer to what is to be found alongside rivers, is purely equivocal, or so Aquinas would say. It is a linguistic accident that "bank" is used of things that bear no resemblance to each other whatsoever (as it is a linguistic accident that, for example, the word "date" is used to refer to what can be eaten and to someone whom one might take out for a romantic evening). The same can be said with an eye on, for example, "pen" as in "I keep my pen in my pocket" and "I keep my pigs in a pen."

With these distinctions in mind, Aquinas asks whether words applied both to God and creatures should be thought of as univocal (meaning exactly the same) or purely equivocal (having no meaning in common). And he rejects both alternatives.

Words applied to creatures, he argues, cannot mean exactly the same when applied to God, since God is not something distinct from his nature. The reasoning goes roughly like this: (1) To say, for example, that John is wise is to note that he has various attributes, not that he *is* these attributes; (2) To say that God is wise is not to say that he has a collection of attributes distinct from what he (considered as an individual) is; in God, wisdom is not something different from God; (3) Clearly, therefore, "wise" in "John is wise" and "God is wise" does not signify (pick out) exactly the same thing. As used of John, it signifies an attribute distinct from an individual. As used of God, it signifies the individual that God is. Or, in Aquinas's words, and focusing on the adjective "wise":

> When we say that a man is wise, we signify his wisdom as something distinct from the other things about him—his essence, for example, his powers, or his existence. But when we use "wise" when talking about God we do not intend to signify something distinct from his essence, power or existence.... So it is clear that we do not use "wise" in the same sense of God and people, and the same goes for all other words. So we cannot use them univocally of God and creatures.[2]

On the other hand, Aquinas also wants to say, words applied to creatures cannot mean something entirely different when applied to God. According to Aquinas, we have positive reasons (philosophical ones) for saying that God is, for example, active, powerful, living, and good, reasons based on what we know of creatures. Yet, so he reasons, this could not be so if words like "active," "powerful," "living," and "good," as used to talk about God, have no meaning in common with our use of these words when we apply them to creatures. Or as Aquinas again puts it: "Although we never use words in exactly the same sense of creatures and of God, we are not merely equivocating when we use the same word...for if this were so we could never argue from statements about creatures—any such argument would be invalidated by the Fallacy of equivocation."[3]

Analogy

Immediately following the above observation, Aquinas writes: "So, we must say that words are used of God and of creatures in an analogical way." But what does he mean here? His basic thought is that, when we apply words signifying perfections to God (words that we learn in the first place when taught to speak about creatures), the words in question (a) are truly applicable to God, and (b) do not mean exactly what they do when used to talk about creatures.

Note the word "perfections" here. When he says that words are used of God and creatures in an analogical way Aquinas is not saying that *all* that we might say of God is to be construed analogically. He does not, for example, think that "The Lord is my shepherd" uses "shepherd" analogously. Analogical predication is, for Aquinas, *literal* predication (is literally true, not figuratively or metaphorically true). To say that Smokey is a cat is to say what is literally true of him. And to say that I am alive is to say what is literally true of me (as I write now). For Aquinas, though, to say that God is a shepherd is not to say what is literally true of him, for God is not literally someone in a field who looks after sheep. But, Aquinas also wants to say, we can predicate certain terms literally of God if the terms in question do not have some irreducibly creaturely meaning built into them. "Shepherd" means something irreducibly creaturely (a shepherd is a human being with a particular job at a particular time and a particular place). But what of words like "good," "living," "wise," and "powerful"? Can we use these words (and similar ones) when speaking of what is not a creature? Aquinas thinks that we can, and it is from here that his teaching on God and analogy takes off.

A central element in it is the conviction that we can use certain words without meaning exactly the same thing on various occasions while also not meaning something entirely different. And the conviction here is a sound one. Consider, for example: "I love my family," "I love my job," and "I love chicken curry." Does "love" mean exactly the same in each of these sentences? Hardly. But neither does it mean something entirely different. And, notice, there is no problem in supposing that people who utter these sentences are speaking literally. What we need to note is that love can (literally) take different forms. Again, consider the sentences "My baby is strong," "My horse is strong," and "The FBI is strong." These can all be thought to express literally true propositions. Yet the strength of babies is hardly equal to the strength of horses, and the strength of the FBI goes well beyond that of either babies or horses. What we need to note is that strength (power) can take different forms.

With thoughts like these in mind Aquinas argues that we can use certain words when talking of God and that we can understand them literally. He would, however, want to add that we need to recognize how these words do not mean just what they do when used to talk about creatures. Hence, for example, he would find no problem in saying that the FBI is powerful and that God is powerful. But, he would add, God is not a collection of material individuals, as the FBI is. He would say that God's power goes well beyond that of the FBI, while also being comparable to it. Actually, he would say that God's power runs to creating the FBI (while not being an attribute that he has distinct from himself).

Does Aquinas have some rule of thumb for determining what we can and cannot take God to be? Yes, since he thinks that words signifying perfections can always be used when talking of God so long as the perfections in question are not such as to be had only by a creature of God. Being able to purr is a perfection in the feline world. Perfect cats are purring cats. A cat who cannot purr is sick or in some way thwarted. Yet Aquinas would not want to say that God is able to purr. He would, however, say that God is, for example, good. To call something good is not to categorize it as a creature of some kind. Things of many different kinds can be thought of as good. Goodness, we might say, can be had by anything that exists. So, thinks Aquinas, goodness, considered as a perfection, can be ascribed to God. Something is good, says Aquinas, insofar as it is desirable. But God is desirable. So God is good.[4]

On the other hand, however, when it comes to much talk about God Aquinas does not have a rule of thumb. Frequently, his line is that we are justified in speaking of God with some words that we normally use to talk about creatures just because we have one or another reason to do so. Should we, for example, say that God is something that acts? Yes, replies Aquinas, since we have reason to suppose that God has produced something and that he continues to do so.[5] Again, should we say that God is alive? Yes, replies Aquinas, since we have reason to suppose that God acts of himself and not as moved by something else.[6] In general, Aquinas seeks to show that words *X*, *Y*, or *Z* can be used when talking truly (and literally) of God by trying to show that we have reason to use the words in question.

Question 13 of the *Prima Pars* is instructive when it comes to all of this. Here Aquinas defends the claim that we can speak of God analogously with words that we normally use when talking of creatures. But he does not suggest (as some seem to have taken him to do) that we therefore have a calculator that allows us mechanically to determine what can and cannot be truly said of God. Commenting on Aquinas's view that talk about God uses words "analogically," Peter Geach observes: "It would be better to say that it turns out to be analogical: what happens, on Aquinas's view, is that we first call God "wise"; then discover that "the wisdom of God" is a designation of God himself, whereas the like does not hold of any other being whom we rightly call "wise"; and thus reflecting upon this, we see that "wise" cannot be applied to God in the same way as to other beings."[7] With respect to *Prima Pars* 13, Geach is exactly right. That question of the *Summa theologiae* is best read as what Americans refer to as a "State of the Union Speech." In such speeches U.S. presidents tell their country where things stand now given what has recently happened. In *Prima Pars* 13 Aquinas is doing something like that with an eye on what he has written beforehand. He has argued for the truth of "Deus est" ("God exists"); he has then noted ways in which God must differ from creatures; then he has argued that certain words that we use when talking of creatures can, for various reasons, be used when talking of God; then he notes how these words, though not to be thought of as used in a purely equivocal sense, are also not to be thought of as used univocally.

In general, Aquinas's mature view of "God talk" holds that terms we use when speaking of creatures can be used to talk truly of God *if we have reason* for using them with respect to God. And their sense, when used to talk about God, is to be gleaned from the reasons we have for using them when talking of God. So critics of Aquinas on talk about God do not need to worry about a "theory of analogy." They simply need to ask themselves if Aquinas delivers good reasons for saying that God is *X*, *Y*, or *Z*, while also bearing in mind, and, of course, evaluating, his reasons for denying that God is this, that, or the other.[8] "We cannot," says Aquinas, "speak of God at all except in the language we use of creatures."[9] Yet, he thinks, language we use of creatures can be used to talk literally of God. Why? Because, thinks Aquinas, we have a variety of reasons to use it in this way. To evaluate the truth of this conclusion, readers will need to examine Aquinas's many arguments for the truth of the many propositions about God which he claims to be literally true.

NOTES

1. Statements (2) and (3) here are what Aquinas has in mind when saying that God is entirely simple. Aquinas's doctrine of divine simplicity is discussed in this volume by Eleonore Stump, so I shall not labor to expound it in any more detail.

2. *ST* I q.13 a.5. I should say that in this section of the present volume I am concentrating on what Aquinas has to say about talking of God in the *Summa theologiae*, in which his most mature treatment of the topic is to be found.

3. *ST* I q.13 a.5.

4. *ST* I q.6 a.1.

5. Here, of course, Aquinas's causal arguments for the truth of "God exists" (*Deus est*) are relevant.

6. *ST* I q.18 a.3.

7. G. E. M. Anscombe and P. T. Geach, *Three Philosophers* (Blackwell: Oxford, 1961), 122 f.

8. In Appendix 4 to vol. 3 of the Blackfriars edition of the *Summa Theologiae* (London and New York: Eyre and Spottiswoode, 1964), Herbert McCabe writes, "Too much has been made of St Thomas's alleged teaching on analogy. For him, analogy is not a way of getting to know about God, nor is it a theory of the structure of the universe, it is a comment on our use of certain words" (106). McCabe seems to me to hit the nail on the head here.

9. *ST* I q.13 a.5.

PART VII

PHILOSOPHICAL THEOLOGY

CHAPTER 29

PROVIDENCE AND THE PROBLEM OF EVIL

ELEONORE STUMP

Introduction

The problem of evil is raised by the combination of certain traditional theistic beliefs and the acknowledgement that there is evil in the world. If, as the major monotheisms claim, there is a perfectly good, omnipotent, omniscient God who creates and governs the world, how can the world such a God created and governs have evil in it? In medieval philosophy in the Latin-speaking west, philosophical discussion of evil is informed by Augustine's thought.[1] Readers who have some acquaintance with the history of Christian thought in general and with Augustine in particular may expect Aquinas's position as regards the problem of evil to be some version of what is often understood, mistakenly, as Augustine's theodicy.[2] It will save confusion to set this mistaken expectation aside at the outset.

Augustine struggled with the question of the metaphysical status of evil; and his ultimate conclusion, that evil is a privation of being, was shared by many later medieval philosophers, including Aquinas. "*Privation*" here is a technical term of medieval logic and indicates one particular kind of opposition; its correlative is *possession*. A privation is the absence of some characteristic in a thing that naturally possesses that characteristic. So, on Augustine's views, evil is not nothing, as he is sometimes believed to have maintained. Rather, it is a lack or deficiency of some sort of being in something in which that sort of being is natural. This position of Augustine's is an attempt to explain, as it were, the ontology of evil. Nothing about this ontological position constitutes a solution to the problem of evil, nor did Augustine or any later medieval philosophers suppose it did.[3] Aquinas himself would certainly not have supposed that anything about the metaphysical status of evil provided a reason for God's permitting human suffering to occur.[4]

Augustine is also known for his suggestion that the evil permitted by God contributes to the beauty and goodness of the whole universe, just as a dark patch may contribute to the lightness and beauty of a painting. Some people also mistakenly interpret this suggestion on Augustine's part as an attempt at theodicy. But taking Augustine's point in this way is to suppose that, for Augustine, the answer to the question of why God allows suffering is that suffering has an aesthetic value for God. The moral repulsiveness of such a position strikes many people as obvious; it would most certainly have been obvious to Aquinas.[5] Aquinas himself explicitly repudiates the idea that God would allow the suffering of human persons for any reason other than benefit to the sufferers. So, for example, Aquinas says,

> Whatever happens on earth, even if it is evil, turns out for the good of the whole world. Because as Augustine says in the *Enchiridion*, God is so good that he would never permit any evil if he were not also so powerful that from any evil he could draw out a good. But the evil does not always turn out for the good of the thing in connection with which the evil occurs, because although the corruption of one animal turns out for the good of the whole world—insofar as one animal is generated from the corruption of another—nonetheless it does not turn out for the good of the animal which is corrupted. The reason for this is that the good of the whole world is willed by God for its own sake, and all the parts of the world are ordered to this [end]. The same reasoning appears to apply with regard to the order of the noblest parts [of the world] with respect to the other parts, because the evil of the other parts is ordered to the good of the noblest parts. But what ever happens with regard to the noblest parts is ordered only to the good of those parts themselves, because care is taken of them for their own sake, and for their sake care is taken of other things.... But among the best of all the parts of the world are God's saints.... He takes care of them in such a way that he does not allow any evil for them which he does not turn into their good.[6]

Aquinas's Scale of Value

With this possible confusion set aside, we can begin the examination of what Aquinas's theodicy actually is by considering the standard of value he accepts for human flourishing. Any discussion of the problem of evil presupposes some standard of value, in accordance with which the existence of suffering is judged at least prima facie inconsistent with the existence of a good God.

It is easiest to begin with the extrinsic lower limit to human flourishing. What is the worst thing that can happen to a human being? On Aquinas's views, the worst thing that can happen to a person is to become alienated from God; it is to be endlessly isolated from God's redemptive goodness. What underlies Aquinas's adoption of this characterization of the worst thing for human beings is the conviction

Aquinas shares with other thinkers in the Christian tradition that personal relationship is the genus within which the greatest goods for human beings fall. On this conviction, the greatest good for human beings—the greatest flourishing of human beings—consists in personal relationships of a certain sort. For Aquinas, God has a mind and a will; and so, in our sense of the word "person,"[7] God is a person, on Aquinas's views of God. A union of love with God is thus a personal relationship, too; on Aquinas's views, it is the greatest of personal relationships. The best thing for human beings, the intrinsic upper limit on human flourishing, is to be in a union of love with God. And so the worst thing for human beings and the best thing for human beings are correlatives.

Put this way, the point is not exactly right. That is because, on Aquinas's views, the hallmark of a great good is that it is shareable, that it is not diminished by being distributed. The union of love with God, which is the greatest of goods for a human being and the best of personal relationships, is consequently also the most shareable. The love of one human being for another is also a shareable good, and human loves can themselves be woven into the shareable love between God and human persons. So the shared union of love among human beings and God is the best thing for human beings, on Aquinas's scale of value.

Furthermore, on Aquinas's views, human beings are permanent and not transitory things. For this reason, the best thing and the worst thing for human beings can also be permanent things. For Aquinas, heaven is the best thing made permanent and unending. The permanent shared union of loving personal relationship with God in heaven is thus, finally, the truly best thing for human beings. The worst thing is the permanent absence of that shared union. For Aquinas, because a human will is free in a libertarian sense,[8] it is possible for a human being never to want or to achieve real closeness or love with God or with any human persons either. A human being is capable of being in such a condition forever; and this is hell.[9] On Aquinas's worldview, then, not only is loneliness hellish, in the sense that it is one of the worst things for a human being, but also hell, which is the worst thing made permanent and unending, is lonely.[10]

As these remarks make clear, it is part of Aquinas's worldview that a human being's life is divided into two unequal portions, one very little portion before death and another, infinitely enduring, after death.[11] For reasons having to do not with his theology but with his philosophical psychology,[12] Aquinas holds that the state of a person at the end of the little portion of his life determines his state in the infinitely extended portion of his life after death. For any human person, the degree of his flourishing in perpetuity is set by his condition at the end of the first, little portion of his life.[13]

Aquinas's views of the best thing and the worst thing for human beings mark out a scale of value on which human suffering and the benefits which might be thought to redeem it can be measured. Aquinas himself thinks that acceptance of the view that there is an afterlife and that true happiness consists in union with God in that afterlife is essential to his theodicy. Without it, he thinks, the theodicy he adopts will appear senseless. So, for example, he says,

> If there is no resurrection of the dead, it follows that there is no good for human beings other than in this life. And if this is the case, then those people are more miserable who suffer many evils and tribulations in this life. Therefore, since the apostles and Christians [generally] suffer more tribulations, it follows that they, who enjoy less of the goods of this world, would be more miserable than other people.[14]

What Aquinas goes on to say spells out explicitly the difference between the commonly accepted worldview of his society and that of the popular culture of our own. He says,

> If there were no resurrection of the dead, people would not think it was a power and a glory to abandon all that can give pleasure and to bear the pains of death and dishonor; instead they would think it was stupid.

So, in order to see human suffering as Aquinas does in his theodicy, in order not to see the acceptance of human suffering or the justification of God's allowing such suffering as senseless, it is essential to Aquinas's theodicy also to include the doctrine that human beings are capable of everlasting union with God in the afterlife.

It is also important to recognize that the best thing, the upper limit of Aquinas's scale of value for human lives, comes in degrees.[15] This may appear paradoxical, but a moment's thought will dissipate the appearance. As regards physical condition, the best state for human beings is to be in peak physical condition. But human beings will differ greatly in what constitutes peak physical condition for them. The peak physical condition for a professor will be considerably less impressive as regards physical condition than the peak physical condition of a professional athlete. Analogously, on Aquinas's views, human beings differ greatly in what constitutes for them the peak human condition of union with God.[16]

That is because it is possible to have more or less of a loving relationship in union with any person. It is possible to have more or less of a loving relationship in union with God, too. The love and presence of omnipresent God are fully and equally available to all human beings.[17] But there are differences in the willingness and the capacity to receive God's love even on the part of those human beings who are in union with God. Even in heaven, then, the best thing for human beings, their glory, as Aquinas would call it, comes in degrees. For this reason, what constitutes the most excellent state for human beings is itself a degreed state; it is not had equally by all those who are in that state.

The Good of the Sufferer

With this much description of Aquinas's scale of value for a human life, we can now turn to what Aquinas sees as the morally sufficient reason for God to allow suffering.[18] On Aquinas's theodicy, God is justified in allowing the suffering by one or the other of two possible benefits, where Aquinas's scale of value is the measure of the benefits.[19]

Which of the two possible benefits goes to a particular sufferer on any given occasion depends on the condition of the sufferer herself at that time. Aquinas takes a person of faith to be someone who has committed herself to living a life like that of Christ, with the explicit recognition that such a life includes suffering for the sake of greater spiritual good. And so a person of faith has in effect given consent to living a life which includes suffering. Any particular suffering on the part of a person of faith may in fact be involuntary; but, in virtue of the fact that she has voluntarily chosen a course of life in which (involuntary) suffering has a central role, her suffering is not involuntary *simpliciter*. Because of her commitment to the life of faith, her suffering is involuntary only *in a certain respect*. By contrast, when a sufferer who is not a person of faith involuntarily endures the sufferings of life,[20] his suffering is involuntary *simpliciter*. A person who does not have faith, who is not committed to a Christian life, has not given consent for suffering in any sense.

On Aquinas's views, the benefit that defeats suffering has to be understood differently for these two groups. So, for example, in his commentary on the Apostles' Creed, Aquinas says,

> If all the pain a human being suffers is from God [as Aquinas thinks it is], then he ought to bear it patiently, both because it is from God and because it is ordered toward good; for pains purge sins, bring evildoers to humility, and stimulate good people to love of God.[21]

For a person who does not have faith, whose suffering is involuntary *simpliciter*, God is justified in allowing suffering and suffering is defeated because of the contribution suffering makes to warding off a greater harm for the sufferer. On the other hand, for a person who is committed to a life of faith, whose suffering is involuntary only in a certain respect, God is justified in allowing suffering and suffering is defeated because of the contribution of suffering to providing a greater good for the sufferer.[22] Union with God features in each of these benefits. The greater harm warded off is the permanent absence of shared union with God; and the greater good provided is the increased degree of everlasting shared union with God.

Since it is an extrinsic lower limit on the scale of human flourishing, the negative value of the permanent absence of union with God outweighs the negative value of suffering of any kind. And since union with God is the intrinsic upper limit to human flourishing, the greater good of this union outweighs the good of the avoiding of suffering. The main question for Aquinas's theodicy therefore is not whether the good of the benefit outweighs the suffering in any given case but rather whether the suffering is appropriately connected to one or the other of these benefits. Even if we weigh the relative value of the benefits and the suffering as Aquinas does, the question arises why Aquinas would suppose that suffering is connected to these benefits in the way it needs to be for the purposes of theodicy.

The Obstacles to Human Flourishing

It helps in trying to find the answer to this question to see what Aquinas takes to be the impediments to union with God. For Aquinas, the obstacle to any person's flourishing in union with God comes from dispositions in that person's will, which incline him to prefer his own short-term pleasure and power over greater goods. On Aquinas's understanding of the doctrine of original sin, all human beings have a sort of cancer of the will,[23] a proneness to evil, which invariably eventuates in moral wrongdoing sooner or later and which in the right circumstances blows up into moral monstrosity.[24] No human being who remains uncured of the disease of the will can be united with God. For Aquinas, then, the obstacle to a person's having the best thing for human beings, shared union with God, is that person's condition in the will.[25] Since the best thing for human beings and the worst thing for human beings are jointly exhaustive, warding off the worst thing for any human person is also a matter of healing this internal condition.

Aquinas takes the justification and sanctification of postlapsarian human beings to be the means by which a person becomes healed of the disease in the will. (The full story of Aquinas's account of redemption lies outside the scope of this entry; it includes not only Aquinas's understanding of grace but also his theory of the incarnation, passion, death, and resurrection of Christ.[26])

Justification occurs when a human person recognizes and rejects the moral evil in himself and yearns for the goodness of God.[27] It includes most centrally an act of will that is a global second-order desire for a will that wills the good. Aquinas thinks of this as the volitional component of the act of faith. On Aquinas's account of faith, a person who forms such an act of will is in effect forming a volition for God to alter her will by making it progressively more and more internally integrated in the good.[28] Aquinas takes this act of will to be the sole necessary and sufficient condition for warding off the worst thing for human beings. While this act of will remains in a person, permanent isolation from God is ruled out for her. Warding off for a person the greater harm of permanent absence of union with God is thus a matter of bringing about and maintaining this volition in her.[29]

For Aquinas, then, the morally sufficient reason for God's allowing suffering that is involuntary *simpliciter* for a person is the role of such suffering in bringing that person to the act of will in faith constitutive of justification.

When a person forms the act of will constitutive of justification, this act of will is only the beginning of a process of healing the will for that person. The ongoing healing is the process of sanctification. In this process, God works together with the will of a human person in a cooperative enterprise that gradually integrates her more and more in goodness.[30] Sanctification brings a person into as deep a union with God as she is willing to have. Insofar as her greatness is correlative with her union with God, sanctification also transforms her into something glorious.

For those human beings who are committed to the cooperative enterprise of sanctification, then, the morally sufficient reason for God's allowing their suffering, which is involuntary only *in a certain respect*, is the role of that suffering in their sanctification.

The Role of Suffering in Warding off the Worst Thing

Because Aquinas thinks of justification and sanctification as healing for a human psyche, he often speaks of suffering as God's medicine for the psychic disorder of postlapsarian human beings.[31] In his commentary on Thessalonians, he says,

> As water extinguishes a burning fire, so tribulations extinguish the force of concupiscent desires, so that human beings don't follow them at will. . . . Therefore, [the Church] is not destroyed [by tribulations] but lifted up by them, and in the first place by the lifting up of the mind to God, as Gregory says: the evils which bear us down here drive us to go to God.[32]

Aquinas comments in great detail on the line in Hebrews: "whom the Lord loves he chastens."[33] He says, for example,

> Since pains are a sort of medicine, we should apparently judge correction and medicine the same way. Now medicine in the taking of it is bitter and loathsome, but its end is desirable and intensely sweet. So discipline is also. It is hard to bear, but it blossoms into the best outcome.[34]

The same general point appears recurrently in Aquinas's commentary on Job. Arguing that temporal goods such as those Job lost are given and taken away according to God's will, Aquinas says,

> someone's suffering adversity would not be pleasing to God except for the sake of some good coming from the adversity. And so although adversity is in itself bitter and gives rise to sadness, it should nonetheless be agreeable [to us] when we consider its usefulness, on account of which it is pleasing to God. . . . For in his reason a person rejoices over the taking of bitter medicine because of the hope of health, even though in his senses he is troubled.[35]

In commenting on a line in Job containing the complaint that God sometimes does not hear a needy person's prayers, Aquinas says,

> Now it sometimes happens that God hearkens not to a person's pleas but rather to his advantage. A doctor does not hearken to the pleas of the sick person who requests that the bitter medicine be taken away (supposing that the doctor doesn't

> take it away because he knows that it contributes to health); instead he hearkens to [the patient's] advantage, because by doing so he produces health, which the sick person wants most of all. In the same way, God does not remove tribulations from the person stuck in them, even though he prays earnestly for God to do so, because God knows these tribulations help him forward to final salvation. And so although God truly does hearken, the person stuck in afflictions believes that God hasn't hearkened to him.[36]

For Aquinas, then, suffering is medicinal for the parts of a person's psyche in need of healing.[37] For those who are already healed to a certain extent, the experience of suffering enables them to open in a deeper way to the love of God, as Aquinas says in the commentary on the Creed. But for those who are very far from being healed, suffering is medicinal in the sense that, as Aquinas puts it, it helps the sufferer forward to salvation. For those very alienated from themselves and from God, suffering contributes to warding off from the sufferer the worst thing for human beings.

The Role of Suffering in Providing the Best Thing

Given Aquinas's view of suffering as medicinal for the human psyche, one might be tempted to think that Aquinas would also take the degree of a person's suffering to be in direct proportion to her need for psychic healing. One might suppose, that is, that since for Aquinas suffering is medicinal, he would also think that a person who was more advanced in healing would need and so would get less suffering. But, in fact, Aquinas's position is just the opposite.

On Aquinas's theodicy, the more a person is healed, the more advanced she is in the process of drawing near to God, the more likely it is that she will experience suffering. In explicating two metaphors in one of Job's speeches,[38] comparing human beings in this life to soldiers on a military campaign and to employees, Aquinas makes the point in this way:

> It is plain that the general of an army does not spare [his] more active soldiers dangers or exertions, but as the plan of battle requires, he sometimes lays them open to greater dangers and greater exertions. But after the attainment of victory, he bestows greater honor on the more active soldiers. So also the head of a household assigns greater exertions to his better servants, but when it is time to reward them, he lavishes greater gifts on them. And so neither is it characteristic of divine providence that it should exempt good people more from the adversities and exertions of the present life, but rather that it reward them more at the end.[39]

Aquinas's sense that the inner wholeness of a person renders her more, rather than less, likely to suffer can be understood in light of his taking suffering as medicinal.

Strenuous medical regimens are saved for the strongest patients, in the hopes of bringing them to the most robust health and functioning. On Aquinas's theodicy, for those people who are psychically healthier, the benefit that justifies suffering is the connection between suffering and glory. So, for example, he says,

> All the saints who have pleased God have gone through many tribulations by which they were made the sons of God.[40]

In his commentary on Thessalonians, Aquinas makes the same point in a slightly different way:

> Many who are alive [in the eschaton] will be tried in the persecution of Antichrist, and they will surpass in greatness the many who had previously died.[41]

Elsewhere he puts the point in a more general way. He says,

> from sufferings borne here a person attains to glory.[42]

These and many other passages make it clear that Aquinas thinks there is a connection between suffering, on the one hand, and glory in shared union with God, on the other. It is not surprising, then, to find that Aquinas sees a person's enduring severe suffering as a sign of the spiritual greatness of the sufferer.

Aquinas does not lose sight of the fact that any particular involuntarily endured suffering is real suffering, lamentable, sorrowful, execrable, and to be avoided or remedied if at all possible. But because Aquinas thinks that the suffering for those able and willing to receive it as sanctifying contributes to the best thing for human beings, he also thinks that there is something to exult in as regards such suffering. So, for example, he says,

> It is a sign of the ardent hope which we have on account of Christ that we glory not only because of [our] hope of the glory to come, but we glory even regarding the evils which we suffer for it. And so [Paul] says that we not only glory (that is, in our hope of glory), but we glory even in tribulations, by which we attain to glory.[43]

Suffering and Consolation

Even with this much clarification, Aquinas's theodicy is still not presented in full. What is yet missing is his understanding of the role of divine consolation.

Because God is omnipresent and perfectly loving, Aquinas thinks that all suffering is encompassed even in this life by the love of God. The experience of the personal presence of God is not reserved just for mystics.[44] On the doctrine of omnipresence, God's personal presence is always available to every human being. A person has only to be wholeheartedly willing to receive God's love and presence in order to have them, to one degree or another.[45] For those who are open to God's presence, the minimal omnipresence of God becomes presence in love; and this presence brings consolation with it.

In fact, Aquinas thinks that, for sufferers who are open to God's presence, the consolation of that presence is felt with increased intensity in direct proportion to their sufferings. At the start of his commentary on 1 Thessalonians, Aquinas quotes with approval the line in 2 Corinthians, which says that "as the sufferings of Christ abound in us, so our consolation also abounds by Christ" (2 Cor. 1:5).

It should also be said that Aquinas's notion of consolation is not abstract or anemic; rather, it emphasizes the role of personal presence in relationship with God. So, for example, Aquinas says,

> the ultimate perfection, by which a person is made perfect inwardly, is joy, which stems from the presence of what is loved. Whoever has the love of God, however, already has what he loves, as is said in 1 John 4:16: "whoever abides in the love of God abides in God, and God abides in him." And joy wells up from this.[46]

Elsewhere, commenting on a text in the epistles of Paul, Aquinas puts the point this way:

> When [Paul] says "the Lord is near," he points out the cause of joy, because a person rejoices at the nearness of his friend.[47]

Moreover, on Aquinas's views, the joy that comes from such personal presence between God and a human person is essential to a religious life of a believer; and he expects that all persons of faith will have such joy.[48] As Aquinas sees it, without the joy of this relationship, no progress is possible for anyone in the life of faith.[49]

Someone might object that suffering interferes with the joy of loving relations and that Aquinas simply fails to appreciate this point. In response to such an objection, Aquinas would grant that loving relationship even with the deity does not prevent or take away suffering.[50] On the other hand, however, Aquinas would reject the objection itself. Aquinas thinks that no sort of suffering, not even pain, can destroy the good of the loving personal relationship between God and a human being open to God's presence.[51]

Conclusion: The Mysteriousness of Suffering

Finally, a word should be said about the mysteriousness of suffering. In recent years, a substantial literature has developed that contends on the basis of epistemological considerations that a theodicy is not needed in order to rebut the argument from evil. This response to the problem of evil has come to be called "skeptical theism," and it is centered on the limitedness of human cognitive capacities. On the view of skeptical theism, we can know that we are not in an epistemic position to recognize morally sufficient reasons for God's allowing suffering,[52] because we can see that finite human minds cannot comprehend the infinite mind of God or cannot evaluate the intricacies of probabilistic reasoning or cannot calculate complicated modal claims.[53] Since we can know that our minds are limited in one or more of these ways, the response of skeptical theism goes, then the argument from evil is undermined.[54]

Aquinas would suppose skeptical theism to be false.[55] He takes it to be true that human beings are in a position to know what God's reasons are for allowing suffering—that is, the suffering of fully functional adult human beings, to which the theodicy under discussion in this entry is limited. But Aquinas would suppose that this theodicy is applicable only in general or in theory. For any particular case of suffering, because of the opacity of the benefits defeating suffering, human beings will typically not be in a position to know what justifies God in permitting that suffering. The epistemic problem for Aquinas is not the inscrutability of God's mind (as skeptical theism alleges) but the inscrutability of the human heart and the complexity of a human life. On Aquinas's views, then, there is a mundane reason for being doubtful about our ability to discern the morally sufficient reason justifying any particular case of human suffering: the particular benefits that could defeat that particular suffering are not transparent to us. So, for example, in explaining why some things are not known to some cognizers, Aquinas says,

> [one reason why something is not known is that] it is obscured by being inside something [else]. The things most obscured in this way are the things hidden in the [human] heart, which is exceedingly deep and inscrutable.[56]

What requires healing about a particular person, what role a particular instance of suffering plays or might play in that person's redemption and glory—these are things which no human being, including the sufferer, may be in a position to know. The role of any particular case of suffering in contributing to bringing a particular person closer to God can be evident only to a person in a position to see more than human persons typically can see.

For this reason, the inference in any particular instance of suffering to the absence of a benefit defeating suffering from the appearance of the absence of such a benefit is not valid. On Aquinas's account, the nature of a particular benefit able to defeat suffering in any given case is such that reason may not be able to see it. Unlike the agnosticism of skeptical theism, however, this is not an agnosticism about the general nature of the morally sufficient reasons for God's allowing suffering. Consequently, this agnosticism does not militate against the possibility of theodicy in general, as skeptical theism does. Rather, Aquinas's views about the benefits that could defeat suffering constitute an argument only against confidence in human abilities to evaluate the application of the general claims of theodicy to any particular case of suffering. If in some particular case of human suffering we can see no particular benefit that justifies that suffering, we are not thereby entitled to claim that in that case there is none.

And so, although Aquinas supposes that there is available to human beings a good and acceptable theodicy, it remains the case that, on his views, any particular case of suffering is likely to remain a mystery to us. A theodicy, as Aquinas understands it, cannot give a specific answer to the question why Aunt Sallie was hit by a car.[57]

It should also be said here that, in the same way and for analogous reasons, Aquinas's theodicy cannot give a specific answer to questions about suffering of large-scale societies. If we want to know why God allowed the suffering of the western world during World War I, or what benefits in particular defeated the great communal suffering elicited by that social convulsion, then it is important to recognize that, on Aquinas's account, we are not in a position to give an answer to the question.

For Aquinas, such an answer would have to fall within the general outlines of his theodicy. That is, the benefits would have to go primarily to the sufferers, as measured by Aquinas's scale of value for human flourishing. Furthermore, because the question asks about the communal suffering of many nations taken together, the benefit would have to be commensurate in scope and size. That is, the benefit would have to affect many societies, and it would also have to impact society as a whole, influencing the entire community in such a way as to ward off the worst thing for human beings or contribute to the best thing for human beings taken communally. Only someone in a position to be aware of the trajectory of whole societies could answer the question about suffering of this magnitude. It seems clear that human beings are very rarely in a position to grasp things of this sort.

And so although there is no answer to the question about suffering affecting whole societies, on Aquinas's theodicy we can see that we are rarely if ever able to see the things about such extensive organizations of people, which we would have to see in order to apply Aquinas's theodicy to suffering on that scale.[58]

NOTES

1. The literature on Augustine's reflections on goodness is vast; but see, e.g., Christopher Kirwan, *Augustine* (London: Routledge, 1989) and G. R. Evans, *Augustine on Evil* (Cambridge: Cambridge University Press, 1982) for helpful introductions. For more recent discussion, see Norman Kretzmann and Eleonore Stump, eds., *The Cambridge Companion to Augustine* (Cambridge: Cambridge University Press, 2001). For a good overview of the problem in the context of medieval philosophical theology, see Ingolf Dalferth, *Malum: Theologische Hermeneutik des Bösen* (Tübingen: Mohr Siebeck, 2008).

2. For some further discussions of the issues in this section, see my "The Problem of Evil," in Robert Pasnau, ed., *The Cambridge History of Later Medieval Philosophy* (Cambridge: Cambridge University Press, 2009).

3. For a general discussion of this Augustinian position in later medieval philosophy, see, e.g., Scott MacDonald, ed., *Being and Goodness: The Concept of the Good in Metaphysics and Philosophical Theology* (Ithaca, N.Y.: Cornell University Press, 1991).

4. In this essay, I am limiting consideration not just to human suffering but in fact to the suffering of normally functioning adult human beings. The reasons for such a limitation on the description of Aquinas's theodicy and the possibility of extrapolating

from that theodicy to other cases of suffering not covered in it are explored in detail in my *Wandering in Darkness: Narrative and the Problem of Suffering* (Oxford: Oxford University Press, 2010).

5. Augustine would also have found such a position unacceptable, in my view. For a discussion of this issue, see my "The Problem of Evil," in Robert Pasnau, ed., *The Cambridge History of Later Medieval Philosophy* (Cambridge: Cambridge University Press, 2009). Some parts of this entry are taken from that essay.

6. *In Rom* 8.6.

7. In Aquinas's terms, the point has to be put differently, of course; on the doctrine of the Trinity, in medieval terms, there is one God in three persons. But this is a technical sense of "person," drawn from Boethius's formulation: a person is an individual substance of a rational nature. Nonetheless, the technical sense as it is used in the doctrine of the Trinity is compatible with the claim that God is a person, in our sense of the word "person." There is just one will and one intellect in the triune God, on the orthodox views Aquinas accepts. Insofar as, in our sense of "person," something having one mind and one will is a person, it is true to say that for Aquinas God is a person. Some readers will also want to object to the claim that for Aquinas God has a will and a mind, on the grounds that for Aquinas God is simple and therefore has no parts that can be distinguished from one another as mind is distinguished from will. But although it is true that Aquinas's God is simple, Aquinas himself talks about the intellect and the will of God. Formulating claims about God in order to bring the doctrine of simplicity to the fore requires so much clumsiness in locution that Aquinas himself regularly omits it. For defense of Aquinas's views on simplicity, see the relevant chapter in my *Aquinas* (London: Routledge, 2003).

8. For an explanation of Aquinas's kind of libertarianism, see the chapter on free will in my *Aquinas*.

9. There is more to hell than simply the loss of God's presence, on Aquinas's views, because there is also penalty or punishment; but Aquinas supposes that the loss of God's presence is sufficient for hell.

10. For examination of Aquinas's view that the union of love is possible only in integration around goodness, see my "Love, By All Accounts," *Proceedings and Addresses of the American Philosophical Association* 80:2 (November 2006): 25–43.

11. For Aquinas's position on the separated soul, see my entry in this volume.

12. Because of the connection he accepts between the intellect and the will, Aquinas thinks that there is no major change of heart possible after a person has his first experience of the afterlife and sees whatever of God he can see. For explanation of Aquinas's moral psychology, see the chapters on freedom and on wisdom in my *Aquinas*.

13. Aquinas supposes that there is no traffic between heaven and hell; that is, no person who was really in heaven ever goes to hell, and no person who was really in hell ever goes to heaven. (The qualifier "really" is needed to handle some theological complexities, such as the harrowing of hell, which are not relevant to the topic of this essay.) It is clear enough why the inability to lose heaven would be essential to peace and joy in heaven. But it is less easy to see why a person in hell could not repent and come to heaven. The reasons Aquinas gives for his view that it is not possible have to do with his understanding of the conditions needed for changing one's mind. If he were wrong on this score, the error would necessitate only a redescription of the extrinsic lower limit of the scale of value for human flourishing.

14. Aquinas, *In I Cor* 15.2.

15. It is also the case that, for Aquinas, the extrinsic lower limit on flourishing comes in degrees. The state of everlasting distance from God is a degreed state too, on his views.

As far as I can see, this part of his worldview makes no significant difference to the lineaments of his theodicy, and so I am leaving it out of account here, for the sake of keeping complications to a minimum. But if in fact someone supposes that this part of Aquinas's worldview does make a difference to his theodicy, it can be added in at no cost except that of complexity. In that case, the lower limit of flourishing would have to be dealt with in the same way as the upper limit.

16. Cf., e.g., *ST* I-II q.112 a.4 ad 2, where Aquinas addresses the objection that there cannot be greater or lesser grace in one person than in another, either in this life or in heaven. In the reply to that objection, Aquinas makes clear that there are differences of degree even, as he says, in final glory.

17. For further discussion of Aquinas's position on God's grace and its role in human salvation, see the chapters on faith and on grace and free will in my *Aquinas*.

18. Some readers will suppose that by speaking of a morally sufficient reason for God to allow evil, one attributes moral obligations to God; and they will resist such attribution. It is important to recognize that this position is not entailed by a theodicy; a theodicy does not require anyone to posit moral obligations for God. A morally sufficient reason for God to allow suffering is only a reason which, by the moral standards of human beings considering the problem of evil, is sufficient to justify God in our eyes for his permission of human suffering.

19. In what follows, the discussion is limited to the suffering of fully functional adult human beings, for the sake of brevity. For a consideration of the reasons for this limitation and suggestions for ways in which Aquinas's basic theodicy as presented here might be extended, see my *Wandering in Darkness*.

20. The point of the clumsy phrase "the sufferings of life" is, of course, to exclude some sorts of partly voluntary suffering, such as the suffering experienced by athletes or soldiers in the course of their activities as athletes or soldiers.

21. For an annotated translation of the text, see Nicholas Ayo, *The Sermon-Conferences of St. Thomas Aquinas on the Apostles' Creed* (Notre Dame, Ind.: University of Notre Dame Press, 1988). Although I have preferred to use my own translation, I found Ayo's helpful, and for this work I give citations both to the Latin and to Ayo's translation. Thomas Aquinas, *Collationes Credo in Deum*, sec. III; Ayo, *Sermon-Conferences*, 40–42.

22. Of course, the same person might at one time not be a person of faith and at another time might be a person of faith. So the benefit defeating suffering has to be relativized not only to a person but also to the condition of that person at a particular time.

23. Strictly speaking, this claim needs to be slightly qualified for reasons having to do with the Incarnation.

24. Aquinas, *Super ad Hebraeos*, chap. 12, lect. 2.

25. To say that this is the only obstacle is not to say that a human being can achieve this union on her own without help from God. But since, on Aquinas's views, the apostle Paul is correct in claiming that God desires to save all human beings, the *obstacle* to union with God comes only from human beings.

26. For discussion of these topics, see the relevant chapters in my *Aquinas*.

27. For the connection between this claim and Aquinas's theory of the atonement, see the chapters on faith and on atonement in my *Aquinas*.

28. For the role of grace in the formation of this act of will, see the chapter on grace in my *Aquinas*.

29. For more discussion of justification, see the relevant chapters in my *Aquinas*.

30. For a discussion of the sort of cooperation at issue here, see the chapters on faith and on grace in my *Aquinas*.

31. For futher discussion of suffering as medicinal in the thought of Thomas Aquinas, see the chapter on providence and suffering in my *Aquinas*.

32. There is a translation of this commentary: *Commentary on Saint Paul's First Letter to the Thessalonians and the Letter to the Philippians by St. Thomas Aquinas*, trans. F. R. Larcher and Michael Duffy (Albany, N.Y.: Magi Books, 1969). Although I have preferred to use my own translations, I found the Larcher and Duffy translation helpful. Thomas Aquinas, *Super ad Thessalonicenses I*, prologue; Larcher and Duffy, *Commentary*, 3.

33. *Super ad Hebraeos*, chap. 12, lect. 1.

34. *Super ad Hebraeos*, chap. 12, lect. 2.

35. Aquinas, *Expositio super Job*, chap. 1, sec. 20–21; Thomas Aquinas, *The Literal Exposition on Job: A Scriptural Commentary concerning Providence*, trans. Anthony Damico and Martin Yaffe, The American Academy of Religion Classics in Religious Studies (Atlanta: Scholars Press, 1989), 89.

36. Aquinas, *Expositio super Job*, chap. 9, sec. 15–21; Damico and Yaffe, *Literal Exposition on Job*, 174.

37. To say that it is medicinal for all sufferers is not to say that all sufferers are justified and sanctified by it; not all things that are medicinal are efficacious for cure.

38. Only one of the two metaphors is in the text translated in the Revised Standard Version, the King James, and the Anchor Bible.

39. Aquinas, *Expositio super Job*, chap. 7, sec. 1; Damico and Yaffe, *Literal Exposition on Job*, 146.

40. *Super ad Hebraeos*, chap. 12, lect. 2.

41. Aquinas, *Super ad Thessalonicenses* I, chap. 4, lect. 2; Larcher and Duffy, *Commentary*, 39.

42. Aquinas, *Super ad Philippenses*, chap. 3, lect. 2; Larcher and Duffy, *Commentary*, 102.

43. Aquinas, *Super ad Romanos*, chap. 5, lect. 1.

44. It is clear that there are degrees of such experience. For human beings in this life, the religious experience of mystics no doubt is an upper bound. At the lower bound, it is possible to receive something of the consolation of God's presence and love without recognizing it as such. The consolation of love, and its opposites, need not operate at the level of full consciousness. Perhaps it is possible even for a person who believes of himself that he is alienated from God or an atheist to receive some kind of consolation from God's presence, provided that, contrary to what he believes of himself, he has not closed God out entirely. There is a poignant description of such a complicated psychic state in the autobiographical work, *Grace Abounding to the Chief of Sinners*, by the seventeenth-century Puritan writer John Bunyan. So perhaps there are people who believe of themselves that they have no religious experiences but who are wrong in that claim.

45. The notable exception to this claim has to do with the dark night of the soul, a complicated religious phenomenon that has to be left aside here.

46. There is an English translation of this work: *Commentary on Saint Paul's Epistle to the Galatians by St. Thomas Aquinas*, trans. F. R. Larcher and Richard Murphy (Albany, N.Y.: Magi Books, 1966). Although I have preferred to use my own translations, I found the Larcher and Murphy translation helpful. *Super ad Galatas*, chap. 5, lect. 6; Larcher and Murphy, *Commentary*, 179–80.

47. *Super ad Philippenses*, chap. 4, lect. 1; Larcher and Duffy, *Commentary*, 113.

48. For Aquinas, joy is one of the fruits of the Holy Spirit, and it is the state resulting from the gifts of the Holy Spirit that are necessary to salvation. See, e.g., *ST* I-II q.70 a.3.

49. *Super ad Philippenses*, chap. 4, lect. 1; Larcher and Duffy, *Commentary*, 112.

50. See, e.g., Aquinas's interpretation of the suffering of Christ in his commentary on the Gospel of John.

51. We ourselves share this view when it comes to relationships between human persons. That is why we do not leave a person in pain to himself. We suppose that there is some great consolation for him, which even pain cannot take away, in having someone who loves him near him in his suffering.

52. As pointed out by William Rowe, in his classic formulation of the argument from evil, it is also possible to rebut the argument from evil effectively without a theodicy by employing on it what Rowe calls "the G. E. Moore shift" (William Rowe, "The Problem of Evil and Some Varieties of Atheism," *American Philosophical Quarterly* 16 [1979]; reprinted in Daniel Howard-Snyder, *The Evidential Problem of Evil* [Bloomington: Indiana University Press, 1996], 1–11). As Rowe explains it, the G. E. Moore shift consists in taking as a premiss the negation of the conclusion of an opponent's argument and deriving as a conclusion the negation of one of the premisses in the opponent's argument. In the case of the argument from evil, the G. E. Moore shift is a matter of taking as a premiss the existence of God and concluding that there is a morally sufficient reason for God to allow evil. This response to the argument from evil depends on some support for the premiss that God exists, support which is not effectively undercut by the problem of evil itself. The G. E. Moore shift has not received much attention by contemporary philosophers because they suppose that support for the premiss that God exists would have to come from arguments for the existence of God, and few people now have much confidence that such arguments can be adequately defended. So, e.g., Peter van Inwagen says that a response of this sort to the argument from evil is "unappealing, at least if 'reasons' [for preferring the claim that God exists to the rival claim of atheism] is taken to mean 'arguments for the existence of God' in the traditional or philosophy-of-religion-text sense. Whatever the individual merits or defects of those arguments, none of them but the 'moral argument' (and perhaps the ontological argument) purports to prove the existence of a morally perfect being. And neither the moral argument nor the ontological argument has many defenders these days" (Peter van Inwagen, "The Problem of Evil, the Problem of Air, and the Problem of Silence," in Daniel Howard-Snyder, ed., *The Evidential Argument from Evil* [Bloomington: Indiana University Press: 1996], 154). Even if none of the arguments for the existence of God is successful, however, it might still be the case that for any particular individual belief in God is rooted in religious experience or is in some other way a properly basic belief. In that case, the G. E. Moore shift would be an adequate response to the argument from evil for such a person. On the other hand, even if it were successful, the G. E. Moore shift would not obviate the usefulness of a theodicy, because a theodicy contributes an explanation of evil, as the G. E. Moore shift does not.

53. Skeptical theism comes in different varieties, some considerably different from or more complicated than the short description in the text here indicates. For a good introduction to the varieties of skeptical theism and objections to them, see Paul Draper, "The Skeptical Theist," in Daniel Howard-Snyder, ed., *The Evidential Argument from Evil* (Bloomington: Indiana University Press, 1996), 175–92.

54. See, e.g., William Alston, "The Inductive Argument from Evil and the Human Cognitive Condition"; Stephen Wykstra, "Rowe's Noseeum Arguments from Evil"; Peter van Inwagen, "The Problem of Evil, the Problem of Air, and the Problem of Silence"; Paul Draper, "The Skeptical Theist"; and Peter van Inwagen, "Reflections on the Chapters by

Draper, Russell, and Gale," in Daniel Howard-Snyder, ed., *The Evidential Argument from Evil* (Bloomington: Indiana University Press, 1996), 97–125, 126–50, 151–74, 175–92, 219–43, respectively.

55. Aquinas would agree with skeptical theism that a limited human mind cannot comprehend the infinite mind of God. But Aquinas accepts the idea that God can communicate his purposes to human beings through revelation. So even if skeptical theism is right about what unaided human intellects can understand, Aquinas would suppose that human intellects are not always unaided.

56. *Super ad Hebraeos*, chap. 4, lect. 2.

57. I say "specific" in this context because, of course, Aquinas's theodicy provides a general answer which applies in an abstract way to every case of human suffering.

58. I am grateful to Brian Davies for helpful comments on an earlier draft.

CHAPTER 30

THE TRINITY

GILLES EMERY

Aquinas places the Trinity at the heart of the Christian faith: "The Christian faith chiefly consists in confessing the holy Trinity."[1] The revelation of the Trinity is thus of central importance: "To know the divine persons was necessary for us for two reasons. First, in order to have a right view of the creation of things... The other and principal reason is so that we may have the right view of salvation of mankind, accomplished by the Son who became flesh and by the gift of the Holy Spirit."[2] Faith in Christ intrinsically implies faith in the Trinity.[3] Final beatitude consists in the vision of the Holy Trinity, and, "moreover, what brings us to beatitude is the mission of the divine persons."[4] Aquinas's account of Christian faith is Trinitarian in nature.[5] "The vision of the Father (*visio Patris*) is the end of all our desires and actions."[6]

Exposition of Speculative Trinitarian Theology

Faith in the Trinity depends exclusively on Revelation whose center is the Incarnation of the Son, his life in the flesh and the sending of the Holy Spirit. Aquinas not only rules out the possibility of natural reason attaining to knowledge of the Trinity[7] but also refuses to consider God's personal plurality as the fruit of an essential fecundity of the divine being.[8] He draws a clear distinction between our knowledge of the divine essence and our knowledge of personal plurality in God: this straightforward distinction is one of Aquinas's most salient features, particularly in comparison to Bonaventure. For Bonaventure, the plurality of divine persons is held by faith, but even so the believing mind can show this plurality by means of "reasons" (drawn on God's simplicity, primacy, perfection, happiness, charity, and actuality) that have the force of necessity;[9] whereas Aquinas maintains that only the "truth of faith" leads one to affirm the plurality of divine persons: reasons such as those given by Bonaventure do not conclude necessarily.[10]

Concerning Trinitarian faith, arguments advanced by the theologian are thus chiefly of two kinds. The first kind of argument falls under the authority of Holy Scripture, which reveals that the Father, Son, and Holy Spirit are distinct yet perfectly one. The other kind of argument consists of "persuasions" that do not demonstrate the Trinity but seek to render the Trinitarian faith *more articulate* in the minds of believers and that show that what is proposed to faith is not impossible,[11] so that "the mind is lifted up to get some glimpse of the truth that suffices for excluding errors."[12] Thomistic Trinitarian theology is a "spiritual exercise."[13] In order to manifest biblical faith concerning the Trinity, Aquinas exploits numerous sources: creeds, the liturgy, Latin Fathers (chiefly Augustine, Hilary of Poitiers, Ambrose of Milan), Greek Fathers (chiefly John Damascene and Pseudo-Dionysius but others also), and medieval (Boethius, Anselm), as well as philosophical (Aristotle) authors, not to mention the contribution of the Trinitarian debates of the twelfth and the first half of the thirteenth century. First place among these goes to Augustine and his medieval reception: the "manifestation" of the Trinity by the "similitude" of the Word and Love in the human mind explicitly follows the way traced out by Augustine.[14]

Aquinas has supplied several syntheses of Trinitarian doctrine (*Super Sent*, *SCG*, *QDP*, *CT*, and *ST* in particular). The principal elements of his Trinitarian doctrine are present as well in his biblical commentaries (on John and Paul in particular). The *Summa theologiae* offers his most complete synthesis. Concerning the structure of the study of God, Aquinas distinguishes between "first, that which pertains to the divine essence, secondly, that pertaining to the distinction of the persons, and thirdly that concerning the procession of creatures from God."[15] This structure, which does not signify the modern separation between a treatise on the One God and a treatise on the Triune God, seeks to fulfill three fundamental doctrinal exigencies: the distinction between God in himself and in his effects ("theology" and "economy"); the double mode of our access to knowledge of God (reason and faith); and the double perspective of the human grasp of the Trinitarian mystery: the perspective of the common essence and the perspective of the relative properties of the persons. To render account of the faith, Aquinas's speculative Trinitarian theology rests chiefly on two doctrinal pillars: the conception of the divine person as a subsistent relation, as well as the doctrine of the Word and Love.

Processions, Relations, and Persons

Aquinas conceives of the divine person as a "subsistent relation." To grasp the divine person then, it is first of all necessary to clarify what a relation is. Now, in our world, real relations do not suddenly appear from nowhere but come from a foundation that causes them. In the case of the Trinity, this foundation is the procession that our mind conceives as the source of the relation. Thus, the order of the speculative manifestation of divine tripersonality will be: procession, then relation, then person.

Interpreting Aristotle, Aquinas holds that two bases can cause a real relation: quantity and action-passion.[16] Since quantity must be excluded from God, that leaves action and procession. By "procession," one must understand "the drawing out of a reality that issues from a principle."[17] In God, the action that gives rise to the procession of a person consubstantial to its principle can only be an "immanent" action, that is, an action that remains within the agent itself. Aquinas recognizes two kinds of immanent procession in an intellectual nature: that of the intellect and that of the will.[18] In God, the first procession is that of the Word, who proceeds by way of intellect: this procession is properly a generation. The second procession is that of the Spirit, who proceeds by way of love. Aquinas shows that the procession of Love is distinguished from the Word's generation in the real order, because generation takes place through the mode of a *similitude*, while the procession of Love takes place through the dynamic mode of a *principle of impulsion* toward the being that is loved.[19] Aquinas gradually elaborated this doctrine, which appears beginning with the *SCG*. He considers the analogical mode, intellectual and voluntary, according to which the intelligent being is present to itself.

The doctrine of procession takes note of the real relations between the principle of the procession and the term that proceeds: paternity (the Father's relation to the Son), filiation (the Son's relation to the Father), spiration (the relation of the Father and the Son to the Spirit), and procession (the Spirit's relation to the Father and the Son). The reality of these relations flows from their foundation (immanent action) and arises from the fact that those who are related share in the same divine nature and are thus of the same order. In every real relation, Aquinas distinguishes two aspects: the proper essence or "*ratio*" of the relation and the being or "*esse*" of the relation. Under the aspect of its "*ratio*," the divine relation consists of a pure relationship to the other according to origin. But under the aspect of its being, the divine relation is formally identical with the divine essence and thus possesses the "*esse*" of the divine essence. The relations founded on the processions of the Word and of Love thus *integrate* a double aspect in themselves: the real distinction between "opposed relations" (paternity–filiation and spiration–procession) and divine existence, to the extent that these relations possess divine existence.[20]

Aquinas takes up Boethius's definition of a person: "a person is an individual substance of a rational nature." A person is thus defined by three characteristics: individuality, that is, the mode of existence of a real incommunicable singular; subsistence, that is, substantial existence of that which exists distinctly by and in itself; and intellectual nature, that is, the essence of beings endowed with intelligence and freedom. This interpretation of Boethius's definition supplies an *analogical* notion that is applied to God the Trinity differently than to angels and human beings. To grasp the divine person, Aquinas brings the analysis of the divine relation to bear under the double aspect of its "*ratio*" and its "*esse*." He holds that the "divine person," "the distinct subsistent in the divine nature," signifies the relation itself insofar as it subsists, that is, "relation as something subsisting." In other words, a divine person "signifies relation by way of substance, which is a hypostasis subsisting in the divine nature."[21] Aquinas does not apply this conception of a person as relation, to human beings; he reserves it to the divine person: the distinction of created persons is through principles that constitute the essence while in God alone the relations subsist.[22] This doctrine of "subsistent relations," which accounts for both essential unity and personal plurality in the Trinity, constitutes the keystone of Aquinas's Trinitarian doctrine. On one hand, the consistency of this doctrine of "subsistent relations" depends on Aquinas's analysis of relations in the created world. Namely, there are real relations where such relations are accidents with a "*ratio*" and a real "*esse*"; and these relations differ from the other accidents that found them (quantity, action-passion). Aquinas stresses the unique status of the proper "*ratio*" of a relation: this "*ratio*" is not derived from a respect to the subject that bears the relation, but it consists of a pure relationship to the correlative term. On the other hand, divine simplicity and analogy play an important role in the doctrine of subsistent relations. To the objection: "No substance is a relation," Aquinas answers: "The divine essence is not in the genus of substance, but is, rather, above every genus, embracing in itself the perfections of all genera. That is why nothing prevents one from finding that which pertains to relation within it."[23]

In the wake of Albert the Great,[24] and as opposed to Bonaventure (who gives priority not to relation but to "origin," namely generation and procession),[25] Aquinas holds that the divine persons are formally distinguished and constituted by relations: it falls to "personal relation" (paternity, filiation, and procession), which is intrinsic to the divine person, to distinguish and constitute the person,[26] in such a way that if we were to abstract the relations, we would no longer be able to conceive of the divine persons.[27]

The Properties and the Names of the Father, the Son, and the Holy Spirit

The Father is characterized by two properties: paternity and innascibility (with the "notion" of spiration). The word "Father" is not a metaphor but a proper name that distinctly signifies the divine person who is the principle of the Word. Paternity signifies first of all the relation of the Father to the Son, that is, the eternal relation of divine person to divine person: it is in the Father and the Son that the perfection of paternity and filiation resides, "since one is the nature and glory of the Father and the Son."[28] Thus, the person of the Father is known to us only through the revelation of the Son. Paternity also designates, by analogy to this full and principal sense, and at different levels, the relation that God maintains with all creatures (in virtue of creation) and with his adopted children (in virtue of grace). The second property by which we know the Father, is innascibility: the Father is not generated. Unlike other authors

(Bonaventure) for whom innascibility designates the "fontal plenitude" of the Father,[29] Aquinas considers innascibility to be a property whose content is not positive but negative: the Father has no principle. While paternity and spiration show the Father's fecundity as "source," our knowledge of the Father is perfected by innascibility: the Father is the principle *without principle*.[30]

Aquinas manifests the property of the Son around three names that signify him properly: Son, Word, and Image. Beginning with the *Summa contra Gentiles*, it is by means of the notion of the "Word" that Aquinas will show what the names "Son" and "Image" signify. In the human mind, a word is not a "*species intelligibilis*" by which the intellect is reduced to the act of knowledge (this "*species*" is the principle of the act of understanding) but is the concept of the reality known, which the intellect *forms and expresses*; this concept is the *term* of the act of understanding.[31] This analysis shows that the word is a reality relative to its principle. This makes it possible for Aquinas to show analogically that the name "Verbum" properly and exclusively signifies the Son who is conceived by the Father, who remains in the Father and who is of the same nature as the Father. In knowing himself, the Father conceives his Word, who is his perfect expression, and who is distinguished from him by a pure relation of origin.[32] The name "Word" first of all signifies the Son in his relation to the Father and secondarily the Son in his free relation to creatures, in the order of creation and that of grace. The divine Word is "both expressive and causative with respect to creatures."[33] The doctrine of the "Word" thus makes it possible for Aquinas to show that the Son manifests and reveals the Father (expressive dimension of "word"), that the Father accomplishes all things through his Son (operative and expressive dimension of "word"), and that adoptive filiation by which human beings are made children of God is a participation in the filiation of the Word: "He who is adopted as a son of God is conformed to his True Son."[34]

Far from being forgotten, it is the Holy Spirit who in the *Summa theologiae* receives the most developed treatment (three questions).[35] On one hand, Aquinas's pneumatology is characterized by a very firm affirmation of the procession of the Spirit from the Father *and the Son*, the Father and the Son being *one single* principle of the Spirit. The doctrine of relative opposition according to origin obliges the recognition that if the Holy Spirit did not proceed from the Son, the Holy Spirit would not be distinguished personally from the Son (Sabellianism). To Aquinas, who has multiplied arguments on this point and devoted long elaborations to the question, the Byzantine doctrine that the Spirit proceeds from the Father alone and not from the Son appears to be profoundly unintelligible. On the other hand, in a manner comparable to the role played by the notion of "Word" in grasping the Son, it is the property of Love that Aquinas emphasizes in order to manifest the personal identity of the Spirit.[36] By "love," in analogical fashion, he does not mean the act of loving but the "affection" that in the human will is found at the beginning of the act of loving, that is, what "moves and impels the will of the lover towards the beloved."[37] So, here love designates the "imprint of the reality loved" that proceeds in the will when the will loves, that is, the affectionate imprint ("*impressio*") according to which the being loved is present in a dynamic way in him who loves, and that moves the will toward the being that is loved.[38] This "imprint" possesses a relation of origin to the will from which and in which it proceeds: this relation of origin, distinct from the relation of the Word, makes it possible to manifest the Holy Spirit as Love in person, in the Trinity. Aquinas welcomes and reinterprets as well the Augustinian theme of the Spirit as the mutual Love of the Father and the Son. The theme of mutual Love does not signify the Spirit as an intermediary person between the Father and the Son but as proceeding from the Father and the Son who love each other with one same and single love. It is also by means of Love that Aquinas shows that the Spirit is Gift, because "love has the property of being the first gift."[39] When Aquinas considers the Spirit as Gift in person, he does not signify a Gift that the Father makes to the Son and reciprocally, but he shows that in virtue of his property of Love, it belongs properly to the Spirit to be given in person to the angels and to human beings in grace.[40] It is thus by means of the property of Love that Aquinas explains the entire work of the Spirit taught by Scripture, in the order of nature and in that of grace, from creation to final beatitude.[41] As the Father utters himself and every creature by his Word, so he loves himself and every creature by the Holy Spirit.[42] In summary: "The Father and the Son love each other and love us by the Holy Spirit, or Love proceeding."[43]

Today, theologians often reproach Aquinas for having constructed his Trinitarian doctrine on the basis of a "psychological analogy" drawn from an analysis of the human soul rather than from God's action in history, so that his doctrine supposedly obscures the economic dimensions of the Trinitarian mystery. But in reality, a reading of Aquinas reveals that his theology of the Word and Love seeks to illuminate the very foundations of the economy established by God who acts, creates, and saves by his Son and his Holy Spirit.

The Creative and Sanctifying Action of the Trinity

The divine persons act in the world in virtue of their single essence. Following this principle issuing from the Greek and Latin Fathers, the Trinity works inseparably in any action performed on behalf of creatures. In other words, power, divine action, and its effects belong to the whole Trinity.[44] The essential divine attributes, divine action, or effects can be "appropriated" to one person by reason of an affinity with the property of that person: it is thus, for example, that eternity (an attribute of God in his being itself that is without beginning), unity (God in his undividedness), power (the principle of operation), and creation (an originating divine action) are appropriated to the Father because he is the "principle without principle." The divine person, beforehand known by his property, is indirectly manifested by means of essential attributes: such is the procedure of appropriation, which moreover is not limited to divine action in the world but is applied in a general way to what concerns the one single essence of God.[45] Appropriation, which Aquinas exploits abundantly, constitutes a common teaching of the Masters of the thirteenth century.

Nevertheless these elements do not constitute the last word on the Trinitarian dimension of divine action. On one hand, Aquinas explains that the processions of the divine persons, which include divine knowledge and will, are the cause of and reason for the production of creatures. On the other hand, each person engages in the one single divine action according to his personal property. So, for instance, Aquinas explains that it is in a proper manner and not only by appropriation that the Son is he "through whom the Father does all things."[46] Each divine person acts with the others according to his proper and distinct mode of acting, a relative mode of acting that concerns the intratrinitarian relations of divine person to divine person. This personal dimension of divine action implies that an integral understanding of creation and the exercise of providence requires Trinitarian faith.[47]

The life of grace is procured by the mission of the Son and the Holy Spirit. This doctrine of missions constitutes the crowning of Trinitarian theology.[48] The "invisible mission" designates the sending of the Son and the Holy Spirit into souls. This sending consists in the eternal procession of the Son and of the Spirit and in a new mode of presence of the Son and the Spirit in rational creatures. This mode of presence implies that the Son and Spirit, as well as the Father who sends them, "indwell" the souls of the saints. Through the invisible mission of the Son and Spirit, "God is said to be present in the rational creature as the known is in the knower and the beloved in the lover." This invisible mission thus takes place according to the gifts of sanctifying grace.[49] The created gifts of sanctifying grace *dispose* one to receive the divine person *himself* who is sent, the divine person being the source and end of the gifts of grace.[50] These gifts of grace assimilate their beneficiaries to the person sent. Through the gift of wisdom, which is a participation in the personal relation that the Word has with the Father, the just are made like the Son. Through the gift of charity, which is a participation in the personal property of the Holy Spirit, the just are conformed to the Holy Spirit.[51] Thus, through their missions, the Son and Spirit give sanctifying knowledge and the love of God to the saints, through which God makes himself present as the known and beloved. The invisible mission of persons, through which the saints are conformed to God known and loved, brings about their divinization. What Trinitarian doctrine expresses with respect to God himself, the doctrine of man as the image of the Trinity expresses with respect to the human being.[52] When the human mind knows and loves itself, "there is a representation of the uncreated Trinity according to analogy," but when it knows and loves God "the mind itself becomes conformed to God."[53] This is the divinization by which the saints "are in some way transformed into God."[54] We find here again the objective assimilation observed in the doctrine of the invisible missions.

The doctrine of the missions culminates in the exposé of the "visible mission" of the Son (Incarnation) and the "visible missions" of the Holy Spirit

(Baptism and Transfiguration of Christ, Christ's breathing of the Spirit on the Apostles, and Pentecost). The "visible" mission adds to the "invisible mission" the manifestation of the procession of the divine person and the manifestation of the fullness of grace through a tangible sign. In accord with his property of Love, the Holy Spirit is sent as the "Gift of sanctification," that is, as sanctifying Gift in person. Regarding the Son, in accord with his property as Son in virtue of which he is the principle of the Holy Spirit, he is sent visibly as the "Author of sanctification," that is, as him who gives the Holy Spirit with the collaboration of the humanity that he assumes in the Incarnation.[55] Trinitarian doctrine, which enlightens creation, thus supplies the foundations of the economy of grace and Christology. The revelation of the Trinity and the gift of salvation consist in the missions of the divine persons.

Contemporary criticism generally recognizes the metaphysical and logical achievement of Aquinas's Trinitarian theology but often reproaches him for a lack of existential impact for believers, as well as an insufficient consideration of the economy of salvation in the elaboration of speculative themes. The difficulties posed by this criticism suggest that the study of the method and purpose of Aquinas's Trinitarian theology,[56] as well as the study of the biblical foundation and soteriological dimensions of this Trinitarian theology[57] (the place of Trinitarian faith in the whole of theology, in relation to the speculative manifestation of the Trinity), constitute privileged fields of current research.

NOTES

1. *De rationibus fidei*, c.1.

2. *ST* I q.32 a.1 ad 3. Translations of the *ST* are taken, with some modifications, from: St. Thomas Aquinas, *Summa Theologiae*, ed. Thomas Gilby and T. C. O'Brien, 60 vols. (London: Eyre and Spottiswoode; New York: McGraw-Hill, 1964–73). Other translations are mine.

3. *ST* I-II q.2 a.8.

4. *ST* I-II q.2 a.8 ad 3; cf. *Super Sent* I, dist.1, q.2, a.2.

5. Jean-Pierre Torrell, *Saint Thomas Aquinas*, vol. 2, *Spiritual Master*, trans. Robert Royal (Washington, D.C.: Catholic University of America Press, 2003), 23–224: "A Trinitarian Spirituality." Most of the elements outlined in the present contribution are developed at greater length (with a bibliography) in Gilles Emery, *The Trinitarian Theology of Saint Thomas Aquinas*, trans. Francesca Murphy (Oxford: Oxford University Press, 2007).

6. Aquinas, *Super Johan*, c.14, lect.3.

7. *ST* I q.32 a.1.

8. Hans Christian Schmidbaur, *Personarum Trinitas: Die trinitarische Gotteslehre des heiligen Thomas von Aquin* (St. Ottilien: EOS Verlag, 1995).

9. Bonaventure, *Super Sent* I, dist.2, a.1, q.2; *Opera omnia*, vol. 1 (Quaracchi: Ed. Collegii S. Bonaventurae, 1882), 53–54. See Gilles Emery, *Trinity in Aquinas*, 2d ed. (Naples, Fla.: Sapientia Press, 2006), 16–23.

10. Aquinas, *Super Sent* I, dist.2, q.1, a.4; cf. *ST* I q.32 a.1.

11. *ST* II-II q.1 a.5 ad 2.
12. *QDP*, q.9, a.5.
13. Gilles Emery, *Trinity, Church, and the Human Person: Thomistic Essays* (Naples, Fla.: Sapientia Press, 2007), 1–72.
14. *ST* I q.32 a.1 obj. 2; *QDP*, q.9, a.5.
15. *ST* I q.2 prol.; cf. *CT* I, c.2.
16. *ST* I q.28 a.4.
17. *Super Sent* I, dist.13, q.1, a.1.
18. *ST* I q.27 a.5.
19. *ST* I q.27 a.1–4.
20. *ST* I q.28.
21. *ST* I q.29 a.4.
22. *ST* I q.39 a.1 ad 1.
23. *QDP*, q.8, a.2, ad 1.
24. Albert, *Super Dionysium de divinis nominibus*, c.2, §25–26; *Opera omnia* (Cologne edition), vol. 37/1, ed. Paulus Simon (Münster: Aschendorff, 1972), 60. See also Albert, *Super Sent* I, dist.28, a.4; *Opera omnia* (Paris edition), vol. 26, ed. Auguste Borgnet (Paris: Vivès, 1893), 59–61.
25. Bonaventure, *Super Sent* I, dist.26, a.1, q.3; *Opera omnia*, 1:456–58.
26. *ST* I q.40 a.2.
27. *ST* I q.40 a.3.
28. *ST* I q.33 a.3.
29. Bonaventure, *Super Sent* I, dist.27, pars 1, a.1, q.2, sol. and ad 3; dist.28, a.1, q.2; dist.28, dubium 1; *Opera omnia*, 1:469–72, 499–500, and 504.
30. *ST* I q.33 a.4.
31. *SCG* I, c.53; *QDP*, q.8, a.1; *Super Johan*, c.1, lect.1.
32. *SCG* IV, c.11; *ST* I q.34 a.1–2.
33. *ST* I q.34 a.3.
34. *In Rom*, c.8, lect.6; *ST* III q.23. a.3.
35. *ST* I q.36–38.
36. *ST* I q.37 a.1–2; *SCG* IV, c.19.
37. *ST* I q.36 a.1.
38. *ST* I q.37 a.1; I-II q.28 a.2 resp. and ad 1.
39. *ST* I q.38 a.2.
40. *ST* I q.38 a.1.
41. *SCG* IV, c.20–22.
42. *ST* I q.37 a.2 ad 3.
43. *ST* I q.37 a.2.
44. *ST* I q.32 a.1; q.45 a.6.
45. *ST* I q.39 a.7–8.
46. *Super Johan*, c.1, lect.2; *ST* I q.39 a.8.
47. Emery, *Trinity, Church, and the Human Person*, 115–53.
48. *ST* I q.43; *Super Sent* I, dist.14–16.
49. *ST* I q.43 a.3.
50. *Super Sent* I, dist.14, q.2, a.1, quaestiunc.2; cf. *ST* I q.43 a.3 resp. and ad 1.
51. *ST* I q.43 a.5 ad 2; *Super Sent* I, dist.15, q.4, a.1; *In Rom*, c.5, lect.1.
52. *ST* I q.93 a.5 and a.7–8.
53. *QDV*, q.10, a.7.
54. *In II Cor*, c.3, lect.3.

55. *ST* I q.43 a.7; cf. *In Rom*, c.1, lect.3.

56. See, for instance, Timothy L. Smith, *Thomas Aquinas' Trinitarian Theology: A Study in Theological Method* (Washington, D.C.: Catholic University of America Press, 2003).

57. See, for instance, Matthew Levering, *Scripture and Metaphysics: Aquinas and the Renewal of Trinitarian Theology* (Oxford: Blackwell, 2004); Gilles Emery, "*Theologia* and *Dispensatio*: The Centrality of the Divine Missions in St. Thomas's Trinitarian Theology," *The Thomist* 74 (2010): 515–61; Guillermo A. Juárez, *Dios Trinidad en todas las creaturas y en los santos: Estudio histórico-sistemático de la doctrina del Comentario a las Sentencias de Santo Tomás de Aquino sobre la omnipresencia y la inhabitación* (Córdoba, Argentina: Ediciones del Copista, 2008). On the person of the Father, see John Baptist Ku, "St. Thomas Aquinas's Treatment of the Name 'Father' in *ST* I, q. 33, a. 2," *Nova et Vetera* 9 (2011): 433–78. —I owe a special thanks to John Baptist Ku, O. P. who translated the present chapter from French into English.

CHAPTER 31

INCARNATION

MICHAEL GORMAN

Introduction

According to Christian belief, Jesus Christ is a divine person who became "incarnate," that is, who became human. A key event in the second act of the drama of creation and redemption, the incarnation could not have failed to interest Aquinas, and he discusses it in a number of places. A proper understanding of what he thought about it is thus part of any complete understanding of his work. It is, furthermore, a window into his ideas on a variety of other topics: God, human nature, language, substance, and so on. Finally, it forces us to come to grips with what is at stake in acknowledging that Aquinas was not only a philosopher but a theologian as well.

The Incarnation as a Properly Theological Problem

The claim that God became human is, or should be, a surprising one. As a matter of fact, Aquinas thinks it cannot be known by human reason operating alone. Instead, it is revealed by God through Scripture as authoritatively interpreted by the Church. As Aquinas explains, appeal to the authority of revelation establishes *that* something is the case, but it does not provide an understanding of *how* it is so.[1] The theologian's job is to accept what is revealed, an acceptance called "faith," and then to reflect on it in as satisfactory a way as possible by drawing out implications, making comparisons between revealed realities and more familiar things, and so on. This task might even involve modifying philosophical categories and tools to make room for possibilities that show themselves only in theological contexts. There is, to be sure, a point beyond which the human intellect cannot go, at least in this life.[2] But even once that point has been reached, the quest for understanding need not be abandoned altogether: it will at least be possible to give an intelligent characterization of where our understanding falls short.

On the one hand, the attempt to make revelation the basis of theological inquiry is far from incoherent. If there is a God at all, it is to be expected that detailed information about him will be very hard for humans to acquire, but also to be expected that, if he so chooses, God can reveal himself. On the other hand, it cannot be demonstrated that revelation actually has taken place, and some readers of Aquinas will in fact reject the notion of divine revelation outright. For any reader, however, it would be a mistake to expect Aquinas to set out a theory of the incarnation (or of any properly theological topic) that in no way relies on what he takes to be revelation or that resolves all difficulties in a way that is entirely satisfying to reason apart from revelation. Aquinas would consider such attempts to be at once futile and presumptuous.

Some Basic Thomistic Claims about the Incarnation

Christians believe that God wills the salvation of human beings from sin and that his plan to bring this about involves the second person of the Trinity's becoming human and living out a true human life, a life that leads to his atoning death, resurrection from the dead, and further salvific actions such as the sending of the Holy Spirit. Jesus Christ, then, is a divine person, the second person of the Trinity and the eternal Word of the Father, who has become human. After disputes lasting generations, this understanding of Christ was formulated in A.D. 451 by the Council of Chalcedon as the teaching that Christ is one person existing in two natures, divine and human. (Since the word "hypostasis" can usually be used interchangeably with the word "person" in these debates, the union of natures resulting from the incarnation is often called the "hypostatic union.")

Now the Chalcedonian definition did not bring all discussion to an end; more debates and councils brought further refinements, and the history of these councils and their after-effects is complicated. It is safe to say, however, that essentially Chalcedonian ideas served as the context within which Aquinas and his contemporaries worked. In that context, the two most important ideas are nature and person. For present purposes, let us jump straight to Aquinas's understanding of them.

The nature or essence[3] of something is what corresponds to its real definition.[4] A human being, for example, is defined as a rational animal, and that is because its nature or essence is to be just such an entity. And it is worth noting that what Aquinas means by "nature" or "essence" is something narrower than what contemporary analytic philosophers are likely to mean by "essence"; the essential attributes of a thing for Aquinas are not the same as the attributes that the thing cannot exist without. Aquinas holds that something might have attributes without which it cannot exist but which are nonetheless not essential to it—these "flow from" the essence rather than forming part of it.[5]

With regard to the concept "person," Aquinas follows Boethius, who sets out two conditions: a person must be an individual substance (hypostasis, supposit), and it must have a rational nature. To understand the first condition, consider the horse Bucephalus. Bucephalus exists independently, or "subsists": it is not part of his nature to inhere in, or belong to, anything else. By contrast, his accidents depend on him, exist in him, inhere in him, and it is part of their nature to do so.[6] So Bucephalus is an individual substance, but is he a person? He is not, because his nature, horseness, is not a rational one. Socrates, however, also a substance, does have a rational nature, humanity, and for that reason he is not just an ordinary substance or supposit, but a person.[7]

So when Aquinas says that Christ is one person, he means that Christ is one individual rational substance. The incarnation is not a relationship between two rational substances—for example, a relationship by which the Word of God makes Jesus holy. Rather, Christ's humanity is a constituent of the one rational supposit that Christ is. And when Aquinas says that Christ has two natures, he means that there are two kinds of which we could say that Christ is a substance of that kind: if for a moment we make so bold as to speak of defining God, we could say that Christ fits the real definition of God and the real definition of a human being. Humanity is not joined to Christ in a way that results in a merging or blending of humanity and divinity—the two natures remain distinct.[8] Not that they are on a completely equal footing, to be sure: Christ had his divine nature from eternity, and only at a certain point in the world's history did he assume a human nature.

More should be said about Christ's humanity. Aquinas thinks that Christ could have had every possible human perfection, and his list of these is a generous one: in principle, Christ could have known everything a human can know, could have been free of all temptation and all passions, could have been free of every bodily ailment, and so on. Being perfectly human, in short, is not inconsistent with being human. In fact, however, Aquinas attributes only some of these perfections to Christ, depending on whether possessing them or not possessing them furthers his salvific mission.[9]

Christ's human knowledge was as extensive as human knowledge could be: he had the beatific vision, full infused knowledge, and full acquired knowledge.[10] Of his possession of the beatific vision, Aquinas notes that this enabled Christ to be, in virtue of his humanity, the source of truth for other humans.[11] He also had a human will and the ability to perform authentically human actions.[12]

At the same time, Aquinas is clear that Christ did have imperfections or defects both of body and of soul. Bodily defects are usually imposed, as a penalty for sin; this does not apply to Christ, of course. He accepted such defects willingly, as part of his salvific mission. In particular, Aquinas says that Christ took on bodily defects for three reasons: to be able to atone for our sins by taking our punishment upon himself, to make his human nature more believable, and to be able to provide us with an example of patience in the face of suffering.[13] In addition to these defects of body, Christ took on defects of soul; for example, he was liable to physical pain and sorrow. Aquinas is careful to note that the way in which Christ suffered from such defects was different from the way in which we suffer from them: in our case, defects of soul often interfere with the exercise of reason and lead to sin, but in Christ's case they did not.[14]

Aquinas intends what he says about Christ's human defects, and what he says about Christ's human perfections, to be consistent with the central claim that Christ has a human soul and a human body, with human mental and physical powers that allow him to perform true human acts. Mark 10:13–16 portrays Christ as embracing young children. His decision to embrace them was on Aquinas's understanding a real human decision; the arms with which he embraced them were real human arms, animated by a real human soul and folded around the children in a real human greeting. Christ really was (and is) a man, a human being.

But who—that is, *which person*—is Christ? Or to put the question in linguistic terms, which person does the expression "Christ" stand for? It stands for the very same person that expressions like "the Word" or "the Son of God" or "the second person of the Trinity" stand for, and also for the very same person that "Jesus" stands for.[15] The human being at issue is not a different person from the second person of the Trinity but rather the very same person. Christ is one divine-and-human person whose humanity retains its own powers while serving as an instrument of the divinity. Thus, for Aquinas, it is the one Christ who, in one act, both touches a leper by virtue of his human power and heals him by virtue of his divine power.[16]

In line with a long tradition, Aquinas would say that a good test of whether one has correct views in Christology is whether one accepts the "communication of idioms," that is, the sharing of properties. One must be willing to say not only that the Word of God created the stars but also that Jesus created the stars; likewise, one must be willing to say not only that Jesus suffered on the cross but also that the Word of God suffered on the cross. "The Word" and "Jesus" are two names for one person who both created and suffered. At the same time, one must know when and how to qualify such claims when necessary, lest misunderstandings arise; the Word suffers on the cross not in virtue of his divinity, but rather in virtue of his humanity.[17]

A Difficult Issue

So far I have simply laid out some of the many claims that Aquinas makes about the incarnation, without much attempt to indicate where difficulties arise or how Aquinas might address them. In the remainder of this article, I will focus by way of example on one difficult topic. The goal, besides exploring more of Aquinas's views, will be to provide an example of how Thomas uses and adapts philosophical ideas in carrying out his Christological investigations.

Let us begin by briefly stepping back from Christ's humanity and talking instead about Socrates'. Socrates' human nature is a principle in virtue of which he exists in a certain way, as an entity of a certain sort—namely, as a human being.[18] But it is not only for being an entity of a certain sort that he is dependent on having a human nature—he is also dependent on having a human nature for the simple fact that he exists at all, as an individual substance or supposit of any sort.[19] In other words, he depends on his human nature not only for being such-and-such a sort of thing but also for what Aquinas would call his "simple" or "absolute" existence. Without his humanity, Socrates would not only fail to be human, he would fail to be anything at all—he would simply not exist.[20] Let us say henceforth that Socrates' human nature is not only a "humanizing" nature but also a "supposit-supporting" nature.

Now is what is true of Socrates' human nature true of every instance of human nature? If we were to say "yes," implying that Christ's human nature too is not only humanizing but also supposit-supporting, then we would run into problems. Given that there is only one supposit in Christ and that this supposit is the second person of the Trinity, we would be committed to saying that Christ's human nature is supposit-supporting for a divine supposit, that is, that a divine supposit depends for its absolute existence on being human. Obviously, Aquinas is not going to take this route.

So it seems necessary to answer "no," that is, to say that there can be a human nature that is humanizing but not supposit-supporting. And in fact this is just what Aquinas holds: "On the basis of his human nature, the Son of God does not exist absolutely...but only as a human being."[21] The person or supposit of the Son of God is not supported by Christ's human nature. His humanity is a principle in virtue of which he is human, as well as divine, but not a principle in virtue of which he exists as opposed to not existing at all. Indeed, there is no supposit or person that depends for its absolute existence on Christ's humanity.

It might sound wrong to say that Christ's humanity does not account for the absolute existence of any supposit or person. Saying so seems to imply that his human nature is somehow lacking in metaphysical dignity. Worse, it might seem to imply a sheer impossibility, namely, that something could be a human nature and yet not be that on which the absolute existence of a person depends.[22]

Concerning the dignity of Christ's human nature, Aquinas says that "it is more dignified for something to exist in something else that is of greater dignity than for it to exist through itself."[23] To forgo a lower role (being responsible for the existence of a supposit) for the sake of a higher one (being a constituent of a divine–human supposit) is no loss—in fact, it is gain.

Concerning the second and deeper worry, that is, the worry about whether it is even possible for there to be a human nature that is humanizing but not supposit-supporting, Aquinas clearly thinks that it is possible, so long as the nature exists in some pre-existing supposit (it could not exist in no supposit at all). His idea seems to be that it is not a necessary condition of something's being a human nature that it *actually* be a principle upon which a supposit depends for its absolute existence—what is necessary is only that it be the sort of reality to which it is natural to have a supposit thus dependent upon it. This is still true of Christ's human nature, even though it is not supposit-supporting in actual fact.

The same point can be made from the complementary perspective, that of the supposit rather than that of the nature. Everything that possesses a human nature must have absolute existence as a supposit, that is, every human being must be a supposit. But from this it does not follow that everything that possesses a human nature must have absolute existence as a supposit *in virtue of possessing that nature.* It might, as in Christ's case, have it in virtue of possessing some other nature. Before the Son became human, he was already subsistent, already a supposit, and therefore becoming subsistent was not possible for him. Christ's human nature was given no opportunity to be supposit-supporting; from the very first it existed only as a constituent of a supposit that was, so to speak, already supported. But, of course, that does not mean that Christ's human nature does nothing—before the incarnation, the Son was not human, and Christ's human nature serves for him precisely as a humanizing principle, a principle in virtue of which he is not only divine but human as well. Although in the incarnation the Son does not come to be a supposit or person, he does come to be human, to be corporeal and animate in a fully and properly human way.

To say that there can be a human nature that is humanizing but not supposit-supporting is certainly to deviate from the usual way of thinking. Such a deviation might be looked upon as a valuable insight, or it might be looked upon as a desperate ad hoc maneuver. Whether one thinks of it as desperate or not depends, in large part, on whether one thinks it rational to adopt Aquinas's faith-based point of view in the first place. As for its being ad hoc, however, there is a sense in which Aquinas would gladly agree: he is explicit about the fact that the incarnation is a unique case, and so in a sense an ad hoc solution is just what one should expect.[24] As noted at the outset, theology in Aquinas's understanding must not only employ philosophical notions but modify them when necessary.[25]

NOTES

1. *Quodl* 4, q.9, a.3, response.

2. See, e.g., *ST* I q.12 a.12–13.

3. For "essence" and other synonyms of "nature," see, e.g., *DEE*, c.1.

4. See, e.g., *Super Sent* 3, d.5, q.1, a.2; *SCG* 4, c.35; *QDP*, q.9, a.1, response; *QDV*, a.1; *ST* III q.2 a.1.

5. For helpful remarks on some of Aquinas's views here, see Matthew J. Kelly (1976), "'Subject,' 'Substance,' and 'Accident' in St. Thomas," *New Scholasticism* 50 (1976): 232–36. For a partial attempt to recapture the same sort of approach in a contemporary

framework, see Michael Gorman, "The Essential and the Accidental," *Ratio* 18 (2005): 276–89.

6. That last claim would need to be qualified in light of Aquinas's understanding of transubstantiation, but such concerns lie beyond the scope of this chapter.

7. See *Super Sent* 3, d.5, q.1, a.3; *Super Sent* 3, d.6, q.1, a.1, qa.1, response; *QDP*, q.9, a.1–2; *DUI*, a.1–2; *ST* I q.29 a.1–2; *ST* III q.2 a.2–3. Lafont has laid stress on the fact that for Aquinas the divine persons are subsisting relations (e.g., *ST* I q.28 a.2), and he thinks that the Boethian notion of person as rational substance is not always adequate for Christological purposes. The particular problems that Lafont is concerned with are not at issue here, however, so the point will not be pursued further. See Ghislain Lafont, *Peut-on connaître Dieu en Jésus Christ?* (Paris: Cerf, 1969), 107–57. For further complications, see John Wippel, *The Metaphysical Thought of Thomas Aquinas* (Washington, D.C.: Catholic University of America Press, 2000), 228–37.

8. *ST* III q.2 a.1–3; see also *SCG* 4, c.41; *QDVUI*, a.1–2.

9. A good discussion of Aquinas on Christ's human nature from just this perspective can be found in Marilyn McCord Adams, *What Sort of Human Nature? Medieval Philosophy and the Systematics of Christology* (Milwaukee: Marquette University Press, 1999), 49–68.

10. For an overview of Christ's human knowledge, see *ST* III q.9. For details on Christ's possession of the beatific vision, see *ST* III q.10; for details on his infused knowledge, see *ST* III q.11; for details on his acquired knowledge, see *ST* III q.12.

11. See *ST* III q.9 a.2.

12. See *ST* III q.18–19.

13. *ST* III q.14 a.1; for more on Christ's bodily defects, see the whole of *ST* III q.14.

14. *ST* III q.15 a.4; for more on Christ's sinlessness, see *ST* III q.15 a.1–2; for physical pain, see *ST* III q.15 a.5; for sorrow, see *ST* III q.15, a.6.

15. For a sustained reflection on some of the linguistic issues concerning the incarnation, and on the metaphysical issues that lie behind them, see Henk J. M. Schoot, *Christ the "Name" of God: Thomas Aquinas on Naming Christ* (Leuven: Peeters, 1993).

16. *ST* III q.19 a.1 ad 5; see also *ST* III q.18 a.1 ad 2.

17. See *ST* III q.16.

18. See, e.g., *DEE*, c.1.

19. See, e.g., *QDVUI*, a.4.

20. Here it is worth comparing Socrates' humanity with one of his accidental forms: in virtue of his whiteness, Socrates is the sort of thing that is white, but he does not depend on his whiteness for his absolute existence (cf. *QDVUI*, a.4).

21. "Non enim ex natura humana habet Filius Dei quod sit simpliciter... sed solum quod sit homo" (*ST* III q.3 a.1 ad 3), my translation. See also *Super Sent* 3, d.6, q.1, a.1, qa.4, ad 1. *QDVUI*, a.1, ad 15, as it appears in the Marietti edition, seems to undermine or even contradict the idea that Christ is humanized by his human nature, but the text of that edition is flawed there: see Michael Gorman, "Christ as Composite according to Aquinas," *Traditio* 55 (2000): 143–57, at 150 n.12. For a few more relevant passages, not all of them easy to interpret, see *Super Sent* 3, d.10, q.1, a.2, qa.1, ad 1–2; *Super Sent* 3, d.10, q.1, a.2, qa.2, ad 1; *Super Sent* 3, d.12, q.1, a.1, ad 2; *ST* III q.2 a.2 ad 2; *ST* III q.2 a.3 ad 3; *ST* III q.16 a.6 ad 1; *ST* III, q.16 a.12 resp. and ad 1.

22. Here it is worth mentioning a distinct but related problem. According to Aquinas's canonical way of speaking, a human nature is but one principle of a human being, and human beings are not identical to their natures. From this perspective it makes sense to consider the possibility that Christ's human nature is unique inasmuch as it fails to *support*

a human supposit, but it does not make sense to consider the possibility that Christ's human nature is unique inasmuch as it fails to *be* a human supposit—such is true of every human nature. But there is another way of using the expression "human nature," also found in Aquinas, in accordance with which it might indeed make sense to say that ordinary human natures are human persons but that Christ's human nature, uniquely, is not. If we did say that, then we would face the analogous difficulty of explaining how it could be true at all, and how it could be true without Christ's human nature being inadequate in some way. For discussion, see, e.g., Othmar Schweizer, *Person und Hypostatische Union bei Thomas von Aquin* (Freiburg [Schweiz]: Universitätsverlag, 1957); Michael Gorman, "Uses of the Person–Nature Distinction in Thomas's Christology," *Recherches de théologie et philosophie médiévales* 67 (2000): 58–79; Richard Cross, *The Metaphysics of the Hypostatic Union* (Oxford: Oxford University Press, 2002), 246–56; Eleonore Stump, *Aquinas* (London and New York: Routledge, 2003), 409–10. Although I do not think that Aquinas's views on this problem have yet received a fully adequate interpretation, I do think it safe to say that the right path is the one laid out by Schweizer and Stump.

23. "Dignius autem est alicui quod existat in aliquo se digniori, quam quod existat per se" (*ST* III q.2 a.2 ad 2), my translation.

24. For example, in *QDVUI*, a.3, response, Aquinas notes that in the case of the Trinity there is one nature with three supposits, and in the case of the incarnation two natures with only one supposit, but that in every other case, the correspondence between natures and supposits is one-to-one. See also *ST* III q.2 a.6 ad 1, where Aquinas quotes John Damascene to the effect that the incarnation is not wholly like anything else.

25. I would like to thank Anne-Marie Gorman and Thomas Weinandy for helpful comments on earlier drafts of this paper.

CHAPTER 32

THE SAVING WORK OF CHRIST

RIK VAN NIEUWENHOVE

Introduction

How we have been saved in Christ is undoubtedly one of the most central questions for any Christian theologian, and it is not any different with Aquinas.[1] In recent years Aquinas's soteriology has not enjoyed the same attention as his theology of the Trinity, or his virtue ethics. Nevertheless, in my view Aquinas's soteriology deserves more consideration, not only because it is a fairly sophisticated one, central to all his theological endeavors, but also because it differs rather considerably in inspiration, presuppositions, and issues it addresses from those of modern-day theologians. It is exactly because of these differences (which often evoke criticism) that it can begin to challenge us at a more fundamental level.

Theologians of a liberal mindset, for instance, may want to question a soteriology that (allegedly) attributes saving significance to the innocent suffering of Jesus of Nazareth. It has been argued that the Anselmic theory of satisfaction that Aquinas adopts (with modifications) comes dangerously close to turning God into a vindictive, punitive God who needs a bloody sacrifice before he becomes reconciled with this sinful world. The theory of satisfaction, so it is further alleged, is legalistic, transactional, more indebted to feudal categories than to the Scriptures, and effectively glorifies innocent suffering, instead of providing us with resources to challenge it. In this vein E. Schillebeeckx has famously argued that we have been saved "despite the Cross."[2] He writes, "Many existing theories of our redemption through Jesus Christ deprive Jesus, his message and career of their subversive power, and even worse, sacralize violence to be a reality within God. God is said to call for a bloody sacrifice which stills or calms his sense of justice."[3] I will argue that Aquinas is very much aware of the concerns that Schillebeeckx raises and is perfectly capable of dealing with them.[4] Moreover, I am in little doubt that Aquinas would be ill at ease with the disturbingly unscriptural stance that is implied in Schillebeeckx's disparagement of the Cross as the central event in Christian salvation.

Other theologians, such as J. Moltmann, have developed an influential and popular theology of suffering that does pay attention to the Cross as the supreme saving event but rather than interpreting it in terms of a salvation from evil it is interpreted in terms of a salvation from suffering: in the Cross God suffers and dies for us, and this is the only viable theodicy that can meet the challenges of the atheist critique.[5] Now Aquinas is perfectly happy to state that God suffers and dies for us on the Cross in the humanity of the incarnate Word—but unlike Moltmann he explicitly rejects the view that this suffering and death can be attributed to the divinity: "The Lord of glory is said to be crucified, not as the Lord of glory, but as a man capable of suffering."[6] This traditional view, which Aquinas represents here, does not go far enough for Moltmann who criticizes it (erroneously in my view) on the grounds that this emphasis upon the impassibility of God is due to the influence of Aristotelian philosophy (the unmoved mover). Now Moltmann's theopaschite theology has, in turn, come in for a sharp critique from a number of thinkers who argue that a suffering God may perhaps give us some psychological solace—we are not alone in our suffering—but from a mature religious point of view it will not do: if even God is subject to suffering and in need of salvation there is no hope left. That is not to say that the issue of suffering is not relevant to Aquinas; but he approaches it by focusing our attention on the God-man, the Word-become-human, as I hope to show in this contribution, and not on the intratrinitarian life, as Moltmann does.[7]

In what follows I will outline Aquinas's soteriology by examining the following themes: the saving significance of the Passion of Christ, the Body of Christ, and the role of the Eucharist. Given the systemic nature of Aquinas's theological enterprise, these themes are deeply interwoven with one another.

Christ, the Sacrament of Our Salvation

A good place to start is the *Compendium of Theology*.[8] Here Aquinas describes how Christ's death was "a salutary means of satisfaction," freeing us from the debt of penalty—a topic which I will discuss in the next section. His death "was also appropriate as a sacrament. Christ wished to make clear by his death that we ought so to die in our carnal life that our spirit might be raised to higher things. Hence He himself says, in John 12:32: 'I, if I be lifted up from the Earth, will draw all things to myself.'" Finally, Christ's death is an example of perfect virtue, exemplifying perfect virtue (John 15:13), obedience, fortitude, and patience. In this section I will examine the second element.

It is only very rarely that Aquinas calls the death of Christ a sacrament of our salvation *(salutis sacramentum)*.[9] However, the theological notion it expresses does receive considerable attention in Aquinas's later works. By adopting the notion of the humanity of Christ as the instrument of his divinity,[10] Aquinas can argue that every aspect of Christ's life, death, and resurrection has a sacramental meaning and power.[11] Aquinas puts it with unrivalled clarity in his Commentary on St. Paul's Letter to the Romans (*In Rom*): "as the humanity of Christ was so to speak the instrument of his divinity, as John Damascene says, all the sufferings and works of the humanity of Christ have saving value for us, as they are derived from his divine power."[12] The phrase "instrument of the divinity" should not be taken to imply that the significance of Christ's humanity is undervalued. It is the exact opposite: while the divine and human natures of Christ retain their distinctiveness they nevertheless act in unison, thereby bestowing upon every aspect of the life and death of the man Jesus a sacramental power: "the principal efficient cause of man's salvation is God. But since Christ's humanity is the instrument of the Godhead as stated above [*ST* III q.43 a.2], therefore all Christ's actions and sufferings operate instrumentally in virtue of His Godhead for the salvation of men."[13] This explains the saving power of Christ's body, both historically (in his healings), through his death and resurrection, and in the sacraments in the strict sense. Through Baptism, for instance, we are made conformable to Christ's Passion and Resurrection, insofar as we die to sin and begin to live anew to righteousness.[14] Through faith, hope, and love, we become incorporated in Christ, so as to die to sin through his death, and to live for God through his resurrection.[15] I will now examine in some more detail how Christ's death in particular has saving value for us.[16]

The Death of Christ, the Universal Cause of Salvation (cf. *SCG* IV, 55.29)

In his earlier works, Aquinas refers mainly to the notion of "making satisfaction" to describe the saving meaning of Christ's death. In *ST* the picture becomes more diverse, and he appeals also to a number of other key categories, including the more biblical notion of "sacrifice."[17] Nevertheless, the notion of making satisfaction remains important for Aquinas in his mature works, and it is this notion we will examine first. I will also deal with a number of objections that have been raised against this notion.

It was Anselm of Canterbury who developed the so-called theory of satisfaction in his work *Cur Deus Homo*—although the notion has patristic roots and cannot be simply associated with the feudal context in which he was working.[18] The following quotation from *CT* summarizes the doctrine quite well:

> If God had decided to restore man solely by an act of His will and power, the order of divine justice would not have been observed. Justice demands satisfaction for sin. But God cannot render satisfaction, just as he cannot merit. Such a service pertains to one who is subject to another. Thus God was not in a position to satisfy for the sin of the whole of human nature; and a mere man was unable to do so.... Hence divine Wisdom judged it fitting that God should become man, so that thus one and the same person would be able both to restore man and to offer satisfaction.[19]

While the onus was on humanity to restore the relationship with God, we could not do so, infected as we are by sin. Therefore, it was necessary that somebody who was both human and divine (and thus sinless) would restore this relationship (i.e., make satisfaction). I would like to make a number of comments.

First, it is a gross misreading to understand "making satisfaction" in terms of retribution and punishment. Aquinas repeatedly points out that there are two major differences between punishment and making satisfaction. The first difference is that punishment is inflicted upon the sinner against his will, while making satisfaction is something we *freely* undertake to restore a broken relationship with somebody: grieving for the offence we committed we are anxious to become reconciled with, or make satisfaction to, our friend.[20] Hence, for Aquinas, as for Anselm, satisfaction excludes punishment. Incidentally, the language of friendship Aquinas uses here suggests a personalist rather than a judicial or legalistic paradigm for understanding salvation. This is further confirmed by the link between the satisfaction Christ makes on the Cross, and the sacrament of penance.[21] Given the fact that penance is described as "a spiritual healing of a sort"[22] or as "a spiritual medicine"[23] and that sin is called "a sickness of the soul" (*infirmitas animae*),[24] it is clear that "making satisfaction" too should be understood in medicinal terms. It comes therefore as no surprise to find that Aquinas describes Christ as a doctor.[25] These metaphors reveal, of course, a world of difference: whereas a judge punishes, a doctor heals.

The second major difference between punishment and making satisfaction is that one person can make satisfaction for *another* if the two are united in *charity*.[26] By drawing on the Pauline notion of the Church as the mystical Body of Christ,[27] Aquinas argues that Christ's saving activity benefits all the faithful. I will come back to this important point in the next section.

Some readers might perhaps be wondering whether Aquinas's soteriology is not excessively subjectivist: has the Cross actually made an objective difference in the world? Undoubtedly, Aquinas puts a very strong emphasis upon our need to somehow "appropriate" the saving work of Christ: Christ's Passion, which is a kind of universal cause of merit and of the forgiveness of sins, still needs to be applied to each individual for the cleansing of personal sins.[28] Similarly, as a doctor prepares a medicine, we still need to apply it through faith, love, and the sacraments of the Church.[29] However, although there is undoubtedly a strong personalist or subjectivist element to Aquinas's soteriology, this should not be taken to imply that the saving work of Christ has nothing to do with the restoration of justice in "objective" terms. The order of the world, as created by God, was distorted by sin.

This needs to be rectified, and if it had not been for Christ's saving work this distortion and alienation would have been perpetuated indefinitely (an alienation that would involve, according to Aquinas, the punishments of hell). In that sense there is something "objectively" changed in the world in that the disorder that sin has caused is being rectified through the redeeming and meritorious work of Christ. Sin cannot have the last word: it needs to be cancelled out by the overarching mercy of God.

This restoration of the order of justice in the world should not be taken to mean, as is sometimes alleged, that God somehow subjects his mercy to his justice in the redemptive work of Christ. In agreement with Anselm, Aquinas argues that in the divine self-gift that is the life and death of Christ the divine mercy and justice are in perfect harmony with one another.[30] Also, when I speak of an "objective" dimension of Aquinas's soteriology, I mean that something is changed in the world—not in God. Aquinas, like other medieval theologians before him, rejects the view that God is somehow "changed" by the life and death of Christ:[31] the Cross is the expression and manifestation of God's love, not the cause of it.[32]

But some readers might still share Schillebeeckx's reservations: is it appropriate to attribute saving significance to the suffering of an innocent man? Should we not see the Cross for what it is: a horrible crime inflicted upon a defenceless victim, rather than the way in which God reconciles the world? Aquinas, however, argues that this is a false dilemma. Given his understanding of providential care and divine causality, which implies that God is such a powerful efficacious Cause that he can attain his goals by genuinely contingent events,[33] Aquinas suggests that it is not incoherent to state that the slaying of Christ was a most grievous sin, and yet in accordance—on a more transcendent level, if you like—with God's providential plan.[34]

Of course, God could have forgiven us without Christ's saving work, but this would have been less "fitting."[35] Examining the reasons why this is the case reveals a lot about how much Aquinas values human dignity and the reciprocity of the relationship between humanity and God: if we had simply been forgiven by a divine *fiat*, we would not have been allowed to participate, through Christ and in union with him (as members of his Body), in the restoration of our relationship with God (i.e., making satisfaction).[36]

But what exactly is the source of merit in Christ's saving work? It is not his sufferings as such but rather what these sufferings reveal: his obedience and love. Thus, not the sufferings per se but the willingness with which Christ took them upon himself are a source of merit that can be shared with all the faithful.[37] The emphasis upon the voluntary nature of Christ's saving activity allows Aquinas to state in *ST* that making satisfaction needs to be understood in terms of a *gift of self* by Christ (*Christus autem satisfecit... dando... seipsum*).[38] This is an important observation for two reasons: first, because, again, it dispels the specter of a revengeful God and instead reveals a self-giving God;[39] second, because this teaches us something about the way we should approach our own afflictions: we should refrain from attributing any intrinsic value to them as such; rather, if borne with obedience and love, they can become an occasion for us to become more Christ-like. I will come back to this in the next section.

In summary, Aquinas adopts the notion of making satisfaction to explain how Christ, as the God-man, restores a broken relationship between humanity and God: while the onus to restore the relationship was on humanity (as we were the guilty party), only God, as the sinless source of all merit, could make satisfaction for the whole human race.[40] As I tried to make clear, this theory should not be construed in legalistic or penal terms. Nor should it be construed in terms of substitution. To explain why this is the case we need to examine in more detail the theme of our participation in Christ's redemptive work as members of his Body.

Our Participation in Christ as Members of His Body

The key presupposition governing Aquinas's soteriology, and to which I have alluded a number of times, is the intimate union between Christ and his faithful. This element, which had been left underdeveloped by Anselm in his work *Cur Deus Homo*, receives major attention in Aquinas's exposition. In *ST* we read for instance: "The head and members are as one mystic person; and therefore Christ's satisfaction belongs to all the faithful as being his members."[41] Similarly, dealing with the issue of how we have been redeemed from sin by the Passion of Christ, Aquinas writes:

> For since He is our head, then, by the Passion which he endured from love and obedience, He delivered us as his members from our sins, as by the price of his Passion: in the same way as if a man by the good industry of his hands were to redeem himself from a sin committed with his feet. For, just as the natural body is one, though made up of diverse members, so the whole Church, Christ's mystic body (*mysticum corpus Christi*), is reckoned as one person with its head, which is Christ.[42]

This does not simply mean that Christ is in union with us; it also means that we are in union with Christ. Thus, it is not just the case that Christ suffers for us; but also: our own sufferings can be seen as a sharing in those of Christ. Commenting on John 20:21, Aquinas writes: "He [= Christ] says *As the Father has sent me, so too I sent you*, which means: as the Father who loves me has sent me in the world to suffer the Passion for the salvation of the faithful... so too I love you, and I send you to endure tribulations for my sake."[43] The view that our own sufferings are a way of becoming more Christ-like was a prominent theme amongst the early Church Fathers. Augustine, for instance, had put it at the heart of his *Exposition on the Psalms* and had actually stated in this work[44] that the risen Christ himself continues to suffer in the members of his Body, the Church.[45] Aquinas does not make such a radical statement, and it is revealing that he hardly ever refers to the crucial text, Colossians 1:24, which at first sight seems to suggest that the sufferings of Christ are somehow deficient and need to be completed in the faithful.[46] Thus, although he does not go as far as stating that the risen Christ continues to suffer in his members, Aquinas does adopt the notion that our sufferings can be interpreted as a means of growing in conformity with Christ. In *SCG*, for instance, when dealing with the objection that it seems odd to claim that Christ saved us while death and other penalties are still with us,[47] he writes that the afflictions that remain allow us to achieve conformity to Christ as members to the head:

> It was both fitting and useful to have the penalty remain even when the fault was taken away. First, indeed, to achieve conformity of the faithful to Christ as members to the head; hence, just as Christ bore many sufferings, and thus arrived at the glory of immortality, it was also becoming to his faithful first to undergo sufferings and so to arrive at immortality, bearing in themselves, so to say, the marks of the passion of Christ, in order to achieve likeness to his glory. So the Apostle says: "Heirs, indeed of God, and joint-heirs with Christ: yet so, if we suffer with him, that we might also be glorified with him" (Rom 8:17).[48]

Thus, Christ does not take away our afflictions here and now. Rather, we should regard our continuing afflictions as a way of sharing in his saving work, as a way of becoming more Christ-like.[49] Although Aquinas does not share the view that the risen Christ continues to suffer in the members of his Body, he does make room for the notion that Christ's saving work continues for all eternity. He does so by developing the idea of Christ's eternal priesthood and by pointing out the significance of the sacramental economy.[50]

The Priesthood of Christ, Sacrifice, and the Lord's Supper

As suggested earlier, in the *ST* Aquinas retains the notion of making satisfaction but he also pays attention to a number of other concepts to describe the saving work of Christ, including "sacrifice."[51] This concept has the advantage that it is more biblical; it also allows Aquinas to link in a more cohesive manner the sacrifice of Christ on the Cross with the sacramental economy (especially the Eucharist[52]). This connection is strengthened by Augustine's definition of sacrifice from Book X of *De Civitate Dei* (*The City of God*), which Aquinas repeatedly quotes: "the visible sacrifice is the sacrament, i.e., the sacred sign, of the invisible sacrifice."[53] This text proves fruitful for a number of reasons. First, as we have already noted, it reiterates the view that saving value is not to be found in Christ's sufferings as such but rather in the obedience and love that they manifest: it is not the external but the interior sacrifice that matters. Second, it makes clear how the faithful can share in this sacrifice by offering themselves up, mirroring the self-gift of Christ, as we saw in the previous section.[54] Third, this offering is continued in the sacrament of the Lord's Supper, which contains "Christ crucified"[55] and which is called "Christ's sacrifice."[56] Let us examine this connection between Christ's sacrifice on the Cross and his sacrifice during the Mass in some more detail.

When discussing the priesthood of Christ, Aquinas (again quoting Augustine) points out that Christ was both priest and offering.[57] A priest is a mediator between God and the people, somebody who bestows divine things upon the people:[58] as priest, Christ freely offers himself to suffer on our behalf. Through this sacrifice of Christ, we become reconciled with God and partakers of the divine nature.[59] As we will see, Aquinas attributes the same benefits to the Lord's Supper.

The notions of sacrifice and priesthood allow Aquinas to cover the same material as that covered by the notion of *satisfactio*, and sometimes his terminology reverts to "making satisfaction" when discussing priesthood.[60] All the faithful, for instance, can participate in the priesthood of Christ through faith and love, and by offering themselves up[61]—a theme I have already mentioned.[62] The notion of sacrifice and priesthood, however, open up a number of vistas that had been left unexplored in the theory of satisfaction. Drawing on his commentary on St. Paul's Letter to the Hebrews (*In Heb*), written in the late 1260s, Aquinas states, for instance, that Christ's priesthood lasts eternally[63] and that the resurrected Christ still carries the scars of his Passion, so as to allow him to intercede on our behalf with the Father for all eternity.[64] However, it is especially in the Lord's Supper that the saving efficacy of Christ's sacrifice on the Cross is continued.

In a beautiful article,[65] Aquinas makes clear that the Lord's Supper has a threefold significance. In relation to the past it is a *sacrifice*, commemorative of the Passion of our Lord; in relation the present, it establishes union amongst the faithful through participation in Christ and is therefore called *communion*; while in relation to the future, it is called *Eucharist* or Viaticum: this is the eschatological meaning, referring to the fact that it anticipates the union with God that we will enjoy in heaven, a foreshadowing of our enjoyment of God in the afterlife *(hoc sacramentum est praefigurativum fruitionis Dei)*. Thus, in the Lord's Supper we receive grace (*Eucharistia*, meaning good grace, *bona gratia*); the Church as the Body of Christ is constituted (*communio*); and the sacrifice that Christ offered on Calvary is being re-enacted for the forgiveness of sins (*sacrificium*).[66] Through the Lord's Supper, the Church as the Body of Christ is established and Christ's saving deeds become universally present. As Aquinas puts it in his *Commentary on John*:

> because this sacrament is that of the Passion of our Lord, it contains within itself the suffering of Christ; therefore, all the beneficiary effects of the Passion of our Lord reside plentifully in this sacrament. This sacrament is nothing else but the Passion of our Lord that is communicated to us.... The destruction of death that Christ has effected by his death and the renewal of life that he effected through his resurrection are also the effects of this sacrament.[67]

Commenting on John 6:54, Aquinas states that through the Eucharistic food we become Christ-like; it is the Eucharistic food that transforms us into Christ, makes us members of his Body, deifies us, and inebriates us with the divinity.[68] Because the Word resides in this sacrament according to his divinity and his humanity, it is the cause of our spiritual and bodily resurrection.[69]

Conclusion

This is a balanced and beautiful soteriology, utterly faithful to the biblical witness; it does justice to the reality of sin, the need to tackle the disorder it causes, and the overwhelming mercy of God. Given the sacramental understanding of Christ, it is Aquinas's view that every aspect of Christ's life, death, and resurrection has saving meaning. The salvation that Christ effected, particularly through his redeeming death, continues to reside in the sacraments, especially in the Lord's Supper, through which the Church is established as one Body. This notion of the Church as the Body of Christ is pivotal in everything that Aquinas has to say about how we appropriate the salvation Christ accomplished. This suggests the organic unity of Aquinas's "theory" of Christ's saving activity, and his sacramentology. But perhaps we should not call Aquinas's soteriology a "theory" of salvation, for it is much more than that. It offers us spiritual guidance as to how we should live and die in Christ.

NOTES

1. I developed some of the ideas in this chapter elsewhere, such as in "'Bearing the Marks of Christ's Passion'—Aquinas' Soteriology," in Rik Van Nieuwenhove and Joseph Wawrykow, eds., *The Theology of Thomas Aquinas* (Notre Dame, Ind.: University of Notre Dame Press, 2005), 277–302; and Rik Van Nieuwenhove, "St Anselm and St Thomas Aquinas on 'Satisfaction': Or How Catholic and Protestant Understandings of the Cross Differ," *Angelicum* 80 (2003): 159–76.

2. Edward Schillebeeckx, *Christ: The Christian Experience in the Modern World* (London: SCM, 1980), 729.

3. Edward Schillebeeckx, *The Church: The Human Story of God* (London: SCM, 1990), 125.

4. For instance, in *SCG* IV, 53.16, we find the objection that it seems "impious and cruel to command an innocent to be led to death, especially on behalf of the impious who are worthy of death. But the man Christ Jesus was innocent. Therefore it would have been impious if at the command of God the Father He had undergone death." In Saint Thomas Aquinas, *Summa contra Gentiles, Book Four: Salvation*, trans. Charles O'Neil (Notre Dame, Ind.: University of Notre Dame Press, 1975), 226. For a reply, see *SCG* IV, 55.18–19; *ST* III q.47 a.3 ad 1 and III q. 47 a.4 ad 2.

5. See Jürgen Moltmann, *The Crucified God* (London: SCM, 1976), esp. ch. 6.

6. All translations from *ST* are from the Benzinger edition, St Thomas Aquinas, *Summa Theologica*, trans. Fathers of the English Dominican Province (Westminster, Md.: Christian Classics, 1981). *ST* III q.46 a.12 ad 1.

7. For an excellent critique of Moltmann's theology, see Thomas Weinandy, *Does God Suffer?* (Edinburgh: T & T Clark, 2000).

8. *CT* I, 227–28.

9. We do not find the expression in either the *SCG* or *ST*.

10. See *ST* III q.19 a.1.

11. I deliberately write that every aspect of Christ's life has sacramental "meaning and power" because for Aquinas causation and signification are not opposed but mutually enrich one another. This is important to keep in mind as some recent critics (such as L.-M. Chauvet) have artificially played out a supposedly more "existentialist" *signification* against a supposedly more "metaphysical" *causation*, preferring the first to the second. Unfortunately, this runs the risk of reducing God's sacramental power to our understanding or experience of it. For a more in-depth discussion of this issue, see Liam Walsh's searching contribution on the "Sacraments" in Rik Van Nieuwenhove and Joseph Wawrykow, eds., *The Theology of Thomas Aquinas* (Notre Dame, Ind.: University of Notre Dame Press, 2005), 326–64, esp. 329–30.

12. *In Rom* 4:25, no. 380. My translation from the Marietti edition.

13. *ST* III q.48 a.6; see also *ST* III q.49 a.1.

14. *ST* III q.66 a.2.

15. *In Rom* 6:11, no. 491.

16. Within the confines of this contribution I cannot develop Aquinas's theology of the resurrection. For this, see Van Nieuwenhove, "'Bearing the Marks of Christ's Passion,'" esp. 294–95.

17. In *ST* III q.48, Aquinas describes how the Passion of Christ effects our salvation by way of merit, by way of making satisfaction, by way of sacrifice, and by way of redemption.

18. I have dealt with this in Van Nieuwenhove, "St Anselm and St Thomas Aquinas on 'Satisfaction,'" 169–70.

19. *CT* I, 200, in *The Light of Faith: The Compendium of Theology*, trans. by C. Vollert (Manchester: Sophia Institute Press, 1993), 229–30. See also *SCG* IV, 54.9 and *ST* III q.48 a.2.

20. Cf. *ST* III q.85 a.3 ad 3 and *ST* III q.84 a.5 ad 2. Some editions (such as the Editio Altera Romana, 1894) have "et quod amico homo studeat *satisfacere*"; others have "et quod amico homo *reconciliari* studeat."

21. Cf. *SCG* IV, 72.14. The sacrament of penance consists of three elements: confession, contrition, and making satisfaction (see *SCG* IV, 72). It is only the element of making satisfaction (*satisfactio*) that applies to Christ's redemptive activity through the union with his members (see *ST* III q.48 a.2 ad 1).

22. *SCG* IV, 72.1.

23. *ST* III q.84 a.10 ad 5.

24. *ST* I-II q.88 a.1.

25. In *ST* III q.49 a.1 ad 3.

26. *SCG* III, 158, 7 and *ST* III q.48 a.2 ad 1.

27. *ST* III q.49 a.1; III q.48 a.2 ad 1.

28. *ST* III q.49 a.1 ad 4.

29. Cf. *ST* III q.49 a.1 ad 3; *ST* III q.49 a.3 ad 1.

30. *ST* III q.46 a.1 ad 3.

31. Cf. *ST* III q.1 a.1 ad 1.

32. *ST* III q.49 a.4 ad 2.

33. Cf. *ST* I q.19 a.8; *SCG* III, 72.

34. Cf. *ST* III q.47 a.4 ad 2; *ST* III q.47 a.3 ad 1.

35. Cf. *ST* III q.46 a.1 and a.3.

36. Cf. *SCG* IV, 54.8.
37. See *ST* III q.48 a.1; *SCG* IV, 55, 25–26.
38. *ST* III q.48 a.4.
39. Cf. *In Rom* 5:8–9, no. 399.
40. *SCG* IV, 54, 9.
41. *ST* III q.48 a.2 ad 1; see also *ST* III q.8 a.1 and a.3.
42. In *ST* III q.49 a.1.
43. *Super Johan*, no. 2527, my trans.
44. Augustine, *Expos. on the Psalms*, 62, 2.
45. See *Ennerationes in Psalmos* 62, 2, in *Exposition on the Psalms*, vol. 3, trans. Maria Boulding (New York: New City Press, 2001), 230–31: "This solidarity [between the Head and the Body] meant that when Christ suffered, we suffered in him; and it follows that now that he has ascended into heaven, and is seated at the right hand, he still undergoes in the person of his Church whatever it may suffer amid the troubles of this world." See Rik Van Nieuwenhove, "The Christian Response to Suffering, and the Significance of the Model of the Church as Body of Christ," *Angelicum* 82 (2005): 605ff.
46. He refers to the text only twice outside the *Commentary on Colossians* itself (no. 61), namely in *ST* III q.48 a.5 obj. 3 and in *In I Cor* 1:13, no. 32. In each case he points out that the Passion of Christ is the sole cause of our salvation and that the sufferings of the saints do not have any redemptive but only an exemplary value.
47. *SCG* IV, 55.28.
48. *Summa contra Gentiles*, trans. by O'Neil, 245.
49. Cf. *ST* III q.49 a.3 ad 3; *ST* III q.79 a.2 ad 1; *ST* I-II q.85 a.5 ad 2; *ST* III q.56 a.1 ad 1; *In Rom* 8:17, no. 651.
50. "Sacramental economy" refers to the communication (esp. through the sacraments) of the fruits of Christ's paschal mystery into our world.
51. Cf. *ST* III q.48 a.3.
52. Cf. *ST* III q.83 a.1; but also *ST* III q.63 a.6 ad 1.
53. *ST* III q.22 a.2; III q.48 a.3 obj. 2; III q.60 a.1; II-II q.81 a.7 ad 2.
54. Cf. *In Rom* 12:1–2, nos. 957–67; *ST* II-II q.85 a.2; *ST* II-II q.85 a.3 ad 2; *Lectura super Epistolam Pauli ad Ephesos* 5:2, no. 270.
55. *ST* III q.73 a.5 ad 2.
56. *ST* III q.83 a.1.
57. *ST* III q.22 a.2.
58. *Sacerdos* [priest] is derived from *sacra dans*, to give sacred things, as Aquinas explains in *ST* III q.22 a.1.
59. *ST* III q.22 a.1. Christ's priesthood fulfils the priesthood of the *OT* in its threefold aspect, namely as offerings for sins, peace offerings, and burnt offerings (*ST* III q.22 a.2). For an illuminating discussion as to how Christ fulfils the hopes of Israel, see Matthew Levering, *Christ's Fulfillment of Torah and Temple: Salvation according to Aquinas* (Notre Dame, Ind.: University of Notre Dame, 2002).
60. For instance, in *ST* III q.22 a.1, we find that Christ in his role as priest is the mediator who "offers up the people's prayers to God, and, in a manner, makes satisfaction to God for their sins" *(et pro eorum peccatis Deo aliqualiter satisfacit)*. Similarly, *ST* III q.22 a.3.
61. *ST* III q.82 a.1 ad 2.
62. See the brilliant contribution by Gilles Emery, "Le Sacerdoce spirituel des fidèles chez Saint Thomas d'Aquin," *Revue Thomiste* 99 (1999): 211–43.
63. *ST* III q.22 a.5.

64. *ST* III q.54 a.4.

65. *ST* III q.73 a.4.

66. Aquinas states that the sacrifice that is offered every day in the Church is not distinct from that which Christ himself offered, but is a commemoration (*commemoratio*) of it (*ST* III q.22 a.3 ad 2). It is clear from his stance on the Real Presence of Christ in the Eucharistic Bread and Wine that "commemoration" should not be misunderstood in terms of mere remembrance.

67. *Super Johan*, no. 963. My translation. A similar view can be found in *ST* III q.73 a.5 ad 2: "The Eucharist is the perfect sacrament of our Lord's Passion, as containing Christ crucified."

68. *Super Johan*, no. 972.

69. *Super Johan*, no. 972–73.

CHAPTER 33

SACRAMENTS

DOMINIC HOLTZ, O.P.

It is an ancient, and some would say original, conviction of the Church that the redemption won in the deeds, sufferings, and glorification of Jesus Christ is communicated to the Christian faithful in the enacting of certain ritual practices understood in some sense to have been instituted by Jesus Christ himself. Said differently, the universal tradition of the Church has attributed to what have been called the *sacraments* or *mysteries* the role in Christian life of making manifest and effective here and now the universal salvation effected by the Word made flesh. Thomas Aquinas is no different in this regard, nor does he intend to be. He recognizes as sacraments instituted by Christ those rites so recognized by the Latin Church in the thirteenth century: above all Baptism and Eucharist, but also Confirmation, Penance, Extreme Unction, Order, and Matrimony.

Sacraments as Worship

Aquinas understands worship, and not simply the internal love shown in mind and will of a rational creature to its Creator but also the use of material objects, words, and bodily gestures, to be a natural obligation of all human beings.[1] As a matter of justice, creatures must honor their Creator, even as children must honor their parents and citizens their city and must also do so in ways proper to their nature.[2] Furthermore, to succeed at its task, any human religion must include means of designating those who are able to perform the rites, those who may benefit from them, as well as a means to restore to right relationship those who have been rendered unfit for worship, whether unfit to minister or to receive the blessings of ministry.[3] That is, worship, for Aquinas, while at heart directed to God, nonetheless requires the constitution of a people rightly ordered to one another and to God. As with many other features of the natural law, the specifics of such natural worship are not, on Aquinas's view, necessary, and there are many ways by which a human creature might rightly devise rites, prayers, festivals, and sacrifices to fulfill the natural obligation of worship.

However, the worship that derives from a human response to the natural law will necessarily fall short of its goal. In part, this is because of the effects of sin on human knowledge and desire. Being subject to the corruption of sin, knowledge of God is dimmed and the authentic desire to be rightly related to God is bent, and thus human persons will misconceive not only God's nature but also the kind of worship pleasing to him. This false worship will in turn orient the worshippers either to nothing at all or to some other being unworthy of divine worship. Moreover, even the best rites of natural worship will fail to bring the believer to God precisely because, as natural activities, they are insufficient for their end, which is supernatural. This, Aquinas holds, is the reason God both revealed the rites of the Tabernacle and Temple for the Old Covenant and the sacraments of faith for the New. Since the worship of God found in the Old and New Covenant directs the believer to God as to a supernatural end, an end that exceeds all unaided human efforts both to know fully and to achieve, no natural worship originating from human ingenuity will as such succeed.[4] In addition, for such worship to be not merely rightly oriented but also succeed in accomplishing what it promises, that is to draw the worshipper into the mystery of the divine interpersonal communion that is God himself, it must be in important ways an act of God himself, since only a divine act is proportionate to a divine end. It is uniquely that worship of God offered by the God-man, the Word Incarnate, Jesus Christ, through all of his theandric acts and experiences, but most especially in his death on the Cross,[5] that succeeds at being worship in spirit and in truth, the reasonable or spiritual worship of the New Covenant. Indeed, it is only insofar as the worship of the Church is the worship of Christ himself, the acts of his body of which he is the head, and only insofar as the prayer of the Church is the prayer of the Holy Spirit, that the rites of the Church are acceptable as true worship and effective for directing and bringing the believer to eternal life.

Sacraments as Signs

Aquinas is rightly credited with asserting that the sacraments are better understood as signs than as causes, and that even as causes, they have their effect by means of their signifying.[6] Of course, to see the sacraments as signs is nothing new of itself. The earliest discussions of the Christian sacraments distinguished between what was seen and touched, the words spoken and the rites performed, on the one hand, and the sacred reality imparted, on the other hand. In Aquinas's day, the distinction between sign (*sacramentum*) and reality (*res*) was well established. Moreover, the response in the eleventh century to the sacramental teachings of Berengar of Tours and subsequent developments in the twelfth century equipped Aquinas with a threefold way of discussing the sacraments.[7] In every sacrament, there is something that is only a sign, the dynamic ritual action by members of the faithful rightly constituted as recipients and dispensers of God's grace in the Church (*sacramentum tantum*), that which is both sign and signified reality, the healing and sanctifying work of Christ applied to the recipient here and now (*res et sacramentum*), and that which is only a signified reality, that ultimate possession of the reality, inaugurated and experienced in part through the sacrament, but of which the effect here and now is only a foretaste and a pledge (*res tantum*).

The purpose of this analysis of the sacraments is meant to do justice to the fullness of the sacramental teaching that Aquinas has inherited from the early centuries of the Church. Aquinas, like other Christians, holds that there is more to Baptism, for example, than getting someone wet, more to Eucharist than what appears to the eye and taste as bread and wine, more to penance than comforting words and admirable or ascetical deeds, and yet that these ritual actions disclose important features of that reality which they impart. Yet, while early and Medieval Christians asserted that these human rites had divine effects, they also accepted that the effect, the reality associated with each did not always obtain. Not everyone baptized in fact remains dead to sin. Not all who share in the Eucharist maintain that union of charity in which the Body of Christ consists, and so on. By the twelfth century in the Latin West, the threefold schema of sacramental language was thus a means of upholding all three aspects of this common and ancient wisdom, that not all the sacraments promise is true here and now, nor perhaps even in the future, but that no sacrament rightly enacted goes without a real effect.

At the same time, the signification that is true of the sacraments is true also of other ritual activity that does not pretend to have a direct spiritual, which is to say supernatural, effect. There is, in other words, a broader way to speak of sacraments, namely as signs of sacred realities. Taken at its broadest, it might be possible to claim that everything created, insofar as it is what it is, insofar as it participates in some way in God's perfection, is a sign of a sacred thing, namely, of God's own being. Aquinas, however, is not inclined to use the term "sacrament" in this way.[8] Similarly, while Aquinas takes the worship of God to be a natural obligation of human beings as rational animals, he does not generally speak of the rites of human religion in general as sacraments. He is, however, willing to speak of the sacraments of the Old Law, including not only the ceremonies, festivals, and sacrifices but also those rites that constitute the community of Israel as sacred, as set apart for worship of the Lord, especially circumcision and the anointing of priests. While Aquinas asserts that these sacraments of the Old Law signified sacred realities, and specifically that they presignified the reality of the saving work of the Incarnate Word,[9] Aquinas held that they did not effect what they signified. It was the faith of the people of Israel in the redemption signified by these rites, not the rites themselves, which Aquinas takes to be the basis of the salvation of those who believed in the true God before the coming of Jesus Christ.[10] Still, while this distinguishes the sacraments of the Old Covenant from those of the New, it also admits a continuity between them.[11]

Curiously, while Aquinas has a high view of the rites of the Old Law, and indeed devotes a fair number of questions in his *Summa theologiae* to the very topic, he holds celebration of these same rites now, and indeed in any time since the promulgation of the Gospel by the apostles, to be sinful. Why should this be so? On Aquinas's view, ritual activity, ritual signification, is fundamentally communicative: it "says" something.[12] Moreover, it does so in a "tensed" way. The grammar of rites includes, on Aquinas's view, a past, present, and future.[13] According to Aquinas, the rites of the Old Law are all in the future tense. They speak, admittedly in shadow and figured ways, of the *future* coming of the Lord. While one could have "said" that the Lord *will* come in the flesh and *will* suffer and die prior to the Incarnation of the Word and the life, death, resurrection, and glorification of the Son of God, after these events, such rites will no longer be true.

Since the sacraments, the signification of enacting the rites themselves, depend on this kind of contextual meaning, and since the sacraments are effective only insofar as they succeed in signification, some recent theologians have wondered whether the seven sacraments recognized by Thomas Aquinas might not be too deeply enmeshed in the cultural framework of the classical Mediterranean and the inheritor cultures of the Greco-Roman world, that is, the culture of Europe and the European Diaspora.[14] Can a Eucharist with wheat bread and wine of the grape have an effect if the signification of wheat and grape wine is altogether different from its meaning in Europe, say in sub-Saharan Africa or East Asia? Might not a different cultural framework require a different, even radically different, kind of signification, in both matter and ritual word and act (i.e., form) to succeed in signifying meaningfully?

Aquinas is not unaware that one might imagine both different matter and different form, particularly different words, to enact the sacraments. In certain respects, Aquinas is willing to admit a range of signification. Any wine of the grape, for example, will do.[15] Any kind of wheaten bread, leavened or unleavened, will succeed for the celebration of the Eucharist.[16] Any water will do for Baptism,[17] whether in a small pool or a running stream, a lake or the ocean. Likewise, Aquinas is aware that the ritual actions that surround the sacrament admit to a wide variety, even change. The words that are used in the sacraments, while not infinitely plastic, likewise may be subject to legitimate variety and change. Aquinas is keenly aware of the ways in which the ritual words used by Orthodox Christians in the East differ from those used by Latin Christians in the West, and he admits that, while the Latin forms are simply speaking better, the "Greek" (i.e., Orthodox) ritual forms are no less valid, no less true in their signification.[18] Even errors in speech do not, for Aquinas, necessarily vitiate the signification that is important for the sacraments to be effective. So long as the intended meaning of the words is not altogether lost by the error, the signification is preserved.[19]

Nonetheless, Aquinas rejects any radical departure from the matter or the ritual forms accepted by the Church. He notes, for example, that while Eucharist with barley loaves or a lamb rather than bread of wheat may have a kind of logic, no rite so celebrated would be a true sacrament. Similarly, to baptize in the name of the Father who creates, the Son who redeems, and the Spirit who sanctifies, would be valid and effective, while to baptize in the name of the Mother, the Daughter, and the Spirit would not.[20] What permits the variety in some sense, but does not allow change in another? Aquinas recognizes that objects and ritual actions are ambiguous as signs. They generally require words to locate the meaning that they have here and now. Moreover, on Aquinas's view, the signification in the sacraments is located not principally in the culture in which the sacraments are celebrated, but in the historical particularities of the earthly life of the Incarnate Word. This means that the critical question is not, for example, what wheat and wine of the grape "mean" semantically in Osaka, but whether sake and rice cakes adequately signify in the way Jesus Christ intended when he instituted the Eucharist at the Last Supper. The question for Baptism is not whether "Son" and "Father" have the same signification in North America in the early twenty-first century that they had in the first in Palestine, but why, in God's providence, his Son was Incarnate in first-century Palestine and chose to reveal himself as the Son of the Father.

Sacraments as Causes

While Aquinas is rightly credited, especially in his later works, with a refined and enriched conception of the sacraments as signs, it would be a mistake to overlook the crucial ways that Aquinas wanted to safeguard understanding the sacraments as true causes of grace. At first glance, one can see why several of Aquinas's precursors, and some of his contemporaries as well, were anxious about the claim that the sacraments cause what they signify. The sacraments are signs of supernatural effects, of the various participations in the healing of sin and more importantly of the perfection, the completion of the human person through a sharing in the life of the Incarnate Word, Jesus Christ. However, since this is a divine effect, it is difficult to see how the act of a creature could produce it. Indeed, some of Aquinas's contemporaries argued just that, namely, that the sacraments are only signs of what God does independently of them.[21] They are, so they claimed, like a lead coin that a king has decreed to have commercial value. One can truly buy things with the coin, not because the coin has value in itself, but merely by the power of the royal decree. These theologians conceived the sacraments then as occasions of grace, that God promised to produce certain effects of grace concurrently with the sacraments, of which the sacraments were however only the signs.

Others, including Aquinas himself in his early career, were dissatisfied with this approach. The sacraments, he argued, really produce some effect. Why? Fundamentally, the early Aquinas and others were convinced from the language of the Scriptures as understood through the heritage of the Fathers of the Church that the sacraments did something. Seeing the occasionalist explanation as a denial of any causality for the sacraments, they rejected it as unfaithful to the received Tradition. Nonetheless, there remained the problem of associating a supernatural effect with a natural, and thus finite and disproportionate, cause. Aquinas's early solution was to assert that the sacraments indeed had an effect, but only so as to dispose the recipient to receive the grace of the sacrament, which grace God imparts directly, without mediation.[22] Since this disposing effect was understood to be proportionate to the sacraments as finite signs, it was seen as a way to assert, on the one hand, that the sacraments were indeed efficient signs and, on the other hand, that it was God, and not created activities, who imparted to believers the gift of eternal life. Ultimately, Aquinas will abandon this disposing view of the effect of the sacraments for a more robust claim that the sacraments in fact, without nuance, impart the grace that they signify, but that in doing so they do not violate the claim that a finite, physical cause cannot, of itself, produce a divine, spiritual effect.[23] This shift is possible through an appeal to the notion of instrumental causality, itself enriched not only by an engagement with the Christological writings of the Christian East, especially John of Damascus, but also in general of a more comprehensive sense of the relationship between God's primary causality and secondary causes in the created world.

It is also worth noting that, fundamentally, Aquinas's incentive to hold his position arises from his conviction that the sacraments are received in faith as handed on from Jesus Christ, who instituted them, and passed them on to the apostles, who themselves handed them on to their successors, and through them to the Church throughout the ages. The sacraments are, for Aquinas, a theological *datum*, part of the revelation given in Christ. They are neither the product of human ingenuity nor can they be derived from prior principles. There is no more foundational category, "sacramentality," that can be used to then discover or produce some new set or ordering of the sacraments of faith other than the seven sacraments received from Christ by the Church.[24] Aquinas does consider the hypothetical possibility, for example, that Christ might have authorized the apostles to produce new sacraments, or sacramental effects, in their own name rather than his.[25] Likewise, he accounts for the number of sacraments and what they do on the basis of anthropology (in light of the origin, growth, maintenance, and restoration of human beings both as individuals and as social animals) and the virtues (moral and theological).[26] However, in both of these cases, Aquinas is keen to demonstrate the *convenientia*, the fittingness of the sacraments as they have been received. They have an order and a reason to them, but only in the way that all of the works of God are characterized by wisdom. One could no more invent a new sacrament on Aquinas's view than write a new inspired book of Scripture. One could no more restructure the sacramental system than one could rewrite the events of Christ's life.

A more recent worry about Aquinas's presentation of the sacraments responds to his understanding of the sacraments as causes. Specifically, the worry has taken the form of a Heideggerian critique of metaphysics and "ontotheology," especially in the work of Chauvet.[27] Chauvet, following Heidegger, worries about the project of seeking a single foundation for all instances of being, for some indeterminate and unspecified being shared by all, and then identifying this ground of being with God. As a result, so the critique goes, while, on the one hand, the richness of individual things as primary is lost to the vagueness of foundational "being," so also God is misrepresented as knowable, as sharing the same kind of being as any other thing, albeit maximally. God thus becomes the subject of human rational projects, as opposed to being the One encountered in the world but as always escaping the capacity of the world to anticipate or categorize. As related to classic sacramental thought exemplified in Thomas Aquinas, this ontotheological project is accused of depersonalizing and objectifying the sacraments, making what should be understood as the creative, self-producing power of ritual words in an encounter with God who escapes all human anticipations into a mechanistic scheme of "grace" in which the actions of God, being capable of categorization in the sphere of being, are safely known, deprived of mystery.

This is not the place to provide a full response to Chauvet's critique, much less to Heidegger's critique of ontotheology, as they relate to Thomas Aquinas.[28] However, it may be helpful to consider Chauvet's worry that Aquinas's account depersonalizes the sacraments, subordinating them to a productionist scheme of impersonal objects. On the face of it, the worry does not seem altogether unfounded. After all, Aquinas does admit that the sacraments are causes of grace. Even granting that they cause by signing or through their signification, they are nonetheless causes. Indeed, because they produce the effects of grace in the recipient, they are efficient causes, and because they produce their saving effects not of their own materiality or their intentional ritual use (i.e., their form) but by God's use of them to produce an effect properly divine, they are instrumental causes.

Now, efficient causality is not generally how we conceive of the interaction of persons as persons. The loving encounter between persons is, one might insist, precisely opposed to producing an effect in the other directly, as opposed to moving the other by loving example through a kind of exemplar or final causality. Similarly, if the minister in the ritual enacting of the sacrament is understood to act as an instrument, and Aquinas's preferred analogy for instrumental causality is the saw in the hand of a carpenter,[29] we might rightly worry here that not only the recipient of the sacrament, but also the minister, is reduced to something inert, an object on which God effects a change rather than a person invited into the encounter with mystery.

Given these unhappy implications, why would Aquinas assert that sacraments are instrumental causes? Fundamentally, Aquinas is committed to the claim that the sacraments are not human acts pointing to God, but divine acts, God applying the work of salvation effected by the deeds and experiences of the Incarnate Word to the faithful in the Church, which is itself the body of the Incarnate Word. They are, in other words, not merely interpersonal, but in crucial ways intrapersonal, the realization in each of the members of the body what is fully realized in the head, Jesus Christ, by means materially and numerically different from the *acta et passa Christi*, but which communicate the same power and person those theandric activities accomplished in the earthly ministry of the Incarnate Word.[30]

Even so, how should instrumentality not undermine the very personal reality Aquinas seeks to uphold? The answer lies in the richness Aquinas sees in the notion of instrumental causality, a richness he has expanded well beyond its brief discussion in Aristotle, even as Aquinas's sacramental thought as a whole enriches and expands the whole understanding of causality itself.[31] The most excellent and pertinent case of instrumental causality is, for Aquinas, the human nature assumed by the Son of God in the Incarnation. In this most intimate of all unions, more than even the union of a hand with its body, the Word of God employs the human nature, an animate, rational nature, as his own, such that even the simplest of human acts or experiences of the Incarnate Word is theandric, the human act or experience of God. Because this fully rational human nature is the human nature of a divine person, all of the human activity of Jesus Christ is therefore of infinite value, overflowing with divine charity and sufficient for the salvation of the whole human race, even if this is all the more evident and effected in those deeds most clearly enacted out of love for the human race, most especially his death on the Cross. Thus, in the economy of salvation, all of God's saving work is accomplished through the instrumentality of the humanity of the Incarnate Word and the joining of believers to that saving instrumentality through the Spirit ordinarily through the instrumentality of the sacraments.

So, in highlighting the instrumentality both of the minister and recipient of the sacraments, Aquinas is committed neither to a project of depersonalization nor to the mechanization of the work of grace. The notion of sacramental character, far from a theological curiosity to distinguish sacraments that cannot be repeated in the same individual from those that can, serves to account for how both the reception of the sacraments and their administration is not merely a human act occasioning or preparing for a divine act, but a real knowing and loving participation in the personal, theandric, saving work of the Incarnate Word.[32] Indeed, this is why Aquinas insists that the sacraments do effect what they sign, that they are efficient causes. To know and love as we ought, to know and love as Christ knows and loves, to breathe with the same breath that is the Holy Spirit, to be in other words divinized, is not traceable, reducible, or derivable from any created nature. No account of semiotics and the power of signs, nor any kind of formal or final causality alone, can speak meaningfully of what it means for a created agent to be drawn into the life of the Trinity through the saving work of the Son of God made flesh. In the end, whatever ways it may also be the work of the believer, it must necessarily be principally the work of God.

For Aquinas, in line with the historical consensus of Christendom, while the sacraments share much not only with human religious ceremonies in general and the offices and sacrifices of the Old Testament in particular, these sacraments take their origin, institution, meaning, and effect directly from Jesus Christ in his earthly ministry and as handed on to the Apostles and their successors. That is, while the sacraments may be said to be *ecclesial* (to be *sacramenta ecclesiae*) insofar as they both constitute the Church as such and are, especially in the Eucharist, the fundamental activity of the Church, for Aquinas they are essentially *dominical* in nature. The sacraments flow from God's freedom, from the divine will and plan to draw his elect to himself by the saving work of the Incarnate Word and the sending forth of the Holy Spirit. Thus, like any other part of the economy of salvation, and especially the mysteries of the Incarnation to which they are intimately linked, the sacraments cannot be deduced by reason, reduced to a set of principles, or produced by human ingenuity.[33] They are irreducibly the works of Jesus Christ, to be contemplated and explored for deeper understanding, to be sure, but like all else in the divine economy, explored not for necessity, but for their fittingness (*convenientia*) with the eternal wisdom made manifest in God's work of salvation in Jesus Christ.

NOTES

1. *SCG* 3, q.119; *ST* II-II q.85 a.1.
2. *ST* II-II q.81 a.2.
3. *ST* I-II q.102 a.5.
4. *ST* I-II q.99 a.3.
5. *ST* III q.48 a.3.
6. *ST* III q.60 a.1; John P. Yocum, "Sacraments in Aquinas," in Thomas Weinandy, Daniel Keating, and John Yocum, eds., *Aquinas on Doctrine: A Critical Introduction* (London and New York: T & T Clark International, 2004), 160–64.
7. Edward J. Kilmartin, *The Eucharist in the West* (Collegeville, Minn.: Liturgical Press, 1998), 97–102, 120ff.
8. *ST* III q.60 a.2 ad 1.
9. *ST* I-II q.102 a.2.
10. *ST* III q. 62 a. 6.
11. *ST* I-II q.107 a.1.
12. Yocum, "Sacraments in Aquinas," 165–68.
13. *ST* II-II q.93 a.1.
14. See Phillip Tovey, *Inculturation of Christian Worship: Exploring the Eucharist* (Aldershot and Burlington, Vt.: Ashgate Publishing, 2004), 33–55.
15. *ST* III q.74 a.5 ad 3.
16. *ST* III q.74 a.4.
17. *ST* III q.66 a.4.
18. *ST* III q.60 a.8; *ST* III q.66 a.5 ad 1.
19. *ST* III q.60 a.7 ad 3.
20. *ST* III q.60 a.7 ad 3; *ST* III q.60 a.8.
21. *ST* III q.62 a.1.
22. *Super Sent* 4, d.1, q.1, a.4, qc.1, co.
23. *ST* III q.62 a.1.
24. In all his works, Aquinas only uses the word *sacramentalitas* once, *Super Sent* 4, d.31, q.1, a.2, ad 7. Here he seeks to distinguish different understandings of marriage. While marriage is a sacrament, it is also a form of life arising from human nature (*officium naturae*), and so it can be understood in this latter way, and not only in terms of its signification of, among other things, inseparability.

25. *ST* III q.64 a.4.

26. *ST* III q.65 a.1.

27. Louis-Marie Chauvet, *Symbole et sacrement: Une relecture sacramentelle de l'existence chrétienne* (Paris: Les Éditions du Cerf, 1988). See also Kenan B. Osborne, *Christian Sacraments in a Postmodern World: A Theology for the Third Millennium* (New York and Mahwah, N.J.: Paulist Press, 1999).

28. For a recent critique of Chauvet's engagement with Aquinas, see Bernard Blankenhorn, "The Instrumental Causality of the Sacraments: Thomas Aquinas and Louis-Marie Chauvet," *Nova et Vetera* 4:2 (2006): 255–94.

29. *ST* III q.62 a.1.

30. *ST* III q.8.

31. Mark D. Jordan, *Rewritten Theology: Aquinas after His Readers* (Malden, Mass. and Oxford: Blackwell Publishing, 2006), 163–68.

32. *ST* III q.63 a.2.

33. *ST* III q.64 a.2 ad 3.

CHAPTER 34

RESURRECTION AND THE SEPARATED SOUL

ELEONORE STUMP

The Soul as Substantial Form

Aquinas takes human beings to be material things, and he takes the human soul to be the form of the human body.[1] Although Aquinas thinks that not all forms are forms of material objects, on his view all material things are composites of matter and form. In the case of human beings, the soul is the substantial form of the whole. A substantial form of a material object such as a human being is that in virtue of which the material object is a member of the species to which it belongs. In general, form for Aquinas is not static but dynamic. And a substantial form is the configuration or organization that gives a thing its species-specific causal powers. According to Aquinas, at death, the human soul is replaced in the body by a different, non-animating substantial form that takes the place of the soul. In consequence of its configuration by that form, the matter of the dead body is substantially different.[2] That is why after death the body can be called 'a human body' only equivocally. For the same reason, Aquinas thinks that when we use the names of the parts for the dead body, we use those words equivocally. Once a human being dies and the soul is gone, Aquinas says, we use words such as 'flesh' or 'eye' equivocally if we apply them to parts of the corpse.[3]

For Aquinas, the individuation of a substance is also a function of its substantial form. Any given particular substance is *this* thing just in virtue of the fact that the form which configures it is *this* form. For example, a material substance such as Socrates is this human being in virtue of having *this* substantial form. What is necessary and sufficient for something to be identical to Socrates is that its substantial form be identical to the substantial form of Socrates.[4]

But how are the substantial forms of material objects such as human beings individuated? The answer is expressed in Aquinas's line that matter individuates.[5] The line is well known, but its meaning is less evident.

For Aquinas, the substantial form of any material substance configures *prime* matter, that is, matter that is devoid of every form, without any configuration. On the other hand, when Aquinas attempts to explain the concept of matter relevant to individuation, he tends to speaks of it as matter under *indeterminate* dimensions,[6] that is, matter which is extended in three dimensions but where the degree of extension in any dimension is not specified. Any actually existing matter has *determinate* dimensions. But the particular degree of extension in a dimension is one thing; the materiality, as it were, of matter is another thing. The determinate dimensions of a material thing have to do with exactly what space that thing occupies. On the other hand, matter under indeterminate dimensions, that is, the *materiality* of the matter, is responsible for the space-occupying feature itself. Matter is the sort of thing that is *here* now, in a way that numbers, for example, are not. But this feature of matter, its space-occupying character, can be considered without specifying the precise spatial locations that any particular material thing occupies. Matter is *this* matter in virtue of occupying *this* space, even if the dimensions of that space are indeterminate.[7]

And so because matter has an irreducible space-occupying character, we can distinguish one substantial form from another by its association with matter. This substantial form is the configuration of this matter, and that one is the configuration of that matter.[8] For Aquinas, all the matter of a material substance is configured directly by a particular substantial form. That is, the substantial form of a substance such as a cat does not weave together the integral parts of the cat—the legs and trunk and so on—or any other matter-form composites in the cat. Rather, every material part of the cat is a cat-ish part, which is what it is in virtue of being informed by the substantial form *cat*. But what makes a substantial form *cat* this particular substantial form *cat* is that there is some particular materiality, *now* and *here*, which is informed by that form. In the case of human beings, Aquinas's idea is the same. What individuates Socrates is *this* substantial form of a human being; and a substantial form of a material substance such as Socrates is *this* substantial form in virtue of the fact that it configures *this* matter. On this way of understanding the form that is the human soul, it is easier to see why Aquinas thinks that the soul makes matter to be not just human but also this human being. The soul configures prime matter, whose basic materiality or extensibility then differentiates this form with its spatio-temporal location from any other. In fact, Aquinas thinks that, for human beings, each soul is, as it were, handcrafted by God to inform *this* matter.

Aquinas holds that the separated soul can exist independently of the body after death, but Aquinas's way of individuating the substantial forms of material substances has seemed to some people to pose a problem for this claim of his. It is true that the separated soul of Socrates will differ from the separated soul of Plato in virtue of having configured the body of Socrates rather than the body of Plato. But some philosophers suppose that, even so, Aquinas is stuck with an incoherent position. So, for example, Richard Swinburne says,

> If Aquinas' view is to be spelled out coherently, it must be done.... [in terms of intrinsic properties of the soul]. What did happen to a soul in the past, namely that it was united to a certain body, and will happen to it in future cannot make it the soul it is now. That must be something internal to it now. Religious believers who believe that humans can exist without their bodies, even if only temporarily, must hold that. So too must any believer who holds that there is life after death, even if souls do not exist separately from bodies.[9]

For Aquinas, however, there *will* be intrinsic differences between the separated soul of Socrates and the separated soul of Plato. On Aquinas's position,

> everything has its being and its individuation from the same source.... Therefore, as the being of the soul is from God as from an active principle... so also the individuation of the soul, even if it has a certain relationship to the body, does not perish when the body perishes.[10]

One reason for his holding this position is that there is continuity of cognitive and conative faculties, with their dispositions and occurrent conditions, between an embodied person such as Socrates and his subsisting separated soul. For example, the separated soul of Socrates has the memories of Socrates rather than those of Plato.[11] As far as that goes, all the intellectual faculties, including the rational will, of Socrates are preserved in his separated soul. But what is contained in these faculties of the separated soul of Socrates, including the habits of the will, as well as the mind's memories and knowledge, will be different from those in the faculties of the separated soul of Plato. And so there are these intrinsic differences between the separated souls of Socrates and Plato: the things known, willed, and remembered by the separated soul of Socrates are different from those known, willed, and remembered by the separated soul of Plato. Consequently, on Aquinas's view, there are intrinsic characteristics that differentiate one separated soul from another.

Constitution and Identity

In addition to this much of Aquinas's basic metaphysics of the nature of substantial forms in general and the substantial form that is the human soul in particular, it is also important to understand that on Aquinas's views constitution is not identity.[12] Or, to put the same point another way, for Aquinas a whole is greater than the sum of its parts. In many places in his texts, Aquinas makes plain that, in virtue of having its elements configured by the form of the whole, a whole has emergent properties not had by any of its parts, so that a sum of the parts and the properties of the parts will not be equivalent to the whole. So, for example, Aquinas says, "a composite is not those things out of which it is composed... [as, for example,] flesh is not identical to fire and earth [the elements of which it is composed]."[13] In fact, Aquinas's views of change commit him to the claim that constitution is not identity. On the Aristotelian understanding of change that Aquinas inherits and accepts, a thing that gains or loses an accidental form undergoes change while remaining one and the same thing. Quantities, including quantity of matter, are also accidents. So, on Aquinas's position, a human being who loses a quantity of matter, such as a hand or a leg, for instance, remains one and the same thing while undergoing change. If, however, constitution were identity for Aquinas, then a human being whose material constituents changed would cease to be the thing he was and become some other thing instead. In that case, contrary to Aquinas's position, the gain or loss of an accident such as quantity of matter would not be a change in a human being; it would be the destruction of one thing and the generation of another.

Furthermore, because constitution is not identity for Aquinas, it is also possible for him to suppose that a particular substance survives even the loss of some of its metaphysical constituents, provided that the remaining constituents can exist on their own and are sufficient for the existence of the substance. The point applies especially in the case of human beings. A human being is not identical to either the integral or the metaphysical parts that constitute him. Normally, the integral parts of a human being include two hands, but a human being can exist without being in the normal condition. A human being can survive the loss of a hand or other of his larger integral parts, as well as the elemental bits of which such larger integral parts are composed. That is why the loss of a hand or the amputation of a limb is not the destruction of a human being. Aquinas would therefore repudiate the sort of mereological essentialism that identifies a person as the whole sum of his material parts. Analogously, although the metaphysical constituents of a human being normally include matter and a substantial form, Aquinas thinks that a human being can exist without being in the normal condition in this way, because what constitutes a human being is not the same as that to which a human being is identical. On Aquinas's view, a human being can survive even the loss of his entire body, when the substantial form remains.

The Separated Soul

Since what makes Socrates this individual substance is the individual substantial form that configures him, and since the substantial form can exist independently of the body, then for Aquinas the existence of the substantial form separated from the body is sufficient for the existence of the human being whose substantial form it is. Socrates can continue to exist when all that remains of him is his separated soul. But it does not follow that Socrates is identical to his soul, because constitution is not identity.

Given these views, Aquinas should be interpreted as holding that, in Socrates's disembodied condition, when he is not composed of the normal constituents for human beings, Socrates is nonetheless identical to the same thing he was identical to in his embodied condition: an individual substance in the category *rational animal*.[14]

It is easy to become confused about Aquinas's position here, however, because Aquinas is adamant in his rejection of Platonic dualism (or Cartesian dualism, as we would say). He is at pains to make clear that in his view a human being is not identical to his soul. So, for example, in his commentary on I Corinthians,[15] Aquinas says, "Since a soul is part of a body of a human being, it is not the whole human being, and my soul is not me."[16] In consequence of passages such as this, some scholars take it as evident that for Aquinas the separated soul is not the same as the human being whose soul it was during that person's bodily life. On their interpretation of Aquinas, Aquinas thinks that the soul of Socrates, separated from the body of Socrates, is not a human being and that, for this reason, the soul of Socrates is not Socrates.

If the soul is not *Socrates*, but the soul of Socrates is all that continues to exist after the death of Socrates's body, then it seems to follow, on Aquinas's views as these scholars read him, that *Socrates* does not survive bodily death. Without any doubt, however, Aquinas accepted the Christian doctrine that, after the death and before the resurrection of the body, the soul persists in a separated state. And so, on the views of these scholars, Aquinas has to be read as holding that a human being ceases to exist at bodily death and comes back into existence only with the resurrection of the body.[17] The persisting separated soul is not to be identified with the person who died.

The Consistency of Aquinas's Position

This interpretation, however, is not plausible if Aquinas's views of the separated soul are considered in the context of his theological claims about it.

To take just one example of many that could be given, on Aquinas's theological views, before the general judgment of all humanity, each separated soul is judged, individually, at the moment of the bodily death of the human being whose soul it is. But at that individual judgment, the separated soul is judged on the basis of the actions and dispositions of the human being it informed. The separated soul of Socrates is judged by Christ on the basis of the life of Socrates; and, on the basis of this judgment, the soul either enjoys the blessings of heaven or the pains of the fires of hell. Aquinas says,

> When the soul is separated from the body, it receives its reward or punishment immediately for those things which it did in the body.... In the providence of God, rewards and punishments are due to rational creatures. Since when they are separated from the body, they are immediately capable both of glory and of punishment, they immediately receive one or the other; and neither the reward of

> the good nor the punishment of the bad is put off until the souls take up their bodies again.[18]

But if the soul of Socrates is not Socrates, then what justice is there in assigning to the separated soul either the reward or the punishment merited by Socrates, who is not the soul? Furthermore, at the resurrection Socrates will exist again; and the separated soul-which-is-not-Socrates will cease to exist, since the separated soul will then cease to exist as a separate subsisting thing. But why should the separated soul-which-is-not-Socrates lose its bliss when Socrates is resurrected?

The views implied by the position that a human being fails to exist in the period between bodily death and bodily resurrection are theological gibberish, and they are contradicted in multiple places by explicit claims on Aquinas's part. So, for example, about the nature of the separated soul's bliss, Aquinas says that

> souls immediately after their separation from the body become unchangeable as regards the will.... [B]eatitude, which consists in the vision of God, is everlasting.... But it is not possible for a soul to be blessed if its will did not have rectitude.... And so it must be that the rectitude of the will in the blessed soul is everlasting.[19]

This text and many others like it make plain the unacceptability of the interpretation that assigns to Aquinas the view that a human being ceases to exist at death and that a separated soul is not the same human being as the person whose soul it is. That interpretation has to attribute to Aquinas views that make his theological position bizarre and that he explicitly denied in one place or another. It is abundantly clear therefore that for Aquinas the existence of the separated soul is sufficient for the existence of the human being whose soul it is.

But, then, we need to ask, how can Aquinas also hold that a human being is a material composite? It seems as if, for Aquinas, either a human being is identical to his soul, in which case a human being is not a material composite, or else a human being is a material composite, in which case he is not identical to his soul. How is it possible for a human being to be a material composite and yet to continue to exist in the absence of his body?

The consistency of Aquinas's position is manifest if we give proper weight to the distinction between constitution and identity in his thought. A human person is not identical to his soul; rather, a human person is identical to an individual substance in the species *rational animal*. A particular of that sort is normally, naturally, composed of form and matter configured into a human body. Because constitution is not identity for Aquinas, however, a particular can exist with less than the normal, natural complement of constituents. It can, for example, exist when it is constituted only by one of its main metaphysical parts, namely, the soul. And so although a person is not identical to his soul, the existence of the soul is sufficient for the existence of a person. Once we are clear about Aquinas's distinction between constitution and identity, we can see that a rejection of the Platonic position that a human being is identical to a soul is not equivalent to the acceptance of the position that a human being cannot exist without a body.

Resurrection, Reassembly, and Reconstitution

Some philosophers and theologians suppose that resurrection is a matter of the reassembly of the atoms of a person's earthly body, but this is not Aquinas's view at all. For Aquinas, preservation of identity is not something that has to be guaranteed by recomposing the human being of the same bits of matter-form composites, such as atoms, as before. Rather, on Aquinas's account, the soul is what makes unformed prime matter into this human being by configuring prime matter in such a way that the matter is this living animal capable of intellective cognition. In the resurrection of the body, by informing unformed matter, the soul makes unformed matter this human being again. And so puzzles about what happens when the same atoms have been part of more than one human being are avoided.

Furthermore, the material and causal continuity between the matter that composed Socrates' at the moment of his death and the matter that at any subsequent time composes him is provided by the substantial form itself. For Aquinas, the individuation and identity of anything at all is provided by its substantial form. And so the matter configuring Socrates's resurrected body is the same as the matter configuring Socrates's earthly body in virtue of the fact that it is configured by the same particular substantial form, which is the soul of Socrates.

For these reasons, on Aquinas's views, God's resurrecting Socrates is not like bringing back the snows of yesteryear,[20] because, unlike the snows of yesteryear, Socrates never ceased to exist. The re-embodiment of Socrates is not a reassembly of those atoms still available as constituents for Socrates's new body. On Aquinas's account, resurrection is not so much reassembly of integral parts as it is reconstitution of metaphysical parts. The constituents of Socrates in his resurrected state are the same as those of Socrates during his earthly life: this substantial form, the soul, and the prime matter that is configured by the soul into a body. Unlike the snows of yesteryear or the atoms of Socrates's earthly life, prime matter has no form of its own. It exists only in potentiality; and in order to be the same matter as it was before, it needs only to be configured by the same form as it was before.

The Thomistic synthesis of Aristotelian hylomorphism and Christian theology therefore yields a doctrine of the resurrection less open to objection than some of its critics suppose.[21]

NOTES

1. For further discussion of the metaphysical issues raised here and in subsequent sections in connection with Aquinas's theory of forms, see the chapter on Aquinas's theory of things in my *Aquinas* (London: Routledge, 2003).

2. *In DA* II.11.226.

3. *QDA* un.9.

4. *In BDT* 2.4.2; cf. also *ST* I q.119 a.1 and *QDP* 9.1.

5. Perhaps the most detailed exposition of this view of his is in his *In BDT* 2.4.2.

6. *In BDT* 2.4.2. Aquinas does not always describe his position on this score in the same way, and the variation in terminology suggests to some scholars either a development in his thought or a series of changes of mind. The issue is complicated, and so I am leaving it to one side here. For the discussion of the scholarly controversy, see John Wippel, *The Metaphysical Thought of Thomas Aquinas: From Finite Being to Uncreated Being* (Washington, D.C.: Catholic University of America Press, 2000), 357–73.

7. But see also Jeffrey Brower's contribution to this volume.

8. Cf., e.g., *ST* III q.3 a.7 ad 1, where Aquinas says that a substantial form is multiplied in accordance with the division of matter.

9. Richard Swinburne, "Soul, Nature and Immortality of the," in *Routledge Encyclopedia of Philosophy* (London: Routledge, 1999).

10. *QDA* un.1 ad 2.

11. In fact, for Aquinas, there are two memory capacities, one which is dependent on the senses and phantasia, and one which is dependent on the intellect. The second is the memory at issue here. For further discussion of Aquinas's views of human cognitive capacities, see the chapter on the mechanisms of cognition in my *Aquinas* (London: Routledge, 2003).

12. See, e.g., *In Metaphysica* VII.17.1672–1674. There Aquinas says that in cases in which the composite is one thing, the composite is not identical with its components; rather the composite is something over and above its components. For interesting contemporary arguments against the reduction of wholes to their parts, see Mark Johnston, "Constitution is Not Identity," *Mind* 101 (1992): 89–105, and Lynne Rudder Baker, "Why Constitution is Not Identity," *Journal of Philosophy* 94 (1997): 599–621. For an excellent discussion of the constitution relation, see Lynne Rudder Baker, "Unity Without Identity: A New Look at Material Constitution," *Midwest Studies in Philosophy* 23 (1999): 144–65. Cf. also Lynne Rudder Baker, *Persons and Bodies: A Constitution View* (Cambridge: Cambridge University Press, 2000).

13. *In Metaphysica* VII.17.1673–1674.

14. For more defense of this position, see my "Resurrection, Reassembly, and Reconstitution: Aquinas on the Soul," in Bruno Niederberger and Edmund Runggaldier, eds., *Die menschliche Seele: Brauchen wir den Dualismus?* (Frankfurt a. M.: Ontos Verlag, 2006).

15. I am grateful to Brian Leftow for calling this passage to my attention.

16. *In I Cor*, ch. 15, l.2.

17. So, e.g., Peter van Inwagen says, "Aquinas. . . . sees the human person as essentially a composite of a human soul and a human body. According to the 'composite' theory, a person cannot exist without a body: to exist is for one's soul (always numerically the same) to animate some human body or other. (In the interval between one's death and one's receiving a new body at the time of the general resurrection, one's soul exists and thinks and has experiences, but *one* does not, strictly speaking, exist)" (Peter van Inwagen, "Resurrection," in *Routledge Encyclopedia of Philosophy* [London: Routledge, 1999]). Robert Pasnau also argues that for Aquinas a separated soul is not a human being and therefore that a human being ceases to exist at death, on Aquinas's position. As one example supporting this interpretation, Pasnau cites a passage from Aquinas's *Sentence* commentary in which Aquinas is discussing the separated soul of Abraham. In that place, as Pasnau rightly points out, "Aquinas remarks . . . that 'Abraham's soul is not, strictly speaking,

Abraham himself' " (the passage is cited by Pasnau as *Super Sent* IV 43.1.1.1 ad 2). Pasnau claims that Aquinas "insists on this point precisely so as to argue that bodily resurrection is necessary for human immortality. Hence [Aquinas] immediately concludes: 'So Abraham's soul's having life would not suffice for Abraham's being alive.' " In Pasnau's view, this passage shows that Aquinas cannot have supposed that "the persistence of the soul 'is sufficient for the existence' of the human being." Rather, in Pasnau's view, the passage makes plain that Aquinas "would deny that a human soul could constitute a human being." See Robert Pasnau's review of my *Aquinas* in *Mind* 114 (2005): 203–6.

18. *SCG* IV.91.

19. *SCG* IV.92.

20. The phrase is Van Inwagen's; see Van Inwagen, "Resurrection."

21. I am grateful to Brian Davies for helpful comments on an earlier draft of this paper.

CHAPTER 35

PRAYER

BRIAN DAVIES

AQUINAS wrote on prayer (*oratio*) in a time following some confusion on the topic, a confusion that seems to prevail even today. In keeping with what seems to be the New Testament approach, early Christian authors understood prayer as a matter of petition.[1] For them, to pray is primarily to ask God for things that one wants, and this understanding of prayer survived well into the Middle Ages. However, prior to Aquinas's time, and during it, other senses of "prayer" emerged among theologians. In 1 Thessalonians 5:17, St Paul tells us to "pray without ceasing," so there were authors who felt obliged to understand prayer as encompassing much that clearly does not seem like asking. St. Bonaventure, for example, says that, in its broadest sense, prayer means "every good deed."[2] Other authors began to talk about different *parts* and *kinds* of prayer—the idea being (a) that prayer should be formally subdivided into temporally sequential and ordered stages comparable to the structure of a liturgy, and (b) that one can "progress" from an inferior form of prayer to another—from petitionary prayer to "contemplative prayer" (considered as having nothing to do with anything as lowly as asking for something). As Simon Tugwell has said, "by the time of St. Thomas . . . it is far from clear quite what the word 'prayer' means."[3] As Tugwell goes on to emphasize, however, Aquinas's most mature and extended discussion of prayer comes in the *Summa theologiae*,[4] and, though some of his earlier writings on prayer do not unequivocally do so, the treatment in the *Summa* makes it clear that prayer, as in its traditional Christian sense, should be taken to be petition. In what follows, therefore, it is on the *Summa theologiae*'s treatment of prayer that I shall focus.[5]

Aquinas, Prayer, and the Nature of God

One will never understand what Aquinas says on prayer if one does not recognize that, like so much else that he writes, it flows from his conviction that God is *Ipsum Esse Subsistens* ("Subsisting Being Itself") and the source of the existence or being (*esse*) of everything other than himself. According to Aquinas, every individual in the universe, and every operation of every individual in the universe, is being made to be by, is being created by, is being caused by God.

In various places, Aquinas asks whether or not the universe began to be. He denies that we can prove that it did, but goes on to say that, even if the universe had no beginning, it should still be thought of as made to be by God. For Aquinas, God accounts for the sheer existence of everything other than himself. So if something is, then, thinks Aquinas, it *is*, and it is *what* it is, and it *does* what it does, because God is bringing this about—not as a temporal agent acting on things in the universe, but as the eternal and unchanging cause of there being any universe at all (as, so we might say, accounting for the fact that there is, at any time, something rather than *nothing*).

Aquinas believes that we should ask, and try to answer, a variety of causal questions concerning how things come to be in the universe. He also believes that we can seek to answer such questions by appealing to increasingly more general levels of explanation—that we can, for example, explain how a particular cat exists by referring to its parents, we can explain how cats come to exist by referring to conditions on earth favoring the emergence and continued existence of cats, that we can go on to account for the emergence of these conditions, and so on. But, Aquinas insists, when we are done with what we might refer to as "scientific explanations" we are still left with the question "How come any universe at all?" This is obviously not a scientific question (since it is asking about the universe as a whole, and since scientific questions and answers have to do with what are parts of the universe). Yet Aquinas takes it to be a valid question to which there must be an answer, and he gives the name "God" to whatever the answer is. God is not part of the universe. He accounts for it being there at all and at any time. Since changes that occur in the universe are as real as anything else to be found in it, Aquinas consequently concludes that all changes, all "operations," in the universe are also God's doing.

In short, Aquinas has an understanding of God according to which everything created is at all times made to be what it is by God. Some people have objected to this understanding, since, so they have said, it seems to embrace a radical determinism according to which nothing that happens in the world could fail to happen: if divinity is what Aquinas takes it to be, does it not follow that everything that happens in the universe is *forced* to be what it is by God? This objection to Aquinas, however, is based on a misunderstanding of how he thinks. When it comes to things in the universe, Aquinas believes that various events can be determined by their causes. He would say, for example, that, when sulfuric acid burns my skin, the changes occurring in my skin are determined by the acid (indeed, he would say, the changes in my skin *are* the acid at work). In general, Aquinas holds that if an agent acts on something so as to oblige it to become thus and so, then we have an instance of determinism. However, Aquinas adds, God's creative causality is not such that God acts *on* something so as to *determine* that it becomes thus and so. For Aquinas, God creates something (brings it about that something has *esse*) not by *modifying* it but by simply making it to be whatever it is. As he puts it in his commentary on Aristotle's *Peri Hermeneias*:

> God's will is to be thought of as existing outside the realm of existents (*extra ordinem entium existens*), as a cause from which pours forth everything that exists in all its various forms. Now *what can be* and *what must be* are variants of being, so that it is from God's will itself that things derive whether they must be or may or may not be and the distinction of the two according to the nature of their immediate causes. For he prepares causes that must cause for those effects that he wills must be, and causes that might cause but might fail to cause for those effects that he wills might or might not be. And it is because of the nature of their causes that some effects are said to be effects that must be and others effects that need not be, although all depend on God's will as primary cause, a cause which transcends this distinction between *must* and *might not.*[6]

In other words, Aquinas thinks that God's omni-causality *does not act as a rival to* the causality of creatures, since it actually empowers this or makes it to exist.

With this thought in mind, Aquinas draws the conclusion that God is omnipotent. Unlike some authors, by "God is omnipotent" Aquinas does not mean that we can stick the expression "God can..." before any expression signifying any logically possible feat. He does not mean that God is omnipotent, since, for example, God can ride a bicycle, or fly to Germany, or sin. Aquinas's account of omnipotence is tied to his notion of God as bringing it about that things have *esse*. His rule is: if it can be thought (without contradiction) to be, then God can make it to be. And this rule takes us to the notion of petitionary prayer. For people who pray want it to be the case that certain things, states, or processes come to be. And, so one might ask, if Aquinas is right on the topic of God as Creator, then is it not reasonable for such people to ask God to bring it about that these things, states, or processes actually do come to be?[7]

Prayer and Practical Reason

We can, of course, be reasonable in different ways. One way of being reasonable is to work our way through a series of proofs in logic or mathematics, or to demonstrate, on the basis of his symptoms, that Fred has scarlet fever. Here, so Aquinas would say, we would be exercising our theoretical reasoning. But he also believes that we can engage in practical reasoning—reasoning with respect to how to achieve our goals, how to get what we want. And, thinks Aquinas, (a) one reasonable way of getting what we want is to ask for this from one who is able to provide it, and (b) prayer is a reasonable practice to engage in given that God is able to provide what we might reasonably ask for.

Aquinas's idea here is ridiculously simple. If I want people to help me, then it is reasonable to ask them to do so (assuming that I know that they are in a position to oblige). If Mary wants a kitten for her birthday, then she is reasonable in asking her parents for one. And so on. By the same token, Aquinas argues, it is reasonable to ask God for things, so long as what one is asking for is what God is able to provide. Some authors on prayer have thought of it primarily in emotional or affective terms—the basic idea being that prayer is all about our feelings and not about our reason. Yet Aquinas rejects this conclusion. For him, prayer is first of all an example of practical reasoning. It springs from knowing what we want and recognizing how we might obtain it.[8]

This, of course, means that Aquinas thinks of prayer as exactly on a par with much that we go in for in day to day life. Treatises on prayer, especially in recent years, have evidently left readers wondering what on earth they have to do in order to pray. Is there some "state" into which they ought to get themselves? If so, what is that state? And how should they sustain it? Is prayer something "mystical"? If so, how does one become "mystical"? Some writers on prayer have lauded something called "mental prayer," and their readers have often wondered what that might be, how they might practice it, and how long it should last (advocates of mental prayer commonly recommend two half hours a day). Aquinas, however, just does not get sucked down into questions like these. His approach to prayer is, we might say, an attempt to demystify it, to view it as a regular exercise of practical reason, as a matter of asking for something one wants (which everyone knows how to do).[9] And his basic reason for offering this approach is his conviction that God is the Creator who can bring about anything that can be thought to be. Do you want such and such? Then, thinks Aquinas, it is reasonable to ask for it from God.[10]

Objections to Prayer

But is it? Not according to many people. Some of these would object to the notion of petitionary prayer on the ground that there is no God to pray to, and, if that is so, then petitionary prayer is obviously misguided. More commonly, however, critics of petitionary prayer argue that there is something unreasonable about engaging in it because of what God is commonly taken to be. God is said to be good and omniscient. In that case, however, would he not know what we want or need without us telling him, and would he not provide for us without being asked? And does it not, therefore, follow that prayer is redundant? Given God's goodness and omniscience, many have suggested that this is exactly what it is. Others have held that petitionary prayer makes no sense given the traditional claim that God is immutable. If God is immutable, so it has been argued, then he changelessly wills what he wills from eternity and nothing that we can do or say can make any difference when it comes to what God wills.

These objections to petitionary prayer, though often voiced today, are ancient ones. You can find them documented in, for example, chapter 3 of Origen's *De Oratione* (written around A.D. 233).[11] And Aquinas is aware of them. As they emerge in his formulation:

> Prayer seems to be needed to give information about what we want to the person we are asking for something. But, as it says [Matthew 6:32] "Your Father knows that you need all these things"...Prayer is a way in which we change the mind of the person to whom we are praying, so that he will do what is being asked of him. But God's mind cannot be changed or deflected....It is more generous to give something without waiting to be asked than it is to give something to someone who asks for it....But God is extremely generous. So it is apparently not appropriate that we should pray to God.[12]

Yet Aquinas rejects these objections. And his basic response to them is:

> Divine providence does not merely arrange what effects are to occur; it also arranges the causes of these effects and the relationships between them. And among other causes, some things are caused by human acts. So human beings have to do certain things, not so as to change God's plans by their acts, but in order to bring about certain effects by their acts, according to the pattern planned by God....We do not pray in order to change God's plans, but in order to obtain by our prayers those things which God planned to bring about by means of prayers.[13]

You shall, I hope, see how this response of Aquinas fits in with what I reported above concerning his take on God as Creator. But let me try to spell things out a bit.

Given what he says of God in general, Aquinas clearly cannot think of prayer as having a causal effect on God. In his way of thinking, the source of the *esse* of creatures cannot be modified by a creature. So Aquinas does not think of prayer in magical terms—as a way of manipulating God. Consequently, he does not think of it as informing God or as changing him in any way. But he still thinks of prayer as a significant activity, since, so he believes (and regardless of how good or generous God is), it matters that we should recognize God for what he is and turn to him for what we need. "We do not," he observes, "have to present our prayers to God in order to disclose to him our needs and desires, but in order to make ourselves realize that we need to have recourse to his help in these matters."[14]

What, then, of the causality of prayer? Evidently, Aquinas cannot say that my praying causes God to do something in the sense that, say, my tossing a salad causes its ingredients to become covered in dressing. And yet, so Aquinas would presumably add, my responding to a request from you is not caused in this sense either. Aquinas holds that people have freedom of choice (*liberum arbitrium*) and, so he would say, a good example of this being exercised would be someone giving people something for which they ask. Of course, I might give you what you ask for because you coerce me (because you force some money out of my hand, say). For Aquinas, though, I would not really be giving or acting here. I would be operating under duress. On his account, people freely responding to requests are not being caused by the requests or the petitioners in the way in which a salad gets caused to be dressed by one tossing it.

One might, of course, reply that, even if we accept this point, prayer, on Aquinas's account cannot really make any difference. The argument might go like this: If Fred asks John for some money, and if John gives him some, Fred's asking might be thought to have made a difference in that John might not have given Fred money had he not asked for it. If Aquinas is right, however, God is immutable. So he brings about what he has decreed from eternity to bring about. What room is there in this picture for a prayer making any difference at all? And if prayer makes no difference, why bother with it?

To understand Aquinas's position with respect to this argument, it is important to note that he genuinely believes that creatures have causal powers. He thinks, for example, that we actually do digest food, or hit tennis balls, or build houses. His claim that God acts in every operation is not meant to deny that creatures genuinely act. It is meant to put the causal activity of creatures into a deeper context—that of God as Creator. For Aquinas, in causing the *esse* of all creatures, God is also empowering their creaturely causality. And with this thought in mind, Aquinas insists that, for example, when I act it is true *both* that I act *and* that I act only as God is bringing it about that I do so.

Now consider the case of someone deciding, for example, to build a house. And imagine this person reasoning thus: "Well, it's actually pointless for me to get started since, if Aquinas is right in what he says about God, I can't make any difference. If God has from eternity decreed that the house shall be built, then it will get built and I can spare myself some effort." This argument, of course, clearly rests on the assumption that creatures are not genuine causal agents and that God is an omnipotent puppet master, an assumption that Aquinas denies. He would say that, as God in his providence has arranged things, houses do not get built unless people get on with building them. He would, indeed, agree that whether people build houses, and whether or not houses come to exist, depend on God's changeless will as the Maker of all things. But he would not take this to mean that people do not make a difference when it comes to what happens.

That said, we can return to the notion of prayer making a difference. In Aquinas's view (if I understand his teaching on miracles correctly), God could have brought it about that the British Houses of Parliament came to be by the direct action of God and of nothing else. Yet what in fact happened, so Aquinas would say, is that God brought them about by the action of people. By the same token, so Aquinas thinks, God could bring it about that, say, I recover from an illness without anyone praying that I do so. Yet, Aquinas also thinks, what might in fact come to pass is that God brings it about that I recover as having been prayed for—that my improved state of health is an *answer* to someone's concern for me and not just a mere matter of getting better. "God," says Aquinas, "gives us many things out of sheer generosity, without being asked. The reason why he wants to give us some things in response to our petition is that it is profitable for us to acquire a certain confidence in running to him and to recognize that he is the source of all that is good for us."[15]

Prayer and Christian Practice

That last quotation should make it obvious that Aquinas sees value in prayer regardless of whether or not we obtain what we specifically ask for. Prayer, he thinks, is an expression of trust in God and is, therefore, intrinsically meritorious and an "act of religion." The purpose of religion, thinks Aquinas, is "offering reverence and honor to God," and that, he believes is what we do by praying. "By praying," he observes, "we offer God reverence, inasmuch as we subject ourselves to him and profess, by praying, that we need him as the author of all that is good for us."[16] Prayer, Aquinas also insists, is an act of charity, for we can pray for others. Indeed, he says, we *should* pray for others. "We ought," he explains, "to desire good things not only for ourselves, but also for others.... Therefore charity requires us to pray for other people."[17]

And what should we pray for? With an eye on this question, and in keeping with his view of prayer as an exercise of practical reasoning, Aquinas avoids high-minded generalities. He does not suggest that we should only vaguely ask for what is good. To be sure, he is clear that prayer should be directed to union with God and should be offered by us as seeking to achieve this. He is also clear that we might just be wrong when it comes to identifying what is good for us.[18] With those provisos made, however, Aquinas argues that "it is lawful to pray for what it is lawful to desire."[19] So, as with any mundane asking of things from people, Aquinas holds that, when we pray, we can specify what we want. We can, for example, pray for particular temporal things, for forgiveness of specific sins, or for the well-being of our neighbors (understood in concrete terms). And, thinks Aquinas, we can be confident in praying. We might not obtain what we specifically ask for, he agrees, for God's will for us may not exactly coincide with our will for ourselves.[20] Yet, Aquinas also says, God sometimes wants to give us what we desire *because* we have asked for it. And, Aquinas adds, insofar as we are asking for what leads to beatitude, we are guaranteed what we ask for as long as we persevere.[21]

As I have said, Aquinas's most mature discussion of prayer can be read as an attempt to demystify it. It does not confuse prayer with Christian goodness in general. It does not make prayer out to be something for which we need a manual. It does not confuse prayer with the acquiring of "techniques" or the entering into of "states." It locates prayer among one of the most ordinary and unpuzzling of human activities while also explaining how it elevates those who pray into the less than ordinary business of seeking to get to God. Given the complexity and unclarity that some theologians have introduced when seeking to say what prayer is and why it matters, Aquinas's treatment of it surely represents something of an achievement.

NOTES

1. For some history of the term "prayer" in Christian circles, see Michel Dupuy, "Oraison," in *Dictionnaire de Spiritualité*, vol. 11 (Paris: Beauchesne Editions, 1982).

2. Bonaventure, quoted in *Super Sent* IV, d.15, p.2, a.1, q.4.

3. Simon Tugwell, O.P., *Albert and Thomas: Selected Writings* (New York and Mahwah, N.J.: Paulist Press, 1988), 275. See also Simon Tugwell, O.P., "Prayer, Humpty Dumpty and Thomas Aquinas," in Brian Davies, ed., *Language, Meaning and God* (London: Geoffrey Chapman, 1987).

4. *ST* II-II q.83.

5. In *Super Sent* IV, d.15, q.1, a.4, Aquinas seems prepared to take seriously the suggestion that "prayer" is to be used in more than one sense. By the time he writes on prayer in the *ST*, however, his focus is entirely on prayer as petition. Texts in which Aquinas deals with *oratio* include: *Super Sent* IV, d.15, q.4; *QDV*, q.6, a.6; *SCG*, III, 95–96; *In 1 Cor* 14:13–15. Reliable translations of these texts, and other texts by Aquinas on prayer, can be found in Tugwell, *Albert and Thomas*, 363–523.

6. *In Peri herm*, 1:14. I quote from Timothy McDermott, ed., *Aquinas: Selected Philosophical Writings* (Oxford: Oxford University Press, 1993), 282f.

7. In *ST* II-II q.83 a.4, Aquinas argues that it is appropriate to address prayer to the saints and angels, but only insofar as we ask them to join their prayers to ours. "We address prayer to the angels and the saints," he says, "not because we want them to let God know what we want, but because we want our petitions to be successful through their intercession and merits."

8. This is the main point made in *ST* II-II q.83 a.1.

9. So Aquinas denies that nonrational creatures pray. Cf. *ST* II-II q.83 a.10.

10. What if I want all babies born within the next twenty-four hours to be murdered by gangsters? Then, Aquinas would say, I would have no business asking for this from God, since he is the highest good (the source of all creaturely goods) and can hardly be called upon to produce what is obviously evil. That said, however, Aquinas's position is that if you want it, and if God can provide it, it makes sense to ask him for it.

11. For a translation of this text, see Origen, *On Prayer*, trans. E. G. Jay (London: S.P.C.K., 1954).

12. *ST* II-II q.83 a.2. I quote from Tugwell, *Albert and Thomas*, 479–80.

13. *ST* II-II q.83 a.2. Tugwell, *Albert and Thomas*, 481.

14. *ST* II-II q.83 a.2 ad 1. Tugwell, *Albert and Thomas*, 481.

15. *ST* II-II q.83 a.2 ad 3. Tugwell, *Albert and Thomas*, 481.

16. *ST* II-II q.83 a.3. In *ST* II-II q.83 a.15, Aquinas goes on to note that prayer is an expression of humility, faith, and devotion, and is, therefore, meritorious (meaning that it brings us closer to God).

17. *ST* II-II q.83 a.7. In *ST* II-II q.83 a.4, Aquinas goes on to say that we should pray for our enemies.

18. *ST* II-II q.83 a.5.

19. *ST* II-II q.83 a.6.

20. Curiously, Aquinas does not note the obvious point that it might be logically impossible for God to grant what everyone prays for since different people might (and do) pray for things that are mutually exclusive (e.g., "a fine day for my garden party" and "rain for my crops"). Perhaps he does not note the point since it is, indeed, obvious.

21. *ST* II-II q.83 a.15.

CHAPTER 36

THE GIFTS AND FRUITS OF THE HOLY SPIRIT

ANDREW PINSENT

Introduction

Recent scholarship has suggested the need to reconsider the validity of an Aristotelian reading of Aquinas's virtue ethics. The recognition that there are certain differences between the virtues described by Aristotle and Aquinas is not, of course, anything new. Even a cursory examination of Aquinas's vast treatise on the virtues in *Summa theologiae*[1] reveals many perfective qualities, such as humility, which Aristotle never mentions. Nevertheless, the general approach of much Thomistic scholarship has been to view Aquinas's treatise as following an Aristotelian framework with certain extrinsic additions. The cardinal virtues in Aquinas's treatise have long been treated, in particular, in more or less the same way as their homonymous counterparts in the *Nicomachean Ethics*.

The principal motivation for doubting the continued validity of this approach is a growing recognition of the differences between Aristotle and Aquinas regarding what is meant by "virtue" in the proper sense.[2] Aquinas does recognize that we can acquire virtues in the Aristotelian manner by repeated good actions; he calls such virtues *acquired virtues*. Aquinas also claims, however, that proper or perfect virtues are not acquired, but *infused* in us by God.[3] These infused virtues include counterparts of many of the acquired moral and intellectual virtues. So, for example, as well as acquired justice, there is infused justice, which is the proper sense of the virtue of justice. Similarly, besides acquired prudence, there is infused prudence, which is the proper sense of the virtue of prudence, and so on.[4]

While defining the relationship between the acquired and the infused virtues has proved difficult, it is clear that acquired and infused virtues are distinct in several important ways. First, Aquinas argues that only the infused virtues are perfect and deserve to be called "virtues" simply.[5] Second, acquired and infused virtues differ in species, distinguished, according to Aquinas, by their proper objects and the kinds of flourishing to which they are directed.[6] Third, as Jean Porter has noted, all human beings have the capacity to receive infused virtues, even those, such as children, who lack the intellectual training required for Aristotelian virtues.[7] Fourth, as Porter and Bonnie Kent have observed, an infused virtue, unlike an acquired virtue, can be present with a previously acquired contrary disposition.[8] Fifth, Aquinas claims that infused virtues are connected together, unlike specific acquired tendencies to do good actions.[9] Sixth, as Jeffrey Hause argues, the difference between acquired and infused virtues cannot be reduced to a proportional change in the good established by reason, such as greater asceticism, since such a change does not require a different virtue.[10] Seventh, even if a person possesses *all* the acquired virtues, if he lacks the infused virtues he cannot enter heaven.[11]

Besides these important distinctions, the structure of *ST* II-II q.1–170 provides additional evidence of a non-Aristotelian approach to virtue ethics. It should occasion some wonder that, despite having the greatest respect for Aristotle and a detailed knowledge of the structure of the *Nicomachean Ethics*,[12] Aquinas organized his own treatise on the virtues in such a different way from that of Aristotle. Furthermore, the difference in Aquinas's approach is not just that he has added novel virtues, like the theological virtues and humility, hallowed by Christian tradition. Even his articles on the Greek cardinal virtues of prudence, justice, courage, and temperance, interleave these virtues with other attributes that are not virtues at all and which lack any Aristotelian counterpart.

Consider, for instance, the virtue of courage. Following his treatise on courage as a virtue,[13] Aquinas appends a further question describing an entirely new quality, the *Gift* (*donum*) of Courage.[14] Although this Gift of Courage is infused, Aquinas claims that a Gift is a different kind of quality from an infused virtue.[15] Even the addition of the Gift of Courage is not the end of the story, though, because Aquinas claims that this Gift is linked to a further attribute, a *Beatitude* (*beatitudo*) called "Hungering and thirsting for justice."[16] This Beatitude is in turn associated with two final and distinct attributes, the *Fruits* (*fructus*) of Patience and Long-suffering.[17] So Aquinas appends a network with one Gift, one Beatitude, and two Fruits to the virtue of courage. Similar networks can be found for the other cardinal and theological virtues, giving the impression of an intricate and even "organic" structure different from that of the *Nicomachean Ethics*.[18]

This non-Aristotelian structure implies that the cardinal virtues Aquinas examines in *ST* IIaIIae are not the acquired versions of these virtues, even if they exhibit many parallels with the acquired virtues and even though Aquinas often cites Aristotle. *ST* II-II q.47 a.14 clarifies, in fact, that the prudence being examined is infused prudence, and there are similar clarifications for the other cardinal virtues.[19] If, then, the cardinal virtues in *ST* II-II q.1–170 are infused rather than acquired, a further inference follows. To grasp what Aquinas means by an infused virtue, it is also important to study what he means by a Gift, a Beatitude, and a Fruit. These attributes appear to be interconnected with the virtues, both in *ST* IIaIIae and according to a claim Aquinas makes when he introduces the genus of virtue in *ST* IaIIae: "We must speak in the first place of the good *habitus*, which are virtues, and of other matters connected with them, namely the Gifts, Beatitudes and Fruits."[20]

In this chapter I focus on the first and last of these three kinds of attributes that Aquinas appends to the virtues: the Gifts and the Fruits of the Holy Spirit. As I shall show, Aquinas claims that the Gifts are, in fact, essential and connected to the virtues, while Fruits feature as the terminating attributes of the entire network. Given these pivotal roles, understanding the Gifts and Fruits is, therefore, an important step toward grasping Aquinas's virtue ethics as a whole.

The Gifts

What is a Gift of the Holy Spirit, and how do Gifts relate to virtues and other perfecting attributes? There are seven Gifts, which Aquinas appends to various theological and cardinal virtues in *ST* IIaIIae. The cognitive Gifts are Understanding (*Intellectus*) and Knowledge (*Scientia*), which are appended to the virtue of faith, Wisdom (*Sapientia*), appended to the virtue of *caritas*,[21] and Counsel (*Consilium*), appended to the virtue of prudence. The appetitive Gifts are Fear (*Timor*), appended to the virtue of hope, Piety (*Pietas*), appended to the virtue of justice, and Courage (*Fortitudo*), appended to the homonymous virtue of courage.[22] Aquinas also examines the genus of Gift in *ST* I-II q.68, immediately following his treatise on the genus of virtue, *ST* I-II q.55–67.

ST I-II q.68 a.2 claims that the Gifts are essential to salvation, an explicit confirmation that they are not adventitious in Aquinas's account of human flourishing. *ST* I-II q.68 a.8 adds that, while the theological virtues are more excellent than the Gifts, the Gifts are more excellent than the moral and intellectual virtues, thereby taking precedence over any of the qualities described in the *Nicomachean Ethics*.[23] Aquinas even claims, in *ST* II-II q.19 a.9 ad 4, that the Gifts are the origins or foundations (*principia*) of the intellectual and moral virtues.

The function of the Gifts is, however, more difficult to grasp than the fact of their importance. *ST* I-II q.68 a.4 states that the Gifts extend to all those things to which the virtues, both intellectual and moral, extend. Yet if the work of the Gifts parallels that of the virtues, why are the Gifts necessary? Aquinas's response is a principle set out in *ST* I-II q.68 a.1:

> Now it is manifest that human virtues perfect man according as it is natural for him to be moved by his reason in his interior and exterior actions. It is fitting, therefore, for there to exist in man higher perfections, whereby he is disposed to be moved by God in a divine way. These perfections are called Gifts, not only because they are infused by God, but also because by them man is disposed to be made readily moveable by divine inspiration.[24]

In this passage, Aquinas claims that what is specific about a Gift is not that it is infused, since perfect virtues are also infused, but that, by means of a Gift, we are disposed to be moved by God. What, however, does being "moved" by God mean in this context? Aquinas clarifies elsewhere that such movement is not coercive.[25] Furthermore, it can be inferred that what is given by means of the Gifts is not reducible to some propositional description of the world, a description that could, in principle, be communicated in some other way.[26] In what, then, does Gift-based movement consist?

A partial answer to this question can be inferred from the notion of a "participated likeness" (*participativa similitudo*), a phrase that Aquinas uses when describing the Gift of Knowledge. Aquinas claims that the Gift of Knowledge enables a "participated likeness" of God's knowledge, knowledge that is absolute and simple rather than discursive, as for the homonymous intellectual virtue.[27] A similar notion of participation can be found in Aquinas's descriptions of the other Gifts. By the Gift of Piety, we are moved to regard other persons as God regards them, namely as potential or actual children, and thereby our brothers and sisters.[28] By the Gift of Courage, we regard present dangers and potential future dangers with the kind of confidence with which God regards such difficulties.[29] By the Gift of Fear, we regard ourselves as God regards us, as adopted children with whom God desires to be united, and so shrink from the loss of our own good from God's perspective.[30] By the Gift of Counsel, we are "directed as though counseled by God," implying that we take on God's stance toward possible courses of action.[31] By the Gift of Understanding, we grasp what is proposed to us by God.[32] Finally, by the Gift of Wisdom, we are enabled to judge aright about divine things on account of a "connaturality" with them.[33] In all these cases, the movement enabled by the Gifts can be characterized as a sharing or appropriation of God's stance toward some object.

Such appropriations of God's stance cannot, however, be reduced to mere imitations, as Aquinas shows, for example, in his description of the Gift of Wisdom: "Wisdom as a Gift is more excellent than wisdom as an intellectual virtue, since it attains to God more intimately by a kind of union of the soul with him (*unio animae ad ipsum*)."[34] The idea of a union or oneness of the soul with God in this passage is reflected in other texts about the Gifts, especially Aquinas's claim that whoever has *caritas*, which unites us to God, has all the Gifts, none of which can be possessed without *caritas*.[35] So Gift-based movement is not a mere imitation of God's stance but implies a union of the soul with God, a union based on *caritas*.

Aquinas's descriptions of Gift-based movement therefore express two main principles. First, he describes a situation in which a person's stance toward some object involves a participation in God's stance toward the same object. Second, Gift-based movement involves what Aquinas describes as a union or oneness of the soul with God. Expressed in these terms, Aquinas's descriptions of the operation of the Gifts seem analogous to the phenomenon of *joint attention*, the subject of a new field of experimental psychology and philosophy.[36] While the precise definition of joint attention remains a matter of some debate, the phenomenon has at least the following basic characteristics. First, joint attention takes place in a person-person-object situation in which both persons share a stance toward the object that is the focus of their attention. In the context of parent–child interactions, activities manifesting joint attention can include, for example, referential use of eye contact, offering and giving objects to others, pointing at objects and following others' points. Second, joint attention involves sharing an awareness of the sharing of focus *with* the other person,[37] an experience commonly described as a "meeting of minds." Both these characteristics of joint attention with another person have clear parallels with Aquinas's descriptions of Gift-based movement.

So a description of the Gifts seems clear and the phenomenon of joint attention may provide an analogy for their operation. Nevertheless, to show the function of the Gifts does not, in itself, explain their importance. Why, exactly, are the Gifts so essential to Aquinas's conception of human flourishing? If joint attention is a correct analogy for Gift-based movement, then it may be possible to answer this question by examining the role of joint attention in interactions between human persons. In particular, by examining what happens when joint attention between persons is inhibited, it may be possible to highlight what is so important about joint attention for human relationships, and, in turn, what is important about Gift-based movement with regard to one's relationship with God.

As it turns out, there is a condition that is characterized by lack of engagement in joint attention with other human persons. This condition is autism, the characteristics of which have been both an incentive and a means to investigate joint attention in recent years. In the following passage, Peter Hobson, a professor of developmental psychopathology, describes the outcome of an experiment designed to highlight how autistic children interact with other persons:

> In two respects, then, the children with autism were not moved to adopt the orientation of the person they were watching. They did not adopt the style with which the experimenter executed the actions, nor did they identify with him and copy his self-orientated actions so that these actions became orientated towards themselves. On the other hand, they were perfectly able to perceive and copy the strategies by which he achieved the goals in each demonstration. So they were able to learn something from watching what the experimenter did.... Yet what they learned seemed to be available from their position as a kind of detached observer of actions and goals. They were not "moved."[38]

The experiment described in this passage showed that autistic children were perfectly capable of recognizing other persons and following instructions given by another person.[39] Furthermore, they were also able to imitate the actions and goals of another. What the children with autism did not do, however, was to appropriate another person's psychological orientation or to "identify" with the other person.[40] Indeed, in the passage above, Hobson articulates what is missing from autistic behavior by the same language that Aquinas uses to describe the Gifts: the children with autism were not "moved."

So joint attention provides a possible analogy for Gift-based movement, and autism provides a corresponding analogy for a person's condition, in relationship to God, when the person lacks the Gifts. Now the analogy of autism with a lack of the

Gifts does not imply that the condition of autism precludes possession of the Gifts. On the contrary, unlike the acquired virtues, Aquinas is clear that anyone can possess the infused virtues and Gifts.[41] Nevertheless, the analogy between the condition of autism and the absence of the Gifts gives some indication of why the Gifts are important.

Furthermore, there is another intriguing characteristic of autism that sheds light on the role of the Gifts in relationship to God. As Leo Kanner noted in his original description of the syndrome, and many subsequent studies have confirmed, children with autism often refer to themselves as "you" and the person they are speaking with as "I."[42] For example, the question, "How are you?" might elicit the response, "You are fine." Such instances of pronoun reversal are not, however, common to children with other kinds of retarded learning conditions, such as Down Syndrome.[43] The fact that those with autism find it especially hard to grasp the rules for second-personal pronouns suggests that those with autism have difficulties relating to others in a specifically *second-personal sense*. Indeed, if the capacity to engage in joint attention is inhibited, as in the case of autism, it is hard to see how an intuitive grasp of the "I"–"you" relationship can be acquired easily in human development.[44]

The connection between joint attention and the second person therefore implies a further way of showing why the Gifts are important for Aquinas's understanding of human flourishing. If joint attention enables a second-personal relationship to other human persons, the Gifts, by analogy, enable a specifically second-personal relationship with God. If, therefore, virtues can be classified as *first-personal habitus*, by which a person is moved easily by his or her own reason, the Gifts, by contrast, are the *second-personal habitus*, by which a person is moved by God in a manner analogous to joint attention. Such a conclusion is consistent with the intrinsic connection that Aquinas makes between the Gifts and *caritas*, given that Aquinas describes *caritas* as friendship with God and friendship implies the ability to relate to one's friend in a second-personal way.[45]

The Fruits

Aquinas introduces the Fruits by means of a material analogy. Using the example of a plant, Aquinas observes that a material fruit is "the product of a plant when it comes to perfection, and has a certain sweetness."[46] These qualities also characterize the ethical attribute that he calls a "Fruit": "The notion of Fruit implies two things: first that it should come last; second, that it should calm the appetite with a certain sweetness and delight... that which is last simply, and in which one delights as in the last end, is properly called a Fruit; and this it is that one is properly said to enjoy."[47] Consistent with the notion of a Fruit coming last, Aquinas generally assigns the Fruits of each virtue last in the *ST* II-II q.1–170, after the appended Gifts and

Beatitudes. Aquinas also examines the genus of Fruit in *ST* I-II q.70, after examining the genus of Gift and Beatitude.

What, however, does Aquinas understand by the term "Fruit"? According to *ST* I-II q.70 a.3, the Fruits of *Caritas*, Joy (*Gaudium*), Peace (*Pax*), Patience (*Patientia*), and Long-suffering (*Longanimitas*) pertain to the good ordering of the mind. The Fruits of Goodness (*Bonitas*), Benignity (*Benignitas*), Meekness (*Mansuetudo*), and Faith (*Fides*) pertain to one's neighbor. The Fruits of Modesty (*Modestia*), Continency (*Continentia*), and Chastity (*Castitas*) pertain to the body. The twelve Fruits therefore extend to many, and perhaps all, of the same things to which the virtues and the Gifts extend. Why, therefore, is there yet another set of attributes, distinct from the virtues and the Gifts?

The mystery of the Fruits is deepened by Aquinas's claim that they are not *habitus* in the manner of Gifts or virtues.[48] On the contrary, Aquinas describes the Fruits variously as *actus* or *operationes* or *opera* of the virtues and as the last and congruous products of the Gifts.[49] The implication is that a Fruit is some kind of actualization or manifestation of the virtues and Gifts. Some of the Fruits, such as *Caritas*, have homonymous counterparts among the virtues, whereas others, such as Joy and Peace, are unique to the category of Fruit. How, then, is the attribute of Fruit to be understood?

Aquinas implies an answer to this question in his description of the Fruit of Peace, which he classifies as an *actus* of *caritas*:

> Peace implies a twofold union. . . . The first is the result of one's own appetites being ordered toward one thing; while the other results from one's own appetite being united with the appetite of another: and each of these unions is effected by *caritas* . . . hence it is reckoned a sign of friendship if people "make choice of the same things" (*Ethic.* ix, 4), and Tully says (*De Amicitia*) that friends like and dislike the same things.[50]

In the article cited above, Aquinas highlights the interpersonal aspect of the Fruit of Peace and its connection with friendship, observing that Peace implies a harmony between two persons, an alignment in which one chooses the same things as one's friend and with one's friend.[51] Aquinas also describes other Fruits in interpersonal terms: he associates Joy with the experience of God abiding in a person, and the Fruit of *Caritas* with both a union of affections and a union of persons.[52]

These interpersonal descriptions are consistent with Aquinas's claim that the Fruits are the last and congruous products of the Gifts. Since, as argued previously, the Gifts are second-personal *habitus*, one would expect the Fruits, as *actus* of these Gifts, to have a second-personal aspect as well. Nevertheless, in Aquinas's network of perfecting attributes, not all *actus* of the Gifts are Fruits. The *actus* of Counsel, for example, are not Fruits, but only means for bringing about Fruits.[53] Furthermore, the Fruits are also consequent upon the Beatitudes, as Aquinas states in *ST* II-II q.139 a.2,[54] implying some intermediate step between Gift-based *actus* in general and the special class of *actus* that are Fruits. By what measure, then, are the Fruits perfect or complete compared to Gift-based *actus* in general?

Some poetic inspiration to help answer this question may be found in a scene from Dante's *Paradiso*, during which Dante the traveler encounters the soul of Aquinas in heaven,

> And he will have some shadowing forth of that
> True constellation and the double dance
> That circled round the point at which I was;[55]

The idea of "stars," that is, souls in paradise, revealing their interpersonal union to Dante by the image of a perfect dance, suggests that it is important to examine not only what it means to be moved by another person, but the manner in which such movements are perfected. Orchestras, choirs, or dancers, for example, do not always harmonize very well and can experience discords, mistimings, and mistakes. When their joint operation becomes second nature, however, with the participants being near-perfectly attuned to one another, there is often a sudden, disproportionate improvement in the objective quality of the activity. Subjectively, musicians or dancers may also experience the pleasurable exhilaration of "flying along," accompanied by the sense of being "one" with the other persons. This harmonized operation appears similar to the phenomenon of *resonance* in physics, when two systems engage in close to perfect joint operation with disproportionate ease and intensity.[56] In the case of the joint operation of two persons, when activities in union with the other person have become second nature, the phenomenon could be described as an *interpersonal resonance.*

Can the Fruits be regarded as resonances? A resonance is a perfected joint operation, matching the description of the Fruits as *actus* that are also perfections, the terminating attributes of the entire network of Gifts, virtues, and Beatitudes. An interpersonal resonance also needs at least two persons, matching the inference that the Fruits, based on the Gifts, are intrinsically second-personal. A resonance in joint human activity, such as musicians playing in perfect harmony, is also pleasurable, matching Aquinas's material analogy of a Fruit as having "sweetness." Finally, a resonance indicates that some aspect of a second person is sealed or imprinted on oneself, knowledge which is no longer mediated but immediate.[57] Within the context of a piece of music, for example, the musicians can be said to know one another perfectly and immediately, analogous to the way in which Aquinas associates the Fruits with having an immediate experience of God being with oneself or even abiding in oneself.[58] I therefore conclude that the Fruits, as Aquinas describes them, can be characterized as resonances.

Conclusions

To grasp what Aquinas means by an infused or perfect virtue, it is also important to study what he means by a Gift, a Beatitude, and a Fruit. Aquinas claims that the seven Gifts are necessary for true human flourishing and appends these to the theological and cardinal virtues. The twelve Fruits, by way of the Beatitudes, are the terminating attributes of the "organic" network of *ST* II-II q.1–170.

The essential characteristic of the Gifts is that they enable a person to be "moved" by God in a second-personal manner. In other words, the Gifts enable us to share in God's stance toward something, in union with God in an "I"–"You" relationship. To lack the Gifts does not preclude all knowledge of God or interaction with God, but it is analogous to being autistic with respect to God, so that second-personal interaction with God is inhibited. The Fruits are the perfect *actus* of the Gifts and virtues. These *actus* also have a second-personal basis, according to the descriptions Aquinas gives of certain Fruits and insofar as they conclude a network of attributes in which the Gifts play a foundational role. Those *actus* that are Fruits may be characterized as interpersonal resonances, in which a person's activity is aligned and united perfectly with God in a harmonized manner.

It seems, therefore, that Aquinas regards infused virtue ethics as intrinsically second-personal, both in terms of the foundations of the virtues, in which the Gifts play an essential role, and the Fruits or interpersonal resonances to which all perfective attributes are ordered.[59]

NOTES

1. *ST* II-II q.1–170.

2. In answering the question of how to define virtue, *ST* I-II q.55 a.4, Aquinas defends the definition, "Virtue is a good quality of the mind, by which we live righteously, of which no one can make bad use, which God works in us, without us." Mark Jordan has drawn attention to the fact that this definition of virtue, the only one Aquinas sets out to defend explicitly, is drawn from Peter Lombard's *Sentences* rather than from Aristotle. This choice is an early indication in the *ST* of Aquinas's non-Aristotelian approach to virtue in the proper or perfect sense. See Mark Jordan, "Theology and Philosophy," in Norman Kretzmann and Eleonore Stump, eds., *The Cambridge Companion to Aquinas* (Cambridge: Cambridge University Press, 1993), 237–41.

3. According to Aquinas, only the acquired virtues are caused in an Aristotelian manner, that is, by repeated good actions, whereas infused virtues, that is, virtues in the proper sense, are caused by the action of God. See, e.g., *QDVCom* a.2, ad 18, in which Aquinas claims that, just as acquired virtues are increased and fostered by the same sort of acts that caused them, so the infused virtues are increased by the action of God, by whom they are caused.

4. Aquinas differentiates acquired and infused justice in *ST* I-II q.100 a.12, claiming that only the latter is true justice. In *ST* I-II q.47 a.14, he distinguishes acquired and infused prudence. In *ST* I-II q.63 a.4, he describes acquired and infused temperance as distinct species of temperance. Acquired and infused courage are mentioned as distinct virtues in *QDVCom* a.10, ad 10. John Inglis, "Aquinas's Replication of the Acquired Moral Virtues," *Journal of Religious Ethics* 27:1 (1999): 3–27, has drawn attention to Aquinas's introduction of infused counterparts of the acquired moral virtues and to the need for greater study of the impact of infused virtues on Aquinas's ethics as a whole. Robert C. Miner, "Non-Aristotelian Prudence in the Prima Secundae," *The Thomist* 64:3 (2000): 401–22, has examined prudence

in *ST* I-II and argued that Aquinas's descriptions differ strikingly from Aristotelian *phronêsis*. Most of the intellectual virtues are, however, replicated as Gifts rather than virtues (*ST* II-II q.8, 9, 45), a point made by Eleonore Stump, "Wisdom: Will, Belief, and Moral Goodness," in Scott Charles MacDonald and Eleonore Stump, eds., *Aquinas's Moral Theory: Essays in Honor of Norman Kretzmann* (Ithaca, N.Y.: Cornell University Press, 1999), 48.

5. *ST* I-II q.65 a.2: "It is therefore clear from what has been said that only the infused virtues are perfect, and deserve to be called virtues simply: since they direct a person well to the ultimate end. But the other virtues, those, namely, that are acquired, are virtues in a restricted sense, but not simply: for they direct a person well in respect of the last end in some particular genus of action, but not in respect of the last end simply." Aquinas is clear, therefore, that only the infused virtues are virtues properly speaking. This clarification further suggests that, when Aquinas refers to a virtue without qualification, he is referring to an infused rather than an acquired virtue.

6. In *ST* I-II q.63 a.4, Aquinas claims that acquired and infused virtues differ in species, both in relation to their proper objects and to their respective ends, "those infused moral virtues, whereby persons behave well in respect of their being 'fellow-citizens with the saints, and of the household of God,' differ from the acquired virtues, whereby a person behaves well in respect of human affairs." Aquinas makes a similar distinction in *ST* I-II q.65 a.2: "It is possible by means of human works to acquire moral virtues, in so far as they produce good works that are directed to an end not surpassing the natural power of man: and when they are acquired thus, they can be without *caritas*, even as they were in many of the Gentiles. But in so far as they produce good works in proportion to a supernatural last end, thus they have the character of virtue, truly and perfectly; and cannot be acquired by human acts, but are infused by God."

7. Jean Porter, "The Subversion of Virtue: Acquired and Infused Virtues in the 'Summa theologiae,'" *Annual of the Society of Christian Ethics* (1992), 34. Citing *ST* II-II q.47 a.14, Porter points out that infused prudence is present, according to Aquinas, in all who have grace, even those who cannot exercise independent thought and judgment. She concludes that the infused virtues function in a way that is significantly different from the way in which the acquired virtues function, "so much so that they can be described as virtues only in a carefully qualified sense" (ibid. 20).

8. Ibid. 30; Bonnie Kent, "Does Virtue Make It Easy to be Good? The Problematic Case of St. Paul," in Bernardo C. Bazán, Eduardo Andújar, and Leonard G. Sbrocchi, eds., *Les Philosophies morales et politiques au Moyen Âge: Actes du IXe Congrès International de Philosophie Médiévale, Ottawa, 17–22 Août 1992* (Ottawa: Legas, 1995), 728. The article from which these observations are taken is *ST* I-II q.65 a.3 ad 2: "Sometimes the *habitus* of moral virtue experience difficulty in their works, by reason of certain ordinary dispositions remaining from previous acts. This difficulty does not occur in respect of acquired moral virtue: because the repeated acts by which they are acquired, remove also the contrary dispositions." See also ibid. ad 3: "Certain saints are said not to have certain virtues, in so far as they experience difficulty in the acts of those virtues, for the reason stated; although they have the *habitus* of all the virtues."

9. Jordan, "Theology and Philosophy," 240, points out that Aquinas's view of the unity of the virtues is nuanced. If an acquired moral virtue is regarded simply as an acquired tendency to carry out a particular kind of good action, then such virtues are not connected, "since we find men who, by natural temperament or by being accustomed, are prompt in doing deeds of liberality, but are not prompt in doing deeds of chastity" (*ST* I-II q.65 a.1). Infused virtues, on the other hand, are infused together with *caritas* and connected on account of *caritas* (*ST* I-II q.65 a.3).

10. Jeffrey Hause, "Aquinas on the Function of Moral Virtue," *American Catholic Philosophical Quarterly* 81:1 (2007): 16. Hause's argument is important because Aquinas's example of infused temperance (*ST* I-II q.63 a.4) seems to suggest that the difference between acquired and infused temperance is simply that the latter is more ascetic, promoting fasting rather than moderate consumption. From this example, it might be thought that the infused virtues are proportionally harder or more demanding versions of the acquired virtues. This is the understanding implied by Réginald Garrigou-Lagrange, who exemplifies the neo-Thomist school of the first half of the twentieth century. Garrigou-Lagrange conflates the definitions of the acquired and infused versions of the cardinal virtues, holding that the same definition holds proportionally for both categories. See Réginald Garrigou-Lagrange, *La Synthèse Thomiste*, Bibliothèque française de philosophie (Paris: Desclée de Brouwer, 1946), 529, 530, 532, and 536. Hause, however, argues that such an approach cannot be correct. Acquired temperance could also be constituted in a mean that pursues fasting and chastising. Infused and acquired virtues must be different in kind and not merely in degree.

11. Acquired virtues imply moral and intellectual maturity, yet once a person has achieved such maturity, she will tend, among other things, to deliberate about herself. If this deliberation leads her to direct herself to her due end, she will, by means of grace, receive the remission of original sin, together with *caritas* and the infused virtues (*ST* I-II q.89 a.6). If, however, a person does not direct himself to the due end, and as far as he is capable of discretion at that particular age, "he will sin mortally, for through not doing that which is in his power to do" (*ST* I-II q.89 a.6) and if unrepentant, he will end in hell (*ST* I-II q.89 a.6; *QDM*, q.7, a.10, ad 10). Similarly, if he accepts grace, and subsequently rejects it by mortal sin, he will again forfeit the infused virtues, without necessarily losing the acquired virtues. Once again, if he persists in mortal sin without repentance, he will end in hell. So to be in a state of possessing only the acquired virtues is of no true benefit to the moral agent. Indeed, to possess acquired virtues without infused virtues may even be a sign of the rejection of grace arising from some conscious decision, arguably a worse state than one in which a person lacks the maturity to choose.

12. Evidence for Aquinas's detailed appropriation of the *Nicomachean Ethics* can be seen in his analysis of the structure of Aristotle's work. Aquinas subdivides the text into a complex nested structure with some fifteen hundred functionally distinct parts. For an English translation of his commentary, see St Thomas Aquinas, *Commentary on Aristotle's Nicomachean Ethics*, trans. C. I. Litzinger (Notre Dame, Ind.: Dumb Ox Books, 1993).

13. *ST* II-II q.123–38.

14. Aquinas introduces the Gift of Courage in *ST* II-II q.139 a.1, at the conclusion of his treatment of the virtue of courage. Since Courage and certain other attributes have homonymous counterparts among the virtues in Aquinas's network, I capitalize references to the Gifts, Beatitudes, and Fruits in this chapter to distinguish them from the virtues.

15. Aquinas devotes *ST* I-II q.68 a.1; q.69 a.1; and q.70 a.2 to arguments that the virtues, Gifts, Beatitudes, and Fruits are distinct kinds of attributes from one another.

16. Aquinas argues that courage is about difficult things and, since it is difficult to do virtuous deeds with an insatiable desire, which may be signified by "hunger and thirst for justice," this Beatitude is properly assigned to the virtue of courage (*ST* II-II q.139 a.2), as well as to the virtue of justice (*ST* II-II q.121 a.2).

17. *ST* II-II q.139 a.2 ad 3.

18. Aquinas's network is described as an "organic unity" in Servais Pinckaers, *Morality: The Catholic View* (South Bend, Ind.: St. Augustine's Press, 2001), 87. By contrast, most commentators on the non-Aristotelian aspects of Aquinas's network of attributes have

tended to concentrate on the Gifts, paying little attention to the virtue-Gift-Beatitude-Fruit network as an organic whole. The pattern of this approach was set in the seventeenth century in a classic work by John of St. Thomas. As its title implies, John of St. Thomas concentrates almost exclusively on the Gifts, devoting ten out of eleven chapters to commentaries on their general or particular operations. While he makes occasional references to the Beatitudes and Fruits in these chapters, it is only in chapter 9 that he considers the Beatitudes as a distinct group of qualities and it is only in the last two paragraphs that he mentions the Fruits. For an English translation of this work, see John of St. Thomas, *The Gifts of the Holy Ghost*, trans. Dominic Hughes, O.P. (New York: Sheed & Ward, 1951).

19. In much of the *ST* II-II q.1–170, Aquinas does not state explicitly whether he is describing an acquired or an infused virtue. Nevertheless, *ST* I-II q.65 a.2 makes clear that "virtue" taken simply means infused virtue. Furthermore, in *ST* II-II q.47 a.14, Aquinas shows that the prudence he is examining is infused prudence, since it is infused along with grace and *caritas*, in contrast to acquired prudence, the acquisition of which is "caused by acts" and which demands "experience and time." In *ST* II-II q.123, he argues that the principal act of courage is martyrdom, involving the virtues of faith and *caritas*, underlining that this is the infused rather than the acquired virtue of courage. In *ST* II-II q.141 a.1 ad 2, he refers to the temperance that he is describing, that is, the perfect sense, as not acquired through habituation, implying that "temperance" taken simply means infused temperance. In the case of justice, the many theological concepts Aquinas annexes to justice, such as the act of prayer (*ST* II-II q.83), provide corroborating evidence that he is examining an infused rather than an acquired virtue. So unless Aquinas explicitly states otherwise, the cardinal virtues of *ST* II-II q.1–170 appear to be the infused rather than acquired versions of these virtues.

20. *ST* I-II q.55 prol. I am grateful to Fr Kevin Flannery, S.J. for the opportunity to discuss the most appropriate way of expressing certain ideas in Aquinas's texts. In this passage, the term *habitus* is sometimes translated as "habit" or as "disposition," but both words are slightly misleading for the senses in which Aquinas uses the word *habitus*. I have therefore left the term untranslated.

21. The word *caritas* is sometimes translated as "love" or "charity." Since, in Aquinas's work, *caritas* denotes the unique love pertaining to divine friendship (*ST* II-II q.23 a.1), I have left the word untranslated.

22. The questions devoted to the specific Gifts are *ST* II-II q.8 (Understanding), q.9 (Knowledge), q.19 (Fear), q.45 (Wisdom), q.52 (Counsel), q.121 (Piety), and q.139 (Courage).

23. Whether Aquinas is referring to acquired or infused virtues, his claim that the Gifts take precedence over the moral and intellectual virtues means that the Gifts take precedence over any of the qualities described in the *Nicomachean Ethics*.

24. *ST* I-II q.68 a.1. Descriptions of the Gifts as enabling us to be moved by God can also be found in *ST* I-II q.68 a.4; II-II q.52 a.1; q.52 a.3; III q.7 a.5.

25. Aquinas argues in *ST* I-II q.10 a.4 that the will is not moved of necessity by God. In whatever manner, therefore, God does cause our acts of will (and this is a point of some debate), it is generally acknowledged that, according to Aquinas, God's action on the will is "not coercive" (cf. Brian J. Shanley, "Divine Causation and Human Freedom in Aquinas," *American Catholic Philosophical Quarterly* 72:1 [1998]: 113).

26. In *ST* II-II q.8 a.5, Aquinas refers to the Holy Spirit enlightening the mind without the Gifts, in regard to truths that are preambles of faith. Nevertheless, he also states that such enlightenment, no matter how extensive, is no substitute for movement by means of the Gift of Understanding. He confirms this point in *ST* II-II q.9 a.3 ad 3, in which he says that not everyone who understands, has the Gift of Understanding, but only the one who

understands from a *habitus* of grace (cf. *ST* II-II q.9 a.3 ad 3 on Knowledge). So what is communicated by means of the Gifts cannot be reduced to propositions, since propositions could, in principle, be communicated in some other way besides the Gifts.

27. *ST* II-II q.9 a.1 ad 1. Note that none of the cognitive Gifts are deliberative, despite the fact that three of them share names with intellectual virtues that pertain to discursive reasoning. The operations of the cognitive Gifts are, therefore, consistent with understanding them as enabling participation in God's absolute, "simple" cognition.

28. In *ST* II-II q.121 a.1, Aquinas describes the Gift of Piety as moving us to have a filial affection toward God, and, as a consequence, to pay veneration and service to all people on account of their relationship to God.

29. *ST* II-II q.139 a.1. The Gift of Courage could be said to "cement" the virtue of courage, because the virtue adequate for current difficulties might still be feared inadequate for hypothetical future difficulties. The Gift, however, enables a sharing in God's standpoint, a confidence that any future challenge can also be overcome with divine assistance.

30. In *ST* II-II q.19 a.9, Aquinas describes the Gift of Fear as moving us to revere God and avoid separating ourselves from him. This Gift enables "filial fear," the kind of fear a child has to disappoint a father whom he loves, not the fear of loss or pain for oneself, which is "servile fear" (*ST* II-II q.19 a.5). So the Gift of Fear disposes one to shrink from separation from God, not from the point of view of one's own good as desired by oneself, but from the point of view of one's own good as desired by God with whom one is united by *caritas*.

31. *ST* II-II q.52 a.1 ad 1.

32. *ST* II-II q.8 a.4. The relational aspect of the Gift of Understanding is a point of distinction between the Gift and the homonymous virtue.

33. *ST* II-II q.45 a.2.

34. *ST* II-II q.45 a.3.

35. *ST* I-II q.68 a.5.

36. Naomi Eilan, "Joint Attention, Communication, and Mind," in Naomi Eilan et al., eds., *Joint Attention: Communication and Other Minds: Issues in Philosophy and Psychology* (New York: Oxford University Press, 2005), 1.

37. Peter Hobson, "What Puts Jointness into Joint Attention?" in Eilan et al., eds., *Joint Attention*, 185. Hobson is a professor of developmental psychopathology who has developed experiments to study joint attention and autism.

38. Ibid. 200.

39. An autistic child is, therefore, able to respond to another person in Darwall's sense of the "second-person standpoint," that is, "the perspective that you and I take up when we make and acknowledge claims on one another's conduct and will." See Stephen Darwall, *The Second-Person Standpoint: Morality, Respect, and Accountability* (Cambridge, Mass.: Harvard University Press, 2006). For an introduction to the main ideas and examples from everyday life, see pp. 3–38. Douglas Lavin has provided a helpful review and critique of Darwall's thesis for the *Notre Dame Philosophical Review*, January 2008.

40. Such findings are consistent with other symptoms of autism in young children, such as a failure to follow the gaze of an adult toward an object, failing, in other words, to appropriate and track a second person's stance.

41. Cf. *ST* II-II q.47 a.14 ad 3.

42. Leo Kanner, "Autistic Disturbances of Affective Contact," *Nervous Child* 2:220 (1943); reprinted in *Acta Paedopsychiatrica* 35:4 (1968): 100–36.

43. For a comparison of pronoun reversal in autistic and Down syndrome children, see, e.g., Helen Tager-Flusberg, "Dissociations in Form and Function in the Acquisition of

Language by Autistic Children: Studies of Atypical Children," in Helen Tager-Flusberg, ed., *Constraints on Language Acquisition* (Hillsdale, N.J.: Lawrence Erlbaum, 1994), 184.

44. Johannes Roessler, "Joint Attention and the Problem of Other Minds," in Eilan et al., eds., *Joint Attention*, 247.

45. *ST* II-II q.23 a.1; see also, e.g., *QDC*, q.2, a.4, ad 11; q.2 a.8, ad 16 and *QDM*, q.5, a.5. The centrality of friendship with God as a principle of Aquinas's work highlights another distinction between the virtue ethics of Aquinas and that of Aristotle. Although Aristotle suggests the possibility of attaining a kind of similitude of divine activity, he denies that a human being can be friends with any god. See *Nicomachean Ethics*, X, 8, 1159a3–9.

46. *ST* I-II q.70 a.1.

47. *ST* I-II q.11 a.3.

48. Aquinas argues, e.g., that certain specific Fruits, such as Joy and Peace, are *operationes* and not virtues (*ST* II-II q.28 a.4; q.29 a.4).

49. *In Gal*, 5.6. Regarding terminology, Aquinas uses the word *actus*, e.g., when he argues that Joy and Peace are *actus* of *caritas*, and when he describes a Fruit as an *actus* of virtue rather than a virtue (*ST* II-II q.28 a.4). Aquinas uses the word *operatio*, e.g., when he argues that Counsel has no assigned Fruit (*ST* II-II q.52 a.4 ad 3) and when he describes a Fruit as a kind of perfect *operatio* (*In Gal*, 5.6). Sometimes Aquinas will use the term *opus*, when, for example, he describes the Fruits as *opera* of the virtues and of the Spirit (*opera virtutum et spiritus*) (*In Gal*, 5.6). As the usual translations (such as "act," "operation," or "work") can be misleading when discussing the Fruits, I have not translated these words, especially as the determination of the nature of the Fruits is one of the goals of the chapter.

50. *ST* II-II q.29 a.3.

51. In *ST* II-II q.29 a.3, Aquinas is principally referring to the alignment involved in the friendship of two human persons, but *caritas* also signifies friendship with God (I-II q.65 a.5), implying that the Peace involved in the love of God is also a kind of alignment.

52. *ST* II-II q.28 a.1; *ST* II-II q.27 a.2.

53. In *ST* I-II q.52 a.4, Aquinas assigns no Fruits to the Gift of Counsel, even though Counsel helps direct or bring about the actions of other Fruits, such as Goodness and Benignity. Counsel is, therefore, an instance of a Gift for which the corresponding *actus* are not Fruits.

54. In the case of Peace, e.g., the Beatitude of Peacemaking precedes the Fruit of Peace (*ST* II-II q.45 a.6).

55. Dante Alighieri, *The Divine Comedy*, trans. Henry Wadsworth Longfellow (Boston, 1867), *Paradiso*, Canto XIII, 19–21.

56. When a playground swing, e.g., is given a periodic push at a certain frequency, the natural frequency of the swing, it is very easy to make the swing go higher. In the terminology of the physical sciences, the two systems, the swing and the person pushing, are said to be in resonance.

57. The notion of resonance and *habitus* matching is also hinted at by Aquinas's description of the Fruit of Benignity. Aquinas twice explains that "Benignity" means "good fire" (*bonus ignis*), one by which a person "melts" to relieve the needs of others (*ST* I-II q.70 a.3; *In Gal*, 5.6). Given that a "good fire" is also one of the most common symbols of the Holy Spirit, Aquinas seems to imply that the person becomes *like* God in the manner in which she loves others.

58. *ST* II-II q.29 a.3; *ST* I-II q.65 a.5.

59. I am most grateful to Eleonore Stump and Brian Davies for reviewing earlier drafts of this chapter. I also thank Theodore Vitali for encouraging me to pursue research in this field. I explore these issues in more detail in a forthcoming book, *The Second-Person Perspective in Aquinas's Ethics: Virtues and Gifts* (Routledge, 2012).

PART VIII

AQUINAS'S INTELLECTUAL PROGRESS AND THE INFLUENCE OF HIS THINKING

CHAPTER 37

THE DEVELOPMENT OF AQUINAS'S THOUGHT

GIORGIO PINI

SOME years after Aquinas's death, the Augustinian theologian, Giles of Rome, allegedly derided those who were looking for inconsistencies in Aquinas's writings by drawing the following contrast between Aquinas and the masters of the next generation, to which Giles himself belonged:

> It is a clear sign of the subtle intelligence and certain judgment of this admirable and memorable teacher, brother Thomas Aquinas, that, after he became a master of theology, when teaching or writing, he did not change the original views and arguments he had endorsed as a bachelor, except in a few cases. By contrast, we modern authors, as suits people of uncertain and doubtful judgment, change the views we once endorsed any time an objection is raised against them, no matter how weak.[1]

It is not sure whether Giles of Rome actually uttered these words. But the claim attributed to him is fairly accurate. Even though Aquinas's teaching stretched over a period of twenty years, his thought is remarkably consistent. Indeed, some events may have caused him to refine his opinions on a few topics. For example, his direct confrontation with Averroës's followers around 1270 may have induced him to reconsider a few issues in his theory of the soul and cognitive psychology.[2] And it has been suggested that his increasingly critical attitude toward Maimonides may have resulted in a more nuanced endorsement of negative theology.[3] Furthermore, Aquinas's relatively late exposure to some important theological and philosophical writings left a mark in the development of his thought. For example, in 1268 William of Moerbeke's translation of Proclus's *Elements of Theology* (*Elementatio theologica*) gave new impetus to Aquinas's understanding of Neoplatonism.[4] Also, Aquinas's exposure to the proceedings of ancient ecumenical councils at the papal court in

1261–65, and more specifically the proceedings of the Council of Chalcedon, is likely to have influenced the development of his views on Christ.[5] As a final example, Aquinas's reading in the 1260s of two of Augustine's late writings, *On the Predestination of the Saints* (*De praedestinatione sanctorum*) and *On the Gift of Perseverance* (*De dono perseverantiae*), probably played a key role in the development of his views on grace and merit.[6] With the possible exception of the last case, however, none of these events and readings resulted in a major shift in Aquinas's thought.

Accordingly, it is not surprising that Aquinas has often been presented as a monolithic figure, whose system leaped fully formed from his head. The very possibility of development has sometimes been rejected as an attempt to diminish the perfection of Aquinas's achievement. This attitude may have been fostered by the understandable and deeply entrenched tendency to regard the *Summa theologiae* as the standard or even the only place to look for Aquinas's opinion about any given topic. It is quite clear, however, that it would be unfair, to say the least, to dismiss such masterpieces as his commentary on the *Sentences* and the questions *De veritate* as merely youthful works—not to speak of the *Summa contra Gentiles*, the Aristotelian commentaries and the later disputed questions, most notably *De Potentia* and *De malo*. Once these and other writings are taken into account, it is difficult to escape the conclusion that Aquinas's thought did develop and that he did change his mind about a number of topics. What is more, the view of Aquinas's unhesitatingly embracing a certain opinion at the beginning of his career and sticking to it in all his writings does not fit with what can be gathered from the autograph of two of his works, namely the third book of his commentary on the *Sentences* and the *Summa contra Gentiles*. As emerges from the study of those portions of these works that are still extant in his handwriting, in many cases Aquinas revised and rewrote up to four times what he had originally written.[7] Many of these revisions cannot be dismissed as merely cosmetic improvements. Rather, they allow us to get a glimpse at Aquinas's hesitations and developments about some key topics in his thought.

Aquinas himself explicitly claimed to have changed opinion about at least three issues, namely, Christ's acquired knowledge, the effects of the Empyrean Heaven on other bodies, and the healing effects of circumcision before Christ's incarnation.[8] But several other instances have long been known to both Aquinas's adversaries and followers and have been investigated by modern interpreters.

The most remarkable and still most useful tool to investigate the development of Aquinas's thinking is the list compiled by some members of the Dominican order around 1280 to indicate several topics about which Aquinas changed his mind between writing his early commentary on the *Sentences* to drafting his later works. To the original 32 topics listed in 1280, some more were added in the following years to arrive at a total of 80 topics about which Aquinas held a "better opinion" in the *Summa* than in the *Sentences*.[9]

I will not here give an exhaustive treatment of all or even the most important topics about which Aquinas changed his mind. Rather, I intend to document the evolution of Aquinas's thought by focusing on four cases and merely mentioning a few other shifts in Aquinas's views. Most of the cases I will take into consideration have both a theological and a philosophical side. The two criteria I have followed in my selection are, first, that the evidence for Aquinas's change of mind is textually solid and generally undisputed among modern interpreters and, second, that the topics addressed are particularly significant from a philosophical and/or a theological point of view.

Sensory Images in Intellectual Cognition: Christ and Separated Souls

A remarkable change can be documented with regard to Aquinas's views on the role sensory images (*phantasmata*) play in human intellectual cognition. From the very beginning of his career, Aquinas claimed that sensory images have a twofold function in intellectual cognition. First, sensory images are the source from which the content of intellectual cognition is abstracted. Second, sensory images are that toward which the intellect turns back in order to pass from dispositional to occurrent knowledge (by way of the so-called *conversio ad phantasmata*).[10] Let me illustrate this twofold function with an example.[11] Suppose I do not know what a horse is. According to Aquinas, my learning what a horse is can be described as my intellect's action of forming a mental representation of what a horse is (which Aquinas calls "intelligible species") on the basis of the sensory images of horses with which I am acquainted. This mental representation or intelligible species is both *formed* by my intellect and *received* and *stored* in my intellect. In its function of forming a mental representation, the intellect is called "agent intellect." In its role of subject in which a mental representation is received and stored, the intellect is called "possible intellect." The agent intellect's act of producing a mental representation out of sensory images is called "abstraction." Once my intellect has carried out this operation of abstraction, I know what a horse is. This does not mean, however, that I am also thinking about what a horse is. Rather, it often happens that I know what a horse is but do not actually think about it. In order to pass from dispositional knowledge (i.e., the state of knowing what a horse is) to actual knowledge (i.e., actually thinking about what a horse is), Aquinas held that my intellect must turn back toward sensory images of horses, in order to reactivate the mental representation (i.e., the intelligible species) of a horse previously abstracted and stored in the so-called possible intellect. In Aquinas's jargon, when the intellect turns back toward the phantasm, the intelligible species passes from incomplete to complete actuality.[12]

Throughout his career, Aquinas endorsed this account of the role of sensory images in intellectual cognition. He changed his mind, however, about an important point. Specifically, in the first stage of his career, Aquinas held that there are two instances of human cognition (i.e., the knowledge possessed by Christ and by separated souls after death) that make exception to the general rule of the twofold function of sensory images. Later on, however, he rejected the view that cognitive acts occurring without abstraction from sensory images or without turning back toward sensory images can count as genuinely *human* acts. Thus, in his later years, Aquinas clearly adopted the view that sensory images are necessary not only to what *typically* counts as human cognition, but to *any* act of human intellectual cognition whatsoever, in any possible state (i.e., before and after the Fall and before and after death).

This shift can be documented in Aquinas's treatment of two apparently unrelated topics, that is, the sort of knowledge possessed by Christ and by separated souls, respectively. When addressing the first topic, Aquinas wondered whether human beings *necessarily* acquire their information by abstraction from sensory images. When addressing the second topic, Aquinas wondered whether human beings *necessarily* turn back toward sensory images in order to actually think about something. In his early commentary on the *Sentences*, Aquinas answered "no" to both questions. In the *Summa theologiae*, he answered "yes" to both questions.

With regard to Christ's knowledge, Aquinas's earlier position was that Christ had only infused, not acquired knowledge.[13] This means that Christ knew the essences of all things from birth and did not learn any of them from experience. Since Christ was born already provided with this knowledge, he never acquired a single concept from sensory images. Like any human being, however, Christ also had sensory images of the things he experienced. But for him, these sensory images were not the sources of new information; rather, they only served as that toward which his intellect turned in order to actually think about what he already knew. As a consequence, sensory images did not increase Christ's knowledge; they only added to the certainty with which Christ knew what he already knew.[14]

The view that Christ was born with innate knowledge of all the kinds of things that exist and consequently did not have to acquire any new concept from experience was the standard opinion in Aquinas's time. By adopting it, however, Aquinas had to pay a very high price. He had to concede that, in the case of Christ, sensory images are not sources of new information. Accordingly, Christ's agent intellect never carried out an act of abstraction; its only function was that of turning back toward sensory images in order to recover information that had been infused directly by God.[15] Since Christ was in all respects a human being, Aquinas had to concede that human beings (albeit in a very special case) do not necessarily cognize by acquiring new information from sensory images.

Some years afterwards, however, Aquinas adopted the view that Christ did not have innate knowledge of all and every essence. By contrast, Christ genuinely learned from experience something about essences he was ignorant of and consequently progressed in knowledge during his life on earth. Thus, Christ's intellect carried out the operation of abstraction from sensory images just like any other human intellect.[16]

This is one of the three cases in which Aquinas explicitly remarked that he had previously held a different position.[17] Aquinas's view that Christ acquired genuine knowledge in this life (which seems to have been unprecedented among medieval theologians)[18] has a clear theological significance, as it stresses Christ's humanity in all and every aspect of his nature and activity. Behind the theological point, an important philosophical point was also at stake. Aquinas recognized that the agent intellect's role of abstracting new information from sensory images is a defining aspect of what human cognition is. Correspondingly, the role of sensory images as the only source of new information is a necessary element in any act of human cognition. The case of Christ constitutes no exception.

With regard to the sort of the knowledge possessed by separated souls after death and before resurrection, Aquinas always held that separated souls cannot acquire new information by abstracting intelligible species from sensory images, since separated souls are not united with their bodies and as a consequence have no access to sensory information. Separated souls, however, can acquire new information by receiving intelligible species directly from God. But this is a *supernatural* way of acquiring information, because separated souls require God's special intervention over and above their natural capacities in order to acquire new information in that way.[19]

Separated souls, however, can also think about what they learned when they were united to their bodies. But the key question is: how can separated souls carry out this act of thinking about information previously acquired?

It seems possible to distinguish three stages in Aquinas's development with regard to this issue.

In his commentary on the *Sentences*, Aquinas held the view that only when united with a body does a soul need to turn toward sensory images in order to think about what it already knows. Once a human soul is separated from its body, nothing in that soul's nature prevents it from recovering the intelligible species it had previously acquired when united to its body. Thus, in order to think about what they learned when united with their bodies, separated souls only need the habit of previously acquired knowledge; they do not need any extra help from God's part. The important philosophical point here is that Aquinas held that it is within the *natural* capacities of a human soul to think without sensory images. That ordinarily we *do* think by turning back to sensory images only depends on the burden that the current union with the body puts on our souls' natural capacities. Aquinas even noticed that the view that souls, when separated from their bodies, cannot think about what they already know is a position that fits well with the opinion of those who hold that human souls are mortal, that is, that they are destroyed once the body is destroyed. For, given the link between what something is and its activity, it is appropriate to say that, if a soul is incapable of carrying out any activity without its body, then it is also incapable of existing without its body.[20]

In the immediately following years, Aquinas maintained the basic elements of this view but he introduced some important precision. He argued that human souls keep their own nature whether they are united to their bodies or are separated from them. In those two conditions, however, souls have two distinct modes of existing. To each of these two modes of existing there corresponds a distinct mode of thinking. When souls are united with the body, they think through sensory images. By contrast, when they are separated from the body, they can think by themselves, without any need of sensory images. Specifically, sensory images are needed neither as sources of new information nor in order to bring back to mind what was previously learned. First, sensory images are not needed as sources of new information because, when human souls are separated from the body, they can receive more easily the influence of separated substances, such as angels and God himself, and thus can receive new intelligible species directly from those substances. Thus, we should conclude that the state of being united with the body prevents a human soul from receiving a more perfect form of knowledge. Second, separated souls do not need sensory images to think about what they learned when they were united with the body because a soul has a natural capacity to access all the information it already possesses. When united to the body, a human soul maintains this capacity to recover previously acquired information, but it cannot *exercise* this capacity without sensory images. The need for sensory images, however, merely depends on a soul's union with a body. Once the body is removed, the soul can exercise its capacity to recover previously acquired information without the help of sensory images.[21]

Finally, in the *Summa theologiae*, Aquinas maintains the view that souls have two modes of existing and two corresponding modes of thinking, when they are united with the body or when they are separated from it, respectively. But he now claims that the only *natural* mode of existing for a human soul is for it to be united to the body. Correspondingly, the only *natural* mode of thinking for a human soul is through sensory images. For a human soul, to think about what it already knows without turning back toward a sensory image is beyond its natural capacities. Consequently, it is something that can be achieved only thanks to God's supernatural intervention. Left to itself, a separated soul is incapable both of acquiring new information and of thinking about what it learned when united with the body.[22] Contrary to what he had previously implied, Aquinas even argues that the supernatural mode of thinking without sensory images is, for a human soul, *worse* than the mode of thinking by way of sensory images, for to think without sensory images is less fitting to a human soul's nature.[23]

Behind this technical issue there is again an important philosophical point. Aquinas came to realize that, in any instance of human cognition, sensory images are necessary not just as the source of information but also as what triggers the recovery of information previously acquired. Thus, human thinking is necessarily and essentially thinking by images. There can be no exception to this rule. Since separated human souls are not united with a body, they cannot think by images. As a consequence, they cannot think at all unless God, by a supernatural intervention, allows them to recover the information they had acquired when they were united to their bodies.

Most probably, Aquinas progressively shifted his views about the necessity of sensory images in any instance of human cognition because he only gradually came to realize all the consequences that the view that human beings are essentially compound of a soul and a body (his so-called "hylomorphism") had on his theory of cognition. Since a human being is essentially a composite of soul and body, the body is essentially involved in the process of human cognition via sensory images. At some point, Aquinas toyed with the idea of different states and of corresponding different modes of thinking pertaining to a human soul when it is united to a body and when separated from it. By the time he wrote the first part of his *Summa theologiae*, however, Aquinas had reached the uncompromising view that the only natural state for a human soul is to be united with a body. Consequently, the only natural mode of cognition for a soul is by way of sensory images, both in order to acquire new information and in order to think about what it has previously learned.[24]

Mental Words

An important and particularly well-documented development in Aquinas's thought concerns the notion of mental word.[25]

This shift has both a theological and a philosophical side to it. With regard to the theological side, in his commentary on the *Sentences* Aquinas held that the term "word" can be said both personally and essentially of the Trinity. In the first sense, the term "word" refers exclusively to the second person of the Trinity. In the second sense, the term "word" refers to the divine essence. It is this second sense that is controversial. Aquinas illustrated this point by a parallelism with human intellectual cognition. According to Aquinas's earlier position, there are only two items involved in human intellectual cognition in addition to the object of thought. First, there is an intelligible species that makes the intellect actual with regard to the cognition of a certain object and provides the content of thought. Second, there is the act of thinking itself, that is, the activity that the intellect carries out once it has been actualized by the intelligible species. For example, suppose that I am thinking about what a horse is (i.e., the essence of horses). According to Aquinas's account in the *Sentences*, this intellectual activity can be analyzed into the presence of the intelligible species that my intellect abstracts from sensory images of horses, on the one hand, and, on the other hand, my intellect's act of thinking about what a horse is. Since these are the only two elements into which thinking can be broken down, when we apply the term "word" to the activity of human cognition we may be referring to either the intelligible species or the act of thinking (Aquinas leaves this option open). As far as God's intellectual activity is concerned, however, there is neither an intelligible species nor an act of thinking distinct from the divine essence itself, due to God's simplicity. As a consequence, when applied to God, if the term "word" is taken to refer to God's intellectual activity, that term is said essentially of God, that is, it refers to the entire divine essence and not only to the second person of the Trinity, since God's intellectual activity is identical with his essence.[26]

Some years afterwards, however, Aquinas became dissatisfied with this view both theologically and philosophically. The process through which he reached his mature position was particularly tortured. Some elements of a new solution can already be found in *De veritate*, q.4, a.2. But Aquinas's mature view emerged only after he drafted a key chapter of the *Summa contra Gentiles* no fewer than three times between 1259 and 1264–65.[27] By the time he completes the fourth book of the *Summa contra Gentiles*, the questions *De Potentia*, the first part of the *Summa theologiae* and the commentary on St. John's Gospel, the contours of Aquinas's definitive position are clear.[28] From a theological point of view, Aquinas rejects the view that the term "word" can be said of the entire divine essence. Rather, there is only one sense of the term "word," and that is the personal sense by which that term refers only to the second person of the Trinity.[29] From a philosophical point of view, Aquinas rejects the view that the process of human cognition can be analyzed into only two elements, that is, the intelligible species and the act of thinking. He now adds a third factor, namely, a concept (*conceptio*) produced by the act of thinking. Thus, when I think about what a horse is, in addition to the object I am thinking about, there is, first, an intelligible species abstracted from sensory images of horses; second, there is my intellect's act of thinking; and finally, there is also a concept produced by my act of thinking. It is this concept that is called a "mental word." To think about something is to *produce* a concept of that thing.[30]

The difference between Aquinas's first and second account of the process of intellectual cognition can also be expressed in the following terms. Both in his earlier and in his later account, Aquinas held that acts of thinking are what he called "immanent actions," that is, actions that do not produce effects distinct from the agents that perform those actions. In that respect, thinking is different from actions such as building, which produces houses, and heating, which results in something's becoming hot. So far, Aquinas did not change his mind. But whereas in his earlier account he held that thinking is an action that does not produce anything at all, in his later account he claims that thinking is an action that produces a result distinct from the process of thinking, that is, a concept or inner word. That concept or inner word, however, does not get outside the intellect. As a consequence, Aquinas can still claim that thinking is an immanent action, but the reason is not that the act of thinking produces nothing, as he had previously claimed, but that its product remains within the intellect.

Possibly the most significant philosophical outcome of Aquinas's new position on mental words is that he can now introduce a more stringent parallelism between acts of thinking and natural actions. In both cases, an agent *produces* something. Just as the act of building produces a house, so the act of thinking produces a concept. When considered as a *productive* act, an act of thinking can be compared more easily to natural actions such as heating and cooling and thus be interpreted within the framework of natural philosophy.[31]

Analogy

Some modern interpreters have called attention to a significant development in Aquinas's treatment of analogy and the relation of likeness holding between creatures and God.[32] How can we account for our predicating of God terms such as "being," "good," "wise," and so on? Aquinas's answer was that we can do so because, in some respect, creatures are like God. All along his career, Aquinas's constant effort was to account for the relationship of likeness linking the created world to God while at the same time contending that there is no common feature shared by both God and creatures. Because there is a similitude between creatures and God, it is possible to attribute to God some terms that are ordinarily attributed to creatures (such as "being," "good," "wise," and the like). Because there is no common feature between God and creatures, however, these terms do not have exactly the same meaning when applied to God and when applied to creatures.[33]

Granted that Aquinas always subscribed to these claims, it is possible to distinguish three stages in his understanding of analogy.[34]

First, in his commentary on the *Sentences*, Aquinas distinguished between two kinds of analogy. The first kind of analogy is grounded on a relationship between two (or more) things that share the same feature according to different degrees. The second kind of analogy is grounded on the relationship holding between two (or more) things of which one imitates the other within the limits of its own essence even though there is no common feature shared by both the imitating and the imitated thing. According to Aquinas's earlier view, the first kind of analogy holds among all created things, which all share the same feature (i.e., being), even though some things (i.e., accidents) are beings only because they inhere in other things (i.e., substances). By contrast, the second kind of analogy holds between creatures and God. Creatures imitate God within the limits of their own nature and are therefore like God in some respect. Notwithstanding this likeness between creatures and God, however, there is no common feature shared by both God and creatures. Aquinas assumed as primitive the relation of imitation on which the analogy between God and creatures is grounded and did not make any attempt to explain it.[35]

Second, in his *De veritate*, Aquinas adopted a unique view. He rejected the position he had previously endorsed, according to which creatures are directly related to God by a primitive relation of imitation. By contrast, he argued that no relation can directly tie creatures and God, because the distance between creatures and God is infinite, and any relation holding between two things presupposes that there is a determined, that is, measurable and finite, distance between them. Thus, to say that creatures and God are directly related to each other would entail that there is a finite distance between creatures and God. But if there were a finite distance between creatures and God, God would be one of the things of this world. This would just eliminate God's transcendence. In order to avoid this result, Aquinas posited a peculiar kind of analogy, which is based not on a relation holding between two *things* but between two *proportions*. Aquinas called the relation on which this second kind of analogy is based "agreement of proportionality" (*convenientia proportionalitatis*) and contrasted it to the relation holding between two or more things, which he called "agreement of proportion" (*convenientia proportionis*). For example, the number six is related to the number three just as the number four is related to the number two. Six and three, on the one hand, and four and two, on the other hand, are related to each other by the relation of "being the double of." This relation, however, holds between two proportions. The terms of each proportion are not directly related to each other. Similarly, sight is related to the body just as the intellect is related to the soul, and a pilot is related to a ship just as a prince is related to a city. Sight is in some way similar to the intellect, but only by virtue of sight's being related to the body and the intellect's being similarly related to the soul. Sight and intellect are not similar to each other by virtue of any intrinsic property present in either sight or the intellect. The same holds for a pilot and a prince. Aquinas contended that the analogy holding between creatures and God is of this kind. For example, God's goodness is related to God's infinite being just as a creature's goodness is related to that creature's finite being. A creature's goodness, however, is not directly related to God's goodness. In this way, Aquinas could give a detailed analysis of the relation of imitation, which he had previously assumed as primitive in his commentary on the *Sentences*. That creatures imitate God within the limits of their essence only means that the properties of creatures are related to their being just as God's attributes are related to his being. This solution, however, came at a very high cost. Aquinas had to give up the view that there is any direct relationship holding between creatures and God. As several commentators have noted, this comes very close to saying that there is complete equivocity between what we say of creatures and what we say of God.[36]

Third and finally, in his most mature works, Aquinas recovers his first idea that there is a relation holding directly between creatures and God. Contrary to what he had done in the *Sentences*, however, he now gives an analysis of the relation by which each creature is directly linked to God. Creatures are related to God and imitate God because they are *caused* by God. Specifically, Aquinas holds that it is efficient causality that grounds the relationship of likeness holding between creatures and God. He now recognizes that the relation of likeness between creatures and God is just a consequence of the principle according to which every agent produces something like itself (*omne agens agit sibi simile*). This principle holds even when no common feature is shared by the agent and its effect.[37] Furthermore, Aquinas can now give a unified account of the analogy holding among creatures, on the one hand, and between creatures and God, on the other hand. With regard to the former sort of analogy, there is no common feature shared by accidents and substances. Contrary to what he had previously claimed, Aquinas now thinks that being is not a common feature shared by created things.[38] All the same, accidents are attributed to substances as to their cause (presumably, their efficient and material cause). Similarly, with regard to the latter analogy, there is no feature common to both creatures and God. All the same, creatures are in some way like God because they are caused by God. As a consequence of this likeness, terms such as "being," "good," "wise," and the like, can be literally (i.e., nonmetaphorically) predicated of both creatures and God.

The Necessity of Grace

A significant change can be noticed in Aquinas's views concerning the necessity of grace both in order to avoid committing mortal sin and in order to carry out the precepts of the divine law (i.e., the ten commandments).[39]

With regard to the necessity of grace in order to avoid mortal sin, in his commentary on the *Sentences* Aquinas claimed that human beings can avoid committing mortal sins even without grace. Some people, Aquinas noticed, held that human beings, even without grace, can avoid committing only some individual mortal sins, but they cannot avoid sinning altogether; moreover, those people held that human beings can exceptionally abstain from sinning even without grace, but only for a short time. Against those people, Aquinas argued that sin does not destroy human nature and the will's natural capacity to choose the good and avoid evil (i.e., its freedom). Consequently, no matter how badly we sinned in the past, we are always capable of abstaining from sinning in the future. To the argument that this may be true occasionally but not for a long time, Aquinas retorted that the more the will refrains from evil the stronger it becomes in its resistance to sin. Thus, time works in favor, not against our capacity to avoid sinning mortally.[40]

Already in the *De veritate*, however, Aquinas abandoned this optimistic position.[41] In the *Summa theologiae*, he distinguishes between the human condition before and after the Fall. He flatly denies that in the present, postlapsarian condition it is possible for those who are without grace to avoid committing mortal sins. Aquinas actually adopts the position he had rejected in the *Sentences*. Only occasionally and for a short time, he now argues, can human beings abstain from mortal sins if they are not provided with grace. Interestingly, Aquinas quotes Aristotle's emphasis on habit in support of his new position. Such is the force of habit that the original freedom of the will turns out to be severely impaired. No matter how perseverant in its efforts, a will without God's supernatural help will sooner or later revert to sin.[42]

A similar shift in Aquinas's position can be observed with regard to the mirror question, that is, the necessity of grace in order to carry out the precepts of the divine law. In his commentary on the *Sentences*, Aquinas argued that grace is necessary to carry out the precepts of the divine law only with regard to the mode of the law, not with regard to the substance of the law. This means that human beings do not need grace to do what the divine law commands (e.g., to honor one's own parents, to refrain from stealing, etc.). Grace is only needed to carry out those precepts according to the lawgiver's intention, that is, as God himself wanted those precepts to be obeyed. According to God's intention, his precepts should be not just obeyed, but obeyed out of charity, that is, out of infused love for God himself. Since charity is God's gift, grace is necessary in order to carry out the precepts of the divine law according to God's own intention. But what those precepts command can be done by mere free will.[43] Already in the *De veritate*, Aquinas seems to have embraced this position with much more hesitation.[44] In the *Summa theologiae*, he just reverses his earlier view. Adopting the same strategy that he had followed when addressing the question whether it is possible not to sin mortally without grace, he now distinguishes between the state of nature and the fallen state. In the state of nature, grace was not necessary to do what the divine law commanded, even though grace was still required to abide by the divine law out of charity. In the fallen state, however, healing grace is necessary even to do what the divine law commands.[45]

Thus, it seems that for the mature Aquinas somebody deprived of grace, for example, an atheist or a pagan, is both inevitably prone to sin mortally and incapable of carrying out what the divine precepts command.[46]

Other Issues

There are several other issues about which Aquinas's thought evolved. Here I will list only a few cases.[47]

(1) Whether God can communicate the power to create to his creatures. In his commentary on the *Sentences*, Aquinas claimed that God can communicate to creatures the power to create by virtue of his own causality, that is, as instruments of his action. Aquinas noticed that it is in this way that some philosophers (e.g., Avicenna) thought that separated substances create something. Aquinas remarked that this position is heretical. But at that stage of his career, he did not seem to have any philosophical objection to it. In his later works, however, Aquinas rejects the view that creatures can be given the power to create, even if only as instruments of God's causality, on the ground that to create is to give being, and being is God's proper effect.[48]

(2) Whether there is a divine idea of prime matter distinct from the idea of composites of matter and form. In the *Sentences*, Aquinas claimed that there is such an idea. In the *Summa theologiae*, he argues that there is not.[49]

(3) Whether pain is located in the senses (and specifically in touch) or in the soul (and specifically in that part of the soul that Aristotle called "appetitive," which is connected with bodily desires). In the *Sentences*,

Aquinas claimed that pain is located in touch. In the *Summa theologiae*, he argues that pain is located in the appetitive soul.[50]

(4) Whether God can dispense human beings from the commandments contained in the second tablet (i.e., those commandments that do not concern our dealings with God but our dealings with other human beings). In his commentary on the *Sentences*, Aquinas argued that God can dispense us from obedience from the commandments contained in the second tablet. In the *Summa theologiae*, he argues that this is impossible.[51]

(5) Whether Christ's resurrection is the cause of human salvation. In his commentary on the *Sentences*, Aquinas held the traditional view that Christ's resurrection plays no causal role in human salvation, for salvation is caused directly by the divine essence. In the *Summa theologiae*, however, he adopts the novel view that Christ's resurrection is not only an example but the genuine cause of our own salvation.[52]

(6) How charity increases when the body is reunited with the soul after resurrection. In the *Sentences*, Aquinas held that after resurrection charity increases both intensively and extensively. In the *Summa theologiae*, he claims that after resurrection charity increases only extensively, not intensively.[53]

Conclusion

As I have said at the beginning of this chapter, Aquinas's thought is remarkably consistent. Any suggestion that Aquinas may have changed his mind about a certain topic should be assessed with extreme care. Sometimes, this suggestion does not stand the test of an attentive consideration of Aquinas's writings. A case in point is Aquinas's alleged passage from an intellectualist to a voluntaristic position in his theory of the will. This hypothesis, once popular among scholars, is most probably one to be rejected.[54] More often than not, however, students of Aquinas (probably because of a misplaced urge to defend their master) have refused to contemplate the very possibility that Aquinas ever changed his mind about any topic whatsoever. This attitude, however, clashes with textual evidence. As well known already to his contemporaries and first interpreters, Aquinas did change his mind about a certain number of topics. When taken together, these changes do not amount to any major turn or reversal in Aquinas's thought. Nevertheless, each one of them deserves careful consideration. As once remarked by Cajetan (possibly the most enthusiastic and influential among Aquinas's interpreters), it is not detrimental on Aquinas's dignity to have reached his definitive view only step by step, because "it is natural for the human intellect to be perfected in the course of time."[55]

NOTES

1. William of Tocco, *Ystoria sancti Thome de Aquino de Guillaume de Tocco (1323)*, ed. Claire le Brun-Gouanvic (Toronto: Pontifical Institute of Mediaeval Studies, 1996), 170. I have adopted the following chronology of Aquinas's writings: *Scriptum super libros Sententiarum* (= *Super Sent*): 1252–56; *Quaestiones disputatae De Veritate* (= *QDV*): 1256–59; *Expositio in librum Boethii De trinitate* (= *In BDT*): 1257–58/59; *Summa contra Gentiles* (= *SCG*): 1259/60–64/65; *Quaestiones disputatae De Potentia* (= *QDP*): 1265–66; *Quaestiones de disputata anima* (= *QDA*): 1266–67; *Sententia Libri De anima* (= *In DA*): 1267–68; *Quaestio disputata De spiritualibus creaturis* (= *QDSC*): 1267–68; *Summa theologiae* (= *ST*) I: 1265/66–68; I-II: 1271; II-II: 1271–72; III, incomplete: 1272–73; *Quaestiones de quodlibet I–XII* (= *Quodl*) I: 1269; II: 1269; III: 1270; VI: 1270; XII: 1272; *Sententia super Metaphysicam* (= *In Meta*): 1270–72; *Quaestio disputata De unione verbi incarnati* (= *QDUVI*): 1272. Unless otherwise indicated, the translations from Aquinas's writings are my own.

2. J.-P. Torrell, *Saint Thomas Aquinas*, vol. 1, *The Person and His Work*, rev. ed., trans. Robert Royal (Washington, D.C.: Catholic University of America Press, 1996), 191–96.

3. J. F. Wippel, *Metaphysical Themes in Thomas Aquinas* (Washington, D.C.: Catholic University of America Press, 1984), 229–40; "Thomas Aquinas on What Philosophers Can Know about God," *American Catholic Philosophical Quarterly* 66 (1992): 279–97, esp. 286–88; *The Metaphysical Thought of Thomas Aquinas: From Finite Being to Uncreated Being* (Washington, D.C.: Catholic University of America Press, 2000), 540–41.

4. Torrell, *Saint Thomas Aquinas*, 221–22.

5. G. Geenen, "En marge du Concile de Chalcédoine: Les textes du quatrième Concile dans les oeuvres de S. Thomas," *Angelicum* 19 (1952): 43–59; "Doctrinae concilii Chalcedonensis usus et influxus in theologia S. Thomas Aquinatis," *Divus Thomas* (Pl.) 56 (1953): 319–42; D. Ols, *Le cristologie contemporanee e le loro posizioni fondamentali al vaglio della dottrina di S. Tommaso* (Città del Vaticano: Libreria Editrice Vaticana, 1991), 161–62, n. 17.

6. H. Bouillard, *Conversion et grace chez S. Thomas d'Aquin: Étude historique* (Paris: Aubier, 1944), 92–122; J. P. Wawrykow, *God's Grace and Human Action: "Merit" in the Theology of Thomas Aquinas* (Notre Dame, Ind. and London: University of Notre Dame Press, 1995), 266–76.

7. P.-M. Gils, "Textes inédits de S. Thomas: Les Premières Redactions du *Scriptum super Tertio Sententiarum*," *Revue des sciences philosophiques et théologiques* 45 (1961): 201–28; 46 (1962): 445–62 and 609–28; "S. Thomas écrivain," in Sancti Thomae de Aquino *Super Boetii De Trinitate. Expositio libri Boetii de hebdomadibus*, Opera omnia, 50, Commissio Leonina, Rome and Les Éditions du Cerf (Paris, 1992), 173–209, esp. 191–209.

8. On Christ's knowledge, *ST* III q.9 a.4: "And thus, although elsewhere I wrote differently (*quamvis aliter alibi scripserim*), it must be said that in Christ there was acquired knowledge"; and q.12,a.2: "Therefore, if in the soul of Christ there were no habit of acquired knowledge in addition to the habit of infused knowledge, as it seems to some and sometime seemed to me (*ut quibusdam videtur, et mihi aliquando visum est*)." On the Empyrean Heaven, *Quodl* 6, q.11, art. un. [19]: "some think that the Empyrean Heaven has no influence on the other bodies.... And so at some time it seemed to me (*Et hoc quidem mihi aliquando visum est*)." On circumcision, *ST* III q.62 a.6 ad 3: "And thus others say that circumcision conferred grace also with regard to a certain positive effect, namely by making human beings worthy of eternal life, but not so as to repress the concupiscence that makes human beings prone to sin. And so at one time it seemed to me (*Quod aliquando mihi visum est*)." See Ols, *Le Cristologie*, 160–61; T. Litt, *Les Corps célestes dans*

l'univers de saint Thomas d'Aquin (Louvain and Paris: Publications universitaires and Béatrice-Nauwelaerts, 1963), 260, n. 2. I wish to thank Adriano Oliva and Ruedi Imbach for these indications.

9. R.-A. Gauthier, "Les 'Articuli in quibus frater Thomas melius in Summa quam in Scriptis,'" *Recherches de théologie ancienne et médievale* 19 (1952): 271–326. This list of topics was known as "Articles in which brother Thomas held a better opinion in his *Summa* than in his *Commentary on the Sentences*" (*Articuli in quibus frater Thomas melius in Summa quam in Scriptis*" [= *Articuli*]). For other concordances and similar documents, see ibid. 292–93.

10. *Super Sent* II, d.20, q.2, a.2, ad 3; *Super Sent* III, d.31, q.2, a.4; *QDV*, q.10, a.2, ad 7; q.10, a.8, ad 1; *SCG* II, 73; *ST* I q.84 a.7; q.85 a.1; *Quodl* XII, q.9, a.1. See R. Pasnau, *Thomas Aquinas on Human Nature: A Philosophical Study of* Summa theologiae *Ia 75–89* (Cambridge: Cambridge University Press, 2002), 278–95.

11. In what follows, I focus exclusively on the acquisition of simple concepts such as the concept *horse*, the concept *human being*, etc., and on the acts of understanding and thinking about the real essences that correspond to those concepts. Aquinas referred to these acts as *actus intelligendi* or *intellectiones* and he used the verb *intelligere* to indicate the intellect's operation of performing those acts. I translate these expressions by "acts of thinking" and "thinking." "Acts of understanding" and "understanding" are also possible translations.

12. *QDV*, q.10, a.2, ad 4; q.19, ad 1; *SCG* II, 74; *ST* I q.79 a.6 ad 3; *Quodl* III, q.9, a.1.

13. *Articuli*, art. 29, in Gauthier, "Les 'Articuli in quibus,'" 312–13.

14. *Super Sent* III, d.14, q.1, a.3, qla 5: "Christ's knowledge never increased with regard to the kind of cognition he had... nor did it increase with regard to the number of things He knew, because from the first instant of His conception He knew all that pertains to such knowledge. But [Christ's knowledge] increased with regard to the mode of certitude"; d.18, a.1, ad 5: "it must be said that Christ did not have any knowledge received from the senses; rather, He had infused knowledge." See Ols, *Le Cristologie*, 154–56; J.-P. Torrell, *Recherches thomasiennes: Études revues et augmentés* (Paris: Vrin, 2000), 202, n. 1.

15. *Super Sent* III, d.14, q.1, a.3, qla 5, ad 3: "by virtue of the light of the agent intellect, no new species was received in His possible intellect; rather, there occurred a new turning back to the species that were already in His imagination, just as it happens to somebody who already has the habit of knowledge with regard to what he imagines or sees."

16. *ST* III q.9 a.4: "Thus is it necessary to say that in Christ there were some intelligible species received in the possible intellect by the action of the agent intellect—which is just to say that in Him there was acquired knowledge, which some call 'experiential knowledge'"; q.12 a.2: "Christ is thought to have acquired knowledge... because of what is fitting to the agent intellect, so that its action, which is to make things actually intelligible, will not be useless." Aquinas started questioning his earlier position already in *QDV*, q.20, a.3. See Ols, *Le cristologie*, 156–59. Of course, the question of acquired versus infused knowledge only concerns Christ as a human being, not Christ as God.

17. See above, note 8.

18. Torrell, *Recherches thomasiennes*, 202. By "knowledge" I refer here to knowledge of essences. Thus, the point is not whether Christ learned that A.D. January 20, 30 was a sunny day. Rather, the question is whether Christ learned what a horse is, what a dog is, and so on. See above, note 11.

19. *Super Sent* III, d.31, q.2, a.4; *Super Sent* IV, d.50, q.1, a.1; *QDV*, q.19, a.1; *SCG* II, 80–81; *QDA*, q.15; *ST* I q.89 a.1; *ST* I-II q.67 a.2; *Quodl* III, q.9, a.1.

20. *Super Sent* III, d.31, q.2, a.4: "Therefore, a soul separated from its body will still retain its nature, but will lose its actual union with a body. And thus that soul, considered just in its

nature, will need no sensory image in order to consider what it already knew [before being separated from the body]. Rather, it will need sensory images only in order to consider those things that it must learn for the first time. And thus, [that soul] will be able to consider those things that it already knew not by using a sensory image, but by virtue of the habit of knowledge that it acquired previously.... For to say that a soul, in accordance with what *now* that soul has in its nature, won't be able to think at all without its body, is a claim typical of those who hold that the soul ceases to exist with the body, because, as is said in the first book of *On the Soul*, if none of the soul's operation can exist without the body, then the soul itself could not exist without the body, since natural operations follows nature."

21. *QDV*, q.19, a.1: "But when the soul will be separated from the body, just as it will have its being neither dependent on the body nor existing in the body, so, too, it will receive an influx of intellectual cognition in such a way that it will neither be confined to the body, as though it had to be exercised through the body, nor will it have any ordination to the body at all. Therefore, when at its creation the soul is infused in the body, the only intellectual cognition that is given it is ordained to the powers of the body. Thus, through the agent intellect it can make sensory images that are only potentially intelligible *actually* intelligible, and through the possible intellect it can receive the intelligible species thus abstracted. And this is also the reason why, as long as it has being united to the body in the state of this life, it does not know even those things whose species are preserved in it except by insight into sensory images.... But when it will have its being free of the body, then it will receive the influx of intellectual cognition in the way in which angels receive it, without any ordination to the body. Thus, it will receive species of things from God Himself, and it won't be necessary to turn back to any image in order to actually think by virtue of those species or of those that it acquired previously." The English translation is taken, with some modification, from St. Thomas Aquinas, *Truth*, vol. 2, trans. J. V. McGlynn (Chicago: Henry Regnery Company, 1953), 390. See also *SCG* II, 81.

22. *ST* I q.89 a.1: "Therefore with respect to the mode of existence by which the soul is united to a body, the appropriate mode of thinking for the soul is to turn toward the sensory image of bodies, sensory images that exist within bodily organs. But once it has been separated from its body, the appropriate mode of thinking for the soul is to turn toward intelligible things straightaway—just as is appropriate for other separate substances. So turning toward sensory images is, for the soul, its natural mode of thinking, just as being united to a body is natural. But being separated from its body is foreign to the character of its nature, and thinking without turning toward sensory images is likewise foreign to its nature. So it is united to a body in order to exist and operate in keeping with its nature." The English translation is taken, with a few modifications, from Thomas Aquinas, *The Treatise on Human Nature:* Summa Theologiae *1a 75–89*, trans. Robert Pasnau (Indianapolis and Cambridge: Hackett Publishing Company, 2002), 205–6.

23. Ibid.: "One need to consider, then, that although thinking by turning toward higher things is in itself loftier than thinking by turning toward sensory images, still that first mode of thinking was less perfect considered as it was possible for the soul." (Pasnau's translation with some modifications.) Aquinas had already anticipated this position in *QDA*, q.15, where he had granted that the knowledge obtained by separated souls is not as good and precise as that obtained by way of sensory images. Contrary to what he would say in *ST*, however, in *QDA* Aquinas still maintained that separated souls do not need any supernatural help to think without sensory images. The *QDA* are thought to precede immediately or be roughly contemporary to the first part of *ST*.

24. Possibly connected to the role of sensory images in human cognition is the question whether it is possible to see God in this life without the light of glory (*lumen*

gloriae). In *QDV*, q.10, a.11, Aquinas held that this is possible. By contrast, in *ST* II-II q.175 a.3 ad 2, he argued that this is not possible, because the human intellect can be actualized only by an intelligible species abstracted from a sensory image; as a consequence, the human intellect cannot be actualized directly by God, as is the case in the beatific vision, without being supernaturally predisposed by the light of glory, which replaces the agent intellect's act of abstraction. See *Articuli*, art. 75 in Gauthier "Les 'Articuli in quibus,'" 325.

25. H. Paissac, *Théologie du Verbe: Saint Augustine et saint Thomas* (Paris: Éditions du Cerf, 1951), 117–218; A. F. von Gunten, "*In principio erat verbum*: Une évolution de saint Thomas en théologie trinitaire," in C.-J. Pinto de Oliveira, ed., *Ordo Sapientiae et Amoris: Hommage au Professeur Jean-Pierre Torrell OP à l'occasion de son 65e anniversaire* (Fribourg, Suisse: Éditions universitaires, 1993), 119–41; *Articuli*, art. 8, in Gauthier, "Les 'Articuli in quibus,'" 303.

26. *Super Sent* I, d.27, q.2, a.2, qla 1. In addition to the studies indicated in the previous note, see J. Chênevert, "Le *Verbum* dans le Commentaire sur le Sentences de Saint Thomas d'Aquin," *Sciences ecclésiastiques* 13 (1961): 191–233; 359–90. There are two versions of the relevant part of this question. See von Gunten "*In principio erat verbum*," 212–28; A. Oliva, *Les débuts de l'enseignement de Thomas d'Aquin et sa conception de la* sacra doctrina, *avec l'édition du prologue de son commentaire des* Sentences (Paris: Vrin, 2006), 123–29.

27. *SCG* I, 53. The third and definitive version is the one printed in the editions of the *SCG* commonly available. The first and second versions are given in the appendix to vol. 13 of the Leonine edition, 20*–21*. See L.-B. Geiger, "Les rédactions successives de *Contra Gentiles I*, 53 d'après l'autographe," in *Saint Thomas d'Aquin aujourd'hui* (Paris: Desclée de Brouwer, 1963), 221–40.

28. *SCG* IV, 11; *QDP*, q.8, a.1; q.9, a.5; *ST* I q.27 a.1 and a.2; q.28 a.4 ad 1; q.34 a.1; q.85 a.2 ad 3; *Super Johan* I, 1.

29. According to Roger Marston's testimony, the position Aquinas held in the commentary on the *Sentences* was excommunicated around 1271–72 in the course of a disputation attended by Aquinas himself. See Roger Marston, *De emanatione aeterna*, q.6, in *Quaestiones disputatae* (Ad Claras Aquas, 1932), 117. For the debate on the theological issue of mental word, see G. Pini, "Henry of Ghent's Doctrine of *Verbum* in Its Theological Context," in *Henry of Ghent and the Transformation of Scholastic Thought: Studies in Memory of Jos Decorte* (Leuven: Leuven University Press, 1993), 307–26.

30. *QDP*, q.8, a.1: "And that concept (*conceptio*) differs from the three other things I have mentioned. It differs from the thing thought about.... It differs from the intelligible species.... It also differs from the intellect's action, because that concept is considered as the *term* of the action and as something produced by it, as it were.... This concept of the intellect is properly called 'word' in us." On Aquinas's mature doctrine of mental words, see C. Panaccio, "From Mental Word to Mental Language," *Philosophical Topics* 20 (1992): 125–47, esp. 126–28; R. Pasnau, *Theories of Cognition in the Later Middle Ages* (Cambridge: Cambridge University Press, 1997), 256–71; C. Panaccio, *Le Discours intérieur de Platon à Guillaume d'Ockham* (Paris: Éditions du Seuil, 1999), 177–92; Pasnau, *Thomas Aquinas on Human Nature*, 327–28; E. Stump, *Aquinas* (London and New York: Routledge, 2003), 266–68.

31. G. Pini, "Two Models of Thinking: Thomas Aquinas and John Duns Scotus," in G. Klima, ed., *Intentionality, Cognition and Representation in the Middle Ages* (New York: Fordham University Press, forthcoming).

32. B. Montagnes, *The Doctrine of the Analogy of Being according to Thomas Aquinas*, trans. E. M. Macierowski and P. Vandevelde (Milwaukee: Marquette University Press, 2004). See also G. P. Klubertanz, *St. Thomas Aquinas on Analogy: A Textual Analysis and Systematic Synthesis* (Chicago: Loyola University Press, 1960).

33. Wippel, *The Metaphysical Thought*, 543–72.

34. Montagnes, *The Doctrine of the Analogy*, 65–93.

35. *Super Sent* prol., q.1, a.2, ad 2; I, d.19, q.5, a.2; d.35, q.1, a.4; d.48, q.1, a.1; II, d.16, q.1, a.1, ad 3.

36. *QDV* I, q.2, a.11.

37. On the likeness obtaining between creatures and God: *SCG* I, 29; *ST* I q.4 a.3. Specifically on analogy: *SCG* I, 32 and 34; *QDP*, q.7, a.7; *ST* I q.13 a.5: "So, whatever we say of both God and creatures we say in virtue of the order that creatures have to God as to their source and cause, in which all the perfections of things pre-exist most excellently." The English translation is from Aquinas, *Summa Theologiae, Questions on God*, ed. Brian Davies and Brian Leftow (Cambridge: Cambridge University Press, 2006), 149. On the principle that every agent produces something like itself, which Aquinas takes to be entailed by the very nature of causality, see Wippel, *The Metaphysical Thought*, 517–18, 558–59.

38. *SCG* I, 34.

39. *Articuli*, art. 16 and art. 17, in Gauthier, "Les 'Articuli in quibus,' " 306–7. On Aquinas's shift concerning grace, probably due to his increased familiarity with Augustine's writings, see Bouillard, *Conversion et grace*, 92–122; J.-P. Torrell, *Nouvelle recherches thomasiennes* (Paris: Vrin, 2008), 125, n. 2. See also A. E. McGrath, *Iustitia Dei: A History of the Christian Doctrine of Justification*, 3d ed. (Cambridge: Cambridge University Press, 2005), 132–38. For a similar shift concerning merit and the role of predestination from the *Sentences* to the *Summa theologiae*, see Wawrykow, *God's Grace and Human Action*. In general on nature and grace in Aquinas, see Torrell, *Nouvelle recherches thomasiennes*, 99–129.

40. *Super Sent* II, d.28, q.1, a.2: "Others, however, with the intention of preserving the nature of free will, say that human beings, in keeping with their natural virtue, have been created in such a way that they can avoid sin; but as a consequence of sin virtue is so changed that one who is already in a state of sin cannot avoid sin but falls into another sin unless he is freed by grace. But because they do not want to appear to say that it is absolutely impossible not to sin, they add that somebody who is in mortal sin can avoid this or that particular sin, but not all sins. And the same is true of venial sins. They also state that somebody who is in a state of mortal sin can avoid sinning for some time, but not for a long time. This position, however, seems false in several respects. First, it is false because, just as sin reduces but does not remove the natural goods, a human being cannot lose what pertains to the nature of a natural power, even though he can become weak in that respect. Therefore, since the free choice or avoidance of good or evil pertains to the nature of free will, the capacity to avoid sin cannot be taken away from a human being. Rather, it can only be reduced, namely in such a way that one can avoid only with difficulty that sin that previously he could have avoided easily. . . . And it cannot even be said that somebody can avoid sinning for some time but not for long, because a free will that resists evil becomes much stronger in resisting evil, not weaker; and so it is much more capable of avoiding sinning after than before."

41. *QDV* I, q.24, a.12.

42. *ST* I-II q.109 a.8: "But in the state of corrupted nature human beings need grace to heal their nature in order that they may entirely abstain form sin. . . . So, too, before a human being's reason, wherein is mortal sin, is restored by justifying grace, that human being can avoid each mortal sin, and for some time, since it is not necessary that he should always be actually sinning. But it cannot be that he remains for a long time without mortal sin. . . . And thus, just as inordinate movements of the sensitive appetite cannot help occurring when the lower appetite is not subject to reason, so likewise, when a human

being's reason is not entirely subject to God, the consequence is that many disorders occur in the acts themselves of reason. For when a human being's heart is not so fixed on God as to be unwilling to be parted from Him for the sake of finding any good or avoiding any evil, many things happen for the achieving or avoiding of which a human being strays from God and breaks His commandments, and thus sins mortally; especially since, when surprised, a human being acts according to his preconceived end and his pre-existing habits, as the Philosopher says, although with the premeditation of his reason a human being may do something outside the order of his preconceived end and the inclination of his habit. But because a human being cannot always have this premeditation, it cannot help occurring that he acts in accordance with his will turned aside form God, unless, by grace, he is quickly brought back to the due order." The English translation is taken, with some modifications, from *Basic Writings of Saint Thomas Aquinas*, ed. Anton C. Pegis, vol. 2 (New York: Random House, 1945), 991–92. Around 1280, Roger Marston, while noticing Aquinas's development on this topic, did not hesitate to label Aquinas's earlier position as Pelagian ("Istud manifeste est de errore Pelagii"). See Roger Marston, *De statu naturae lapsae*, q.2, ad 28, in *Quaestiones disputatae*, p. 200, as quoted in Gauthier, "Les 'Articuli in quibus,'" 277–78, n. 17.

43. *Super Sent* II, d.28, q.3, a.1: "Therefore, it must be said that somebody can observe the precepts of the law by free will, with regard to what falls directly under a precept, and without gratuitously given or sanctifying grace (*sine gratia gratis data vel gratum faciente*), as long as grace is taken to mean some infused habit. But with regard to the lawgiver's intention, the precepts of the law cannot be observed in the absence of grace, because the gift of charity cannot become present in us through our own forces but is infused by God."

44. *QDV*, q.24, a.15, ad 2.

45. *ST* I-II q.109 a.4: "I answer that there are two ways of fulfilling the commandments of the Law. The first regards the substance of works, as when somebody does works of justice, fortitude, and of other virtues. And in this way a human being in the state of integral nature could fulfill all the commandments of the Law; or otherwise he would have been unable not to sin in that state, since to sin is nothing else than to transgress the divine commandments. But in the state of corrupted nature, a human being cannot fulfill all the divine commandments without healing grace." The English translation is taken, with some modifications, from *The Basic Writings of Saint Thomas Aquinas*, 2:985.

46. There seems to be a similar shift in Aquinas's position concerning the necessity of grace in order to carry out the commandment of loving God above everything else (grace is not necessary: *Super Sent* II, d.28, q.1, a.3; grace is necessary: *ST* I-II q.100 a.10), as well as in order to prepare ourselves to the reception of healing grace (grace is not necessary: *Super Sent* II, d.28, a.4; grace is necessary: *QDV*, q.24, a.15; *Quodl* I, q.4, a.2; *ST* I-II q.109 a.6). See *Articuli*, art. 18 and art. 39, in Gauthier, "Les 'Articuli in quibus,'" 307 and 317, and, on the latter issue, Roger Marston, *De statu naturae lapsae*, q.2, ad 11, 195–96, in *Quaestiones disputatae*, as quoted in Gauthier, "Les 'Articuli in quibus,'" 287, n. 39. A close reading of Aquinas's text, however, seems to cast some doubts on Aquinas's shift especially concerning the latter issue.

47. Sometimes Aquinas hesitated between two views, but it is not possible to detect a clear evolution in his position. The question whether supposit and essence are identical in angels is a case in point. In several places, Aquinas argued that supposit and essence are identical in angels. See *Super Sent* I, d.25, q.1, a.1, ad 3; *Super Sent* II, d.3, q.1, a.2; *Super Sent* III, d.5, q.1, a.3; *SCG* IV, 55; *QDP*, q.7, a.4; *QDP*, q.9, a.1; *QDA*, q.17, ad 10; *In DA* 3, 2; *ST* I q.3 a.3; q.39 a.3 ad 3; *QDSC* 5, ad 9; *In Meta* VII, 5 and 11; VIII, 3. In other places, however, Aquinas claimed that supposit and essence are really different in any creature, angels

included. See *Super Sent* I, d.5, q.1; d.34, q.1, a.1; *SCG* II, 54; *Quodl* II, q.2, a.2; *QDUVI*, 1; cf. also *ST* III q.17 a.1. See *Articuli*, art. 36, in Gauthier, "Les 'Articuli in quibus,'" 316–17; Wippel, *The Metaphysical Thought*, 238–53. Similarly, Aquinas's wavered in his opinion about the role that determinate or indeterminate dimensions play in the individuation of material things. See *Super Sent* II, d.3, q.1, a.4; *Super Sent* II, d.30, q.2, a.2; *In BDT*, q.4, a.2 (the individuating principle is matter considered under indeterminate dimensions); *Super Sent* III, d.1, q.2, a.5; *In DA* 2, c.12; *QDA*, q.9 (the individuating principle is matter considered under determinate dimensions). See Wippel, *The Metaphysical Thought*, 356–73.

48. *Super Sent* II, d.1, q.1, a.2; *SCG* II, 21; *QDP*, q.3, a.4; *ST* I q.45 a.5. See *Articuli*, art. 12, in Gauthier, "Les 'Articuli in quibus,'" 305. John of Naples noticed this development. See Gauthier, "Les 'Articuli in quibus,'" 287, n. 41.

49. *Super Sent* I, d.36, q.2, a.3, ad 2; *ST* I q.15 a.3 ad 3. See *Articuli*, art. 56, in Gauthier, "Les 'Articuli in quibus,'" 321.

50. *Super Sent* III, d.15, q.2, a.3, sol.1; *ST* I-II q.35 a.1. See *Articuli*, art. 30, in Gauthier, "Les 'Articuli in quibus,'" 313–14. Giles of Rome noticed this development. See Gauthier, "Les 'Articuli in quibus,'" 278, n. 18.

51. *Super Sent* I, d.47, q.1, a.4; *ST* I-II q.100 a.8. See *Articuli*, art. 10, in Gauthier, "Les 'Articuli in quibus,'" 304.

52. *Super Sent* IV, d.43, q.1, a.2; *ST* III q.56 a.1 ad 3. Aquinas's evolution concerns the notion of instrumental causality and can be documented also in *QDV*, q.27, a.4. See Torrell, *Recherches thomasiennes*, 214–41.

53. *Super Sent*, IV, d.49, q.1, a.4, sol. 1; *ST* I-II q.4 a.5 ad 5. See F. Pelster, "Das Wachstum der Seligkeit nach der Aufestehung, um die Auslegung von S. Th. I-II, q. 4 a. 5 ad 5," *Scholastik* 27 (1952): 561–63; Torrell, *Recherches thomasiennes*, 195–96, n. 3.

54. The view that Aquinas changed his mind about the will was first proposed in O. Lottin, "La date de la Question Disputée *De Malo* de Saint Thomas d'Aquin," *Revue d'histoire ecclésiastique* 24 (1928): 373–88. It was then endorsed in many other studies, both by Lottin and other scholars, including B. Lonergan, "St. Thomas's Thought on *Gratia Operans*," *Theological Studies* 2 (1941): 289–324; 3 (1942): 69–88, 375–402, 533–78, reprinted as *Grace and Freedom: Operative Grace in the Thought of Thomas Aquinas*, ed. F. E. Crowe and R. M. Doran (Toronto: University of Toronto Press, 2000). Serious doubts have been cast on this hypothesis in D. Westberg, "Did Aquinas Change His Mind about the Will?" *The Thomist* 58 (1994): 41–60; and esp. P. Eardley, "Thomas Aquinas and Giles of Rome on the Will," *Review of Metaphysics* 56 (2003): 835–62.

55. This remark, which concerns Aquinas's development on mental words, is taken from the commentary on the first part of the *Summa theologiae by* Thomas de Vio, Cardinal Cajetan, as printed in vol. 4 of the Leonine edition, 368, and quoted in von Gunten, "*In principio erat verbum*," 119, n. 2.

I wish to express my gratitude to Adriano Oliva, O.P. (Commissio Leonina) and Russell Friedman (Katholieke Universiteit Leuven) for their suggestions and help. I also wish to thank Brian Davies for many useful comments on a first draft of this paper.

CHAPTER 38

THE INFLUENCE OF AQUINAS

CHRISTOPHER UPHAM

To INQUIRE about the influence of Aquinas is to ask whether his thought produced any important effects. Aquinas himself would suggest that there are four questions to consider when trying to measure something's effects: (1) whether any effect exists; (2) what is the form of the effect; (3) what is its intensity; and (4) what is its duration.[1] It goes without saying that the first question should be answered in the affirmative, so this chapter will be devoted to probing the remaining three. What has been the nature of Aquinas's influence? To what degree has this influence been felt? During which periods of history has this influence been more significant?

Doubtless, the most salient effects of Aquinas's doctrines are to be found in the medieval university setting. Indeed, he would come to be known as "the Angel of the Schools." Yet, before he gained this title, he was referred to as the *Doctor Communis*.[2] Whether this was meant to evoke the affability of his temperament or the generality of his acceptance, it is difficult to ascertain. What is clear is that his teaching was not so friendly that it avoided censure, nor was his authority so well-accepted, as a commentator on Aristotle and as an orthodox (i.e., Catholic) theologian, that it was beyond reproach. In the wake of Aquinas's passing, a number of controversies emerged, but these are almost entirely confined to the walls of European universities. For this reason, I will address these conflicts as part of the backdrop for the burgeoning school of Thomists, in the second section. First, however, I will mention a few branches of Aquinas's legacy that deserve more attention, especially insofar as they illustrate some ways in which his teaching was quite common, both because it extended beyond the university and because it affected many ordinary people.

Common Doctor: Aquinas outside the Schools

Among the People

If the singular focus on European universities smacks of elitism, this might be remedied by noting the popular transmission of Aquinas's work. Obviously, the vast majority of people being illiterate, Aquinas could only be known indirectly to most during the High Middle Ages. Notwithstanding this impediment, even an uneducated commoner could meet with Aquinas's influence in two venues: first, in the confessional booth; second, in public lectures.

Perhaps a surprising, and certainly austere, means of dispensing Aquinas's teaching is to be found in the confessional. The medium by which Aquinas's moral theology reached confessors was often at a degree of remove: rather than consulting the *Secunda Secundae*, priests would have resorted to a casuist manual for help identifying or addressing particular sins. However, as Boyle meticulously documents, Aquinas was recorded quite faithfully and copiously in at least one such casuist manual. Through the widely circulated *Summa confessorum* of John of Freiburg, the Common Doctor exerted a fairly direct sway over pastoral care in the fourteenth and fifteenth centuries.[3] However, it is difficult to offer a succinct description of the precise nature of Aquinas's influence or to assess the degree to which Aquinas's systematic moral treatises, such as those found in the *Summa theologiae*, survived the reconfiguration into case-based manuals. Complicating matters more, the *Summa confessorum* draws heavily on more occasional works, like some of Aquinas's *Quaestiones Quodlibetales*, and even the obscure letter to the Duchess of Brabant, *De regimine Iudaeorum* (On the Government of the Jews).

Outside of the practical concerns of the Church, the public disputations and lectures of medieval scholars presented a more detailed and, for that reason, less accessible mode of diffusion for Aquinas's thought. Indeed, these public disputations could be diffusive in a double sense: they both disseminated and, at times, diluted the intellectual force of Aquinas's arguments. With such scant evidence often in the form of *reportationes* (student notes) and *ordinationes* (notes edited by the *magister*), it seems futile to conjecture about the exact nature of the influence Aquinas may have exerted in these forums, even among his most docile students. Doubtless, the effect would be even more diminished in cases where a Thomist publicly defended theses in harmony with Aquinas's conclusions. All the same, this venue is the most likely point of contact between the Common Doctor and Dante Alighieri, who appears to have received his exposure to Thomist doctrines in a public setting—not in a university—from a student of Aquinas himself, Dominican Friar Remigio of Girolami.[4] As with John of Freiburg, Dante was most interested in the moral theology of Aquinas. A perusal of Dante's *Commedia* suggests the impact of many of Aquinas's moral doctrines, namely, concerning the nature and severity of sins, the relationship between grace and merit, as well as the characterization of beatitude in visual terms.[5] Admittedly, Aquinas's hold on Dante's mind was far from exclusive. Yet, in a poignant example of Aquinas's influence, the *Doctor Communis* would be immortalized in Dante's heaven before the Church completed his canonization in 1323.

Among the Byzantines

At the time of Aquinas's death, the Western Church was attempting to repair the rift with the Eastern Orthodox. Despite the significant barriers between the Latin West and Greek Byzantium, Aquinas earned an unmistakable authority among some Orthodox theologians, an authority that is evident not long after his passing in 1274. Although some would refer to the rise of Byzantine Thomism, this is certainly too triumphalist, since those who appropriated Aquinas in the Eastern Church were rarely, if ever, unequivocal proponents of his theological doctrines. With this caveat in mind, however, it is obvious that Aquinas received serious attention from Eastern Orthodox theologians during the late Byzantine renaissance of the fourteenth and first half of the fifteenth century. At least, the fact that Aquinas had any Byzantine advocates seems noteworthy, especially in this era when the Vatican was making efforts at reunification with the East.

Unfortunately, a more detailed account of Aquinas's influence in Byzantium before the fall of Constantinople (1453) seems to have received only passing notice at the present, so it is difficult to summarize his impact. Still, a brief overview of some extant texts carried over to the Greek offers some suggestive insights into the interests of these Byzantine translators, but these are mere proposals. One of the earliest conveyors of Aquinas into Byzantium was Maximus Planudes (1260–1310), who translated a *reportatio* of Aquinas, *Expositio in symbolum apostolorum* (An Exposition of the Apostle's Creed).[6] On the face of it, this lends itself well to ecumenical uses, especially because this earliest of creeds predates the Nicene formulation with the controversial "filioque" clause.[7] Another of Aquinas's writings suitable to more conciliatory purposes, the *Summa contra Gentiles*, was translated into Greek in the mid-fourteenth century by Demetrius Cydones (c. 1320–1400). This piece of philosophical theology also takes on particular relevance for Byzantine Christians due to their uneasy proximity to the rising Ottoman Empire.[8] With his brother Prochorus, Demetrius even took up portions of the *Summa theologiae* into Greek, though it would require a much more involved treatment of these matters to suggest motives for their selections. Provisionally, it seems safe to conclude that one important aspect of Aquinas's influence concerned Trinitarian theology, especially since the precise characterization of the relationships between Divine Persons was a hotly disputed topic.[9]

By the fifteenth century, Aquinas was familiar enough in Eastern Christianity that exceptional Byzantine theologians, such as George Courtesis (c. 1405–1472), would study Aquinas closely and manifest open respect for his thinking.[10] In the case of Courtesis, there seems to have been, in his early adulthood at least, a deep conviction that Aquinas's doctrines could eventually make possible a reconciliation between the East and West, though political expediency may have also played a role in this optimism.[11] The encroaching Ottomans were becoming more hostile, and the hope for military assistance from Catholic princes may have rendered all forms of rapprochement—even with Latin theology—more appealing. Whatever Courtesis's motives were, reconciliation never came, and when Constantinople fell to the Turks, he was their selection as the new Patriarch of Constantinople, Gennadius II Scholarius, whose job description involved keeping the peace between Christian subjects and Muslim rulers.[12] If nothing else, this is another illustrative example of Aquinas appearing in the midst of a complex conflict, where unity could only be achieved through a tense juxtaposition of opposites.

Among the Rabbis

We have seen some ways that Aquinas influenced thinkers outside the university, both in Christian Europe and in Byzantium. But his works also reached beyond Christian audiences, finding favor with certain Jewish rabbis, for example, Hillel of Verona (c. 1220–c. 1295) and Judah Romano (c. 1280–c. 1325). These Italian Jews sought to interpret Moses Maimonides' *Guide for the Perplexed* without adopting the radical Averroistic Aristotelianism of some of their contemporaries.[13] As a decidedly anti-Averroist reader of Aristotle, Aquinas was an ally in opposing doctrines like the possibility of affirming two contradictory truths (one based on reason and one on faith), the necessity of eternal creation, the immortality of the soul in an unindividuated state, or the human intellect as a separate and unified faculty. To speak of "Jewish Thomism" in reference to these rabbis would be misleading at best, even less apt than the term "Byzantine Thomism." For these rabbis, Aquinas was not an unquestioned philosophical authority, much less a theological master. Rather than defending and advancing the whole scheme of Aquinas's views, these rabbis very selectively translated the Common Doctor into Hebrew,[14] finding in him a superb commentator on Aristotle and a rich source of arguments against Averroists.

This sweeping review of Aquinas's influence outside the university reveals that his works were reaching some unlikely audiences within a few decades of his death. Yet, in these diverse contexts the Common Doctor was known for different aspects of his thought, whether it be his moral theology, Trinitarian theology, or Aristotelian anti-Averroism. Hence, it is not obvious that any single thread of Aquinas's thinking drew all of his divergent readers to his lights. With this concession, however, the title of *Doctor Communis* takes on new significance: rather than picking out Aquinas's authoritative status within the schools, perhaps this shorthand more fittingly connotes his influence outside the European university. Although Scotists and Ockhamists did not share Aquinas in common with the Thomists, he was a common doctor in the sense that his doctrines were studied and applied beyond the walls of the schools, among the common people, among the Byzantines, and even among the rabbis.

Angelic Doctor: Aquinas and Some Thomists

In addition to his renown as the *Doctor Communis*, Aquinas acquired the title *Doctor Angelicus*, bringing to mind the unblemished character of his life and the seemingly superhuman penetration of his intellect. This denomination came into currency long after his passing,[15] marking more than respect but an outright adoration of Aquinas by his most ardent defenders and expounders, those who would form the Thomist school of theology in the medieval university. While these Thomists would debate for centuries with Scotists and also nominalists (to mention just two broad categories), the pluralism of medieval schools of thought would not prevent later generations from remembering Aquinas as the singular "Angel of the Schools". For this reason, it seems most appropriate to discuss his influence within the schools under this heading.

The remainder of this chapter will recount the highlights of the Thomist tradition, but in order to do this, it is first necessary to clarify, as much as possible, just what constitutes a Thomist. Rather than undertake the problematic task of defining Thomism by a set of common doctrines or beliefs,[16] this brief history will instead identify Thomists by their actions, considering Thomists to be those particular scholars who self-consciously devoted themselves to carrying on a theological and philosophical tradition inaugurated by Thomas Aquinas.[17] The aim of this much-abridged history will not be to catalogue the names and dates of prominent Thomists;[18] indeed, many noteworthy Thomists will be entirely ignored. Still, I hope to provide enough detail to show that, to the extent that there ever has been a single, orthodox Thomism, its vitality has depended upon the activity of the Thomists, who followed Aquinas by taking up the challenges of contemporary scholarship.

Aquinas's Fitful Rise to Authority: From Condemnation to Canonization

In spite of an active life filled with teaching, writing, and traveling, or perhaps because of these preoccupations, Aquinas had few staunch disciples when he came to his final rest at Fossanova. There is evidence that the University of Paris mourned his death, in the form of a letter of condolence from the faculty of arts to the General Chapter of Dominicans in 1274;[19] however, conspicuously lacking from the historical record is any sign of sorrow in the theology faculty, of which Aquinas had been a member. Still, if Paris was equivocal in its commemoration of Aquinas, Lyon surely had a unique and poignant sense of his absence, when the Second Council of Lyon commenced in May 1274. For, Aquinas had been expected to participate in these sessions, and had been en route from Italy when he caught ill.[20]

During the immediate aftermath of Aquinas's burial, little evidence survives to indicate what we might call an embryonic Thomist school. Yet, exactly three years post-mortem, unmistakable birth pangs signal a forthcoming theological movement. On March 7, 1277, Étienne Tempier, Bishop of Paris, issued to the arts faculty at the university a condemnation of 219 propositions, making plain to its members that "on pain of excommunication, they are prohibited to dogmatize, disseminate, or sustain in any way" (*dogmatizare, aut defendere seu sustinere quoquo modo*)[21] the articles comprised in the document. At Oxford, Archbishop Robert Kilwardby published a similar condemnation that same year. Ostensibly, these condemnations were just the latest installment in a decades-long controversy, especially rife at Paris, over the proper relationship between faith and reason, namely, the theology and arts faculties.

For, it had only been a few years prior in 1255 that the ban on reading and lecturing from Aristotle's natural philosophy (i.e., *Physica*, *De anima*, etc.) was lifted at Paris.[22] With access to so much new material, the scope envisioned for human reason unaided by Divine revelation began to exceed former limits; if theology was still the unquestioned superior, the extent of this superiority was now put into question. In this context, though it is difficult to imagine today, much of Aquinas's work, involving Aristotle so frequently and deferentially, was controversial and cutting edge, especially since he was a theologian. Doubtless, this goes a long way toward explaining why the arts faculty mourned Aquinas so openly, whereas the theologians were more reserved.

Against this background, the clear message of the Paris condemnation was to diminish any hubris rising from the arts: reason cannot gainsay faith; human capacities are constrained, and God transcends the limits of reason. Yet, besides this explicit intention, a close examination reveals that no less than sixteen of the censured propositions may be attributed to Aquinas,[23] though Tempier made no mention of his sources. However quietly, official Church authorities had cast a shadow upon the bold synthesis forged in Aquinas's writings.

If the condemnations fit all too well into a familiar narrative of ecclesiastic obscurantism, the Franciscan criticisms of Aquinas elicit comparisons to modern academic infighting. This second front of attacks upon the late theologian was less covert than the Bishops', and almost scathingly (or, from our current vantage point, comically) provocative. Englishman William de la Mare (d. c. 1285) composed the exemplar of these Franciscan anti-Thomist tracts in 1278—both summarizing and rebutting Aquinas on 118 of his conclusions—and published his polemic as a *Correctorium Fratris Thomae* (A Correctory of Brother Thomas). The patronizing, diminutive tone still rings through today. With good will already strained between the Franciscans and Dominicans, this *Correctorium* fomented a wave of counter-*Correctoria*: the pro-Thomist *Correctoria corruptorii Thomae* (Correctories of the corruptions of Thomas),[24] which argued that critics had not properly understood Aquinas—hence, they corrupted him—and which defended his Aristotelian philosophical bent as entirely faithful to Christian dogma.

As so often is the case, this conflict sharpened the attention of many scholars, with many lending a critical eye to Aquinas's writings. These critical treatments sometimes led to objections, and other times resulted in careful interpretations of

Aquinas. What is more, these early debates give the contemporary reader insight into the most contentious, and perhaps the most innovative, aspects of Aquinas's thought. The fraught metaphysical questions regarding the unity of substantial form within each singular being, designated matter as the principle of individuation within a species, and the real distinction in creatures between the *esse* and *essentia*, these all became focused topics of disputation. Far from inconsequential, defending Aquinas on these articles could be dangerous. One early Dominican Thomist in England, Richard [Clapwell] Knapwell (fl. 1284–1286) died in exile after circulating arguments in favor of the unity of substantial form.[25]

Despite ecclesiastic and scholastic opponents, no other contemporary Thomists seem to have met such a dire end as Knapwell. For instance, his confrère Thomas Sutton[26] (c. 1250–1315) produced extensive works that defended Aquinas and responded to influential critics, one of whom was the famous Oxford Franciscan, John Duns Scotus[27] (c. 1266–1308). Indeed, for every powerful and vocal anti-Thomist—such as Henry of Ghent[28] (d. 1293) or Durandus of St. Pourçain[29] (c. 1275–1334)—there appeared to be an equally able pro-Thomist—like Hervaeus [Harvey] Natalis[30] (c. 1250–1323) or Nicolai Medensis (fl. 1325–1330), usually called "Durandellus" because of his opposition to Durandus of St. Pourçain.[31]

One upshot of these earliest defenses was a growing consensus that Aquinas's interpretations of Aristotle needed to be distinguished from those of the Latin Averroists, something that the initial condemnations seemed to overlook. Once Aquinas was no longer under suspicion of being Averroist, his readings of Aristotle would prove to be formidable for opponents, both for their cogency and for their compatibility with Christian doctrine. As a result, theologians of all persuasions would begin engaging with Aristotle rather than ignoring him. Although Aristotle may have gained ascendancy in the European university without the patronage of the Thomist school, Aquinas's particular blend of Christian faith and pagan understanding was a luminous example that the human mind could attain worldly knowledge without contradicting supernatural revelation.

It would be wrong to give the impression that Aquinas's influence in the schools was only, or even primarily, at the intersection between theology and philosophy. History records that "Aquinas the philosopher" was certainly an object of controversy, but he did not draw attention only for going beyond (or beneath) his purview, as it were, dabbling in philosophy when his vocation was theology. "Aquinas the theologian" also drew criticism for some of his distinctive theological claims. For example, at a time when Popes were consolidating power, John (Quidort) of Paris[32] (c. 1255–1306) would discover in Aquinas the basis for distinct (though not necessarily separate) papal and regal dominion within society.[33] Whereas this represents a somewhat chastened ecclesiology, Aquinas supplemented this concession to secular rule with a radically uncompromising Christology, Christ being the one from whom all authority derives and to whom all allegiance is due. In fact, Thomists—notably Hervaeus Natalis and John of Naples[34] (d. 1331)—would reserve for Christ such a preeminence that they would even reject the Scotist position on the immaculate conception of Mary.[35]

With such avid supporters, there was little chance that Aquinas would be consigned to obscurity. However, he may have continued as just one scholastic theologian among many, if it were not for some major Thomist victories in the first decades of the fourteenth century. First, in a blow to supporters of the plurality of substantial forms, the Council of Vienne (1311) confirmed that psychological unity was more compatible with the doctrines of Christian faith than rival formulations. In addition to this triumph of Aquinas's work, the Church went on to validate his person and life, canonizing him as a saint in 1323. While this did not remove St. Thomas' writings from scrutiny,[36] his canonization seems to have lent his teaching a newfound weight of authority, especially within the Dominican order. Prior to 1323, Thomists fought against suspicions of heterodoxy, often from a position of rhetorical weakness. A sampling of texts from after 1323 illustrates a significant shift. For example, in Durandellus's *Evidentiae contra Durandum*,[37] one finds a calm enumeration of arguments in favor of Aquinas, conspicuously lacking a defensive tone. Even at Cologne, where Albert the Great held greater sway than Aquinas, Henry of Lübeck (d. 1336) would record that his thinking aspired to follow "the venerable Blessed Thomas Aquinas."[38]

Just as Thomists were achieving a semblance of security, Aquinas having attained an authoritative status by the mid-fourteenth century, another scholastic opponent began to emerge with force: English Franciscan William Ockham[39] (c. 1285–1349), next to Scotus and Aquinas the most reputed scholastic of the High Middle Ages, and perhaps the most original and iconoclastic figure, bar none. Ockham's outspoken nominalist semantics and logic, with its concomitantly parsimonious ontology, would clear a path for a drastically new approach to teaching and discussing topics in metaphysics, philosophical psychology, and natural philosophy in general. This *via moderna*, pitting itself against the putatively abstruse and onerous *via antiqua*, would threaten to do worse than refute the intricacies of Aquinas's thinking; it would move to make him irrelevant. Aside from the nominalist challenge, the decline of this first phase of Thomists is due to the bubonic plague that decimated Europe around 1348–1350. With the social and political fabric of life in tatters, the universities in Europe were likewise worn thin, being short on students and qualified faculty.

Thomistic Renaissance: From Plague to Prominence

Europe recovered slowly from the plague, and the Great Western Schism (1378–1417) only enhanced the instability in all facets of life during this time. After the Black Death of the plague, this second period, spanning the fifteenth century, can be fittingly described as a Thomist renaissance. Building on the authority won for Aquinas during the early polemics, fifteenth-century Thomists would be responsible for putting the *Summa theologiae* into some universities' curricula. Moreover, without the pressure to defend Aquinas from pariah status, this period sees Thomists devoting volumes to more detailed expositions. Since the purpose of these writings was not only to counteract misinterpretations, the Thomist literature of this period rewards its readers with fruitful developments upon Aquinas's doctrines.

One of the first to sow the seeds for this season of new life among the Thomists was the rather unlikely Henry of Gorkum[40] (c. 1386–1431). Not a Dominican, but a secular priest from what is now Gorinchem, in the Netherlands, Henry would earn the title *Thomistarum Coloniensium monarcha* (Monarch of the Thomists at Cologne). He penned treatises on predestination and just war, and even finished a compendium on the *Summa theologiae*, which was probably the first commentary on Aquinas's magnum opus. However, this seems to have been largely overlooked by his contemporaries. Indeed, Henry's impact as a scholar seems to have derived less from his writing and more from his teaching. While on the faculty of the University of Cologne, Henry dispensed with the tradition of lecturing from Peter Lombard's *Sentences*, placing Aquinas's *Summa theologiae* on his lectern instead.[41]

The implications of this shift were immediate and enduring. Whereas Cologne had always been known as a stronghold of Albertist (i.e., Albert the Great's) disciples, the fifteenth century saw many active Thomists emerge from Cologne. For instance, one student at Cologne during Henry's tenure was none other than Denis the Carthusian[42] (c. 1403–1471), an encyclopedic writer with an unmistakable debt to Aquinas. Even toward the end of the fifteenth century, Thomists at Cologne fostered a prolonged debate with the Albertist faculty, eliciting a finely nuanced discussion in the philosophy of mind.[43]

Yet, perhaps the most important Thomist of this period hailed from the University of Paris. Known as the *Princeps Thomistarum* (Prince of the Thomists), John Capreolus (c. 1380–1444) composed his *Defensiones theologiae divi Thomae Aquinatis* (Defenses of the Theology of Thomas Aquinas),[44] a commentary on the *Summa theologiae* that aspired to elucidate Aquinas's doctrines and refute his critics. His final work was so comprehensive and successful that it would invite imitators, thus founding the genre of direct commentaries on Aquinas's major works. This commentary, a high-water mark of the Thomist renaissance, is certainly a far cry from the low point when bishops were condemning Aquinas's conclusions.

Yet, not every aspect of this second period is worth celebrating. With the aid of hindsight, one can discern the first signs of decay in Scholasticism during this period, even as these Thomists were enjoying a relative heyday. In short, scholastic professors, and Thomists among them, seemed drawn to insularity. With the fall of Constantinople and the influx of Byzantine Christians, many Europeans were faced with uncertainty, as well as new ideas. Adding to this furor, Gutenberg's press—in operation at mid-century—was making more information accessible to the average European, and allowing for more rapid sharing of ideas. Perhaps we can overlook the fact that scholastic professors missed an opportunity to adapt their methodologies to this new technology.[45] But, what deserves censure is that, rather than embrace or even inquire into any contemporary alternatives, the Thomists of this era seemed singularly interested in upholding their master. To wit, perusing Capreolus's commentary, one can discover refutations of Henry of Ghent, John

Duns Scotus, Durandus of St. Pourçain, William Ockham, but no mention of any living critics. Similarly, though the Thomists at Cologne interacted with their Albertist colleagues, neither of these parties (whose differences were remarkably slight) went outside their narrow circle to grapple with the burgeoning ideas beyond the schools. The doctrines of the Angelic Doctor may have survived among the Thomists, but his spirit of conquest, of reining in truth under the standard of faith, seemed long forgotten.[46]

Thus, even as Aquinas gathered an increasing number to his following during the fifteenth century, these Thomists remained limited to a specialized class of university scholars. In a review of medieval libraries, Jocelyn Hillgarth confirms this narrow demographic of Thomists, inasmuch as one could hardly be considered a Thomist without access to some of his works:

> Aquinas appealed, as we have seen, to many friars, monks, university teachers, and students, to relatively few high ecclesiastics, and, among the laity, to some jurists and doctors. Popes and princes might not read him themselves but, by 1500 at least, considered him a necessary part of a great library. He did not, it seems, appeal to the general intelligent lay person who had not been educated in a university. . . . Nobles or rich bourgeois could have acquired the works of Aquinas but they were not interested in doing so.[47]

Thomists Enter the Baroque: From Eminence to Decadence

On my assessment, the Thomist renaissance displayed a dual nature: Thomists were flourishing internally but, viewed from the outside, they were gradually becoming ossified. This trend continued through this third period of Thomists, though the authority of Aquinas would reach a new pinnacle. Arguably, at the utmost peak of his influence, Aquinas would be pivotal in the Catholic counterreformation, with his doctrines being decisive at the Council of Trent (1545–1563) in defining Rome's responses to Protestant "heresies." Notwithstanding Aquinas's active and often authoritative role in shaping Catholic thought during this period, Thomists during the third period—in its entirety, encompassing the years 1500 to 1650—were preoccupied with problems that were meaningful to only a select few, even during their own time. For this reason, I find it instructive to juxtapose the eminence of these Thomists within Catholic Europe with the decadence manifested by their relative seclusion from concerns in the wider culture.

Continuing the trends among Thomists in the fifteenth century, this period would reap the harvests of the renaissance, as it were. One superbly gifted lecturer, Peter Crockaert[48] (d. 1514) would make a mid-life conversion from Ockhamist to Thomist, and subsequently, his students would read the *Summa theologiae* as their textbook at the University of Paris. Crockaert would effectively export this practice to Spain, when his pupil, Francisco de Vitoria[49] (1492/93–1546), returned to his native country and obtained the principle chair in theology at Salamanca in 1526.

Aside from the impact of using Aquinas's work as a textbook, Vitoria made some significant contributions with his own applications of Aquinas's moral and legal doctrines to the political questions of his day. Vitoria published few works during his own lifetime, but his lectures were immensely popular and he also had the ear of Emperor Charles V. During a time when European rulers were vying with each other and with papal power, as well as beginning to colonize the newly discovered Americas, Vitoria expounded Thomistic theories of national sovereignty, the laws of peace and war, and even international law.[50] Vitoria's emphasis on natural rights and on political authority as rightly limited by universal norms—though not entirely original—certainly deserved attention. Indeed, his published lectures would become a touchstone for much subsequent political thinking. For instance, in part through Vitoria's mediation, Thomist doctrines would inform aspects of Hugo Grotius's seminal treatise of 1625, *De jure belli ac pacis* (The Law of War and Peace), with the Dutch scholar often citing Aquinas directly.[51]

In another development of earlier trends, the third period of Thomists boasts the two paradigmatic commentaries on Aquinas's major works, both devised by Italians. Thomas de Vio Cajetan[52] (1469–1534) took up the *Summa theologiae*, and the resulting volumes remain to this day as the standard commentary on Aquinas's masterpiece, published along with the *Summa theologiae* in the Leonine edition. Cajetan's compatriot, Francesco Sylvester of Ferrara (1474–1528), followed suit by commenting on Aquinas's *Summa contra Gentiles*. Of these two, there is no question that Cajetan produced a more remarkable imprint in his own lifetime and in the centuries to follow.

Besides the *Summa theologiae* commentary, Cajetan penned a perspicuous defense of Aquinas's metaphysics in the form of an exposition of the *De ente et essentia*. He also composed the noteworthy treatise *De nominum analogia* (On the Analogy of Names), which synthesizes Aquinas's disparate remarks regarding analogy. The result goes beyond a mere summary of Aquinas and is perhaps best regarded as an original theory of analogy in its own right, though certainly inspired by Thomistic theses.[53] As influential as Cajetan was through his writing, he earned an even greater reputation for his skills in debate. Most famously, after being made cardinal in 1517, Pope Leo X sent Cajetan to the Diet of Augsburg with the charge of examining the teachings of Martin Luther. Although Cajetan would ultimately play a role in excommunicating Luther, the cardinal was impressed by the reformer, to whom he was willing to make certain concessions. Perhaps because of this encounter with Luther, Cajetan primarily devoted the latter part of his career to biblical exegesis, as opposed to his previous work in more speculative theology.

During this period when the proponents of Aquinas reached the height of their influence, changes in the broader culture of Europe would signal the demise of Scholasticism, namely, the rise of humanism and the advent of the Reformation. Interestingly, Cajetan seemed aware of these important developments, and he worked to preserve the Thomistic tradition while he opened himself to insights from new perspectives. Nevertheless, these two major movements in the sixteenth century would begin to undermine the authority of Aquinas.

First, the humanist movement of the early sixteenth century, with its devotion to ancient Greco-Roman achievements in the arts and rhetoric, would foster a corresponding disdain for medieval modes of education and argumentation.[54] Humanists rejected not only the form of scholastic thought, but often much of its content. Marius Nizolius of Modena (1498–1575), author of *Contra pseudophilosophos*, would recommend that the art of rhetoric replace the pseudo-sciences of dialectic (logic) and metaphysics.[55] Those humanists who did not contemn Aristotle frequently favored a revival of the ancient philosopher himself, eschewing the subtleties of the scholastic Aristotelians.[56]

Second, and most obviously, the Protestant Reformation would instigate a general upheaval in previous authorities, all but confining Aquinas's influence to Catholic countries by the seventeenth century.[57] Thomists thrived especially in the Iberian Peninsula, as this region would avoid the ravages of the Thirty Years War (1618–1648). Yet, even during the Council of Trent (1545–1563), well-poised Thomists would bring about significant triumphs for Aquinas's theological doctrines, with certain key definitions from the Council following Aquinas closely. To mention perhaps one of the most bitterly contested between Catholics and Protestants, the Council's decree on the doctrine of justification, its preconditions and its causes, is nearly a paraphrase of certain passages in the *Summa theologiae*.[58]

Since this third period is rife with important Thomists, it is simply impossible to give more exhaustive treatment of their disputes and contributions.[59] What follows is only a glimpse of prolific activity in this Baroque phase. Besides the long-standing tradition of Dominican and Carmelite Thomists, St Ignatius of Loyola added to the ranks of the Thomists in the mid-sixteenth century, when he singled out Aquinas as the preferred author for instructing the newly founded Society of Jesus in "scholastic doctrine."[60] A sort of Thomist rivalry between Dominicans and the Jesuits would goad each to outdo the others. Among the Jesuits, Luis de Molina[61] (1535–1600), Francisco Suárez[62] (1548–1617), and Gabriel Vasquez[63] (1549–1604) would stand out, and often stand against, Dominicans like Bartholomew of Medina (1527–1581) and Dominic Báñez[64] (1528–1604). Most notably, Medina initiated the probabilist moral theory based on a reading of Aquinas's *Summa theologiae*, I-II q.19 a.5, according to which people can legitimately follow a moral maxim shown to be merely probable, even if they know of a more probable one. With regard to theological innovation, Molina would propose middle knowledge, God's foreknowledge of unrealized future contingents, as a resolution to the theological problem of reconciling efficacious grace with human free will. In the area of metaphysical speculation, Báñez attended to Aquinas's thoughts regarding *esse*, elucidating the importance in holding that *esse* "signifies the actuality of every form commonly."[65] Finally, flourishing at the close of this period, the Portuguese Dominican John (Poinsot) of St. Thomas[66] (1589–1644) serves as a suitable last word. His arguments against Jesuit Thomists, particularly Suárez, are interesting from the standpoint of the history of philosophy. For, one founder of modern philosophy, René Descartes, being educated by Jesuits, had read Suárez but not Poinsot. For this reason, the latter's major contributions, a *Cursus philosophicus Thomisticus* (published in installments from 1631 to 1635) and a *Cursus theologicus*, are worth attention as a sort of missing link between the late scholastic and early modern eras.[67]

Although the accomplishments of Thomists during this period endure as the classic expressions of the Thomist school, they failed to answer the challenges by humanists, remained foreign to Protestant intellectual formation, and seemed totally ignorant of the advances in the new science. When Francis Bacon, in his 1623 treatise *De augmentis scientiarum* (On the Advancement of Learning), subjected scholastic thinkers to ridicule,[68] the absence of a Thomist rebuttal spoke volumes. By the mid-seventeenth century, Aquinas suffered three counts against him, each a considerable limit upon the reach of his influence: (1) he was Scholastic in method and language; (2) his religious affiliation was decidedly Catholic; (3) his authority in philosophy was Aristotle, and an Aristotle often read in conjunction with Muslim commentators.

Late Thomists: The Death of Thomistic Traditionalism and the Birth of the Neo-Thomists

What was previously an active tradition of teaching, discussing, and writing on the doctrines of Aquinas became rigid and traditionalist as the modern era captured Europe's minds. The tendency toward insularity, the detachment from historical developments in arts and sciences, finally overcame the Thomists in this fourth and final period. Although there are examples of Thomist scholars throughout the eighteenth century, their intellectual efforts would remain cloistered in Catholic seminaries. Even within the deferential context of the seminary, historian Étienne Gilson has suggested that Catholic theological instruction would become infiltrated by modern metaphysical assumptions (i.e., those of Leibniz and, later, Wolff), currents that would subvert the most profound insights of Aquinas's doctrines.[69] The effect of all these malignant forces, as James Weisheipl so bluntly puts it, was that "by the middle of the 18th century the Thomistic school was dead."[70] Hence, Aquinas's influence waned during this period, whether we look to his friends or his foes. Within Catholic circles, Aquinas was a revered but distant figure; among Enlightenment thinkers, he was more often ignored or dismissed outright. Somewhat paradoxically, even among the emergent Neo-Thomists around the turn of the twentieth century, which marks the central focus of activity in this stage of the history, efforts to revive the study of Aquinas would unwittingly play a role in furthering the demise of his influence.

If one turns to the groundbreaking philosophers at the outset of this period, both among rationalists and empiricists, already one can barely discover any connection to Aquinas. Descartes (1596–1650) and Leibniz (1646–1716), to be sure, seemed bound to pay their respects to Aquinas, not willing to declare themselves against such an authority. But their deference to Aquinas amounts to so much lip service; their philosophical positions depend very little upon Aquinas, and often run counter to his teachings. Despite Descartes's protests that the presuppositions of his ontological argument "do not differ from the Angelic Doctor in any respect," Descartes quite tellingly goes on to urge that "existence *belongs to* [God's] true and immutable nature."[71] In the case of Leibniz, his formulation of God as a necessary being should not be confused with Aquinas's claims in the *Tertia Via*. For, Leibniz was dealing with *logical* necessity, whereas Aquinas relied on no such notion in his arguments for the truth of "*Deus est*." Quite the contrary, Aquinas held that logic alone could definitely not solve the question of God's existence.[72]

Outside of these rationalist contexts, Aquinas was no longer held in esteem, even nominally. In his *Leviathan*, Hobbes (1588–1679) would mention Aquinas only to spurn the value of appeals to authority, as long as the source is a mere human being.[73] In characteristic modern fashion, Locke (1632–1704), in his *Essay*, would dismiss the insights of the entire scholastic age, whose contributions he caricatures rather than criticizes.[74] By the time of Hume (1711–1776), British empiricism—and modern philosophy as a whole—was all but a self-contained conversation, hardly concerned to engage seriously with medieval masters such as Aquinas, even for the sake of ridicule.

By the late-nineteenth century, the Catholic Church turned to its Angelic Doctor in order to remedy the theological challenges of the day, all the more dire against a background of dependence on modern philosophy. Thus, in 1879 the Papal encyclical *Aeterni Patris* encouraged the "restoration of Christian philosophy" in the vein of the scholastic doctors, among whom "the chief and master of all towers [was] Thomas Aquinas."[75] The ensuing Neo-Thomist revival among Catholics would receive official support from the Vatican. After a 1914 letter from Pope Pius X (*Doctoris Angelici*), the Sacred Congregation of Studies determined twenty-four Thomistic theses for use in seminaries.[76] Years later, Pius XI clarified (in *Studiorum Ducem* of 1923) that the doctrines of Aquinas were not merely suggestive hypotheses: "if we are to avoid the errors which are the source and fountain-head of all the miseries of our time, the teaching of Aquinas must be adhered to more religiously than ever."[77]

At a first glance, the aim of restoring Christian philosophy with Aquinas as the guiding luminary may appear a success. These years gave rise to numerous Thomists. Beyond their prolific writing on Aquinas and other medieval theologians, all of these Thomists would assist later generations to appreciate the context and complexity of the scholastic period by founding medieval institutes and establishing journals dedicated to medieval studies.[78] However, the single label "Thomist" masks the diversity among these disciples of Aquinas. To better appreciate this diversity, let us consider some of the general categories into which they fall.

Some, known as Aristotelian Thomists (e.g., James Weisheipl[79] [1923–1985]), stressed Aquinas's dependence upon Aristotle for his philosophical project, seemingly avoiding the problems of modernity by recourse to a prior consensus. Others, like the transcendental Thomists[80] (e.g., Joseph Maréchal[81] [1878–1944], Karl Rahner[82] [1904–1984], and Bernard Lonergan[83] [1904–1984]), sought to preserve the basic elements of Kantian philosophy alongside the major tenets of Aquinas. Unlike Aristotelian Thomists, the transcendental Thomists were wary of rejecting all modern philosophy on the basis of premodern thought. Surely, they might contend, naïve realism can no longer be a viable option after the skeptical arguments of Descartes and Hume. Hence, transcendental Thomists would deny a purely passive cognitive power in favor of a more active construal of the mind's relation to the world.[84]

Finally, there were those who would emphasize Aquinas's originality, at least in his characterization of the *actus essendi*. These were the existential Thomists (e.g., Jacques Maritain[85] [1882–1973] and Étienne Gilson[86] [1884–1978]), raised in the school of Bergson and drawn to Aquinas's metaphysics of *esse*. For them, Aquinas had helpfully gone further than Aristotle, positing *esse* as a perfection created by God alone and irreducible to forms.

Besides the interminable issue of how to interpret Aquinas, these more recent Thomists often varied widely on which of Aquinas's doctrines were most important and which might be overlooked as contingent upon his medieval perspective. Of course, another question often debated was the extent to which Aquinas may be compatible with other philosophical systems. Interestingly, the fault lines among Neo-Thomists lay in the fields of metaphysics and philosophy of mind, often centering around Aquinas's thoughts about *esse*, essence, and intentionality. Modern preoccupations were often in the foreground, involving dichotomies like realism and idealism, or direct realism versus representationalism. John Knasas[87] and Fergus Kerr[88] provide some excellent studies of the twentieth-century Neo-Thomists and help to navigate the intricacies of their debates, as well as to assess their contributions.

Without denying the benefits afforded by the Neo-Thomist movement—perhaps especially in sharpening the critique of modern philosophy among Catholic intellectuals—there is an important sense in which the papal directives backfired. For one thing, attention to Aquinas's own distinction between sacred doctrine (believed on faith) and scientific understanding (known by rational demonstration) leaves one to wonder what would constitute a *Christian* philosophy. Certainly much of what is philosophical in the work of the Aquinas derives from pagan or at least non-Christian thinking. Moreover, if philosophy differs from positive or revealed theology inasmuch as the former involves an exploration of what the human mind can know by reasoning without appeals to the supernatural (certainly a plausible reading of *ST* I q.1 a.5 ad 2), then presumably the truths attainable in such a pursuit would be essentially common to all humans, not unique to some particular community of the faithful.

Aside from the inherent tension between Aquinas's own teaching and the aims of developing a Christian philosophy, the Neo-Thomists too often labored under the seeming contradiction that they were to forge a *philosophy* from a preestablished set of doctrines. Again, if *religious* adherence to doctrines implies that belief is not based on reasons, which seems a plausible interpretation of this phrase, then the assent proper to a *philosophy* would seem to require, at the very least, an initially indifferent attitude. Hence, in a way, the papal sponsorship of Neo-Thomists contravened their concerted endeavors to enliven the philosophical insights of Aquinas, turning the vital cord of his delicate synthesis into a sort of noose.[89]

The Second Vatican Council (1962–1965) marked a transition, one might even call it an impasse, for the Neo-Thomists. Clearly, after this period the Church ceased to prop up a Christian philosophy by enforcing any kind of rigid Thomist "orthodoxy." Without institutional support, Neo-Thomists have been forced to survive on their own merits, and they have not dropped out of existence. Nevertheless, current interest in Aquinas is not exclusively or even primarily based on the efforts of Neo-Thomists. Instead, a growing number of scholars today find that Aquinas is worth reading and understanding in his own right, apart from any ulterior religious motivation to circumvent modern philosophy. For, more and more now recognize that there are independent, even philosophical (as opposed to religious) reasons to consider many modern assumptions about the mind, about human action, and about human nature in general to be mistaken or confused. For example, in the English-speaking world, some disciples of Wittgenstein, notably Peter Geach and Anthony Kenny, have learned to critique modernity from Wittgenstein and have discovered an alternate way of thinking in Aquinas.[90] Kenny has gone on the record with his opinion that Aquinas is "one of the dozen greatest philosophers of the western world."[91]

This recent interest, which often extends to many medieval thinkers, means that current scholarship in Aquinas characteristically exhibits a desire to judge his teaching on its own merits, and not based on preconceived doctrines of faith nor on how well he measures up to contemporary intuitions. As scholars better understand Aquinas within his own historical context, they are also increasingly able to apply his theories to contemporary philosophical problems. While this approach has earned Aquinas high esteem among certain thinkers today, many of these no longer would consider themselves to be Thomists. Their goal is not to defend Aquinas at all costs or to hold him aloft as some sort of angelic messenger of Truth. Instead, perhaps it is even more impressive that present-day scholars such as those found in this volume, though they often subject his teaching to rigorous criticism, still find much to commend in Aquinas after more than seven hundred years.

NOTES

1. *Summa theologiae* I q.42 a.1 ad 1.

2. This is reported by Aidan Nichols in *Discovering Aquinas* (Grand Rapids, Mich.: Eerdmans, 2003), 130.

3. Leonard Boyle, "The *Summa Confessorum* of John of Freiburg," in *Facing History: A Different Thomas Aquinas* (Louvain: La Neuve, 2000), 37–64.

4. Eugenio Garin, *History of Italian Philosophy*, tran. Giorgio A. Pinton, vol. 1 (Amsterdam: Rodopi, 2008), 86.

5. The introductions and notes to Esolen's translation of the *Commedia* draw out these connections well. See Dante, *Inferno*, *Purgatory*, and *Paradise*, tran. Anthony Esolen (New York: Random House Publishing Group, 2004).

6. Romanus Cessario, O.P., *A Short History of Thomism* (Washington, D.C.: Catholic University of America Press, 2003), 57.

7. The Eastern Church denies that the Holy Spirit proceeds from the Father *and the Son*, and never consented to its presence in the Nicene symbol. Aquinas's exposition of the Apostle's Creed does not evade this controversy, since he does include a very succinct defense of the Nicene inclusion.

8. Charles L. Stinger, *Humanism and the Church Fathers: Ambrogio Traversari (1386–1439) and Christian Antiquity in the Italian Renaissance* (Albany, N.Y.: SUNY Press, 1977), 90.

9. Cf. op. cit.: Lending further support to this, Stinger reports that Planudes also translated Augustine's *De Trinitate*.

10. Steven Runciman, *The Last Byzantine Renaissance* (Cambridge: Cambridge University Press, 1970), 80.

11. J. Gill, "Gennadius II Scholarius, Patriarch of Constantinople," *New Catholic Encyclopedia*, 2d ed., vol. 6 (Detroit: Gale, 2003), 136–37.

12. Ibid.

13. Seymour Feldman, "Maimonides—A Guide for Posterity," in Kenneth Seeskin, ed., *The Cambridge Companion to Maimonides* (Cambridge: Cambridge University Press, 2005), 332–35.

14. Cf. Jean-Pierre Torrell, *Saint Thomas Aquinas*, vol. 1, *The Person and His Work*, tran. Robert Royal (Washington, D.C.: Catholic University of America Press, 1996), 316. Among the texts translated into Hebrew, Torrell mentions the first part of the *De unitate intellectus*, extracts from the *Summa theologiae*, and the *Super de causis*.

15. Cf. Nichols, *Discovering Aquinas*, 130.

16. To be sure, there are certain doctrines almost ubiquitous among Thomists (here one might mention the real distinction in creatures between *esse* and *essentia*), so that it is not nonsense to speak of Thomism. For an example of a definition of Thomism based on shared beliefs, see J. A. Weisheipl, "Thomism," *New Catholic Encyclopedia*, 2d ed., vol. 14 (Detroit: Gale, 2003), 40–52. Cessario's *Short History of Thomism* follows Weisheipl's formulation.

17. Here, I am taking my cue from Freddoso in his review of Cessario, accessed online at: <http://www.nd.edu/~afreddos/pubs.htm>.

18. Such a catalogue already exists. Cf. L. A. Kennedy, *A Catalogue of Thomists, 1270–1900* (Notre Dame, Ind.: University of Notre Dame Press, 1987).

19. Fergus Kerr, *After Aquinas: Versions of Thomism* (Oxford: Blackwell Publishing, 2002), 10.

20. His polemic tract *Contra errores Graecorum* (Against the Errors of the Greeks) served in his stead, but one can only imagine that Aquinas in person would have argued his case more persuasively.

21. As quoted by Hans Thijssen, "Condemnation of 1277," *The Stanford Encyclopedia of Philosophy* (Fall 2008 edition), ed. Edward N. Zalta, accessed online at: <http://plato.stanford.edu/archives/fall2008/entries/condemnation/>.

22. For a helpful guide to these controversies, see Edward Grant, *The Foundations of Modern Science in the Middle Ages: Their Religious, Institutional, and Intellectual Contexts* (Cambridge: Cambridge University Press, 1996), 70–85.

23. A list of these can be found in Gyula Klima, with Fritz Allhoff and Anand Jayprakash Vaidya, eds., *Medieval Philosophy: Essential Readings with Commentary* (Oxford: Blackwell Publishing, 2007), 180–89.

24. Five pro-Thomist correctories remain to this day: D. A. Callus, "Correctoria," *New Catholic Encyclopedia*, 2d ed., vol. 4 (Detroit: Gale, 2003), 274–78.

25. Simon Tugwell, *Albert & Thomas* (Mahwah, N.J.: Paulist Press, 1988), 241.

26. J. J. Przezdziecki, "Thomas of Sutton," *New Catholic Encyclopedia*, 2d ed., vol. 14 (Detroit: Gale, 2003), 37.

27. Allan Wolter, "Duns Scotus, John (c. 1266–1308)," *Encyclopedia of Philosophy*, ed. Donald Borchert, 2d ed., vol. 3 (Detroit: Macmillan Reference USA, 2006), 133–45.

28. Eugene Rairweather, "Henry of Ghent (??–1293)," *Encyclopedia of Philosophy*, ed. Donald Borchert, 2d ed., vol. 4 (Detroit: Macmillan Reference USA, 2006), 312–15.

29. James Weisheipl, "Durandus of Saint-Pourçain (c. 1275–1334)," *Encyclopedia of Philosophy*, ed. Donald Borchert, 2d ed., vol. 3 (Detroit: Macmillan Reference USA, 2006), 148–49.

30. Roland Teske, "Hervaeus Natalis (c. 1250–323)," *Encyclopedia of Philosophy*, ed. Donald Borchert, 2d ed., vol. 4 (Detroit: Macmillan Reference USA, 2006), 343–44.

31. Isabel Iribarren, *Durandus of St Pourcain: A Dominican Theologian in the Shadow of Aquinas* (Oxford: Oxford University Press, 2005). Two recent studies of Durandellus are worth attention: Gilles Emery, "La Théologie trinitaire des *Evidentiae contra Durandum* de Durandellus," *Revue Thomiste* 97:1 (1997): 173–218; M. Lanczowski and R. Wittwer, "Les *Evidentiae contra Durandum* de Durandellus," *Revue Thomiste* 97:1 (1997): 143–56.

32. James Weisheipl, "John of Paris (c. 1255–1306)," *Encyclopedia of Philosophy*, ed. Donald Borchert, 2d ed., vol. 4 (Detroit: Macmillan Reference USA, 2006), 842.

33. Argued in John's *De Potestate Regia et Papali* (On royal and papal power) of 1302. See John of Paris, *On Royal and Papal Power: A Translation, with Introduction, of De potestate Regia et Papali of John of Paris*, tran. Arthur P. Monahan (New York: Columbia University Press, 1974); or John of Paris, *On Royal and Papal Power*, tran. J. A. Watt (Toronto: Pontifical Institute of Mediaeval Studies, 2002).

34. Edward Bouverie Pusey, *First Letter to the Very Rev. J. H. Newman* (London: Rivingtons, 1869).

35. Scotus defended the immaculate conception in his *Lectura in III Sent.*, dist.3, q.1.

36. Aquinas would not be declared officially a "Doctor of the Church" until 1567, under Pope Pius V.

37. According to Iribarren, a specialist on Durandus of St. Pourçain, this exhibits the authoritative status of Thomism within the Dominican order by 1325, when he penned the *Evidentiae contra Durandum*, 2 vols., ed. P. T. Stella, critical edition prepared by M. Lanczkowski and R. Imbach, *Corpus Philosophorum Medii Aevi: Opera Philosophica Mediae Aetatis Selecta* (Tübingen and Basle: A. Francke Verlag, 2003).

38. Martin Grabmann, *Mittelalterliches Geistesleben: Abhandlung zur Geschichte der Scholastik und Mystic*, vol. 1 (Munich: Max Hueber, 1926), 421.

39. Ernest Moody, "William of Ockham (c. 1285–1349)," *Encyclopedia of Philosophy*, ed. Donald Borchert, 2d ed., vol. 9 (Detroit: Macmillan Reference USA, 2006), 770–85.

40. C. R. Meyer, "Henry of Gorkum," *New Catholic Encyclopedia*, 2d ed., vol. 6 (Detroit: Gale, 2003), 753.

41. M. Grabmann, *Mittelalterliches Geistesleben, Abhandlungen zur Geschichte der Scholastik und Mystik*, vol. 2, (München, 1936), 443; vol. 3 (1956), 412. Cf. Thomas Franklin O'Meara, *Thomas Aquinas Theologian* (Notre Dame, Ind.: University of Notre Dame Press, 1997), 158. Cf. also, Paul van Geest, Harm Goris, and Carlo Leget, eds., *Aquinas as Authority: A Collection of Studies Presented at the Second Conference of the Thomas Insituut te Utrecht, December 14–16, 2000* (Leuven, Belgium: Peeters Publishers, 2002), 31.

42. a.k.a. Denys van Leeuwen, of Rijkel/Ryckel, Belgium. For more, see B. Du Moustier, "Denis the Carthusian," *New Catholic Encyclopedia*, 2d ed., vol. 4. (Detroit: Gale, 2003), 661–62. For primary sources: "Doctoris ecstatici Dionysii Cartusiani," *Opera Omnia*, 42 vols. (Montreuilsur-Mer: Tournai Parkminster, 1896–1913, 1935). This is a noncritical, slightly corrected reissue of the sixteenth-century Cologne edition. Also, see Kent Emery, *Dionysii Cartusiensis Opera selecta: prolegomena Bibliotheca manuscripta/auctore Kent Emery Jr* (Turnholti [Turnhout, Belgium]: Typographi Brepols, 1991). For secondary sources: Kent Emery, "Twofold Wisdom and Contemplation in Denys of Ryckel (Dionysius Cartusiensis, 1402–71)," *Journal of Medieval and Renaissance Studies*, 18 (1988): 99–134; David C. Steinmetz, *Luther in Context* (Bloomington, Ind.: Indiana University Press, 1986); Anselme Stoelen, "Denys the Carthusian," in James Walsh, ed., *Spirituality through the Centuries* (New York: Kenedy & Sons, 1964), 220–32.

43. For details, see Leen Spruit, *Species Intelligibilis*, vol. 1, *Classical Roots and Medieval Discussions* (Leiden: E. J. Brill, 1994), 360–68.

44. John Capreolus, *Defensiones Theologiae divi Thomae Aquinatis* (Turonibus: Sumptibus Alfred Cattier, 1900).

45. The format of lectures and disputations makes sense in an oral culture, where books are not available to all students and lengthy, repetitive arguments offer the surest means to cover all aspects of a question. Print media, of course, allow for perfect recall without the need for memorization by repetition.

46. I should acknowledge one glaring exception to the insularity of this period: Christopher Columbus's protector, Diego de Deza, was a Dominican Thomist, and according to the renowned explorer in a letter dated December 21, 1504, "It is he [Diego de Deza] who was the cause of their Majesties' possessing the Indies." One Thomist, namely, de Deza, had a vital role in Columbus's voyage across the Atlantic, though this can hardly be considered a direct result of Aquinas's influence. Quote taken from *The Catholic Historical Review*, vol. 1 (Washington, D.C.: Catholic University of America Press, 1915), 105. Also, cf. P. Mandonnet, *Les Dominicains et la découverte de l'Amérique* (Paris: P. Lethielleux, 1893).

47. J. N. Hillgarth, "Who Read Thomas Aquinas?" in *The Gilson Lectures on Thomas Aquinas* (Toronto: Pontifical Institute of Mediaeval Studies, 2008), 46–73. The quote is from page 70.

48. J. F. Hinnebusch, "Crockaert, Peter," *New Catholic Encyclopedia*, 2d ed., vol. 4 (Detroit: Gale, 2003), 374.

49. Felix Alluntis, "Vitoria, Francisco de (1492/1493–1546)," *Encyclopedia of Philosophy*, ed. Donald Borchert, 2d ed., vol. 9 (Detroit: Macmillan Reference USA, 2006), 698–99.

50. His most famous lectures were collected in *relectiones*, and include *De Indis*, *De Iure Belli*, *De Potestate Civili* among the most important. See Gregory M. Reichberg, "Francisco De Vitoria, De Indis and De Iure Belli Relectiones (1557): Philosophy Meets War," in Jorge J. E. Gracia, ed., *The Classics of Western Philosophy: A Reader's Guide* (Malden, Mass.: Blackwell Publishing, 2003).

51. Hugo Grotius, *The Law of War and Peace*, tran. Francis W. Kelsey (New York: Bobbs-Merrill Company, Inc., 1925).

52. Joshua Hochschild, "Cajetan, Cardinal (1469–1534)," *Encyclopedia of Philosophy*, ed. Donald Borchert, 2d ed., vol. 2 (Detroit: Macmillan Reference USA, 2006), 6–7.

53. Cf. Joshua Hochschild, *The Semantics of Analogy: Rereading Cajetan's De Nominum Analogia* (Notre Dame, Ind.: University of Notre Dame Press, 2010).

54. For example, consider Desiderius Erasmus, *Moriae Encomium (The Praise of Folly)* (London: Hamilton, Adams & Co., 1887), 142–43. Originally written in 1509: "Do not wonder, therefore, that at public disputations they bind their heads with so many caps one over another; for this is to prevent the loss of their brains, which would otherwise break out from their uneasy confinement. It affords likewise a pleasant scene of laughter, to listen to these divines in their hotly managed disputations. To see how proud they are of talking such hard gibberish, and stammering out such blundering distinctions, as the auditors perhaps may sometimes gape at, but seldom apprehend. [paragraph] And they take such a liberty in their speaking of Latin, that they scorn to stick at the exactness of syntax or concord; pretending it is below the majesty of a divine to talk like a pedagogue, and be tied to the slavish observance of the rules of grammar. Finally, they take a vast pride, among other citations, to allege the authority of their respective master."

55. Leibniz would edit this work in 1670.

56. Peter de la Ramée (1515–1572) is indicative of this tendency: "Let us ignore all these Aristotelians and return to Aristotle, the author of such a noble discipline [i.e., philosophy], and to Cicero, who tries to emulate Aristotle's teaching and to imitate him." As quoted by Erland Sellberg, "Petrus Ramus," *The Stanford Encyclopedia of Philosophy* (Fall 2008 edition), ed. Edward N. Zalta, accessed online at: <http://plato.stanford.edu/entries/ramus/>. Ramée's popularity seems to have exceeded his insights.

57. However, some recent scholarship has suggested some occult influences that Aquinas may have exerted within the *via moderna*, as characterized by Gabriel Biel and transmitted to Martin Luther. See van Geest et al., eds., *Aquinas as Authority*.

58. For the preparation for justification, compare *ST* III q.85 a.5 with the decrees of the Council of Trent, Session VI, chapter 6. For the causes of justification, compare *ST* I-II q.112 a.4 and II-II q.24 a.3 with Session VI, chapter 7.

59. For a more complete, if somewhat apologetic, summary of Thomists during this period, see Réginald Garrigou-Lagrange, *Reality: A Synthesis of Thomistic Thought*, tran. Patrick Cummins (St. Louis: B. Herder, 1958), ch. 3.

60. Thomas Franklin O'Meara, *Thomas Aquinas Theologian* (Notre Dame, Ind.: University of Notre Dame Press, 1997), 162.

61. Michael Griffin, "Molina, Luis de (1535–1600)," *Encyclopedia of Philosophy*, ed. Donald Borchert, 2d ed., vol. 6 (Detroit: Macmillan Reference USA, 2006), 321–23.

62. John Mourant, "Suárez, Francisco (1548–1617)," *Encyclopedia of Philosophy*, ed. Donald Borchert, 2d ed., vol. 9 (Detroit: Macmillan Reference USA, 2006), 282–85.

63. Vernon Bourke, "Vasquez, Gabriel (1549–1604)," *Encyclopedia of Philosophy*, ed. Donald Borchert, 2d ed., vol. 9 (Detroit: Macmillan Reference USA, 2006), 649–50.

64. Vernon Bourke, "Báñez, Dominic (1528–1604)," *Encyclopedia of Philosophy*, ed. Donald Borchert, 2d ed., vol. 1 (Detroit: Macmillan Reference USA, 2006), 476.

65. Cf. Aquinas's commentary on the *De Interpretatione*, Bk. I, lect.5.

66. Vernon Bourke, "John of St. Thomas (1589–1644)," *Encyclopedia of Philosophy*, ed. Donald Borchert, 2d ed., vol. 4 (Detroit: Macmillan Reference USA, 2006), 843–44.

67. For more on this suggestive possibility, see John N. Deely, *Four Ages of Understanding: The First Postmodern Survey of Philosophy from Ancient Times to the Turn of the Twenty-first Century* (Toronto Studies in Semiotics) (Toronto: University of Toronto Press, 2001), 447–84.

68. Francis Bacon, *The Advancement of Learning* (Rockville, MD: Serenity Publishers, 2008), 31. Take the following critical passage: "Surely, like as many substances in nature, which are solid, do putrefy and corrupt into worms; so it is the property of good and sound knowledge, to putrefy and dissolve into a number of subtle, idle, unwholesome, and, as I may term them, vermiculate questions, which have indeed a kind of quickness, and life of spirit, but no soundness of matter, or goodness of quality. This kind of degenerate learning did chiefly reign amongst the schoolmen: who having sharp and strong wits, and abundance of leisure, and small variety of reading, (but their wits being shut up in the cells of a few authors, chiefly Aristotle their dictator, as their persons were shut up in the cells of monasteries and colleges,) and knowing little history, either of nature or time, did, out of no great quantity of matter, and infinite agitation of wit, spin out unto us those laborious webs of learning, which are extant in their books."

69. Gilson rejects these assumptions as "essentialist," basing metaphysics on the abstract notions of the human mind, rather than the transcendent character of all actual, existent things.

70. James A. Weisheipl, "Thomism," *New Catholic Encyclopedia*, 2d ed., vol. 14 (Detroit: Gale, 2003), 40–52.

71. René Descartes, *The Philosophical Writings of Descartes*, vol. 2, tran. John Cottingham, Robert Stoothoff, and Dugald Murdoch (Cambridge: Cambridge University Press, 1984), 82–83, emphasis mine.

72. Cf. *ST* I q.2 a.1. Importantly, Aquinas does not think that a nominal definition of "God," such as "that than which nothing greater can be conceived," or perhaps "the necessary being" is sufficient by itself to prove that God exists. For Aquinas, these premises only result in a mental existence, or conception of God. But Aquinas wants to arrive at a mind-independent reality for God.

73. Cf. *Leviathan*, Part I, ch. 4, "necessities of definitions."

74. Cf. *An Essay Concerning Human Understanding*, Bk. III, ch. X, §§6–10.

75. *Aeterni Patris*, accessed online at: <http://www.vatican.va/holy_father/leo_xiii/encyclicals/documents/hf_l-xiii_enc_04081879_aeterni-patris_en.html>.

76. For the contents of this list, see <http://www.catholicapologetics.info/catholicteaching/philosophy/thomast.htm>.

77. *Studiorum Ducem*, accessed online at: <http://www.ewtn.com/library/ENCYC/P11STUDI.HTM>.

78. On this front, one thinks of the Leonine Commission, which has worked since 1879 to produce critical editions of the entire body of Aquinas's writings. Institutes devoted to all aspects of medieval study have been formed throughout Europe (e.g., at the University of St Thomas in Rome, the Thomas-Institut of Cologne, the Grabmann-Institut of Munich, the Thomas Instituut of Utrecht, and the Thomist Institue of Warsaw, to name just a few). In North America, I must mention the Pontifical Institute of Medieval Studies in Toronto, created in 1929 at the suggestion of Gilson. Journals include the *Revue Thomiste*, *The Modern Schoolman*, and *The Thomist*. Finally, an excellent resource for any scholar of Aquinas is Roberto Busa's electronic index of Aquinas's works, accessed online at <http://www.corpusthomisticum.org/>.

79. N. E. Fenton, "Weisheipl, James Athanasius," *New Catholic Encyclopedia*, 2d ed., vol. 14 (Detroit: Gale, 2003), 672–73.

80. W. J. Hill, "Thomism, Transcendental," *New Catholic Encyclopedia*, 2d ed., vol. 14 (Detroit: Gale, 2003), 52–57.

81. James Conway, "Maréchal, Joseph (1878–1944)," *Encyclopedia of Philosophy*, ed. Donald Borchert, 2d ed., vol. 5 (Detroit: Macmillan Reference USA, 2006), 707–10.

82. Elizabeth Galbraith, "Rahner, Karl (1904–1984)," *Encyclopedia of Philosophy*, ed. Donald Borchert, 2d ed., vol. 8 (Detroit: Macmillan Reference USA, 2006), 231–34.

83. F. G. Lawrence, "Lonergan, Bernard," *New Catholic Encyclopedia*, 2d ed., vol. 8 (Detroit: Gale, 2003), 772–75.

84. For Rahner, this activity would most poignantly be expressed in terms of *excessus*, which Aquinas mentions in his *De divinis nominibus expositio*, c.7, lect.4.

85. Joseph Evans, "Maritain, Jacques (1882–973)," *Encyclopedia of Philosophy*, ed. Donald Borchert, 2d ed., vol. 5 (Detroit: Macmillan Reference USA, 2006), 712–17.

86. Robert Miller, "Gilson, Étienne Henry (1884–1978)," *Encyclopedia of Philosophy*, ed. Donald Borchert, 2d ed., vol. 4 (Detroit: Macmillan Reference USA, 2006), 91–93.

87. John F. X. Knasas, *Being and Some Twentieth-Century Thomists* (New York: Fordham University Press, 2003).

88. Kerr, *After Aquinas*.

89. Theologian Karl Rahner seems to have been well aware of this problem. In 1980, his response when asked to say a few words about his philosophy was "Ich habe keine Philosophie" (I have no philosophy). See William V. Dych, *Karl Rahner*, Outstanding Christian Thinkers series (New York: Continuum International Publishing Group, 2000).

90. For a sampling of Geach on Aquinas, see *Three Philosophers: Aristotle, Aquinas, Frege* (Oxford: Blackwell Publishing, 1973). Kenny has many notable works, but for an introduction to his thinking on Aquinas, see *Aquinas on Mind* (London: Routledge, 1993); and *Aquinas on Being* (Oxford: Oxford University Press, 2002).

91. Anthony Kenny, *Aquinas: A Collection of Critical Essays* (Notre Dame, Ind.: University of Notre Dame Press, 1976), 1.

Chronological List of Aquinas's Writings

Works sometimes ascribed to Aquinas may well be texts of which he was not the author in any sense. What follows is a list of Aquinas's writings with respect to which there is not too much scholarly controversy concerning their authenticity. They are cited by the Latin titles commonly used for them, together with English translations of these. But note that we cannot always be sure of the titles that Aquinas gave to his writings (notably, in the case of the *Summa theologiae* and the *Summa contra Gentiles*). Within each category below, works are cited in roughly chronological order of composition, though in some cases this order is uncertain. For detailed discussions concerning the dating of Aquinas's writings, see Jean-Pierre Torrell, *Saint Thomas Aquinas: The Person and His Work* (Washington, D.C.: Catholic University Press of America, 1996).

GENERAL THEOLOGICAL TREATISES

Scriptum super libros Sententiarum (*Comentary on the Sentences of Peter Lombard*: c.1252–1257).
Summa contra Gentiles, sometimes referred to as *Summa contra Gentes* (*Summary against the Pagans* [sc. people neither Jewish or Christian]: c.1259–1265).
Summa theologiae, sometimes referred to as *Summa theologica* (*Summary of Theology*: c.1265–1273).
Compendium theologiae (*Compendium of Theology*: c.1265–1273).

DISPUTED QUESTIONS

Quaestiones disputatae De veritate (*Disputed Questions on Truth*: c.1256–1259).
Quaestiones disputatae De potentia (*Disputed Questions on the Power [of God]*: c. 1265–1266).
Quaestio disputata De anima (*Disputed Question on the Soul*: c.1265–1266).
Quaestio disputata De spiritualibus creaturis (*Disputed Question on Spiritual Creatures*: c.1267–1268).
Questiones disputatae De Malo (*Disputed Questions on Evil*: c.1266–1270).
Quaestiones disputatae De virtutibus (*Disputed Questions on the Virtues*: c.1271–1272).
Quaestio disputata De unione verbi incarnati (*Disputed Question on the Union of the Incarnate Word*: c. 1271–1272).

Quaestiones de quodlibet I–XII (*Quodlibetal Questions I–XII* [concerning a very large range of topics]: c.1252–1256 and c.1268–1272).

BIBLICAL COMMENTARIES

Expositio super Isaiam ad litteram (*Commentary on Isaiah*: c.1248–1254).
Super Ieremiam et Threnos (*Commentaries on Jeremiah and Lamentations*: c.1248–1252).
Expositio super Job ad litteram (*Commentary on Job/Literal Exposition on Job*: c.1261–1265).
Catena aurea (*The Golden Chain*: c.1262–1264 [commentary on the Gospels drawing on quotations from the Church Fathers]).
Lectura super Matthaeum (*Commentary on Matthew*: c.1269–1270).
Lectura super Ioannem (*Commentary on John*: c.1270–1272).
Expositio et Lectura super Epistolas Pauli Apostoli (*Commentaties on the Letters of St. Paul*: dating very difficult to establish, possibly 1265–1273).
Postilla super Psalmos (*Commentary on the Psalms*: c.1273).

COMMENTARIES ON ARISTOTLE

Sententia Libri De anima (*Commentary on Aristotle's On the Soul*: 1267–1268).
Sententia Libri De Sensu et sensato (*Commentary on Aristotle's On Sense [and On Memory]*: c.1268–1269).
Sententia super Physicam (*Commentary on Aristotle's Physics*: c.1268–1269).
Sententia super Meteora (*Commentary on Aristotle's Meteorology*: c.1268–1270).
Sententia Libri Politicorum (*Commentary on Aristotle's Politics*: c. 1269–1272).
Expositio Libri Peri hermeneias (*Commentary on Aristotle's On Interpretation [De Interpretatione]*: c.1270–1271).
Expositio Libri Posteriorum (*Commentary on Aristotle's Posterior Analytics*: c. 1270–1272).
Sententia Libri Ethicorum (*Commentary on Aristotle's Nichomachean Ethics*: 1271–1272).
Sententia super Metaphysicam (*Commentary on Aristotle's Metaphysics*: c.1270–1272).
Sententia super librum De caelo et mundo (*Commentary on Aristotle's On the Heavens*: c. 1272–1273).
Sententia super libros De generatione et corruptione (*Commentary on Aristotle's On Generation and Corruption*: c.1272–1273).

OTHER COMMENTARIES

Expositio super librum Boethii De trinitate (*Commentary on Boethius's De Trinitate*: c.1257–1259).
Expositio in librum Boethii De hebdomadibus (*Commentary on Boethius's Hebdomads* [actually, Boethius's third theological tractate]: c. 1257–1259).

Expositio super Dionysium De divinis nominibus (*Commentary on [Pseudo-] Dionysius's The Divine Names*: c.1261–1268).
Expositio super librum De causis (*Commentary on the Book of Causes*: c.1272).

POLEMICAL WRITINGS

Contra impugnantes Dei cultum et religionem (*Against those who Impugn the Cult of God and Religion*: 1256).
De perfectione spiritualis vitae (*On the Perfection of the Spiritual Life*: 1269–1270).
De unitate intellectus contra Averroistas (*On the Unicity of the Intellect Against the Averroists*: 1270).
Contra doctrinam retrahentium a religione homines a religionis ingressu [commonly referred to as *Contra retrahentes*] (*Against the teachings of those who prevent men entering the religious life*: 1271).
De aeterntate mundi (*On the Eternity of the World*: c.1271).

TREATISES AND OTHER WORKS ON ASSORTED TOPICS

De ente et essentia (*On Being and Essence*: c.1252–1256).
De principiis naturae (*On the Principles of Nature*: c.1252–1256, possibly earlier).
De regno ad regem Cypri (*On Kingship, to the King of Cyprus*: c.1267).
De substantiis separatis (*On Separate Substances*: c. 1271).
Contra errores Graecorum (*Against the Errors of the Greeks*: c.1263–1264).
De mixtione elementorum (*On the Mixture of Elements*: c.1270).

LITURGICAL AND RELATED WORKS

Collationes in decem praecepta (*Homilies on the Ten Commandments*: c.1261–1273).
Officium de festo Corporis Christi (*Office for the Feast of Corpus Christi*: c.1264).
Hymn *Adoro Te* (commonly referred to by its Latin title: date unknown).
Collationes in orationem dominicam, in Symbolorum Apostolorum, in salutatem angelicam (*Homilies on the Lord's Prayer, the Apostles's Creed, and the Angelic Greeting*: c.1268–1273).

Editions and Translations

1. PRIMARY SOURCES

The most authoritative listing of Aquinas's works in English is I. T. Eschmann, "A Catalogue of St. Thomas's Works: Bibliographical Notes," in E. Gilson, *The Christian Philosophy of St. Thomas Aquinas* (New York: Random House, 1956). It is supplemented by "A Brief Catalogue of Authentic Works" in James A. Weisheipl, *Friar Thomas D'Aquino* (Oxford: Basil Blackwell, 1974; republished with Corrigenda and Addenda, Washington D.C.: Catholic University of America Press, 1983).

The definitive edition of Aquinas's writings is currently being published by the Leonine Commission, established by Pope Leo XIII in 1880, which has now produced volumes containing Aquinas's most important works (*Sancti Thomae Aquinatis Doctoris Angelici. Opera Omnia. Iussu Leonis XIII*, Rome: Vatican Polyglot Press, 1882–). Publications of Aquinas's writings prior to the Leonine edition include the Parma edition (*Opera Omnia*, Parma: Fiaccadori, 1852–73) and the Vivès edition (*Opera Omnia*, Paris: Vivès, 1871–82). Most of Aquinas's writings have also been published in manual size by the Casa Marietti (Torino-Rome).

Students of Aquinas should also consult R. Busa, *Index Thomisticus* (Stuttgart-Bad Cannstatt: Frommann-Holzboog, 1974–80), which provides a text of Aquinas's writings and a useful, if somewhat unwieldy, way to search for terms used by him.

A substantial amount of Aquinas's writings still remains untranslated into English. There are, however, some currently available English editions of a number of his more important works.

To date, the best English edition of the *Summa theologiae* (with notes and commentaries) is the Blackfriars edition (61 vols., Latin and English with notes and introductions, London: Eyre & Spottiswoode, and New York: McGraw-Hill Book Company, 1964–80). Unfortunately, however, this translation is sometimes unreliable. For a more literal rendering of the text, see *St. Thomas Aquinas Summa Theologica* (translated by the Fathers of the English Dominican Province, originally published by Burns, Oates, and Washbourne in London in 1911 and now available from Christian Classics, Westminster, Md., 1981). This edition may be found on the Internet at: <http://www.newadvent.org/summa>. A searchable concordance to it can be found on the Internet at: <http://www.intratext.com/IXT/ENG0023/_FA.HTM>. Also worth consulting is Timothy McDermott (ed.), *St Thomas Aquinas, Summa Theologiae: A Concise Translation* (London: Eyre and Spottiswoode, 1989). A Latin concordance of Aquinas's full corpus can be found at the Corpus Thomisticum website: <http://www.corpusthomisticum.org/it/index.age>.

For a reliable translation of the *Summa contra Gentiles*, see *On the Truth of the Catholic Faith*, translated by Anton Pegis, James F. Anderson, Vernon J. Bourke, and Charles J. O'Neil (New York: Doubleday, 1955–57, reprinted as *Summa Contra Gentiles*, Notre Dame, Ind. and London: University of Notre Dame Press, 1975). An annotated translation of the *Summa contra Gentiles* (by Joseph Rickaby, with some abridgements) is available on the Internet at: <http://www.nd.edu/departments/maritain/etext/gc.html>.

Other English translations of Aquinas's writings include:

(a) *Disputed Questions*

Truth (*Quaestiones disputatae De veritate*), translated by Robert W. Mulligan, J. V. McGlynn, and R. W. Schmidt (3 vols., Chicago: Henry Regnery Company, 1952–54).

On the Power of God (*Quaestiones disputatae De potentia*), translated by the English Dominican Fathers (3 vols., London: Burns, Oates, and Washbourne, 1932–34).

The Soul (*Quaestio disputata De anima*), translated by J. H. Robb (Milwaukee, Wis.: Marquette University Press, 1984).

On Spiritual Creatures (*Quaestio disputata De spiritualibus creaturis*), translated by M. C. Fitzpatrick and J. J. Wellmuth (Milwaukee, Wis.: Marquette University Press, 1949).

On Evil (*Quaestiones disputatae De Malo*), translated by Richard Regan (New York and Oxford: Oxford University Press, 2001).

Disputed Questions on Virtue (*Quaestio disputata De virtutibus in communi* and *Quaestio disputata De virtutibus cardinalibus*), translated by Ralph McInerny (South Bend, Ind.: St. Augustine's Press, 1999).

On Charity (*Quaestio disputata De caritate*), translated by Lottie H. Kendzierski (Milwaukee, Wis.: Marquette University Press, 1984).

Quodlibetal Questions 1 and 2, translated by Sandra Edwards (Toronto: Pontifical Institute of Medieval Studies, 1983).

(b) *Commentaries on Scripture*

The Literal Exposition on Job (*Expositio super Job as litteram*), translated by Anthony Damico (Atlanta, Ga.: Scholars Press, 1989).

Commentary on the Gospel of John (*Lectura super Ioannem*), translated by James A Weisheipl and F. R. Larcher (2 vols., Albany, N.Y.: Magi Books, 1980, and Petersham, Mass.: St. Bede's Publications, 1998).

Commentary on Saint Paul's First Letter to the Thessalonians and the Letter to the Philippians, translated by F. R. Larcher and Michael Duffy (Albany, N.Y.: Magi Books, 1969).

Commentary on Saint Paul's Epistle to the Ephesians, translated by Matthew L. Lamb (Albany, N.Y.: Magi Books, 1966).

Commentary on Saint Paul's Epistle to the Galatians, translated by F. R. Larcher (Albany, N.Y.: Magi Books, 1966).

(c) *Commentaries on Aristotle*

A Commentary on Aristotle's De anima (*Sententia Libri De anima*), translated by Robert Pasnau (New Haven, Conn. and London: Yale University Press, 1999).

Commentary on Aristotle's Physics (*Sententia super Physicam*), translated by R. Blackwell (New Haven, Conn.: Yale University Press, 1963).

On Interpretation (*Expositio Libri Peri hermenias*), translated by Jean T. Oesterle (Milwaukee, Wis.: Marquette University Press, 1962).

Commentary on the Posterior Analytics of Aristotle (*Expositio Libri Posteriorum*), translated by F. R. Larcher (Albany, N.Y.: Magi Books, 1970).

Commentary on Aristotle's Nicomachean Ethics (*Sententia Libri Ethicorum*), translated by C. I. Litzinger (2 vols., Notre Dame, Ind.: University of Notre Dame Press, 1964).

Commentary on Aristotle's Metaphysics (*Sententia super Metaphysicam*), translated by John P. Rowan (Notre Dame, Ind.: University of Notre Dame Press, 1995).

(d) *Other Commentaries*

Saint Thomas Aquinas, Faith, Reason, and Theology. Questions I–IV of his Commentary on the De Trinitate of Boethius (*Expositio super librum Boethii De trinitate*), translated by A. Maurer (Toronto: Pontifical Institute of Medieval Studies, 1987).

Saint Thomas Aquinas, The Divisions and Methods of the Sciences. Questions V and VI of his Commentary on the De Trinitate of Boethius (*Expositio super librum Boethii De trinitate*), translated by A. Maurer (Toronto: Pontifical Institute of Medieval Studies, 1986).

Saint Thomas Aquinas, An Exposition of the "On the Hebdomads" of Boethius, Introduction and translation by Janice L. Schultz and Edward A. Synan (Washington, D.C.: Catholic University of America Press, 2001).

Commentary on the Book of Causes (*Expositio super librum De causis*), translated by Vincent A. Guagliardo, Charles R. Hess, and Richard C. Taylor (Washington, D.C.: Catholic University of America Press, 1996).

(e) *Other Writings*

On Being and Essence (*De ente et essentia*), translated by Joseph Bobik (Notre Dame, Ind.: University of Notre Dame Press, 1965).

Aquinas on Matter and Form and the Elements (translations of *De principiis naturae* and *De mixtione elementorum*), translated by Joseph Bobik (Notre Dame, Ind.: University of Notre Dame Press, 1998).

On There Being Only One Intellect (*De unitate intellectus contra Averroistas*), translated by Ralph McInerny in *Aquinas Against the Averroists* (West Lafayette, Ind.: Purdue University Press, 1993).

Compendium of Theology (*Compendium theologie*), translated by Richard J. Regan (Oxford and New York: Oxford University Press, 2009).

The Sermon Conferences of St. Thomas Aquinas on the Apostle's Creed (*Collationes in Symbolorum Apostolorum*), translated by Nicholas Ayo (Notre Dame, Ind.: University of Notre Dame Press, 1988).

Readers might like to note that Thérese Bonin maintains an updated web site listing currently available English translations of Aquinas at: <http://www.home.duq.edu/~bonin/thomasbibliography.html>.

The Thomas Institute in Utrecht also lists translations into English of Aquinas and provides one of the most helpful of internet research sites for students of Aquinas. It can be found at: <http://www.thomasinstituut.org/>.

2. USEFUL SELECTIONS FROM AQUINAS IN ENGLISH

Steven E. Baldner and William E. Carroll, *Aquinas on Creation* (Toronto: Pontifical Institute of Medieval Studies, 1997).
Mary T. Clark, *An Aquinas Reader*, revised edition (New York: Fordham University Press, 2000).
Christopher Martin (ed.), *The Philosophy of Thomas Aquinas* (London: Routledge, 1988).
Timothy McDermott (ed.), *Aquinas: Selected Philosophical Writings* (Oxford and New York: Oxford University Press, 1993).
Ralph McInerny, *Thomas Aquinas: Selected Writings* (Harmondsworth: Penguin Books, 1998).
Anton C. Pegis (ed.), *Introduction to St. Thomas Aquinas* (New York: The Modern Library, 1945).

3. BIBLIOGRAPHICAL WORKS

P. Mandonnet and J. Destrez, *Bibliographie Thomiste*, 2d ed., revised by M.-D. Chenu (Paris: Vrin, 1960).
Vernon J. Bourke, *Thomistic Bibliography: 1920–1940*, *The Modern Schoolman*, 1921.
Richard Ingardia, *Thomas Aquinas: International Bibliography 1977–1990* (Bowling Green, Ohio: Philosophy Documentation Center, 1993).
Terry L. Miethe and Vernon J. Bourke, *Thomistic Bibliography, 1940–1978* (Westport, Conn.: Greenwood Press, 1980).
The *Bulletin Thomiste* (1940–65), continued in *Rassegna di Letteratura Tomistica* (1966–), receives all Thomistic publications and is a useful research tool with respect to Thomistic bibliography.

Bibliography

Adams, Marilyn McCord. *What Sort of Human Nature? Medieval Philosophy and the Systematics of Christology*. Milwaukee, Wis.: Marquette University Press, 1999.

———. *William Ockham*. Notre Dame, Ind.: University of Notre Dame Press, 1987.

Adamson, Peter, and Richard Taylor, eds. *The Cambridge Companion to Arabic Philosophy*. Cambridge: Cambridge University Press, 2005.

Aertsen, Jan A. "Aquinas and the Human Desire for Knowledge." *American Catholic Philosophical Quarterly* 79 (2005): 411–30.

———. "Good as Transcendental and the Transcendence of the Good." In Scott MacDonald, ed., *Being and Goodness: The Concept of the Good in Metaphysics and Philosophical Theology*, 56–73. Ithaca, N.Y. and London: Cornell University Press, 1991.

———. *Medieval Philosophy and the Transcendentals: The Case of Thomas Aquinas*. Brill Studien und Texte zur Geistesgeschichte des Mittelalters 52. Leiden, New York, and Köln: Brill Academic Publishers, 1996.

Aillet, M. *Lire la Bible avec S. Thomas: Le Passage de la littera à la res dans la Somme théologique*. Studia friburgensia 80. Fribourg: Éditions universitaires, 1993.

Albert the Great. *Opera omnia* (Cologne edition). Münster: Aschendorff, 1951ff.

———. *Opera omnia* (Paris edition), ed. Auguste Borgnet. Vol. 26. Paris: Vivès, 1893.

———. *Super Dionysium de divinis nominibus*, c.2, §25–26. In *Opera omnia* (Cologne edition), ed. Paulus Simon. Vol. 37/1, Münster: Aschendorff, 1972.

Albertus Magnus. *Super Ethica commentum et quaestiones*. In *Opera omnia*, ed. W. Kübel. Vol. 14/1–2. Cologne: Aschendorff, 1968–72 and 1987.

Alexander of Hales. *Glossa in quatuor libros Sententiarum Petri Lombardi*. Vol. 2. Quaracchi: Collegium S. Bonaventura, 1952.

———. *Summa theologiae*. Quaracchi: Collegium S. Bonaventurae, 1928.

Alluntis, Felix. "Vitoria, Francisco de (1492/1493–1546)." In Donald Borchert, ed., *Encyclopedia of Philosophy*. 2d ed. Vol. 9: 698–99. Detroit, Mich., Mich.: Macmillan Reference USA, 2006.

Alston, William. "The Inductive Argument from Evil and the Human Cognitive Condition." In Daniel Howard-Snyder, ed., *The Evidential Argument from Evil*, 97–125. Bloomington: Indiana University Press, 1996.

Anscombe, Elizabeth. *Human Life, Action and Ethics*. Exeter: Imprint Academic, 2005.

Anscombe, G. E. M. *Intention*. Cambridge, Mass.: Harvard University Press, 2000.

———. "'Whatever Has a Beginning of Existence Must Have a Cause': Hume's Argument Exposed." *Analysis* 34:5 (1974): 145–51.

Anscombe, G. E. M., and Peter Geach. *Three Philosophers: Aristotle, Aquinas, Frege*. Oxford: Basil Blackwell, 1961.

Articuli in quibus frater Thomas melius in Summa quam in Scriptis. In R.-A. Gauthier, "Les 'Articuli in quibus frater Thomas melius in Summa quam in Scriptis.'" *Recherches de théologie ancienne et médiévale* 19 (1952): 271–326.

Ashworth, E. J. "Analogy and Equivocation in Thirteenth-Century Logic: Aquinas in Context." *Mediaeval Studies* 54 (1991): 94–135.

———. "Medieval Theories of Analogy." *The Stanford Encyclopedia of Philosophy* (Winter 2004 edition), ed. Edward N. Zalta. <http://plato.stanford.edu/archives/win2004/entries/analogy-medieval/>.

Augros, Michael. "Aquinas's *Tertia Via.*" *Angelicum* 83 (2006): 767–92.

Aumann, J. "Thomistic Evaluation of Love and Charity." *Angelicum* 55 (1978): 534–56.

Averroës. *Commentarium in Ethicorum*, in *Moralem totam philosophiam complectentes cum Averrois Cordubensis in Moralia Nicomachia expositione*, Vol. 3 of *Aristotelis Stagiritae Libri* (Venice: Juncta); reprint Frankfurt am Main: Minerva G.m.b.H., 1962.

———. *In I Physicam*, com. 83. In his *Opera omnia* (Venice: 1562–1574), vol. 4, fol. 47rb-vb; *In VI Metaphysicam*, com. 2–3, vol. 8, fols., 146rb–147ra.

Avicebron. *Fons vitae*. In C. Baeumker, ed., *Beiträge zur Geschichte der Philosophie des Mittelalters*. Bd. 1, H. 2–4. Münster: Aschendorff, 1892.

Avicenna. *Liber de anima seu sixtus de naturalibus*. In S. Van Riet, ed., G. Verbeke, intro., *Avicenna Latinus*. 2 vols. Vol. 1, Louvain/Leiden: Peeters/Brill, 1968. Vol. 2, Louvain/Leiden: Éditions Orientalistes/Brill, 1972.

———. *The Metaphysics of Healing*. Trans. Michael Marmura. Provo, Utah: Brigham Young University Press, 2005.

Ayo, Nicholas. *The Sermon-Conferences of St. Thomas Aquinas on the Apostles' Creed*. Notre Dame, Ind.: University of Notre Dame Press, 1988.

Bacon, Francis. *The Advancement of Learning*. Rockville, MD: Serenity Publishers, 2008.

Baisnee, Jules. "St. Thomas Aquinas's Proofs of the Existence of God Presented in Their Chronological Order." In John K. Ryan, ed., *Philosophical Studies in Honor of the Very Reverend Ignatius Smith, O.P.*, 29–64. Westminster, Md.: Newman Press, 1952.

Baker, Lynne Rudder. *Persons and Bodies: A Constitution View*. Cambridge: Cambridge University Press, 2000.

———. "Unity Without Identity: A New Look at Material Constitution." *Midwest Studies in Philosophy* 23 (1999): 144–65.

———. "Why Constitution is Not Identity." *Journal of Philosophy* 94 (1997): 599–621.

Bazán, Bernardo Carlos. "The Human Soul: Form *and* Substance? Thomas Aquinas' Critique of Eclectic Aristotelianism." *Archives d'histoire doctrinale et littéraire du Moyen Age* 64 (1997): 95–126.

Bazán, Bernardo Carlos, G. Fransen, J. F. Wippel, and D. Jacquart. *Les Questions disputées et les questions quodlibétiques dans les facultés de théologie, de droit et de médecine*. Typologie des sources du moyen âge occidental 44–45. Turnhout: Brepols, 1985.

Berceville, Gilles. "Le Sacerdoce du Christ dans le *Commentaire de l'épître aux Hébreux* de saint Thomas d'Aquin." *Revue Thomiste* 99 (1999): 143–58.

Berger, D. *Thomas von Aquins "Summa Theologiae."* Darmstadt: Wissenschaftliche Gesellschaft, 2004.

Bernard, C.-A. *Théologie de l'espérance selon Saint Thomas d'Aquin*. Paris: Vrin, 1961.

Berndt, Rainer. "La Théologie comme système du monde: Sur l'évolution des sommes théologiques de Hugues de Saint-Victor à Saint Thomas d'Aquin." *Revue des sciences philosophiques et théologiques* 78:4 (1994): 555–72.

Beuchot, Mauricio. "Saint Thomas' Third Way: Possibility and Necessity, Essence and Existence." In Adolfo García de la Sienra, ed., *The Rationality of Theism*, 93–108. Atlanta, Ga.: Rodopi, 2000.

Beumer, Johannes. "Ein nicht-authentischer Text im Prolog zum Sentenzenkommentar des hl. Thomas von Aquin (q.1a.3.sol.2)." *Scholastik* 33 (1958): 247–52.

Bianchi, L. *L'Errore di Aristotele: La polemica contro l'eternità del mondo nel XIII secolo.* Firenze: La nuova Italia, 1984.
Biffi, I. *I Misteri di Cristo in Tommaso d'Aquino.* Milano: Jaca Book, 1994.
Blanchette, Oliva. *The Perfection of the Universe According to Aquinas: A Teleological Cosmology.* University Park: Pennsylvania State University Press, 1992.
Blankenhorn, Bernard. "The Instrumental Causality of the Sacraments: Thomas Aquinas and Louis-Marie Chauvet." *Nova et Vetera* 4:2 (2006): 255–94.
Blund, Johannes. *Tractatus de anima*, ed. D. A. Callus and R. W. Hunt. London: Oxford University Press, 1970.
Bobik, Joseph. "Aquinas's Fourth Way and the Approximating Relation." *Thomist* 51 (1987): 17–36.
Bochenski, Joseph M. "The Five Ways." In Adolfo García de la Sienra, ed., *The Rationality of Theism*, 61–92. Atlanta, Ga.: Rodopi, 2000.
Boland, Vivian. *Ideas in God According to Saint Thomas Aquinas: Sources and Synthesis.* Brill Studies in the History of Christian Thought 69. Leiden and New York: E. J. Brill, 1996.
Bonaventure. *Commentaria in quatuor libros Sententiarum.* In *Opera omnia.* Vols. 1–4. Quaracchi: Collegium S. Bonaventurae, 1882–1902.
———. *Opera omnia.* Quaracchi: Typographia Collegii S. Bonaventurae, 1882–1902.
Bonino, S.-T. *Thomas d'Aquin, De la vérité Question 2 (La science en Dieu).* Introduction, traduction, et commentaire, "Vestigia 17". Paris/Fribourg: Cerf/ Éditions universitaires, 1996.
Bouillard, H. *Conversion et grace chez S. Thomas d'Aquin: Étude historique.* Paris: Aubier, 1944.
Bourgeois, Daniel. "'Inchoatio vitae eternae': La Dimension eschatologique de la vertu théologale de foi chez saint Thomas d'Aquin." *Sapienza* 27 (1974): 272–314.
Bourke, Vernon J. "The Background of Aquinas' Synderesis Principle." In Lloyd P. Gerson, ed., *Graceful Reason*, 345–60. Toronto: Pontifical Institute of Mediaeval Studies, 1983.
———. "Báñez, Dominic (1528–1604)." In Donald Borchert, ed., *Encyclopedia of Philosophy.* 2d ed. Vol. 1: 476. Detroit, Mich.: Macmillan Reference USA, 2006.
———. "John of St. Thomas (1589–1644)." In Donald Borchert, ed., *Encyclopedia of Philosophy.* 2d ed. Vol. 1: 843–44. Detroit, Mich.: Macmillan Reference USA, 2006.
———. *St. Thomas and the Greek Moralists.* Milwaukee, Wis.: Marquette University Press, 1947.
———. "Vasquez, Gabriel (1549–1604)." In Donald Borchert, ed., *Encyclopedia of Philosophy.* 2d ed. Vol. 1: 649–50. Detroit, Mich.: Macmillan Reference USA, 2006.
Bowlin, John. *Contingency and Fortune in Aquinas' Ethics.* Cambridge: Cambridge University Press, 1999.
Boyle, Leonard E. "Notes on the Education of the *Fratres communes* in the Dominican Order in the Thirteenth Century." In R. Creytens and P. Künzle, eds., *Xenia medii aevi historiam illustrantia oblata Th. Käppeli O.P.* Vol. 1: 249–67. Storia e Letteratura, Raccolta di Studi e Testi 141. Rome: Edizioni di storia e letteratura, 1978. Reprinted in Leonard E. Boyle, *Pastoral Care, Clerical Education and Canon Law, 1200–1400.* Etude VI. London: Variorum Reprints, 1981.
———. *Pastoral Care, Clerical Education and Canon Law, 1200–1400.* London: Variorum Reprints, 1981.
———. "The Quodlibets of St. Thomas and Pastoral Care." In Leonard E. Boyle, *Facing History: A Different Thomas Aquinas*, 13–35. Louvain-La-Neuve: Federation Internationale des Instituts d'Etudes Medievales, 2000. (Cf. *The Thomist* 38 (1974): 232–56.)

———. *The Setting of the* Summa theologiae *of Saint Thomas*. The Etienne Gilson Series 5. Toronto: P.I.M.S., 1982.

———. "The Setting of the *Summa theologiae*—Revisited." In Stephen J. Pope, ed., *The Ethics of Aquinas*, 1–16. Washington, D.C.: Georgetown University Press, 2002.

———. "The Setting of the *Summa Theologiae*." In Brian Davies, O.P., ed., *Aquinas's* Summa Theologiae: *Critical Essays*, 1–25. Lanham, Md.: Rowman & Littlefield Publishers, 2006.

———. "The *Summa Confessorum* of John of Freiburg." In Leonard E. Boyle, *Facing History: A Different Thomas Aquinas*, 37–64. Louvain-La-Neuve: Federation Internationale des Instituts d'Etudes Medievales, 2000.

Bradley, Denis. *Aquinas on the Twofold Human Good: Reason and Happiness in Aquinas's Moral Science*. Washington, D.C.: Catholic University of America Press, 1997.

Brent, James R., O. P. "The Epistemic Status of Christian Beliefs in Thomas Aquinas." Ph.D. diss., Saint Louis University, 2008.

Bright, Michael. *Intelligence in Animals*. New York: Reader's Digest Association, Ltd., 1997.

Brock, Steven L. *Action and Conduct: Thomas Aquinas and the Theory of Action*. Edinburgh: T & T Clark, 1998.

Brower, Jeffrey. "Making Sense of Divine Simplicity." *Faith and Philosophy* 25 (2008): 3–30.

Brower, Jeffrey, and Susan Brower-Toland. "Aquinas on Mental Representation: Concepts and Intentionality." *Philosophical Review* 117 (2008): 193–243.

Brown, Patterson. "St. Thomas' Doctrine of Necessary Being." In Anthony Kenny, ed., *Aquinas: A Collection of Critical Essays*, 157–74. Notre Dame, Ind.: University of Notre Dame Press, 1976.

Brown, Stephen F. "The Theological Virtue of Faith (IIa IIae, qq.1–16)." In Stephen J. Pope, ed., *The Ethics of Aquinas*, 221–31. Washington, D.C.: Georgetown University Press, 2002.

Burnyeat, Myles F. "Aristotle on Understanding Knowledge." In Enrico Berti, ed., *Aristotle on Science: The "Posterior Analytics."* Proceedings of the Eighth Symposium Aristotelicum, 97–139. Padua: Editrice Antenore, 1981.

Burrell, David. "Act of Creation with Its Theological Consequences." In Thomas Weinandy, Daniel Keating, and John Yocum, eds. *Aquinas on Doctrine*. London and New York: T&T Clark, 2004.

———. *Aquinas: God and Action*. Notre Dame, Ind.: University of Notre Dame Press, 1979.

———. *Freedom and Creation in Three Traditions*. Notre Dame, Ind.: University of Notre Dame Press, 1993.

———. "God's Knowledge of Future Contingents: A Reply to William Lane Craig." *The Thomist* 58:2 (April 1994): 317–22.

———. "Islamic Philosophical Theology and the West." *Islamochristiana* 33 (2007): 75–90.

———. *Knowing the Unknowable God: Ibn Sina, Maimonides, Aquinas*. Notre Dame, Ind.: University of Notre Dame Press, 1986.

Butera, Guiseppe. "The Moral Status of the First Principle of Practical Reason in Thomas's Natural Law Theory." *The Thomist* 71 (2007): 609–31.

Cahn, Steven M., and Christine Vitrano, eds. *Happiness: Classic and Contemporary Readings in Philosophy*. New York and Oxford: Oxford University Press, 2008.

Cajetan. *Thomas de Vio Caietani In De Ente et Essentia D. Thomae Aquinatis*. Turin: Marietti, 1934.

———. *Thomas de Vio: Scripta Philosophica: Commentaria in Praedicamenta Aristotelis*, ed. M. H. Laurent. Romae: Angelicum, 1939.

Callus, D. A. "Correctoria." In *New Catholic Encyclopedia*. 2d ed. Vol. 4: 274–78. Detroit, Mich.: Gale, 2003.

Cartwright, Richard. "The Second Way." *Medieval Philosophy and Theology* 5 (1996): 189–204.
Casey, G. "An Explication of the *de Hebdomadibus* of Boethius in the Light of St. Thomas's Commentary." *The Thomist* 51 (1987): 419–34.
Catao, Bernard. *Salut et Rédemption chez S. Thomas d'Aquin*. Paris: Desclée, 1965.
Cates, Diana. *Aquinas on the Emotions: A Religious-Ethical Inquiry*. Washington, D.C.: Georgetown University Press, 2009.
Cessario, Romanus, O.P. *The Godly Image: Christ and Salvation in Catholic Thought from Anselm to Aquinas*. Petersham, Mass.: St. Bede's Publications, 1990.
———. *A Short History of Thomism*. Washington, D.C.: Catholic University of America Press, 2003.
———. "The Theological Virtue of Hope (IIa IIae, qq. 17–22)." In Stephen J. Pope, ed., *The Ethics of Aquinas*, 232–43. Washington, D.C.: Georgetown University Press, 2002.
Chardonnens, Dennis. "Éternité du sacerdoce du Christ et effet eschatologique de l'eucharistie." *Revue Thomiste* 99 (1999): 159–80.
———. *L'Homme sous le regard de la Providence*. Providence de Dieu et condition humaine selon l'*Exposition littérale sur le Livre de Job* de Thomas d'Aquin, Bibliothèque thomiste 50. Paris: Vrin, 1997.
Chauvet, Louis-Marie. *Symbole et sacrement: Une relecture sacramentelle de l'existence chrétienne*. Paris: Les Éditions du Cerf, 1988.
Chênevert, J. "Le *Verbum* dans le Commentaire suer le Sentences de Saint Thomas d'Aquin." *Sciences ecclésiastiques* 13 (1961): 191–233, 359–90.
Chenu, Marie-Dominique, O.P. *Aquinas and His Role in Theology*. Trans. Paul J. Philibert, O.P. Collegeville, Minn.: Liturgical Press, 2002.
———. *Introduction à l'étude de Saint Thomas d'Aquin*. 2d ed. Montréal/Paris: Institut d'Études Médiévales/Vrin, 1954.
———. *La Théologie comme science au XIIIe siècle*. 3d ed. Paris: Vrin, 1957.
Conlon, G. M. "The Certitude of Hope." *The Thomist* 10 (1947): 76–119, 226–52.
Conway, David. "Possibility and Infinite Time: A Logical Paradox in St. Thomas' Third Way." *International Philosophical Quarterly* 14:2 (1974): 201–9.
Conway, James. "Maréchal, Joseph (1878–1944)." In Donald Borchert, ed., *Encyclopedia of Philosophy*. 2d ed. Vol. 1: 707–10. Detroit, Mich.: Macmillan Reference USA, 2006.
Copleston, Frederick. *A History of Philosophy*. Vol. 1–3. Garden City, N.Y.: Doubleday, 1985.
Cosgrove, Matthew R. "Thomas Aquinas on Anselm's Argument." *Review of Metaphysics* 27 (1974): 513–30.
Côté, Antoine. "Siger and the Skeptic." *Review of Metaphysics* 60 (2006): 305–25.
Craig, William Lane. "Aquinas on God's Knowledge of Future Contingents." *The Thomist* 54:1 (January 1990): 33–79.
———. *The Problem of Divine Foreknowledge and Future Contingents from Aristotle to Suarez*. Leiden: E. J. Brill, 1988.
Cross, Richard. *The Metaphysics of the Hypostatic Union*. Oxford: Oxford University Press, 2002.
———. *The Physics of Duns Scotus: The Scientific Context of a Theological Vision*. Oxford: Clarendon Press, 1998.
Crowe, Michael. "Synderesis and the Notion of Law in Saint Thomas." In *L'Homme et son destin, d'après les penseurs du moyen âge*, 601–609. Leuven: Nauwelaerts, 1960.
D'Alverny, Marie-Therese. *La Transmission des textes philosophiques et scientifiques au Moyen Age*, ed. C. Burnett. Aldershot: Variorum, 1994.
D'Ancona Costa, C. "La Notion de l'un dans Thomas d'Aquin: Une confrontation des commentaires sur les Noms divins et sur la Métaphysique." *Recherches de théologie et philosophie médiévales* 64 (1997): 315–51.

———. "Saint Thomas lecteur du *Liber de Causis*: Bilan des recherches contemporaines concernant le *De Causis* et analyse de l'interprétation thomiste." In C. D'Ancona Costa, *Recherches sur le Liber De Causis*. Études de philosophie médiévale 72, 229–58. Paris: Vrin, 1995.

Dales, Richard. *The Problem of the Rational Soul in the Thirteenth Century*. Leiden: E. J. Brill, 1995.

Dalferth, Ingolf. *Malum: Theologische Hermeneutik des Bösen*. Tübingen: Mohr Siebeck, 2008.

Dante Alighieri. *The Divine Comedy*. Trans. John Ciardi. New York: New American Library, 2003.

Darwall, Stephen. *The Second-Person Standpoint: Morality, Respect, and Accountability*. Cambridge, Mass.: Harvard University Press, 2006.

Dauphinais, M., and M. Levering, eds. *Reading John with St. Thomas Aquinas*. Washington, D.C.: Catholic University of America Press, 2005.

Dauphinais, M., B. David, and M. Levering. *Aquinas the Augustinian*. Washington, D.C.: Catholic University of America Press, 2007.

Davies, Brian, O.P. "Aquinas's Third Way." *New Blackfriars* 82 (2001): 450–66.

———. "Simplicity." In Chad Meister and Charles Taliaferro, eds., *The Cambridge Companion to Christian Philosophical Theology*. Cambridge: Cambridge University Press, 2009.

———. *The Thought of Thomas Aquinas*. Oxford: Clarendon Press, 1992.

Dawkins, Richard. *The God Delusion*. New York: Bantam Press, 2006.

De Couesnongle, V. "Le 'Dieu de l'espérance' de saint Thomas Aquinas." *Studia Theologica Varsaviensis* 12 (1974): 103–20.

De Koninck, Charles. *De la primauté du bien commun contre les personalistes*. Québec/ Montréal: Éditions de l'Université Laval/Éditions Fides, 1943.

De Nys, Martin. "If Everything Can Not-Be There Would Be Nothing: Another Look at the Third Way." *Review of Metaphysics* 56 (2002): 99–122.

De Wulf, Maurice. "L'Augustinisme 'avicennisant.'" *Revue néoscolastique de philosophie* 33 (1931): 11–39.

Deloffre, M.-H., ed. and trans. *Thomas d'Aquin, Question disputée: L'Union du Verbe incarné* (*De unione Verbi incarnati*). Texte latin, Introduction, traduction, et notes. Paris: Vrin, 2000.

Deely, John N. *Four Ages of Understanding: The First Postmodern Survey of Philosophy from Ancient Times to the Turn of the Twenty-First Century*. Toronto Studies in Semiotics, 447–84. Toronto: University of Toronto Press, 2001.

Dermine, Francois. "Razionalitá e fede." *Divus Thomas* 95 (1992): 126–44.

Descartes, René. *The Philosophical Writings of Descartes*. Vol. 2. Tran. John Cottingham, Robert Stoothoff, and Dugald Murdoch. Cambridge: Cambridge University Press, 1984.

Desiderius Erasmus. *Moriae Encomium (The Praise of Folly)*. London: Hamilton, Adams & Co., 1887.

Dewan, Lawrence, O.P. "St. Thomas, James Ross, and Exemplarism: A Reply." *American Catholic Philosophical Quarterly* 65 (1991): 221–34.

Doig, James C. *Aquinas on Metaphysics: A Historico-doctrinal Study of the Commentary on the Metaphysics*. The Hague: Nijhoff, 1972.

———. *Aquinas's Philosophical Commentary on the Ethics*. Dordrecht: Kluwer, 2001.

Donagan, Alan. "Thomas Aquinas on Human Action." In Norman Kretzmann, Anthony Kenny, and Jan Pinborg, eds., *The Cambridge History of Later Medieval Philosophy*, 642–54. Cambridge: Cambridge University Press, 1982.

Doolan, Gregory T. *Aquinas on the Divine Ideas as Exemplar Causes*. Washington, D.C.: Catholic University Press of America, 2008.

Draper, Paul. "The Skeptical Theist." In Daniel Howard-Snyder, ed., *The Evidential Argument from Evil*, 175–92. Bloomington: Indiana University Press, 1996.

Drost, Mark. "Intentionality in Aquinas's Theory of Emotions" *International Philosophical Quarterly* 31 (1991): 449–60.

———. "In the Realm of the Senses: St. Thomas Aquinas on Sensory Love, Desire, and Delight." *The Thomist* 59 (1995): 47–58.

Du Moustier, B. "Denis the Carthusian." In *New Catholic Encyclopedia*. 2nd ed.Vol. 4: 661–62. Detroit, Mich.: Gale, 2003.

Dufeil, M.-M. "Évolution ou fixité des institutions ecclésiales: Une controverse universitaire. L'édition critique de trois oeuvres polémiques de saint Thomas d'Aquin." *Revue des sciences philosophiques et théologiques* 55 (1971): 464–79.

———. *Guillaume de Saint-Amour et la polémique universitaire parisienne 1250–1259*. Paris: Picard, 1972.

Duns Scotus. *Ordinatio* 3, d.36, nn.72–100. Vatican edition. Vol. 10: 249–61. Vatican City: Typis Vaticanis, 2007.

Dupuy, Michel. "Oraison." *Dictionnaire de Spiritualité*. Vol. 11. Paris: Beauchesne Editions, 1982.

Durandellus. *Evidentiae contra Durandum*. Ed. P. T. Stella, critical edition prepared by M. Lanczkowski and R. Imbach. *Corpus Philosophorum Medii Aevi: Opera Philosophica Mediae Aetatis Selecta*. 2 vols. Tübingen and Basle: A. Francke Verlag, 2003.

Duroux, Benoit. *La Psychologie de la foi chez S. Thomas d'Aquin*. Tournai: Desclée de Brouwer, 1963.

Dych, William V. *Karl Rahner*. Outstanding Christian Thinkers series. New York: Continuum International Publishing Group, 2000.

Eardley, P. "Thomas Aquinas and Giles of Rome on the Will." *Review of Metaphysics* 56 (2003): 835–62.

Eilan, Naomi. "Joint Attention, Communication, and Mind." In Naomi Eilan, et al., *Joint Attention: Communication and Other Minds. Issues in Philosophy and Psychology*, 1–33. New York: Oxford University Press, 2005.

Eisen Murphy, Claudia. "Aquinas on Voluntary Beliefs." *American Catholic Philosophical Quarterly* 74 (2000): 569–97.

Elders, Leo J. "La Doctrine de la conscience de Saint Thomas d'Aquin." *Revue Thomiste* 83 (1983): 533–57.

———. *The Philosophical Theology of St. Thomas Aquinas*. Leiden, New York, København, and Köln: E. J. Brill, 1990.

Emery, Gilles, O.P. "Biblical Exegesis and the Speculative Doctrine of the Trinity in St. Thomas Aquinas's Commentary on St. John." In id., *Trinity in Aquinas*, 271–319.

———. "Key Themes in St. Thomas' Theology of the Trinity." In Henk H. M. Schoot, ed., *Jaarboek 2008 Thomas Institut te Utrecht*, 9–34. Utrecht: Thomas Instituut, 2009.

———. "Le Sacerdoce Spirituel des Fidèles chez Saint Thomas d'Aquin" *Revue Thomiste* 99 (1999): 211–43.

———. "La Théologie trinitaire des *Evidentiae contra Durandum* de Durandellus." *Revue Thomiste* 97:1 (1997): 173–218.

———. "The Treatise of St. Thomas on the Trinity in the Summa Contra Gentiles." In id., *Trinity in Aquinas*, 71–120.

———. *The Trinitarian Theology of Saint Thomas Aquinas*. Trans. Francesca A. Murphy. Oxford: Oxford University Press, 2007.

———. *La Trinité Créatrice: Trinité et création dans les commentaires aux* Sentences *de Thomas d'Aquin et de ses précurseurs Albert le Grand et Bonaventure*. Bibliothèque thomiste 57. Paris: Vrin, 1995.

———. *Trinity, Church, and the Human Person: Thomistic Essays*. Naples, Fla.: Sapientia Press, 2007.

———. *Trinity in Aquinas*. 2d ed. Ypsilanti, Mich. and Naples, Fla.: Sapientia Press, 2003; 2006.

Emery, Gilles, O.P., ed. Thomas d'Aquin, *Traités: Les raisons de la foi. Les articles de la foi et les sacrements de l'Église*. Introduction, traduction, et annotation. Paris: Cerf, 1999.

Emery, Kent. *Dionysii Cartusiensis Opera selecta: Prolegomena Bibliotheca manuscripta/ auctore Kent Emery Jr*. Turnhout: Brepols, 1991.

———. "Twofold Wisdom and Contemplation in Denys of Ryckel (Dionysius Cartusiensis, 1402–71)." *Journal of Medieval and Renaissance Studies* 18 (1988): 99–134.

Emery, Kent, and Joseph Wawrykow, eds. *Christ among the Medieval Dominicans: Representations of Christ in the Texts and Images of the Order of Preachers*. Notre Dame, Ind.: University of Notre Dame Press, 1998.

Eschmann, I. T. "A Catalogue of St. Thomas' Works." In E. Gilson, ed., *The Christian Philosophy of St. Thomas Aquinas*, trans. by L. K. Shook, 381–437. New York: Random House, 1956.

Evans, Gillian R. *Augustine on Evil*. Cambridge: Cambridge University Press, 1982.

———. "The Discussions of the Scientific Status of Theology in the Second Half of the Twelfth Century." In Matthias Lutz-Bachmann, Alexander Fidora, and Andreas Niederberger, eds., *Metaphysics in the Twelfth Century: On the Relationship among Philosophy, Science and Theology*, 161–83. Turnhout: Brepols, 2004.

Evans, Joseph. "Maritain, Jacques (1882–1973)." In Donald Borchert, ed., *Encyclopedia of Philosophy*. 2d ed. Vol. 1: 712–17. Detroit, Mich.: Macmillan Reference USA, 2006.

Fabro, Cornelio. *La nozione metafisica di partecipazione secondo S. Tommaso d'Aquino*. Turin: Società editrice internazionale, 2d rev. ed. 1950; 3d ed. 1963.

Falanga, A. J. *Charity: The Form of the Virtues according to Saint Thomas*. Washington, D.C.: Catholic University of America Press, 1948.

Farthing, John Lee. "The Problem of Divine Exemplarity in St. Thomas." *The Thomist* 49 (1985): 183–222.

Feldman, Seymour. "Maimonides—A Guide for Posterity." In Kenneth Seeskin, ed., *The Cambridge Companion to Maimonides*, 332–35. Cambridge: Cambridge University Press, 2005.

Fenton, N. E. "Weisheipl, James Athanasius." In *New Catholic Encyclopedia*. 2d ed. Vol. 14: 672–73. Detroit, Mich.: Gale, 2003.

Fidora, Alexander. *Die Wissenschaftstheorie des Dominicus Gundissalinus: Voraussetzungen und Konsequenzen des zweiten Anfangs der aristotelischen Philosophie im 12. Jahrhundert*. Berlin: Akademie Verlag, 2004.

Finnis, John. *Aquinas: Moral, Political, and Legal Theory*. Oxford: Oxford University Press, 1998.

———. *Natural Law and Natural Rights*. Oxford: Clarendon Press, 1980.

———. "Object and Intention in Moral Judgments according to Aquinas." *The Thomist* 55 (1991): 1–27.

Finnis, John, and Germain Grisez. "The Basic Principles of Natural Law: A Reply to Ralph McInerny." *American Journal of Jurisprudence* 26 (1981): 21–31.

Flannery, Kevin L., S.J. *Acts Amid Precepts: The Aristotelian Logical Structure of Thomas Aquinas's Moral Theory*. Washington, D.C.: Catholic University of America Press, 2001.

Floyd, Shawn. "Aquinas on Emotion: A Response to Some Recent Interpretations" *History of Philosophy Quarterly* 15 (1998): 161–75.
Fox, Rory. *Time and Eternity in Mid-Thirteenth Century Thought*. Oxford: Oxford University Press, 2006.
Funkhouser, Eric. "On Privileging God's Moral Goodness." *Faith and Philosophy* 23 (2006): 409–22.
Galbraith, Elizabeth. "Rahner, Karl (1904–1984)." In Donald Borchert, ed., *Encyclopedia of Philosophy*. 2d ed. Vol. 1: 231–34. Detroit, Mich.: Macmillan Reference USA, 2006.
Galeazzi, Umberto. "Le passioni secondo Tommaso d'Aquino: *De veritate* q. 26." *Aquinas* 47 (2004): 547–70.
Gallagher, David. "Free Choice and Free Judgment in Thomas Aquinas." *Archiv für Geschichte der Philosophie* 76 (1994): 247–77.
Galluzzo, Gabriele. "Aquinas on the Structure of Aristotle's *Metaphysics*." *Documenti e studi sulla tradizione medievale* 15 (2004): 353–86.
Garin, Eugenio. *History of Italian philosophy*. Tran. Giorgio A. Pinton. Vol. 1. Amsterdam: Rodopi, 2008.
Garrigou-Lagrange, Réginald, O.P. *La Synthèse Thomiste*. Bibliothèque française de philosophie. Paris: Desclée de Brouwer, 1946.
———. *Reality: A Synthesis of Thomistic Thought*. Trans. Patrick Cummins. St. Louis: Herder, 1958.
Gauthier, R. A. "Les 'Articuli in quibus frater Thomas melius in Summa quam in Scriptis.'" *Recherches de théologie ancienne et médievale* 19 (1952): 271–326.
———. "Le Cours sur l'*Ethica nova* d'un maitres es arts de Paris (1235–1240)." *Archives d'histoire doctrinale et litteraire du moyen age* 43 (1975): 71–141.
———. *"Introduction" à Saint Thomas d'Aquin, Somme contre les Gentils*. Paris: Éditions universitaires, 1993.
———. "Notes sur les débuts (1225–1240) du premier "averroïsme." *Revue des sciences philosophiques et théologiques* 66 (1982): 327–74.
———. *"Praefatio," Sententia libri Ethicorum*, in *Sancti Thomae de Aquino Opera Omnia*, T. XLVII. Vol. 1. Rome: Sancta Sabina, 1969.
Geach, Peter. *Providence and Evil*. Cambridge: Cambridge University Press, 1977.
Geenen, G. "Doctrinae concilii Chalcedonensis usus et influzus in theologia S. Thomas Aquinatis." *Divus Thomas* (Pl.) 56 (1953): 319–42.
———. "En marge du Concile de Chalcédoine: Les Textes du quatrième Concile dans les oeuvres de S. Thomas." *Angelicum* 19 (1952): 43–59.
Geiger, Louis Bertrand. "Abstraction et separation d'après s. Thomas *In De Trinitate* q. 5, a. 3." *Revue des sciences philosophiques et théologiques* 31 (1947): 3–40.
———. *La Participation dans la philosophie de S. Thomas d'Aquin*. 2d ed. Bibliothèque thomiste 23. Paris: Vrin, 1953.
———. "Les Rédactions sucessives de *Contra Gentiles I*, 53 d'après l'autographe." In Jean-Yves Jolif, O.P., et al., eds., *Saint Thomas d'Aquin aujourd'hui*, 221–40. Paris: Desclée de Brouwer, 1963.
Gerson, Lloyd P. *God and Greek Philosophy*. London and New York: Routledge, 1990.
Ghazali, Abu Hamid al. *Ihya' Ulum ad-Din* (Book 35): *Book of Faith in Divine Unity [tawhid] and Trust in Divine Providence [tawakkull]*. Trans. D. Burrell. Cambridge/Louisville, Ky.: Islamic Texts Society/Fons Vitae, 1996.
———. *The Incoherence of the Philosophers [Tahāfut al-falāsifah]*. Trans. Michael E. Marmura. Provo, Utah: Brigham Young University Press, 2000.
Gill, J. "Gennadius II Scholarius, Patriarch of Constantinople." In *New Catholic Encyclopedia*. 2d ed. Vol. 6: 136–37. Detroit, Mich.: Gale, 2003.

Gilson, Étienne. *Being and Some Philosophers*. Toronto: Pontifical Institute of Mediaeval Studies, 1952.

———. *The Christian Philosophy of St. Thomas Aquinas*. Notre Dame, Ind.: University of Notre Dame Press, 1994.

———. "Pourquoi Saint Thomas a critiqué Saint Augustin." *Archives d'histoire doctrinale et littéraire du Moyen Âge* 1 (1926): 1–127.

Glorieux, P. "Pour la chronologie de la Somme." *Mélanges de science religieuse* 2 (1945): 59–98.

Gorevan, Patrick. "Aquinas and Emotional Theory Today: Mind–Body, Cognitivism, and Connaturality." *Acta Philosophica* 9 (2000): 141–51.

Goris, Harm. "Divine Foreknowledge, Providence, Predestination, and Human Freedom." In Rik van Nieuwenhove and Joseph Wawrykow, eds., *The Theology of Thomas Aquinas*, 99–122. Notre Dame, Ind.: University of Notre Dame Press, 2005.

———. *Free Creatures of an Eternal God*. Nijmegen: Stichting Thomasfonds, 1996.

Gorman, Michael. "Christ as Composite according to Aquinas." *Traditio* 55 (2000): 143–57.

———. "Uses of the Person–Nature Distinction in Thomas's Christology." *Recherches de théologie et philosophie médiévales* 67 (2000): 58–79.

———. "The Essential and the Accidental." *Ratio* 18 (2005): 276–89.

Grabmann, Martin. *Mittelalterliches Geistesleben: Abhandlung zur Geschichte der Scholastik und Mystic*. Munich: Max Hueber, 1926 (Vol. 1); 1936 (Vol. 2); 1956 (Vol. 3).

Grant, Edward. *The Foundations of Modern Science in the Middle Ages: Their Religious, Institutional, and Intellectual Contexts*. Cambridge: Cambridge University Press, 1996.

Green, Keith. "Aquinas on Attachment, Envy, and Hatred in the *Summa theologiae*." *Journal of Religious Ethics* 35 (2007): 403–28.

Griffin, Michael. "Molina, Luis de (1535–1600)." In Donald Borchert, ed., *Encyclopedia of Philosophy*. 2nd ed. Vol. 1: 321–23. Detroit, Mich.: Macmillan Reference USA, 2006.

Grisez, Germain. "The Structures of Practical Reason: Some Comments and Clarifications." *The Thomist* 52 (1988): 269–91.

Gundisalvus, Dominicus. "The Treatise *De anima* of Dominicus Gundissalinus," ed. J. T. Muchkle, intro. E. Gilson. *Mediaeval Studies* 2 (1940): 23–103.

Guzie, Tad W. "The Act of Faith according to St. Thomas: A Study in Theological Methodology." *The Thomist* 29 (1965): 239–80.

Hankey, Wayne John. "*Ab uno simplici non est nisi unum*: The Place of Natural and Necessary Emanation in Aquinas' Doctrine of Creation." In Michael Treschow, Willemien Otten, and Walter Hannam, eds., *Divine Creation in Ancient, Medieval, and Early Modern Thought: Essays Presented to the Rev'd Dr Robert D. Crouse*. Studies in Intellectual History, 309–33. Leiden: Brill, 2007.

———. "Aquinas and the Platonists." In Stephen Gersh and Martin Hoenen, eds., *The Platonic Tradition in the Middle Ages: A Doxographic Approach*, 279–324. Berlin and New York: de Gruyter, 2002.

———. "Aquinas, Pseudo-Denys, Proclus and Isaiah VI.6." *Archives d'histoire doctrinale et littéraire du Moyen Âge* 64 (1997): 87–90.

———. *God in Himself: Aquinas' Doctrine of God as Expounded in the Summa Theologiae*. Oxford Theological Monographs/Oxford Scholarly Classics. Oxford: Oxford University Press, 1987.

———. "*Participatio divini luminis*, Aquinas' Doctrine of the Agent Intellect: Our Capacity for Contemplation." *Dionysius* 22 (2004): 149–78.

———. "Self and Cosmos in Becoming Deiform: Neoplatonic Paradigms for Reform by Self-Knowledge from Augustine to Aquinas." In Christopher Bellitto and Louis

Hamilton, eds., *Reforming the Church before Modernity: Patterns, Problems and Approaches*, 39–60. Aldershot: Ashgate, 2005.
———. "*Theoria versus Poesis*: Neoplatonism and Trinitarian Difference in Aquinas." *Modern Theology* 15 (1999): 387–415.
———. "Thomas' Neoplatonic Histories: His Following of Simplicius." *Dionysius* 20 (2002): 153–78.
———. "Why Philosophy Abides for Aquinas." *Heythrop Journal* 42:3 (2001): 329–48.
Harrington, Larry Michael, ed. *A Thirteenth-Century Textbook of Mystical Theology at the University of Paris*. Paris/Leuven and Dudley: Peeters, 2004.
Hasse, Dag Nikolaus. *Avicenna's De Anima in the Latin West: The Formation of a Peripatetic Philosophy of the Soul, 1160–1300*. London/Turin: The Warburg Institute/Nino Aragno, 2000.
———. "The Soul's Faculties." In R. Pasnau, ed. *The Cambridge History of Medieval Philosophy*, 305–19. Cambridge: Cambridge University Press, 2010.
Hause, Jeffrey. "Aquinas on the Function of Moral Virtue." *American Catholic Philosophical Quarterly* 81 (2007): 1–20.
———. "Thomas Aquinas and the Voluntarists." *Medieval Philosophy and Theology* 6 (1997): 167–82.
Henle, Robert John, S.J. *Saint Thomas and Platonism: A Study of the Plato and Platonici Texts in the Writings of Saint Thomas*. The Hague: Martinus Nijhoff, 1956.
Hergan, Jeffrey. *St. Albert the Great's Theory of the Beatific Vision*. New York: Peter Lang, 2002.
Hibbs, Thomas S. "Aquinas, Virtue, and Recent Epistemology." *Review of Metaphysics* 52 (1999): 573–94.
———. *Virtue's Splendor: Wisdom, Prudence and the Human Good*. New York: Fordham University Press, 2001.
Hill, Daniel. *Divinity and Maximal Greatness*. London: Routledge, 2005.
Hill, Thomas E., Jr. "Four Conceptions of Conscience." In Ian Shapiro and Robert Adams, eds., *Integrity and Conscience*, 13–52. New York and London: New York University Press, 1998.
Hill, W. J. "Thomism, Transcendental." In *New Catholic Encyclopedia*. 2d ed. Vol. 14: 52–57. Detroit, Mich.: Gale, 2003.
Hillgarth, J. N. "Who Read Thomas Aquinas?" In *The Gilson Lectures on Thomas Aquinas*, 46–73. Toronto: Pontifical Institutre of Mediaeval Studies, 2008.
Hinnebusch, J. F. "Crockaert, Peter." In *New Catholic Encyclopedia*. 2d ed. Vol. 4: 374. Detroit, Mich.: Gale, 2003.
Hissette, Roland. *Enquête sur les 219 articles condamnés à Paris le 7 mars 1277*. Louvain: Publications universitaires, 1977.
Hittinger, Russell. *A Critique of the New Natural Law Theory*. Notre Dame, Ind.: University of Notre Dame Press, 1987.
Hobson, Peter. "What Puts Jointness into Joint Attention?" In Naomi Eilan, et al., *Joint Attention: Communication and Other Minds: Issues in Philosophy and Psychology*, 185–204. New York: Oxford University Press, 2005.
Hochschild, Joshua P. "Cajetan, Cardinal (1469–1534)." In Donald Borchert, ed., *Encyclopedia of Philosophy*. 2d ed. Vol. 1: 6–7. Detroit, Mich.: Macmillan Reference USA, 2006.
———. *The Semantics of Analogy: Rereading Cajetan's De Nominum Analogia*. Notre Dame, Ind.: University of Notre Dame Press, 2010.
Hoffmann, Tobias. "Aquinas on the Moral Progress of the Weak Willed." In Tobias Hoffmann, Jörn Müller, and Matthias Perkams, eds., *The Problem of Weakness of Will in Medieval Philosophy*, 221–47. Leuven: Peeters, 2006.

Hughes, Christopher. *A Complex Theory of a Simple God.* Ithaca, N.Y.: Cornell University Press, 1989.

Hugo Grotius. *The Law of War and Peace.* Trans. Francis W. Kelsey. New York: Bobbs-Merrill Company, Inc., 1925.

Humbrecht, Thierry-Dominique, O.P. "L'Eucharistie, 'représentation' du sacrifice du Christ, selon saint Thomas." *Revue Thomiste* 98 (1998): 355–86.

———. *Théologie négative et noms divins chez saint Thomas d'Aquin.* Bibliothèque thomiste 57. Paris: Vrin, 2005.

Inglis, John. "Aquinas's Replication of the Acquired Moral Virtues." *Journal of Religious Ethics* 27:1 (1999): 3–27.

Iribarren, Isabel. *Durandus of St Pourcain: A Dominican Theologian in the Shadow of Aquinas.* Oxford: Oxford University Press, 2005.

Irwin, Terence. "Will, Reponsibility and Ignorance: Aristotelian Accounts of Incontinence." In Tobias Hoffmann, Jörn Müller, and Matthias Perkams, eds., *The Problem of Weakness of Will in Medieval Philosophy*, 40–58. Leuven: Peeters, 2006.

Jean de La Rochelle. *Summa de anima.* Ed. J. S. Bougerol. Paris: J. Vrin, 1995.

Jenkins, John I. *Knowledge and Faith in Thomas Aquinas.* Cambridge: Cambridge University Press, 1997.

Jeβberger, Ludwig. *Das Abhängigkeitsverhältnis des hl. Thomas von Aquin von Albertus Magnus und Bonaventura im dritten Buche des "Sentenzenkommentars."* Ph.D. diss., Würzburg, 1936.

John Capreolus. *Defensiones Theologiae divi Thomae Aquinatis.* Turonibus: Sumptibus Alfred Cattier, 1900.

John of Paris. *On Royal and Papal Power: A Translation, with Introduction, of De potestate Regia et Papali of John of Paris.* Tran. Arthur P. Monahan. New York: Columbia University Press, 1974.

———. *On Royal and Papal Power.* Tran. J. A. Watt. Toronto: Pontifical Institute of Mediaeval Studies, 2002.

John of St. Thomas. *The Gifts of the Holy Ghost.* Trans. Dominic Hughes, O.P. New York: Sheed & Ward, 1951.

Johnson, Mark F. "Aquinas' Changing Evaluation of Plato on Creation." *American Catholic Philosophical Quarterly* 66:1 (1992): 81–88.

Johnston, Mark. "Constitution is Not Identity." *Mind* 101 (1992): 89–105.

Jordan, Mark D. *The Alleged Aristotelianism of Thomas Aquinas.* The Etienne Gilson Series 15. Toronto: Pontifical Institute of Mediaeval Studies, 1992.

———. "The Names of God and the Being of Names." In Alfred J. Freddoso, ed., *The Existence and Nature of God*, 161–90. Notre Dame, Ind.: University of Notre Dame Press, 1983.

———. *Rewritten Theology: Aquinas After His Readers.* Malden, Mass., and Oxford: Blackwell Publishing, 2006.

———. "Theology and Philosophy." In Norman Kretzmann and Eleonore Stump, eds., *The Cambridge Companion to Aquinas*, 232–51. Cambridge: Cambridge University Press, 1993.

Kanner, Leo. "Autistic Disturbances of Affective Contact." *Nerv. Child* 2:220 (1943); reprinted in *Acta Paedopsychiatrica* 35:4 (1968): 100–36.

Keenan, James F. *Goodness and Rightness in Thomas Aquinas's* Summa Theologiae. Washington, D.C.: Catholic University of America Press, 1992.

Kelly, Matthew J. " 'Subject,' 'Substance,' and 'Accident' in St. Thomas." *The New Scholasticism* 50 (1976): 232–36.

Kennedy, L. A. *A Catalogue of Thomists, 1270–1900*. Notre Dame, Ind.: University of Notre Dame Press, 1987.

Kenny, Anthony. *Aquinas on Being*. Oxford: Oxford University Press, 2002.

———. *Aquinas on Mind*. London: Routledge, 1993.

———. "Divine Foreknowledge and Human Freedom." In Anthony Kenny, ed., *Aquinas: A Collection of Critical Essays*, 255–70. London: MacMillan, 1969.

———. *The Five Ways: Saint Thomas Aquinas' Proofs of God's Existence*. London: Routledge & K. Paul, 1969.

———. *What is Faith? Essays in the Philosophy of Religion*. Oxford: Oxford University Press, 1992.

———. *Will, Freedom, and Power*. Oxford: Basil Blackwell, 1975.

Kenny, Anthony, ed. *Aquinas: A Collection of Critical Essays*. Notre Dame, Ind.: University of Notre Dame Press. 1976.

Kent, Bonnie. "Does Virtue Make It Easy to be Good? The Problematic Case of St. Paul." In Bernardo C. Bazán, Eduardo Andújar, and Leonard G. Sbrocchi, eds., *Les Philosophies morales et politiques au Moyen Âge: Actes du IXe Congrès International de Philosophie Médiévale, Ottawa, 17–22 Août 1992*, 723–32. Ottawa: Legas, 1995.

———. *Virtues of the Will: The Transformation of Ethics in the Late Thirteenth Century*. Washington, D.C.: Catholic University of America Press, 1995.

Kerr, Fergus, O.P. *After Aquinas: Versions of Thomism*. Oxford: Blackwell Publishing, 2002.

———. "Theology in Philosophy: Revisiting the Five Ways." *International Journal for Philosophy of Religion* 50 (2001): 115–30.

Kilmartin, Edward J. *The Eucharist in the West*. Collegeville, Minn.: Liturgical Press, 1998.

King, Peter. "Aquinas on the Passions." In Scott MacDonald and Eleonore Stump, eds., *Aquinas's Moral Theory*, 101–32. Ithaca, N.Y.: Cornell University Press 1998.

———. "Dispassionate Passions." In Martin Pickave and Lisa Shapiro, eds., *Reason and Emotion in Medieval and Early Modern Philosophy*. Oxford: Oxford University Press, 2011.

———. "Emotions in Medieval Thought." In Peter Goldie, ed., *The Oxford Handbook of Philosophy of Emotion*, 167–87. Oxford: Oxford University Press, 2010.

Kirk, Kenneth. *The Vision of God: The Christian Doctrine of the Summum Bonum*. New York: Harper Torchbooks, 1966.

Kirwan, Christopher. *Augustine*. London: Routledge, 1989.

Klima, Gyula. "Aquinas on the Materiality of the Human Soul and the Immateriality of the Human Intellect." *Philosophical Investigations* 32 (2009): 163–82.

———. "Aquinas' Theory of the Copula and the Analogy of Being." *Logical Analysis and History of Philosophy* 5 (2002): 159–76.

———. "The Changing Role of Entia Rationis in Medieval Philosophy: A Comparative Study with a Reconstruction." *Synthese* 96 (1993): 25–59.

———. "Peter of Spain, the Author of the Summulae." In J. Gracia and T. Noone, eds., *Blackwell's Companion to Philosophy in the Middle Ages*, 526–31. Oxford: Blackwell Publishing, 2003.

———. "Review of C. Panaccio: Le Discours intérieur de Platon à Guillaume d'Ockham." *History and Philosophy of Logic* 23 (2002): 71–73.

———. "The Semantic Principles Underlying Saint Thomas Aquinas's Metaphysics of Being." *Medieval Philosophy and Theology* 5 (1996): 87–141.

———. "Syncategoremata." In Keith Brown, ed., *Elsevier's Encyclopedia of Language and Linguistics*. 2d ed. Vol. 12: 353–56. Oxford: Elsevier, 2006.

Klima, Gyula, Fritz Allhoff, and Anand Jayprakash Vaidya, eds. *Medieval Philosophy: Essential Readings with Commentary*. Oxford: Blackwell Publishing, 2007.

Klubertanz, George P. *St. Thomas Aquinas on Analogy: A Textual Analysis and Systematic Synthesis*. Chicago: Loyola University Press, 1960.

Kluxen, Wolfgang. "Thomas von Aquin: Das Seiende und seine Prinzipien." In J. Speck, ed., *Grundprobleme der großen Philosophen*, 174–214. Göttingen: Vandenhoeck & Rupprecht, 1972.

Knasas, John F. X. "Ad Mentem Thomae: Does Natural Philosophy Prove God?" *Proceedings of the American Catholic Philosophical Association* 61 (1987): 209–19.

———. *Being and Some Twentieth-Century Thomists*. New York: Fordham University Press, 2003.

Knuutila, Simo. *Emotions in Ancient and Medieval Philosophy*. Oxford: Oxford University Press, 2004.

———. *Modalities in Medieval Philosophy*. New York: Routledge, 1993.

———. "The 'Statistical' Interpretation of Modality in Averroes and Thomas Aquinas." *Ajatus* 37 (1978): 79–98.

Kondoleon, Theodore J. "God's Knowledge of Future Contingent Singulars: A Reply." *The Thomist* 56:1 (January 1992): 117–39.

Kretzmann, Norman. "Evidence Against Anti-Evidentialism." In Kelly J. Clark, ed., *Our Knowledge of God: Essays on Natural and Philosophical Theology*, 17–38. Dordrecht, Boston, and London: Kluwer Academic Publishers, 1992.

———. "Infallibility, Error, and Ignorance." In Richard Bosley and Martin Tweedale, eds., *Aristotle and His Medieval Interpreters*, 159–94. Calgary: University of Calgary Press, 1991.

———. *The Metaphysics of Theism: Aquinas's Natural Theology in* Summa contra Gentiles *I*. Oxford: Clarendon Press, 1997.

Kretzmann, Norman, and Eleonore Stump, eds. *The Cambridge Companion to Augustine*. Cambridge: Cambridge University Press, 2001.

Kries, Douglas. "Origen, Plato, and Conscience (*Synderesis*) in Jerome's Ezekiel Commentary." *Traditio* 57 (2002): 67–83.

Kronen, John D., Sandra Mennsen, and Thomas D. Sullivan. "The Problem of the Continuant: Aquinas and Suarez on Prime Matter and Substantial Generation." *Review of Metaphysics* 53 (2000): 863–85.

Labourdette, M-Michel. "Connaissance practique et savoir moral." *Revue Thomiste* 48 (1948): 142–79.

Lafont, Ghislain. *Peut-on connaître Dieu en Jésus Christ?* Paris: Cerf, 1969.

Lagerlund, Henrik. *Rethinking the History of Skepticism: The Missing Medieval Background*. Leiden: Brill, 2010.

Lanczowski, M., and R. Wittwer. "Les *Evidentiae contra Durandum* de Durandellus." *Revue Thomiste* 97:1 (1997): 143–56.

Lauer, Rosemary. "The Notion of Efficient Cause in the Secunda Via." *The Thomist* 38 (1974): 754–67.

Lawrence, F. G. "Lonergan, Bernard." In *New Catholic Encyclopedia*. 2d ed. Vol. 8: 772–75. Detroit, Mich.: Gale, 2003.

Le Boulluec, Alain. "Recherches sur les origines du thème de la syndérèse dans la tradition patristique." In Christian Trottmann, ed., *Vers la contemplation: Études sur la syndérèse et les modalités de la contemplation de l'Antiquité à la Renaissance*, 61–77. Paris: Librairie Honoré Champion, 2007.

Leftow, Brian. "Aquinas, Divine Simplicity and Divine Freedom." In Kevin Timpe, ed., *Metaphysics and God*. London: Routledge, forthcoming.

———. "Aquinas on God and Modal Truth." *Modern Schoolman* 82:3 (2005): 171–200.

———. "Divine Simplicity." *Faith and Philosophy* 23 (2006): 365–80.
———. "Omnipotence." In Thomas Flint and Michael Rea, eds., *The Oxford Handbook of Philosophical Theology*. Oxford: Oxford University Press, forthcoming.
———. *Time and Eternity*. Ithaca, N.Y.: Cornell University Press, 1991.
Levering, Matthew. *Christ's Fulfillment of Torah and Temple: Salvation according to Aquinas*. Notre Dame, Ind.: University of Notre Dame Press, 2002.
———. *Scripture and Metaphysics: Aquinas and the Renewal of Trinitarian Theology*. Oxford: Blackwell, 2004.
Libera, Alain de. La *Querelle des universaux: De Platon à la fin du Moyen Age*. Paris: Des travaux, 1996.
Libera, Alain de, ed. Thomas d'Aquin, *L'Unité de l'intellect contre les averroïstes, suivi des Textes contre Averroès antérieurs à 1270*. Texte latin. Traduction, introduction, bibliographie, chronologie, notes et index. GF 713. Paris: Flammarion, 1994.
Libera, Alain de, and Cyrille Michon, ed. and trans. Thomas Aquinas–Dietrich de Freiberg, *L'Etre et l'essence: Le Vocabulaire médiéval de l'ontologie*. Commentary by Alain de Libera and Cyrille Michon. Point: Essais. Paris: Seuil, 1996.
Lisska, Anthony. *Aquinas's Theory of Natural Law: An Analytic Reconstruction*. Oxford: Clarendon Press, 1996.
Litt, T. *Les Corps célestes dans l'univers de saint Thomas d'Aquin*. Louvain and Paris: Publications universitaires and Béatrice-Nauwelaerts, 1963.
Lonergan, Bernard. "St. Thomas's Thought on *Gratia Operans*." *Theological Studies* 2 (1941): 289–324; 3 (1942): 69–88, 375–402, 533–78. Reprinted as *Grace and Freedom: Operative Grace in the Thought of Thomas Aquinas*, ed. F. E. Crowe and R. M. Doran. Toronto: University of Toronto Press, 2000.
Lottin, Odon, O.S.B. "La Date de la Question Disputée *De Malo* de Saint Thomas d'Aquin." *Revue d'histoire ecclésiastique* 24 (1928): 373–88.
———. *Psychologie et morale aux XII et XIII siècles*. Vol. 3/1 and 2. Paris: Louvain, 1949.
———. "Syndérèse et conscience aux XIIe et XIIIe siècles." In *Psychologie et morale aux XIIe et XIIIe siècles*. Vol. 2/1: 103–349. Leuven/Gembloux: Abbaye du Mont César/J. Duculot, 1948.
Loughlin, Stephen. "*Tristitia et dolor*: Does Aquinas Have a Robust Understanding of Depression?" *Nova et Vetera* 3 (2005): 761–83.
Luna, C. "Quelques précisions chronologiques à propos de la controverse sur l'unité de l'intellect." *Revue des sciences philosophiques et théologiques* 83 (1999): 649–84.
Lutz-Bachmann, Matthias. "Die Einteilung der Wissenschaften des Thomas von Aquin. Ein Beitrag zur Rekonstruktion der Epistemologie in Quaestio 5, Artikel 1 des Kommentars von Thomas zum Trinitätstraktat des Boethius." In Rainer Berndt and Matthias Lutz-Bachmann, eds., *"Scientia" und "Disciplina": Wissenstheorie und Wissenschaftspraxis im 12. und 13. Jahrhundert*, 235–47. Berlin: Akademie Verlag, 2002.
MacDonald, Scott. "Aquinas's Libertarian Account of Free Choice." *Revue Internationale de Philosophie* 2 (1998): 309–28.
———. "Aquinas's Parasitic Cosmological Argument." *Medieval Philosophy and Theology* 1 (1991): 119–55.
———. "The Metaphysics of Goodness and the Doctrine of the Transcendentals." In Scott MacDonald, ed., *Being and Goodness: The Concept of the Good in Metaphysics and Philosophical Theology*, 31–55. Ithaca, N.Y. and London: Cornell University Press, 1991.
———. "Practical Reasoning and Reasons-Explanations: Aquinas's Account of Reason's Role in Action." In Scott MacDonald and Eleonore Stump, eds., *Aquinas's Moral Theory: Essays in Honor of Norman Kretzmann*, 133–60. Ithaca, N.Y.: Cornell University Press, 1998.

———. "The Relation between Being and Goodness." In Scott MacDonald, ed., *Being and Goodness: The Concept of the Good in Metaphysics and Philosophical Theology*, 1–30. Ithaca, N.Y. and London: Cornell University Press, 1991.

———. "Theory of Knowledge." In Norman Kretzmann and Eleonore Stump, eds., *The Cambridge Companion to Aquinas*, 160–95. Cambridge: Cambridge University Press, 1993.

———. "Ultimate Ends in Practical Reasoning: Aquinas's Aristotelian Moral Psychology and Anscombe's Fallacy." *Philosophical Review* 100 (1991): 31–66.

MacDonald, Scott, ed. *Being and Goodness: The Concept of the Good in Metaphysics and Philosophical Theology*. Ithaca, N.Y.: Cornell University Press, 1991.

MacIntosh, J. J. "Aquinas on Necessity." *American Catholic Philosophical Quarterly* 72 (1998): 371–404.

———. "St. Thomas on Angelic Time and Motion." *The Thomist* 59 (1995): 547–75.

Magister Artium. *Lectura in librum De anima a quodam discipulo reportata* (Ms. Roma Naz. V. E. 828). Ed. R. A. Gauthier. Grottoferrata: Collegium S. Bonaventurae, 1985.

———. *Sententia super II et III De anima* (Oxf. Bod. Lib. Lat. Misc. C. 70, f. 1ra–25b; Roma, Bibl. Naz. V. E. 828, f. 46vb, 48ra–52ra). Ed. B. Carlos Bazan. Louvain-la neuve and Louvain-Paris: Peeters, 1998.

Maillard, P. Y. *La Vision de Dieu chez Thomas d'Aquin: Une lecture de l'*In Ioannem *à la lumière de ses sources augustiniennes*. Bibliothèque thomiste 53. Paris: Vrin, 2001.

Mandonnet, P. *Les Dominicains et la découverte de l'Amérique*. Paris: P. Lethielleux, 1893.

Mansini, G. "Similitudo, Communicatio, and the Friendship of Charity in Aquinas." *Thomistica, Recherches de théologie ancienne et médiévale*, Supplement 1 (Leuven, 1995): 1–26.

Manzanedo, Marcos. "Efectos y propriedades de la delectación." *Studium* 29 (1989): 107–39.

———. "El deseo y la aversión según Santo Tomás." *Studium* 27 (1987): 189–233.

———. "El dolor y sus causas." *Studium* 31 (1991): 63–97.

———. "La audacia según Santo Tomás." *Studium* 34 (1994): 437–53.

Marenbon, John. *The Philosophy of Peter Abelard*. Cambridge: Cambridge University Press, 1997.

Markosian, Ned. "Simples, Stuff, and Simple People." *The Monist* 87 (2004): 405–28.

Marmo, Costantino. "*Hoc etiam etsi potest tollerari*… Egidio Romano e Tommaso d'Aquino sulle passioni dell'anima." *Documenti e studi sulla tradizione filosofica medievale* 2 (1991): 281–315.

Marrone, Steven. *The Light of Thy Countenance: Science and Knowledge of God in the Thirteenth Century*. 2 vols. Leiden: Brill, 2001.

Martin, C. F. J. *Thomas Aquinas: God and Explanations*. Edinburgh: Edinburgh University Press, 1997.

Masiello, Ralph J. "Reason and Faith in Richard of St. Victor and St. Thomas." *New Scholasticism* 48 (1974): 233–42.

Masnovo, Amato. *Da Guglielmo d'Auvergne a S. Tommaso d'Aquino*. 3 vols. Milan: Società Editrice Vita e Pensiero, 1930–45.

Maurer, Armand A. "James Ross on the Divine Ideas: A Reply." *American Catholic Philosophical Quarterly* 65 (1991): 213–20.

McCabe, Herbert. Appendix 4 in *Summa Theologiae*. Vol. 3. London and New York: Eyre and Spottiswoode, 1964.

———. *Faith Within Reason*. Ed. Brian Davies. New York: Continuum, 2007.

———. *God and Evil in the Theology of St. Thomas Aquinas*. Ed. Brian Davies. New York: Continuum, 2010.

———. *The Good Life: Ethics and the Pursuit of Happiness*. Ed. Brian Davies. London and New York: Continuum, 2005.
———. *Law, Love, and Language*. New York: Continuum, 2003.
———. *On Aquinas*. Ed. Brian Davies. London and New York: Continuum, 2008.
McDermott, Timothy, ed. *Aquinas: Selected Philosophical Writings*. Oxford: Oxford University Press, 1993.
McInerny, Ralph. *Aquinas on Human Action: A Theory of Practice*. Washington, D.C.: Catholic University of America Press, 1992.
———. *Boethius and Aquinas*. Washington, D.C.: Catholic University of America Press, 1990.
———. *Ethica Thomistica: The Moral Philosophy of Thomas Aquinas*. Washington, D.C.: Catholic University of America Press, 1982; revised 1997.
———. "The Principles of Natural Law." *American Journal of Jurisprudence* 25 (1980): 1–15.
———. "Saint Thomas on De hebdomadibus." In Scott MacDonald, ed., *Being and Goodness: The Concept of the Good in Metaphysics and Philosophical Theology*, 74–97. Ithaca, N.Y. and London: Cornell University Press, 1991.
McQueen, Donald. "What is Aquinas' Second Way?" *History of Philosophy Quarterly* 11:1 (1994): 23–35.
Meyer, C. R. "Henry of Gorkum." In *New Catholic Encyclopedia*. 2d ed. Vol. 6: 753. Detroit, Mich.: Gale, 2003.
Meyer, Michel. "Le Problème des passions chez saint Thomas d'Aquin." *Revue Internationale de Philosophie* 48 (1994): 363–74.
Michon, Cyrille, ed. *Thomas d'Aquin et la controverse sur L'éternité du monde*. Traités sur l'éternité du monde de Bonaventure, Thomas d'Aquin, Peckam, Boèce de Dacie, Henri de Gand et Guillaume d'Ockam. GF Flammarion 1199. Paris: Flammarion, 2004.
Miller, Robert. "Gilson, Étienne Henry (1884–1978)." In Donald Borchert, ed., *Encyclopedia of Philosophy*. 2d ed. Vol. 1: 91–93. Detroit, Mich.: Macmillan Reference USA, 2006.
Miner, Robert. *Thomas Aquinas on the Passions*. Cambridge: Cambridge University Press, 2009.
———. "Non-Aristotelian Prudence in the Prima Secundae." *The Thomist* 64 (2000): 401–22.
Moltmann, Jürgen. *The Crucified God*. London: SCM, 1976.
Montagnes, B. *La Doctrine de l'analogie de l'être d'après saint Thomas d'Aquin*. Louvain: Nauwelaerts, 1963; repr. Paris: Éditions du Cerf, 2008. English translation: *The Doctrine of the Analogy of Being according to Thomas Aquinas*. Trans. E. M. Macierowski and P. Vandevelde. Milwaukee: Marquette University Press, 2004.
Moody, Ernest. "William of Ockham (c. 1285–1349)." In Donald Borchert, ed., *Encyclopedia of Philosophy*. 2d ed. Vol. 1: 770–85. Detroit, Mich.: Macmillan Reference USA, 2006.
Morard, M. "Thomas d'Aquin lecteur des Conciles." *Archivum Franciscanum Historicum* 98 (2005): 213–365.
Mourant, John. "Suárez, Francisco (1548–1617)." In Donald Borchert, ed., *Encyclopedia of Philosophy*. 2d ed. Vol. 1: 282–85. Detroit, Mich.: Macmillan Reference USA, 2006.
Mulchahey, M. M. *"First the Bow is Bent in Study . . .": Dominican Education before 1350*. Studies and Texts 132. Toronto: P.I.M.S., 1998.
Murphy, Claudia. "Aquinas on Our Responsibility for Our Emotions." *Medieval Philosophy and Theology* 8 (1999): 163–205.
Narbonne, Jean-Marc. *Hénologie, ontologie et Ereignis (Plotin-Proclus-Heidegger)*. Paris: Les Belles Lettres, 2001.
Naus, John. *The Nature of the Practical Intellect*. Rome: Libreria Editrice dell' Universita Gregoriana, 1959.

Nederman, Cary. "Aristotelianism and the Origins of 'Political Science' in the Twelfth Century." *Journal of the History of Ideas* 52 (1991): 179–94.

Nelson, Daniel Mark. *The Priority of Prudence: Virtue and Natural Law in Aquinas and Its Implications for Modern Ethics*. University Park: Pennsylvania State University Press, 1992.

Nichols, Aidan, O.P. *Discovering Aquinas*. Grand Rapids, Mich.: Eerdmans, 2003.

Niederbacher, Bruno. "Erläuterungen des Prologs zum Sentenzenkommentar des Thomas von Aquin." In Bruno Niederbacher and Gerhard Leibold, eds., *Theologie als Wissenschaft im Mittelalter: Texte, Übersetzungen, Kommentare*, 268–89. Münster: Aschendorff, 2006.

———. *Glaube als Tugend bei Thomas von Aquin: Erkenntnistheoretische und religionsphilosophische Interpretationen*. Stuttgart: Kohlhammer, 2004.

———. "Immediate Cognition of God: Aquinas on Rapture." *Disputatio Philosophica* 2 (2000): 71–88.

Noone, T. B. "The Originality of St. Thomas's Position on the Philosophers and Creation." *The Thomist* 60 (1996): 275–300.

Nuchelmans, Gabriel. *Late Scholastic and Humanist Theories of the Proposition*. Amsterdam: North Holland Publishing Co., 1980.

———. *Theories of the Proposition: Ancient and Medieval Conceptions of the Bearers of Truth and Falsity*. Amsterdam: North Holland Publishing Co., 1973.

O'Daly, G. "Dionysius Areopagita." *Theologische Realenzyklopädie* 8 (1981): 772–80.

O'Meara, Thomas Franklin, O.P. *Thomas Aquinas Theologian*. Notre Dame, Ind.: University of Notre Dame Press, 1997.

O'Rourke, Fran. *Pseudo-Dionysius and the Metaphysics of Aquinas*. Studien und Texte zur Geistesgeschichte des Mittelalters 32. Leiden: Brill, 1992.

Oliva, A. *Les Débuts de l'enseignement de Thomas d'Aquin et sa conception de la* sacra doctrina, *Avec l'édition du prologue de son commentaire des* Sentences. Paris: Vrin, 2006.

———. "Quelques éléments de la *doctrina theologiae* selon Thomas d'Aquin." In M. Olszewski, ed., *What is "Theology" in the Middle Ages? Religious Cultures of Europe (11th–15th Centuries) as Reflected in Their Self-Understanding*, 167–93. Münster: Aschendorff, 2007.

Ols, D. *Le Cristologie contemporanee e le loro posizioni fondamentali al vaglio della dottrina di S. Tommaso*. Città del Vaticano: Libreria Editrice Vaticana, 1991.

Origen. *Origen On Prayer*. Trans. E. G. Jay. London: S.P.C.K., 1954.

Osborne, Kenan B. *Christian Sacraments in a Postmodern World: A Theology for the Third Millennium*. New York and Mahwah, N.J.: Paulist Press, 1999.

Osborne, Thomas M., Jr. *The Love of Self and Love of God in Thirteenth-Century Ethics*. Notre Dame, Ind.: University of Notre Dame Press, 2005.

———. "Perfect and Imperfect Virtues in Aquinas." *The Thomist* 71 (2007): 57–62.

———. "The Threefold Referral of Acts to the Ultimate End in Thomas Aquinas and His Commentators." *Angelicum* 85 (2008): 715–36.

Owens, Joseph, C.Ss.R. "Aquinas and the Five Ways." *The Monist* 58 (1974): 16–35; reprinted in John Catan, ed., *St. Thomas Aquinas on the Existence of God: Collected Papers of Joseph Owens*, 132–42. Albany: State University of New York Press, 1980.

Paissac, H. *Théologie du Verbe: Saint Augustine et saint Thomas*. Paris: Éditions du Cerf, 1951.

Panaccio, Claude. "Aquinas on Intellectual Representation." In D. Perler, ed., *Ancient and Medieval Theories of Intentionality*, 185–201. Leiden: Brill, 2001.

———. *Le Discours intérieur de Platon à Guillaume d'Ockham*. Paris: Éditions du Seuil, 1999.

———. "From Mental Word to Mental Language." *Philosophical Topics* 20 (1992): 125–47.
Pasnau, Robert. *Metaphysical Themes 1274–1671*. Oxford: Clarendon Press, 2010.
———. "Science and Certainty." In Robert Pasnau and Christina Van Dyke, eds., *The Cambridge History of Medieval Philosophy*, 357–68. Cambridge: Cambridge University Press, 2010.
———. *Theories of Cognition in the Later Middle Ages*. Cambridge: Cambridge University Press, 1997.
———. *Thomas Aquinas on Human Nature: A Philosophical Study of* Summa theologiae *Ia 75–89*. Cambridge: Cambridge University Press, 2002.
———. *Thomas Aquinas: The Treatise on Human Nature*. Summa theologiae *1a 75–89*. Indianapolis, Ind.: Hackett, 2002.
Pasnau, Robert, and Christopher Shields. *The Philosophy of Aquinas*. Boulder, Colo.: Westview Press, 2004.
Pawl, Timothy. "A Thomistic Account of Truthmakers for Modal Truths." Ph.D. diss., Saint Louis University, 2008.
Pegis, Anton C. *St. Thomas and the Problem of the Soul in the Thirteenth Century*. Toronto: Pontifical Institute of Mediaeval Studies, 1934.
Pelster, Franz. "Das Wachstum der Seligkeit nach der Aufestehung, um die Auslegung von S. Th. I–II, q. 4 a. 5 ad 5." *Scholastik* 27 (1952): 561–63.
Penelhum, Terence. "The Analysis of Faith in St Thomas Aquinas." *Religious Studies* 3 (1977): 133–54.
Perler, Dominik. "Late Medieval Ontologies of Facts." *The Monist* 77 (1994): 149–69.
———. *Zweifel und Gewissheit: Skeptische Debatten im Mittelalter*. Frankfurt a.M.: Klostermann, 2006.
Peter of Spain. *Commentarium in De anima*. Ed. M. A. Alonso. In *Obras Filosóficas*, n. 2. Madrid, 1944.
———. *Scientia libri De anima*. Ed. M. A. Alonso. 2d ed. Barcelona: Flors, 1961.
———. *Syncategoreumata*. Ed. L. M. De Rijk and trans. J. Spruyt. Leiden: E. J. Brill, 1992.
———. *Tractatus* (called afterwards *Summule Logicales*). Ed. L. M. De Rijk. Assen: Van Gorcum, 1972.
Pfürtner, S. *Luther and Aquinas on Salvation*. Trans. E. Quinn. New York: Sheed and Ward, 1964.
Pinckaers, Servais, O.P. *Morality: The Catholic View*. South Bend, Ind.: St. Augustine's Press, 2003.
———. *The Sources of Christian Ethics*. Washington, D.C.: Catholic University of America Press, 1995.
Pini, Giorgio. "Henry of Ghent's Doctrine of *Verbum* in Its Theological Context." In *Henry of Ghent and the Transformation of Scholastic Thought: Studies in Memory of Jos Decorte*, 307–26. Leuven: Leuven Univesity Press, 1993.
———. "Two Models of Thinking: Thomas Aquinas and John Duns Scotus." In Gyula Klima, ed., *Intentionality, Cognition and Representation in the Middle Ages*. New York: Fordham University Press, forthcoming.
Plantinga, Alvin. *Does God Have a Nature?* Milwaukee, Wis.: Marquette University Press, 1980.
———. *The Nature of Necessity*. Oxford: Clarendon Press, 1974.
———. "Warranted Christian Belief: The Aquinas/Calvin Model." In Godehard Brüntrup and Ronald C. Tacelli, eds., *The Rationality of Theism*, 125–43. Dordrecht: Cluwer Academic Publishers, 1999.
———. *Warranted Christian Belief*. New York: Oxford University Press, 2000.

Pope, Stephen J., ed. *The Ethics of Aquinas*. Washington, D.C.: Georgetown University Press, 2002.

Porter, Jean. *Nature as Reason: A Thomistic Theory of the Natural Law*. Grand Rapids, Mich.: Eerdmans, 2005.

———. *The Recovery of Virtue: The Relevance of Aquinas for Christian Ethics*. Louisville, Ky.: Westminster/John Knox Press, 1990.

———. "The Subversion of Virtue: Acquired and Infused Virtues in the 'Summa theologiae.'" *Annual of the Society of Christian Ethics*, 1992.

———. "The Unity of the Virtues and the Ambiguity of Goodness: A Reappraisal of Aquinas's Theory of the Virtuous." *Journal of Religious Ethics* 21 (1993): 137–63.

Potts, Timothy C. "Aquinas on Belief a nd Faith." In James F. Ross, ed., *Inquiries into Medieval Philosophy: A Collection in Honor of Francis P. Clarke*, 3–22. Westport, Conn.: Greenwood, 1971.

———. *Conscience in Medieval Philosophy*. Cambridge: Cambridge University Press, 1980.

Proclus. *Elements of Theology*. 2d ed. Ed. Eric Robertson Dodds. Oxford: Clarendon, 1963.

Przezdziecki, J. J. "Thomas of Sutton." In *New Catholic Encyclopedia*. 2d ed. Vol. 14: 37. Detroit, Mich.: Gale, 2003.

Pseudo-Augustinus. *De spiritu et anima*. In *Patrologia Latina*. Vol. 40: 779–832. Paris: J. P. Migne, 1870.

Pseudo-Peter of Spain. *Expositio libri De anima*. Published as: *Pedro Hispano, Obras Filosóficas*. Ed. M. Alonso. Vol. 3. Madrid: Instituto Luis Vives, 1954.

Questiones in tres libros De anima. In *Ein anonymer Aristoteleskommentar des XIII. Jarhunderts*. Ed. J. Vennebusch. Paderborn: F. Schöningh, 1963.

Rairweather, Eugene. "Henry of Ghent (??–1293)." In Donald Borchert, ed., *Encyclopedia of Philosophy*. 2d ed. Vol. 1: 312–315. Detroit, Mich.: Macmillan Reference USA, 2006.

Reichberg, Gregory M. "Francisco De Vitoria, De Indis and De Iure Belli Relectiones (1557): Philosophy Meets War." In Jorge J. E. Gracia, ed., *The Classics of Western Philosophy: A Reader's Guide*, 197–203. Malden, Mass.: Blackwell Publishing, 2003.

———. "The Intellectual Virtues (Ia IIae, qq. 57–58)." In Stephen J. Pope, ed., *The Ethics of Aquinas*, 131–50. Washington, D.C.: Georgetown University Press, 2002.

Reinhardt, Elisabeth, and Josep-Ignasi Saranyana. "La configuración de la ciencia teológica. De Hugo de San Víctor a Tomás de Aquino." *Veritas* 43:3 (1998): 549–62.

Reith, Herman. *The Metaphysics of St. Thomas Aquinas*. Milwaukee, Wis.: Bruce, 1958.

Remy, Gérard. "Sacerdoce et médiation chez saint Thomas." *Revue Thomiste* 99 (1999): 101–18.

Reynolds, Philip. "Properties, Causality, and Epistemic Optimism in Thomas Aquinas." *Recherches de théologie et philosophie médiévales* 68 (2001): 270–309.

Rhonheimer, Martin. *Natural Law and Practical Reason*. Trans. Gerarld Malsbary. New York: Fordham University Press, 2000.

Ricken, Friedo. "Aristotelische Interpretationen zum Traktat *De passionibus animae* (*Summa theologiae* I II *22–48*) des Thomas von Aquin." In Martin Thurner, ed., *Die Einheit der Person: Beiträge zur Anthropologie des Mittelalters*, 125–40. Stuttgart: Kohlhammer, 1998.

———. *Glauben weil es vernünftig ist*. Stuttgart: Kohlhammer, 2007.

Robert, Aurélien. *Penser la substance: Étude d'une question médiévale (XIIIe–XIVe siècles)*. Paris: Vrin, forthcoming.

Roberts, Robert C. *Emotions: An Essay in Aid of Moral Psychology*. Cambridge: Cambridge University Press, 2003.

Roessler, Johannes. "Joint Attention and the Problem of Other Minds." In Naomi Eilan, et al., *Joint Attention: Communication and Other Minds: Issues in Philosophy and Psychology*, 230–59. New York: Oxford University Press, 2005.

Roger Marston. *Quaestiones disputatae*. Quaracchi, Florence: Ad Claras Aquas, 1932.
Ross, James. "Aquinas' Exemplarism; Aquinas' Voluntarism." *American Catholic Philosophical Quarterly* 64 (1990): 171–98.
———. "Response to Maurer and Dewan." *American Catholic Philosophical Quarterly* 65 (1991): 235–43.
Ross, James F. "Aquinas on Belief and Knowledge." In William Frank and Girard J. Etzkorn, eds., *Essays Honoring Allan B. Wolter*, 245–69. New York: Franciscan Institute St. Bonaventure, 1985.
———. "Justice is Reasonableness: Aquinas on Human Law and Morality." *The Monist* 58:1 (January 1974): 86–103.
Rota, Michael. "Substance and Artifact in Thomas Aquinas." *History of Philosophy Quarterly* 21 (2004): 241–59.
Rowe, William. *The Philosophy of Religion: An Introduction*. Belmont, Calif.: Wadsworth, 1993.
———. "The Problem of Evil and Some Varieties of Atheism." *American Philosophical Quarterly* 16 (1979); reprinted in Daniel Howard-Snyder, ed., *The Evidential Problem of Evil*, 1–11. Bloomington: Indiana University Press, 1996.
Royce, Josiah. *The Religious Aspect of Philosophy: A Critique of the Basis of Conduct and of Faith*. Boston: Houghton, Mifflin, and Co., 1885.
Ruello, Francis. *La Christologie de Thomas d'Aquin*. Paris: Beauchesne, 1987.
Runciman, Steven. *The Last Byzantine Renaissance*. Cambridge: Cambridge University Press, 1970.
Ryan, Peter F. "Must the Acting Person Have a Single Ultimate End?" *Gregorianum* 82 (2001): 325–56.
———. "Revisiting Affective Knowledge and Connaturality in Aquinas." *Theological Studies* 66 (2005): 49–68.
———. "A Single Ultimate End Only for 'Fully Rational' Agents? A Critique of Scott MacDonald's Interpretation of Aquinas." *American Catholic Philosophical Quarterly* 75 (2001): 433–38.
Ryle, Gilbert. *The Concept of Mind*. London: Hutchinson, 1949.
Salamucha, Jan. "The Proof 'Ex Motu' for the Existence of God: Logical Analysis of St. Thomas' Arguments." *New Scholasticism* 32 (1958): 334–72.
Schabel, C., ed. *Theological Quodlibeta in the Middle Ages: The Thirteenth Century*. Brill's Companion to the Christian Tradition, I. Leiden and Boston: Brill, 2006.
Scheffczyk, L., "Die Stellung des Thomas von Aquin in der Entwicklung der Lehre von den Mysteria Vitae Christi." In M. Gerwing and G. Ruppert, eds., *Renovatio et Reformatio*, 44–70. Münster: Aschendorff, 1986.
Schenk, Richard. "Perplexus supposito quodam: Notizen zu einem vergessenen Schlüsselbegriff thomasischer Gewissenslehre." *Recherches de Théologie ancienne et médiévale* 57 (1990): 62–95.
Schillebeeckx, Edward. *Christ: The Christian Experience in the Modern World*. London: SCM, 1980.
———. *The Church: The Human Story of God*. London: SCM, 1990.
Schmidbaur, Hans Ch. *Personarum Trinitas: Die trinitarische Gotteslehre des heiligen Thomas von Aquin*. St. Ottilien: EOS Verlag, 1995.
Schockenhoff, E. "The Theological Virtue of Charity (IIa IIae, qq.23–46)." In Stephen J. Pope, ed., *The Ethics of Aquinas*, 244–58. Washington, D.C.: Georgetown University Press, 2002.
Schoot, Henk J. M. *Christ the "Name" of God: Thomas Aquinas on Naming Christ*. Leuven: Peeters, 1993.

Schweizer, Othmar. *Person und Hypostatische Union bei Thomas von Aquin*. Freiburg, Schweiz: Universitätsverlag, 1957.

Scully, John P. E. "Reality and Truth in Thomas of York." Ph.D. diss., University of Toronto, 1960.

Seidl, Horst. "Über die Erkenntnis erster, allgemeiner Prinzipien nach Thomas von Aquin." In Albert Zimmermann, ed., *Thomas von Aquin: Werk und Wirkung im Licht neuerer Forschungen*, 103–116. Miscellanea Mediaevalia 19. Berlin: De Gruyter, 1988.

Sellberg, Erland. "Petrus Ramus." *Stanford Encyclopedia of Philosophy*. Fall 2008 edition. Ed. Edward N. Zalta, accessed online at: <http://plato.stanford.edu/entries/ramus/>.

Sertillanges, A. G. *Foundations of Thomistic Philosophy*. Trans. Godfrey Anstruther. Springfield, Ill.: Templegate Publishers, 1956.

Shanley, Brian, O.P. "Divine Causation and Human Freedom in Aquinas." *American Catholic Philosophical Quarterly* 72 (1998): 99–122.

———. "Eternal Knowledge of the Temporal in Aquinas." *American Catholic Philosophical Quarterly* 71:2 (Spring 1997): 197–224.

Sherwin, Michael S., O.P. *By Knowledge and By Love: Charity and Knowledge in the Moral Theology of St. Thomas Aquinas*. Washington, D.C.: Catholic University of America Press, 2005.

Simon, Yves R. *Philosophy of Democractic Government*. Chicago: University of Chicago Press, 1951.

Simplicius. *Commentaire sur les Catégories d'Aristote, Traduction de Guillaume de Moerbeke*. Ed. Adrien Pattin. Vol. 1. Louvain: Publications universitaires de Louvain, 1971.

———. *On Aristotle On the Soul*. Trans. Henry Blumenthal. London: Duckworth, 2000.

Smalley, Beryl. *The Gospels in the Schools c.1100–c.1280*. London and Ronceverte: Hambledon, 1985.

———. *The Study of the Bible in the Middle Ages*. 3d ed. Oxford: Blackwell, 1983.

———. "William of Auvergne, John of La Rochelle and St. Thomas Aquinas on the Old Law." In *St. Thomas Aquinas, 1274–1974: Commemorative Studies*, foreword by Étienne Gilson. 2 vols. Vol. 2: 11–71. Toronto: Pontificial Institute of Mediaeval Studies, 1974.

Smit, Houston. "Aquinas's Abstractionism." *Medieval Philosophy and Theology* 10 (2001): 85–118.

Smith, Quentin. "Can Everything Come to Be Without a Cause?" *Dialogue: Canadian Philosophical Review* 33:2 (1994): 313–23.

———. "The Uncaused Beginning of the Universe." *Philosophy of Science* 55:1 (1988): 39–57.

Smith, Timothy L. *Thomas Aquinas' Trinitarian Theology: A Study in Theological Method*. Washington, D.C.: Catholic University of America Press, 2003.

Sober, Elliott. *Core Questions in Philosophy*. New York: Macmillan Library Reference, 1991.

Sokolowski, Robert. *The God of Faith and Reason*. Notre Dame, Ind.: University of Notre Dame Press, 1982; Washington, D.C.: Catholic University of America Press, 1996.

Speer, Andreas. "The Hidden Heritage: Boethian Metaphysics and its Medieval Tradition." In Pasquale Porro, ed., *Metaphysica—sapientia—scientia divina* (= *Quaestio* 5), 161–79. Turnhout: Brepols, 2005.

Speer, Andreas, ed. *Thomas von Aquin, Die Summa theologiae: Werkinterpretationen*. Berlin: Walter de Gruyter, 2005.

Spruit, Leen. *Species Intelligbilis: From Perception to Knowledge*. Classical Roots and Medieval Discussions. Vol. 1: 360–68. Leiden: E. J. Brill, 1994.

Steinmetz, David C. *Luther in Context*. Bloomington, Ind.: Baker Academic, 1986.

Stinger, Charles L. *Humanism and the Church Fathers: Ambrogio Traversari (1386–1439) and Christian Antiquity in the Italian Renaissance*. Albany, N.Y.: SUNY Press, 1977.

Stoelen, Anselme. "Denys the Carthusian." In James Walsh, ed., *Spirituality through the Centuries*, 220–32. New York: P. J. Kenedy, 1964.
Stufler, Johann. "Zur Analyse des Glaubensaktes." *Zeitschrift für Katholische Theologie* 66 (1942): 183–95.
Stump, Eleonore. *Aquinas*. London and New York: Routledge, 2003.
———. "Faith and Goodness." In Godfrey Vesey, ed., *The Philosophy in Christianity*, 167–91. Cambridge: Cambridge University Press, 1989.
———. "Love, By All Accounts." *Proceedings and Addresses of the American Philosophical Association* 80:2 (November 2006): 25–43.
———. "The Problem of Evil." In Robert Pasnau, ed., *The Cambridge History of Medieval Philosophy*, 773–84. Cambridge: Cambridge University Press, 2009.
———. "Resurrection, Reassembly, and Reconstitution: Aquinas on the Soul." In Bruno Niederberger and Edmund Runggaldier, eds., *Die menschliche Seele: Brauchen wir den Dualismus?* 153–74. Frankfurt a. M.: Ontos Verlag, 2006.
———. *Wandering in Darkness: Narrative and the Problem of Suffering*. Oxford: Oxford University Press, forthcoming.
———. "Wisdom: Will, Belief, and Moral Goodness." In Scott MacDonald and Eleonore Stump, eds., *Aquinas's Moral Theory: Essays in Honor of Norman Kretzmann*, 28–62. Ithaca, N.Y.: Cornell University Press, 1999.
Stump, Eleonore, and Norman Kretzmann. "Absolute Simplicity." *Faith and Philosophy* 2 (1985): 353–82.
———. "Eternity." *Journal of Philosophy* 78 (1981): 429–58.
———. "Eternity and God's Knowledge: A Reply to Shanley." *American Catholic Philosophical Quarterly* 72:3 (Summer 1998): 439–45.
———. "Eternity, Awareness, and Action." *Faith and Philosophy* 9 (1992): 463–82.
———. "God's Knowledge and Its Causal Effects." In Thomas Senor, ed., *The Rationality of Belief and the Plurality of Faith*, 94–124. Ithaca, N.Y.: Cornell University Press, 1995.
Sullivan, Thomas D. "Coming to Be Without a Cause." *Philosophy* 65 (1990): 261–70.
———. "On the Alleged Causeless Beginning of the Universe: A Reply to Quentin Smith." *Dialogue: Canadian Philosophical Review* 33:2 (1994): 325–36.
Summa Halensis. Quaracchi: Typographia Collegii S. Bonaventurae, 1924–48.
Sweeney, Eileen C. "Three Notions of *Resolutio* and the Structure of Reasoning in Aquinas." *The Thomist* 58:2 (1994): 197–243.
Synan, E. "Brother Thomas, the Master, and the Masters." In *St Thomas Aquinas 1274–1974: Commemorative Studies*. Vol. 2: 219–42. Toronto: PIMS, 1974.
Tager-Flusberg, Helen. "Dissociations in Form and Function in the Acquisition of Language by Autistic Children." In H.-T. Flusberg, ed., *Constraints on Language Acquisition: Studies of Atypical Children*, 175–94. Hillsdale, N.J.: Lawrence Erlbaum, 1994.
Taylor, Richard. *Metaphysics*. 4th ed. Englewood Cliffs, N.J.: Prentice Hall, 1992.
Te Velde, Rudi. "The Concept of the Good according to Thomas Aquinas." In Wouter Goris, ed., *Die Metaphysik und das Gute: Aufsätze zu ihrem Verhältnis in Antike und Mittelalter*, 81–103. Leuven: Peeters, 1999.
———. *Participation and Substantiality in Thomas Aquinas*. Studien und Texte zur Geistesgeschichte des Mittelalters xlvi. Leiden: E. J. Brill, 1995.
Telfer, Elizabeth. *Happiness*. London and Basingstoke: Macmillan Press, 1980.
Teske, Roland. "Hervaeus Natalis (c. 1250–1323)." In Donald Borchert, ed., *Encyclopedia of Philosophy*. 2d ed. Vol. 1: 343–44. Detroit, Mich.: Macmillan Reference USA, 2006.

Thijssen, Hans. "Condemnation of 1277." *Stanford Encyclopedia of Philosophy*. Fall 2008 edition. Ed. Edward N. Zalta, accessed online at: <http://plato.stanford.edu/archives/fall2008/entries/condemnation/>.

Thomas, Rudolf. "Die Präfiguration thomistischen Denkens bei Petrus Abaelardus." In *Tommaso d'Aquino nella storia del pensiero I: Le fonti del pensiero di S. Tommaso (Atti del congresso internazionale Tommaso d'Aquino nel suo settimo centenario)*, 392–98. Naples: Edizioni Domenicane Italiane, 1975.

Torrell, Jean-Pierre, O.P. *Aquinas's* Summa: *Background, Structure, and Reception*. Trans. Benedict M. Guevin, O.S.B. Washington, D.C.: Catholic University of America Press, 2005.

———. "La Causalité salvifique de la resurrection du Christ selon saint Thomas." *Revue Thomiste* 96 (1996): 179–208.

———. *Le Christ en ses mystères: La Vie et l'œuvre de Jésus selon saint Thomas d'Aquin*. Jésus et Jésus-Christ 78–79. 2 vols. Paris: Desclée, 1999.

———. *Initiation à saint Thomas d'Aquin: Sa personne et son oeuvre*. Fribourg Suisse/Paris: Éditions universitaire/Cerf, 1993. English Translation: *Thomas Aquinas: The Person and His Work*. Washington, D.C.: Catholic University of America Press, 2005.

———. *Nouvelle recherches thomasiennes*. Paris: Vrin, 2008.

———. "Philosophie et théologie d'après le Prologue de Thomas d'Aquin au *Super Boetium de Trinitate*: Essai d'une lecture théologique." *Documenti e Studi sulla tradizione filosofica medievale* 10 (1999): 299–353.

———. *Recherches thomasiennes: Études revues et augmentés*. Paris: Vrin, 2000.

———. "Le Sacerdoce du Christ dans la *Somme de théologie*." *Revue Thomiste* 99 (1999): 75–100.

———. *Saint Thomas Aquinas*. Vol. 1, *The Person and His Work*. Revised edition. Washington, D.C.: Catholic University of America Press, 1996.

———. *Saint Thomas Aquinas*. Vol. 2, *Spiritual Master*. Trans. Robert Royal. Washington, D.C.: Catholic University of America Press, 2003.

———. "Le Savoir théologique chez saint Thomas." In *Recherches thomasiennes*, 121–57. Bibliothèque thomiste 52. Paris: Vrin, 2000.

———. "Thomas d'Aquin." *Dictionnaire de spiritualité* 15 (1991): 718–73.

———. *Thomas d'Aquin: Abrégé de théologie (Compendium theologiae)*. Introduction, Texte latin, trad. française et annotations. Paris: Cerf, 2007.

Torrell, Jean-Pierre, O.P., ed. and trans., *Thomas Aquinas, Le Verbe incarné*. Vol. 3, Summa theologiae *IIIa Questions 7–15*. Paris: Cerf, 2002.

Tovey, Phillip. *Inculturation of Christian Worship: Exploring the Eucharist*. Aldershot and Burlington, Vt.: Ashgate Publishing, 2004.

Treiger, Alexander. "The Arabic Version of Pseudo-Dionysius the Areopagite's Mystical Theology, Chapter 1: Introduction, Critical Edition, and Translation." *Le Muséon* 120:3–4 (2007): 365–93.

Tugwell, Simon, O.P. *Albert and Thomas: Selected Writings*. New York and Mahwah, NJ: Paulist Press, 1988.

———. "Prayer, Humpty Dumpty and Thomas Aquinas." In Brian Davies, ed., *Language, Meaning and God*, 24–50. London: Geoffrey Chapman, 1987.

Tuninetti, Luca. *"Per se notum": Die logische Beschaffenheit des Selbstverständlichen im Denken des Thomas von Aquin*. Leiden: Brill, 1996.

Turbessi, R. "Denys l'Aréopagite." *Dictionnaire de spiritualité* 3 (1954): 349–56.

Twetten, David. "Clearing a 'Way' for Aquinas: How the Proof from Motion Concludes to God." *Proceedings of the American Catholic Philosophical Association* 70 (1997): 259–78.

———. "Really Distinguishing Essence from Existence." In Peter A. Kwasniewski, ed., *Wisdom's Apprentice: Thomistic Essays in Honor of Lawrence Dewan, O.P.*, 40–84. Washington, D.C.: Catholic University of America Press, 2007.

Uffenheimer-Lippens, Elisabeth. "Rationalized Passions and Passionate Rationality: Thomas Aquinas on the Relation between Reason and the Passions." *Review of Metaphysics* 56 (2003): 525–58.

Urban, Linwood. "Understanding St. Thomas's Fourth Way." *History of Philosophy Quarterly* 1:3 (1984): 281–95.

Valkenberg, W. G. B. M. *Words of the Living God: Place and Function of Holy Scripture in the Theology of St. Thomas Aquinas*. Leuven: Peeters, 2000.

Van Geest, Paul, Harm J. M. J. Goris, Carlo Leget, and Mishtooni Bose. *Aquinas as Authority: A Collection of Studies Presented at the Second Conference of the Thomas Insituut te Utrecht, December 14–16, 2000*. Leuven: Peeters Publishers, 2002.

Van Gunten, A. F. "*In principio erat verbum*: Une évolution de saint Thomas en théologie trinitaire." In C. J. Pinto de Oliveira, ed., *Ordo Sapientiae et Amoris. Hommage au Proferreus Jean-Pierre Torrell OP à l'occaions de son 65e anniversaire*, 119–41. Fribourg, Suisse: Éditions universitaires, 1993.

Van Inwagen, Peter. *Metaphysics*. 2d ed. Boulder, Colo.: Westview Press, 2002.

———. "The Problem of Evil, the Problem of Air, and the Problem of Silence." In Daniel Howard-Snyder, ed., *The Evidential Argument from Evil*, 151–74. Bloomington: Indiana University Press: 1996.

———. "Reflections on the Chapters by Draper, Russell, and Gale." In Daniel Howard-Snyder, ed., *The Evidential Argument from Evil*, 219–43. Bloomington: Indiana University Press, 1996.

———. "Resurrection." In *Routledge Encyclopedia of Philosophy*. London: Routledge, 1999.

Van Nieuwenhove, Rik. "'Bearing the Marks of Christ's Passion': Aquinas' Soteriology." In Rik Van Nieuwenhove and Joseph Wawrykow, eds., *The Theology of Thomas Aquinas*, 277–302. Notre Dame, Ind.: University of Notre Dame Press, 2005.

———. "The Christian Response to Suffering, and the Significance of the Model of the Church as Body of Christ." *Angelicum* 82 (2005): 595–610.

———. "St Anselm and St Thomas Aquinas on 'Satisfaction': Or how Catholic and Protestant Understandings of the Cross Differ." *Angelicum* 80 (2003): 159–76.

Van Nieuwenhove, Rik, and Joseph Wawrykow, eds. *The Theology of Thomas Aquinas*. Notre Dame, Ind.: University of Notre Dame Press, 2005.

Van Steenberghen, Fernand. *La Philosophie au XIIIe siècle*. Louvain/Paris: Publ. Univ. Louvain/Béatrice-Nauwelaerts, 1966.

Vansteenkiste, Clemens. "S. Bernardo nell'opera di San Tommaso." *Rassegna di letteratura tomistica* 10 (1978): 35–47.

Verger, J. "L'Exégèse de l'Université." In *Le Moyen Age et la Bible*, sous la dir. de P. Riché et G. Lobrichon, 199–232. Paris: Beauchesne, 1984.

Wadell, P. *The Primacy of Love: An Introduction to the Ethics of Thomas Aquinas*. New York: Paulist Press, 1992.

Wallace, William. "Newtonian Antinomies Against the 'Prima Via'." *The Thomist* 19 (1956): 151–92.

Walsh, Liam. "Sacraments." In Rik van Nieuwenhove and Joseph Wawrykow, eds., *The Theology of Thomas Aquinas*, 326–64. Notre Dame, Ind.: University of Notre Dame Press, 2005.

Walzer, Richard. *Al-Farabi on the Perfect State*. Oxford: Clarendon Press, 1985.

———. *Greek into Arabic: Essays in Islamic Philosophy*. Columbia: University of South Carolina Press, 1962.

Wang, Stephen. *Aquinas and Sartre on Freedom, Personal Identity, and the Possibility of Happiness*. Washington, D.C.: Catholic University of America Press, 2009.

Wawrykow, Joseph. *God's Grace and Human Action: "Merit" in the Theology of Thomas Aquinas*. Notre Dame, Ind.: University of Notre Dame Press, 1995.

Weigel, Peter. *Aquinas on Simplicity: An Investigation into the Foundations of His Philosophical Theology*. Frankfurt: Peter Lang, 2008.

Weinandy, Thomas G., OFM Cap. *Does God Suffer?* Edinburgh: T & T Clark, 2000.

Weinandy, Thomas G., OFM Cap., D. A. Keating, and J. P. Yocum, eds. *Aquinas on Scripture: An Introduction to the Biblical Commentaries*. London and New York: T. & T. Clark International, 2005.

Weisheipl, James A., O.P. "Durandus of Saint-Pourçain (c. 1275–1334)." In Donald Borchert, ed., *Encyclopedia of Philosophy*. 2d ed. Vol. 1: 148–49. Detroit, Mich.: Macmillan Reference USA, 2006.

———. *Friar Thomas d'Aquino: His Life, Thought and Works*. Garden City, N.Y.: Doubleday, 1974; 2d ed. with Corrigenda and Addenda, 1983.

———. "Thomism." In *New Catholic Encyclopedia*. 2d ed. Vol. 14: 40–52. Detroit, Mich.: Gale, 2003.

———. "John of Paris (c. 1255–1306)." In Donald Borchert, ed., *Encyclopedia of Philosophy*. 2d ed. Vol. 1: 842. Detroit, Mich.: Macmillan Reference USA, 2006.

Westberg, Daniel. "Did Aquinas Change His Mind about the Will?" *The Thomist* 58 (1994): 41–60.

———. *Right Practical Reason: Aristotle, Action, and Prudence in Aquinas*. Oxford: Clarendon Press, 1994.

White, Kevin. "The *Quodlibeta* of Thomas Aquinas in the Context of His Work." In C. Schabel, ed., *Theological Quodlibeta in the Middle Ages: The Thirteenth Century*, 49–133. Leiden: Brill, 2006.

———. "The Passions of the Soul." In Stephen Pope, ed., *Essays on Aquinas's Ethics*, 103–15. Washington, D.C.: Georgetown University Press, 2002.

Wieland, Georg. *Ethica—Scientia Practica: Die Anfänge der philosophischen Ethik im 13. Jahrhundert*. Münster: Ashendorff, 1981.

———. "Secundum naturam vivere: Über den Wandel des Verhältnisses von Natur und Sittlichkeit." In Bernhard Fraling, ed., *Natur im ethischen Argument*, 20–26. Freiburg: Herder, 1990.

———. "Happiness." In Stephen J. Pope, ed., *The Ethics of Aquinas*, 57–68. Washington, D.C.: Georgetown University Press, 2002.

Wielockx, R. "Poetry and Theology in the *Adoro Te deuote*: Thomas Aquinas on the Eucharist and Christ's Uniqueness." In Kent Emery and Joseph Wawrykow, eds., *Christ among the Medieval Dominicans: Representations of Christ in the Texts and Images of the Order of Preachers*, 157–74. Notre Dame, Ind.: University of Notre Dame Press, 1998.

Wilcox, John. "The Five Ways and the Oneness of God." *The Thomist* 62 (1998): 245–68.

William of Auvergne. *Tractatus de anima*, in *Guilielmi Alverni Opera Omnia*. Vol. 2. Paris, 1674; reprinted: Frankfurt am Main: Minerva GMBH, 1963.

William of Ockham. *Opera Theologica*. Vol. 8. St. Bonaventure, N.Y.: St. Bonaventure University, 1984.

William of Tocco. *Ystoria sancti Thome de Aquino de Guillaum de Tocco (1323)*. Ed. Claire le Brun-Gouanvic. Toronto: Pontifical Institute of Mediaeval Studies, 1996.

Wippel, John F. *Metaphysical Themes in Thomas Aquinas*. Washington, D.C.: Catholic University of America Press, 1984.

———. *The Metaphysical Thought of Thomas Aquinas: From Finite Being to Uncreated Being*. Washington, D.C.: Catholic University of America Press, 2000.

———. "Norman Kretzmann on Aquinas's Attribution of Will and of Freedom to Create to God." *Religious Studies* 39 (2003): 287–98.
———. "Thomas Aquinas on God's Freedom to Create or Not." In John F. Wippel, *Metaphysical Themes in Thomas Aquinas II*, 218–39. Washington, D.C.: Catholic University Press of America, 2007.
———. *Thomas Aquinas on the Divine Ideas*. The Etienne Gilson Series, no.16. Toronto: Pontifical Institute of Mediaeval Studies, 1993.
———. "Thomas Aquinas on What Philosophers Can Know about God." *American Catholic Philosophical Quarterly* 66 (1992): 279–97.
———. "Truth in Thomas Aquinas." *Review of Metaphysics* 43:2 (1989): 295–326.
———. "Truth in Thomas Aquinas." *Review of Metaphysics* 43:3 (1990): 543–67.
Wisnovsky, Robert. *Avicenna's Metaphysics in Context*. London: Duckworth, 2003.
Wolter, Allan. "Duns Scotus, John (c. 1266–1308)." In Donald Borchert, ed., *Encyclopedia of Philosophy*. 2d ed. Vol. 1: 133–45. Detroit, Mich.: Macmillan Reference USA, 2006.
Wolterstorff, Nicholas. "Faith." In Edward Craig, ed., *The Routledge Encyclopedia of Philosophy*. Vol. 3: 538–44. London: Routledge, 1998.
Wykstra, Stephen. "Rowe's Noseeum Arguments from Evil." In Daniel Howard-Snyder, ed., *The Evidential Argument from Evil*, 126–50. Bloomington, Ind.: Indiana University Press, 1996.
Yocum, John P. "Sacraments in Aquinas." In Thomas Weinandy, Daniel Keating, and John Yocum, eds., *Aquinas on Docrine: A Critical Introduction*, 160–64. London and New York: T & T Clark International, 2004.
Young, William. "From Describing to Naming God: Correlating the Five Ways with Aquinas' Doctrine of the Trinity." *New Blackfriars* 85 (2004): 527–41.
Zeis, John. "The Epistemic Passage of the Five Ways." *Proceedings of the American Catholic Philosophical Association* 68 (1994): 73–84.
Zimmermann, Albert. *Ontologie oder Metaphysik? Die Diskussion über den Gegenstand der Metaphysik im 13. und 14. Jahrhundert*. Leuven: Peeters, 1998.

Index

CPSIA information can be obtained at www.ICGtesting.com
Printed in the USA
LVOW05s0620231113

362333LV00006BA/10/P